Dieter Bös · Manfred Rose
Christian Seidl (Eds.)

Welfare and Efficiency in Public Economics

With 28 Figures

Springer-Verlag
Berlin Heidelberg New York
London Paris Tokyo

Professor Dr. Dr. Dieter Bös, Institute of Economics, University of Bonn
Adenauerallee 24-42, D-5300 Bonn 1, West Germany

Professor Dr. Manfred Rose, Alfred-Weber-Institute,
University of Heidelberg, Grabengasse 14, D-6900 Heidelberg,
West Germany

Professor Dr. Christian Seidl, Institute of Public Economics,
University of Kiel, Olshausenstraße 40, D-2300 Kiel 1, West Germany

This volume is a selection of papers presented at a seminar in public economics, Bad Neresheim 1986. We gratefully acknowledge financial support by the Hanns Martin Schleyer-Stiftung and the Deutsche Forschungsgemeinschaft.

ISBN-13:978-3-642-73372-7 e-ISBN-13:978-3-642-73370-3
DOI: 10.1007/978-3-642-73370-3

Softcover reprint of the hardcover 1st edition 1988

Typeset by Heinz-Dieter Ecker on TEX, under assistance of Sfb 303 at the University of Bonn.

2142/7130-543210

Table of Contents

Introduction

Hans-Werner Sinn, Munich, West Germany

This book contains 15 papers presented at a conference in Neresheim, West Germany, in June 1986. The articles were selected by anonymous referees and most of them have undergone substantial revisions since their presentation.

The common topic is measurement of welfare, both from efficiency and from equity perspectives. For many economists, welfare is a diffuse, arbitrary and ambiguous concept. The papers collected in this book show that this view is not justified. Though not beyond all doubt, welfare theory today is crisp and clear, offering fairly straightforward measuring concepts. It even comes up with numbers that measure society's advantage or disadvantage from specific policy options in monetary units. Politicians get something they can intuitively understand and argue with, and they do not have to be afraid that all this is metaphysics or the result of the scientist's personal value judgements.

Some economists, whom I would classify as belonging to the "everything is optimal" school, would claim that providing politicians with numerical welfare measures is superfluous or even dangerous. The world is as it is, and any attempt to give policy advice can only make things worse. I do not share this view. There are good policies and there are bad ones, but it may not be easy to distinguish between them. There is a role for consulting politicians, Dr. Pangloss, or do you go shopping without thinking because you believe whatever you are going to buy is what you wanted anyway? Certainly, everyone knows that political decision processes are not all that rational and that there is a lot of slack in the public sector. This does not imply, however, that no attempt should be made to bring a bit more rationality and objectivity into public policy debates. Measurement of welfare helps to do that.

George McKenzie, whose paper is the first in this volume, discusses what we can measure and what not. Reconsidering the theory of Ragnar Frisch, he provides a stimulating exercise in the comparison between cardinal and ordinal utility. A number of authors have tried, in recent years, to establish cardinal properties of utility by using data on observed demand behavior. McKenzie takes up their examples one by one and demonstrates their inappropriateness. Given that we are all ordinalists today, it is a pleasure to eat the remaining red herrings of the cardinalist school that he has been able to fish out of some of the shallow and remote waters of preference theory. His exercise should not be misinterpreted though. While it may be true that objective interpersonal utility comparisons are impossible, it is not impossible to detect the cardinal properties of introspective utility Frisch was talking about. The psychophysical interval measure procedures have demonstrated this very clearly. If people are able, on request, to identify the increments of income or wealth that generate subjectively equal increments of utility then, for example, Frisch's utility flexibility measure is well defined. But green herrings do not taste as good as red herrings. McKenzie is certainly right in pointing out that there is no way whatsoever to infer any cardinal properties of utility from observed demand behavior and it is good that he reminds us that the money metric welfare measures that are used in welfare theory do not require cardinal properties of utility, let alone interpersonal utility comparisons. The most popular money metric welfare measure nowadays is the Hicksian equivalent variation. This measure expresses the welfare change resulting from the transition from one allocation of resources in the economy to another, the transition being induced perhaps by a government policy measure. To be more specific, the equivalent variation is defined as an income change at new prices that changes consumers' utility levels just as much as the actual variation in the allocation of resources being evaluated. By way of contrast, the compensating variation is an income change that restores each consumer's utility level at old prices. McKenzie points out that only the equivalent variation will always correctly rank the variations in the allocation of resources according to consumer preferences, i.e., according to the Pareto principle.

The favorable view of the equivalent variation is shared by *Udo Ebert* who discusses alternative concepts of excess burden of taxation. In principle, the excess burden of a tax is an income equivalent of the utility loss that results from the tax payer's avoidance reactions and the resulting distortion in the allocation of resources. However, the precise definition of excess burden depends very much on whether it is based on the compensating or the equivalent variation. In the former case, the excess burden is the amount of lump sum rebate in excess of the tax revenue someone would have to receive in order to be restored to his pre-tax utility level. In the latter, the excess burden is the additional tax revenue the government could collect by switching to lump-sum taxation given the tax payers' utility levels. Ebert offers a simple and straightforward axiomatic approach for evaluating alternative excess burden measures and he shows that only the excess burden based on the equivalent variation can meaningfully be used in optimal taxation theory. Only with this definition will the minimization of the excess burden result in a Pareto optimal tax structure given the tax revenue, and this is true regardless of whether homogeneous consumers are assumed or not.

The usual measures of the compensating and equivalent variation are based on the assumption that the consumers' marginal rates of substitution are equal to price ratios. This assumption is rather special since it excludes the case of rationing equilibria. For example, the economy may be in a Keynesian underemployment equilibrium where people are forced to consume more leisure than they wish. To repair this deficiency, *Wilfried Pauwels* introduces a new distance function into consumer theory. Given any vector of non-numéraire commodities, this distance function specifies the quantity of a numéraire commodity the consumer requires to obtain a given utility level. Some important dual relationships exist between the new function and the usual expenditure function. Both functions can be obtained as optimal values of two closely related mathematical programming problems. By solving these problems, the direct and inverse Hicksian compensated demand functions are obtained. Pauwels shows that his function can be used to define and analyze the Hicksian equivalent and compensating variations in a very natural and straightforward way regardless of whether consumers are quantity constrained or not.

Among the rivals of the Hicksian measures is the so-called Debreu coefficient. This coefficient is defined as the percentage to which the resource consumption of an economy could be reduced by abolishing all of its distortions while maintaining every person's utility level. The introduction of a tax system into a Pareto efficient economy, for example, reduces the Debreu coefficient from one to a value lower than one if, and only if, this tax system creates an excess burden. The properties of the Debreu coefficient are thoroughly analyzed by *Michael Ahlheim*. He shows that with a given resource endowment and with identical individuals, the Debreu coefficient is a perfect welfare indicator. In fact, he demonstrates that the coefficient is a strictly monotonic transformation of consumer utility. In the realistic case of different individuals and varying resource endowments however, the Debreu coefficient loses its theoretical virtues. Moreover, there seem to be insurmountable difficulties in measuring the value of the coefficient empirically. Ahlheim therefore concludes that the Debreu coefficient cannot be recommended for welfare comparisons.

By way of contrast, calculating the Hicksian equivalent variation empirically does not involve any comparable problems. The empirical general equilibrium models of the Shoven-Whalley variety have demonstrated this for a great many policy issues. But anyone who has tried to understand how, in detail, this literature proceeds in deriving its results, will probably have been disappointed. Due to the complexity of the calculation procedures involved and the page constraints journals impose, the authors usually abstain from presenting their models formally, but concentrate on verbal descriptions and policy discussions. The editors of this volume therefore have provided space for *Wolfgang Wiegard* and *Georg Hirte* to give a detailed introduction to the Shoven-Whalley approach. Wiegard visited Whalley and learned all the little tricks necessary to actually carry out the calculations. The paper that emerged is the clearest description of empirical "GE" models that I have seen. Technologies, preferences, and the optimization problems of firms and households are carefully described and there remain no ambiguities about the nature of the calibration process by which the benchmark equilibrium is calculated. Glasnost is good, if only because it makes weaknesses of a system visible and helps to improve it. For example, Hirte and Wiegard's description relentlessly reveals that the Shoven-Whalley model does not incorporate a theory of the firm and hence is unable to handle policy issues relating to capital formation, profit taxation, interest rates and the like. Firms are certainly not corporate consumers of capital goods. Much can be done here in the future, but much has been achieved already. The authors successfully demonstrate that the approach, as it stands, can already be meaningfully used to give policy advice for other types of problems. The example they analyze in detail is a substitution of a uniform value-added tax for a number of specific trade taxes in West Germany, and their result is that this will create a welfare loss. This is surprising, as the model used involves utility functions that are separable in commodity consumption and leisure, which usually calls for uniform commodity taxation. The reason that the result nevertheless emerges is that the removal of the trade taxes reduces the world prices of German exports and thereby undermines the monopoly position that these taxes implicitly help the German economy to maintain in world commodity markets. Despite fewer distortions in the labor leisure choice, uniform taxation may therefore not be desirable from the national point of view, notwithstanding, of course, the possibility that it is an efficiency requirement from a world wide perspective.

Another variant of the Shoven-Whalley model is presented by *Manfred Rose*, *Bernhard Kühn*, and *Hans Kungl*. The aim of these authors is to measure the welfare and incidence effects of alternative variants of the income tax reform Germany plans for 1988. The reform will change the degree of progression and the revenue of income taxation, and it will either require an increase in the value-added tax rate or a reduction of government expenditure to balance the budget. To capture these aspects, Rose and co-workers set up a model with four income categories and, as in the Wiegard model, much attention is paid to what happens to foreign trade flows. In fact, the authors even formulate an explicit two-country model where one country carries out the tax reform and the agents in both countries react in line with their individual optimization approaches. The model generates a rich number of detailed results on income and welfare incidence for the four consumer groups distinguished, demonstrating once again that the impact effects of tax reforms to which the public discussion is usually confined say nothing about the long run effects that result when the economy has settled down to a new equilibrium. With some reservations, the authors daringly publish a numerical welfare evaluation of the planned reform. They expect that the sum of equivalent compensations will amount to DM 5.6 billion per year.

Yet another variant of an empirical general equilibrium model is presented by *Klaus Conrad* and *Iris Henseler-Unger*. Unlike the Shoven-Whalley models, this variant is derived from input output analysis, and it places more weight on the description of the production sector. Input output models like that of Conrad and Henseler-Unger are no longer of the fixed-coefficient variety. They have flexible, price dependent input coefficients and, in principle, the behavior of households and firms is compatible with individual optimization. Like the Shoven-Whalley models, they do not describe a Walrasian intertemporal equilibrium, but they incorporate a more explicit description of the process of capital accumulation than those do. The special characteristic of the model presented by Conrad and Henseler-Unger is that it allows for sluggish factor redistributions among the industries after an exogenous demand shock. This aspect makes the model suitable for measuring the welfare loss from an economic recession. The welfare loss results from the fact that firms' production levels deviate from the minima of their average cost curves and consumers buy commodities different from those they would buy if factor movements were not sluggish. For the 1986 recession of the West German economy, the authors calculate an overall annual welfare loss of DM 164 billion, again in terms of equivalent variations. A second objective of the paper of Conrad and Henseler-Unger is to measure the welfare gain from a general tax cut like that currently discussed in Germany. In this respect, the paper parallels that of Rose, Kühn, and Kungl, but unlike these authors, Conrad and Henseler-Unger assume the government budget to be balanced by a cut in spending rather than an increase of the value-added tax. The authors find that a cut in the average income tax rate by 10 percentage points will create a gross welfare gain of DM 45 billion due to an improved allocation of resources in the private sector.

Income tax changes accompanied by changes in government spending are also the topic of *Wilhelm Pfähler* who provides a theoretical analysis of the relevant welfare aspects and reviews the existing literature. His precise question is what are, in monetary equivalents, the welfare changes associated with one additional dollar of public expenditure. There is by now an extensive literature on this topic, and the usual result is that one dollar of public expenditure "costs" one dollar fifty, or so. Pfähler rightly points out, however, that most of this literature neglects the welfare aspects of government expenditure. The direct tax burden resulting from one dollar of government expenditure is one dollar, and there may be an excess burden of taxation that amounts to some additional fifty cents. But, in addition, the dollar of expenditure creates direct benefits that, in money terms, may or may not be equal to one dollar. These direct benefits are precisely one dollar if the size of the government sector is optimized according to the Samuelson-Lindahl rule, but they fall short of one dollar if the government sector is larger, and, vice versa, they exceed one dollar if the government sector is smaller. Moreover, there are indirect benefits or losses from government expenditure that result from the fact that consumers' utility functions may not be separable with regard to private and public consumption. This is an important aspect. If, for example, government expenditure and private consumption of market commodities are complements, then there is a positive indirect welfare effect of government expenditure that counteracts the negative indirect welfare effects of taxation. Conversely, of course, if government expenditure and leisure are complements, then the indirect welfare effect is negative, reinforcing the distortions from income taxation. Pfähler's analysis is theoretical, and not empirical. Nevertheless, he is able to make useful comments on the existing empirical literature, demonstrating the sensitivity of its results. The existence of a marginal excess burden of taxation clearly does not mean that a reduction of government expenditure and taxation is necessarily welfare increasing!

It may be permissable to add that the case for reducing the size of the government sector is even less obvious if the insurance effect of income taxation in an uncertain world is taken into account. This effect has been analyzed by various authors in recent years. It clearly diminishes the net welfare gain from a policy of reducing the size of the government sector, provided there is any such gain at all.

Pfähler's question was whether it pays to increase or reduce government expenditure at the margin, given that this expenditure was different in kind from the rival private expenditure. An alternative question is whether any given kind of commodity provided by the government could be privately produced. This question is discussed by *Dieter Bös*, who shows us how to measure the social costs and benefits from privatization. Privatization is clearly impossible for pure public goods with non-rival demand, and, in fact, this is not what Bös discusses. His problem instead is whether it pays to privatize a government monopoly that produces non-rival, "private" goods and that, for technical reasons other than increasing returns to scale, must remain a monopoly even after privatization. In previous papers, the author discussed the issue under the aspect of rent maximization. The case for privatization was then made where the loss in consumer and producer rents resulting from the monopolistic price increase was being overcompensated by the increase in producer rents resulting from the cost decrease due to an improved efficiency. In the paper contained in this volume, Bös experiments with a different welfare objective where welfare is negatively related to output prices (or consumer rents) and, to concentrate on his favorite case, positively to the capital gains the new owners of the privatized firm make when the shares are sold below their market price (the present value of dividends). The optimal degree of privatization is reached where the marginal "efficiency" loss from the price increase just balances the marginal "distributional" gain from selling more shares. Bös also analyzes a further variant, where the government budget constraint is explicitly considered. The case for privatization is now typically increased as the government is willing to accept higher profits of the privatized firm which can be used for higher public expenditure. Due to the non-Paretian efficiency concept underlying the welfare function, the model may have few normative implications for the privatization debate. However, it certainly is a useful attempt to develop a positive theory of government behavior with regard to privatization.

The privatization issue discussed by Bös concerns market failure due to excessive barriers to entry. Another type of market failure results from negative externalities such as air and water pollution or noise production. In a sense, the barriers to entry are too low in this case. This volume contains two papers that deal with this issue.

One is *Werner Pommerehne*'s empirical analysis of the marginal social value of noise reduction. Up to now, there have been two separate and distinct kinds of empirical approaches to measuring the value of noise reduction — the hedonic approach that derives this value indirectly from house price differentials between quiet and noisy areas and the contingent valuation method, basically a skilled way of asking people about their willingness to pay. Pommerehne's paper seems to be the first study where an attempt is made to reconcile these two methods. Applying the methods simultaneously to the city of Basle, he is able to compare their predictions and find out about the biases they involve. The a priori expectation certainly is that, because of strategic behavior on the part of the interviewed, the contingent valuation method produces lower values than the hedonic approach. After all, people might be afraid that their revealed marginal willingness to pay could some day be used to assess what they really have to pay. Surprisingly, however, this a priori expectation is only confirmed for the case of traffic noise, not, however, for aircraft noise. This is an interesting finding that yet has to be explained, although it should not be overemphasized. Despite the differences, I find the fit between the two kinds of estimates quite remarkable. They always give roughly the same order of magnitude, and I suspect for most real life policy issues this is all we want.

The second study dealing with negative externalities is that of *Gunter Stephan*.

Stephan presents a multi-regional intertemporal equilibrium model where each sector produces a specific commodity from labor and capital that can be consumed, invested, traded with other regions and used as an input into the treatment of waste water which is a by-product of industrial activity. His aim is to study the flexibility of market economies in reacting to the imposition of effluent standards, for example the precept to reduce the biochemical oxygen demand of waste water by 95 % before it is released into the environment. For this, he assumes a neo-Austrian time-to-build technology for capital goods which, in addition, is of the putty-clay variety. These realistic features exclude immediate adjustments, but leave enough flexibility for the production technology to optimally react to the effluent standards in the long run. To demonstrate the working of his model, Stephan presents some empirical predictions based on the example mentioned, reaching to the year 1995. They have in common that, after the imposition of the effluent standards, the production of waste water continues to grow for a while but will then strongly decline despite the continuing growth of the economies considered.

Measurement requires norms, and one of the most frequently used norms in tax theory is the neutrality norm. For example, it is very important for tax authorities to know the design of tax systems that do not affect private risk taking, capital investment or asset evaluation. It is certainly not true that neutrality can always be identified with optimality. For example, it might be argued that a tax system that acts as an insurance against income risks should not be neutral, but stimulate risk taking because it reduces the social price of risk compared to a situation where no such system is available. However, for this very reason, the neutrality idea is important. It helps the policy maker to design the tax system so that it deviates from neutrality in the direction he prefers. There are two papers in this volume that deal with the problem of neutral taxation.

The first is that of *Wolfgang Buchholz*. Extending previous analyses of Schneeweiß and Feldstein, and the even earlier work of Domar and Musgrave, he determines wealth tax schedules that, given the decision maker's von Neumann-Morgenstern utility function, are just neutral with regard to private risk taking. The paper is exclusively concerned with fiscal taxation, not redistributive taxation. With fiscal taxation, neutrality results from the interaction of wealth and substitution effects. The substitution effect usually implies more risk taking, but, in the realistic case of decreasing absolute risk aversion, the wealth effect implies less risk taking. It is therefore plausible that, unlike the Domar-Musgrave model that neglects the wealth effect, in general, a shape of the tax schedule that implies neutrality should exist. In the case of constant relative risk aversion, proportional taxes are neutral, but not only proportional taxes. When the Pratt-Arrow measure of relative risk aversion exceeds unity, even increasing marginal tax rates can be neutral. Moreover, neutrality is compatible with increasing marginal and average tax rates when relative risk aversion is increasing, and absolute risk aversion is falling with the level of wealth, the case so strongly advocated by Arrow.

The second paper on the neutrality issue is by *Wolfram Richter*. He discusses the question of how taxation affects an investor's choice between real and financial assets. Both assets are characterized by constant returns to scale, but, due to a progressive tax schedule combined with the assumption that the tax base of the real asset may deviate from the economic base, there is, in general, an interior solution to the portfolio problem. Richter's main problem is to find how the economic tax base for the real asset should be defined so as to imply tax neutrality with regard to portfolio choice or — to use the technical term — to imply investment neutrality of taxation. As is well known, the Johansson-Samuelson theorem implies that investment neutrality prevails under true economic depreciation, i.e., if the decline in the remaining present value of the cash flow generated by an asset can be deducted from the income tax base. However, the theorem refers exclusively to the case of certainty. Under uncertainty, there is a difference between deducting realized depreciation ex post or expected depreciation ex ante. Assuming risk neutrality, Richter shows that proportional taxes could be based both on the ex ante and the ex post concept, but progressive taxes would be neutral only with the ex ante concept. He applies his finding to the taxation of (uncertain) life annuities, showing that ex ante taxation would imply a substantially different tax base from ex post taxation. Richter's analysis complements that of Buchholz. The latter assumes ex post taxation and identifies the shapes of the tax schedule that would imply neutrality given the decision maker's risk preferences. The former shows that tax schedules which are non-neutral when applied ex post may well be neutral when applied ex ante.

Measuring efficiency has been the main topic of the papers presented so far. However, some papers, including those of McKenzie, Rose et al., and Bös, do explicitly address distributional aspects in addition to taxation. McKenzie even points out the formal analogies between efficiency and equity measurement, applying the concept of equivalent variations to the construction of a poverty index. Many hundreds of millions of people in this world suffer from starvation, certainly more than live in the OECD countries. Measuring poverty deserves the attention of the non-panglossian economist. Last, but not least, I now refer to the two papers in this volume that are concerned with this problem.

The first is by *Christian Seidl*, who gives an excellent overview and synthesis of the growing literature in this field. Starting from possible conceptions of poverty, he proceeds by the way of discussing food income ratios, head counts and subjective poverty lines, to the more ambitious axiomatic approach to the measurement of poverty. Measuring without an axiomatic foundation by arbitrarily postulating some formula for condensing the fate of the poor into one number runs the risk of omitting important distributional aspects and indicating counter-intuitive poverty changes after income transfers among the population. For example, the popular income gap ratio, the relative differences between the poverty line income and the average income of those people below it, will increase after a redistribution programme that lifts some people from the range slightly below the poverty line into the range above this line. The axioms have the task of eliminating this and similarly awkward conclusions and of singling out and helping to develop in a logically consistent way those poverty indices that provide more reliable information on the "true" situation of the poor. Seidl thoroughly develops a general axiom system and uses it to examine no less than 10 different poverty indices that have been proposed in the literature. By establishing impossibility theorems that point out inconsistencies between the axioms he clarifies that none of the indices can satisfy all of the axioms presented, but he also shows why some axioms clearly dominate others. Interesting relationships between global poverty dominance and utility poverty indices which are detected in the paper help perform this task.

The second paper on poverty measurement is by *David Cowell.* Cowell tries to shed more light on the relationship between the various kinds of poverty indices by showing that some plausible axioms, similar to those of Seidl, imply that the poverty index can be written as a function of three sub-indices: one measuring the inequality among the poor, the second the inequality between the poor and the rich, and the third the absolute poverty of the poor. A number of popular indices can be subsumed under this general structure, including those of Blackorby-Donaldson, Sen, Anand, and Thon, for example. One crucial assumption made by Cowell is decomposability of the measure of inequality among the poor, which means that this measure can be written as a function of similar measures for subgroups of the poor. While this assumption is not perfectly plausible, it turns out to be extremely useful. Cowell is able to show that it implies that poverty in non-destitute societies, societies whose average income is above the poverty line, can be measured without any reference to absolute poverty. This result establishes a counterposition to Sen who stressed the significance of absolute as opposed to relative poverty and it certainly implies a substantial simplification of some of the recent literature on poverty indices.

Summarizing, I find that this volume contains an interesting and stimulating collection of papers in the field of welfare economics. Those who do not share the views of Dr. Pangloss will certainly benefit from reading it.

Applied Welfare Economics and Frisch's Conjecture

George McKenzie, Southampton, U.K.

I. Introduction

My objective in this paper is to consider a number of ambiguities which have arisen in modern applied welfare economics. At a technical level, I am not proposing to say anything new. Rather I will be concerned with the interpretation and critical assessment of some recent literature and the direction in which I believe this area of research should proceed in the future.

My point of departure is the "conjecture" offered by Ragnar Frisch (1959) about the income elasticity of the marginal utility of money, here denoted by the symbol ω:

> We may, perhaps, assume that in most cases the money flexibility has values of the order of magnitude given below:
>
> $\omega = -10$ for an extremely poor and apathetic part of the population
>
> $\omega = -4$ for the slightly better off but still poor part of the population with a fairly pronounced desire to become better off
>
> $\omega = -2$ for the middle income bracket, "the median part" of the population
>
> $\omega = -0.7$ for the better off part of the population
>
> $\omega = -0.1$ for the rich part of the population with ambitions towards "conspicuous consumption".
>
> It would be a very promising research project to determine ω for different countries and for different types of populations; a universal "atlas" of the values of ω should be constructed. It would serve an extremely useful purpose in demand analysis.

Frisch's call for a "universal atlas" has not gone unheeded, attracting interest from both applied demand analysts and public finance economists. In 1980 Theil has emphasized the importance of verifying Frisch's conjecture and has concluded that "a fair degree of consensus has developed that $\emptyset$ (the inverse of Frisch's ω)

is of the order of $-\frac{1}{2}\ldots$". Previously, Phlips (1974) had written that ω can be interpreted as "a welfare indicator — the more a country is developed, the smaller ω is likely to be..." (p. 130). Lluch, Powell, and Williams in their 1977 World Bank study argue that their results confirm Phlips' suggestion, specifically that ω is "negative, declines in absolute value with G.D.P. per capita, and lies in the interval $(-10, -0.1)$". In a similar vein, Houthakker and Taylor (1970, p. 230) write that "a major premise of the classical theory of consumer's choice is declining marginal utility of income, and since our dynamic model in its limiting long-run is consistent with classical theory, we should expect λ to decline as total expenditure increases".

Indeed all of these comments are consistent with the classical theory of public finance. Writing in 1897 Edgeworth argued that the total utility of society could only be maximized if the marginal utility of income were equal for all individuals. If he had been armed with Frisch's universal atlas the immediate policy recommendation would have been to tax the rich and give the proceeds to the poor — or more specifically, for the rich countries to extend considerable foreign aid to the poorer nations of the world. In a more modern context, public finance economists have attempted to utilize assumptions about the marginal utility of money in order to evaluate the benefits of government expenditure on public goods (e.g. Aaron and McGuire, 1969, 1970; Maital, 1973; Neuberger and Foster, 1974; and Recktenwald and Grüske, 1980).

It is my contention that Frisch's universal atlas is not the mechanism for evaluating alternative economic and social policies or for comparing individuals or nations. Indeed as we shall see below the income elasticity of the marginal utility of money is completely indeterminant. To appreciate why this is so, let us re-examine some first principles.

Perhaps the most profound development for the theory of consumer behaviour, applied demand analysis, and the theory of applied welfare analysis was the Hicks-Samuelson observation that we do not require notions of measurable utility but simply the concept of indifference. Indifference surfaces could be drawn but no longer required cardinal labelling. All we needed to know was whether the consumer preferred one bundle of goods to another or was simply indifferent between them. Of particular significance for the applied economist was the result that consumer demand functions and by implication the associated price and income elasticities were independent of any monotonic, increasing transformation of consumer preferences. An infinite number of cardinal numbering schemes could be consistent with observed consumer behaviour.

Despite this important breakthrough, however, cardinality has not simply become a chapter in treatises dealing with the history of economic thought. As teachers of economics we find it difficult to avoid terms like "utility" or level of "satisfaction" when teaching the theory of consumer behaviour. The desire for some absolute value becomes overwhelming. This trap becomes most apparent when we set about the algebra of deriving well-behaved demand functions. An objective function must be maximized subject to the budget constraint. However, to do this we must express the objective function in terms of measurable units and hence we retreat into a cardinal world in which "utility" or the "level of satisfaction" is maximized. One leading advanced textbook speaks of "preference maximization".[1] Preferences are of course ordinal but alas it is nonsense to say that we are maximizing an ordering. Even the modern reparameterization of the theory of consumer behaviour into expenditure functions is not able to avoid this dilemma. Do we not define this function as measuring the cost of achieving a given level of utility or satisfaction on the basis of a vector of commodity prices?

The purpose of the preceding discussion has simply been to remind ourselves how difficult it is to purge the vocabulary of consumer theory of cardinal concepts. We could, of course, simply treat it as a semantic problem. We are all ordinalists; since there is an infinity of cardinal representations or ordinal preferences, it doesn't matter which one we take to maximize. However, in my opinion, the basic issue is more than a semantic one. In the every day, real world of public policy making, decision takers rightly or wrongly require a cardinal measure of the economic effects of tax policies, proposed public works projects, *et cetera*. Not only do they require a cardinal measure, but they require that it should be expressed in monetary units. It is perhaps for this reason that many applied welfare economists are willing to abandon the logical purity of the ordinal theory of consumer behaviour for a cardinal approach which appears to be policy relevant (cf. Theil, 1980, p. 4).

II. Frisch's Income Flexibility: Some Red Herrings

Let us now turn our attention to some of the specific points which have motivated the development of this paper. I shall present them as a set of "red herrings".[2]

---

[1] Cf. Varian (1978).

[2] I use the term "red herring" to refer to something that is rather ambiguous. Frank Cowell has informed me that in reality, "red herrings" were actually kippers which nineteenth century English villains would distribute in order to put the police hounds on the wrong track. Of course, I do not wish to infer that those who believe that Frisch's conjecture is valid are consciously misleading us.

Red Herring 1: Frisch's income flexibility measure can be uniquely determined from the parameters of ordinary demand functions.

Consider any well-behaved preference function

$$U = U(F(X_1, \ldots, X_n)) \tag{1}$$

where U is an increasing monotonic function of F and X_i is the quantity consumed of commodity i. The first order conditions for the maximization of F with respect to the budget constraint yield

$$\frac{\partial F}{\partial X_i} = \lambda P_i, \qquad i = 1, \ldots, n. \tag{2}$$

Also valid representations of the first order conditions are those associated with the infinitely large set of feasible transformations denoted by U:

$$\frac{\partial U}{\partial X_i} = \frac{\partial U}{\partial F}\frac{\partial F}{\partial X_i} = \lambda' P_i. \tag{3}$$

By combining (2) and (3) we find that

$$\lambda' = \frac{\partial U}{\partial F}\lambda \tag{4}$$

where λ' and λ are the marginal utilities of income associated with U and F respectively. The value of λ' will vary according to whatever positive value that $\partial U/\partial F$ takes on. Since this transformation is independent of observable behaviour, then so is the associated marginal utility of income. This result is really sufficient to disprove the first "red herring". However, further insights can be obtained if we proceed a few steps further. First, let us compare Frisch's money flexibility measures generated by the function F and its transform U:

$$\omega' = \frac{\partial \lambda'}{\partial Y}\frac{Y}{\lambda'} = \frac{\partial \lambda}{\partial Y}\frac{Y}{\lambda} + \lambda Y \frac{\partial^2 U/\partial F^2}{\partial U/\partial F} = \omega + \lambda Y \frac{\partial^2 U/\partial F^2}{\partial U/\partial F} \tag{5}$$

where ω' and ω are the money flexibilities associated with U and F respectively. Although $\partial U/\partial F$ must be positive there is no sign restriction on $\partial^2 U/\partial F^2$. Consequently, Frisch's money flexibility measure may assume any value. In other words its value is dependent not upon observable consumer behaviour but upon the choice of U, something which is entirely arbitrary.

Red Herring 2: The money flexibility measure is always negative.

This alleged property is, of course, fundamental to the welfare implications of Frisch's universal atlas, for it implies that the richer you are, the less satisfaction you receive from each additional Deutsche Mark of income. However, this property can easily be shown to be independent of observable behaviour by referring back to equation (5). Since there is no sign restriction on the second-derivative of the transformation function ω' may be either positive or negative even if ω was negative. A simple example will confirm this. Let

$$F = \frac{Y - a(p)}{b(p)} \tag{6}$$

which is the general form for an indirect utility function exhibiting linear Engel curves. Then consider the following monotonic, increasing transformation of F

$$\begin{aligned} U &= a + dF^{\alpha} \\ &= a + d\left[\frac{Y - a(p)}{b(p)}\right]^{\alpha} \end{aligned} \tag{7}$$

where $d > 0$, $\alpha > 0$. The marginal utility of money associated with U is

$$\lambda = \frac{\partial U}{\partial Y} = d\alpha\left[\frac{Y - a(p)}{b(p)}\right]^{\alpha-1} \Big/ \, b(p) \tag{8}$$

which is clearly positive. To calculate Frisch's money flexibility measure we also require

$$\frac{\partial \lambda}{\partial Y} = \frac{\partial^2 U}{\partial Y^2} = d\alpha(\alpha - 1)\left[\frac{Y - a(p)}{b(p)}\right]^{\alpha-2} \Big/ \, [b(p)]^2. \tag{9}$$

Consequently,

$$\omega = \frac{Y}{\lambda}\frac{\partial \lambda}{\partial Y} = \frac{(\alpha - 1)Y}{Y - a(p)} \tag{10}$$

which can be of any sign, viz.

if	$0 < \alpha < 1$	$\omega < 0$
	$\alpha = 1$	$\omega = 0$
	$\alpha > 1$	$\omega > 0.$

This reasoning accounts for Van Praag's (1971) calculations in which he discovered the apparently counter-intuitive result that the marginal utility of money increases with income. These illustrations may appear to some readers as being extremely superfluous. Perhaps this would indeed be the case were it not for the fact that Theil has provided us with a deceptively compelling proof that $\partial\lambda/\partial Y$ is always negative.

Theil develops his "result" on the basis of the so-called Fundamental Matrix Equation

$$\begin{bmatrix} U & P \\ P' & 0 \end{bmatrix} \begin{bmatrix} \partial X/\partial Y & \partial X/\partial p' \\ -\partial\lambda/\partial Y & -\partial\lambda/\partial p' \end{bmatrix} = \begin{bmatrix} 0 & \lambda I \\ 1 & -X' \end{bmatrix} \tag{11}$$

where U is the matrix of second-order derivatives of the preference function, i.e. $\partial^2 U/\partial X_i \partial X_j$, $\partial X/\partial Y$ is a vector of income effects and $\partial X/\partial p'$ is a matrix of price effects. Equation (11) is most frequently utilized to derive the Slutsky substitution terms. However, it is a straightforward matter to derive a formula for $\partial\lambda/\partial Y$, viz.

$$\frac{\partial\lambda}{\partial Y} = \frac{1}{p'U^{-1}p}. \tag{12}$$

Theil then argues that since the matrix U must be negative semi-definite as a condition for the maximation of U, $p'U^{-1}p$ will be negative with the result that $\partial\lambda/\partial Y$ will be negative. In other words Theil would have us believe that the conditions derived from the maximization of the preference function place an observable restriction on $\partial\lambda/\partial Y$ which we have not taken into account so far.

This is a red herring of the highest quality. Consider the case of an individual consuming two commodities. The first-order condition for utility maximization is, of course,

$$\frac{\dfrac{\partial U}{\partial X_1}}{\dfrac{\partial U}{\partial X_2}} = \frac{\dfrac{\partial U}{\partial F}\dfrac{\partial F}{\partial X_1}}{\dfrac{\partial U}{\partial F}\dfrac{\partial F}{\partial X_2}} = \frac{\dfrac{\partial F}{\partial X_1}}{\dfrac{\partial F}{\partial F_2}} = \frac{P_1}{P_2}. \tag{13}$$

Equation (12) simply confirms that this condition is independent of the transformation U on F. The second-order condition for a maximum requires that the determinant of the following λ bordered Hessian matrix is positive, viz.

$$|H| = \begin{vmatrix} U_{11} & U_{12} & -P_1 \\ U_{21} & U_{22} & -P_2 \\ -P_1 & -P_2 & 0 \end{vmatrix} > 0. \tag{14}$$

Applying the transformation this determinant can be written as

$$\begin{vmatrix} \dfrac{\partial U}{\partial F}F_{11} + \dfrac{\partial^2 U}{\partial F^2}F_1^2 & \dfrac{\partial U}{\partial F}F_{12} + \dfrac{\partial^2 U}{\partial F^2}F_1F_2 & -P_1 \\ \dfrac{\partial U}{\partial F}F_{21} + \dfrac{\partial^2 U}{\partial F^2}F_1F_2 & \dfrac{\partial U}{\partial F}F_{22} + \dfrac{\partial^2 U}{\partial F^2}F_2^2 & -P_2 \\ -P_1 & -P_2 & 0 \end{vmatrix} \tag{15}$$

which in turn equals

$$\lambda \begin{vmatrix} F_{11} & F_{12} & -P_1 \\ F_{21} & F_{22} & -P_2 \\ -P_1 & -P_2 & 0 \end{vmatrix} \tag{16}$$

and which, of course, must also be positive, since λ, the marginal utility of money, is positive. The sign of the second-order condition is thus invariant under increasing, monotonic transformations.

Theil's quadratic condition $p'U^{-1}p$ can be rewritten as

$$p'[\text{adj } U]p \;/\; |U| \tag{17}$$

or

$$|H| \;/\; |U|. \tag{18}$$

We have just shown that the sign of $|H|$ is unaffected by the appropriate transformations. However such is not the case for $|U|$, viz.

$$\begin{aligned} |U| &= U_{11}U_{22} - U_{21}U_{12} \\ &= \left(\frac{\partial U}{\partial F}F_{11} + \frac{\partial^2 U}{\partial F^2}F_1^2\right)\left(\frac{\partial U}{\partial F}F_{22} + \frac{\partial^2 U}{\partial F^2}F_2^2\right) - \\ &\quad - \left(\frac{\partial U}{\partial F}F_{12} + \frac{\partial^2 U}{\partial F^2}F_1 F_2\right)^2 \\ &= \frac{\partial U}{\partial F}(F_{11}F_{22} - F_{12}F_{21}) + \frac{\partial U}{\partial F}\frac{\partial^2 U}{\partial F^2}\lambda |H|. \end{aligned} \tag{19}$$

Hence $p'U^{-1}p$ as well as $\partial\lambda/\partial Y$ may be of either sign. Indeed, for the well known metric, the equivalent variation which we shall be examining later in this paper $\frac{\partial\lambda}{\partial Y} = 0$, given base prices. The basic problem with Theil's approach is that he has attempted to introduce a sign restriction on the determinant $|U|$ whereas in point of fact such restrictions are only relevant for the bordered Hessian H.

Red Herring 3: The assumption that consumer preferences are additive in form enables us to objectively measure Frisch's money flexibility coefficient.

The analysis of the previous sections was sufficiently general for us to realize that special restrictions upon the structure of consumer preferences will have no impact on the proposition that the money flexibility measure is not independent of valid monotonic transformations of preferences. However, there is an important sense in which ω appears to come into its own.

Associated with any general preference function is the matrix of Slutsky substitution terms $\{S_{ij}\}$ where

$$S_{ij} = \frac{\partial X_i}{\partial p_j} + X_j \frac{\partial X_i}{\partial Y} = \frac{\partial X_j}{\partial p_i} + X_i \frac{\partial X_j}{\partial Y} = S_{ji}. \tag{20}$$

We can reparameterize (20) in terms of elasticities and propensities by multiplying S_{ij} and S_{ji} by $P_i P_j / Y$, viz.,

$$\begin{aligned} \sigma_{ij} &= S_{ij} \frac{Y}{P_i P_j} = W_i E_{ij} + W_j C_j \\ &= W_j E_{ji} + W_i C_i = S_{ji} \frac{Y}{P_i P_j} \end{aligned} \tag{21}$$

where E_{ij} is the ordinary elasticity of demand for commodity i with respect to the price of commodity j, C_i is the marginal propensity to consume i and W_i is the budget share $p_i X_i / Y$. We may now define the Pearce separability coefficient as

$$\Pi_{ij} = \frac{\sigma_{ij}}{C_i C_j} = \frac{\sigma_{ji}}{C_i C_j} = \Pi_{ji}. \tag{22}$$

Consider any other commodity K. Then in general

$$\Pi_{ij} \neq \Pi_{ik} \neq \Pi_{jk}$$

since

$$\sigma_{ij} \neq \sigma_{ik} \neq \sigma_{jk}$$

for all values of the commodities being consumed. However, a number of special cases are worth consideration.[3]

a) If preferences are additively separable

$$U = U(F) = U[f_1(q_1) + f_2(q_2) + \ldots + f_n(q_n)] \tag{23}$$

then

$$\Pi_{ij} = \Pi \tag{24}$$

for all n commodities.

---

[3] Cf. Byron (1970) who has designed statistical tests for the various restrictions.

b) Let $Q_A, \ldots, Q_m$ represent m vectors of individual commodities. Preferences will be called groupwise additively separable if preferences are of the form

$$U = U(F) = U[F_A(Q_A) + F_B(Q_B) + \ldots + F_M(Q_M)]. \tag{25}$$

If this is the case, then there will exist separate Pearce separability coefficients between each group,[4] that is

$$P_{AB} = \frac{\sigma_{ij}}{C_i C_j} \quad \text{where } i \in A, \; j \in B, \; A \neq B. \tag{26}$$

c) If each of the branches of b) is itself additively separable then the condition (25) holds for all pairings including $A = B$.

Whether we are considering the general definition of the Pearce separability coefficients or the more special representations noted above, we can obtain from them important, objective information about the structure of consumer preferences. They are dependent only upon observable elasticities, propensities and budget shares and hence are independent of transformations of the preference function. If we can find coefficients such that they satisfy one of a), b) or c) then we have a logical procedure for grouping commodities (Pearce, 1964).

A confusion however arises between this objectivity and Frisch's claim to be able to measure ω as σ_{ij}/C_iC_j. As Samuelson (1947, p. 175) has emphasized this will be possible only if

a) The preference function is additively separable, an assumption which places a priori restrictions on the parameters of consumer demand functions;

and

b) $U = a + bF$. In other words, not all increasing, monotonic transformations of F are admitted.

These two conditions are clearly unacceptable.

Red Herring 4: Frisch's money flexibility measure is a welfare indicator.

Having thrown out the previous three "red herrings", it immediately follows that this one cannot possibly exist as a feasible proposition either.

[4] This is the computation suggested by Pearce (1964).

III. The Equivalent Variation

The previous sections have been negative in tone in that their emphasis has been upon highlighting the inherent weaknesses of a particular strategy that many applied welfare economists have adopted. However, criticism alone is not sufficient. We require procedures which do not suffer from the above weaknesses. Indeed, applied economists have frequently criticized theorists with being too free with negative comments without offering superior alternative methods. It is this concern that has undoubtedly motivated the "new" cardinalism. Fortunately, however, there is an alternative which is not only theoretically sound but also operational.

To motivate this part of the discussion I would like to restate the five criteria which I recently suggested should be met by any operational welfare indicator (1983, p. 2).

1. For an individual or homogeneous group of individuals the measure must be capable of ranking all relevant price/quantity situations according to the preferences of the individual or homogeneous group.
2. The measure must take the form of a single metric or scale.
3. The metric or scale must be expressed in monetary units.
4. The welfare indicator must be amenable to calculation in terms of the parameters of ordinary, observable demand functions.
5. Any indicator meeting the preceding four criteria must also be capable of aggregation across individuals or homogeneous groups so as to obtain an overall indicator of the social desirability of alternative states.

The implications of these criteria are as follows. First, they rule out of consideration Marshallian *consumer surplus* and the notion of "willingness-to-pay" referred to more technically as the *compensating variation*. Both of these measures have formed the basis of applied welfare economics until recent years. In general, the Marshallian consumer surplus measure does not satisfy the first criterion since it is not ordinal. The compensating variation can be utilized to make binary comparisons but can only be utilized as the basis for an ordinal, metric scale if preferences are homothetic. The character of these measures has been the subject of considerable debate, particularly since Hicks' famous (1940) attempt to rehabilitate consumer surplus. It has also been responsible in large measure for diverting attention from the measure which does satisfy the five criteria, the *equivalent variation*.[5]

[5] The characteristics of the equivalent variation as well as other welfare indicators are discussed in McKenzie (1983), Ahlheim and Rose (1984), and McKenzie and Ulph (1986).

Suppose that we perceive a change in prices and income which improves the well-being of an individual consumer. We then ask the question: what variation in income will generate the same improvement but on the basis of the initial set of prices? It is convenient to define this notion more formally in terms of the cost function. Let $U(F(Y^0, p^0))$ represent the consumer's satisfaction (expressed in indirect form) in the original situation and $U(F(Y, p))$ the satisfaction in the new situation. Then, the equivalent variation EV may be written

$$EV = C[U(F(Y,p)); p^0] - C[U(F(Y^0, p^0)); p^0] \tag{27}$$

where the function C indicates the cost of supporting the level of satisfaction indicated, given the vector of base prices p_0.

Equation (27) has several important properties. First, the equivalent variation is independent of increasing, monotonic transformations and thus suffers none of the problems posed by the approach of the "new" cardinal school. No matter how we relabel the consumer preference ordering, the cost function is unchanged. Second, the equivalent variation is itself an increasing, monotonic transformation of consumer preferences and hence is an ordinal welfare indicator. Given base prices we can rank all alternative price/quantity situations. Third, it is expressed in monetary units in a manner which has intuitive appeal. Hence it can easily be appreciated by policy makers with little or no formal training in economics. Fourth, it can be expressed in terms of the parameters of ordinary consumer demand functions which are observable, in principle.

Before proceeding to identify a correct method for making social welfare comparisons, it is desirable to deal with two further red herrings. These relate to the properties of the equivalent variation.

5) *The equivalent variation cannot act as a welfare indicator since it is transitive only when preferences are homothetic*;

and

6) *The equivalent variation is a cardinal measure of satisfaction.*

Both are mutually contradictory claims, of course, a situation which undoubtedly reflects a certain disarray in this area of work.

Red Herring 5: This "red-herring" derives from the arguments contained in the important paper by Samuelson and Swamy in which they attempt to establish a set of criteria which index numbers should satisfy. As I have argued elsewhere (1983) the problem resides with the "circular test" which Irving Fisher had proposed and which Samuelson and Swamy have claimed "is as required as the property of transitivity itself" (1974, p. 576). The circular test appears deceptively like a transitivity test but in point of fact is much stronger. Consider Fisher's own description:

> By the so-called "circular test", taking New York as base (= 100) and finding Philadelphia 110, then taking Philadelphia as base (= 100) and finding Chicago (115), we ought, when we complete the circuit and take Chicago as base (= 115), to find, by direct comparison, New York 100 again. Or again, if Chicago is found to be 115 via Philadelphia, it ought consistently to be 115 when calculated directly [1922, p. 270].

The implications of this restriction can be appreciated if we rewrite the equivalent variation, defined by equation (27), in ratio form

$$A = \frac{C[U(F(Y,p));p^0]}{C[U(F(Y^0,p^0));p^0]} \tag{28}$$

where A is otherwise known as the Allen quantity index. For the indicator to be independent of the reference situation as implied by Fisher's "circular test" preferences must be homothetic, a situation which is empirically unrealistic (cf. Samuelson and Swamy, 1974; and McKenzie, 1983).

A question must then be asked as to whether the circular test should really be used as a criterion in the construction of applied welfare indicators. Fisher himself subsequently rejected it as "erroneous". He argued that if we were interested in comparing price/quantity situations in Norway with those in Egypt we should not utilize weights based on events in the United States. Or to paraphrase this argument into terms more relevant to the problem at hand, all that we require for welfare comparisons is the choice of a base or benchmark price/quantitiy situation. All alternative comparisons can be made with respect to this benchmark by utilizing the equivalent variation. Not only do we posses a monetary measure in the form of an equivalence scale but it is an ordinal welfare indicator. However, to require that the value of EV or A calculated in this way should also equal the value calculated by utilizing a new or alternative price/quantity situation simply does not provide us with any additional information. We should clearly abandon the circular test as superfluous.

Red Herring 6: The equivalent variation, which I am arguing should form the basis of modern applied welfare ecomomics, is, of course, expressed in monetary units. It indicates that a particular policy or event has brought about a change in satisfaction which is *equivalent* to a gain or loss in income. However, despite the fact that the equivalent variation is also an ordinal welfare indicator does not mean that we have in some sense a cardinal measure of satisfaction. We must be more careful than Mervyn King who recently argued that modern welfare economics requires "a cardinalization of utilities" (1983, p. 6). The English language can be deceptively vague at times, so let us clarify the notion of *cardinality*. A *cardinal* number is one which answers the question "how many?" whereas an *ordinal* number is one which answers the different question "what order?". It is thus clear that the equivalent variation is a cardinal metric since it indicates in deutsche marks or pounds or dollars the amount of money required to generate a particular level of satisfaction given initial prices. However, it is necessary to emphasize, as Morey (1984) has recently done, that calculation of the equivalent variation does not imply that we are able to measure the intensity of consumer preferences (cf. McKenzie and Ulph, 1986).

IV. Social Welfare Functions

An important implication of the criteria set out at the beginning of the previous section is that they introduce a dichotomy between a) the characterization of the well-being of an individual or homogeneous group of individuals and b) the process of aggregating these data into a format which can be utilized to make public policy decisions. This method is in contrast to the Frisch approach which treats the exercise as involving but one step: draw social welfare implications from the behaviour of individual consumers. Fortunately, the use of equivalent scales in conjunction with social welfare functions has now become a relatively popular approach to study the problem of income distribution. In the United Kingdom the pioneering work of Atkinson (1970) stands out along with the more recent studies of King (1984). And in the United States Jorgenson and his colleagues (1980, 1981) have taken the innovative step of measuring equivalence scales for homogeneous groups and then examining the implications of alternative public policies.

Despite these and other advances in applied welfare economics, discussions of policy issues frequently involve a confusion between the goals of economic efficiency and a desirable distribution of income. In theory a well-designed policy should be capable of achieving both maximum efficiency and an optimum distribution of income. In practice institutional conventions and market imperfections may render impossible such an outcome with the result that market efficiency can only be achieved at the cost of a sub-optimal distribution of income and vice-versa (e.g. the Common Agricultural Policy of the EEC). Thus it becomes very important that we carefully define our concepts of efficiency and social welfare and do not confuse them. Such confusion is particularly possible in attempting to interpret Harberger's third postulate of applied welfare economics (1971): when evaluating the net benefits or costs of a given action (project, program, or policy), the costs and benefits accruing to each member of the relevant group (e.g. a nation) should normally be added without regard to the individual(s) to whom they accrue.

This criterion will be the seventh and final red herring that we shall consider. The resulting indicator that is obtained by applying Harberger's third postulate is open to two possible, mutually inconsistent interpretations. First, it may be considered as an indicator of the gains or losses in *social welfare* that arise from a particular action. Second, it may be considered as an indicator of gains or losses in *efficiency* associated with that action.

If we utilize the measure in the former sense, it is necessary to make explicit the very strong value judgement implied, namely that we are indifferent between all possible distributions of income. A situation whereby individual A receives 50 Deutsche Marks and individual B receives 950 is considered to be socially equivalent to a situation where both receive 500 Deutsche Marks. In the face of criticism that he was advocating an unacceptably, value-loaded criterion, Harberger (1974, pp. 1–4) replied that he meant that his third postulate should be utilized only as an indicator of efficiency.

However, as Boadway (1974) has correctly emphasized, such an interpretation is not possible: the summation of individual compensating or equivalent variations can lead to paradoxical situations whereby one efficient distribution of consumption goods can appear to be inferior to another efficient distribution. Consider figure 1 which depicts a utility possibility frontier ZW defined in terms of individual preference functions transformed into their money metrics and with base income levels chosen as Y_1^a and Y_2^a. The total income of this two person economy is $\overline{Y}$. If we compare an alternative efficient distribution of income, such as that denoted by B, with the base situation we find the following. Individual one has enjoyed a gain equivalent to an increase in income $Y_1^b - Y_1^a$. However, the position of individual two has been made worse off, equivalent to a loss of income $Y_2^a - Y_2^b$. If we sum the two equivalent variations we find that there has been an overall "loss" even though A and B are both efficient. Hence the paradox and hence the conclusion that the sum of equivalent variations associated with any action cannot be utilized to measure efficiency.

However, if we were willing to re-interpret Harberger's third postulate as representing a social welfare measure then we will obtain a "correct" ordering. Situation A is clearly to be preferred to B. Of course, we probably would not

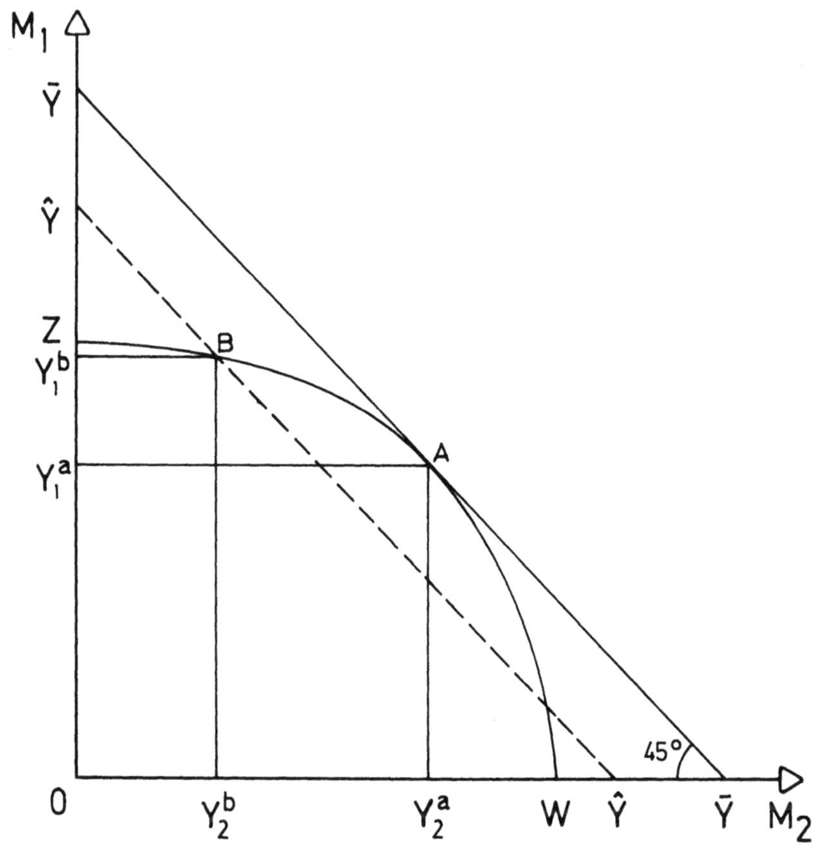

Figure 1

wish to adopt this rule as a social welfare function. However, any well-behaved social welfare function defined in terms of the money metric, or its relative, the equivalent variation, will always enable the ordering of alternative social states in a format that has a monetary interpretation.

The question then arises: is it possible to construct an indicator of efficiency which is expressable in monetary units? Consider figure 2 which involves the same utility possibility frontier as depicted in figure 1. However, let us now assume a Bergson-type social welfare function that involves a diminishing rate of substitution between the welfare of individual 1 and individual 2. Let us suppose that the initial situation is represented by point *A* and that the individual money metric indicators are defined with respect to this situation.

An improvement in efficiency can be achieved by moving from *C* to *B*. This is equivalent to a gain in income for individual 1 of $Y_1^b - Y_1^c$ and for individual 2 of $Y_2^b - Y_2^c$. Both individuals can be made better off without anyone being made worse

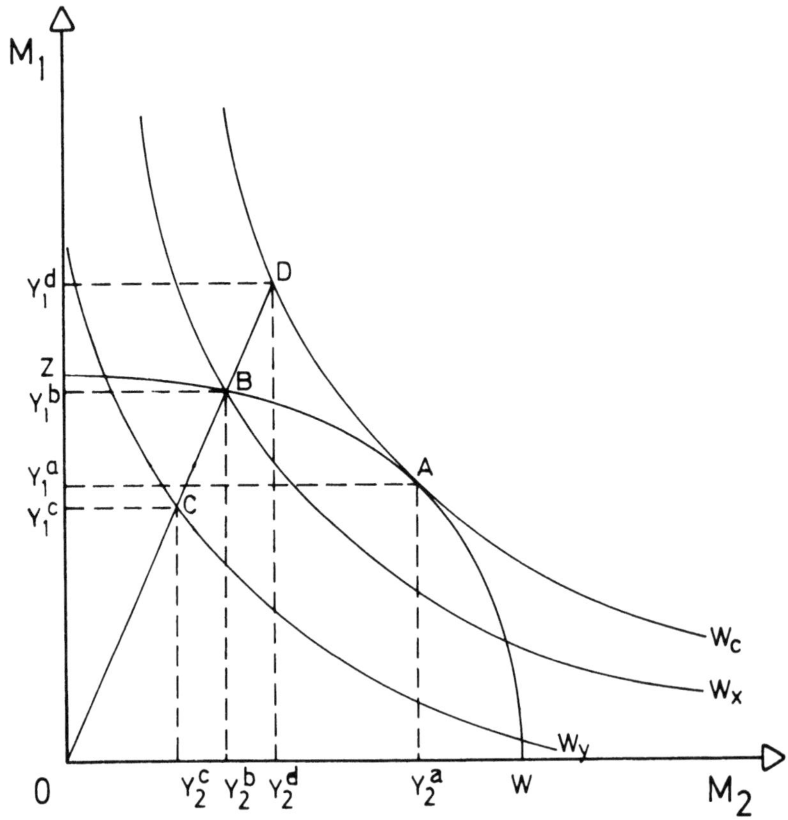

Figure 2

off. An index of this gain in Pareto efficiency is the ratio of the distance $0B/0C$. In essence, this procedure involves normalizing the utility possibility frontier such that

$$\emptyset(M_1, M_2) = \emptyset_{max}$$

where $\emptyset_{max}$ equals $0B$ and $\emptyset$ indicates the various combinations of M_1 and M_2 that are consistent with efficiency. Thus if we moved from C to A instead, this index would remain unchanged since it is impossible to make someone better off without making someone else worse off.

It should also be noted that this procedure enables us to circumvent the Boadway paradox. Summing $(Y_1^b - Y_1^c)$ and $(Y_2^b - Y_2^c)$ gives us a measure of efficiency independent of whether we move from C to B or from C to A since all distributions along the utility possibility frontier are viewed as being equivalent, but only in terms of efficiency.

However, in terms of social welfare, B is clearly inferior to situation A even though individual 2 is better off at the expense of individual 1. What we now require is an index defined *not* with respect to $\emptyset_{max}$ but with respect to W_0. Thus a move from C to A is equivalent to a move from C to D and hence to a gain in income of $Y_1^d - Y_1^c$ for individual 1 and $Y_2^d - Y_2^c$ for individual 2. From a social welfare point of view A is clearly to be preferred to B even though both A and B are equally efficient.

The above analysis suggests that any public policy action can be divided into two components:

i) an efficiency effect,

and ii) a redistribution effect.

Thus the move from C to A has an efficiency effect associated with the move from C to B whereas the redistribution effect involves a move along the utility possibility frontier from B to A. In monetary terms, the efficiency gain is $(Y_1^b - Y_1^c)+(Y_2^b - Y_2^c)$, as defined above, whereas the redistribution gain is $(Y_1^d - Y_1^b)+(Y_2^d - Y_2^b)$.

Conceptually, the above arguments are fairly straightforward. However, the question remains: how should we construct the required social welfare function in practice? The answer is that there can be no single welfare function that we can all agree upon. To the extent that we come from different religious, cultural and social heritages, we will probably have different objectives. To the extent that we share similar objectives we will probably attach different weights or importance to them. However, this is the fundamental problem of public policy formulation. By clearly identifying objectives and their relative importance, policy makers are taking a first step in dealing with contentious issues between different groups or nations. Indeed, intellectual experiments designed to identify the logical implications of alternative policies can be a first step in reducing the wooly arguments that frequently characterize public debate.

VI. Conclusions

In this paper we have compared two divergent approaches to applied welfare economics. We have shown that despite its intuitive appeal work based upon Frisch's money flexibility possesses inherent logical defects and hence has no operational value. In contrast, utilization of the equivalent variation in the context of a social welfare function not only should satisfy the theorist but also possesses an ease of interpretation which will be appealing to policy makers. And, of course, like the Frisch approach it requires estimation of the parameters of demand systems to enable calculation of the equivalent variation. Empirical demand studies will thus remain an integral part of applied welfare economics.

References

Aaron, H., (1970): "Public Goods and Income Distribution." *Econometrica* 38: 907–920.

Aaron, H., and **McGuire, M.** (1969): "Efficiency and Equity in the Optimal Supply of a Public Good." *Review of Economics and Statistics* 51: 31–39.

Ahlheim, M., and **Rose, M.** (1984): "Alte und neue Maße individueller Steuerlasten." *Finanzarchiv* 42: 274–349.

Allen, R. G. D. (1949): "The Economic Theory of Index Numbers." *Economica* 16: 197–203.

Atkinson, A. B. (1970): "On the Measurement of Inequality." *Journal of Economic Theory* 2: 224–263.

Boadway, R. (1974): "The Welfare Foundations of Cost-Benefit Analysis." *Economic Journal* 84: 926–939.

Byron, R. P. (1970): "A Simple Method for Estimating Demand Systems Under Separable Utility Assumptions." *Review of Economic Studies* 37: 261–274.

Clements, K. W.; **Finke, R.**; and **Theil, H.** (1984): "Frisch's Conjecture and the Own-Price Elasticity of the Demand for Food." *Economics Letters* 15: 1–4.

Debreu, G. (1951): "The Coefficient of Resource Utilization." *Econometrica* 19: 273–292.

Debreu, G. (1954): "A Classical Tax-Subsidy Problem." *Econometrica* 22: 14–22.

Edgeworth, F. Y. (1897): "The Pure Theory of Taxation." Economic Journal 7: 550–571.

Finke, R.; **Lu, W.**; and **Theil, H.** (1984): "A Cross-Country Tabulation of Own-Price Elasticities of Demand." *Economics Letters* 14: 137–142.

Frisch, R. (1932): *New Methods of Measuring Marginal Utility*. Tübingen: G. Mohr.

Frisch, R. (1959): "A Complete Scheme for Computing all Direct and Cross Demand Elasticities in a Model with Many sectors." *Econometrica* 27: 177–196.

Harberger, A. (1971): "Three Basic Postulates for Applied Welfare Economics." *Journal of Economic Literature* 9: 785–797.

Harberger, A. (1974): *Taxation and Welfare.* Boston: Little, Brown and Co.

Hicks, J. R. (1981): *Value and Capital.* Oxford: Oxford University Press.

Houthakker, H. S., and **Taylor, L. D.** (1970): *Consumer Demand in the United States, 1929-1970.* Cambridge, Mass.: Harvard University Press.

Jorgenson, D. W.; **Lau, L. J.**; and **Stoker, T. M.** (1980): "Welfare Comparison Under Exact Aggregation." *American Economic Review* 70: 268–272.

Jorgenson, D. W.; **Lau, L. J.**; and **Stoker, T. M.** (1981): "Aggregate Consumer Behaviour and Individual Welfare." In *Macroecomomic Analysis*, edited by D. Currie, R. Nobay, and D. Pell. London: Croom-Helm, pp. 35–61.

King, M. A. (1984): "Tax Policy and Family Welfare." (Second Annual Sir Eric Roll Lecture.) Discussion Papers in Economics and Econometrics No. 8314, Southampton: University of Southampton.

Lluch, C.; **Powell, A. A.**; and **Williams, R. A.** (1977): *Patterns in Household Demand and Saving.* Oxford: Oxford University Press.

McKenzie, G. W. (1983): *New Methods for Measuring Economic Welfare.* Cambridge: Cambridge University Press.

McKenzie, G. W., and **Pearce, I. F.** (1976): "Exact Measures of Welfare and the Cost of Living." *Review of Economic Studies* 43: 465-468.

McKenzie, G. W., and **Ulph, D.** (1986): "Exact Welfare Measures." *Economic Perspectives* 4: 7–49.

Maital, S. (1973): "Public Goods and Income Distribution: Some Further Results." *Econometrica* 41: 561–568.

Morey, E. R. (1984): "Confuser Surplus." *American Economic Review* 74: 163–173.

Neuburger, H., and **Foster, C.** (1974): "The Ambiguity of the Consumer's Surplus Measure of Welfare Change." *Oxford Economic Papers* 26: 66–77.

Pearce, I. F. (1964): *A Contribution to Demand Analysis.* Oxford: Oxford University Press.

Phlips, L. (1974): *Applied Consumption Analysis.* Oxford: Oxford University Press.

Recktenwald, H., and **Grüske, K.-D.** (1980): "Justiva Distributiva durch Umverteilung? Eine Analyse der personalen Budgetinzidenz." *Kyklos* 33: 16–62.

Samuelson, P. A. (1947): *Foundations of Economic Analysis.* Cambridge, Mass.: Harvard University Press.

Samuelson, P. A. (1974): "Complementarity — An Essay on the 40th Anniversary of the Hicks-Allen Revolution in Demand Theory." *Journal of Economic Literature* 12: 1255–1289.

Samuelson, P. A., and **Swamy, S.** (1974): "Invariant Economic Index Numbers and Canonical Duality: Survey and Synthesis." *American Economic Review* 64: 566–593.

Theil, H. (1980): *The System-Wide Approach to Microeconomics.* Oxford: Basil Blackwell.

Van Praag, B. (1971): "The Welfare Function of Income in Belgium: An Empirical Investigation." *European Economic Review* 2: 337–369.

Varian, H. (1978): *Microeconomic Analysis.* New York: Norton.

Vartia, Y. O. (1983): "Efficient Methods of Measuring Welfare Change and Compensated Income in Terms of Demand Functions." *Econometrica* 51: 79–98.

A Reconsideration of Debreu's "Coefficient of Resource Utilization"

Michael Ahlheim, Heidelberg, West Germany*

I. Introduction

Since Gerard Debreu introduced his "Coefficient of Resource Utilization" to the economic literature in 1951 this measure has always been present there in footnotes, "notes in the margin", and so on, but there are only very few articles in which this measure played more than a mere tangential role. The main reason for this is, as I think, that many economists have the strong feeling that "there is something in it", but that it is not quite clear what this really is. The intention of this paper is to review the Debreu Coefficient by first giving it an explicit mathematical form and then investigating its technical and economic properties in some detail.

The scope of the paper is as follows: chapter II gives a description of the model which is a simple general equilibrium model with one representative consumer and several (different) producers. The assumption that consumer behaviour can be described in terms of one single consumer allows us to disregard problems of distribution here in favour of other points which seem to be of greater importance in this context. The extension of the model to a many-consumer economy is rather simple and will be discussed in chapter VI. In section 2 of chapter II a specific mathematical form of the Debreu Coefficient is defined and introduced to the model.

In chapter III the most significant mathematical properties of the Debreu Coefficient are investigated in more detail to facilitate further work with this measure. The second part of this chapter is dedicated to the analysis of the relationship between the Debreu Coefficient and the Shephard distance function of household and production theory.

In chapter IV it is checked whether the Debreu Coefficient has the most important properties of a welfare measure for a one-consumer economy as assumed here, while in chapter V we investigate the applicability of the Debreu Coefficient as a measure of (social) efficiency. Of course, in a one-consumer economy an in-

* I am grateful to Egbert Dierker and to George McKenzie for many helpful comments and suggestions.

crease in efficiency implies an increase in welfare and vice versa but, nevertheless, welfare and efficiency are two completely different concepts with different economic meanings. For that reason they are treated separately here. Debreu himself designed his coefficient as a measure of efficiency, but the analysis in chapter IV shows that in the case of a one-consumer economy it is not worse a (theoretical) welfare measure than any other which is discussed in the literature.

In chapter V three different concepts of social efficiency are introduced and for each of them it is shown under which special set of assumptions (concerning consumption and production) the Debreu Coefficient is a "true" indicator of the respective kind of efficiency.

The last chapter is dedicated to the extension of the analysis to a many-consumer economy and to the problems arising in this context. One possibility for such an extension consists in the introduction of a social welfare function to the model. In this case the analysis remains the same as for the one-consumer economy. If one does not like the concept of a social welfare function one is forced to argue on the basis of the so-called Scitovsky indifference curves, and it is shown in chapter VI that in this case the Debreu Coefficient is not a true indicator of welfare nor of Pareto efficiency.

II. Description of Debreu's "Coefficient of Resource Utilization" for an Economy With One Representative Consumer

II.1 The model

As indicated in the introductory remarks the consumption sector of our model consists of only one ("representative") consumer. This simplification makes it possible to abstract from all problems of distribution and to extend the scope of possible applications of the Debreu Coefficient as will be shown below.

The consumption activity of the representative consumer in a situation k ($k \in \{0, 1, 2, \ldots, K\}$) is given by his consumption vector $x^k \in \mathbf{X}$, where $\mathbf{X} \subset \mathbb{R}^N$ is the set of all consumption vectors possible for the consumer. It has the following properties:

(II–1) The consumption set $\mathbf{X} \subset \mathbb{R}^N$ is closed, bounded from below, and convex.

The positive components of x^k are quantities consumed while its negative components are quantities produced by the consumer (e.g. different kinds of labour). The preference ordering of the consumer is characterized by the binary relation "$\succeq$" ("is at least as desired as") and has the following properties:

(II–2) The preference ordering of the representative consumer is a given complete preordering "$\succeq$" on the consumption set $\mathbf{X}$, which is reflexive, transitive, continuous, monotonic,[1] and convex.

From (II–2) we can derive the upper contour sets

(II–3) $$\mathbf{B}(x^k) = \{x \mid x \in \mathbf{X},\ x \succeq x^k\}$$

for any consumption bundle $x^k \in \mathbf{X}$. The set $\mathbf{B}(x^k)$ has the following properties:

(II–4)
a) $\mathbf{B}(x^k) \subset \mathbf{X}$.
b) $\mathbf{B}(x^k) \neq \emptyset$.
c) $\mathbf{B}(x^k)$ is closed.
d) $\mathbf{B}(x^k)$ is convex.
e) $\mathbf{B}(x^k)$ is bounded from below.
f) $x \in \mathbf{B}(x^k) \ \Rightarrow\ x + x' \in \mathbf{B}(x^k),\ \forall\, x' \in \mathbb{R}^{N+}$.[2]
g) $x^k \succeq x^j \iff \mathbf{B}(x^k) \subset \mathbf{B}(x^j),\ \forall\, x^k, x^j \in \mathbf{X}$.

The production activity of the whole economy is represented by a production vector $y \in \mathbf{Y}$, where $\mathbf{Y} \subset \mathbb{R}^N$ is the set of all production vectors possible for the economy. The positive components of y are inputs while its negative components are outputs.[3] The production possibility set $\mathbf{Y}$ of the whole economy has the following properties:

(II–5)
a) $\mathbf{Y} \subset \mathbb{R}^N$.
b) $\mathbf{Y} \neq \emptyset$.
c) $\mathbf{Y}$ is closed.
d) $\mathbf{Y}$ is convex.
e) $\mathbf{Y} \cap \{-\mathbf{Y}\} = \{0_N\}$.
f) $y \in \mathbf{Y} \ \Rightarrow\ y + y' \in \mathbf{Y},\ \forall\, y' \in \mathbb{R}^{N+}$.
g) $\mathbf{Y} \cap \mathbb{R}^{N--} = \emptyset$.

---

[1] I.e. $x^k > x^j \ \Rightarrow x^k \succeq x^j,\ \forall\, x^k, x^j \in \mathbf{X}$.
We use the following notations for inequalities among vectors:
$x^k \geq x^j \iff x^k_n \geq x^j_n,\ \forall\, n \in \{1, 2, \ldots, N\}$,
$x^k > x^j \iff (x^k \geq x^j) \wedge (x^k \neq x^j)$,
$x^k \gg x^j \iff x^k_n > x^j_n,\ \forall\, n \in \{1, 2, \ldots, N\}$.

[2] By $\mathbb{R}^{N+}$ ($\mathbb{R}^{N++}$) we mean the non-negative (positive) orthant of the N-dimensional Euclidean space. Analogously we mean its non-positive (negative) orthant by $\mathbb{R}^{N-}$ ($\mathbb{R}^{N--}$).

[3] The fact that $\mathbf{X} \subset \mathbb{R}^N$ and $\mathbf{Y} \subset \mathbb{R}^N$ does not necessarily imply that consumption vectors and production vectors must have the same dimension in our model since some of the elements of a consumption vector x may be equal to zero.

These assumptions are rather common and do not need any further explanation. We assume that there are M individual production units in our economy and that the production possiblity set of each of these production units is given by $\mathbf{Y}_m$ $(m = 1, 2, \ldots, M)$ with

$$\text{(II–6)} \qquad \mathbf{Y} = \sum_m \mathbf{Y}_m,$$

i.e. the family of individual production possibility sets $\mathbf{Y}_m$ is a decomposition of the overall production possibility set $\mathbf{Y}$. From this it follows that the production vector y for the whole economy equals the sum of all individual production vectors y_m; i.e. in a situation k we have

$$\text{(II–7)} \qquad y^k = \sum_m y_m^k, \qquad y_m^k \in \mathbf{Y}_m,$$

where y_m^k is the individual production vector of the mth production unit in situation k.

It should be emphasized that $\mathbf{Y}$ gives us the technical production possibilities of our economy and, therefore, is independent of the limitation of physical resources. A vector y represents the net output of the economy, where a single commodity can be an input for some individual production units and an output for some others, i.e., the existence of intermediary goods is not excluded here.

Fig. II–1 shows the set $\mathbf{Y}$ for the two-commodity case, where commodity 1 is an output while commodity 2 is an input.

If we add up the consumption vector x^k of a situation k and the respective production vector y^k we get the vector $z^k \in \mathbb{R}^N$ of *utilized* physical resources:

$$\text{(II–8)} \qquad z^k = x^k + y^k.$$

The vector z^k represents the total net consumption of the whole economy in situation k. Under the assumption that our economy is closed, this net consumption must come from the preexisting stock of available resources which is represented by the vector $z^0 \in \mathbb{R}^{N++}$. We call z^0 the vector of *utilizable* physical resources.

It follows that there are two restrictions for the consumption possibilities of our economy: one is the existing technology (which is represented by the production possibility set $\mathbf{Y}$), and the other is the stock of utilizable resources (which is represented by the vector z^0). The set of realizable consumption vectors x is therefore given by:

$$\text{(II–9)} \qquad \mathbf{C}(\mathbf{Y}, z^0) = \{x | x \in \mathbf{X},\ x = z - y,\ y \in \mathbf{Y},\ z \leq z^0\}.$$

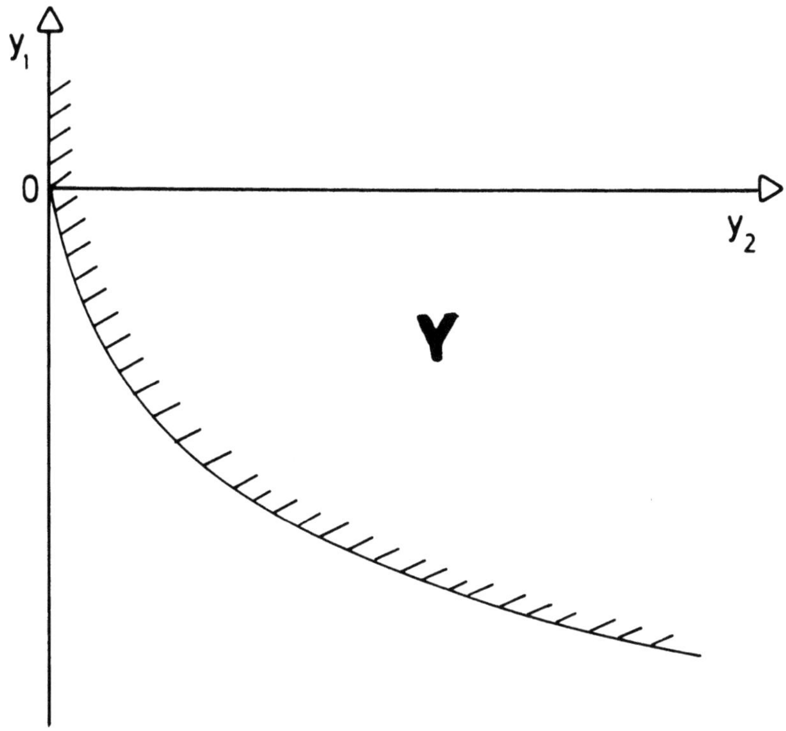

Figure II–1

From the relation between consumption on the one hand and technology and the utilization of resources on the other it follows that a consumption bundle x^k can be produced by utilizing any resources vector z out of the set $\{x^k + \mathbf{Y}\}$. Therefore, each vector x from consumption space can be represented by the set $\{x + \mathbf{Y}\}$ in the resources space, where $z \notin \{x + \mathbf{Y}\}$ means that x cannot be realized with the resources vector z.

By this procedure we can map each upper contour set $\mathbf{B}(x^k)$ point by point from the consumption space into the resources space. There we get a system of upper contour sets $\mathbf{Z}(x^k)$ in resources space with

$$\text{(II–10)} \qquad \mathbf{Z}(x^k) = \mathbf{B}(x^k) + \mathbf{Y}.$$

A set $\mathbf{Z}(x^k)$ is the set of all resources vectors z, the utilization of which permits the production of a consumption bundle that is at least as desired as the bundle x^k. The system of all sets $\mathbf{Z}(x)$ represents the preference ordering of our consumer in the resources space.

From (II–10) and from (II–4), (II–5) we can derive the following typical properties of an upper contour set

(II–11) $$\mathbf{Z}(x^k) = \{z | z = x + y,\ y \in \mathbf{Y},\ x \in \mathbf{B}(x^k)\}$$

in the resources space:

(II–12)
a) $\mathbf{Z}(x^k) \subset \mathbb{R}^N$.
b) $\mathbf{Z}(x^k)$ is closed. [4]
c) $\mathbf{Z}(x^k)$ is convex. [5]
d) $z \in \mathbf{Z}(x^k) \implies z + z' \in \mathbf{Z}(x^k), \quad \forall\, z' \in \mathbb{R}^{N+}$. [6]
e) $x^k \succeq x^j \iff \mathbf{Z}(x^k) \subset \mathbf{Z}(x^j)$. [7]

The exact form of the sets $\mathbf{Z}(x^k)$ depends on the preference ordering of the consumer (as represented by the system of his upper contour sets $\mathbf{B}(x^k)$) and on the available technology (as represented by the production set $\mathbf{Y}$).

It can be shown that for each boundary point $z^{k*} \in bd\,\mathbf{Z}(x^k)$[8] there is a non-negative price vector $p^{k*} \neq 0_N$ and an income so that the consumer realizes the most desired consumption bundle possible under the respective budget restriction and each production unit $m \in \{1, 2, \ldots, M\}$ maximizes its profit (i.e. minimizes $p^{k*} y_m$): [9]

A convex set has a non-zero normal at each of its boundary points, i.e., in each of its boundary points it is supported by a hyperplane with a non-zero normal.[10] Moreover, from (II–12) it follows that the normals to a set $\mathbf{Z}(x^k)$ are non-negative (resp. non-positive, but they never have positive and negative components simultaneously). So for each point $z^{k*} \in bd\ \mathbf{Z}(x^k)$ there is a vector $p^{k*} > 0_N$ which is such that

$$p^{k*} z \geq p^{k*} z^{k*}, \qquad \forall\, z \in \mathbf{Z}(x^k)$$

or

(II–13) $$p^{k*}[z - z^{k*}] \geq 0, \qquad \forall\, z \in \mathbf{Z}(x^k).$$

[4] The set $\mathbf{Z}(x^k)$ is the sum of the non-empty, closed, and convex sets $\mathbf{B}(x^k)$ and $\mathbf{Y}$. There is no direction of recession of one of these sets, the opposite of which is a direction of recession of the other (the recession cone of any set $\mathbf{B}(x^k)$ equals $\mathbb{R}^{N+}$ since $\mathbf{B}(x^k)$ is bounded from below; the opposite of the set $\mathbb{R}^{N+}$ is the set $\mathbb{R}^{N-}$ which does not contain any direction of recession of $\mathbf{Y}$ because of (II–5f) and (II–5d)). Therefore, the sum of $\mathbf{B}(x^k)$ and $\mathbf{Y}$ must be a closed set, too (cf. Rockafellar, 1970, p. 75).

[5] The sum of two convex subsets of $\mathbb{R}^N$ is convex, too (cf. Takayama, 1974, p. 17).

[6] This follows from (II–4e) and (II–5e).

[7] This follows from (II–4f).

[8] By "$bd\,\mathbf{Z}(x^k)$" we mean the set of all finite boundary points of the set $\mathbf{Z}(x^k)$.

[9] Cf. Debreu (1951, pp. 280–281).

[10] Cf. Rockafellar (1970, p. 100).

From (II–11) it follows that

$$\text{(II–14)}\quad p^{k*}[x - x^{k*}] + \sum\nolimits_m p^{k*}[y_m - y_m^{k*}] \geq 0, \qquad \forall\, x \in \mathbf{B}(x^k),\ y_m \in \mathbf{Y}_m,$$

where

$$x^{k*} + \sum\nolimits_m y_m^{k*} = z^{k*}, \qquad x^{k*} \in \mathbf{B}(x^k),\ y_m^{k*} \in \mathbf{Y}_m.$$

This condition is fulfilled if and only if each summand of (II–14) is non-negative, for if one of them were negative, as all the others could be made zero, the whole sum could be made negative. Therefore, $z^{k*} \in bd\,\mathbf{Z}(x^k)$ if and only if

$$\text{(II–15)}\qquad p^{k*}y_m^{k*} \leq p^{k*}y_m, \qquad \forall\, y_m \in \mathbf{Y}_m,\ (m = 1, 2, \ldots, M),$$

and

$$\text{(II-16)}\qquad p^{k*}x^{k*} \leq p^{k*}x, \qquad \forall\, x \in \mathbf{B}(x^k).$$

This is equivalent to saying that y_m^{k*} and x^{k*} are boundary points of the sets $\mathbf{Y}_m$ $(m = 1, 2, \ldots, M)$ and $\mathbf{B}(x^k)$ respectively.

If we interpret p^{k*} as a price vector (II–15) says that each production unit m reaches its profit maximum over its feasible production set $\mathbf{Y}_m$ for the price vector p^{k*} at the production vector y_m^{k*}. Analogously, it follows from (II–16) that with prices p^{k*} the consumption bundle x^{k*} is the cheapest of all consumption bundles that are at least as desired by the consumer as x^k; i.e. x^{k*} solves the consumer's cost minimization problem under the restriction that he shall consume a bundle at least as desired as x^k. If we rewrite (II–16) as

$$x \in \mathbf{B}(x^k) \implies p^{k*}x^{k*} \leq p^{k*}x,$$

we see that this is equivalent to

$$p^{k*}x < p^{k*}x^{k*} \implies x \notin \mathbf{B}(x^k), \qquad (\text{i.e. } x^k \succ x).^{11}$$

This means that with prices p^{k*} all consumption bundles that are cheaper than x^{k*} are less desired than x^k, so that there is no consumption bundle in the set $\{x | p^{k*}x \leq p^{k*}x^{k*}\}$ that is more desired than x^{k*}. Therefore, (II–16) is equivalent to the fact that x^{k*} maximizes the consumer's satisfaction under the budget restriction $p^{k*}x \leq p^{k*}x^{k*}$.

It has been shown that for every boundary point $z^{k*} \in bd\,\mathbf{Z}(x^k)$ of an upper contour set $\mathbf{Z}(x^k)$ in resources space there is a non-negative price vector $p^{k*} \neq 0_N$ (that is the normal of a supporting hyperplane to the set $\mathbf{Z}(x^k)$ through z^{k*})

---

[11] $x^k \succ x \iff (x^k \succeq x) \wedge (x \not\succeq x^k)$. Analogously, we have $x^k \sim x \iff (x^k \succeq x) \wedge (x \succeq x^k)$.

and an income $p^{k*}x^{k*}$ such that all production units m maximize their profits $p^{k*}y_m$ under the restriction of their feasible production sets $\mathbf{Y}_m$ and the consumer chooses the consumption bundle most desired by him under the budget restriction $p^{k*}x \leq p^{k*}x^{k*}$.

After this general description of our model we are now ready to introduce Debreu's "Coefficient of Resource Utilization".

II.2 The Debreu Coefficient

We assume that there is a vector $z^0 \in \mathbb{R}^{N++}$ which represents the stock of all available resources of the economy under consideration. Debreu calls it the "*vector of utilizable resources*". This vector gives us the quantities of all resources that — in our case of a closed economy — are available to realize a consumption bundle x^k ($k \in \{1, 2, \ldots, K\}$). The utilization of the resources z^0 for the realization of the consumption bundle x^k is optimal in the sense of Debreu if there is no consumption bundle x^{k*} that is at least as desired as x^k and that could be realized by utilizing a resources vector z^{k*} which is a fraction smaller than one of the utilizable resources vector z^0 (i.e. $z^{k*} \doteq \gamma z^0$, $\gamma \in [0,1)$); therefore, an optimal allocation of the available resources z^0 in a situation k implies that z^0 is the smallest fraction of itself that allows the production of a consumption bundle that is at least as desired as x^k. In all other cases there is a waste of resources that could be caused, e.g., by underemployment of physical resources (in this case we would have $z^{k*} \ll z^0$ and $z^k < z^0$, where z^k is the vector of resources actually utilized in situation k) or by inefficiencies in production and/or in economic organization like distortionary indirect taxation, tariffs or the existence of imperfections of trade like monopolies (in these cases we would have $z^k = z^0$, but still $z^{k*} \ll z^0$) or by both.

As an indicator of the extent of this economic waste, Debreu introduced his "*Coefficient of Resource Utilization*" which equals *the smallest fraction of the vector of utilizable resources z^0 that would permit the realization of a consumption bundle that is at least as desired as the actually realized consumption bundle x^k*. For given technology $\mathbf{Y}$ the Debreu Coefficient is a function of the vector of utilizable resources $z^0 \in \mathbb{R}^{N++}$ and of the actually realized consumption bundle $x^k \in \mathbf{X}$. So, for a situation k it can be expressed in terms of a function δ which is defined by

$$\text{(II–17)} \qquad \delta(z^0, x^k) = \min_{\gamma \in \mathbf{\Gamma}(z^0, x^k)} \gamma, \qquad \mathbf{\Gamma}(z^0, x^k) = \{\gamma | \gamma \in \mathbb{R}^+,\ \gamma z^0 \in \mathbf{Z}(x^k)\}.$$

The Debreu Coefficient D^k for a situation k is therefore given by

$$\text{(II–18)} \qquad D^k = \delta(z^0, x^k).$$

By definition (II–17) it follows that the Debreu Coefficient takes on the value one if and only if the actual resource utilization is optimal in the sense described above. In all cases of non-optimal resource utilization the value of the Debreu Coefficient is smaller than one. This can also be seen from figure II–2 below:

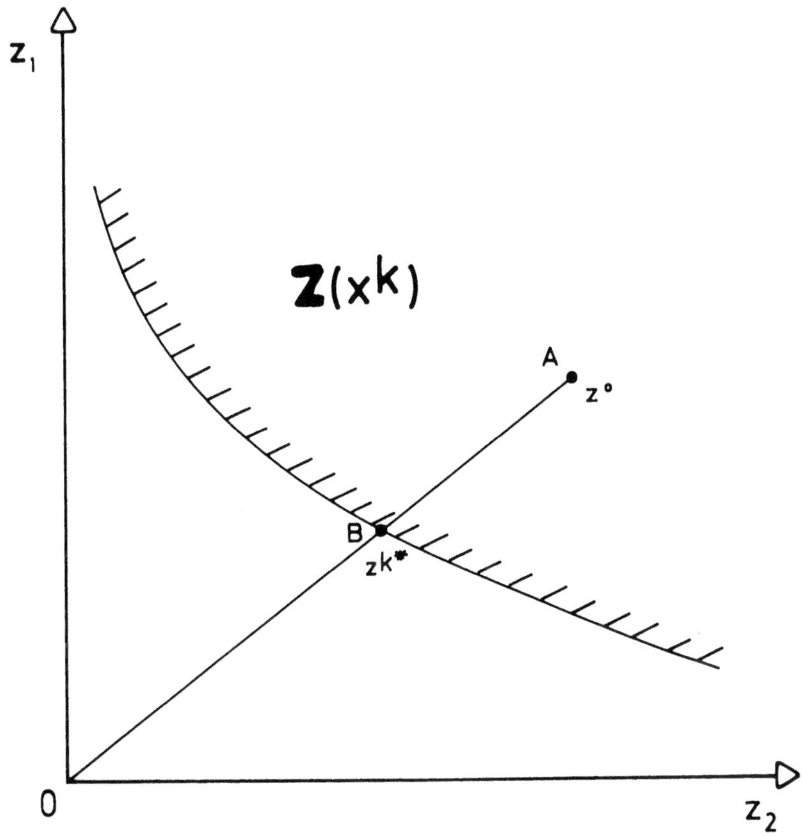

Figure II–2

Here the Debreu Coefficient for the situation k equals the ratio of the norms of the vectors z^{k*} and z^0, i.e.

(II–19) $$D^k = \|z^{k*}\| \;/\; \|z^0\| = 0B/0A.$$

From (II–17) it follows that z^{k*}, the smallest resources vector with direction z^0 that permits the realization of a consumption bundle x^{k*} not less desired than

x^k, is given by

$$z^{k*} = D^k \cdot z^0. \tag{II–20}$$

From the definition of D^k it follows that z^{k*} must be a boundary point of the upper contour set $\mathbf{Z}(x^k)$. Further, it must be an element of $\mathbb{R}^{N++}$ because $z^0 \in \mathbb{R}^{N++}$. Therefore, we have

$$z^{k*} \in bd^{++}\, \mathbf{Z}(x^k), \tag{II–21}$$

where

$$bd^{++}\, \mathbf{Z}(x^k) = bd\, \mathbf{Z}(x^k) \cap \mathbb{R}^{N++}$$

is the set of all positive finite boundary points of $\mathbf{Z}(x^k)$.

While D^k is a dimensionless indicator of economic inefficiency the so-called *Economic Loss*, i.e. the vector

$$l^k = [z^0 - z^{k*}] = (1 - \delta(z^0, x^k))z^0 \tag{II–22}$$

gives us the extent of this inefficiency in physical units of the several kinds of resources that could be saved without making the consumer worse off.

If one prefers to argue in monetary terms, Debreu (1951, p. 288) recommends to multiply the Economic Loss l^k with the actually observed price vector p^k to get the *Monetary Value of the Economic Loss*:

$$M^k = p^k[z^0 - z^{k*}] = (1 - \delta(z^0, x^k))p^k z^0. \tag{II-23}$$

It is evident that these two measures are only minor variations of the same idea that can be expressed in physical units by the "Economic Loss", in monetary units by the "Monetary Value of the Economic Loss", or as a dimensionless index number by the "Coefficient of Resource Utilization" itself. Therefore, in what follows we shall concentrate on the properties of the Debreu Coefficient alone, since the properties of the other two measures can easily be derived from that.

III. The Main Characteristics of the Debreu Coefficient

III.1 General Characteristics

From the previous chapter it follows that the Debreu Coefficient can be represented by a function $\delta : \{\mathbf{X} \times \mathbb{R}^{N++}\} \to \mathbb{R}^+$ with

(III–1) $\delta(z,x) =$

$$= \begin{cases} \min\limits_{\gamma \in \mathbf{\Gamma}(z,x)} \gamma, \quad \mathbf{\Gamma}(z,x) = \{\gamma | \gamma \in \mathbb{R}^{++},\ \gamma z \in \mathbf{Z}(x),\ z \in \mathbb{R}^{N++}\} & , x \in \mathbf{X}^+, \\ 0 & , x \in \{\mathbf{X} \setminus \mathbf{X}^+\}, \end{cases}$$

where[12]

$$\mathbf{X}^+\{x | x \in \mathbf{X},\ 0_N \notin \mathbf{Z}(x)\} \subset \mathbf{X}.$$

This definition is equivalent to (II–17) since it was assumed there that $z^0 \in \mathbb{R}^{N++}$ and since it follows from (II–17) that $\delta(z,x) = 0$ for all $x \notin \mathbf{X}^+$, i.e. for all consumption bundles x that can be realized by utilizing non-positive quantities of all available resources. Of course such cases are economically irrelevant and can be neglected in our further analysis. The domain of the function δ has been divided into $\mathbf{X}$ and $\mathbf{X}^+$ just for convenience because some of the properties of this function that shall be considered in this part of the paper are only valid for $x \in \mathbf{X}^+$.

The Debreu Coefficient is defined in a way that the variables z and x are independent of each other. In all cases in which $z \in \mathbf{Z}(x)$ the value of δ is not greater than one. But the general mathematical definition (III–1) includes not only these economically "reasonable" cases but also all other cases in which $z \notin \mathbf{Z}(x)$, i.e. cases in which the consumption bundle x cannot be realized with the available resources z. In particular we have for all $x \in \mathbf{X}^+$:

(III–2)
a) $\delta(z,x) = 1 \iff z \in bd^{++}\,\mathbf{Z}(x)$
b) $0 < \delta(z,x) < 1 \iff z \in int^{++}\,\mathbf{Z}(x)$
c) $\delta(z,x) > 1 \iff z \notin \mathbf{Z}(x)$,

where

$$int^{++}\,\mathbf{Z}(x) = int\,\mathbf{Z}(x) \cap \mathbb{R}^{N++}$$

is the set of all positive interior points of $\mathbf{Z}(x)$. From (III–1) and (III–2) it follows that

(III–3) The Debreu Coefficient is homogeneous of degree (-1) in $z \in \mathbb{R}^{N++}$, i.e. for all $\alpha > 0$ and $x \in \mathbf{X}^+$ we have $\delta(\alpha z, x) = \alpha^{-1}\delta(z,x)$.

---

[12] By $\{\mathbf{X} \setminus \mathbf{X}^+\}$ we mean the complement of $\mathbf{X}^+$ relative to $\mathbf{X}$.

Proof: Let (i) $\delta(z,x) = \alpha\ (>0)$ for some $z \in \mathbb{R}^{N++}$, $x \in \mathbf{X}^+$.
$\Longrightarrow\ \alpha z \in bd^{++}\,\mathbf{Z}(x)$ [by def. (III–1)] $\Longrightarrow\ \delta(\alpha z, x) = 1$ [by (III–2)] $\Longrightarrow\ \delta(\alpha z, x) = \alpha^{-1}\delta(z,x)$ [by (i)].

Summing up one has:

(III–4) $\qquad \delta(z,x^k) = \gamma^k \iff \delta(\gamma^k z, x^k) = 1 \iff \gamma^k z \in bd^{++}\,\mathbf{Z}(x^k).$

It can be shown now that for a given stock of available resources z the Debreu Coefficient classifies different consumption bundles $x \in \mathbf{X}^+$ in the same way the consumer's preference ordering does. I.e.

(III–5) $\qquad \delta(z,x^k) \geq \delta(z,x^j) \iff x^k \succeq x^j, \qquad x^k, x^j \in \mathbf{X}^+,\ z \in \mathbb{R}^{N++}.$

Proof: Let $\delta(z,x^k) = \gamma^k \geq \delta(z,x^j) = \gamma^j \iff \gamma^k z \geq \gamma^j z \iff \mathbf{Z}(x^k) \subset \mathbf{Z}(x^j)$ [by (III-4)] $\iff x^k \succeq x^j$ [by (II–12e)].

Since (III–5) is just the definition of an ordinal utility function[13] we can say that *for a given stock of available resources the Debreu Coefficient is just a certain monotonic transformation of the consumer's direct utility function*, and so it is a utility function itself (with domain $\mathbf{X}^+$). This follows also from the fact that

(III–6) For a given vector of utilizable resources $z \in \mathbb{R}^{N++}$ the upper and lower level sets of the Debreu Coefficient with respect to $x \in \mathbf{X}^+$ are equal to the upper and lower contour sets of the consumer's preference ordering respectively.

Proof: Let $\delta(z,x^k) = \gamma^k$ with $x^k \in \mathbf{X}^+$. From (III–5) we have $\{x | x \in \mathbf{X}^+, \delta(z,x) \geq \gamma^k\} = \{x | x \in \mathbf{X}^+,\ x \succeq x^k\} = \mathbf{B}(x^k)$.

As a consequence of the fact that the Debreu Coefficient is a utility function (for a given stock of available resources) we expect that it has also the typical characteristics of direct utility functions, especially monotonicity and quasiconcavity with respect to x:

(III–7) The Debreu Coefficient is a monotonic, increasing function with respect to $x \in \mathbf{X}^+$, i.e.
$x^k > x^j \Longrightarrow \delta(z,x^k) \geq \delta(z,x^j), \qquad x^k, x^j \in \mathbf{X}^+,\ z \in \mathbb{R}^{N++}.$

---

[13] Cf. Arrow and Hahn (1971, p. 82).

Proof: Let $x^k > x^j \implies x^k \succeq x^j$ [by (II–2)] $\implies \delta(z, x^k) \geq \delta(z, x^j)$ [by (III–5)].

(III–8) The Debreu Coefficient is quasiconcave with respect to $x \in \mathbf{X}^+$, i.e. for $z \in \mathbf{R}^{N++}$ we have
$$\delta(z, x^k) \geq \delta(z, x^j) \implies \delta(z, (1-\alpha)x^k + \alpha x^j) \geq \delta(z, x^j), \quad \alpha \in [0,1].$$

Proof: Let $\delta(z, x^k) \geq \delta(z, x^j) \implies x^k \succeq x^j$ [by (III–5)] $\implies (1-\alpha)x^k + \alpha x^j \succeq x^j$, $\alpha \in [0,1]$ [by (II–2)] $\implies \delta(z, (1-\alpha)x^k + \alpha x^j) \geq \delta(z, x^j)$ [by (III–5)].

After having clarified the properties of the function δ with respect to x we now want to investigate its characteristics with respect to z.

(III–9) The Debreu Coefficient is a monotonic, (semi-strictly) decreasing function with respect to $z \in \mathbf{R}^{N++}$, i.e.
a) $z^1 > z^2 \implies \delta(z^1, x) \leq \delta(z^2, x)$
b) $z^1 \gg z^2 \implies \delta(z^1, x) < \delta(z^2, x)$,
with $x \in \mathbf{X}^+$.

Proof: Let $\delta(z^1, x) = \gamma^1$ and $\delta(z^2, x) = \gamma^2 \implies \gamma^1 z^1 \in bd^{++}\,\mathbf{Z}(x)$ and $\gamma^2 z^2 \in bd^{++}\,\mathbf{Z}(x)$ [by (III–4)] $\implies \gamma^1 z^1 \not\gg \gamma^2 z^2$ [by (II–12)] $\implies (z^1 > z^2 \implies \gamma^1 \leq \gamma^2) \wedge (z^1 \gg z^2 \implies \gamma^1 < \gamma^2)$.

So for a given standard of living $x \in \mathbf{X}^+$ the value of the Debreu Coefficient is the greater, the smaller the stock of utilizable resources is, i.e. an economy is "appreciated" more by the Debreu Coefficient than another if it generates a certain standard of living with less available resources than the other. At this point the efficiency aspect of the Debreu Coefficient becomes obvious while in (III–5) its welfare aspect was emphasized. So for a given stock of utilizable resources the Debreu Coefficient has some characteristics of a welfare measure, while for a given standard of living it has certain characteristic features of an efficiency measure. The appropriateness of the Debreu Coefficient as a welfare or an efficiency measure will be investigated below while here we shall concentrate on the more technical properties of the function δ.

From (III–2) it follows immediately that

(III–10) $$\mathbf{Z}(x)^{++} = \{z | z \in \mathbf{R}^{N++},\ \delta(z, x) \leq 1\}, \qquad x \in \mathbf{X}^+,$$

with

$$\mathbf{Z}(x)^{++} = \mathbf{Z}(x) \cap \mathbf{R}^{N++}\ [\subset \mathbf{Z}(x)],$$

i.e. the positive part of the upper contour set in resources space $\mathbf{Z}(x)$ for a given standard of living $x \in \mathbf{X}^+$ equals the lower level set for the level $\delta = 1$ of the function δ with respect to $z \in \mathbb{R}^{N++}$ for the same standard of living.

Because of the homogeneity property (III–3) we have the following relation between the lower level sets of δ with respect to z for a given standard of living $x \in \mathbf{X}^+$:

(III–11)
$$\{z|z \in \mathbb{R}^{N++},\ \delta(z,x) \leq \alpha\} = \\ = \alpha^{-1}\{z|z \in \mathbb{R}^{N++},\ \delta(z,x) \leq 1\} = \alpha^{-1}\mathbf{Z}(x)^{++}.$$

Proof: $\alpha^{-1}\{z|z \in \mathbb{R}^{N++}, \delta(z,x) \leq 1\} = \{z|z \in \mathbb{R}^{N++}, z = \alpha^{-1}\hat{z}, \delta(\hat{z},x) \leq 1\}$ $= \{z|z \in \mathbb{R}^{N++},\ \delta(\alpha z,x) \leq 1\} = \{z|z \in \mathbb{R}^{N++},\ \alpha^{-1}\delta(z,x) \leq 1\}$ [by (III–3)] $= \{z|z \in \mathbb{R}^{N++},\ \delta(z,x) \leq \alpha\}$.
The second equality of (III–11) follows from (III–10).

This means that for a given standard of living $x \in \mathbf{X}^+$ all lower level sets of δ with respect to z are radial blow-ups or reductions of each other. So if we know the characteristics of one of them we know them all.

The convexity of the lower level sets of δ that follows from (III–10), (III–11), and (II–12c) is equivalent to the quasiconvexity of δ with respect to z.[14] Therefore, we have:

(III–12) The Debreu Coefficient is a quasiconvex function with respect to $z \in \mathbb{R}^{N++}$, i.e. for each $\alpha \in [0,1]$
$$\delta(z^1,x) \geq \delta(z^2,x) \implies \delta((1-\alpha)z^1 + \alpha z^2, x) \leq \delta(z^1,x), \quad x \in \mathbf{X}^+.$$

From the quasiconvexity of the Debreu Coefficient it follows that[15]

(III–13) If the function $\delta(z,x)$ is differentiable with respect to $z \in \mathbb{R}^{N++}$ at $[\hat{z},x]$, $\hat{z} \in \mathbb{R}^{N++}$ and $x \in \mathbf{X}^+$, then
$$\delta(z,x) \leq \delta(\hat{z},x) \implies \text{grad}_z\, \delta(\hat{z},x)[z-\hat{z}] \leq 0,$$

where $\text{grad}_z \delta(\hat{z},x)$ is the gradient vector of $\delta(z,x)$ with respect to z at $[\hat{z},x]$.

For a given consumption bundle $x^k \in \mathbf{X}^+$ the set $\mathbf{Z}(x^k)^{++}$ equals the lower level set of the function $\delta(z,x^k)$ for the level $\delta = 1$, as was shown in (III–10). From (III–2) we know that for any boundary point $z^{k*} \in bd^{++}\,\mathbf{Z}(x^k)$ it holds that

(III–14)
$$\delta(z,x^k) \leq \delta(z^{k*},x^k) \quad [=1], \qquad \forall\, z \in \mathbf{Z}(x^k)^{++}.$$

[14] Cf. Mangasarian (1969, p. 133).
[15] Cf. Mangasarian (1969, p. 134).

If δ is differentiable at $[z^{k*}, x^k]$ then it follows from (III–13) that

(III–15) $$\text{grad}_z\, \delta(z^{k*}, x^k)[z - z^{k*}] \leq 0, \qquad z \in \mathbf{Z}(x^k)^{++}.$$

This means that there is a supporting hyperplane

$$\mathbf{H}(z^{k*}, x^k) = \{z | z \in \mathbb{R}^N,\ \text{grad}_z\, \delta(z^{k*}, x^k) z \leq \beta, \quad \forall\ z \in \mathbf{Z}(x^k)^{++}\}$$

with

$$\beta = \text{grad}_z\, \delta(z^{k*}, x^k) z^{k*}$$

to the set $\mathbf{Z}(x^k)^{++}$ (and therefore to $\mathbf{Z}(x^k)$) through the boundary point $z^{k*} \in bd^{++}\,\mathbf{Z}(x^k) \subset bd\,\mathbf{Z}(x^k)$ where $\text{grad}_z\, \delta(z^{k*}, x^k)$ is the normal of that hyperplane. In chapter II.1 it was shown that any non-negative normal vector p^{k*} of a supporting hyperplane to the set $\mathbf{Z}(x^k)$ through a boundary point z^{k*} can be interpreted (in combination with (non-profit) income $I^k = p^{k*} z^{k*} = p^{k*}[x^{k*} + \sum_m y_m^k])$ as a general equilibrium price vector of our model. Observing that $\text{grad}_z \delta(z^{k*}, x^k)$ is non-positive [by (III–9)] we can, therefore, conclude that the gradient of the function δ at $[z^{k*}, x^k]$ with respect to z equals the negative of the general equilibrium price vector p^k, that ensures the realization of a consumption bundle not less desired than x^k by optimal[16] utilization of the vector z^{k*}. The (non-profit) income that guarantees the existence of an equilibrium of our model at prices $p^{k*} = -\text{grad}_z\, \delta(z^{k*}, x^k)$ is $I^k = -\text{grad}_z\, \delta(z^{k*}, x^k) z^{k*}$ as was shown in chapter II.1.

Because of the homogeneity of δ according to (III–3) it follows by Euler's Theorem that

(III–16) $$-\text{grad}_z\, \delta(z^{k*}, x^k) z^{k*} = 1.$$

I.e. the income that corresponds to the general equilibrium price vector $p^k = -\text{grad}_z\, \delta(z^{k*}, x^k)$ is identical one so that p^k can be interpreted also as the normalized general equilibrium price vector of our model. Therefore, as *a result we have that the gradient of the function δ at $[z^{k*}, x^k]$ with respect to z equals the negative of the normalized general equilibrium price vector which makes sure that a consumption bundle not less desired than x^k is realized by optimally utilizing the resources vector z^{k*}*, i.e.

(III–17) $$-\text{grad}_z\, \delta(z^{k*}, x^k) = p^{k*}/I^k = p^{k*}.$$

So, there is a direct relation between our functional representation of the Debreu Coefficient and the general equilibrium of our model in the sense that we can

[16] By "optimal" we mean that it would not be possible to realize a consumption bundle at least as desired as x^k by utilizing a fraction smaller than one of the resources vector z^{k*}.

generate the general equilibrium price vector for the (optimal) realization of any standard of living x^k by taking the first derivatives of δ at a point $[z^{k*}, x^k]$, where $z^{k*} \in bd^{++}\,\mathbf{Z}(x^k)$.

Because of the formal similarity of the function δ to the Shephard distance function this result reminds us of a well-known theorem of household theory, the so-called Shephard-Hanoch Lemma. This lemma tells us that the gradient of the Shephard distance function equals the vector of the normalized compensated inverse demand functions of the consumer. So, one could be tempted to interpret the gradient of δ as the vector of some sort of inverse market demand functions. This would be wrong, of course, since the relation (III–17) is true only for boundary points of $\mathbf{Z}(x^k)^{++}$, i.e., it is not a general functional relation but applies only to some single elements of the domain of δ. For all points $[z, x^k]$ where z is not a boundary point of $\mathbf{Z}(x^k)^{++}$ there is no comparable interpretation of $\operatorname{grad}_z \delta(z, x^k)$. The fact that the gradient of δ is no compensated inverse demand function becomes obvious for formal reasons, too, if one recalls that such demand functions must be homogeneous of degree zero with respect to all commodities, while $\operatorname{grad}_z \delta$ is homogeneous of degree (-2) in z because of (III–3).[17]

The question arises whether there would be another result if we described the Debreu Coefficient in terms of the Shephard distance function. This function can be defined on our system of upper level sets $\mathbf{Z}(x^k)$ in resources space by:[18]

$$\text{(III–18)} \qquad d(z,x) = \\ = \max_{\sigma \in \mathbf{S}(z,x)} \sigma, \quad \mathbf{S}(z,x) = \{\sigma | \sigma \in \mathbb{R}^{++},\ [z/\sigma] \in \mathbf{Z}(x),\ z \in \mathbb{R}^{N++},\ x \in \mathbf{X}^{+}\}.$$

From this definition and from (III–1) it becomes obvious that

$$\text{(III–19)} \qquad D^k = \delta(z,x) \equiv 1/d(z,x), \qquad z \in \mathbb{R}^{N++},\ x \in \mathbf{X}^{+},$$

i.e., the Debreu Coefficient is just the reciprocal of the distance function. Therefore,

$$\text{(III–20)} \qquad \operatorname{grad}_z \delta(z,x) = -\operatorname{grad}_z d(z,x)/(d(z,x))^2, \qquad z \in \mathbb{R}^{N++},\ x \in \mathbf{X}^{+}.$$

From definition (III–18) it follows that for all positive boundary points of a set $\mathbf{Z}(x^k)$ the value of the distance function is equal to one so that (III–20) becomes

$$\text{(III–21)} \quad \operatorname{grad}_z \delta(z^{k*}, x^k) = -\operatorname{grad}_z d(z^{k*}, x^k), \qquad z^{k*} \in bd^{++}\,\mathbf{Z}(x^k),\ x^k \in \mathbf{X}^{+}.$$

[17] If a function is homogeneous of degree h its partial derivatives are homogeneous of degree $(h-1)$. Cf. Sydsæter (1981, p. 128).

[18] Normally the distance function is defined on a utility index u which is a function of consumption goods x (cf. Ahlheim, 1985, pp. 298 ff.) instead of defining it directly on x, but the definition chosen here seems to be more appropriate for our problem.

Furthermore it follows from definition (III–18) that $\mathbf{Z}(x^k)^{++}$ equals the upper level set of the function $d(z, x^k)$ for the level $d = 1$, so that $\text{grad}_z\, d(z^{k*}, x^k) \geq 0_N$ is the normal of a supporting hyperplane to the set $\mathbf{Z}(x^k)$ through z^{k*}. Therefore, by the same argument as above, the gradient of the distance function $\text{grad}_z\, d(z^{k*}, x^k)$ can be interpreted as the general equilibrium price vector p^{k*} of our model for (non-profit) income $I^k = \text{grad}_z\, d(z^{k*}, x^k) z^{k*}$. Since d is positively linear homogeneous in z this income is equal to one and the gradient of the Shephard distance function with respect to z is a normalized general equilibrium price vector of our model, i.e.

$$\text{(III-22)} \qquad \text{grad}_z\, d(z^{k*}, x^k) = p^{k*}/I^k = p^{k*} = -\text{grad}_z\, \delta(z^{k*}, x^k).$$

So we have again that the gradient of the Debreu Coefficient at a positive boundary point of $\mathbf{Z}(x^k)$ with respect to z equals the negative of a normalized general equilibrium price vector of our model.

But again, as in the case of the function δ, this relation holds only for boundary points of the set $\mathbf{Z}(x^k)^{++}$ and not for the whole domain of the distance function. For all points $z \notin bd^{++}\, \mathbf{Z}(x^k)$ the value of $d(z, x^k)$ in (III–20) is not equal to one, so that (III–22) does not hold in these cases. Furthermore the general expression for the gradient of the Debreu Coefficient in terms of the distance function is given by (III–20). Since this expression is homogeneous of degree (-2) in z it does not fulfill the integrablility conditions for compensated inverse demand functions.[19] Therefore the gradient of the Debreu Coefficient in terms of the distance function cannot be interpreted as a vector of inverse compensated demand functions. So there would be no advantage in using this version of a functional representation of the Debreu Coefficient. On the contrary, this version is not only mathematically more complicated than our function δ, but it also implies the risk of misinterpretations because of its formal similarity to the household distance function according to Shephard. All those nice microeconomic properties of the Shephard distance function which are based on the duality implications of household theory are not valid for our function d, because d is defined on a system of upper contour sets which contains not only the preference ordering of the representative consumer but also the whole technology of our economy.

The detection of a direct relation between the Debreu Coefficient and whatever kind of demand function would have been of great interest in view of the empirical determination of the Debreu Coefficient. But unfortunately no such relation could be found.

---

[19] This follows from the linear homogeneity of the distance function (cf. Diewert, 1982, p. 560).

After having shown the most important mathematical properties of the Debreu Coefficient and its functional representation δ in this section we shall now proceed to the investigation of its economic properties, especially of its suitability as a measure of welfare and/or efficiency.

IV. The Debreu Coefficient as a Measure of Individual Welfare

Before we check the suitability of the Debreu Coefficient for the measurement of individual welfare we should formulate some basic criteria which an operational welfare indicator should fulfill.

The first criterion is a rather obvious one: starting from a given initial situation 0 of our economy, the welfare measure W should be capable of indicating whether a new state k ($k \in \{1, 2, \ldots, K\}$) which is represented by the consumption bundle $x^k \in \mathbf{X}^+$ is preferred to the initial state by the consumer or not, i.e.

$$\text{(IV–1)} \qquad W^k \geq W^0 \iff x^k \succeq x^0, \qquad x^0, x^k \in \mathbf{X}^+.$$

The second criterion goes a little farther: a suitable welfare indicator should be capable of ranking simultaneously the welfare changes from the initial situation 0 to several alternative new states k ($k \in \{1, 2, \ldots, K\}$) of our economy according to the preference ordering of the representative consumer, i.e.

$$\text{(IV–2)} \qquad (W^k - W^0) \geq (W^j - W^0) \iff x^k \succeq x^j, \qquad x^k, x^j \in \mathbf{X}^+.$$

So the welfare measure must take the form of a single metric or scale for all relevant projects. A well-known example for a welfare measure that fulfills the first criterion but fails to fulfill the second is the Hicksian Compensating Variation.[20]

Another rather self-evident criterion is

(IV-3) The welfare measure W must be uniquely determined for all relevant states of the economy.

A famous welfare measure that fails to fulfill this criterion is the Dupuit-Marshall-Measure of consumer surplus which depends on line integrals that are not path-independent in general.

[20] Cf. Ahlheim and Rose (1984, p. 300).

Of course one can find many more and more demanding criteria for welfare measures in the literature[21] but we shall confine ourselves to the criteria (IV–1) to (IV–3) that form the absolute minimum standard for a reliable *theoretical* welfare indicator. These three criteria say nothing about the empirical computation of the welfare measure under consideration and thus say nothing about its qualities as a practical or *empirical* welfare indicator. But an operational welfare indicator must be not only a reliable theoretical welfare indicator but also a reasonable empirical welfare indicator. The critical point here is that such a measure should be computable from data which really can be determined by empirical work. So we have:

(IV–4) A reliable *theoretical* welfare indicator is also a reasonable *empirical* welfare indicator if it can be exactly computed on the basis of uncompensated (i.e. observable) direct or indirect household demand functions.

From our results in chapter III we know that for a given vector of utilizable resources z^0 the Debreu Coefficient fulfills the criteria (IV–1) to (IV–3) for a reliable theoretical welfare indicator. But, as was explained at the end of chapter III, there seems to be no convincing way to compute the Debreu Coefficient solely on the basis of household demand functions, since it is based on the representative consumer's preference ordering as well as on the technological possibilities of the M production units of our economy, and since the Debreu Coefficient does not seem to be "decomposable" according to these different influences. Therefore, duality theorems which are important for the empirical computation of a measure like Roy's Identity are not valid for the Debreu Coefficient because it contains not only the household demand functions (like a "normal" utility function) but also the supply functions of the firms and the working of the whole market mechanism (which leads to the normalized general equilibrium price vector as a gradient of the Debreu Coefficient). So, none of these single elements can be identified separately from the Debreu Coefficient as would be necessary to "reconstruct" any kind of demand (or supply) function from it.

Debreu (1954) himself worked out a possibility for a first-order approximation of the "Monetary Value of the Economic Loss" [cf. (II–23)], but this computation is only valid for such states of the economy which are in the neighbourhood of a Pareto optimal initial state. So, these computations are completely unsatisfactory in the light of criterion (IV–4) since they are neither exact under computational nor sufficiently general under theoretical aspects.

---

21 See e.g. McKenzie (1983, p. 2), or Ebert (1984).

To sum up it can be said that for a given vector of utilizable resources the Debreu Coefficient is a reliable *theoretical* welfare indicator. In principle the coefficient can be calculated, however, no satisfactory way for its empirical computation has yet been published.

It is obvious that there is no sense in comparing two or more states of our economy with different stocks of utilizable resources under the welfare aspect since the Debreu Coefficient will show different values for each new vector of utilizable resources even if the relevant consumption bundle stays the same (as can easily be verified from fig. II–2). Comparisons of situations with different vectors of available resources for the realization of one and the same standard of living are a matter of efficiency and not of welfare measurement as will be shown in the following chapter.

V. The Debreu Coefficient as a Measure of Efficiency

When we talk about efficiency in economics we are talking about the relation between a certain economic result and the efforts made to achieve this result. In production theory this means the relation between output and input quantities, while in a general equilibrium model like ours efficiency is a matter of the realized standard of living (or welfare) on the one hand and the quantities of utilizable resources on the other (which are to be regarded as completely "spent" in this context, no matter whether some of them are left idle or not, since idle resources are not used in any utility generating way). Thus, for a given standard of living a certain state of the economy is more efficient the smaller the stock of available resources is, because in this case less available resources mean less waste of resources. Analogously, for a given stock of utilizable resources a situation is more efficient the higher the realized standard of living is, i.e. the more the consumer appreciates the consumption bundle that is realized in this situation.

But efficiency is not only a "relative" property like welfare which allows us to compare certain states of the economy with each other, but also an "absolute" one in the sense that one can determine the degree of efficiency for each single state of the economy. Though there are several different concepts of efficiency, as will be shown below, they all have in common that each of them defines a reference situation, the "efficient" state of the economy, as a yardstick which makes it possible to determine the (absolute) degree of efficiency of each single state of the economy. Thus, efficiency is not only a matter of ranking like (ordinal) utility or welfare but also of absolute measurement and scaling in the sense that one can say, e.g., that efficiency has doubled from one situation to another, while a comparable statement is not possible in the utility/welfare context. This is the most significant difference between the concepts of welfare and efficiency in a one-consumer-economy where all problems of distribution are excluded.

From all that has been said about the concept of efficiency, it follows that an operational efficiency measure should meet the following three requirements: first, it should be able to indicate if a certain situation is an "efficient state" or not; second, it should be able to rank different situations according to their degree of (in)efficiency; third, it should guarantee a consistent scaling of all degrees of (in)efficiency. It should be clear that besides these special conditions, an efficiency measure should also fulfill the general requirements (IV–3) and (IV–4). Since these requirements were already discussed in the context of welfare measurement in chapter IV there is no need to raise this matter here again. From chapter IV we know that the theoretical value of the Debreu Coefficient is determined uniquely but that there seems to be no satisfying way for its empirical computation. Therefore, all that will be said below concerns only the properties of the Debreu Coefficient as a theoretical measure of efficiency.

In the economic literature we find essentially three different concepts of efficiency which can be used in a general equilibrium context: two of them, Koopmans Efficiency and Farell Efficiency, are known from production theory but they can easily be generalized for the application to models of the whole economy, while the third one, the Pareto Efficiency, is a well-known concept of social efficiency which can be applied directly to our model. We shall now define these concepts in turn and check whether the Debreu Coefficient is an operational measure for each of them.

Generalizing Koopmans' concept of technical efficiency[22] for the general equilibrium context, we get for a situation k ($k \in \{0, 1, 2, \ldots, K\}$) which is characterized by a consumption bundle $x^k \in \mathbf{X}^+$ and a vector of utilizable resources $z^{0k} \in \mathbf{Z}(x^k)^{++}$, the following definition:

(V–1) A situation $[z^{0k}, x^k]$ with $z^{0k} \in \mathbf{Z}(x^k)^{++}$ and $x^k \in \mathbf{X}^+$ is *Koopmans efficient* if

$$z < z^{0k},\ z \in \mathbf{R}^{N++} \implies z \notin \mathbf{Z}(x^k).$$

This means that a situation k is Koopmans efficient if the standard of living x^k could not be realized with a resources vector z that is smaller than the vector of available resources z^{0k}.

[22] Cf. Koopmans (1951, p. 60).

To check the suitability of the Debreu Coefficient for indicating Koopmans Efficiency we have to put our above mentioned general criteria for an operational efficiency measure into a concrete form that takes into account the special characteristics of Koopmans Efficiency. Following Färe and Lovell[23] we require that the Debreu Coefficient δ in order to be an operational indicator of Koopmans Efficiency, meet the following conditions for all $z \in \mathbf{Z}(x)^{++}$ and $x \in \mathbf{X}^{+}$:

(V–2) a) $\delta(z,x) = 1 \iff z \in \mathbf{E}(x)^{++}$,
where $\mathbf{E}(x)^{++} = \{z | z \in \mathbf{Z}(x)^{++},\ z' < z \Longrightarrow z' \notin \mathbf{Z}(x)\}$

b) $z' > z \Longrightarrow \delta(z',x) < \delta(z,x)$,

c) $\delta(\alpha z, x) = \alpha^{-1}\delta(z,x), \quad \forall\, \alpha \in [\delta(z,x), \infty)$.

The scaling condition (V–2c) is fulfilled by (III–3) but the ranking condition (V–2b) and the "identification condition" (V–2a) are not fulfilled as can be seen from fig. V–1a:

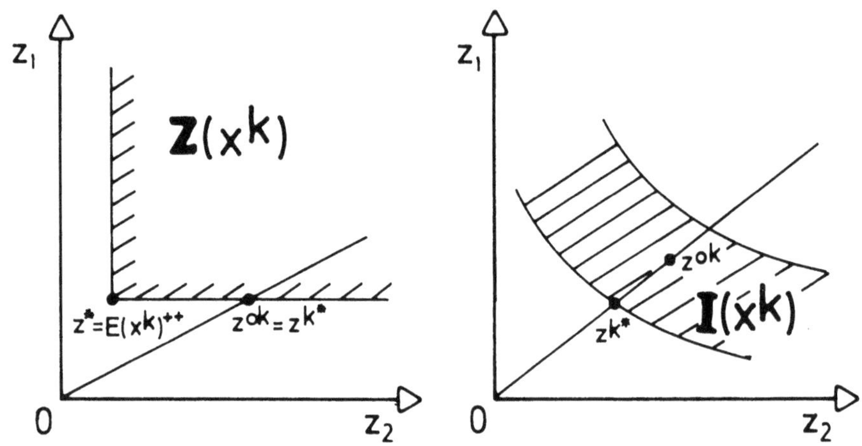

(a) (b)

Figure V–1

In this figure we have the typical Leontief indifference curves. The vector of utilizable resources z^{0k} is just a boundary point of the set $\mathbf{Z}(x^k)$ so that the

[23] Färe and Lovell (1978) presented in a production theory context a catalogue of four requirements a measure of productive efficiency should meet. Russell (1984) showed that one of these four criteria is redundant because, if properly defined, it can be derived from the other three. (V–2) is based on the three remaining Färe-Lovell criteria which are reformulated for our social efficiency context.

Debreu Coefficient takes on the value of one in this case, as follows from (III–2), i.e. $\delta(z^{0k}, x^k) = 1$ because any *proportional* cut of the vector z^{0k} would make it impossible to realize a consumption bundle which is not less desired than x^k (therefore $z^{0k} = z^{k*}$). But obviously the resources vector z^* is smaller than z^{0k} though it is also an element of $\mathbf{Z}(x^k)$. Therefore situation $[z^{0k}, x^k]$ is not efficient in the Koopmans sense because it is possible to realize the standard of living x^k by utilizing the resources vector z^* which is smaller than z^{0k}.

Obviously then there are cases where the Debreu Coefficient identifies situations as "efficient" which are actually inefficient in the Koopmans sense. The reason for this identification error in the case of Leontief indifference curves is that the set of resources vectors which are Koopmans efficient for the realization of a standard of living x^k, i.e. the set $\mathbf{E}(x^k)^{++}$, is only a subset of the positive boundary of the set $\mathbf{Z}(x^k)$ for which the Debreu Coefficient takes on the value of one. In figure V-1a the Koopmans efficient set $\mathbf{E}(x^k)^{++}$ consists only of the vector z^*. Summing up, we can conclude that the Debreu Coefficient fails to meet the Färe-Lovell conditions (V–2a) and (V–2b), and therefore is *not a reliable measure for Koopmans Efficiency.*

Another concept of efficiency that is frequently discussed in the literature on production theory is offered by Farrell (1957). A situation $[z^{0k}, x^k]$ with $z^{0k} \in \mathbf{Z}(x^k)^{++}$ and $x^k \in \mathbf{X}^+$ is Farrell efficient if any proportional cut of the resources vector z^{0k} makes it impossible to realize a consumption bundle which is not less desired than x^k, i.e.

(V–3) A situation $[z^{0k}, x^k]$ with $z^{0k} \in \mathbf{Z}(x^k)^{++}$ and $x^k \in \mathbf{X}^+$ is *Farrell efficient* if

$$z = \beta z^{0k},\ \beta \in [0,1),\ z \in \mathbf{R}^{N++} \implies z \notin \mathbf{Z}(x^k).$$

Reformulating the Färe-Lovell conditions for an operational measure of Farrell Efficiency we get:

(V–4) a) $\delta(z,x) = 1 \iff z \in \mathbf{F}(x)^{++}$,
where $\mathbf{F}(x)^{++} = \{z | z \in \mathbf{Z}(x)^{++},\ \beta z \notin \mathbf{Z}(x),\ \beta \in [0,1)\}$.

b) $z' = \beta z,\ \beta \in [0,1) \implies \delta(z', x) > \delta(z,x)$.

c) $\delta(\alpha z, x) = \alpha^{-1}\delta(z,x), \quad \forall\, \alpha \in [\delta(z,x), \infty)$.

The scaling condition (V–4c) is again fulfilled by (III–3) while the ranking condition (V–4b) is also fulfilled here by (III–9), since $\alpha z \ll z$ for $\alpha \in [0,1)$. From (III–10) and (III–1) it is clear that $\mathbf{F}(x)^{++} = bd^{++}\,\mathbf{Z}(x)$ for all $x \in \mathbf{X}^+$, so that the Debreu Coefficient also meets the identification condition (V–4a) by (III–2). Therefore the *Debreu Coefficient is a reliable measure of Farrell Efficiency.*

Our last concept of social efficiency is the well-known Pareto concept. It assumes a given stock of utilizable resources and asks whether or not it is possible with this given stock of resources to raise the actual standard of living. If this is not possible a Pareto efficient state of the economy is reached. For a one-consumer-economy where no distribution problems exist we have a rather simple version of Pareto Efficiency:

(V–5) A situation $[z^{0k}, x^k]$ with $z^{0k} \in \mathbf{Z}(x^k)^{++}$ and $x^k \in \mathbf{X}^+$ is *Pareto efficient* if
$$x \succ x^k,\ x \in \mathbf{X}^+ \implies z^{0k} \notin \mathbf{Z}(x).$$

Unlike the other two efficiency concepts the Pareto criterion compares situations with different standards of living, i.e. with different levels of utility of the representative consumer. From this it is clear that there is no point in postulating any homogeneity property like (V–2c) and (V–4c) as a scaling requirement for the measure of Pareto Efficiency since this would imply an inadmissible restriction of the consumer's preference ordering. Therefore our Färe-Lovell conditions become here for all $x \in \mathbf{X}^+$, $z \in \mathbf{Z}(x)^{++}$:

(V–6) a) $\delta(z, x) = 1 \iff z \in \mathbf{I}(x)^{++}$,
where $\mathbf{I}(x)^{++} = \{z | z \in \mathbf{Z}(x)^{++} \setminus \mathbf{Z}(x'),\quad \forall\, x' \in \mathbf{X}^+ : x' \succ x\}$.
b) $x \succeq x' \iff \delta(z, x) \geq \delta(z, x'),\quad x' \in \mathbf{X}^+$.

The set $\mathbf{I}(x)^{++}$ is some sort of "indifference curve" in the (positive) resources space. Condition (V–6b) is equivalent to our conditions (IV–1) and (IV–2) for a reliable theoretical welfare measure, while it is the "identification property" (V–6a) that makes the difference between the requirements for a welfare measure and for a measure of Pareto Efficiency.

From chapter IV we know that the Debreu Coefficient fulfills the ranking condition (V–6b), while it becomes clear from fig. V–1b that it does not fulfill the identification condition (V–6a). In this figure we have depicted the special case of a so-called "thick" indifference curve, i.e. an N-dimensional indifference "curve" as it occurs at points of local satiation in the consumer's preference ordering. Since local satiation is not excluded by our assumptions (II–2) we also have to take into account such cases. In fig. V–1b the vector of utilizable resources z^{0k} lies in the interior of the indifference set $\mathbf{I}(x^k)$ so that the value of the Debreu Coefficient is smaller than one (since the consumer could be kept on the same level of satisfaction by utilizing the resources vector z^{k*} which is only a fraction of the vector z^{0k}). Condition (V–6a) requires that a value smaller than one of the Debreu Coefficient indicate that the respective state of our economy is not Pareto efficient. But obviously the situation depicted in fig. V–1b is Pareto efficient in the sense of (V–5) because it is impossible to raise the consumer's level of satisfaction with the vector z^{0k} of available resources. Thus, we have here a case of "misindication" (the Debreu Coefficient does not recognize the Pareto Efficiency of situation k) which is due to the existence of areas of local satiation in the preference ordering of our representative consumer. In such cases the set $\mathbf{F}(x^k)$ of resources vectors for which the Debreu Coefficient takes on the value of one is only a subset of the set of Pareto efficient vectors $\mathbf{I}(x^k)$, as can be seen from fig. V–1b. This example shows that under the assumptions of our model the Debreu Coefficient is *not a reliable indicator of Pareto Efficiency.*

To summarize we can state that the Debreu Coefficient is an operational measure of Farrell Efficiency while it is not a reliable indicator of social efficiency in the sense of Koopmans as well as of Pareto. Of course this result depends on our rather general assumptions with respect to the preference ordering of the representative consumer and the production structure of our economy. If we excluded the possibility of "thick" and Leontief-type indifference curves in resources space we would find that the Debreu Coefficient is a good (theoretical) measure of all three kinds of social efficiency dealt with in this chapter.

VI. The Debreu Coefficient for an Economy with Several Different Consumers

The extension of our model to a many-consumer economy implies the existence of many preference orderings and so the problem arises how these different preference orderings should be aggregated.

The (technically) simplest way to cope with this problem would be to define a social welfare function of the Bergson type so that one gets a uniquely determined system of social upper contour sets. By adding to each of these sets the total production possibility set $\mathbf{Y}$ of our economy one attains a system of social upper contour sets in resources space and the analysis of the Debreu Coefficient stays essentially the same as in the case of a one-consumer economy.

Debreu (1951, p. 277) himself preferred to argue on the basis of the so-called Scitovsky indifference curves. One such indifference curve connects all points in resources space that guarantee a constant level of satisfaction of each consumer. The problem with these indifference curves is that they are not suited to rank different states of the economy according to the level of welfare attained by the consumers because the distribution of welfare between consumers can vary from one such indifference curve to another and without a social welfare function it is not clear which distribution of welfare is the best. Therefore, in all cases in which the levels of satisfaction of several consumers differ on two different Scitovsky indifference curves it is impossible to decide if the points on one such curve are to be socially preferred to points on the other or not.[24] If the Debreu Coefficient, then, is defined on the basis of such Scitovsky indifference curves it is, of course, not a reliable welfare measure.

The same problem arises in the context of Pareto Efficiency: if the economy moves from one Pareto non-optimal state to another it is impossible to determine on the basis of the Debreu Coefficient which state is Pareto superior to the other if the levels of satisfaction of several consumers have changed in different directions.

Moreover, the qualities of the Debreu Coefficient as a measure of efficiency in the sense of Koopmans and Farrell are the same as in the one-consumer case, i.e., also for a many-consumer economy the Debreu Coefficient is a reliable (theoretical) measure of Farrell Efficiency while it is not a reliable indicator of Koopmans Efficiency under the (rather weak) assumptions of our model.

VII. Concluding Remarks

In the framework of a general equilibrium model with one representative consumer it was shown that Debreu's Coefficient of Resource Utilization is just a special monotonic transformation of the direct utility function of the representative consumer if the stock of utilizable resources of our economy is constant. From this it followed that under such circumstances the Debreu Coefficient is a reliable theoretical welfare measure for a one-consumer economy. Unfortunately it was not possible to find a satisfactory procedure for the empirical determination of the Debreu Coefficient, so that it cannot be recommended as a welfare measure without reservation.

Within the same economic framework the suitability of the Debreu Coefficient as a measure of efficiency was analyzed. In this context we had to distinguish between three different kinds of social efficiency: Koopmans Efficiency, Farrell Efficiency, and Pareto Efficiency. It could be shown that under the rather weak assumptions of our model the Debreu Coefficient is not an operational measure of efficiency in the sense of Koopmans and Pareto while it is a reliable (theoretical) measure of Farrell Efficiency.

---

[24] Cf. Sohmen (1976, pp. 48 and 310).

In the last chapter it was asked how our results change if our model is extended to the many-consumer case. It became obvious that such an extension does not imply any additional problems if a social welfare function of the Bergson type is introduced to the model. But if such a solution is rejected and if, instead, the analysis of the many-consumer case is based on a system of Scitovsky indifference curves, then there is no possibility to use the Debreu Coefficient as a welfare measure and, furthermore, severe problems will arise if one takes it as a measure of Pareto Efficiency. Nevertheless, the qualities of the Debreu Coefficient as a measure of efficiency in the sense of Koopmans and Farrell are unchanged by this extension.

Finally it should be emphasized that, of course, it is not at all the intention of this paper to detect any "mistakes" in Debreu's concept of the Coefficient of Resource Utilization — a task which would be as hopeless as it would be disrespectful. The purpose is instead to recall to our mind this nearly forgotten measure by demonstrating its main theoretical properties and by analyzing some of its possible applications in a rather general economic framework.

References

Ahlheim, M. (1985): *Dualitätstheorie als methodischer Ansatz mikroökonomischer Theorien.* Frankfurt etc.: Lang.

Ahlheim, M., and **Rose, M.** (1984): "Alte und neue Maße individueller Steuerlasten." *Finanzarchiv* 42: 274–349.

Arrow, K. J., and **Hahn, F. H.** (1971): *General Competitive Analysis.* San Francisco: Holden-Day, and Edinburgh: Oliver & Boyd.

Debreu, G. (1951): "The Coefficient of Resource Utilization." *Econometrica* 19: 273–292.

Debreu, G. (1954): "A Classical Tax-Subsidy Problem." *Econometrica* 22: 14–22.

Diewert, W. E. (1982): "Duality Approaches to Microeconomic Theory." In *Handbook of Mathematical Economics, Vol. II*, edited by K. J. Arrow and M. D. Intriligator. Amsterdam etc.: North-Holland, pp. 535–599.

Ebert, U. (1984): "Exact Welfare Measures and Economic Index Numbers." *Zeitschrift für Nationalökonomie/Journal of Economics* 44: 27–38.

Färe, R., and **Lovell, C. A. K.** (1978): "Measuring the Technical Efficiency of Production." *Journal of Economic Theory* 19: 150–162.

Farrell, M. J. (1957): "The Measurement of Productive Efficiency." *Journal of the Royal Statistical Society* 120: 253–290.

Koopmans, T. C. (1951): "Analysis of Production as an Efficient Combination of Activities." In *Activity Analysis of Production and Allocation*, edited by T. C. Koopmans. New York: Wiley, pp. 33–97.

Mangasarian, O. L. (1969): *Nonlinear Programming*. New York etc.: McGraw-Hill.

McKenzie, G. W. (1983): *Measuring Economic Welfare: New Methods*. Cambridge: Cambridge University Press.

Rockafellar, R. T. (1970): *Convex Analysis*. Princeton, N.J.: Princeton University Press.

Russell, R. R. (1985): "Measures of Technical Efficiency." *Journal of Economic Theory* 35: 109–126.

Sohmen, E. (1976): *Allokationstheorie und Wirtschaftspolitik*. Tübingen: Mohr.

Sydsæter, K. (1981): *Topics in Mathematical Analysis for Economists*. London: Academic Press.

Takayama, A. (1974): *Mathematical Economics*. Hinsdale: Dryden Press.

Measuring Welfare Changes in Quantity Constrained Regimes

Wilfried Pauwels, Antwerpen, Belgium*

The concepts of compensating and equivalent variation have been widely used both in empirical and in theoretical work. The strengths and weaknesses of these concepts have been carefully investigated, and methods have been proposed to calculate exact measures instead of approximating measures. For a recent survey of the issues involved, see e.g. McKenzie (1983), and Takayama (1984).

One critical assumption which is inherent in the very concept of compensating and equivalent variation is the assumption that, at the given market prices, the consumer can buy any quantity he wants, subject to a linear budget constraint. This implies that the consumer will buy such a bundle of commodities that, for each commodity, his marginal willingness to pay is equal to the market price.

It is clear, however, that there exist situations in which this equality no longer holds. In case the consumer is rationed with respect to some commodities, utility maximization does not imply that equality must hold between price and marginal willingness to pay. More generally, this equality need not hold in the case of a nonlinear budget constraint. In addition, in some cases (e.g. public goods) market prices may not even exist, while the consumer's marginal willingness to pay is perfectly defined.

Proposals have been made to adjust the concepts of compensating and equivalent variation to allow for such cases. In the present paper we will show that, in all the cases referred to, the Hicksian measures of compensating and equivalent surplus can be used in a straightforward way, without making any complicated, or even arbitrary, adjustments to the concepts of the compensating and equivalent variation.

The paper is organized as follows. In the first section we define and analyse two dual distance functions. These functions will play an important role in section 2. Some of the results obtained are also of more general interest. In section two we define and analyse the concept of compensating and equivalent surplus.

* The author would like to thank B. De Borger and two anonymous referees for several helpful comments.

Finally, in section three, some concluding remarks are given. The proofs of some more technical results are given in a separate appendix.

1. Definition and Properties of Two Dual Distance Functions[1]

In this section we will study two distance functions which are, in a sense that will be made precise, dual to each other. One is defined on primal quantity variables and utility, the other on dual price variables and utility. We will show how both functions can be obtained as optimal values of two closely related mathematical programming problems. When solving these problems we also obtain the direct and inverse Hicksian compensated demand functions. As we will see in section two, the inverse Hicksian compensated demand functions will play an important role in the Hicksian surplus measures.

The primal distance function we will introduce is very similar to the distance function introduced by Deaton (1979). See also Gorman (1976), Blackorby, Primont and Russell (1978), and Anderson (1980). However, for our purposes, our definition seems to be more useful.

Let there be $1+n$ commodities, the quantities of which are represented by a vector $(z,x) \in \mathbb{R}_+^{1+n}$ (the nonnegative orthant of $\mathbb{R}^{1+n}$). Let the preferences of a consumer be represented by a direct utility function $U(z,x)$. The *primal distance function* $F(x,V)$ is defined as follows. For any vector $x \in \mathbb{R}_+^n$ and any utility level V, $F(x,V)$ is defined by the equation

$$U[F(x,V),x] = V. \tag{1.1}$$

The function $F(x,V)$ gives, for any vector $x \in \mathbb{R}_+^n$ and for any utility level V, the quantity of z required such that the consumer attains utility level V in the bundle $(F(x,V),x)$. Figure 1 illustrates the definition of F for the case where $x \in \mathbb{R}_+$.

---

[1] We use the following notation. Let x be a vector in $\mathbb{R}^n$. Then $x > 0$ means that all components of x are positive. Similarly, $x \geq 0$ means that all components of x are nonnegative. All vectors are treated as column vectors. Row vectors are denoted as transposed column vectors. The transpose of a matrix A will be denoted by A'. If $g(x,y)$ is a real valued function of two vectors x and y, then $g_x(x,y)$ denotes the vector of partial derivatives of g with respect to the components of x.
If $g(x,y) = (g_1(x,y),\ldots,g_m(x,y))$ is a vector valued function, then $g_x(x,y)$ represents the matrix, the ij-element of which is given by the partial derivation of $g_i(x,y)$ with respect to x_j. Finally, I_n denotes the $n \times n$ identity matrix.

Consider the indifference curve of $U(z,x)$ corresponding to the utility level V. This indifference curve can also be looked upon as the graph of F for a given value of V: for every value of x, the function F gives the amount of z required to attain a utility level V.

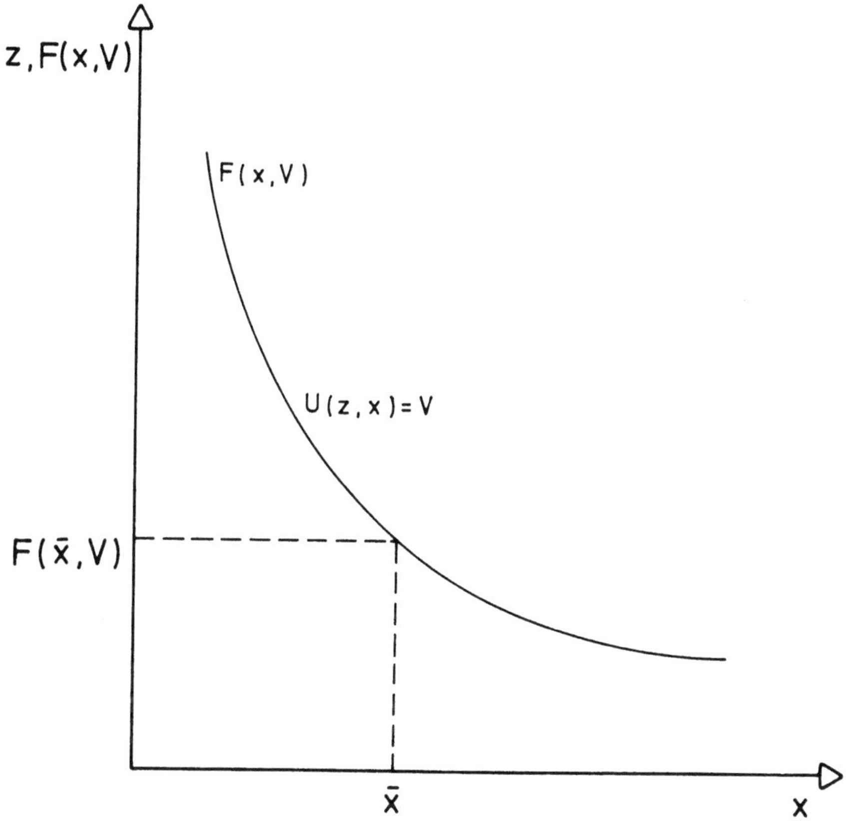

Figure 1

We now define a second distance function. This distance function coincides with the well-known expenditure function, or cost of utility function. Let the price of z be identically equal to one, and let p be the price vector corresponding to the vector x of commodities. Let y be the income of the consumer, and let $v(p,y)$ represent the indirect utility function of the consumer. For any vector p and for any utility level V the *dual distance function* $E(p,V)$ is defined by the equation

(1.2) $$v[p, E(p,V)] = V.$$

The function $E(p,V)$ gives, for any price vector $p \in \mathbb{R}^n_+$ and for any utility level V, the income required such that utility level V is attained at prices p and income $E(p,V)$.

Figure 2 illustrates the definition of E for the case where $p \in \mathbb{R}_+$. Consider the indifference curve of $v(p, y)$ corresponding to the utility level V. For a given value of V, this indifference curve can also be looked upon as the graph of $E(p, V)$: for every value of p, the function E gives the amount of income y required to attain a utility level V.

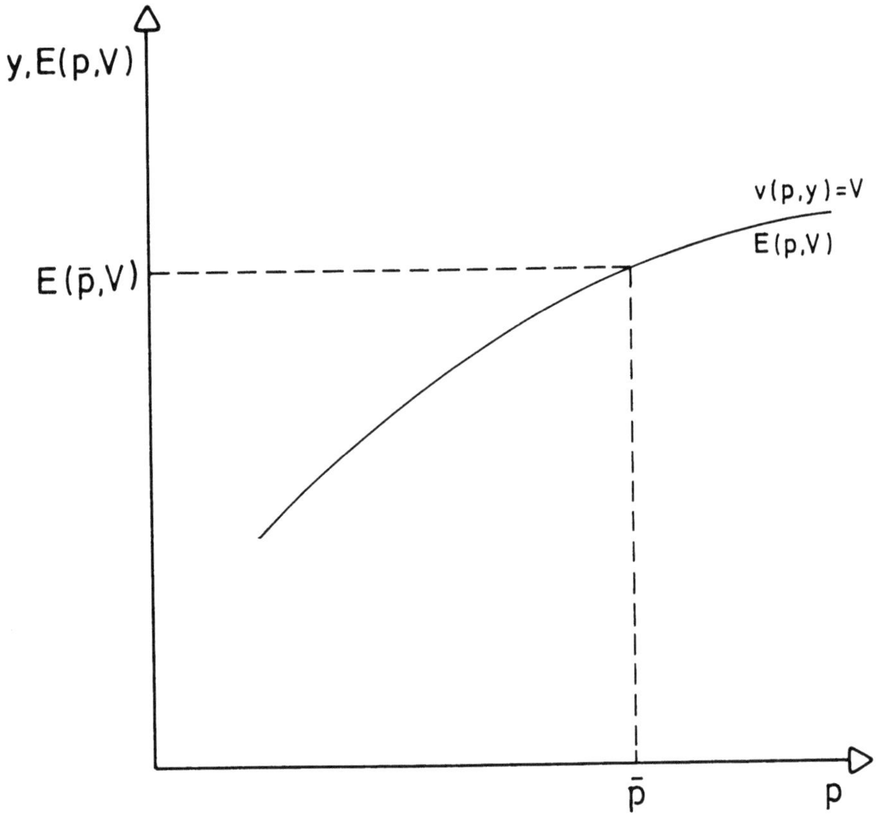

Figure 2

We will now show that both distance functions E and F can be obtained as optimal values of two closely related optimization problems. Consider, to begin with, the bundle of commodities $(F(x, V), x)$ for any vector $x \in \mathbb{R}^n_+$ and any utility level V. Let $p \in \mathbb{R}^n_+$ be any price vector. The cost of bundle $(F(x, V), x)$ at prices p is then given by $F(x, V) + p'x$. It is clear that, given p, the bundle $(F(x, V), x)$ need not be the cheapest way to achieve V. Hence, for any p and V, we have

$$(1.3) \qquad \forall x \in \mathbb{R}^n_+, \quad E(p, V) \leq F(x, V) + p'x.$$

Following Deaton (1979) and Gorman (1976) we say that the vectors $\tilde{p}$ and $\tilde{x}$ are conjugate at V iff the cheapest way to achieve V at prices $\tilde{p}$ is through the bundle $(F(\tilde{x},V),\tilde{x})$. In this case we have

$$E(\tilde{p},V)=F(\tilde{x},V)+\tilde{p}'\tilde{x}. \tag{1.4}$$

Combining then (1.3) and (1.4) we obtain

$$E(p,V)=\min_{x\in\mathbf{R}^n_+}[F(x,V)+p'x]. \tag{1.5}$$

This is illustrated in figure 3.

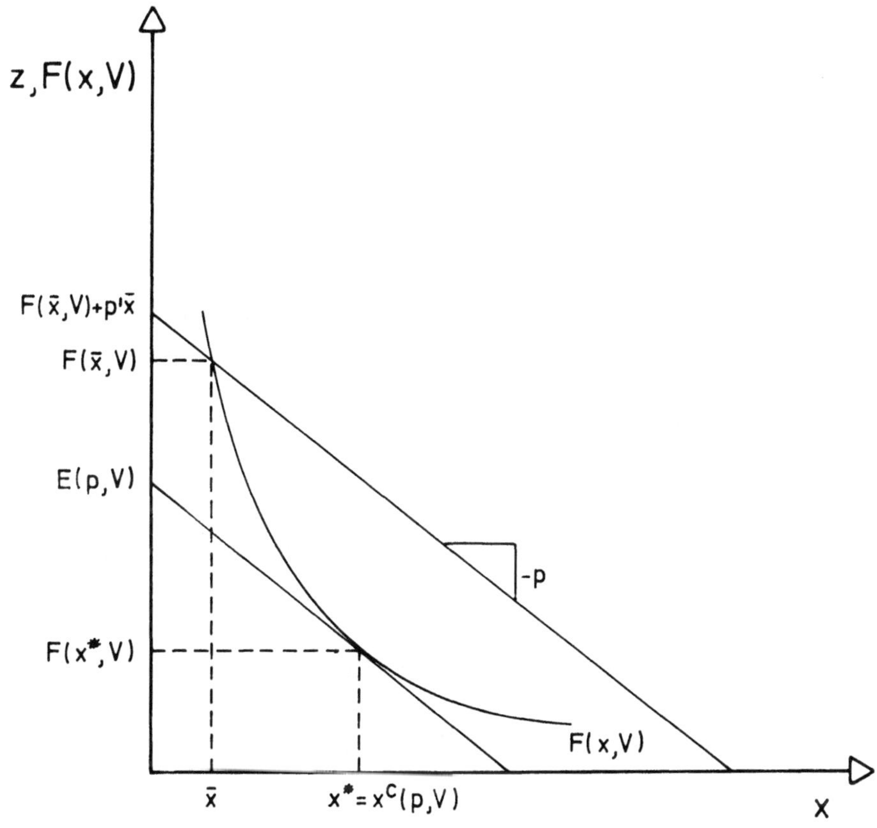

Figure 3

Let x^* be the solution of (1.5). It is clear that x^* will depend on the given values of p and V, so that we can write $x^*=x^c(p,V)$, where $x^c(p,V)$ is the vector of *Hicksian compensated demand functions.* Considering the first order conditions of (1.5), it follows that, in case of an interior minimum, $x^c(p,V)$ must satisfy

$$F_x[x^c(p,V),V]+p=0. \tag{1.6}$$

In figure 3 the slope of F at $x^* = x^c(p,V)$ equals the given value of $-p$. Applying the envelope theorem to problem (1.5) we obtain Shephard's lemma

$$E_p(p,V) = x^c(p,V). \tag{1.7}$$

Differentiation of the equality $v(p, E(p,V)) = V$ with respect to p allows us to write $E_p(p,V)$ as $-v_p(p, E(p,V))/v_y(p, E(p,V))$. (1.7) can then also be written as

$$-\frac{v_p(p, E(p,V))}{v_y(p, E(p,V))} = x^c(p,V). \tag{1.8}$$

Finally, replacing V by $v(p,y)$ in (1.8), and remembering that $E(p, v(p,y)) = y$, we obtain Roy's identity

$$-\frac{v_p(p,y)}{v_y(p,y)} = x(p,y) \tag{1.9}$$

where $x(p,y)$ is the vector of *Marshallian (uncompensated) demand functions*. The results (1.7)–(1.9) are well-known. It is useful, however, to recall them here as we will derive the inverse Hicksian and Marshallian demand functions in an exactly similar way.

In (1.5) we have shown that $E(p,V)$ is the minimal value, over $x \in \mathbb{R}^n_+$, of $F(x,V) + p'x$. We will now show that $F(x,V)$ is the maximal value, over $p \in \mathbb{R}^n_+$, of $E(p,V) - p'x$. For any vector $p \in \mathbb{R}^n_+$ and any utility level V, $E(p,V)$ gives the income required to attain V given p. Take then any vector $x \in \mathbb{R}^n_+$. The difference $E(p,V) - p'x$ represents the quantity of z left over after consuming x at prices p. As the choices of p and x are arbitrary, one may expect in general that the quantity $E(p,V) - p'x$ of z will be insufficient for the consumer to attain utility level V through the bundle $(E(p,V) - p'x, x)$. Hence, for any x and V, we have

$$\forall p \in \mathbb{R}^n_+, \quad F(x,V) \geq E(p,V) - p'x. \tag{1.10}$$

Combining (1.4) and (1.10), we obtain

$$F(x,V) = \max_{p \in \mathbb{R}^n_+} [E(p,V) - p'x]. \tag{1.11}$$

This problem is illustrated in figure 4.

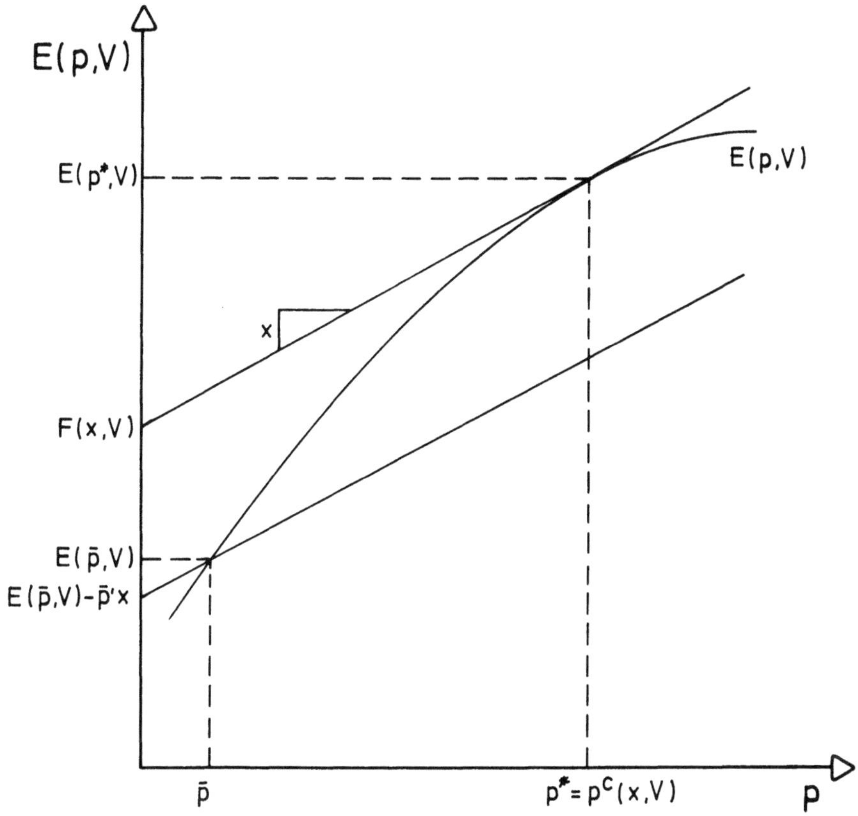

Figure 4

Let p^* be the solution of (1.11). It is clear that p^* will depend on the given values of x and V so that we can write $p^* = p^c(x, V)$, where $p^c(x, V)$ is the vector of *inverse Hicksian compensated demand functions.* Considering the first order conditions of (1.11), it follows that, in case of an interior maximum, $p^c(x, V)$ must satisfy

(1.12) $$E_p[p^c(x, V), V] = x.$$

In figure 4 the slope of E at $p^* = p^c(x, V)$ equals the given value of x. Applying the envelope theorem to problem (1.11) we obtain

(1.13) $$F_x(x, V) = -p^c(x, V).$$

This shows that, given the distance function $F(x, V)$, the inverse Hicksian compensated demand function can be obtained by simple differentiation of F with respect to x.

Differentiation of the equality $U(F(x,V),x) = V$ with respect to x allows us to write $F_x(x,V)$ as $-U_x(F(x,V),x)\ /\ U_z(F(x,V),x)$. (1.13) can then be written as

$$\frac{U_x[F(x,V),x]}{U_z[F(x,V),x]} = p^c(x,V). \tag{1.14}$$

This equality allows us to interpret $p_i^c(x,V)$, the i-th component of $p^c(x,V)$, as the marginal willingness to pay for commodity i as it exists in the bundle $(F(x,V),x)$. In figure 1, $p^c(x,V)$ can be interpreted as the slope of the indifference curve in the point $(x, F(x,V))$. This definition of the inverse compensated demand function seems to be more natural than the definition given by Deaton (1979).

If in (1.14) we replace U by $V = U(z,x)$, and remembering that $F(x,U(z,x)) = z$, we obtain

$$\frac{U_x(z,x)}{U_z(z,x)} = p^c[x,U(z,x)] = p(z,x) \tag{1.15}$$

where $p(z,x)$ is the vector of *inverse Marshallian demand functions.* These functions express the demand prices for the commodities x as a function of (z,x). It is clear from (1.15) that $p_i(z,x)$, the i-th component of $p(z,x)$, is determined by the marginal rate of substitution between z and x_i evaluated in the point (z,x). (1.15) is, of course, very similar to Roy's identity (1.9).

It is well known that, under the usual assumptions, the Hessian matrix

$$E_{pp}(p,V) = x_p^c(p,V) \quad \text{is symmetric and negative definite.} \tag{1.16}$$

$x_p^c(p,V)$ is the Slutsky substitution matrix. In the appendix of the paper it is shown that, under the same assumptions, the Hessian matrix

$$F_{xx}(x,V) \doteq -p_x^c(x,V) \quad \text{is symmetric and positive definite.} \tag{1.17}$$

$p_x^c(x,V)$ is the Antonelli substitution matrix. It is also shown that the functions $x^c(p,V)$ and $p^c(x,V)$ are each other's inverse.

If we differentiate the equality $p(F(x,V),x) = p^c(x,V)$ with respect to x, and if we make use of (1.13), we obtain the "Slutsky-equation" as applied to the inverse demand system $p(z,x)$:

$$p_x(z,x) = p_x^c(x,V) + p_z(z,x)\,p(z,x)' \tag{1.18}$$

where $z = F(x,V)$. See Anderson (1980) for a different formulation of the "Slutsky-equation" for inverse demand systems.

Comparing (1.18) with the usual Slutsky-equation as applied to $x(p,y)$, we expect a close relationship between $p_z(z,x)$ and the income effect $x_y(p,y)$. In the appendix it is shown that the following equalities hold

$$\begin{aligned} x_p^c(p,V)\,p_z(z,x) &= -x_y(p,y) \\ p_x^c(x,V)\,x_y(p,y) &= -p_z(z,x). \end{aligned} \tag{1.19}$$

From the nonsingularity of $x_p^c(p,V)$ and $p_x^c(x,V)$, it then follows that

$$x_y(p,y) = 0 \iff p_z(z,x) = 0. \tag{1.20}$$

Finally, from (1.16), (1.17) and (1.19) it also follows that, for $p_z(z,x) \neq 0$, or for $x_y(p,y) \neq 0$, the inequality

$$x_y(p,y)'\,p_z(z,x) > 0 \tag{1.21}$$

must hold.

2. Hicksian and Marshallian Surplus Measures

In this section we will use the foregoing results to define and analyse the compensating and equivalent surplus measures proposed by Hicks (1956). We will also propose some approximating measures, and some alternative formulations.

Consider a consumer in two different states. The initial state, state 0, is characterized by a vector of quantities consumed (z^0, x^0), and a corresponding utility level $V^0 = U(z^0, x^0)$ so that also $z^0 = F(x^0, V^0)$. Let prices and income be given by p^0, y^0. It is important to note that we do not assume that the consumer is in equilibrium. By this we mean that it is possible that $p^0 \neq p(z^0, x^0)$. Equivalently, we do not require that $x^0 = x(p^0, y^0)$. We do assume, however, that the budget constraint

$$z^0 + p^{0\prime} x^0 = y^0 \tag{2.1}$$

holds. We also consider an alternative state, state 1, characterized by (z^1, x^1) and a utility level $V^1 = U(z^1, x^1)$ so that also $z^1 = F(x^1, V^1)$. Let prices and income be given by p^1, y^1. Again it is possible that $p^1 \neq p(z^1, x^1)$. The equality $x^1 = x(p^1, y^1)$ need not hold. However, the budget constraint

$$z^1 + p^{1'} x^1 = y^1 \tag{2.2}$$

is assumed to hold.

Assume now that the consumer is in state 1. Following Hicks (1956), the *compensating surplus*, denoted by CS, is defined as the decrease in z^1 required to bring the consumer back to utility level V^0, assuming that the quantities x remain fixed at x^1. The following equality defines CS:

$$U[z^1 - CS, x^1] = V^0. \tag{2.3}$$

As we must obviously have that

$$U[F(x^1, V^0), x^1] = V^0$$

it follows that

$$\begin{aligned} CS &= z^1 - F(x^1, V^0) \\ &= z^1 - z^0 + F(x^0, V^0) - F(x^1, V^0) \\ &= z^1 - z^0 + \int_{x^1}^{x^0} F_x(x, V^0)' \, dx. \end{aligned}$$

Using (1.13) this can be written as

$$CS = z^1 - z^0 + \int_{x^0}^{x^1} p^c(x, V^0)' \, dx. \tag{2.4}$$

Note that the line integral in (2.4) is path independent by the symmetry property (1.17).

For the case $n = 1$ the above definitions can be illustrated graphically. See figure 5. Definition (2.3) is illustrated in figure 5a by the indicated vertical distance above x^1. In figure 5b $p^c(x, V^0)$ is drawn. By (1.14) $p^c(x, V^0)$ can be obtained by taking the slope along the indifference curve V^0. From (2.4) it is then also clear that

$$CS = z^1 - z^0 + \text{Area } x^0 B F x^1.$$

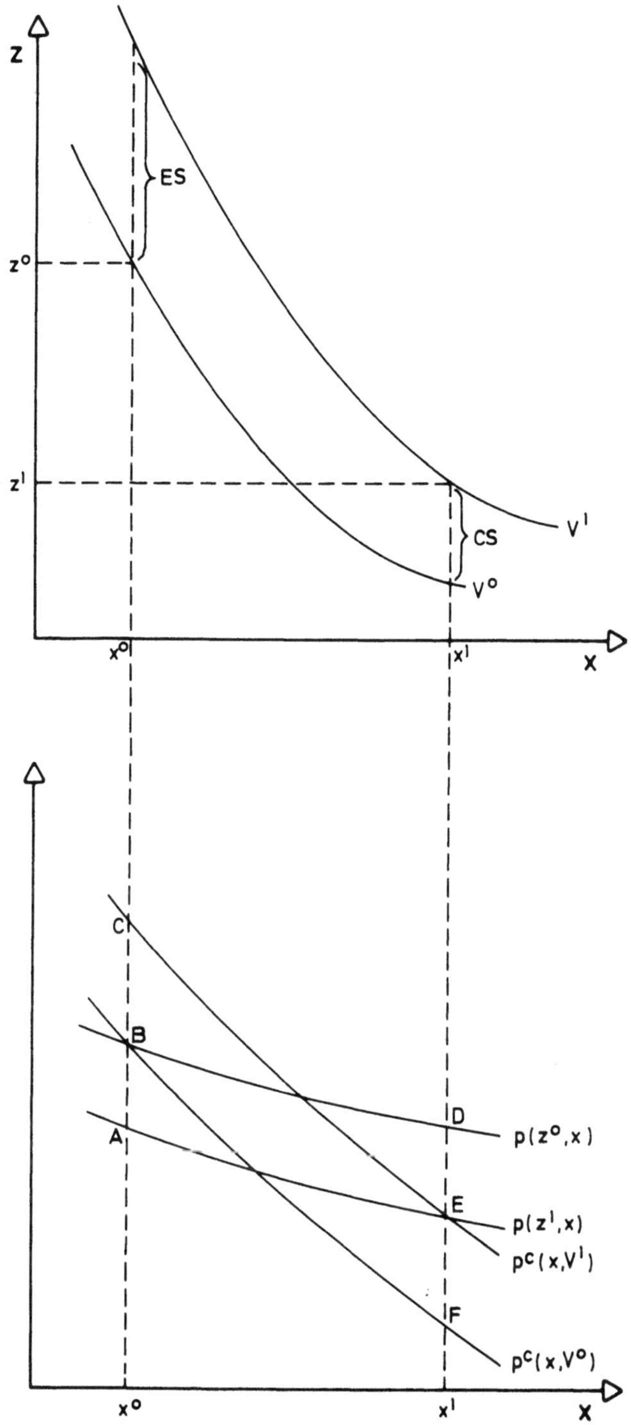

Figure 5, a/b

Instead of calculating the area under the inverse compensated demand curve $p^c(x, V^0)$, one may also, by way of approximation, calculate the area under the inverse uncompensated demand curve $p(z^0, x)$. We then obtain the following measure, approximating the "true" measure CS:

$$H(z^0) = z^1 - z^0 + \int_{x^0}^{x^1} p(z^0, x)' \, dx. \tag{2.5}$$

There are two problems with (2.5): first, the line integral may not be well defined, and, secondly, the question arises how good $H(z^0)$ approximates CS. It is clear that the line integral in (2.5) will be path independent iff $p_x(z^0, x)$ is symmetric. Using the "Slutsky-equation" (1.18) and the symmetry condition (1.17), the symmetry of $p_x(z^0, x)$ is equivalent to the condition that

$$p_z(z^0, x)\, p(z^0, x)' \quad \text{is symmetric.} \tag{2.6}$$

Of course, there is no reason why (2.6) should hold, so that in general $H(z^0)$ is not well defined. Condition (2.6) is trivially satisfied if $p_z(z, x) = 0$ which, by (1.20), is equivalent to $x_y(p, y) = 0$. In case $n = 1$ these integrability problems disappear. For this case $H(z^0)$ is illustrated graphically in figure 5b by

$$H(z^0) = z^1 - z^0 + \text{Area } x^0 B D x^1.$$

The degree to which $H(z^0)$, assuming it exists, approximates CS depends on the importance of the effect $p_z(z, x)$. Considering the case $n = 1$, we see from (1.18) that

$$p_x(z, x) \gtreqless p_x^c(z, x) \quad \text{iff} \quad p_z(z, x) \gtreqless 0.$$

By (1.21) we also have

$$p_z(z, x) \gtreqless 0 \quad \text{iff} \quad x_y(p, y) \gtreqless 0.$$

Comparing then (2.4) and (2.5), we conclude that, for $n = 1$,

$$H(z^0) \gtreqless CS \quad \text{iff} \quad x_y(p, y) \gtreqless 0. \tag{2.7}$$

In figure 5 we have drawn the case when $x_y(p, y) > 0$. (2.7) is, of course, very reminiscent of the well known relationship between Marshallian surplus and the compensating variation.

Let us now define, following again Hicks (1956), the *equivalent surplus*. Assume that the consumer is in state 0. The equivalent surplus, denoted by ES, is defined as the increase in z^0 required to bring the consumer to utility level V^1 assuming that the quantities x remain fixed at x^0. The following equality defines ES:

(2.8) $$U[z^0 + ES, x^0] = V^1.$$

As we must have that

$$U[F(x^0, V^1), x^0] = V^1$$

it follows that

$$\begin{aligned} ES &= F(x^0, V^1) - z^0 \\ &= z^1 - z^0 + F(x^0, V^1) - F(x^1, V^1) \\ &= z^1 - z^0 + \int_{x^1}^{x^0} F_x(x, V^1)' \, dx. \end{aligned}$$

Using (1.13) this can be written as

(2.9) $$ES = z^1 - z^0 + \int_{x^0}^{x^1} p^c(x, V^1)' \, dx.$$

Figure 5 illustrates the above definitions graphically for the case $n = 1$. Definition (2.8) is illustrated in figure 5a by the indicated vertical distance above x^0. On figure 5b $p^c(x, V^1)$ is drawn, so that we know from (2.9) that

$$ES = z^1 - z^0 + \text{Area } x^0CEx^1.$$

As in (2.5) one may want to approximate ES by the following measure

(2.10) $$H(z^1) - z^1 - z^0 + \int_{x^0}^{x^1} p(z^1, x)' \, dx.$$

For the case $n = 1$, this is illustrated in figure 5b by

$$H(z^1) = z^1 - z^0 + \text{Area } x^0AEx^1.$$

It is clear that $H(z^1)$ has the same integrability problems as $H(z^0)$. One also easily derives that, for $n = 1$,

(2.11) $$H(z^1) \lesseqqgtr ES \quad \text{iff} \quad x_y(p, y) \lesseqqgtr 0.$$

Very similar inequalities hold relating Marshallian surplus and the equivalent variation.

How do the CS and ES perform as welfare rankings? When considering the transition from state 0 to state 1 one has

$$CS \gtreqless 0 \quad \text{iff} \quad V^1 \gtreqless V^0 \tag{2.12}$$

$$ES \gtreqless 0 \quad \text{iff} \quad V^1 \gtreqless V^0. \tag{2.13}$$

Indeed, using definitions (2.3) and (2.8) we have

$$V^1 = U(z^1, x^1) \gtreqless U(z^1 - CS, x^1) = V^0 \quad \text{iff} \quad CS \gtreqless 0$$

$$V^0 = U(z^0, x^0) \lesseqgtr U(z^0 + ES, x^0) = V^1 \quad \text{iff} \quad ES \gtreqless 0.$$

Consider now the case when CS and ES are used for ranking more than two states. In particular, suppose that, in addition to state 0 and state 1, there is also a state 2, characterized by the quantities (z^2, x^2) and utility level $V^2 = U(z^2, x^2)$. When considering the transition from state 0 to state i, $i = 1, 2$, we can calculate the compensating surplus, denoted by CS^{0i}, and the equivalent surplus, denoted by ES^{0i}. We then have the following equivalence

$$ES^{01} \gtreqless ES^{02} \quad \text{iff} \quad V^1 \gtreqless V^2. \tag{2.14}$$

Indeed, from definition (2.8) we have

$$V^1 = U(z^1, x^1) = U[z^0 + ES^{01}, x^0]$$
$$V^2 = U(z^2, x^2) = U[z^0 + ES^{02}, x^0].$$

(2.14) then follows from the fact that U is increasing in z. It is worth noting that the equivalence

$$CS^{01} \gtreqless CS^{02} \quad \text{iff} \quad V^1 \gtreqless V^2 \tag{2.15}$$

does *not* hold. As an example, consider the direct utility function

$$U(z, x_1, x_2) = lg(zx_1) + x_2, \quad \text{where } (z, x_1, x_2) \in \mathbb{R}^3_+.$$

Take the following three states

$$\text{State 0, where } (z^0, x^0) = (1,1,2), \text{ and } V^0 = 2;$$

$$\text{State 1, where } (z^1, x^1) = (\frac{1}{2}, 2, 6), \text{ and } V^1 = 6;$$

$$\text{State 2, where } (z^2, x^2) = (\frac{1}{2}, \frac{1}{200}, 18), \text{ and } V^2 = 11.09.$$

We then have $V^1 = 6 < V^2 = 11.09$, while $CS^{01} = .49 > CS^{02} = .2$. The difficulties here are exactly the same as the difficulties one has when using the compensating variation. See Pauwels (1978).

A striking difference between the compensating and equivalent variation on the one hand, and the compensating and equivalent surplus on the other hand, is that in the case of CS and ES we integrate over quantities (see (2.4) and (2.9)) while for the first two measures we integrate over prices. In fact, when deriving (2.4) and (2.9) the prices p^0, p^1 and incomes y^0, y^1 did not play any role, except that we required the budget constraints (2.1) and (2.2) to hold. We will now show how the integrals in (2.4) and (2.9) can be rewritten as integrals over prices.

From (1.11) we can derive that

$$\begin{aligned} F(x^0, V^0) - F(x^1, V^0) &= p^c(x^1, V^0)'x^1 - p^c(x^0, V^0)'x^0 + \\ &\quad + E[p^c(x^0, V^0), V^0] - E[p^c(x^1, V^0), V^0]. \end{aligned} \tag{2.16}$$

Using (1.7) and (1.13), we can rewrite (2.16) as

$$\begin{aligned} \int_{x^0}^{x^1} p^c(x, V^0)'\, dx &= p^c(x^1, V^0)'x^1 - p^c(x^0, V^0)'x^0 + \\ &\quad + \int_{p^c(x^1, V^0)}^{p^c(x^0, V^0)} x^c(p, V^0)'\, dp. \end{aligned} \tag{2.17}$$

This equality is easily checked graphically in figure 5b.

In a similar way we can derive that

$$\begin{aligned} \int_{x^0}^{x^1} p^c(x, V^1)'\, dx &= p^c(x^1, V^1)'x^1 - p^c(x^0, V^1)'x^0 + \\ &\quad + \int_{p^c(x^1, V^1)}^{p^c(x^0, V^1)} x^c(p, V^1)'\, dp. \end{aligned} \tag{2.18}$$

From (2.1) and (2.2) it follows that

$$z^1 - z^0 = y^1 - y^0 + p^{0\prime} x^0 - p^{1\prime} x^1. \tag{2.19}$$

If we then use (2.17) and (2.19) in (2.4) we obtain

$$\begin{aligned} CS = y^1 - y^0 + [p^0 - p^c(x^0, V^0)]' x^0 + [p^c(x^1, V^0) - p^1]' x^1 + \\ + \int_{p^c(x^1,V^0)}^{p^c(x^0,V^0)} x^c(p, V^0)' \, dp. \end{aligned} \tag{2.20}$$

Using (2.18) and (2.19) in (2.9) we obtain

$$\begin{aligned} ES = y^1 - y^0 + [p^0 - p^c(x^0, V^1)]' x^0 + [p^c(x^1, V^1) - p^1]' x^1 + \\ + \int_{p^c(x^1,V^1)}^{p^c(x^0,V^1)} x^c(p, V^1)' \, dp. \end{aligned} \tag{2.21}$$

Expressions (2.20) and (2.21) make it very clear that it is not required that $p^0 = p^c(x^0, V^0)$, nor that $p^1 = p^c(x^1, V^1)$. This property makes the notions of CS and ES well suited to handle situations in which the consumer is rationed, or, in general, situations in which prices do not necessarily reflect the consumer's willingness to pay, or, finally, situations in which market prices may not even exist, e.g. in the case of public goods.

It is clear that (2.20) and (2.21) can also be written as

$$\begin{aligned} CS = y^1 - y^0 \; + \; & \{E[p^c(x^0, V^0), V^0] + [p^0 - p^c(x^0, V^0)]' x^0\} - \\ - \; & \{E[p^c(x^1, V^0), V^0] + [p^1 - p^c(x^1, V^0)]' x^1\} \end{aligned} \tag{2.22}$$

$$\begin{aligned} ES = y^1 - y^0 \; + \; & \{E[p^c(x^0, V^1), V^1] + [p^0 - p^c(x^0, V^1)]' x^0\} - \\ - \; & \{E[p^c(x^1, V^1), V^1] + [p^1 - p^c(x^1, V^1)]' x^1\}. \end{aligned} \tag{2.23}$$

Following Neary and Roberts (1980), we can define a constrained expenditure function $\widetilde{E}$ as

$$\widetilde{E}[x, p, V] = E[p^c(x, V), V] + [p - p^c(x, V)]' x. \tag{2.24}$$

For any vector $x \in \mathbf{R}^n_+$, $p \in \mathbf{R}^n_+$ and utility level V, $\widetilde{E}$ gives the income required by the consumer to attain utility level V, *given* that he has to consume

x at prices p. This income equals the income required to attain V if prices would be equilibrium prices $p^c(x, V)$ (or "virtual" prices in the terminology of Neary and Roberts), plus the extra income which allows for the fact that actual prices need not be equilibrium prices.

If we then use (2.24) in (2.22) and (2.23), we obtain

$$\begin{aligned} CS &= y^1 - y^0 + \widetilde{E}[x^0, p^0, V^0] - \widetilde{E}[x^1, p^1, V^0] \\ ES &= y^1 - y^0 + \widetilde{E}[x^0, p^0, V^1] - \widetilde{E}[x^1, p^1, V^1]. \end{aligned} \tag{2.25}$$

These expressions have been used in the literature to measure welfare changes in rationing situations. See e.g. Lankford (1983) and De Borger (1986). These expressions were intended to generalize the notions of compensating (CV) and equivalent (EV) variation to constrained equilibria. It is well-known that in the unconstrained case

$$\begin{aligned} CV &= y^1 - y^0 + E(p^0, V^0) - E(p^1, V^0) \\ EV &= y^1 - y^0 + E(p^0, V^1) - E(p^1, V^1). \end{aligned} \tag{2.26}$$

Obviously, (2.26) is a special case of (2.25). It is clear, however, that the expressions in (2.25) are a rather complicated way of looking at CS and ES. Our approach, making use of the function $F(x, V)$, is much more straightforward.

3. Summary and Concluding Remarks

In this paper a new distance function is introduced in consumer theory. Some important dual relationships between this new distance function and the expenditure function are fully explored. It is shown how both functions can be obtained as optimal values of two closely related mathematical programming problems. When solving these problems, the direct and inverse Hicksian compensated demand functions are obtained.

The new distance function is then used to define and analyse the Hicksian measures of compensating and equivalent surplus. These concepts allow us to measure the consumer's change in welfare in situations where market prices are no longer equal to the consumer's willingness to pay. It is indicated how these measures can be approximated using inverse Marshallian demand functions. The relationships to some other proposed welfare measures are also explored.

Appendix

In section 1 no explicit assumptions were made with respect to the quasi-concavity, concavity, etc. of the functions U, V, F and E. We will now show how the properties of all these functions depend on each other. Following Ginsberg (1973), we use the following definitions. Let f be a function $f: D \to R$, where D is an open convex set in $\mathbb{R}^n$. Assume that f is twice differentiable in D. We then say that f is strongly concave in D iff

$$\forall x \in D,\ \forall v \in \mathbb{R}^n,\ v \neq 0, \quad v' f_{xx}(x) v < 0.$$

It is well-known (see Ginsberg, 1973, theorem 2) that a strongly concave function is always strictly concave. Also, we say that f is strongly quasi-concave in D iff

$$\forall x \in D,\ \forall v \in \mathbb{R}^n,\ v \neq 0, \quad f_x(x)' v = 0 \Longrightarrow v' f_{xx}(x) v < 0.$$

It can be shown (see Ginsberg, 1973, theorem 7) that a strongly quasi-concave function is always strictly quasi-concave. Finally, a function f is strongly convex or strongly quasi-convex in D iff $-f$ is strongly concave or strongly quasi-concave in D.

We now prove the following important results:

U is strongly quasi-concave in (z, x)

(A.1) $\Updownarrow$

F is strongly convex in x

(A.2) $\Updownarrow$

E is strongly concave in p

(A.3) $\Updownarrow$

v is strongly quasi-convex in (p, y).

To prove (A.1), define a set $A(z, x)$ as

$$A(z,x) = \left\{ v \in \mathbb{R}^{1+n} \;\middle|\; \begin{bmatrix} U_z(z,x) \\ U_x(z,x) \end{bmatrix}' v = 0 \right\}.$$

$A(z, x)$ is a linear subspace of $\mathbb{R}^{1+n}$ of dimension n. It is easy to see that it is spannned by the column vectors of the $(1 + n) \times n$ matrix

$$V(z,x) = \begin{bmatrix} U_x(z,x)' \\ \cdots \\ -U_z(z,x)\ I_n \end{bmatrix}.$$

We can, therefore, rewrite $A(z,x)$ as

$$A(z,x) = \left\{ v \in \mathbb{R}^{1+n} \mid v = V(z,x)w,\ w \in \mathbb{R}^n \right\}.$$

Let $\widetilde{U}(z,x)$ be the Hessian matrix of U, evaluated at the point (z,x). U is then strongly quasi-concave in (z,x) iff for all vectors (z,x) in an open set containing $\mathbb{R}_+^{1+n}$, we have

$$\forall v \in \mathbb{R}^{1+n},\ v \neq 0, \quad v \in A(z,x) \Longrightarrow v'\widetilde{U}(z,x)v < 0$$

which is equivalent to

$$\text{(A.4)} \qquad \forall w \in \mathbb{R}^n,\ w \neq 0, \quad w'V(z,x)'\widetilde{U}(z,x)V(z,x)w < 0.$$

From (1.1) one can calculate the Hessian matrix $F_{xx}(x,V)$ of $F(x,V)$ as

$$\text{(A.5)} \quad F_{xx}(x,v) = -\frac{1}{U_z(F(x,V),x)^3} V(F(x,V),x)'\,\widetilde{U}(F(x,V),x)\,V(F(x,V),x).$$

Comparing then (A.4) and (A.5), we see that the strong quasi-concavity of U is equivalent to the strong convexity of F in x, which proves (A.1).

From (1.13) it follows that

$$F_{xx}(x,V) = -p_x^c(x,V)$$

so that the strong convexity of F is also equivalent to the property that

$$\text{(A.6)} \qquad p_x^c(x,V) \quad \text{is symmetric and negative definite.}$$

It is easy to see now that $p^c(x,V)$ and $x^c(p,V)$ are each other's inverse. From (1.7) and (1.12) it follows that

$$\text{(A.7)} \qquad x^c[p^c(x,V),V] = x.$$

Similarly, from (1.6) and (1.13) it follows that

$$\text{(A.8)} \qquad p^c[x^c(p,V),V] = p.$$

It follows that x^c and p^c are each other's inverse. Differentiating (A.7) with respect to x, and (A.8) with respect to p, we obtain

$$x_p^c[p^c(x,V),V]p_x^c(x,V) = I_n$$

and

$$p_x^c[x^c(p,V),V]x_p^c(p,V) = I_n$$

so that

$$x_p^c[p^c(x,V),V] = [p_x^c(x,V)]^{-1}$$

and

$$x_p^c(p,V) = [p_x^c[x^c(p,V),V]]^{-1}.$$

The following property then easily follows from (A.6)

(A.9) $\quad x_p^c(p,V)$ is symmetric and negative definite.

From (1.7) it follows that

$$E_{pp}(p,V) = x_p^c(p,V)$$

so that by (A.9) and the foregoing arguments it is clear that the strong concavity of E in p is equivalent to the strong convexity of F in x. This proves (A.2). The proof of (A.3) is very similar to the proof of (A.1) and is, therefore, left to the reader.

We have seen that $x^c(p,V)$ and $p^c(x,V)$ are each other's inverse. In a similar way, it is easily seen that the systems

$$\text{(A.10)} \qquad \begin{aligned} z &= z(p,y) = y - p'x(p,y) \\ x &= x(p,y) \end{aligned}$$

and

$$\text{(A.11)} \qquad \begin{aligned} p &= p(z,x) \\ y &= y(z,x) = z - p(z,x)'x \end{aligned}$$

are also each other's inverse. For a given vector (z,x) the solution of (A.10) is given by (A.11), and for a given vector (p,y) the solution (A.11) is given by (A.10). It follows that

$$\text{(A.12)} \qquad \begin{aligned} z &= z[p(z,x),y(z,x)] \\ x &= x[p(z,x),y(z,x)] \end{aligned}$$

and that

$$\text{(A.13)} \qquad \begin{aligned} p &= p[z(p,y),x(p,y)] \\ y &= y[z(p,y),x(p,y)]. \end{aligned}$$

If we differentiate the second line of (A.12) with respect to z, we obtain

$$x_p[p(z,x),y(z,x)]p_z(z,x)+x_y[p(z,x),y(z,x)]y_z(z,y)=0.$$

Using the Slutsky-equation $x_p(p,y)=x_p^c(p,V)-x_y(p,y)x(p,y)'$, this becomes

(A.14) $$x_p^c(p,V)p_z(z,x)=x_y(p,y)[x(p,y)'p_z(z,x)-y_z(z,x)]$$

where $p=p(z,x)$ and $y=E(p,V)=y(z,x)$.

Differentiating the "adding up" condition $y(z,x)=z+p(z,x)'x$ with respect to z, we see that

$$x(p,y)'p_z(z,x)-y_z(z,x)=-1$$

so that (A.14) can be written as

(A.15) $$x_p^c(p,V)p_z(z,x)=-x_y(p,y)$$

where $p=p(z,x)$ and $y=E(p,V)=y(z,x)$.

Similarly, if we differentiate the first line of (A.13) with respect to y, and if we use the "Slutsky-equation" (1.18) and the adding up condition $y=z(p,y)+p'x(p,y)$, we obtain

(A.16) $$p_x^c(x,V)x_y(p,y)=-p_z(z,x)$$

where $x=x(p,y)$ and $z=F(x,V)=z(p,y)$.

References

Anderson, R. W. (1980): "Some Theory of Inverse Demand for Applied Demand Analysis." *European Economic Review* 14: 281–290.

Blackorby, C.; Primont, D., and **Russell, R. R.** (1978): *Duality, Separability, and Functional Structure: Theory and Economic Applications.* Amsterdam etc.: North-Holland.

Deaton, A. (1979): "The Distance Function in Consumer Behavior with Applications to Index Numbers and Optimal Taxation." *Review of Economic Studies* 46: 391–405.

De Borger, B. (1986): "The Relation Between Alternative Benefit Measures for Quantity Constrained Price Subsidies." *European Economic Review* 30: 893–907.

Ginsberg, W. (1973): "Concavity and Quasiconcavity in Economics." *Journal of Economic Theory* 6: 596–605.

Gorman, W. M. (1976): "Tricks with Utility Functions." In *Essays in Economic Analysis*, edited by M. Artis and R. Nobay. Cambridge: Cambridge University Press, pp. 211–243.

Hicks, J. R. (1956): *A Revision of Demand Theory*. London: Oxford University Press.

Lankford, R. H. (1983): "Exact Consumer's Surplus for Changes in Imposed Quantities." Working Paper, State University of New York at Albany.

McKenzie, G. W. (1983): *Measuring Economic Welfare: New Methods*. Cambridge: Cambridge University Press.

Neary, J. P., and **Roberts, K. W. S.** (1980): "The Theory of Household Behavior under Rationing." *European Economic Review* 13: 25–42.

Pauwels, W. (1978): "The Possible Perverse Behavior of the Compensating Variation as a Welfare Ranking." *Zeitschrift für Nationalökonomie / Journal of Economics* 38: 369–378.

Takayama, A. (1984): "Consumer's Surplus, Path Independence, Compensating and Equivalent Variations." *Zeitschrift für die gesamte Staatswissenschaft* 140: 594–625.

Poverty Measurement: A Survey*

Christian Seidl, Kiel, West Germany**

1. The Concept of Poverty

Though poverty is one of the most challenging problems from which mankind has ever suffered to my knowledge only one economist's Nobel Lecture has dealt with this provocative issue. It began with the promising statement: "Most of the people in the world are poor, so if we knew the economics of being poor we would know much of the economics that really matters."[1] But then the curious reader will be rather disappointed discovering that this Nobel Lecture is mostly devoted to agricultural economics.

But though poverty itself is a rather sophisticated and multi-facetted phenomenon, the economics of poverty essentially boil down to "two distinct — but not unrelated — exercises, namely (1) a method of identifying a group of people as poor ('identification'); and (2) a method of aggregating the characteristics of the set of poor people into an over-all image of poverty ('aggregation')."[2] The identification exercise presupposes a viable concept of poverty, or more narrowly, a definition of poverty. Such a definition of poverty allows the specification of a poverty line in terms of income, or alternatively, in terms of individual welfare (individual utility) that separates the poor from the nonpoor. Many authors have specified the poverty line as a singleton concept, but a few others have realized that it should be specified as a multiple concept owing to the different circumstances in individuals' endowments, such as family status, health, or age. But the poverty line means in both cases a rather sharp dichotomization of the population which causes considerable difficulties that will haunt us throughout this paper. This aggregation exercise requires an indicator of poverty as a measurement device, i.e., a poverty index which is usually conceived as being an increasing function of poverty.[3]

---

* This article is dedicated to Professor Willi Albers on the occasion of his seventieth birthday.

** I am indebted to James Foster, Nanak Kakwani, and John Weymark for useful discussions. I am also very much indebted to an anonymous referee whose suggestions proved to be most helpful for the revision of this paper. Elizabeth Harrison has helped to improve my English style.

[1] Schultz (1980, p. 639).

[2] Sen (1981, p. 11).

[3] With the exception of some authors, notably Atkinson (1985a), who defines the poverty index as a decreasing function of poverty.

It is not surprising that we find large varieties both of conceptions of poverty as well as of poverty indices. We shall defer details of poverty aggregation to section 2 and concentrate in this section on different approaches at the identification problem of the poor. Though many concepts of poverty were suggested,[4] they all seem to fall into just two more fundamental categories of poverty concepts, viz. *absolute concepts* of poverty on the one hand, and *relative concepts* of poverty on the other.

As both categories of poverty concepts show typical flaws for the perception of poverty, attempts at a synthesis between these two categories have been made, though these attempts have so far not succeeded in eliminating all problems caused by the respective concepts of poverty. We shall deal with such problems in the third subsection.

1.1 Absolute Concepts of Poverty

Among absolute concepts of poverty we have primarily the *basic needs* approach that may also be termed biological subsistence approach, nutritional approach, or diet approach to poverty, but in the wider sense also the *behaviouristic* or *food ratio* approach of poverty.

The basic needs approach to poverty is the first and oldest attempt at formulating a viable concept of poverty. It has been pioneered by Booth and Rowntree in Britain and — somewhat refined — by Orshansky in the United States. Quite recently, Cutler (1984) has argued in favour of the basic needs approach as the adequate method of characterizing poverty in less developed countries. It was Rowntree's work in particular that laid grounds for the Beveridge report, which in turn proved to be the decisive impact for British social security legislation after World War II.[5] Such nutritional subsistence levels typically look for minimum cost diets that just secure physical survival of an individual. Of course, other indispensable needs of survival, such as clothing and shelter, had also to be allowed for. The minimum cost of such other indispensable needs was either added to the minimum diet cost (Rowntree), or the minimum diet cost was multiplied by the reciprocal of the Engel coefficient for the poor (Orshansky). If the poor spent one third of their household budget on food, the poverty line would thus be three times the amount for the minimum cost diet.

---

[4] Cf., e.g., Sen (1979, pp. 285–289); Sen (1981, pp. 11–21); Sen (1983); Townsend (1979b, chapter 6); Hagenaars (1986, pp. 15–40).

[5] Cf. Fiegehen, Lansley, and Smith (1977, pp. 129–139).

Not unexpectedly, this approach has come under rather heavy attack.[6] It was argued that minimum cost diets not only require excellent managerial skills on the part of the households, which are typically absent in case of the poor, but also that minimum cost diets vary widely among individuals and envisage rather boring, if not in the long run disgusting, nutrition patterns. Further, non-food items of minimum subsistence requirements are not easy to specify, and the level of development of a society is not at all reflected in such biological subsistence approaches to poverty. Such an absolutist stance to the concept of poverty is untenable; in the real world, an individual disposing of some commodity basket may at the same time be considered rich in India and poor in the United States. Rein who has closely investigated this approach to poverty has thus consequently summarized: "Almost every procedure in the subsistence-level definition of poverty can be reasonably challenged."[7]

Although the food ratio approach may also be formulated as a relative concept of poverty,[8] it is mostly shaped as an absolute poverty concept. The first analyses of household budgets undertaken by Engel (1857, 1895) revealed that food expenditures decrease relatively with rising household income, and that this relationship is rather robust. This observation has later on given rise to some definitions of poverty. "A certain food-income ratio is taken to be the poverty threshold: families with an actual food-income ratio higher than this threshold are considered to be poor, and families with a lower food-income ratio are considered to be nonpoor".[9]

This approach, proposed, as it seems, by Watts (1967), soon attracted other scholars. In a study on poverty in Canada, Rose defined "low income families ... as those using 70 per cent or more of their incomes for food, clothing and shelter".[10] Fiegehen, Lansley, and Smith have also used expenditure patterns as an additional device to identify the poor.[11] They argue that "analysis of poor and nonpoor consumption patterns may also help in the measurement and identification of the poor".[12] Following an approach suggested by Oshima (1977), Shari has for his second poverty index defined the poverty line as that decile of income after which the Engel coefficient begins to fall.[13] Rao (1981) has argued that the food ratio approach catches the poverty phenomenon best in less developed countries.

---

6 E.g. Rein (1970); Townsend (1974).
7 Rein (1970, p. 61).
8 If, e.g., a certain quantile of the Engel coefficients in a society is chosen as poverty line.
9 Hagenaars (1986, p. 24).
10 Rose (1969, p. 76).
11 Fiegehen, Lansley, and Smith (1977, chapter 6).
12 Fiegehen, Lansley, and Smith (1977, p. 70).
13 Shari (1979, p. 423).

But, after close empirical examination, Fiegehen, Lansley, and Smith found this approach unsuccessful. They spotted rather disparate consumption patterns within the same income groups which led them to summarize: "There is little doubt that correct information on incomes is more valuable than information on expenditure ...".[14]

In fact, such an approach to the poverty concept would expose the poverty concept to great arbitrariness. Similarity in the food-income ratio may result from differences in tastes rather than from similarities in resource endowments. Consider a family with a rather good income but with a Phaeacian consumption attitude, as it spends most of its income on food, with caviar, gooseliver, and champagne being rather overrepresented in the food basket. This approach would count this family among the poor, which seems, of course, rather strange.

1.2 Relative Concepts of Poverty

Relative concepts of poverty mean first and foremost the perception of poverty as just a phenomenon of inequality. In addition they also comprise less extreme views of poverty, such as the concept of poverty as relative deprivation, poverty as a policy definition, and poverty as a value judgment.

Poverty as Inequality

This approach conceives poverty as a "thorough-going relativity".[15] Its most naive version is bluntly stated, e.g., by Miller and Roby, as follows: "Casting the issues of poverty in terms of stratification leads to regarding poverty as an issue of inequality. In this approach, we move away from efforts to measure poverty lines with pseudo-scientific accuracy. Instead we look at the nature and size of the differences between the bottom 20 or 10 per cent and the rest of society. Our concern becomes one of narrowing the differences between those at the bottom and the better-off in each stratification dimension".[16]

Such concepts of poverty are bound to be misspecified, "for if poverty is defined as a fixed percentage of the income distribution then indeed 'the poor are always with us'".[17] Any war on poverty would be frustrated from the outset

---

[14] Fiegehen, Lansley, and Smith (1977, p. 84).
[15] Sen (1983, p. 155).
[16] Miller and Roby (1970, p. 143).
[17] Fiegehen, Lansley, and Smith (1977, p. 14).

by this very definition of poverty. Following this concept, poverty could only be eliminated by a perfectly egalitarian income distribution.

But there are more refined[18] suggestions of poverty concepts within the relativity approach. Fuchs, e.g., has defined a family whose income is less than one-half the median family income as poor.[19] This approach has also been used by Stark for the United Kingdom,[20] by Taira for Japan,[21] and (as one out of three concepts) by Shari for Malaysia.[22] Even an authority like Townsend is not quite immune to relativistic simplifications, as his statement, "Lacking an alternate criterion, the best assumption would be to relate sufficiency to the average rise (or fall) in real incomes"[23], suggests.

The relativity concept of poverty harbours rather severe repercussions for poverty research. Fiegehen, Lansley, and Smith have observed that "by such a moving criterion poverty is obviously more likely to persist, since there will always be certain sections of society that are badly off in the sense that they receive below-average incomes".[24] It is true that Sen's allegation that the "consequences of taking ... a rigidly relativist view is that poverty cannot — simply cannot — be eliminated, and an anti-poverty programme can never really be quite successful"[25] can be rebutted by arguing that "the adoption of a relative poverty standard does *not* mean that the poor are necessarily always with us. ... it is quite possible to imagine a society in which no one has less than half the average income — in which there is no poverty according to this definition".[26]

But this cannot do away with some rather basic objections against the relativistic concept of poverty. In particular, it is insensitive to growing as well as to shrinking standards of living in the society and among the poor. Suppose families with per capita median income own three Rolls-Royces. Could a family that could afford only one Rolls-Royce then sensibly be termed as poor even if its income were less than half the median income? "Similarly, a general decline in income that keeps the chosen measure of inequality unchanged may, in fact, lead to a sharp

---

18 "More refined" in that sense that poverty may also be wiped out by less than a perfectly egalitarian income distribution.

19 Fuchs (1967, p. 89). Cf. also Rainwater (1974, pp. 41–49); Perlman (1967, pp. 12–16); Plotnick and Skidmore (1975, pp. 37–39).

20 Stark (1972).

21 Following Fiegehen, Lansley, and Smith (1977, p. 14).

22 For his third index of poverty, Shari (1979, p. 424) defined households ranging in the lower half of the per capita income distribution range as poor.

23 Townsend (1979a, p. 18).

24 Fiegehen, Lansley, and Smith (1977, pp. 2 f).

25 Sen (1983, p. 156).

26 Atkinson (1983, p. 228).

increase in starvation, malnutrition and obvious hardship; it will then be fantastic to claim that poverty is unchanged. To ignore such information as starvation and hunger is not, in fact, an abstinence from 'pseudo-scientific accuracy', but blindness to important parameters of the common understanding of poverty".[27]

Relative poverty measures would, e.g., indicate unchanged economic poverty if every individual's income were increased or decreased by the same percentage. This induces us to "argue that inequality is fundamentally a different issue from poverty. To try to analyse poverty 'as an issue of inequality', or the other way round, would do little justice to either. Inequality and poverty are not, of course, unrelated. But neither concept subsumes the other. A transfer of income from a person in the top income group to one in the middle income range must *ceteris paribus* reduce inequality; but it may leave the perception of poverty quite unaffected".[28]

Poverty as Relative Deprivation

The concept of poverty as relative deprivation has been developed among sociologists, notably by Runciman.[29] He suggested that individuals compare themselves with some reference group. They may consider themselves as poor if there is sufficient intensity of feelings of relative deprivation. Therefore, this sociological concept comes close to the concept of poverty as inequality. Translated into economic terminology, this concept of poverty is cast in terms of interpersonally dependent utility rather than in terms of income. Notice that this sociological concept of poverty as relative deprivation does not necessarily imply that there exists a strictly separating poverty line such that the poor compare themselves only with some reference group among the poor. Individuals may well perceive relative deprivation from comparisons with reference groups beyond the poverty line.[30]

But is it really sensible to perceive poverty as relative deprivation? Consider a nomad tribe in the Sahara in which nobody feels relatively deprived, yet all starve. Should this really imply that there is no poverty in this tribe? Le me again quote

---

27 Sen (1981, p. 15). Cf. also the criticism expressed by Fields (1980, pp. 28 f.).

28 Sen (1981, pp. 14 f.).

29 Runciman (1966). — Yitzhaki (1979) has used this concept to show interrelations between relative deprivation, income distribution and the Gini coefficient.

30 This is the decisive difference between the pure concept of poverty as relative deprivation on the one hand, and the use of relative deprivation arguments to provide a rationale for different weights of poverty gaps *among* the poor, on the other hand. This second notion is obviously no thorough application of the relative deprivation argument.

Sen with a passage that is not intended as an objection against relative deprivation, but may well be adduced in the present context: "If I am of a cheerful disposition and enjoy life even without being able to move around, because I succeed in having my heart leap up every time I behold a rainbow in the sky, I am no doubt a happy person, but it does not follow that I have a high standard of living. A grumbling rich man may well be less happy than a contented person, but he does have a higher standard of living than that peasant; the comparison of standard of living is not a comparison of utilities".[31] Imagine for instance a passionate collector of postage stamps. He may spend so much of his income on stamps that he is on the fringe of starving and he may at the same time be relatively deprived as he compares his stamp collection with his much richer friend's collection. But we would hesitate to count this man among the poor because he disposes of income sufficient enough to lift him out of the starvation and relative discomfort if he were not the slave of his own passions. If somebody disposes of the *capability* of not being poor, he should no longer be regarded as poor. Relative deprivation violates this simple postulate.

There are also other interpretations of relative deprivation that might better elucidate the poverty phenomenon. In particular we have to mention Townsend's usage of this concept. He argued that it is the (objective) *conditions* of deprivation which matter, rather than the (subjective) *feelings* of deprivation.[32]

Poverty as a Policy Definition

This approach essentially says that poverty presupposes a consensus in society as to what should be regarded as poverty. Poverty that lacks political recognition as poverty is, by this concept, ruled out as a candidate for poverty. Such a view was expounded by the US President's Commission on Income Maintenance: "If society believes that people should not be permitted to die of starvation or exposure, then it will define poverty as the lack of minimum food and shelter necessary to maintain life. If society feels some responsibility for providing to all persons an established measure of well-being beyond mere existence, for example, good physical health, then it will add to its list of necessities the resources required to prevent or cure sickness".[33] Poverty as a policy definition is a relative concept of poverty that is not, however, automatically in relation with the prevailing income distribution.

[31] Sen (1983, p. 160).

[32] Townsend (1974, pp. 24 ff.).

[33] US President's Commission on Income Maintenance (1969, p. 8).

Its relativity springs from the change in the ruling parties and their respective political ideologies.

The political beliefs concerning poverty precipitate of course in the social security legislation or are published as an official poverty line by the bureau of census or by the official statistical bureau. The official British poverty line is the one given by the Official Supplementary Benefit Scale. Many empirical poverty studies for Britain have indeed used this poverty line.[34] In the United States, the Council of Economic Advisors set up a standard poverty line in 1964, based on estimates by the Social Security Administration of budgets for a non-farm family of four persons. Later a more elaborate poverty standard was introduced which is published annually by the US Bureau of Census. This bureau publishes annually its *Characteristics of the Low Income Population*, which gives an account of the incidence of poverty in the United States. Scores of empirical studies have also been published by the Institute for Research on Poverty at the University of Wisconsin.

There are rather severe objections to the concept of poverty as a policy definition. "First, practical policy-making depends on a number of influences, going beyond the prevalent notions of what should be done. Policy is a function of political organization, and depends on a variety of factors including the nature of the government, the sources of its power, and the forces exerted by other organizations".[35] It is indeed hard to imagine poverty becoming a plaything of lobbyists and vested interests. An uncompromising policy definition of poverty is likely to benefit in the first instance the political clientele of the ruling parties at the cost of the truly poor.

Second, we obviously find "the perversity whereby an increase in the attempts by the State to deal with poverty and low incomes by raising the Supplementary Benefit Scale will tend to increase rather than diminish the measured level of poverty, by raising the poverty line. In this view, *helping* more is read as more help being *needed*. The most effective strategy for the government to adopt to reduce the number of the 'poor', under this approach, is to *cut*, rather than *raise*, the level of assistance through Supplementary Benefits. This can scarcely be right".[36] Poverty should not be open to be defined away by the prevailing policy views.

Third, policy recommendations must of course depend on economic feasibilites. But to acknowledge that a country cannot presently afford to raise assis-

---

[34] Atkinson (1970); Bull (1971); Fiegehen, Lansley, and Smith (1977); Berthoud, Brown, and Cooper (1981); Beckerman and Clark (1982). Abel, Smith, and Townsend (1965) have based their work on the National Assistance Scale (the predecessor of the Supplementary Benefit Scale) plus 40 per cent.

[35] Sen (1981, p. 19).

[36] Sen (1983, p. 158).

tance to the poor is fundamentally different from asserting that poverty does not exist beyond the official assistance thresholds. "If in a country suddenly impoverished, say, by war it is agreed generally that the income maintenance programme must be cut down to a lower level of income, would it be right to say that the country does not have any greater poverty since a reduction of incomes has been *matched* by a reduction of the poverty line?"[37]

Poverty as a Value Judgment

Some authors obviously hold the view that poverty is nothing but a value judgment. Sen has adduced two authorities[38] such as Mollie Orshansky and Eric Hobsbawn with statements such as "poverty, like beauty, lies in the eye of the beholder",[39] and poverty "is always defined according to the conventions of the society in which it occurs".[40] Such a view is closely related to the concept of poverty as a policy definition. We may again raise the objection that poverty does not simply disappear because a different value judgment dictates, e.g., that starvation should no longer be considered as poverty.

1.3 Towards a Synthesis

The two preceding subsections have shown that one cannot close one's eyes to the failures of these two puristic concepts of poverty. But both contain obviously striking features of the phenomenon of poverty. Admitting that poverty is neither a strictly absolute nor a strictly relative concept, there is room for attempts at a synthesis of both concepts.

It was first and foremost Amartya Sen who suggested that poverty be perceived as *absolute deprivation.* I consider his terminology somewhat unsatisfactory, because it may convey the impression that it belongs to the absolute concepts of poverty. Actually, it may express Sen's intention to bring about something like a lexicographic preference for absolute conceptions of poverty in case of severe contradictions between both concepts. In short: Sen rejects relativeness[41] of the poverty line, but recognizes the necessity of its *variation over time*, the latter being the decisive step towards a synthesis of these two concepts.

---

[37] Sen (1981, p. 20).

[38] Notice, however, that both of them did not categorize poverty as being only a value judgment, but the value judgment aspect plays a prominent role in their perception of poverty.

[39] Orshansky (1969, p. 37).

[40] Hobsbawn (1968, p. 398).

[41] This explains the choice of his terminology.

Sen contended that there is "an irreducible absolutist core in the idea of poverty. ... If there is starvation and hunger, then — no matter what the *relative* picture looks like — there clearly is poverty. ... Even if we shift our attention from hunger and look at other aspects of living standard, the absolutist aspect of poverty does not disappear. The fact that some people have a lower standard of living than others is certainly proof of inequality, but by itself it cannot be a proof of poverty unless we know something more about the standard of living that these people do in fact enjoy".[42]

But this should not be misunderstood. Sen does not deny that poverty depends to some extent on the standard of living that prevails within a society. For instance, he recognizes that "in a society in which most families own cars, public transport services might be poor, so that a careless family in such a society might be *absolutely poor* in a way it might not have been in a poorer society. To take another example, widespread ownership of refrigerators and freezers in a community might affect the structure of food retailing, thereby making it more difficult in such a society to make do without having these facilities oneself".[43]

On the other hand, Sen stresses that "there is a difference between achieving *relatively less than others*, and achieving *absolutely less because of falling behind others*".[44] But he argues at the same time that *relativeness should not be confused with variation over time*. Whereas Sen rejects a thorough-going relativist concept of poverty, he recognizes that the poverty line is subject to variations over time such that the poverty line is a function of variables representing the states of society and the economy. As these variables change over time they will induce a corresponding change of the poverty line.

What then should serve as a guideline for the poverty line? It seems that the most appropriate concept of poverty should be mindful of the *individual's financial capability to participate in the activities of the community*. This would give credit to Sen's as well as to Townsend's conceptions of poverty.[45] Of course, such a concept of poverty bears a lot of ambiguity that cannot be eliminated by theoretical considerations alone.[46] Instead we must look for additional footholds coming from the empirical side to be able to settle on definite figures for the poverty line. If we are not primarily interested in the actual extent of poverty, but instead in poverty dominance, we replace the definite figure of a poverty line by an interval of feasible poverty lines. Poverty dominance is dealt with in section 2.3.

[42] Sen (1983, p. 159).
[43] Sen (1983, p. 162).
[44] Sen (1983, p. 155).
[45] Sen (1983, pp. 160 ff.); Townsend (1974, p. 15); Townsend (1979a, p. 18); Townsend (1979b).
[46] Sen (1981, pp. 18 f.).

With respect to the aid coming from empirical studies, the most promising way to demographically capture the perceived poverty line (including its variation over time) is to resort to public opinion polls. Two methods of transforming public opinion poll data into poverty lines have been proposed: the *subjective* poverty line (SPL) approach and the *utility* poverty line (UPL) approach. The SPL approach determines the poverty line from questionnaires concerning the respondents' perceived minimum household income. The UPL approach determines the poverty line by the way of individual utility functions of money and a given individual welfare threshold of utility. Proponents of the UPL approach prefer the terminology *Leyden poverty line*, which refers to the place where this approach was originally developed.

We may illustrate the data generation process for the SPL approach with some examples of public opinion polls. For a rather long period, Gallup presented two questions to a representative sample of Americans:

(1) "How much income a week do you think the average family of four needs for health and comfort in this community?"

(2) "What is the smallest amount of money a family of four needs to get along in this community?"

In the course of 25 years, the average amount of money given in response to these two questions rose in real terms by 50 per cent. The get-along-amount of money was 90 per cent higher on the average than the amount considered appropriate in the first question. Additionally, the get-along-amount did not show a secular pattern over the course of time; it figured rather stably around slightly more than half of the average disposable household income, though there was a marked decrease of the get-along-amount in terms of the disposable median income (from more than 80 per cent in the second half of the forties to 70 per cent in the sixties). Finally, the amounts were positively correlated with the income level of the interviewed persons,[47] with the educational level of the interviewed person, with the food expenditures of the interviewed person, and with the size of the town where the interviewed person resided.[48]

Since 1979, a similar question was included in the Income Survey Development Program Research Panel of the US Social Security Administration.[49] In Austria there have been opinion polls taken by the IMAS Institute since 1972, regarding

[47] Kilpatrick (1973) has estimated the income elasticity of the poverty line of the Gallup poll. It ranges between 0.55 and 0.66.

[48] For details concerning the Gallup poll and related American studies cf. Rainwater (1974, pp. 50 ff.).

[49] Danzinger, van der Gaag, Taussig, and Smolensky (1984, p. 501).

the minimum get-along disposable income of a family of four. Since 1976, the European Community has appended one question concerning minimum income to its so-called Euro-barometer opinion polls, which contain questions on income, living conditions and the perception of poverty. It reads:[50]

> "We would like you to tell us the absolute *minimum* income of money for a household such as yours — in other words, a sum below which you couldn't make ends meet."

A respondent's answer to such a question will be denoted by y_{min}, with y_{min} depending on the respondent's actual net income y and on some other parameters s, among them family composition:

$$y_{min} = f(y, s). \tag{1}$$

Low income families report minimum incomes above their actual net incomes, whereas better-off families report minimum incomes below their actual net incomes. This shows that the responses are systematically influenced by the respondents' own income levels. In order to eliminate this bias, Goedhart *et al.* devised an ingenious computation of y_{min} by setting $y = y_{min}$ in (1)[51] and computing y^*_{min} as:

$$y^*_{min} = f(y^*_{min}, s). \tag{2}$$

This is easily done, using, e.g., a loglinear estimation for $f(\cdot)$. y^*_{min} is then the poverty line in terms of income that will henceforth be denoted by π.

Goedhart *et al.* tested this approach with Dutch data to derive a poverty line for the Netherlands. In particular, they were able to show that the poverty line derived using the SPL approach was well below the official Dutch poverty line, i.e. they found less poverty in the Netherlands compared with the official poverty concept. Related studies applied the SPL approach to find poverty lines for European countries[52] and to contrast SPL's with food poverty lines.[53] Recently Danzinger, van der Gaag, Taussig and Smolensky have applied this approach to the United States using data from the Income Survey Development Program Research Panel.[54] They confirmed the same relationship as that found in the Gallup poll data. However, in contrast to the Dutch studies, they found "that the income

---

[50] van Praag, Goedhart, and Kapteyn (1980, p. 463).

[51] Goedhart, Halberstadt, Kapteyn, and van Praag (1977). Kapsalis (1981) has suggested an alternative method of estimation of their approach.

[52] van Praag, Goedhart, and Kapteyn (1980).

[53] van Praag, Split, and van der Stadt (1982).

[54] Danzinger, van der Gaag, Taussig, and Smolensky (1984).

level associated with 'making ends meet' lies considerably above the [official] US poverty level",[55] but admitted that this might be a consequence of slightly different questions in the US and Europe. Using the Wisconsin Basic Needs Study data, Colasanto *et al.* confirmed, however, the findings of the European studies also for the US, $\pi = y^*_{min}$ being lower than the respective official US poverty lines.[56]

In contrast to the SPL approach, the UPL approach derives the poverty line via a utility function of money and a given individual welfare threshold of utility. This approach was pioneered by the Leyden group of economists. Following a suggestion of van Praag[57] they assume the utility function of money to be best represented by a lognormal distribution function with parameters μ and σ. To be precise, we have to note that the lognormal distribution function is not meant to have a statistical connotation in this context.

The representation of the utility function of money by a lognormal distribution function cannot, however, pass without rather severe critique. First, this function, like any other distribution function, is bounded from above and from below, which, in economic terms, amounts to a *finite bliss, finite agony* assumption.[58] All fortunes of the world, if given to one lucky agent, cannot raise his utility above one (or some other finite number). Second, this utility function is not concave, i.e. the marginal utility of income is not a uniformly nonincreasing function of income. As regarding to the empirical fitting of the lognormal utility function, a logarithmic utility function performs better. This was even admitted by dyed-in-the-wool protagonists of the Leyden approach.[59]

On the other hand, one has to acknowledge that most empirical work has been done in the footsteps of the Leyden school.[60] The data used in the parameter estimations of the utility function were taken from questionnaires where respondents were asked to indicate net incomes they would rate as (1) very bad, (2) bad, (3) insufficient, (4) sufficient, (5) good, and (6) very good[61] (or into some similar categories[62]).

---

[55] Danzinger, van der Gaag, Taussig, and Smolensky (1984, p. 503).

[56] Colasanto, Kapteyn, and van der Gaag (1984).

[57] Van Praag (1968, pp. 74–93). Sometimes one gets the impression that the restrictive conditions of van Praag's analysis have been somewhat neglected by his partisans.

[58] van Herwaarden and Kapteyn (1981, p. 263).

[59] van Herwaarden and Kapteyn (1981).

[60] Cf. van Praag, Hagenaars, and van Weeren (1982); Colasanto, Kapteyn, van de Geer, and van de Stadt (1985); Hagenaars (1986).

[61] Kapteyn and van der Gaag (1984); van Praag, Goedhart, and Kapteyn (1980); Hagenaars (1986, p. 44); van Praag, Hagenaars, and van Weeren (1982, p. 348).

[62] Colasanto, Kapteyn, and van der Gaag (1984, p. 130) distinguish seven income categories, van Herwaarden and Kapteyn (1981) distinguish nine income categories.

Applying the so-called *equal-quantile assumption*[63] the unit interval is calibrated to the income statements, such that "the k-th answer on a six-level scale is associated with a welfare level of"[64]

$$U(y_k) = \frac{k - \frac{1}{2}}{6}, \qquad k = 1, 2, \ldots, 6. \tag{3}$$

This association of income levels with utility levels allows in turn for an empirical estimation of the parameters of the utility function. If a welfare threshold of utility δ is given exogenously,[65] we may derive the money poverty line π from the utility poverty line δ using the inverse of the utility function:

$$\pi = U^{-1}(\delta). \tag{4}$$

We could offer other critiques of the Leyden approach, but space does not permit us to do so.[66]

On the whole, these attempts at an empirical derivation of the poverty line emerge probably as the best implementation of both Sen's and Townsend's concepts of poverty. (My objections to the Leyden approach concern some characteristics of this particular method. They are not aimed against the demographic approach itself.) The empirical poverty lines reflect the basic needs generally considered as necessary to participate in the activities of the community, i.e., of being just able to establish oneself as an integrate member of a given society with its economic endowment. It is not a rigidly relativist concept, but reflects the variation of basic needs over time with respect to prevailing economic conditions. We observe income elasticities of the poverty line ranging from 0.22 to 0.66,[67] which is definitely less than one.

We have to regard these empirical poverty lines rather carefully, however. Though they allow a differentiation according to family size, the scale is relatively flat with respect to family size,[68] which results from serious underreporting of income (which rises with rising family size) and from sample selectivity (low response rates for low income brackets). This should lead us to resort to corrective estimates to reduce the bias of empirical results.[69]

---

[63] This means that the psychometric method of *category scales* [cf., e.g., Luce and Galanter (1963, pp. 261–273)] is applied. This method seems rather unsatisfactory as an experimental framework to estimate utility functions, because it implies the finite-bliss-finite-agony assumption by the very fact that only finitely many categories can be employed. Unfortunately, the economics profession (the Leyden group not excluded) seems to have rather disregarded the advances of psychometricians concerning psychophysical scaling.

[64] Hagenaars (1986, p. 46).

[65] Coming from politicians or from the analyst. Usually $\delta = 0.5$ is used.

[66] Cf. for this Seidl (1987).

[67] Danzinger, van der Gaag, Taussig, and Smolensky (1984, p. 502).

[68] Danzinger, van der Gaag, Taussig, and Smolensky (1984, p. 503).

[69] Cf. first work by Kapteyn, Kooreman, and Willemse (1986).

1.4 Impacts of the Framework of Poverty Characterization on Poverty Measurement

Upon having identified the poor, our next step would be to aggregate the characteristics of the set of the poor into an indicator of poverty within the society, which is usually done by means of a *poverty index*. This computational procedure is not, however, independent of the concept of poverty chosen. The concept of poverty affects poverty aggregation and influences the choice and performance of poverty indices.

Consider, e.g., the concept of poverty as inequality. A poverty index that subscribes to poverty as inequality sets the poverty line also with respect to incomes (or welfare levels) of people who will eventually turn out to be among the nonpoor. This would mean that the income situation of the nonpoor determines to some extent the value of the poverty index, which seems somewhat odd. Following the example provided by Miller and Roby, let us look at the bottom 10 per cent of society. Assume that owing to some generous grant this stratum now disposes of more income than the recipient of the highest income in what was the second decile. The former second decile would then be the poor and the poverty line would shift from the highest income in the former first decile to the highest income in the former second decile. In spite of the fact that all of the former poor have been lifted out of poverty and noone else has lost any income, the extent of poverty remains unchanged in this society. Similar things happen if the poverty line is considered to be some fraction of the median income. Income transfers from the middle income brackets to the high income brackets would decrease median income and would thus cause this poverty line and, incidentally, a poverty index based on this poverty line, to decrease. But, in fact, the income of the former poor would not have changed.

More generally, something like that may also occur for other distribution measures used for deriving the poverty line. But such interrelations between the income situation of the poor and of the nonpoor bears the undesirable effect that a deterioration of the situation of the poor can be outweighed or can even be overcompensated by sufficient increases of the incomes of the nonpoor. Put in other words, poverty within a society can be decreased by making the nonpoor richer. However, we need not stick to the concept of poverty as inequality to point out such inconsistencies. Other specifications among the relative concepts of poverty are plagued by similar effects as well.

To rule out compensation of worse income positions of the poor by sufficient increases of the incomes of the nonpoor, we have to resort to a postulate requiring the poverty index not to decrease if the income of some nonpoor person increases and everything else remains unchanged. But in order to avoid inconsistencies due to path dependence, the poverty index should also not increase if the income of some nonpoor person rises, because to recapture the former value of the poverty index, we must allow the poverty index to decrease if the income of nonpoor persons decreases. This would imply, however, that poverty could be relieved by simply reducing the incomes of the rich while at the same time keeping the poor in their misery. This seems to be an odd result as well, since such envy-driven satisfactions do not reduce material poverty. So we ought to reduce this postulate to the strict form that the poverty index must not be influenced by income changes among the nonpoor as long as noone crosses the poverty line. So specified, this postulate becomes the so-called *focus axiom* suggested by Sen.[70] This axiom, however, rules out other interesting properties of poverty indices (in particular, what proportion of income of the nonpoor would be needed to wipe out poverty altogether).

Absolute concepts of poverty, to the contrary, tend to disregard the environment of poverty completely. Imagine two societies of equal size with equal poverty lines and with exactly the same distribution of all incomes *below* the poverty line, but the incomes *above* the poverty line being much higher in the first society than in the second. Could we then sensibly assert that poverty is equally prevalent in both societies notwithstanding the much better economic potential of the first society to alleviate poverty?

Unfortunately, the attempt at a synthesis between both concepts of poverty suffers also from rather severe deficiencies which are rooted in the sources of this synthesis. The whole approach, to capture the phenomenon of poverty by means of a poverty line separating the poor from the nonpoor and treating both cohorts fundamentally different, is bound to give rise to inconsistencies that cannot possibly be avoided by this poverty-line approach altogether.

Harold Watts has warned "that poverty is not really a discrete condition. One does not immediately acquire or shed the afflictions we associate with the notion of poverty by crossing any particular income line. The constriction of choice becomes progressively more damaging in a continuous manner."[71] The poverty-line approach has largely disregarded this warning and has consequently run into considerable difficulties. It has been argued that a good poverty index should be sensitive to the *incidence* as well as to the *intensity* of poverty, where the head-count ratio (i.e. the fraction of persons below the poverty line) is the

---

[70] Sen (1981, p. 186). — The extensive use of censored income distributions is explained by these difficulties.

[71] Watts (1977/1968, pp. 28 f.).

most common proxy for the incidence of poverty and some measure of dispersion of the incomes of persons below the poverty line is the most common proxy for the intensity of poverty. A poverty index should indicate any increase in the incidence of poverty[72] as well as any increase in the intensity of poverty. But opposite influences may be exerted upon the poverty index if some individuals happen to cross the poverty line. If a former poor person earns some additional income which pushes him to the other side of the poverty line, the head-count ratio decreases and this should also decrease the poverty index. But this one person dropping out from the cohort of the poor may cause the measure of dispersion of incomes among the remaining poor to increase which in turn increases the poverty index. Out of these counteracting influences on the poverty index, the second may well overcompensate the first causing the poverty index to rise, notwithstanding the fact that poverty has virtually decreased in this society.

Amartya Sen recognized this conflict, but has argued that it may well be defended: "There remains, of course, the substantial issue as to whether a poverty measure should always register an increase whenever there is such a transfer even when the transfer actually reduces the number of the poor. In so far as the index of poverty is interpreted to represent the condition of the poor in the nation — their prevalence and their penury — a good case can perhaps be made for permitting the possibility that a reduction of the prevalence of the poor might under some circumstances compensate a rise in the extent of penury of those who remain below the poverty line."[73] But this stance seems to be inconsistent with Sen's plea for the focus axiom.[74] If a fall in the income of the poor can be overcompensated by a decrease in the number of the poor, i.e., in the fixed population case, by an increase in the *number* of the nonpoor, it is hard to understand why this should not also carry over to increases in the *incomes* of the nonpoor. My impression is that in this respect Sen's argument rests on rather shaky ground.

Moreover, incidence and intensity of poverty are *not independent*. They are compound in the sense that in the fixed population case no *ceteris paribus* change in the number of the poor[75] is conceivable. The number of the poor can only change as a consequence of a change of the distribution of incomes also involving incomes of poor persons, though not just any change in the income distribution of the poor gives rise to a concomitant change in the number of the poor. It seems

---

[72] This has led Hagenaars (1986, p. 121) to the explicit formulation of a *proportion-of-poor-axiom*: "An increase in the relative number of the poor should increase the poverty index."

[73] Sen (1979, p. 302); cf. also Sen (1981, pp. 192 f.).

[74] Sen (1981, p. 186).

[75] Thon (1979, p. 438) seems to have that somewhat confused.

hardly convincing that *some* changes in the income distribution of the poor should have an additional (and sometimes counteracting) effect through the number of the poor, whereas other and possibly more substantial changes in the income distribution of the poor do not have this additional effect. The explicit dependence of a poverty index on the number of the poor or some similar measure of the incidence of poverty comes up to an asymmetric treatment of changes of the income distribution among the poor depending on whether they have a concomitant change in the number of the poor or not. But, on the other hand, any abandonment of the poverty-line approach causes the measurement of poverty to boil down to the measurement of inequality, which would, of course, paralyze all attempts at an isolated measurement of poverty altogether. It seems that we have to cope with a rather narrow passage between Scylla and Charybdis in poverty measurement.

In a recent paper, Atkinson has sought to justify both the incidence and the intensity columns of poverty measurement by referring to the two conceptions of poverty as the *standards of living* on the one hand and the *minimum rights to resources* on the other. "On the standards of living approach, we are concerned that people attain a specified level of consumption ... On the rights approach, people are entitled, as citizens, to a minimum income."[76] Though Atkinson is not explicit about that, we may interpret the rights approach as being concerned with the incidence of poverty and the standards of living approach as being concerned with the intensity of poverty.[77] If the poverty line is so low that even survival is at stake for individuals below the poverty line, the head-count ratio and thus the incidence aspect of poverty becomes more important than the intensity aspect of poverty, whereas the intensity aspect of poverty seems to be the really important determinant if the poverty line is rather high in relation to the financial requirements for bare survival. So it is the level of the poverty line that matters. We may well endorse the head-count ratio as the appropriate poverty index for countries such as India and argue at the same time for a poverty index neglecting completely the incidence of poverty as an appropriate poverty index for the OECD countries.

We shall first outline the methodology of poverty measurement under the assumptions that all people are identical in their needs, that the poverty line is the same for all,[78] and that all incomes are given, i.e. that all problems concerning the definition of income, the definition of income receiving units, the sampling and questionnaire frame used in deriving the income data, etc., have been solved.[79]

[76] Atkinson (1985a, p. 4).
[77] Cf. also Atkinson (1985a, pp. 17 f.).
[78] Cf., e.g., Atkinson (1985a, p. 8); Shorrocks (1983, p. 15, note 1).
[79] Cf. Kanbur (1984, p. 403).

These assumptions are not to suggest that problems of this kind are immaterial, but that they are dealt with later in this paper. First, this serves the purpose of concentrating on the bare methodology of poverty measurement stripped from complicating extensions, and, second, gives due consideration to simplifying assumptions that have been made implicitly or explicitly in most work on poverty measurement. If we insisted at the outset on the most realistic framework for poverty measurement, we would have to skip the most important results that have been attained only under more restrictive conditions.

To be forewarned is to be forearmed: this is not a paper on the economics of poverty in general, but a survey of poverty measurement. Therefore, it does neither deal in greater detail with the causes of poverty, nor with its social and economic repercussions, nor with anti-poverty policy. Some such problems which are, however, in close connection with their repercussions on measurement problems of poverty, are alluded to in section 2.6.

2. Poverty Indices

We begin with some notation. Let a society consist of n individuals and let $\{y_i | i \in \{1, \ldots, n\}\}$ denote an ordered distribution of personal incomes. Unless stated otherwise, we shall, for the sake of convenience, also assume that the individuals $\{1, \ldots, n\}$ have been permuted in such a way that $y_i \le y_j$ iff $i < j$, $i, j \in \{1, 2, \ldots, n\}$. π denotes, as we already know, the poverty line. Then $\overline{p} := max\{i | y_i \le \pi\}$ is a strong definition of the number of the poor, $p^0 := max\{i | y_i < \pi\}$ is a weak definition of the number of the poor. Let further $\overline{\Pi}(y, \pi)$ and $\Pi^0(y, \pi)$ denote the respective sets of the poor under the income distribution y.[80] If the exact definition does not matter, we will just use p. $\Pi(y, \pi)$ will then denote the set of the poor in the indiscriminate case. Obviously, p/n is the proportion of poor people in the society. We may also cast this into continuous terms. Let $F(y)$ denote the society's distribution function of income, $F(\pi)$ is the continuous case equivalent to p/n. $P : \mathbb{R}_+^{n+2} \to \mathbb{R}$ defines a poverty index, i.e. $P(y_1, \ldots, y_n, n, \pi)$ is a numerical indicator of poverty of a society consisting of n individuals having the income distribution $\{y_1, \ldots, y_n\}$ and the poverty line π. We will suppress n in the fixed population case.

---

[80] Following Donaldson and Weymark (1986, p. 670).

2.1 Ad Hoc Poverty Indices

Until the development of axiomatic poverty indices by the pioneering work of Sen (1976),[81] there have been essentially only two poverty indices used, viz. the *head-count ratio* H, and the *aggregate poverty gap*. The head-count ratio has been used for most poverty studies since the work of Booth and Rowntree.[82] The aggregate poverty gap is the sum of the differences between the incomes of the poor and the poverty line. It was developed by the US Social Security Administration as a poverty index. While the head-count ratio is the archetypical measure of the incidence of poverty, the aggregate poverty gap is the archetypical measure for the intensity of poverty. The head-count ratio is completely insensitive to changes in the intensity of poverty, and the aggregate poverty gap is completely insensitive to the number of the poor as long as the average income of the poor remains unchanged. These poverty indices may be called ad hoc poverty indices, because they lack a theoretical derivation from some set of explicit assumptions. If we normalize the aggregate poverty gap by the product of the number of the poor and the poverty line, i.e. by the minimum amount of money that would be needed in place of the incomes of the poor to wipe out poverty altogether, we get the so-called *income-gap ratio* I. Obviously,

$$H = \frac{p}{n}, \tag{5}$$

$$I = \sum_{i=1}^{p} \frac{\pi - y_i}{p\pi} = 1 - \frac{\mu}{\pi}, \tag{6}$$

where μ denotes the average income of the poor.

The income-gap ratio is the percentage shortfall of the average income of the poor from the poverty line.[83] Both indices assign positive real numbers to individuals below the poverty line. The head-count ratio assigns $1/n$ to any poor

---

[81] The work of Watts (1977/1968) has in some sense been a precursor of the axiomatic approach to poverty measurement.

[82] Cf. in some similar sense also Bowley (1923, p. 214).

[83] Note the similarity of the structure of the income-gap ratio with Dalton's inequality index D and Atkinson's inequality index A [cf. Hagenaars (1968, pp. 128 f.)]:

$$D = 1 - \frac{W(y)}{W(\tilde{y})}; \quad A = 1 - \frac{U^{-1}\left[\frac{1}{n}\sum_{i=1}^{n} U(y_i)\right]}{\overline{y}}.$$

D is the percentage shortfall of the social welfare of the prevailing income distribution behind the social welfare of the optimal income distribution $\tilde{y}$. A is the percentage shortfall of the equally distributed equivalent level of income behind the average income of the prevailing income distribution. Note also the formal similarity of the income-gap ratio with the second Clark-Hemming-Ulph poverty index to be discussed below.

individual irrespective of how much his income falls short of the poverty line. The income-gap ratio assigns the real number $[\pi - y_i]/[p\pi]$ to any poor individual, thus weighting individuals heavier the poorer they are. Obviously

$$H(p^0) \leq H(\overline{p}); \tag{7a}$$

$$I(p^0) \geq I(\overline{p}); \tag{7b}$$

with equality for $p^0 = \overline{p}$ and inequality for $\overline{p} > p^0$. Notice that even in the case of these two rather crude poverty indices it matters whether we count the individuals just on the poverty line among the poor or among the nonpoor. H and I react adversely if we move from p^0 to $\overline{p}$ and vice versa.

From definitions (5) and (6) we see immediately that if different income distributions give rise to the same p, H will indicate the same poverty level. Whenever different income distributions happen to have the same average income of the poor, I will indicate the same poverty level; I increases only with decreasing average income of the poor and is insensitive to income transfers among the poor, as they would not change μ. If a person with income $y_i > \mu$ is lifted out of poverty, this decreases μ and thus increases poverty. If a person with $y_i < \mu$ is lifted out of poverty, this increases μ and decreases poverty.

These properties led Sen to raise rather severe criticism concerning these two poverty indices: "The income-gap ratio I is completely insensitive to transfers of income among the poor so long as nobody crosses the poverty line by such transfers. It also pays no attention whatever to the number or proportion of poor people below the poverty line, concentrating only on the aggregate shortfall, no matter how it is distributed and among how many. These are damaging limitations.

The head-count measure H is, of course, not insensitive to the number below the poverty line; indeed for a given society it is the only thing to which H is sensitive. But H pays no attention whatever to the extent of income shortfall of those who lie below the poverty line: it matters not at all whether someone is just below the line, or very far from it in acute misery and hunger.

Furthermore, a transfer of income from a poor person to one who is richer can never increase the poverty measure H — surely a perverse feature."[84] This

[84] Sen (1979, p. 295). Notice that this quotation reflects Sen's objections. In section 1.4 above, we remarked critically that the number of the poor cannot change without a simultaneous change in the income distribution among the poor. On the other hand, there are instances where it is first and foremost the number of the poor that matters. Therefore it seems difficult to reject the importance of the influence of the incidence of poverty on an index of poverty altogether.

perversity can easily be shown. Define k by the following inequality:

$$\sum_{i=1}^{k-1} y_i < \sum_{i=k+1}^{p^0} (\pi - y_i) \leq \sum_{i=1}^{k} y_i.$$

Poverty then can be reduced from $\frac{p^0}{n}$ to $\frac{k}{n}$ by taking most if not all income from the remaining k poor to lift the $(p^0 - k)$ richest poor to the poverty line (and, by definition of p^0, out of poverty). Similarly, if there is a fixed budget for an anti-poverty policy, poverty as measured by H would be reduced the most if the anti-poverty budget funds were distributed among the richest poor. But this is hardly the most effective anti-poverty policy.

This should suffice to demonstrate that the ad hoc poverty indices are far from being satisfactory. The more appropriate way is to demand certain properties from satisfactory poverty indices, these properties being nothing less than the axioms a poverty index should satisfy. This more promising approach of deriving a poverty index was pioneered by Sen (1976).[85] It has elicited a lot of follow-up work.

2.2 Axiomatic Poverty Indices

Sen (1976) objected to the head-count ratio, insisting that it violates both a monotonicity axiom and a transfer axiom as formulated by him. He charged that the income-gap ratio violates the transfer axiom. As later discussions have developed more elaborate versions of these axioms, we shall immediately present these more exacting versions.

For the sake of a good representation of axiomatic poverty indices, it is expedient to discuss at the outset not only the monotonicity and transfer axioms, but also the other most commonly used axioms and turn only thereafter to the making of poverty indices proper. We shall first state the axioms formally and then discuss their meaning and their properties.

2.2.1 *Axioms*

Monotonicity Axioms

Weak monotonicity aciom (WM): Let y and x denote two income distributions such that $y_i = x_i$ for all $i \in \{\{1, 2, \ldots, n\} - \{j\}\}$, and $y_j > x_j$ for $j \in \Pi(y, \pi) \cap \Pi(x, \pi)$. Then $P(y, \pi) < P(x, \pi)$.

[85] Cf. also Watts (1977/1968).

Strong monotonicity axiom (SM): Let y and x denote two income distributions such that $y_i = x_i$ for all $i \in \{\{1,2,\dots,n\} - \{j\}\}$, and $y_j > x_j$ for $j \in \Pi(x,\pi)$. Then $P(y,\pi) < P(x,\pi)$.

The weak monotonicity axiom demands that an increase of a poor individual's income, ceteris paribus, reduces the poverty index, *provided this particular individual remains among the poor.* The strong monotonicity axiom demands a decrease of the poverty index whenever the income of a poor individual rises, ceteris paribus. That is, SM ties the decrease of P not to the condition that the (poor) beneficiary of the increase in income remains among the poor. It is obvious that SM implies WM, but WM does not imply SM.

It seems that in the literature there has been almost universal use of the monotonicity axiom in its weak version, Donaldson and Weymark being notable exceptions.[86] Therefore it is not widely known that the strong monotonicity axiom plagues poverty indices with similar difficulties as the strong transfer axiom.[87] The reason is that simply lifting one or more persons out of poverty (what SM allows) changes the set of the poor, i.e. $\Pi(y,\pi) \subset \Pi(x,\pi)$, which means that the income distribution among the poor is not the same as before, because some entries have vanished. But this different income distribution may cause a poverty index to increase, though poverty has in fact decreased, which is surely a perverse result.

Transfer Axioms

Whereas monotonicity axioms consider income changes of one person, everything else remaining unchanged, transfer axioms deal with situations in which redistributions of a fixed amount of total income occur. Most of the literature considers only two transfer axioms, but we shall present the more sophisticated analysis of Donaldson and Weymark which distinguishes four transfer axioms.[88]

Minimal transfer axiom (MT): Let y and x denote two income distributions such that $y_i = x_i$ for all $i \in \{\{1,2,\dots,n\} - \{j,k\}\}$, and $y_j > x_j \geq x_k > y_k$, $y_j - x_j = x_k - y_k$, for $j,k \in \Pi(y,\pi) \cap \Pi(x,\pi)$. Then $P(y,\pi) > P(x,\pi)$.

Weak transfer axiom (WT): Let y and x denote two income distributions such that $y_i = x_i$ for all $i \in \{\{1,2,\dots,n\} - \{j,k\}\}$, and $y_j > x_j \geq x_k > y_k$, $y_j - x_j = x_k - y_k$, for $k \in \Pi(y,\pi) \cap \Pi(x,\pi)$ and $\Pi(y,\pi) = \Pi(x,\pi)$. Then $P(y,\pi) > P(x,\pi)$.

---

[86] Donaldson and Weymark (1986, p. 671). They call weak monotonicity *downward monotonicity* and strong monotonicity *upward monotonicity*, two terms that seem to me to be less pronounced than the terminology suggested here.

[87] Cf. Sen (1977, p. 77, n. 51); Sen (1981, pp. 192 f.); Thon (1983).

[88] Donaldson and Weymark (1986, pp. 672–673).

Strong upward transfer axiom (SUT): Let y and x denote two income distributions such that $y_i = x_i$ for all $i \in \{\{1,2,\ldots,n\} - \{j,k\}\}$, and $y_j > x_j \geq x_k > y_k$, $y_j - x_j = x_k - y_k$, for $k \in \Pi(y,\pi) \cap \Pi(x,\pi)$. Then $P(y,\pi) > P(x,\pi)$.

Strong downward transfer axiom (SDT): Let y and x denote two income distributions such that $y_i = x_i$ for all $i \in \{\{1,2,\ldots,n\} - \{j,k\}\}$, and $y_j > x_j \geq x_k > y_k$, $y_j - x_j = x_k - y_k$, for $k \in \Pi(y,\pi)$. Then $P(y,\pi) > P(x,\pi)$.

Note that the common characteristic of all four transfer axioms is that a *progressive* transfer, i.e. a transfer from a richer to a poorer person (everything else remaining unchanged), should decrease the poverty index, whereas a *regressive* transfer, i.e. a transfer from a poorer to a richer person (everything else unchanged) should increase the poverty index. They differ only with respect to the persons involved. MT demands a decrease (progressive transfer) of P or an increase (regressive transfer) of P only if *both persons* involved in the transfer are and remain poor. WT demands a decrease (progressive transfer) of P or an increase (regressive transfer) of P only if the poorer party to this transfer is and remains poor and if the *set of poor people does not change* [i.e. if the donor of a transfer (progressive transfer) happens to be nonpoor, the transfer must not cause him to cross the poverty line and if the recipient of a transfer (regressive transfer) happens to be among the poor, the transfer must not lift him out of poverty]. SUT demands a decrease (progressive transfer) of P or an increase (regressive transfer) of P only if the poorer party to this transfer is and remains poor. That means that SUT allows also for a decrease of P if the donor (progressive transfer) falls into poverty by the transfer (but is not worse off than the recipient after the transfer), and for an increase of P if the recipient (regressive transfer) is lifted out of poverty by the transfer. Finally, SDT demands that P decrease whenever a person originally poor receives a transfer from someone remaining richer after the transfer, even if the recipient is lifted out of poverty as a consequence of the transfer, and demands that P increase whenever a poor person transfers income to some richer person.

Notice once more the difference between SUT and SDT. Under SUT, only the richer party to a transfer may cross the poverty line if this is to bear relevance for the poverty index, whereas SDT completely ignores crossing the poverty line. SDT insists only that the poorer party to a transfer be among the poor *before* this transfer takes place.

Of course, we have SDT $\Rightarrow$ SUT $\Rightarrow$ WT $\Rightarrow$ MT. Sen had originally chosen

SUT as his transfer axiom[89] but soon found that his poverty index (to be discussed below) violated this axiom, which led him to weaken his transfer axiom to WT.[90] Though it is possible to reconcile poverty indices with weaker versions of the transfer axiom, we are disturbed to find that a transfer from the poorest of the poor to the richest of the poor may indeed reduce the value of the poverty index, provided that the recipient crosses the poverty line. Thon has shown also that the poverty indices (to be discussed below) suggested by Anand (1977), by Takayama (1979), by Kakwani (1980a), and the first poverty index suggested by Clark, Hemming, and Ulph (1981) violate the strong transfer axioms.[91]

Now, what has happened? The same phenomenon present in the discussion of the strong monotonicity axiom is also present here, viz. any crossing of the poverty line changes the set of the poor, which implies simultaneously a change in the income distribution of the poor. But due to the asymmetric treatment of incomes of the poor and nonpoor inherent in most poverty indices, this could cause the poverty index to increase in case of progressive transfers or to decrease in case of regressive transfers, which runs counter to the intentions of the transfer axioms. Poverty indices which satisfy a strong transfer axiom consider "the poverty-alleviating role of crossing the poverty line ... less crucial"[92]. The respective poverty indices stress the distributional aspects of poverty and less the prospect of falling short of the poverty line. But the failure of many poverty indices to satisfy a strong transfer axiom is somewhat disturbing.

Sensitivity Axioms

Sensitivity Axioms are designed to make poverty indices sensitive to the inequality of incomes among the poor by causing the poverty index to be more affected the poorer a person is. It was in particular Kakwani who drew attention to sensitivity axioms in connection with poverty measurement.[93]

---

[89] Sen (1976a, p. 219). — Note that this axiom had indeed already been suggested by Dalton (1920, p. 351) for inequality measures of income distributions, which he called *the principle of transfers*. Dalton himself refers to Pigou concerning this principle. Cf. also Pigou (1932, p. 89): "... any transference of income from a relatively rich man to a relatively poor man of similar temperament, since it enables more intense wants to be satisfied at the expense of less intensive wants, must increase the aggregate sum of satisfaction. ... Any cause which increases the absolute share of real income in the hands of the poor, provided that is does not lead to a contraction in the size of the national dividend from any point of view will, in general, increase economic welfare." Notice, however, Pigou's careful analysis of the conditions under which this principle of transfers will hold: Pigou (1932, pp. 90–97), and part IV of his *Economics of Welfare*.

[90] Sen (1977, p. 77, n. 51); Sen (1981, pp. 186, 192 f.).

[91] Thon (1979, pp. 436 f.); Thon (1983).

[92] Sen (1981, p. 193).

[93] Kakwani (1980a, pp. 438 f.).

Monotonicity sensitivity axiom (MOS): Let $(\Delta P)_i$ denote the increase in the poverty index due to a small reduction δ in the income of the i-th poor. Then $(\Delta P)_i > (\Delta P)_j$ iff $\pi > y_j > y_i$.

Rank transfer sensitivity axiom (RTS): Let $(\Delta P)_{i,i+\rho}$ denote the increase in the poverty index due to a transfer of income δ from the i-th poor to the $(i+\rho)$-th poor. Then $(\Delta P)_{i,i+\rho} > (\Delta P)_{j,j+\rho}$ iff $y_j > y_i$, $y_{j+\rho} > y_{i+\rho}$, and $(j+\rho)$ is among the poor after the transfer.

Distance transfer sensitivity axiom (DTS): Let $\delta > 0$ denote a transfer from the i-th poor with pre-transfer income y_i, to a poor with pre-transfer income $y_i + h$, $h > 0$, and let $[\Delta P(h,\delta)]_i$ denote the increase in the poverty index due to this transfer. Then $[\Delta P(h,\delta)]_i$ decreases with increasing i whenever $y_i + h + \delta \leq \pi$ (or $< \pi$ for the weak definition of the poor).

The next axiom requires first a definition of greater poverty aversion of poverty indices.

Definition: Let P_1 and P_2 denote two poverty indices. Then P_2 is said to be more poverty averse than P_1, if for all $\delta > 0$ the function

$$\varphi(i) := \frac{P_2(y_1,\ldots,y_i-\delta,\ldots,y_n,\pi)}{P_1(y_1,\ldots,y_i-\delta,\ldots,y_n,\pi)}$$

increases with decreasing i for all income distributions and for all $y_i - \delta < \pi$, $y_1 - \delta > 0$, $y_i > y_{i-1}$.

Increasing poverty aversion axiom (IPA): Let π and two poverty indices P_1 and P_2 be given with P_2 being more poverty averse than P_1. Then $P_1 \leq P_2$ for all $(y_1,\ldots,y_n)$.

The first three axioms have been stated by Kakwani (1980a) for the purpose of poverty measurement. They have precursors in the field of the measurement of income inequality. IPA has so far not been suggested in the literature.

MOS demands a poverty index to increase more, the poorer the individual is that has to suffer a certain reduction of income. RTS implies that the sensitivity of the poverty index to transfers should depend on the relative position of the transferer in the ordering of the poor people when the relative positions of the transferer and the recipient of the transfer remain unchanged. The lower the relative position of the transferer in the income ordering among the poor, the higher should be the increase of the poverty index if a certain transfer occurs. DTS focusses on a constant distance of pre-transfer incomes of the transferer and the recipient of a transfer and requires the poverty index to increase all the more for any given transfer amount, the poorer the transferer is. Whereas RTS pays attention to the number of relative income positions between the transferer and the recipient of the transfer, DTS disregards this particularity concentrating instead on equal income intervals.

Notice that MOS, RTS and DTS have been stated only in their weak formulations, in accordance with their formulation in the literature. Like the monotonicity and transfer axioms, these three sensitivity axioms may readily be formulated as strong axioms, allowing also for crossings of the poverty line. As these generalizations have thus far not appeared in the literature, we shall not pursue this digression in greater detail.

IPA is an axiom referring to changes in the poverty index. It demands that a ceteris paribus shift from some poverty index to a more poverty averse poverty index should not decrease the numerical indicator of poverty. IPA is of particular importance for cross-section analysis. Let x and y denote two income distributions and let P_1 and P_2 denote two poverty indices, with P_2 more poverty averse than P_1. Then $P_2(y, \pi)$ should be smaller than $P_1(x, \pi)$ only if there is sufficiently less poverty under y than under x. $P_2(y, \pi)$ must not be smaller than $P_1(x, \pi)$ if $P_2(y, \pi) > P_2(x, \pi)$ or $P_1(y, \pi) > P_1(x, \pi)$, because

$$P_2(y, \pi) > P_2(x, \pi) \geq P_1(x, \pi);$$
$$P_2(y, \pi) \geq P_1(y, \pi) > P_1(x, \pi).$$

Focus Axioms

Focus axiom (F): Let y and x denote two income distributions such that $\Pi(y, \pi) = \Pi(x, \pi)$ and $y_i = x_i$ for all $i \in \Pi(y, \pi)$. Then $P(y, \pi) = P(x, \pi)$.

The focus axiom causes a poverty index to be perfectly independent of income levels and income distributions *above* the poverty line. "One consequence of this is that no fall in the income of the poor can be *outweighed* by any rise — no matter how large — in the incomes of the rich."[94] Conversely, no rise in the income of the poor can be frustrated by any fall in the income of the rich, provided all poor remain poor and all rich remain rich.

Usually, the focus axiom is formulated only with respect to the fixed population case. But it can readily be generalized to populations of different size.

[94] Sen (1981, p. 186). Chakravarty (1983a, p. 308) calls this axiom *independence of the incomes of the rich.*

Generalized focus axiom (GF): Let y and x denote two ordered income distributions, possibly of different size, such that $\Pi(y,\pi) = \Pi(x,\pi)$ and $y_i = x_i$ for all $i \in \Pi(y,\pi)$. Then $P(y,\pi) = P(x,\pi)$.

This means, of course, that GF $\Rightarrow$ F.

Symmetry and Asymmetry Axioms

Symmetry and asymmetry axioms are concerned with responses of the poverty index to replications of identical populations, to permutations of the income distribution, to symmetric changes of income, or to variations in the size of the population.

Size independence axiom (SIN):[95] Let y denote an income distribution and let y^m denote an m-fold replication of y in the sense that any income in y is the income of exactly m persons in y^m. Then $P(y,\pi) = P(y^m,\pi)$.

Anonymity axiom (A):[96] Let y denote an ordered income distribution where, contrary to our usual assumption, the individuals $\{1,2,\ldots,n\}$ have not been permuted such that $i < j$ whenever $y_i < y_j$, $i,j \in \{1,2,\ldots,n\}$. Let y' denote this ordered income distribution where the individuals have been permuted in some way. Then $P(y,\pi) = P(y',\pi)$.

Scale invariance axiom (SI):[97] $P(\lambda y, \lambda\pi) = P(y,\pi)$, $\lambda > 0$.

Translation invariance axiom (TI):[98] $P(y_1+\delta,\ldots,y_n+\delta,\pi+\delta) = P(y_1,\ldots,y_n,\pi)$, $\delta \in \mathbb{R}$, $y_1 + \delta > 0$.

Poverty growth axiom (PG):[99] Let y and y' denote two ordered income distributions of size n and $(n+1)$, respectively, such that $y = (y_1, y_2, \ldots, y_n)$ and $y' = (y_1, y_2, \ldots, x, \ldots, y_n)$ and $x < \pi$. Then $P(y,\pi) < P(y',\pi)$.

Nonpoverty growth axiom (NPG): Let y and y' be defined as in PG, but with $x > \pi$. Then $P(y,\pi) > P(y',\pi)$.

95 This axiom had been suggested in a different context by Sen (1976b, p. 28). Shorrocks (1983, p. 7) makes use of it as an invariance axiom of population replication for measures of income inequality. Hagenaars (1986, p. 121) refers to it as population symmetry axiom for poverty measurement.

96 Chakravarty (1983a, p. 308) calls it *impartiality*, Foster (1984, p. 220) calls it *symmetry*.

97 Chakravarty (1983a, p. 308); Blackorby and Donaldson (1980, p. 1054).

98 Formulated as an axiom following Blackorby and Donaldson (1980, p. 1058).

99 This and the next axiom were suggested by Kundu and Smith (1983, pp. 426 f.

SIN is a self-evident axiom. It simply demands that the poverty index is not allowed to change if two or more populations with identical income distributions are pooled. This axiom is of importance for poverty comparisons among populations of different sizes, say m and n. SIN permits us to compare the values of the poverty index evaluated for a population of mn individuals with an m-fold and an n-fold replication of the respective income distributions.

A demands the poverty index not to change when individuals are associated with different incomes as long as the overall structure of the incomes does not change. This excludes the influence of all personal information whatsoever on the poverty index, beyond the bare amount of income. Innocent as this axiom appears, it has nevertheless rather serious repercussions for the whole issue of inequality and poverty measurement. A more detailed discussion of this is deferred, however, to section 2.6.

SI requires a poverty index not to change if all incomes and the poverty line change by the same factor. TI requires a poverty index not to change if all incomes and the poverty line are increased or decreased by the same amount δ. Of course, the perception of poverty as absolute deprivation, which seems to be the most agreeable concept of poverty, will essentially be incompatible with both SI and TI. It seems that both axioms are inspired by Kolm's *rightist* (SI) and *leftist* (TI) measures of income inequality.[100] Poverty indices satisfying SI are called *relative* poverty indices; poverty indices satisfying TI are called *absolute* poverty indices.[101] Relative poverty indices are thus homogeneous of degree zero in all incomes and in the poverty line. Absolute poverty indices remain unchanged if all incomes and the poverty line are shifted by some constant δ. Obviously both SI and TI will be inconsistent with a conception of poverty as absolute deprivation, as has been agreed upon in section 1.3 above.

PG and NPG consider aspects of population growth: if one additional individual to the population is poor, the poverty index should increase, if he or she is nonpoor, the poverty index should decrease. A greater share of the nonpoor should, according to NPG, cause the poverty index to indicate less poverty in the society, though the poor and their incomes remain unchanged. It is obvious that NPG and GF are inconsistent in the sense that a poverty index satisfying NPG never satisfies GF and vice versa. Kundu and Smith checked seven well known

[100] Kolm (1976).

[101] This terminology was suggested by Blackorby and Donaldson (1980), and was taken up by Chakravarty (1983).

poverty indices and discovered that of these only the head-count ratio satisfies both PG and NPG.[102]

Decomposability Axioms

Decomposability axioms require a poverty index to permit a consistent breakdown of the overall poverty into poverty prevailing in the various strata of society. They ensure that a poverty index is able to answer questions extending, e.g., to the contribution of the old to total poverty, of female-headed households to total poverty, or of families with many children to total poverty. In multi-racial societies one would be interested in the contribution of the various races to total poverty, e.g. in the contribution of Blacks, Whites and Chicanos to total poverty in the USA, or in the contribution of Malays, Chinese, Indians and others to total poverty in Malaysia. One might also be interested in the contribution of various socio-economic groups to total poverty; think of the various professions, blue-collar and white-collar workers, workers and entrepreneurs, unemployed, veterans, urban and rural districts, etc. Decomposition of poverty may, of course, not pretend to uncover any causality of poverty. It is rather a methodological prerequisite for causality analyses of poverty.

Subgroup monotonicity axiom (SUM):[103] Let y and x be distributions of income broken down into K subgroups $k = 1, \dots, K$. If $y^{(k)} = x^{(k)}$ for all subgroups $k \in \{\{1, 2, \dots, K\} - \{\ell\}\}$, and $P(y^{(\ell)}, \pi) > P(x^{(\ell)}, \pi)$ for subgroup ℓ, then $P(y, \pi) > P(x, \pi)$.

Additive decomposability axiom (AD): Let y be an income distribution broken down into K subgroups $y^{(1)}, y^{(2)}, \dots, y^{(K)}$, and let $\tilde{y}^{(k)}$ be defined as[104]

$$(8) \qquad \tilde{y}_i^{(k)} = \begin{cases} y_i^{(k)} & \text{if } i \notin \Pi(y, \pi), \\ \mu_k & \text{if } i \in \Pi(y, \pi), \end{cases}$$

where μ_k denotes the mean income of the poor in group k. Let $\overline{Y}$ denote the K-vector of the mean incomes of $y^{(k)}$, let M denote the K-vector of the mean incomes of the poor μ_k, let N denote the K-vector of $n_k := card\ y^{(k)}$, and let

[102] Kundu and Smith (1983, p. 427).

[103] Suggested by Foster, Greer, and Thorbecke (1984, p. 763).

[104] This may also be formulated for the weak definition of the poor (with possibly different results).

$w_k(\overline{Y}, M, N, K, \pi) \geq 0$ denote coefficients. Then

$$(9) \quad P(y^{(1)}, y^{(2)}, \ldots, y^{(k)}; n, \pi) = \sum_{k=1}^{K} w_k(\overline{Y}, M, N, K, \pi) P(y^{(k)}, n_k, \pi) + P(\tilde{y}^{(1)}, \tilde{y}^{(2)}, \ldots, \tilde{y}^{(K)}; n, \pi).$$

Weighted sum decomposability axiom (WSD): Let y be a distribution of income broken down into K subgroups $k = 1, \ldots, K$ with population shares n_k/n. Then

$$P(y, \pi) = \sum_{k=1}^{K} \frac{n_k}{n} P(y^{(k)}, \pi).$$

Though SUM seems to be a rather weak logical requirement for poverty indices, many poverty indices do not comply with this requirement, which comes as a great surprise. SUM demands that for any partition of two n-dimensional income distributions into K groups such that $K-1$ partial income distributions are equal, and such that the poverty index for the first remaining partial income distribution is higher than the poverty index for the second remaining partial income distribution, the value of the overall poverty index of the first income distribution should exceed the value of the overall poverty index of the second income distribution.

It seems that AD has so far not been suggested in the literature on poverty measurement. It is inspired by Shorrocks' work on additively decomposable inequality measures of income distributions in general.[105] (9) suggests a breakdown of the poverty index into the measurement of "within group" poverty on the one hand and "between group" poverty on the other. The "within group" component of poverty rests on the values of the poverty indices of the various income groups multiplied by positive coefficients. These coefficients should sum to less than 1 in order to leave some room for the "between group" component of poverty. The measurement of the "between group" component of poverty uses the income distribution $\tilde{y}$ defined in (8). $\tilde{y}$ is derived from y, but replaces all incomes on or below the poverty line by the mean income of the poor μ_k for the respective socio-economic group k. $\tilde{y}$ assumes all poor to have exactly the mean income of the poor within the socio-economic group to which they belong. This enables us to isolate $P(\tilde{y}, \pi)$ as the "between group" component of poverty.

[105] Shorrocks (1980, pp. 614 f.). More general notions of decomposability may be formulated following Cowell's (1980) work on additive inequality measures. Cf. also the Hamada-Takayama (1977, pp. 625–628) attempt at a decomposition of poverty indices along these lines. Anand's (1982, pp. 86–92) notion of decomposition, on the contrary, does not lend itself immediately to be applied also to poverty indices.

WSD does not separate the structural "within group" component of poverty from the systematic "between group" component of poverty, but amalgamates both into a weighted average of the poverty indices of the socio-economic groups, the weights being the population shares. As WSD apportions the amount of poverty aliquotly to the socio-economic groups, it is of much help and importance for empirical work, but it does not allow for discrimination of the structural from the systematic components of poverty. Notice that WSD implies SIN.

Other Axioms

Continuity axiom (C): $P(y, \pi)$ is continuous in y and π.

Increasing poverty line axiom (IPL): $P(y, \pi)$ increases with increasing π.

Normalization axiom (N): For all income distributions $y \geq 0$ and all poverty lines $\pi > 0$ we have $0 \leq P(y, \pi) \leq 1$.

The message of these three axioms is rather simple. N reflects a convenient methodological property that a poverty index should possess. C might also be regarded as a convenient methodological property and may be desirable as long as changes δ in y_i below or above the poverty line are involved that are sufficiently small such that $y_i + \delta$ is on the same side of the poverty line as y_i. Given the dichotomous treatment of the poor and the nonpoor in many instances of poverty measurement, the general applicability of C can hardly be endorsed for poverty indices.[106] We may, however, subscribe to a *poverty continuity axiom* (PC): $P(y, \pi)$ is continuous with respect to all $y_i < \pi$ and π.

IPL requires a poverty index to duly register increases in the poverty line. The proportion of poor axiom advanced, e.g., by Hagenaars[107] is not included in our list of axioms because it lacks analytical rigour. We have already mentioned above that there is no ceteris paribus change in the number of the poor, unless we permit sudden changes from the weak to the strong definition of the poor, or vice versa, and assume the presence of individuals with incomes exactly on the poverty line. But it is in particular this rather special case, where the proportion of poor axiom makes little sense. Such an axiom may only become acceptable if changes in the number of the poor are linked to their concomitant changes in the income distribution. But then it is no longer a proper proportion of poor axiom in the strict sense.

---

[106] Cf. in the same sense Donaldson and Weymark (1986, p. 674).
[107] Hagenaars (1986, p. 121).

2.2.2 *Impossibility Theorems*

If we require poverty indices to satisfy a certain set of axioms three cases may possibly arise:

(i) There exists no poverty index that satisfies all required axioms. In this case the set of axioms chosen is too ambitious and we strike upon an *impossibility theorem*.

(ii) There exists either exactly one poverty index or exactly one parametric family of poverty indices which satisfy all required axioms. In this case, the axiom system is just sufficient to single out a particular poverty index or a particular family of poverty indices. We shall characterize this case as the case of a *possibility theorem*, though it is, in the narrower sense, properly the case of a unique possibility theorem.

(iii) There exist different poverty indices or different families of poverty indices which satisfy the set of required axioms. Then these axioms have the nature of conditions that narrow down the set of feasible poverty indices. The set of axioms has been chosen to be too soft. There is still room for strengthening the requirements of a poverty index thus allowing that additional desirable axioms may be satisfied. We may also speak of possibility theorems in a wider sense, though in this case they do not produce unique results. They just insure the consistency of poverty indices with given sets of axioms.

In this section we shall deal with impossibility theorems. Impossibility theorems show inconsistencies of axioms. Once we strike upon an impossibility theorem, this signals us that it makes no sense at all to look for a poverty index joining all those requirements we want it to satisfy. We have to curb our ambitions and settle for some more modest set of axioms. That is, we have to trade off those axioms of major importance for other axioms of less importance for our purpose.

We cannot, of course, examine all combinations of axioms for their mutual compatibility. We will instead present some of the impossibility theorems of poverty indices that have been discussed in the literature or have been immediately noted in the context of this survey. We have, for example, previously referred to the inconsistency of GF and NPG. From this we deduce the following:

Theorem 1: No poverty index satisfies both GF and NPG.

Proof: Let y denote an n-dimensional ordered income distribution and let y' denote an $(n+1)$-dimensional ordered income distribution with $y_i = y'_i \ \forall\ i = 1, 2, \ldots, n$ and $y'_{n+1} > y'_n$. If $P(\cdot)$ satisfies NPG, $P(y', \pi) < P(y, \pi)$, if it satisfies GF, $P(y', \pi) = P(y, \pi)$, obviously a contradiction. □

A series of impossibility theorems were provided by Donaldson and Weymark. For the sake of economy of space we shall present these theorems without proof. They demonstrate that it is the strong definition of the poor as well as the strong monotonicity and transfer axioms that make poverty indices susceptible to impossibility results.

Theorem 2:[108] Using the strong definition of the poor, no poverty index satisfies F, SM and C.

Theorem 3:[109] Using the strong definition of the poor, no poverty index satisfies both F and SDT.

Theorem 4:[110] Using the strong definition of the poor, no poverty index satisfies F, SM, and SUT.

Let us consider some rationale for these impossibility theorems. F demands a poverty index to be independent of the incomes of the nonpoor. Adopting the strong definition of the poor, F combined with C will force the poverty index to be independent of the nonpoor and the borderline poor. But SM requires a poverty index to decrease if someone of the poor (including the borderline poor) receives some additional money, however small this amount may be. This brings about theorem 2.

SDT requires a poverty index to decrease if a poor person (including the borderline poor under the strong definition of the poor) receives some transfer, however small, from some nonpoor person. But if the recipient of this transfer happens to be one of the borderline poor, this transfer produces a different income distribution among the nonpoor without affecting the incomes of the non-borderline poor. But shifts in the income distribution of the nonpoor should, according to F, not affect the value of the poverty index. We arrive at the impossibility result of theorem 3.

SUT demands a poverty index to increase in case of regressive transfers. Suppose a transfer takes place from a poor person below the poverty line to a borderline poor person thus lifting the borderline poor person out of poverty. According to F, this should change the poverty index by the same amount as if the money taken from the transferer had been destroyed. But SM requires the poverty index to be responsive to any amount of money that a poor person (including a borderline

[108] Donaldson and Weymark (1986, p. 681).
[109] Donaldson and Weymark (1986, pp. 681 ff.).
[110] Donaldson and Weymark (1986, p. 684).

poor person under the strong definition of the poor) receives. This produces the impossibility result of theorem 4.

The next impossibility theorem had been put forward by Kundu and Smith.

Theorem 5:[111] Using the weak definition of the poor, no poverty index satisfies F,[112] SUT, PG,[113] and NPG.

Kundu and Smith checked seven well known poverty indices and found only the head-count ratio to satisfy both PG and NPG.[114] The head-count ratio satisfies also F, yet it violates SUT. If a transfer from a poor person to another poor person near the poverty line takes place which is sufficient to push the latter beyond the poverty line, then, according to SUT, the poverty index should increase, whereas the head-count ratio in fact decreases. This particular case is a good illustration of the conflict between SUT on the one hand and PG and NPG on the other. We can imagine a transfer from a poor person to another poor person near the poverty line which lifts the latter out of poverty, to be split into two parts, viz. first into a drop-out of one poor person, and second into an entrance of one nonpoor person. The first move should, according to PG, decrease the poverty index, and the second move should, according to NPG, decrease the poverty index still further. But these two moves, taken together, conflict with SUT which requires the poverty index to increase if a transfer takes place which is simply a combination of those two moves. This contradiction establishes essentially the impossibility result of theorem 5.[115]

NPG is, of course, contradictory to the conception of poverty as absolute deprivation and violates the requirement that a poverty index should not decrease if only the nonpoor become richer. This extends, of course, to the case of rich people entering the population while leaving the poor in their misery. We have thus immediately noted a conflict between NPG and GF in theorem 1. Kundu and Smith, however, contend that "it may be argued that growth of the rich in no way helps the poor, and in fact deteriorates their situation relative to the average citizen. However, if one compares poverty between large countries and small countries having the same absolute number of poor (with respect to some relevant poverty line) then it seems hard to argue that the degree of poverty in the

---

[111] Kundu and Smith (1983, p. 428).

[112] Notice that Kundu and Smith (1983, p. 424) already *define* a poverty index to satisfy F, contrary to the bulk of other work on poverty measurement.

[113] PG may be weakened to the $\geq$ sign. Cf. Kundu and Smith (1983, p. 429).

[114] Kundu and Smith (1983, p. 427).

[115] Cf. also the explanations for this impossibility result by Sen (1981, p. 193, n. 12); Kundu and Smith (1983, p. 431); Foster (1984, pp. 232 f.).

small country is not greater."[116] It seems unwarranted to outrightly turn down their argument.[117]

2.2.3 *Possibility Theorems*

In the preceding section we have been concerned with too demanding combinations of axioms that precipitate impossibility results. Less demanding combinations of axioms will permit one or more of the poverty indices to pass the test and fulfill the required axioms. Sometimes exactly one poverty index (or one parametric family of poverty indices) should be selected from the set of all poverty indices satisfying some set of axioms. This induced many authors to supplement the set of desirable axioms by some other *conditions* that are not on a par with the more fundamental importance of an axiom, but are more or less incidental requirements designed to reduce the set of feasible poverty indices to just one poverty index. Sometimes an indirect route is chosen, i.e., a poverty index is presented rather directly and its compliance with those axioms that are considered to be indispensable is demonstrated thereafter. This approach does not, of course, exclude the existence of other poverty indices which satisfy the same set of indispensable axioms.

In this section we shall discuss the most important poverty indices that rest essentially on an axiomatic basis. In accordance with their structure we will divide them into *generalized poverty gap indices* on the one hand and *distributional poverty indices* on the other. Before delving into a discussion of this work I hasten to say that there is also another line of rather useful work on poverty indices which penetrates the interrelations between the general axioms (and their various versions) of poverty indices. Such meritorious work has recently been done by Donaldson and Weymark (1986), but space does not permit a more intense discussion of this line of research.

2.2.3.1 *Generalized Poverty Gap Indices*

The first group of poverty indices we shall deal with are those that build in some form upon the notion of the poverty gap, i.e. on the differences between the poverty line and the incomes of the poor. The first axiomatic poverty index put forward by Amartya Sen (1976) was exactly of this kind and has elicited much follow-up work.

---

[116] Kundu and Smith (1983, p. 430).

[117] Kundu and Smith (1983, p. 431) favour a fuzzy set definition of poverty that may perhaps overcome their impossibility result.

The Sen Index

Sen's seminal work originated from his critique of the ad hoc poverty indices. He objected to the head-count ratio, saying that it violates both the monotonicity axioms and the transfer axioms and that the income-gap ratio violates the transfer axioms.[118] These axioms were, however, formulated somewhat elusively in Sen's article, as the most general forms of these axioms, viz. SM and SDT, fit completely his description of these axioms. (Notice that Sen stated these axioms only in one version each.)

But, curiously enough, Sen takes the violation of the monotonicity and transfer axioms only as a point of departure. He then formulates a system of conditions[119] that are sufficient to derive a unique index which happens to satisfy coincidently the monotonicity and the transfer axioms.[120]

Sen required the poverty index to be of the general form

$$P(y,\pi) = A(n,p,\pi)\sum_{i=1}^{p}(\pi - y_i)v_i(y,\pi), \tag{10}$$

where $v_i(y,\pi)$, $i \in \{1,2,\ldots,p\}$, denote the weights of the poverty gaps and $A(\cdot)$ denotes a normalizing parameter.

This poverty index should further meet the following two conditions:

Ranked relative deprivation (RRD):[121]

$$v_i(y,\pi) = p + 1 - i. \tag{11}$$

Normalized absolute deprivation (NAP): Let y denote an ordered income distribution and let $\tilde{y}$ be derived from y by setting $\tilde{y}_i = y_i \;\forall\, i > p$ and $\tilde{y}_i = \mu \;\forall\, i \leq p$. Then

$$p(\tilde{y},\pi) = HI. \tag{12}$$

This gives rise to the following:

---

[118] Sen (1976a, pp. 219 f.).

[119] Sen actually calls them axioms.

[120] To be precise, only weaker versions of these axioms are satisfied by the Sen index, which, however, turned out only later.

[121] Sen (1976a, pp. 221 f.) actually demands two axioms, viz. the *ordinal rank weights axiom* and the *monotonic welfare axiom* which, however, boil immediately down to (11) which has directly been stated for the sake of greater simplicity.

Theorem 6:[122] The only poverty index of the shape (10) satisfying the conditions RRD and NAP has the form

$$(13) \qquad P(y,\pi) = \frac{2}{(p+1)n\pi}\sum_{i=1}^{p}(\pi - y_i)(p+1-i),$$

which converges for rising p to

$$(14) \qquad P(y,\pi) = H[I + (1-I)G],$$

where G denotes the Gini coefficient of the income distribution among the poor.

The particular choice of (10) for the poverty index is obviously inspired by the aggregate poverty gap and by the income-gap ratio, respectively. RRD should reflect relative deprivation among the poor.[123] A poor person feels more deprived, the more other poor persons are perceived to be better off than him or her. It is, however, somewhat difficult to swallow why this feeling of relative deprivation should immediately stop at the poverty line and should not also extend to people beyond it. This assumption therefore does not lack ambiguity: if one argues in favour of perceptions of relative deprivation among the poor, one should at the same time also argue for perceptions of relative deprivation vis-a-vis nonpoor incomes. But Sen rejects this latter approach in spite of his acceptance of relative deprivation *within* the poor. An authority like Pigou had argued quite to the contrary: "Now the part played by comparative, as distinguished from absolute, income is likely to be small for incomes that only suffice to provide the necessaries and primary comforts of life, but to be large with large incomes. In other words, a larger proportion of the satisfaction yielded by the incomes of rich people comes from their *relative*, rather than from their absolute, amount."[124] Pigou attributes thus much greater importance to relative deprivation among the rich than among the poor. We may, of course, agree that poverty is relatively more important, the more a person falls below the poverty line. This could provide another rationale for (11) without requiring us to employ the relative deprivation among the poor as an explanation for (11). But this other explanation fails to convince us that the same income shortfall from the poverty line should be judged differently depending on the number of other poor persons with higher incomes.

As Sen himself asserts, (11) is borrowed from Borda's rank-order method for social choice. "This makes the weights equi-distanced, ... choosing equal distances in the absence of a convincing case for any alternative assumption."[125]

---

[122] Sen (1976a, pp. 223 ff.).
[123] Sen (1981, p. 187).
[124] Pigou (1932, p. 90).
[125] Sen (1979, p. 297). Note that the Gini coefficient may be expressed along similar lines; cf. Anand (1983, pp. 311–316).

This expresses Sen's assumption that "individual welfare is taken to be ordinally measurable and level comparable."[126] But this assumption is at variance with the aggregation procedure chosen in (10), as this aggregation by means of summation requires full cardinal comparability of individual welfare, individual welfare obviously being conceived as decreasing linearly with weighted increasing poverty gaps. Such cardinalistic aggregation procedures contradict the chosen ordinal approach to poverty measurement. By this approach, more information is admitted that would allow us to go beyond the mere rank information of the Borda rule. Moreover, the Borda rule has well-known difficulties with some consistency conditions,[127] which may perhaps also prove disturbing for poverty measurement.

The NAP condition was motivated by the observation that H and I together give us adequate information on the level of poverty if all poor people have the same income μ, "since in this special case the two together can tell us all about the proportion of people who are below the poverty line and the extent of the income short-fall of each. To obtain a simple normalization, we make P equal HI in this case."[128] This condition had been criticized for its rather ad hoc character. Foster, e.g., objected that "specifying that a poverty measure must be precisely the product of H and I seems rather restrictive and arbitrary."[129] He argued that any poverty index which satisfies A, SI, and F will only be a function of H and I for the income distribution $\tilde{y}$,[130] though this is not sufficient to warrant the particular functional form HI. Quite recently, Basu has tried to provide an axiomatic basis for NAP,[131] but some of his axioms can hardly claim to be more intuitive than demanding NAP outrightly, as Sen does.

Theorem 6 tells us, that the Sen index converges for rising p to (14) which is a function of only H, I, and G. It is interesting to note that the convergence to (14) is rather speedy with the number of the poor rising, so that (14) may well serve as a good substitute for (13) in empirical work. (13) may, after some manipulations,[132] be expressed as

$$P(y,\pi) = H\left[I + (1-I)G\frac{p}{p+1}\right], \tag{15}$$

which shows that the difference between (13) and (14) is rather small if the number of the poor is in the magnitude of several thousand.

---

126 Sen (1976a, p. 221).
127 Cf. Sen (1977, pp. 78 f.).
128 Sen (1976a, p. 223).
129 Foster (1984, p. 226).
130 Foster (1984, pp. 246, n. 27).
131 Basu (1985).
132 Sen (1976a, pp. 224 f.).

How does the Sen index comply with the more general axioms? It satisfies WM, MT, and WT, but not SM, SUT and SDT. This may readily be verified if we look at (13). Imagine that the richest poor person, being sufficiently close to the poverty line, is lifted out of poverty. On the one hand, this decreases P by $(\pi - y_p)$, and on the other hand increases P, because the denominator in (13) shrinks from $(p+1)n\pi$ to $pn\pi$. This latter effect may overcompensate the former if y_p were sufficiently close to π thereby enabling the additional income or the transfer to become arbitrarily small.

As to the sensitivity axioms, the Sen index satisfies MOS, but neither RTS nor DTS. If \$ 1 is transferred from the i-th poor person to the $(i+\rho)$-th poor person, this increases the Sen index by $2\rho/(p+1)n\pi$, irrespective of i, which violates RTS. If \$ 1 is transferred from a poor person with income y_i to a poor person with income $y_i + h$, and if, alternatively, \$ 1 is transferred from a poor person with income y_j to a poor person with income $y_j + h$, where $j > i$, but with more income ranks between $y_j + h$ and y_j than between $y_i + h$ and y_i, then this will cause the Sen index to increase more for the transfer from y_j to $y_j + h$ than for the transfer from y_i to $y_i + h$, notwithstanding that $j > i$. This violates DTS.

It is readily verified that the Sen index satisfies F, but it violates GF, because rising n decreases P, given the poor and their incomes. For this very reason it satisfies, curiously enough, NPG, but violates PG if the income of the "new" poor is sufficiently close to the poverty line and the number of the poor is small. Simple numerical examples demonstrate that it violates SIN. The Sen index satisfies A and SI, but not TI. Though TI does not change the poverty gaps, nor the weights, it increases the denominator from $(p+1)n\pi$ to $(p+1)n(\pi+\delta)$, which changes the value of the poverty index.

The Sen index violates both SUM and WSD.[133] Consider two subgroup income distributions $y^{(1)} = (3,3,10,11,15)$ and $y^{(2)} = (7,8,8,11,11)$ with $\pi = 10$. The Sen index gives $P(y^{(1)},\pi) = 0.35$ and $P(y^{(2)},\pi) = 0.15$, but $P(y,\pi) = 2/7$ which is greater than $1/4$, the weighted sum of the two subgroup poverty indices. Allow the income distribution now to be transformed into $x^{(1)} = (1,6,9,11,15)$ and $x^{(2)} = (7,7,9,11,11)$, with π remaining the same. Then the Sen index increases for both subgroups to $P(x^{(1)},\pi) = 0.36$ and $P(x^{(2)},\pi) = 0.16$, but the Sen index for the total income distribution decreases by $1/175$!

I suspect that the Sen index also violates AD, but this remains to be shown. It satisfies N, assuming the value $P = 0$ if there are no poor in the society and the value $P = 1$ if everybody has zero income. It does not satisfy C, but it satisfies PC.

---

133 We take Foster's (1984, p. 241) example. — Notice that the violation of SIN implies the violation of WSD.

Anand suggested a poverty index closely related to the Sen index. His index differs in that he normalized the poverty index to the mean income of the society, $\overline{y}$, instead of to the poverty line, as does the Sen index[134] Anand's poverty index is simply the Sen index multiplied by $\pi/\overline{y}$. If we set $y_i = \mu \; \forall \; i \in \Pi(y, \pi)$, we get for the Anand index

$$(16) \qquad P = \frac{p(\pi - \mu)}{n\overline{y}}.$$

This is the ratio of the aggregate income shortfall of the poor and the GDP, in other words, the share of the GDP which, if transferred to the poor, would just suffice to wipe out poverty completely. It is immediately seen that, by its dependence on $\overline{y}$, the Anand index is sensitive to the income of the nonpoor as well and therefore violates F. If a rise in the income of any member of society can be taken as a proxy for the capacity of reduction of poverty (e.g. to indicate a potential for redistribution), the Anand index would indeed do a good job, as the Sen index is insensitive to the incomes of the nonpoor. If, according to Sen, the purpose of measurement is to check a country's potential ability to meet the challenge of poverty, the Anand index has some definite advantages. An index of poverty, however, should, in Sen's view, not allow an income shortfall of the poor to be compensated by a sufficiently high rise in the incomes of the nonpoor.[135]

The Kakwani and Thon Indices

The failure of the Sen index to satisfy RTS and DTS gave rise to a doctored version of the Sen index which was suggested by Kakwani. Kakwani raised the weights of the Sen index to the k-th power[136] and re-normalized the Sen index to allow for this manipulation. He derived the poverty index[137]

$$(17) \qquad P(y, \pi) = \frac{p}{n\pi \sum_{i=1}^{p} i^k} \sum_{i=1}^{p} (\pi - y_i)(p + 1 - i)^k, \qquad k \geq 0.$$

For $k = 0$, the Kakwani index reduces to HI, for $k = 1$ it becomes the Sen index. The Kakwani index essentially satisfies and violates the same axioms as the Sen index with the exception of RTS and DTS. For $k > 1$, the Kakwani index satisfies RTS, and for a sufficiently large k, it also satisfies DTS. If \$ 1 is

[134] Anand (1977, p. 9).

[135] Sen (1981, pp. 189 f.). — Note that Kakwani (1977b) and Kakwani (1980b, pp. 329 ff.) also normalized with respect to $\overline{y}$ instead of to π.

[136] Kakwani (1980a, p. 441).

[137] Kakwani (1980a, p. 442).

transferred from the j-th poor person to the $(j+\rho)$-th poor person, the Kakwani index increases by

$$(18) \qquad (\Delta P)_{j,j+\rho} = \frac{p}{n\pi \sum_{i=1}^{p} i^k}[(p+1-j)^k - (p+1-j-\rho)^k].$$

Of course, $(\Delta P)_{j,j+\rho}$ increases with decreasing j if $k > 1$, which demonstrates that RTS is satisfied. But things are more complicated with respect to DTS, because starting from different j's the number of income positions between j's income y_j and the person with income y_j+h may fluctuate. We may not exclude that there is only one income position between y_j and y_j+h, which means $\rho = 1$. Equation (18) shows that, including such cases, DTS is satisfied only if k is sufficiently large. But this applies for the fixed population case only, as Foster has demonstrated.[138] For any given k there exists, however, a population size n, such that DTS is violated. Even for populations of fixed size, k^* (such that DTS holds for all $k \geq k^*$) depends on the structure of the income distribution.

The failure of the Sen index to satisfy SM, SUT, and SDT led Thon to develop another variant of the Sen index. Thon also suggested a slight change in the weights of the Sen index, which makes his approach methodologically similar to the Kakwani index. He used the rank of the income position of the poor with respect to the *total* ordered income distribution rather than their rank just within the income distribution of the poor (as Sen did). Thus he used the weights:[139]

$$(19) \qquad v_i = (n+1-i).$$

Upon adequate normalization, Thon derived the poverty index

$$(20) \qquad P(y,\pi) = \frac{2}{(n+1)n\pi} \sum_{i=1}^{p} (\pi - y_i)(n+1-i).$$

It can readily be seen that the Thon index, contrary to the Sen index, satisfies SM, SUT, and SDT, but shares with the Sen index the violation of RTS and DTS, as well as it shares all other essential properties of the Sen index. But as to SM, SUT, and SDT, the Sen and the Thon indices may lead to completely contradictory results. Consider, e.g., the distribution of income among the poor given by $y = (5,5,10,15,26)$ with $\pi = 30$. Then any transfer from a poor individual to another poor person pushing the latter beyond the poverty line would cause Sen's P to decrease, but Thon's P to increase.[140]

---

[138] Foster (1984, p. 229 f.).
[139] Thon (1979, p. 438). — Note that Thon has recently presented a doctored version of this index along similar lines. Cf. Thon (1984, pp. 61 f.).
[140] This example is taken from Foster (1984, p. 231).

Kakwani has also suggested another modification of the Sen index, i.e. to take as weights of the poverty-gaps $(\pi - y_i)$ the proportion of income between π and y_i instead of the number of persons between p and i.[141] This should capture the relative deprivation in terms of the incomes of the richer poor. Sen has observed that this index "takes no note of how the aggregate income of those people is divided among them, and, more importantly, no note even of the number of persons among whom this aggregate income is divided."[142] This second Kakwani index, therefore, does not seem to be an improvement on the Sen index.[143]

The Foster-Greer-Thorbecke Index

Another poverty index related to Sen's has been suggested by Foster, Greer, and Thorbecke. Their index differs from the Sen index as they do not introduce separate weights, but use the poverty gaps themselves as weights:[144]

$$P(y,\pi) = \frac{1}{n}\sum_{i=1}^{p}\left(\frac{\pi - y_i}{\pi}\right)^{\alpha}, \qquad \alpha \geq 0. \tag{21}$$

This is a parameterized poverty index which yields for $\alpha = 0$ the head-count ratio and for $\alpha = 1$ the product of the head-count ratio and the income-gap ratio, HI.

The work of Foster, Greer, and Thorbecke was inspired by the challenge to find a parametric class of additively[145] decomposable poverty indices that satisfy most of the basic properties proposed by Sen. The parameter α can be interpreted as an indicator of *aversion to poverty*. Take $i, j \in \Pi(y, \pi)$ with $y_i < y_j$. Then the ratio of the two contributions to the FGT poverty index $\left(\frac{\pi - y_i}{\pi - y_j}\right)^{\alpha}$ increases with rising α, because $(\pi - y_i)/(\pi - y_j) > 1$. That is, the *relative* influence of poorer persons among the poor upon the value of the FGT index increases with rising α. For $\alpha \to \infty$ the FGT index approaches Rawlsian maximin justice.

The FGT index satisfies first and foremost SUM and WSD, SI but not TI, NPG but not PG, A and SIN, PC, IPL, and F but not GF. This is readily seen by inspection. It satisfies WM and SM for $\alpha > 0$, all transfer axioms and MOS for $\alpha > 1$, and DTS and obviously also RTS for $\alpha > 0$.[146] However, the FGT index

141 Kakwani (1980b, p. 337).

142 Sen (1981, p. 190).

143 Cf. in greater detail Thon (1981).

144 Foster, Greer, and Thorbecke (1984, p. 763); Foster (1984, pp. 239 f.).

145 They mean additive decomposability in the sense of WSD, because they consider a "between group" poverty term to be unnecessary (Foster, Greer, and Thorbecke, 1984, p. 761, n. 2). AD shows, however, that a "between group" poverty term may be defined in a meaningful way.

146 Foster, Greer, and Thorbecke (1984, p. 763).

violates IPA, because $1 \geq (\pi - y_i)/\pi \geq 0 \; \forall \; i \in \Pi(y,\pi)$, which makes the FGT index a decreasing function of α.

For $\alpha = 2$ the FGT poverty index is closely related to

$$(22) \qquad P(y,\pi) = H[I^2 + (1-I)^2 C^2]$$

where $C^2 = \sum_{i=1}^{p} \frac{(y_i-\mu)^2}{p\mu^2}$, i.e. C^2 is the squared coefficient of variation of the incomes of the poor.

We thus see that for $\alpha = 2$ this poverty index bears some resemblance to the Sen index. In particular, it "exhibits a 'transfer neutrality' property based on income differences: a regressive transfer [i.e. a transfer from a poorer to a less poor person] of a given amount of income between two poor persons whose incomes are a certain distance apart will always have the same effect on poverty irrespective of the absolute incomes of persons involved."[147] This means, of course, violation of DTS for $\alpha = 2$.

A similar poverty index was suggested by Chakravarty, who derived this index from a normalized aggregate utility gap of the poor assuming an identical, increasing, and strictly concave utility function of income.[148] It has the shape

$$(23) \qquad P(y,\pi) = \frac{1}{n}\sum_{i=1}^{p}\left[1 - \left(\frac{y_i}{\pi}\right)^e\right], \qquad 0 < e < 1.$$

For $e \to 1$, this index approaches HI. e is a parameter of poverty aversion. The poverty aversion of the Chakravarty index increases with decreasing e in the sense that the incomes of the poor near the bottom are given more *relative* attention by this index. This can easily be demonstrated. The ratio

$$\frac{1-(y_i/\pi)^e}{1-(y_j/\pi)^e}, \qquad y_i < y_j, \quad i,j \in \Pi(y,\pi)$$

increases with decreasing e. Unfortunately, the value of the Chakravarty index itself decreases with decreasing e and thus with increasing poverty aversion. Therefore it violates IPA.

The Chakravarty index has properties similar to the Foster-Greer-Thorbecke index, but it satisfies all monotonicity and transfer axioms without further restrictions on the parameter e. In particular, it satisfies also the decomposability axioms SUM and WSD.

---

[147] Foster (1984, p. 240).
[148] Chakravarty (1983a, pp. 309 f.).

2.2.3.2 *Distributional Poverty Indices*

The Sen-Kakwani Index

Sen has opened up *two* avenues to derive poverty indices. His first approach was essentially to construct a poverty index as a function of the individual poverty gaps leading to the prototype index (13). So far, we have reviewed doctored versions of this type of poverty index. The alternative avenue revealed by Sen was to derive a poverty index by the way of an appropriate inequality measure of the income distribution among the poor. This way led to the poverty index (14). Though Sen derived (14) as a limit of (13) for increasing p, (14) could as well serve as a starting point, i.e., poverty indices may be directly specified in terms of an adequate inequality measure of the income distribution among the poor. One simple way of doing that starts from (14) which can be written as:

$$P(y,\pi) = \frac{p}{n\pi}[\pi - \mu(1-G)]. \tag{24}$$

If we agree to make the dependence of P on G more general, we may choose:

$$P(y,\pi) = \frac{p}{n\pi}[\pi - \mu g(G)] \quad \text{with} \tag{25}$$
$$0 \leq g(G) \leq 1, \quad g(G) = 1 \text{ if } G = 0, \quad g'(G) < 0.$$

This was Kakwani's approach to characterize a more general class of poverty indices.[149] He showed that the Sen index emerges if g is specified as $g(G) = 1 - G$, and the second Kakwani index (relative deprivation in terms of incomes below π, but above y_i) emerges if g is specified as $g(G) = \frac{1}{1+G}$. Discussions of the properties of these indices are included in the last section. Here we are concerned only with the distributional varieties of the Sen and of the Kakwani indices.

The Blackorby-Donaldson Index

There is, of course, no a priori reason why of all inequality measures only the Gini coefficient of the income distribution among the poor, G, should serve as a proxy for the intensity of poverty. Blackorby and Donaldson replaced G in (14) and in (24) by a relative, strictly S-convex and homogeneous of degree zero inequality measure of the incomes of the poor of the Atkinson inequality measure type. We shall denote it by K:

$$K = 1 - \frac{\xi}{\mu}. \tag{26}$$

149 Kakwani (1980b, p. 331). Note that Kakwani used $\overline{y}$ instead of π in the numerator of (25).

ξ denotes the representative income of the poor which "is that income, ... which, if enjoyed by each poor person is ranked as socially indifferent to the current distribution."[150] The rationale for the identification of ξ as representative income of the poor rests on recent work relating inequality measures to social evaluation functions which amount to Bergson-Samuelsonian social welfare functions of income distributions.[151] Let $W(\cdot)$ denote such a social welfare function of the income distribution among the poor. We obtain ξ as a solution of the equation

$$(27) \qquad W(\xi, \xi, \dots, \xi) \doteq W[y_i | i \in \Pi(y, \pi)],$$
where $(\xi, \xi, \dots, \xi)$ is a p-dimensional vector.

We re-arrange (26) to

$$(28) \qquad \xi = \mu(1 - K)$$

and plug this into (24), replacing $\mu(1-G)$, which gives[152]

$$(29) \qquad P(y, \pi) = \frac{p}{n}\left(1 - \frac{\xi}{\pi}\right) = HI^*$$
$$\text{where } I^* = 1 - \frac{\xi}{\pi} = \sum_{i=1}^{p} \frac{\pi - \xi}{p\pi},$$

i.e., I^* is an income-gap ratio using the representative income of the poor ξ instead of the mean income of the poor μ.

The Blackorby-Donaldson poverty index satisfies F and, by virtue of the S-convexity of K, also WT. But there are quite a few objections against this index.[153] In one respect, this poverty index is rather restrictive, as K enters only in the functional form as stated in (14) and (24) into the poverty index; there exist many more possibilities to aggregate inequality measures of the incomes of the poor into a poverty index. On the other hand, (29) may violate even WM, and also the strong transfer axioms,[154] because K may decrease when the income of poor persons decreases (e.g., if a poor person had an income above μ). This would indicate reduced poverty, though poverty has in fact increased. The compliance of the Blackorby-Donaldson index with most other axioms depends decisively on the form of $W(\cdot)$ to derive ξ from (27), so that nothing may be said in general unless

150 Blackorby and Donaldson (1980, p. 1054).
151 Cf. Blackorby and Donaldson (1978).
152 Blackorby and Donaldson (1980, p. 1055).
153 Cf. Foster (1984, pp. 234 f.).
154 Cf. Chakravarty (1983b, p. 79).

$W(\cdot)$ is specified. This index is, in general, also not amenable to decomposability, as may be verified from (27).

Blackorby and Donaldson also presented an absolute poverty index, but we will skip it here, as it suffers from the same aforementioned shortcomings.

The First Clark-Hemming-Ulph Index

Clark, Hemming, and Ulph start along similar lines. They observe that the Sen index (14) can be expressed as[155]

$$P(y,\pi) = HI(1+G^*), \tag{30}$$

where G^* is the Gini index of the distribution of the poverty gaps.

They derive a class of poverty indices by replacing G^* by some other inequality measure as defined on the set of poverty gaps. In particular, they choose individual deprivation functions similar to those suggested by Atkinson (1970):

$$\frac{1}{\alpha}(\pi - y_i)^\alpha, \qquad \alpha \geq 1. \tag{31}$$

The aggregate deprivation function is assumed to be the sum of the individual functions:

$$\sum_{i=1}^{p} \frac{1}{\alpha}(\pi - y_i)^\alpha. \tag{32}$$

The equally distributed equivalent poverty gap can then be computed by:

$$\frac{p}{\alpha}(\pi - \xi)^\alpha = \sum_{i=1}^{p} \frac{1}{\alpha}(\pi - y_i)^\alpha, \tag{33a}$$

which yields:

$$(\pi - \xi) = \left[\frac{1}{p}\sum_{i=1}^{p}(\pi - y_i)^\alpha\right]^{\frac{1}{\alpha}}. \tag{33b}$$

Finally, normalizing this by the mean poverty gap $(\pi - \mu)$ and inserting it into (30) in the place of $(1+G^*)$ gives the poverty index:[156]

$$P(y,\pi) = HI\left(\frac{\pi - \xi}{\pi - \mu}\right). \tag{34}$$

155 Clark, Hemming, and Ulph (1981, p. 519).

156 Note that $\xi < \mu$ if the social evaluation function is strictly concave.

Foster has demonstrated that the inequality measure used by Clark, Hemming, and Ulph is closely related to the Atkinson family of inequality measures.[157]

Though this poverty index resembles the Blackorby-Donaldson index, it is more specific, as it chooses the particular social welfare function as stated in (32). This removes many of the ambiguities that plague the Blackorby-Donaldson index. The advantage of the first CHU index is, of course, bought at the cost of less generality of this index, in the sense that it is limited to a particular form.

The values of the CHU poverty index lie in the closed interval $[0,1]$. For $\alpha = 1$ the CHU index becomes $P(y,\pi) = HI$. For $\alpha > 1$, the CHU index satisfies WM and SM,[158] as well as MT and WT, but fails to satisfy SUT,[159] and, thus, also fails to satisfy SDT. It satisfies, however, MOS, RTS, and DTS. α may be conceived of as a parameter of poverty aversion, as P becomes more sensitive to regressive transfers with rising α. But, as P itself rises with rising α, the CHU index, not unexpectedly, also satisfies IPA, which the attentive reader may easily check for simple numerical examples. It satisfies F, but not GF. Formula (33b) shows that SIN is satisfied, and it may be seen from footnotes 158 and 159 that NPG, but not PG is satisfied (though it will comply with PG in most practical instances of population growth). The CHU index also satisfies A and SI, but not TI.

As to decomposability, we write the CHU index in the form

$$P(y,\pi) = \frac{p}{n\pi}\left[\frac{1}{p}\sum_{i=1}^{p}(\pi - y_i)^{\alpha}\right]^{\frac{1}{\alpha}}. \tag{35}$$

If we also do the same for the indices of the partitioned population, we obtain in general:

$$\frac{p}{n\pi}\left[\frac{1}{p}\sum_{i=1}^{p}(\pi - y_i)^{\alpha}\right]^{\frac{1}{\alpha}} \neq \sum_{k=1}^{K}\frac{p_k}{n\pi}\left[\frac{1}{p_k}\sum_{i\in\Pi(y^{(k)},\pi)}(\pi - y_i)^{\alpha}\right]^{\frac{1}{\alpha}}, \tag{36}$$

[157] Foster (1984, p. 237).

[158] This becomes evident if we write P in the form:

$$P(y,\pi) = \frac{p^{1-\frac{1}{\alpha}}}{n\pi}\left[\sum\nolimits_{i=1}^{p}(\pi - y_i)^{\alpha}\right]^{\frac{1}{\alpha}}.$$

As $0 < 1 - 1/\alpha < 1$ for $\alpha > 1$, lifting one person out of poverty reinforces the reduction of the index in the SM case by the reduction of the factor $p^{1-\frac{1}{\alpha}}$.

[159] For the same reason as noted in the previous footnote, if the richer party to a regressive transfer crosses the poverty line, this reduces P by influence of the factor $p^{1-\frac{1}{\alpha}}$, which may overcompensate the increase in P due to the loss in income of the poorer party to the transfer.

because $p^{1-\frac{1}{\alpha}} \neq \sum_{k=1}^{K} p_k^{1-\frac{1}{\alpha}}$. Therefore the CHU index violates WSD, whereas it obviously satisfies SUM.

Clark, Hemming, and Ulph suggested also another index which we shall deal with below.

The Takayama Index

Whereas most poverty indices try to capture the intensity of poverty by being sensitive to relative deprivation with respect to incomes among the poor, the focus axiom F demands a poverty index to be insensitive to relative deprivation of the poor with respect to incomes of the nonpoor, i.e. relative deprivation stops at the poverty line. The focus axiom, on the other hand, commands justification for poverty measurement because, otherwise, poverty might be reduced as a consequence of the nonpoor becoming richer. A suspension of F may allow a greater wealth of the nonpoor to overcompensate a greater misery among the poor, which would reduce the value of a poverty index, notwithstanding that poverty, regarded in isolation, has in fact increased.

This challenge obviously induced Takayama to suggest another poverty index. He contended that "in measuring poverty it seems reasonable that any income variations of the community member above the poverty line do not affect the value of the poverty index so long as they do not drive him below the poverty line. At the same time, we cannot neglect the existence of people above the poverty line,"[160] because "someone in poverty compares his income with that of others in the community as a whole, not only with that of individuals below the poverty line."[161]

Takayama tried to take incomes above the poverty lines into account without, however, violating the focus axiom. His escape from the Scylla of the focus axiom and the Charybdis of neglecting the incomes of the nonpoor altogether was found in the censored income distribution.

Let $y_1, \ldots, y_n$ be an ordered income distribution, its censored income distribution $y_1^*, \ldots, y_n^*$ is defined as

(37) $$y_i^* := min\{y_i, \pi\}, \qquad i = 1, 2, \ldots, n;$$

i.e., all incomes exceeding the poverty line are replaced by π. Takayama's poverty

160 Takayama (1979, p. 752).
161 Takayama (1979, p. 749).

index is then simply the Gini coefficient of the censored income distribution:[162]

$$(38) \qquad P(y,\pi) = 1 + \frac{1}{n} - \frac{2}{n^2\left[\pi - \frac{p}{n}(\pi - \mu)\right]} \sum_{i=1}^{n} (n+1-i) y_i^*,$$

where $\pi - \frac{p}{n}(\pi - \mu)$ is the mean income of the censored income distribution, $\frac{1}{n}\sum_{i=1}^{n} y_i^*$.

Takayama showed that his poverty index may be expressed in the same terms (H, I, and G) as the Sen index (14) in the form:[163]

$$(39) \qquad \begin{aligned} &P(y,\pi) = H[(1-\Phi)I + \Phi G], \\ &\text{where } \Phi := \frac{\mu}{\mu + \frac{n-p}{p}\pi} = H \frac{\mu}{\left[\pi - \frac{p}{n}(\pi - \mu)\right]}. \end{aligned}$$

Φ is the head-count ratio times the ratio of the mean income of the poor and the mean income of the censored income distribution.

The Takayama index takes the same weights as the Thon index (20) but applies them to incomes instead of to poverty gaps. As it also extends to the (censored) incomes of all n individuals, the Takayama index is virtually an inequality measure of an income distribution adjusted to become a poverty index. The Takayama method may, of course, readily be generalized by applying other inequality measures than the Gini coefficient to the censored income distribution. This has consequently been done by Hamada and Takayama. They suggest a utilitarian index of poverty as:

$$(40) \qquad P(y,\pi) = -\frac{1}{n}\sum_{i=1}^{n} U(y_i^*)$$

and show that, by appropriate specification of the utility function, this index may give rise to the Atkinson measure of inequality adjusted to become a poverty index, to the Theil measure, to the squared coefficient of variation, to the average poverty gap, and even to the Domar-Musgrave measure.[164]

The Hamada-Takayama family of poverty indices (40) seems to be pretty general and little can be said about the properties of this family of poverty indices unless the particular form of the utility function $U(\cdot)$ in (40) has been adequately specified.[165] Hamada and Takayama, however, seem to narrow down their more

---

162 Takayama (1979, p. 754).

163 Takayama (1979, p. 756).

164 Hamada and Takayama (1977, pp. 622–624).

165 Hamada and Takayama (1977, p. 622) only require $U(\cdot)$ to be increasing and concave. Foster's (1984, pp. 235 f.) critique can, therefore, not apply to this general form (40) of a poverty index.

general poverty index (40) to inequality measures of the censored income distribution.

Yet the Hamada-Takayama family of poverty indices suffers from rather severe deficiencies if restricted to inequality measures of the censored income distribution, as Hamada and Takayama's work seems to imply.[166] All poverty indices that are merely inequality measures of the censored income distribution are unsuitable as poverty indices. Imagine a society in which everybody is poor, yet poverty is perfectly equally distributed, i.e., $y_i = \mu < \pi$ for all $i = 1, 2, \ldots, n$. Then any inequality measure of the censored income distribution will assume the value zero in spite of universal incidence of poverty in this society![167] If we have $y_i = \gamma < \pi$ for $i \in \{\{1, 2, \ldots, n\} - \{j\}\}$ and $y_j = \gamma + \Delta < \pi$, $\Delta > 0$, we will have a value greater than zero for such a Hamada-Takayama index. Thus, decreasing j's income ceteris paribus by Δ will cause such a Hamada-Takayama index to decrease. This illustrates that these Hamada-Takayama indices violate both monotonicity axioms. More generally, "a person below the poverty line may still be among the relatively richer in the censored distribution of income with an income above the mean and the median of that distribution. A reduction of his income will in an obvious sense reduce the extent of inequality in the censored distribution, but in an equally obvious sense the community must now be having *more* — not less — poverty."[168] It is obvious that the same effect may apply to transfers from the poor to the nonpoor or to transfers lifting somebody out of poverty, which means that such Hamada-Takayama indices also violate both strong transfer axioms.[169] Little can be said about the compliance of the Hamada-Takayama index with most other axioms unless the specific form of the inequality measure of the censored income distribution is known. From the very construction of these poverty indices we know just that they all satisfy F and A. Because of the properties of the Gini coefficient, the simple Takayama index (38) will neither satisfy the decomposability axioms nor the transfer sensitivity axioms RTS and DTS.[170]

The Second Clark-Hemming-Ulph Index

Though it might seem at first sight that censored income distributions lead to a deadlock, Clark, Hemming, and Ulph have managed to derive a rather promising

---

166 Hamada and Takayama (1977, pp. 623 f.).

167 Foster (1984, p. 235).

168 Sen (1981, p. 194). — Notice also that this poverty index may decrease if sufficiently many nonpoor individuals drop below the poverty line, provided the inequality of the censored income distribution is thereby reduced.

169 Notice, however, that there are plausible restrictions to the occurrence of decreasing P with increasing H in the Takayama index; cf. Takayama (1979, p. 757, n. 16).

170 Cf., e.g., Kanbur (1984, p. 417).

poverty index by employing censored income distributions.[171] They assumed a social evaluation function for individual incomes of the Arrow-Pratt-Atkinson-type and applied this function to censored income distributions. This approach assumes thus the following social evaluations for the individual incomes:

$$U(y_i^*) = \frac{1}{\beta}(min\{y_i, \pi\})^\beta, \qquad \beta \leq 1. \tag{41}$$

Then they calculated for the censored income distribution the equally distributed equivalent income, ξ^*, from:

$$\frac{n}{\beta}(\xi^*)^\beta \doteq \sum_{i=1}^{n} \frac{1}{\beta}(min\{y_i, \pi\})^\beta. \tag{42}$$

Now, their poverty index emerged simply as:

$$P(y, \pi) = 1 - \frac{\xi^*}{\pi}. \tag{43}$$

This may also be expressed as:

$$P(y, \pi) = 1 - \{H[(1 - A)(1 - I)]^\beta + (1 - H)\}^{1/\beta}, \tag{44}$$

where $A := 1 - \frac{\left[\frac{1}{p}\sum_{i=1}^{p} y_i^\beta\right]^{1/\beta}}{\mu}$ is the Atkinson inequality index for the distribution of incomes among the poor.

The range of this index is the closed interval $[0, 1]$. It decreases with rising β and reaches finally $P(y, \pi) = HI$ for $\beta = 1$. The second CHU index satisfies, of course, A and F, but not GF. If we write (43) in the more explicit form

$$P(y, \pi) = 1 - \frac{1}{\pi}\left[\sum_{i=1}^{n} \frac{1}{n}(min\{y_i, \pi\})^\beta\right]^{1/\beta}, \tag{45}$$

we can immediately see that this poverty index satisfies both WM and SM, and SUT and SDT as well, as the nonpoor parts of transfers across the poverty line are suppressed by this index. But this also implies compliance with the weak transfer axioms.[172] For $\beta < 1$, the second CHU index satisfies the sensitivity axioms MOS, RTS, and DTS, but, alas, it does not satisfy IPA. This comes as a surprise, as β

[171] Clark, Hemming, and Ulph (1981, pp. 521 f.).

[172] Notice that this holds only if $y_1 > 0$ after possible transfers. Otherwise P becomes 0 for $\beta < 0$ and maintains that value unless y_1 becomes strictly positive again.

looks to be something like a parameter of poverty aversion, causing the index to increase with decreasing β. But let us choose $\beta_2 < \beta_1$ and check

$$\varphi(i) = \frac{P_2(y_1, \ldots, y_i - \delta, \ldots, y_n, \pi)}{P_1(y_1, \ldots, y_i - \delta, \ldots, y_n, \pi)}.$$

In the sense of the above definition of greater poverty aversion, simple numerical examples show that $\varphi(i)$ does not generally increase with decreasing i. Thus the second CHU index does not exhibit increasing poverty aversion with decreasing β, and therefore it cannot satisfy IPA.

From inspection of (45) it is seen at once that the second CHU index satisfies SIN and SI as well as NPG, but not PG, and that it satisfies SUM, but not WSD. Notice that the second CHU index approaches zero as the income of at least one poor person approaches zero and β is chosen to be negative. But this value is a kind of absorbing barrier, tying the index to zero as long as any one income is zero. In this special case the second CHU index violates all axioms that require the index to change without changing at the same time $y_1 = 0$.

As seen in (43) and suggested by Chakravarty,[173] this poverty index may readily be generalized. Chakravarty's generalization retained the shape of the poverty index given by (43), but allowed for continuous, increasing, strictly S-concave, homothetic, but otherwise arbitrary social evaluation functions defined on the censored income distribution. Such functions may replace the social evaluation function given in (41). The equally distributed equivalent income ξ^* is then to be derived from the applied social evaluation function. Not unexpectedly, this more general poverty index essentially satisfies the same axioms as does the second Clark-Hemming-Ulph index. Chakravarty also defined an absolute poverty index $P = \pi - \xi^*$ which satisfies the same set of axioms (the scale invariance axiom being replaced by the translation invariance axiom),[174] but we will not go into details concerning this index. We shall also skip twelve more poverty indices constructed by Donaldson and Weymark,[175] as most of them are only minor variations of indices discussed above.

The Leyden Index

In section 1.3 we noted that we may find a poverty line π by the SPL approach or by the UPL approach. Under both approaches, however, the poverty line was eventually expressed in terms of money, in particular in terms of income.[176]

---

[173] Chakravarty (1983b, pp. 79 ff.).
[174] Chakravarty (1983b, pp. 82 ff.).
[175] Donaldson and Weymark (1986, pp. 677–680).
[176] Cf. (4) above for the UPL approach.

Only recently the UPL approach has taken the last step along the utility line and expressed the poverty index itself in terms of utility.[177] The welfare threshold of utility δ is directly employed as a poverty line, now expressed in terms of utility. Obviously, we have

$$U(\pi) = \delta. \tag{46}$$

To avoid confusion with the poverty line π we shall refer to δ as the *poverty threshold.*

Hagenaars derives her poverty index from the censored distribution of the utilities of the respective incomes:

$$U^*(y_i) := min\{U(y_i), \delta\}, \qquad i = 1, 2, \ldots, n. \tag{47}$$

Her poverty index is just the Dalton welfare inequality index associated with a utilitarian social welfare function for the censored utility distribution of incomes:[178]

$$P[U(y), \delta] = 1 - \frac{\frac{1}{n}\sum_{i=1}^{n} U^*(y_i)}{\delta}. \tag{48}$$

This index describes the relative shortfall of the average censored utility from the poverty threshold.

Whereas the monetary poverty indices that have been discussed so far do not discriminate among income recipients (beyond their different incomes), utility poverty indices may readily be generalized to allow for individual circumstances without having to specify them in the form of equivalent income scales or to express them as different poverty lines. This is accomplished by making the utility function dependent not only on the individual income, but also on a vector of parameters ς specifying the individual circumstances:

$$U = U(y_i, \varsigma_i), \tag{49}$$

where y_i denotes i's income and ς_i denotes the parameter values of i's individual circumstances. This is certainly a definite advantage of utility poverty indices. We will call a Leyden index based on (46) a *simple* Leyden index, whereas we will term a Leyden index based on (49) a *generalized* Leyden index.

Concerning the compliance of the Leyden index with the axioms, much depends on the particular shape of the individual utility function chosen. As most

177 Hagenaars (1986, pp. 139–144).
178 Hagenaars (1986, p. 139).

axioms are defined in monetary expressions, the utility poverty index has to be translated back into monetary terms in order to check its compliance with most axioms.

By immediate inspection, we can see that the Leyden index (48) satisfies the decomposability axioms SUM and WSD. The simple Leyden index satisfies SIN and A, but the generalized Leyden index [based on (49)] violates A, as it matters to whom the respective incomes are assigned. The Leyden index satisfies F if and only if the individual utility function is *independent* of the prevailing income distribution y. However, it violates GF. Provided the individual utility function remains constant and we treat δ as if it were π, the Leyden index satisfies NPG, but not PG.[179] If the individual utility function is increasing with respect to income, the Leyden index satisfies WM and SM, as $\sum U^*(y_i)$ will increase in cases of additional income to some of the poor. If the individual utility function is increasing and strictly concave, the simple Leyden index satisfies all transfer axioms.[180] However, if individual parameters other than income may also exert an influence on the individual utilities, the transfer axioms are no longer satisfied. Thus the generalized Leyden index violates the transfer axioms. It seems that strict concavity of a strictly increasing individual utility function with $U''' > 0$ is sufficient for the simple Leyden index to satisfy the sensivity axioms MOS, RTS, and DTS. As to IPA, still more information on the individual utility function would be needed.

2.3 Global Poverty Dominance

The framework of poverty measurement discussed so far provides a complete ordering of income distributions with respect to poverty. But we encounter considerable differences in opinions as to the right poverty line and as to the appropriate choice of the poverty index. The choice of a particular poverty line and of a particular poverty index may, unfortunately, considerably affect the results obtained and conclusions drawn. Some scholars[181] have therefore bent their interest towards the question of robustness of the results with respect to variations in the poverty line and in the poverty index. Curiously enough, these investigations not only

---

[179] If an individual with an income x and a utility of this income such that $\frac{1}{n}\sum U^*(y_i) < U^*(x) \leq \delta$ enters, the value of the Leyden index decreases, which violates PG.

[180] For a proof cf. Hagenaars (1986, pp. 142 f.). Notice, however, that the Leyden utility function of income being assumed to be S-shaped (lognormal) violates the transfer axioms even for the simple Leyden index, which is one of the inconsistencies of Hagenaars' work. For further details cf. Seidl (1987).

[181] Notably Atkinson (1985a, 1985b); Foster and Shorrocks (1986); Le Breton (1986).

reveal a close relationship between poverty dominance and the social welfare of income distributions, but also between monetary poverty indices and utility poverty indices.

Let us, for the sake of simplicity, start with the head-count ratio as a poverty index. Let us first assume a fixed population of size n and let us consider two ordered income distributions y and x. We define a binary relation $H(\pi_0)$ as follows:

$$(50)\quad yH(\pi_0)x \iff \#\{y_i|i \in \Pi(y,\pi)\} \geq \#\{x_i|i \in \Pi(x,\pi)\} \quad \forall\, \pi \in \mathbb{R}_+,\ \pi \leq \pi_0.$$

$yH(\pi_0)x$ means that there is no less poverty in y than in x in the fixed population case if for *all* poverty lines not exceeding π_0 the head-count ratio of y is not smaller than the head-count ratio of x. This captures the notion of global poverty dominance under the head-count ratio, where the globality is, however, restricted by π_0.

Of course, $H(\pi_0)$ no longer provides a complete ordering of income distributions with respect to poverty, but only a *partial* ordering. However, *if* this relation holds, we can rely on robust results for the range $(0, \pi_0]$ of the poverty line. There is no less poverty in y than in x under the head-count ratio irrespective of which value of the poverty line in the interval $(0, \pi_0]$ is chosen. This result is not endangered by reversals if the poverty line shifts within its feasible range.

Let us now consider the set of increasing utility functions of income:

$$(51)\qquad \mathcal{U}_1 := \{U|\mathbb{R}_+ \to \mathbb{R},\ U' > 0\ \forall\, y \in \mathbb{R}_{++}\}.$$

Let us recall that $y_i^* = min\{y_i, \pi\}$ denotes the censored income distribution. We may now employ a close relative of the Leyden index (48) to define the following relationships:

(52)

$$y\mathcal{U}_1(\pi_0)x \iff 1 - \frac{\frac{1}{n}\sum_{i=1}^{n} U(y_i^*)}{U(\pi)} \geq 1 - \frac{\frac{1}{n}\sum_{i=1}^{n} U(x_i^*)}{U(\pi)} \quad \forall\, U \in \mathcal{U}_1 \text{ and } \pi \leq \pi_0.$$

This means that this relative of the Leyden index should indicate no less poverty for y than for x under all feasible utility functions and for all $\pi \in (0, \pi_0]$. $\mathcal{U}_1(\pi_0)$ is, of course, also a partial ordering of income distributions.

As to the relationship between $H(\pi_0)$ and $\mathcal{U}_1(\pi_0)$, we have the following

Theorem 7: $yH(\pi_0)x \iff y\mathcal{U}_1(\pi_0)x.$

Proof: Let (50) hold. Then we must have $y_i \leq x_i\ \forall\ i \in \Pi(y, \pi_0)$. Assume, to the contrary, $y_k > x_k$, $k \in \Pi(y, \pi_0)$. Then we may choose a $\overline{\pi} < \pi_0$ such that $y_k > \overline{\pi} > x_k$, which gives $\#\{i \in \Pi(y, \overline{\pi})\} < \#\{i \in \Pi(x, \overline{\pi})\}$, i.e. a contradiction.

$y_i \leq x_i \; \forall \; i \in \Pi(y, \pi_0)$ means $\Pi(x, \pi) \subseteq \Pi(y, \pi) \; \forall \; \pi \leq \pi_0$. This means that for any $\pi \leq \pi_0$ we have no more entries in x^* less than π_0 than we have in y^*, and that corresponding entries in y^* are not greater than those in x^*. For increasing utility functions U this implies:

$$\sum_{i=1}^{n} U(y_i^*) \leq \sum_{i=1}^{n} U(x_i^*), \tag{53}$$

which gives, after some re-arrangement, (52).

Conversely, (52) gives (53) immediately. We shall prove that this implies $y_i \leq x_i \; \forall \; i \in \Pi(y, \pi_0)$, which in turn means $yH(\pi_0)x$, as we already know. Assume $x_1 < y_1$. Then we can choose a $\pi < \pi_0$ such that $x_1 < \pi < y_1$. Now we have

$$nU(\pi) > U(x_1) + (n-1)U(\pi),$$

which contradicts (53). Therefore $U(y_1) \leq U(x_1)$ and thus $y_1 \leq x_1$. Let us now assume by induction that $y_i \leq x_i$, $i = 1, 2, \ldots, k$, which implies

$$\sum_{i=1}^{k} U(y_i) \leq \sum_{i=1}^{k} U(x_i).$$

We show $y_{k+1} \leq x_{k+1}$ by contradiction. If $y_{k+1} > x_{k+1}$, we can choose a $U \in \mathcal{U}_1$ such that (notice that U is an increasing but otherwise arbitrary function)

$$U(y_{k+1}) - U(x_{k+1}) > \sum_{i=1}^{k} U(x_i) - \sum_{i=1}^{k} U(y_i). \tag{54}$$

Assume further that we choose a $\pi < \pi_0$ such that $y_{k+1} < \pi < y_{k+2}$. Then (54) violates (53). Therefore $y_{k+1} \leq x_{k+1}$.

□

Notice that this result translates readily to the variable population case. Let n_y and n_x denote the numbers of the individuals in the distributions y and x, respectively. We can modify (50) by dividing the left hand side of the inequality by n_y and the right hand side by n_x, and we can modify (52) by substituting n_x and n_y in the appropriate places. The result remains essentially unchanged for the variable population case.

Theorem 7 reveals many important insights. Its first message is that the head-count ratio conveys exactly the same information regarding global poverty dominance as a Leyden-type poverty index which admits *all* strictly increasing utility functions. This result gives much greater appeal to the head-count ratio than we would attribute to it without this insight. If we cannot settle up on some more specific utility functions than just strictly increasing utility functions, then all the information a Leyden-type index conveys with respect to global poverty dominance is conveyed by the head-count ratio as well.

Second, there is a close relationship between utilitarian welfare dominance of the censored income distribution and the head-count ratio. This is shown in (53) and evolved as an intermediate result from our analysis. If a censored income distribution x has more aggregate welfare than y under all strictly increasing utility functions for all π in some interval $(0, \pi_0]$, x welfare dominates y. This global welfare dominance implies, on the other hand, global poverty dominance of y over x, as expressed by the head-count ratio. Therefore most work in this field is cast in terms of poverty dominance vis-a-vis welfare dominance,[182] though a good case can be made to juxtapose monetary poverty indices to utility poverty indices instead.

Third, notice the close relationship between the head-count-ratio and first order stochastic dominance. If (50) and (52) hold, we must have, by proof of theorem 7,

$$y_i^* \leq x_i^*, \quad i = 1, 2, \ldots, n; \; y \text{ and } x \text{ censored at } \pi_0,$$

and therefore

$$\frac{\#\{y_i^* | y_i^* \leq \pi\}}{n} \geq \frac{\#\{x_i^* | x_i^* \leq \pi\}}{n} \quad \forall\, \pi \in (0, \pi_0]. \tag{55}$$

This means that x is preferred to y by the criterion of first order stochastic dominance.

Our discussion of the compliance of the Leyden poverty index with axioms of poverty measurement has shed some light on the influence of the properties of the utility function on the satisfaction of various axioms. If the utility function is only known to be strictly increasing, the Leyden index satisfies the monotonicity axioms, but not the transfer axioms. It will do so, however, if the utility function is known to be strictly increasing and concave. The concavity requirement is one more restriction on the utility function which allows more specific results. This additional information allows the derivation of a more specific poverty index than the head-count ratio for the analysis of global poverty dominance. Here we shall only sketch these more sophisticated results, but refer to the work of Foster and Shorrocks (1986) for greater detail.

---

182 Such is the line of work done by Foster and Shorrocks (1986) and Le Breton (1986). Atkinson (1985b, p. 33) seems to have laid more stress on the second interpretation.

Let us consider the poverty index HI. Then global poverty dominance for $\pi \in (0, \pi_0]$ is equivalent to global poverty dominance of the Leyden-type index for strictly increasing *concave* utility functions, to welfare dominance for strictly increasing concave utility functions, and to second order stochastic dominance.[183]

If we go still further and employ the Foster-Greer-Thorbecke poverty index with $\alpha = 2$, global poverty dominance for $\pi \in (0, \pi_0]$ is equivalent to global poverty dominance of the Leyden-type index and to welfare dominance for strictly increasing concave utility functions with $U''' > 0$, and to third order stochastic dominance.[184]

Concerning these results, we are, of course, not confined to finite or to discrete income distributions. All results carry over readily to continuous terms analysis. Notice also that all results hold if there is no upper bound π_0 on the poverty line. However, an effective upper bound π_0 strengthens the range of results still further, because all income differences beyond π_0 are ignored. Notice finally that all monetary poverty indices may also be interpreted in utility terms,[185] though this may sometimes seem somewhat artificial.

So far, the analysis of global poverty dominance has produced results only for the poverty indices H, HI, and for the FGT-index with $\alpha = 2$. Further research is necessary to extend this analysis to other poverty indices also. This research would have to concentrate in particular on the class of the individual utility functions that convey exactly the same information in terms of utility poverty indices, and thereby in terms of aggregate welfare, as the particular monetary poverty index.

2.4 Multidimensionality in Poverty Measurement

In accordance with our assumption at the end of section 1.4, we have assumed up to now that all people may be treated alike: the old, the young, the disabled, male and female, people living in different places in households of different size and structure. In short, people with rather different characteristics have been treated as if they all were homogeneous with respect to all characteristics except income. Of course, people do differ in reality. Does this frustrate all theoretical work on poverty measurement as has been expounded above?

There are at least two ways out of this stalemate. First, we may partition the set of individuals into mutually disjoint groups of agents that are homogeneous

183 Cf. Foster and Shorrocks (1986, pp. 13–18). — Notice that, curiously enough, HI does not satisfy the transfer axioms (probably because it is the "least concave" function).

184 Cf. Foster and Shorrocks (1986, pp. 19–25; cf. also a minor restriction noted on p. 27).

185 Cf. Hagenaars (1986, pp. 133–136).

with respect to the characteristics that should explicitly be taken into consideration. Then we may calculate poverty indices for all groups with usually different poverty lines.[186] Our final task is an *aggregation exercise*, viz., to aggregate the values of the poverty indices of the various groups into an overall poverty index. Notice that this aggregation exercise is different from, though somewhat related to, the decomposition of poverty indices. The decomposition exercise traces poverty down to different socio-economic groups using, however, the *same* poverty line for all groups. The aggregation approach places the comparison of different groups' poverty into the aggregation procedure of groups' poverty indices.

The other way out of this stalemate is to make the comparison of poverty of people with different characteristics on the level of the individuals themselves. This is commonly done by computing *equivalent incomes* which refer to some basic type of individuals with reference values of the characteristics. After calibrating the individual incomes in that way, they may readily be compared to a poverty line which is derived for the reference type individual. As the incomes of all other types have been converted to equivalent incomes, all equivalent incomes may readily be compared with the reference poverty line which becomes the unique poverty line in the world of calibrated incomes. The conventional poverty indices may now be applied to the income data that have been processed in this way.

Both approaches are far from being ideal devices. Each one has its merits and its drawbacks. The first approach handles poverty measurement *within* each group in a satisfactory manner, but shifts the rub to the aggregation exercise. It is then up to the aggregation exercise to solve questions such as whether poverty among the disabled would bear heavier on overall poverty, rather than would poverty among the old, etc. This may be expressed in terms of monetary poverty indices or in terms of utility poverty indices. As the utility formulation is of much help for this exercise (utilities being assumed to be cardinal and fully interpersonally comparable), we find the aggregation approach essentially only in connection with utility poverty lines.[187] This approach has, on the other hand, the advantage that monetary group poverty indices are reported in terms of the same monetary units for all, and utility group poverty indices are reported in terms of the same utility units for all.

The equivalence scales approach, on the other hand, has the advantage that all individual incomes are adapted vis-a-vis a common reference group, which allows

[186] Otherwise the partition would be too fine, because the rationale for assigning individuals to different groups lies in their different poverty demarcation line depending on the characteristics of the various groups.
[187] Hagenaars (1986, p. 136).

a common unique poverty line to be applied. Once the data have been processed in this way, we may proceed as if we had only dealt with homogeneous individuals. However, we do not report poverty for all but one group in terms of the same monetary unit. One unit of real money may have a rather different impact on poverty measurement if it is transferred from a member of one socio-economic group to a member of another socio-economic group. In terms of reference income, it may either increase or decrease in importance and may exert rather heavy influence on poverty measurement. Moreover, all axioms refer only to standardized monetary (or utility) units, where there is a *different* factor converting real money into standardized money for each socio-economic group. The equivalence scales approach buys simplicity at the cost of expressing everything in standardized money (utility) units.

Let us, for the simplicity of exposition, illustrate this only for the case of different treatment of households and household composition for poverty measurement.

Concerning the treatment of households, Atkinson has stressed that we could either take the household as the unit, or we could take the individual as the unit and assign the per capita household income to the individuals (the approach that we have chosen so far may implicitly be interpreted this way), or we could express the household members in terms of equivalent adults and express income as per capita income of an equivalent adult.[188] Neither approach is, however, satisfactory for the purpose of poverty measurement.[189] The first approach would consider a household with income $\pi - \epsilon$, $\epsilon > 0$, but arbitrarily small, as poor, irrespective of the number of its members. Moreover, if the composition pattern of poor households differs from the composition pattern of nonpoor households, poverty will either be underestimated or overestimated. The second approach does not allow for scale effects of different household size and different household composition. A household consisting of a couple with 6 children, say, below the age of 10, and only one spouse working with per capita income of $\pi - \epsilon$, $\epsilon > 0$, but very small, may enjoy a satisfactory standard of living, whereas a household consisting of one disabled person with the same per capita income may at the same time be considered as rather poor. The third approach does not treat individuals equally. If the poor happen to have relatively more children, a simple poverty index such as the head-count ratio will underestimate poverty; if they have relatively fewer children, it will overestimate poverty. This carries over to most other poverty indices as well.

---

188 Atkinson (1983, p. 52).
189 Sen (1979, pp. 291 f.).

A more satisfactory approach is to express individual income as *per capita equivalent household income.* The computation of equivalent household income was pioneered by Barten and Muellbauer,[190] building on work by Sydenstricker and King, Friedman, and Prais and Houthakker;[191] credit must also be paid to Kakwani.[192] Space does not permit us to go into details with this sophisticated and sometimes cumbersome approach. To put it in a nutshell, one starts usually with a Stone-Geary utility function and a linear expenditure system. This framework gives rise to an indirect utility function and to parameter estimates. A standard household is then specified and, choosing a standard income level, the income level of another household with a different composition that gives rise to the same utility of the original household is computed. This is the equivalent household income. Expressed in per capita terms we may, e.g., find that the equivalent per capita income of a one-person household is 75 per cent higher than that of a household with two adults and two children, and that the equivalent per capita income of a household with two adults and seven children is only half of that of the standard household (2 adults and 2 children).[193] This makes a ratio of approximately 3.5 : 1 between per capita equivalent incomes of one person households and nine-person households.

Multidimensionality in poverty measurement leads, last but not least, to other entirely new dimensions not encountered in one-dimensional poverty measurement, viz. poverty as a consequence of *inadequate characteristics.* Let us, again, concentrate on household composition and let us assume a ratio of 3.5 : 1 between per capita equivalent incomes of one-person households and nine-person households. Then one might argue that if nine one-person households decided to form one nine-person household, they may at once all be lifted out of poverty due to the great economies of scale of larger households. Of course, this recommendation is not meant to be taken seriously, but it demonstrates the existence of a phenomenon in poverty measurement quite different from just insufficient income, viz. *poverty by structure*, such as inadequate household structure, old age, disability, sex, living in the wrong places, etc. Poverty by structure and poverty by insufficient income exert mutual influence on each other. So far, there are no results which reconcile both influences. Perhaps some methods developed for the investigation of multidimensional inequality measurement,[194] which are, however, still in their infancy,

---

[190] Barten (1964); Muellbauer (1974); cf. also Deaton and Muellbauer (1980, chapter 8).

[191] Sydenstricker and King (1920/21); Friedman (1952); Prais and Houthakker (1971, chapter 9–10).

[192] Kakwani (1977a); Kakwani (1980b, pp. 352 ff.).

[193] Kakwani (1980b, p. 363).

[194] Cf., e.g., Kolm (1977); Atkinson and Bourguignon (1982); Maasoumi (1986).

may also prove to be of some help for multidimensional poverty measurement. This challenge provides much scope for further research.

2.5 Poverty and Measurement Problems of Income

We have thus far implicitly made yet another simplifying assumption, to wit that low income is the best proxy for the incidence of poverty. It has sometimes been argued that low spending rather than low income should be regarded as the better proxy for poverty,[195] where low spending should be understood in the sense of consumption rather than consumption expenditure.[196] The reason put forward is that spending includes *dissaving* and consumption includes also the consumption of durables, in contrast to consumption expenditure, which may either overshoot consumption (if durables are bought) or undershoot consumption (if durables bought in some former period are used).

A related question is the treatment of inter-family and intra-family transfers for poverty measurement. The existence of such transfers could make inter-family and intra-family income distribution quite different from the way it looks if we assume an equal distribution of income per head within a family. It seems that it is in particular the women who are worse off than their husbands in low income families.[197]

The differences between income and consumption as appropriate yardsticks and indicators of poverty are considerably toned down if we transform ordinary monetary income into more doctored versions, as suggested mainly by social aid experts. The very first thing would be the consideration of income components that are not counted as usual income, such as some monetary transfers, or income from the black economy.[198] Next we may impute income components resulting from the agents' endowments with different wealth.[199] We may take a step further and make allowances for different individual talents or other possibilities that might, if adequately utilized, increase money income.[200] As already mentioned, we may adjust the income distribution to reflect the influence of gifts and inter-family

---

[195] Cf. Atkinson (1985b, pp. 7 f.), and the literature quoted there.
[196] Atkinson (1985b, pp. 24 f.).
[197] Atkinson (1985b, pp. 20 f.).
[198] Cf. Plotnick and Skidmore (1975, p. 32); Green (1967, pp. 30 ff.).
[199] Cf. the *income-net worth concept* pioneered by Weisbrod and Hansen (1977, p. 34).
[200] Cf. in particular the *earnings capacity concept* pioneered by Garfinkel, Haveman, and Betson (1977); cf. also Garfinkel and Haveman (1977); Watts (1977, p. 27).

as well as intra-family transfers.[201] Finally, there may occur income in kind,[202] fringe benefits, or home production,[203] which lead to further superimpositions of the original income distribution. Notice, however, that all these refinements for adjusting the income concept to the real disposal of economic resources require detailed information that is typically lacking. The analyst has usually to confine himself with more or less deficient images of such ideal patterns.

But once the concept of income is adequately modified such that it approaches the true disposability of economic resources for the individual, the difference between income, spending and consumption becomes increasingly meaningless. If an individual may dispose of sufficient resources, but, for some reason, refuses to do so, he can hardly be regarded as being poor in some objective sense. The voluntary abstention from making use of economic resources to which an individual has access does not cause him to rank among the poor.

There is hardly any disagreement in the literature that income should be comprehensively measured, but there is considerable disagreement as to the extent of comprehensiveness in income measurement. The effects of more comprehensive concepts of income for inequality measures of the income distribution may well be ambiguous. It depends on whether the high or low income strata experience greater relative increases of comprehensive income as compared with narrower concepts of direct monetary income. But concerning poverty, more comprehensive concepts of income should unequivocally decrease both the incidence and the intensity of poverty. The neglect of more comprehensive income concepts has led to much premature judgment on poverty and to widespread overestimation of the incidence and intensity of poverty.

Another source of over- or underestimation of poverty may be determined to result from *fluctuating incomes*.[204] If the average income of an agent lies above the poverty line, but due to some circumstances such as casual unemployment, the actual income falls below the poverty line for some periods, actual poverty is in fact overestimated by influence of this particular agent. If an agent's average income lies below the poverty line, but, due to casual employment, it exceeds the poverty line for some periods, actual poverty is underestimated by influence of this particular agent. It depends on the relative occurence of agents of the first or of the second kind, whether we encounter overestimation or underestimation of

201 Smeeding (1977a, pp. 162 f.); Smeeding (1977b, p. 363); concerning the old, cf. Moon (1977, pp. 98 ff.).
202 Smolensky, Stiefel, Schmundt, and Plotnick (1977); Smeeding (1977b).
203 Watts (1977, pp. 27 f.); Vickery (1977) devised a (two-dimensional) poverty measure explicitly allowing for home production.
204 Cf. Atkinson (1985b, pp. 23 f.).

poverty in the aggregate. The perturbances of fluctuating incomes with respect to poverty measurement may be reduced by longer assessment periods of income, such as on an annual income basis rather than on a monthly income basis.

Let us finally cast an eye upon the reliability of available data. Data concerning the lower tail of income distributions are notoriously defective. For instance, data on low incomes coming from income tax statistics or from statistics of social security contributions show a marked bias of underestimating income because they ignore incomes and income deductions that are not subject to tax or to contributions, they ignore most transfers (as they are not liable to tax or to contributions), income in-kind, fringe benefits, home productions, income from the black economy, and the value of leisure. The use of data resulting from supplementary benefit scales and similar guidelines from social policy typically suffer from the same defects. Serious estimates of poverty in a society should therefore preferably rely on primary data, not on secondary data of existing statistics that have been devised with some other purpose in mind. But as most scholars (with good reason) eschew the immense work of new data collection (or have not access to micro census data), most empirical studies on poverty exaggerate the true incidence and intensity of poverty.

This is of particular importance if we employ poverty indices that bear an immediate meaning, such as, e.g., the head-count ratio. It certainly differs if we say that 10 per cent of the population is exposed to the misery of poverty, or if we find 30 per cent of the population in poverty. Most axiomatic poverty indices, however, lack such an immediate impression. They are primarily used for the purpose of *comparisons* of poverty, whereas their actual values are difficult to interpret, as intuitive interpretations of such more abstract indices are lacking in most cases. For such poverty indices, the important question refers to the effect on poverty *comparisons* by defective data. If all relevant data happen to be biased in the same direction, it could well be true that poverty is equally understated in each case, whereas the poverty ranking is not affected.

2.6 Poverty Indices, Maximin Justice, and Welfarism: A Reflection

When I considered attempting to gain a foothold on attitudes about poverty aversion using an experimental approach, I posed the following question to some respondents: "Imagine two families of four persons that are identical, except that famliy A disposes of an adjusted annual income of $ 8,000.–, whereas family B disposes of only $ 5,000.–. Let the poverty line amount to $ 10,000.–. Now suppose I make a charity donation of $ 500.– and ask you to distribute this amount justly to these two families. How much would you give each of them?" To my great surprise, the majority of respondents suggested that the whole amount of $ 500.– should be given to the poorer family B. That is evidence that they were led by something like the Rawlsian principle of maximin justice.

Then I posed the same question in the garb of a different story: "Imagine the fate of a Soviet dissident family: Mr. Aleksejovich had been a famous surgeon in Moscow, his wife had been a Professor of philosophy at Moscow university. Both being dissidents, they were persecuted by the KGB, lost their jobs, and finally managed to emigrate to the United States. They have two children. Due to difficulties with the English language and due to the restrictions exerted by the AMA, Mr. Aleksejovich is jobless. His wife is forced to work as a cleaning aid in a public lavatory. This family disposes of an annual adjusted income of $ 8,000.–. Let the poverty line be again $ 10,000.–. Mr. Bold, on the other hand, is a well known drunkard; his wife is a drug addict. Their two half-grown children are members of a youth gang that has committed some burglaries. This family disposes of an adjusted annual income of $ 5,000.–. How would you distribute my charity donation of $ 500.– justly to those two families?" It turns out that the majority of respondents will give the Aleksejovich family the whole amount of $ 500.– and would give nothing to the Bold family, obviously applying something like a leximax principle of justice.

This example captures the main contemporary problem of poverty measurement and inequality measurement, viz. the absence, neglect or outright suppression of any information other than income information. But unequal income positions can only be justified under a welfaristic social welfare function if there is at least one additional variable other than income that may justify different income positions. If this is not the case, then only an *equal* distribution[205] of incomes will maximize welfaristic social welfare, provided the individual utility function[206] is increasing and concave.

This means that poverty measures as well as inequality measures suffer from a normative bias, as they unconditionally endorse a more equal distribution of income (or of income among the poor) vis-a-vis a less equal distribution, irrespective of all other circumstances. This is even made a condition of poverty and inequality

---

[205] Notice that the *equally distributed equivalent income* that plays a prominent role in poverty measurement as well as in inequality measurement is nothing else than the application of this concept. Given total national income, welfaristic social welfare is maximized if incomes are equally distributed. This relates to the Dalton and Atkinson indices of inequality.

[206] Notice that for lack of other factors influencing utility we have to assume an equal utility function of income for all agents.

measurement if we invoke the *anonymity* axiom, because the assignment of given incomes to other individuals should not influence the value of a poverty index or of an inequality index. But precisely this may occur, if the anonymity axiom is dispensed with. When measuring poverty, an assignment of the given incomes to different individuals may, in the absense of the anonymity axiom, not only push some individuals across the poverty line; it may also alter the intensity of poverty among the poor. Thus it will generally affect the value of the poverty index. The same story also holds for inequality measurement. In this respect, poverty and inequality measurement resemble Edgeworthian and other efforts to derive a first best welfaristic taxation formula. Only one rather robust solution emerged, viz. an equal post-tax, post-transfer income for all. It was not until the development of optimal tax theory in the seventies that more sophisticated tax formulae could be presented as solutions of models of second best taxation. The crucial step in accomplishing that was the introduction of work effort as the second parameter into the utility function and the assumption that individuals differ with respect to their ability. Once we abandon the anonymity axiom and allow other information to influence the judgment of the welfare position of an individual, we inevitably enter the realm of multi-dimensional poverty measurement. Considering the difficulties of an empirical derivation of degrees of poverty aversion or inequality aversion without additional information, this is certainly the avenue ahead of us.

No less an authority than Pigou has adduced arguments for different treatment of poor and rich people. He remarked that "it may be maintained that a rich man, from the nature of his upbringing and training, is capable of obtaining considerably more satisfaction from a given income ... than a poor man would be. For, if anybody accustomed to a given standard of living suddenly finds his income enlarged, he is apt to dissipate the extra income in forms of exciting pleasure, which, when their indirect, as well as their direct, effects are taken into account, may even lead to a positive loss of satisfaction. To this argument, however, there is a sufficient answer. It is true that at any given moment the tastes and temperament of persons who have long been poor are more or less adjusted to their environment, and that a sudden and sharp rise of income is likely to be followed by a good deal of foolish expenditure which involves little or no addition to economic welfare. If, however, the higher income is maintained for any length of time, this phase will pass; whereas, if the increase is gradual or, still better, if it comes about in such a way as not to be directly perceived — through a fall in prices, for example — the period of foolishness need not occur at all."[207] Quite recently,

[207] Pigou (1932, pp. 90 f.).

Atkinson has argued along similar lines: "For some people, interdependence between consumption at different dates is seen to be such as to impose a greater cost of poverty on those who had previously enjoyed a high level of living."[208]

It is astonishing to see the economics of poverty undergo a development that somewhat resembles the development of welfare economics. Old welfare economics rested on cardinal and interpersonally comparable utility, an assumption that was strongly opposed by new welfare economics, which was anxious to express utility as an ordinal concept without any interpersonal comparability whatsoever. But, as the discussion of compensation criteria and Pareto optimality shows, new welfare economics proved to be a deadlock. New avenues were only opened up by Amartya Sen's suggestion of social welfare functionals that are more or less based on doctored versions of good old cardinal and interpersonally comparable utility.

There are parallels in the economics of poverty. Davis has shown that until the work of Booth, shortly before the turn of the century, poverty had hardly been dealt with at all without pejorative overtones expressing that the poor were to blame for their misery. (Just think of Malthusian economics!) Booth became the first to separate the *fault of being poor* from a *value-free description of poverty* in a completely statistical way. "His definition of poverty as an inadequate number of calories per day, based on a scientific analysis of the average adult's daily energy need, allowed poverty to be identified, measured, and possibly alleviated. Previous measures of poverty had necessarily always had a degree of subjectivism and moralism about them."[209] The twentieth century has gradually begun to remove "the 'capitalistic-religious' moral stigma attached to poverty and to cause impoverishment to be regarded as largely the result of such forces as economic dislocation and social inequality."[210]

Such is the contemporary state of the art, and it is the present state that has been surveyed. But if we want to rescue the economics of inequality and the economics of poverty from blind and unreflected egalitarianism, we have to allow more information to enter into the judgment of the welfare position of an individual. Such justification of different income positions, however, invariably leads back to consider once again moral principles for the judgment of income positions and of poverty. Personal merits and personal fault concerning the economic positions of individuals are then likely to re-enter poverty and inequality measurement once again.

---

[208] Atkinson (1985b, p. 25).
[209] Davis (1979/80, p. 96).
[210] Davis (1979/80, p. 96).

References

Abel-Smith, B., and **Townsend, P.** (1965): *The Poor and the Poorest.* London: Bell and Sons. (Occasional Papers on Social Administration, No. 17.)

Anand, S. (1977): "Aspects of Poverty in Malaysia." *Review of Income and Wealth* 23: 1–16.

Anand, S. (1983): *Inequality and Poverty in Malaysia, Mesurement and Decomposition.* Oxford etc.: Oxford University Press.

Atkinson, A. B. (1970): *Poverty in Britain and the Reform of Social Security.* Cambridge etc.: Cambridge University Press.

Atkinson, A. B. (1972): "On Measurement of Inequality." *Journal of Economic Theory* 2: 244–263.

Atkinson, A. B. (1983): *The Economics of Inequality.* 2nd. ed. Oxford: Clarendon Press.

Atkinson, A. B. (1985a): "On the Measurement of Poverty." Discussion Paper No. 90. London: Economic and Social Research Council Programme, London School of Economics.

Atkinson, A. B. (1985b): "How Should We Measure Poverty?: Some Conceptual Issues." Discussion Paper No. 82. London: Economic and Social Research Council Programme, London School of Economics.

Atkinson, A. B., and **Bourguignon, F.** (1982): "The Comparison of Multi-Dimensioned Distributions of Economic Status." *Review of Economic Studies* 49: 183–201.

Barten, A. P. (1964): "Family Composition, Prices and Expenditure Patterns." In *Econometric Analysis for National Economic Planning*, edited by P. Hart, G. Mill, and J. Whittaker. London: Butterworth, pp. 277–292.

Basu, K. (1985): "Poverty Measurement: A Decomposition of the Normalization Axiom." *Econometrica* 53: 1439–1443.

Beckerman, W., and **Clark, S.** (1982): *Poverty and Social Security in Britain Since 1961.* Oxford etc.: Oxford University Press.

Berthoud, R.; **Brown, J. C.**; and **Cooper, S.** (1981): *Poverty and the Development of Anti-Poverty Policy in the UK.* London: Heinemann.

Beveridge, W. H. B. (1942): *Social Insurance and Allied Services.* London: Her Majesty's Stationery Office.

Blackorby, C., and **Donaldson, D.** (1978): "Measures of Relative Equality and Their Meaning in Terms of Social Welfare." *Journal of Economic Theory* 18: 59–80.

Blackorby, C., and **Donaldson, D.** (1980): "Ethical Indices for the Measurement of Poverty." *Econometrica* 48: 1053–1060.

Blackorby, C., and **Donaldson, D.** (1984): "Ethically Significant Ordinal Indexes of Relative Inequality." In *Advances in Econometrics, Vol. 3*, edited by R. Basmann and G. Rhodes. Greenwich: JAI Press, pp. 131–147.

Booth, C. (1902): *Life and Labour of the People of London.* London: Macmillan.

Bowley, A. L. (1923): *The Nature and the Purpose of the Measurement of Social Phenomena.* London: P. S. King.

Bull, D. (ed.) (1971): *Family Poverty.* London: Duckworth.

Chakravarty, S. R. (1983a): "A New Index of Poverty." *Mathematical Social Sciences* 6: 307–313.

Chakravarty, S. R. (1983b): "Ethically Flexible Measures of Poverty." *Canadian Journal of Economics* 16: 74–85.

Clark, S.; **Hemming, R.**; and **Ulph, D.** (1981): "On Indices for the Measurement of Poverty." *Economic Journal* 91: 515–526.

Colasanto, D.; **Kapteyn, A.**; and **van der Gaag, J.** (1984): "Two Subjective Definitions of Poverty: Results from the Wisconsin Basic Needs Study." *Journal of Human Resources* 19: 127–138.

Cowell, F. A. (1980): "On the Structure of Additive Inequality Measures." *Review of Economic Studies* 47: 521–531.

Cutler, P. (1984): "The Measurement of Poverty: A Review of Attempts to Quantify the Poor, with Special Reference to India." *World Development* 12: 1119–1130.

Dalton, H. (1920): "The Measurement of the Inequality of Incomes." *Economic Journal* 30: 348–361.

Danzinger, S.; **van der Gaag, J.**; **Taussig, M. K.**; and **Smolensky, E.** (1984): "The Direct Measurement of Welfare Levels: How Much does it Cost to Make Ends Meet?" *Review of Economics and Statistics* 66: 500–505.

Davis, S. P. (1979/80): "The Concept of Poverty in the Encyclopaedia Britannica from 1810 to 1975." *Labor History* 21: 91–101.

Deaton, A., and **Muellbauer, J.** (1980): *Economics and Consumer Behaviour.* Cambridge etc.: Cambridge University Press.

Donaldson, D., and **Weymark, J. A.** (1986): "Properties of Fixed-Population Poverty Indices." *International Economic Review* 27: 667–688.

Engel, E. (1857): "Die Produktions- und Consumptionsverhältnisse des Königreichs Sachsen." *Zeitschrift des Statistischen Bureaus des Königlich Sächsischen Ministeriums des Innern* 8 and 9.

Engel, E. (1895): "Die Lebenskosten belgischer Arbeiterfamilien früher und jetzt. Ermittelt aus Familienhaushaltsrechnungen und vergleichend zusammengestellt." *Bulletin of the International Institute of Statistics* 9: 1–74.

Fiegehen, G. C. (1979): "Problems in Measuring Poverty." In *Social Security Research, The Definition and Measurement of Poverty*, edited by Department of Health and Social Security. London: Her Majesty's Stationery Office, pp. 1–14.

Fiegehen, G. C.; Lansley, P. S.; and **Smith, A. D.** (1977): *Poverty and Progress in Britain 1953–1973.* Cambridge etc.: Cambridge University Press.

Fields, G. S. (1980): *Poverty, Inequality, and Development.* Cambridge etc.: Cambridge University Press.

Foster, J. E. (1984): "On Economic Poverty: A Survey of Aggregate Measures." In *Advances in Econometrics, vol. 3*, edited by R. Basmann and G. Rhodes. Greenwich: JAI Press, pp. 215–251.

Foster, J. E.; Greer, J.; and **Thorbecke, E.** (1984): "A Class of Decomposable Poverty Measures." *Econometrica* 52: 761–766.

Foster, J. E., and **Shorrocks, A. F.** (1983): "Welfare Dominance and Poverty Orderings." Mimeo. London School of Economics.

Foster, J. E., and **Shorrocks, A. F.** (1986): "Poverty Orderings and Welfare Dominance." Mimeo. London School of Economics.

Friedman, M. (1952): "A Method of Comparing Incomes of Families Differing in Composition." *Studies in Income and Wealth* 15: 9–24.

Fuchs, V. R. (1967): "Redefining Poverty and Redistributing Income." *The Public Interest* 5: 88–95.

Garfinkel, I. and **Haveman, R. H.** (1977): "Earnings Capacity, Economic Status, and Poverty." In *Improving Measures of Economic Well-Being*, edited by M. Moon and E. Smolensky. New York etc.: Academic Press, pp. 52–74.

Garfinkel, I.; Haveman, R. H.; and **Betson, D.** (1977): *Earnings Capacity, Poverty, and Inequality.* New York etc.: Academic Press.

Goedhart, T.; Halberstad, V.; Kapteyn, A.; and **van Praag, B.** (1977): "The Poverty Line: Concept and Measurement." *Journal of Human Resources* 12: 503–520.

Green, C. (1967): *Negative Taxes and the Poverty Problem.* Washington, D.C.: Brookings Institution.

Hagenaars, A. J. M. (1986): *The Perception of Poverty.* Amsterdam etc.: North-Holland.

Hamada, K., and **Takayama, N.** (1977): "Censored Income Distributions and the Measurement of Poverty." *Bulletin of the International Statistical Institute* 47: 617–632.

van Herwaarden, F. G., and **Kapteyn, A.** (1981): "Empirical Comparison of the Shape of Welfare Functions." *European Economic Review* 15: 261–286.

Hobsbawn, E. (1968): "Poverty." In *International Encyclopaedia of the Social Sciences, vol. 12.* New York: Macmillan & Free Press, pp. 398–403.

Kakwani, N. (1977a): "On the Estimation of Consumer Unit Scale." *Review of Economics and Statistics* 59: 507–510.

Kakwani, N. (1977b): "Measurement of Poverty and Negative Income Tax." *Australian Economic Papers* 16: 237–248.

Kakwani, N. (1980a): "On a Class of Poverty Measures." *Econometrica* 48: 431–436.

Kakwani, N. (1980b): *Income Inequality and Poverty, Methods of Estimation and Policy Applications.* New York etc.: Oxford University Press.

Kakwani, N. (1984a): "Issues in Measuring Poverty." In *Advances in Econometrics, vol. 3*, edited by R. Basmann and G. Rhodes. Greenwich: JAI Press, pp. 253–282.

Kakwani, N. (1984b): "Welfare Ranking of Income Distributions." In *Advances in Econometrics, vol. 3*, edited by R. Basmann and G. Rhodes. Greenwich: JAI Press, pp. 191–213.

Kakwani, N. (1986): *Analyzing Redistribution Policies, A Study Using Australian Data.* Cambridge etc.: Cambridge University Press.

Kanbur, S. M. R. (1984): "Measurement and Decomposition of Inequality and Poverty." In *Mathematical Methods in Economics*, edited by F. van der Ploeg. New York: Wiley, pp. 403–432.

Kapsalis, C. (1981): "Poverty Lines: An Alternative Method of Estimation." *Journal of Human Resources* 16: 477–480.

Kapteyn, A.; **van de Geer, S.**; and **van de Stadt, H.** (1985): "The Impact of Changes in Income and Family Composition on Subjective Measures of Well-Being." In *Horizontal Equity, Uncertainty, and Economic Well-Being*, edited by M. David and T. Smeding. Chicago, Ill. etc.: The University of Chicago Press, pp. 35–64.

Kapteyn, A.; **Kooreman, P.**; and **Willemse, R.** (1986): "Some Methodological Issues in the Implementation of Subjective Poverty Definitions." Mimeo, Department of Econometrics, Tilburg University.

Kilpatrick, R. W. (1973): "The Income Elasticity of the Poverty Line." *Review of Economics and Statistics* 55: 327–332.

Kolm, S.-C. (1976): "Unequal Inequalities I, II." *Journal of Economic Theory* 12: 416–442; 13: 82–111.

Kolm, S.-C. (1977): "Multidimensional Egalitarians." *Quarterly Journal of Economics* 91: 1–13.

Kundu, A., and **Smith, T. E.** (1983): "An Impossibility Theorem on Poverty Indices." *International Economic Review* 24: 423–434.

Le Breton, M. (1986): "Inequality, Poverty Measurement and Welfare Dominance: An Attempt at Unification." Mimeo. Department of Economics, University of Rennes.

Lewis, O. (1968/69): "The Culture of Poverty." In *On Understanding Poverty, Perspectives from the Social Sciences*, edited by D. P. Moynihan. New York etc.: Basic Books, pp. 187–200.

Luce, R. D., and **Galanter, E.** (1963): "Psychophysical Scaling." In *Handbook of Mathematical Psychology, vol. I*, edited by R. D. Luce, R. R. Bush, and E. Galanter. New York etc.: Wiley, pp. 245–307.

Maasoumi, E. (1986): "The Measurement and Decomposition of Multi-Dimensional Inequality." *Econometrica* 54: 991–997.

Miller, S. M., and **Roby, P.** (1970): "Poverty: Changing Social Stratification." In *The Concept of Poverty*, edited by P. Townsend. London: Heinemann, pp. 124–145.

Moon, M. (1977): "The Economic Welfare of the Aged and Income Security Programs." In *Improving Measures of Economic Well-Being*, edited by M. Moon and E. Smolensky. New York etc.: Academic Press, pp. 88–110.

Moon, M., and **Smolensky, E.** (eds.) (1977): *Improving Measures of Economic Well-Being*. New York etc.: Academic Press.

Muellbauer, J. (1974): "Household Composition, Engel Curves and Welfare Comparisons between Households." *European Economic Review* 5: 103–122.

Nicholson, J. L. (1979): "The Assessment of Poverty and the Information We Need." In *Social Security Research, The Definition and Measurement of Poverty*, edited by Department of Health and Social Security. London: Her Majesty's Stationery Office, pp. 61–76.

Orshansky, M. (1965a): "Counting the Poor: Another Look at the Poverty Profile." *Social Security Bulletin* 28/1: 3–29.

Orshansky, M. (1965b): "Who's Who Among the Poor: A Demographic View of Poverty." *Social Security Bulletin* 28/7: 3–32.

Orshansky, M. (1966): "How Poverty is Measured." *Social Security Bulletin* 29/2: 37–41.

Orshansky, M. (1966): "Recounting the Poor: A Five Year Review." *Social Security Bulletin* 29/4: 20–37.

Oshima, H. T. (1977): "Some Notes on Defining and Estimating Poverty Levels." Mimeo. University of the Philippines.

Perlman, R. (1976): *The Economics of Poverty*. New York etc.: McGraw-Hill.

Pigou, A. C. (1932): *The Economics of Welfare*. 4th. ed. London: Macmillan.

Plotnick, R. D., and **Skidmore, F.** (1975): *Progress Against Poverty, A Review of the 1964–1974 Decade*. New York etc.: Academic Press.

van Praag, B. M. S. (1968): *Individual Welfare Functions and Consumer Behaviour, A Theory of Rational Irrationality*. Amsterdam etc.: North-Holland.

van Praag, B. M. S.; Goedhart, T.; and **Kapteyn, A.** (1980): "The Poverty Line: A Pilot Survey in Europe." *Review of Economics and Statistics* 62: 461–465.

van Praag, B. M. S.; Hagenaars, A. J. M.; and **van Weeren, H.** (1982): "Poverty in Europe." *Review of Income and Wealth* 28: 345–359.

van Praag, B. M. S.; Split, J.; and **van de Stadt, H.** (1982): "A Comparison between the Food Poverty Line and the Leyden Poverty Line." *Review of Economics and Statistics* 64: 691–694.

Prais, S. J., and **Houthakker, H. S.** (1971): *The Analysis of Family Budgets*. 2nd. ed. Cambridge etc.: Cambridge University Press.

Rainwater, L. (1974): *What Money Buys, Inequality and Social Meanings of Income*. New York: Basic Books.

Rao, V. V. B. (1981): "Measurement of Deprivation and Poverty Based on the Proportion Spent on Food: An Exploratory Exercise." *World Development* 9: 337–353.

Rein, M. (1970): "Problems in the Definition and Measurement of Poverty." In *The Concept of Poverty*, edited by P. Townsend. London: Heinemann, pp. 46–63.

Rose, A. "Poverty in Canada: An Essay Review." *Social Service Review* 43: 74–84.

Rowntree, B. S. (1901): *Poverty: A Study of Town Life*. London: Macmillan.

Rowntree, B. S. (1941): *Poverty and Progress*. London: Longmans.

Rowntree, B. S., and **Lavers, G. R.** (1951): *Poverty and the Welfare State*. London: Longmans.

Runciman, W. G. (1966): *Relative Deprivation and Social Justice.* London: Routledge & Kegan Paul.

Russell, R. R. (1985): "A Note on Decomposable Inequality Measures." *Review of Economic Studies* 52: 347–352.

Schultz, T. W. (1980): "Nobel Lecture: The Economics of Being Poor." *Journal of Political Economy* 88: 639–651.

Seidl, C. (1981): "Theoretische Grundlagen der Sozialpolitik." and "Bedürftigkeitsmessung als ökonomisches Problem." In *Sozialpolitik und Umverteilung*, edited by H.-G. Ruppe. Vienna: Signum, pp. 20–127.

Seidl, C. (1987): "A Review of A. J. M Hagenaars' The Perception of Poverty." *Journal of Economics/Zeitschrift für Nationalökonomie* 47: 92–98.

Sen, A. K. (1976a): "Poverty: An Ordinal Approach to Measurement." *Econometrica* 44: 219–231.

Sen, A. K. (1976b): "Real National Income." *Review of Economic Studies* 43: 19–39.

Sen, A. K. (1977): "Social Choice Theory: A Re-examination." *Econometrica* 45: 53–89.

Sen, A. K. (1979): "Issues in the Measurement of Poverty." *Scandinavian Journal of Economics* 81: 285–307.

Sen, A. K. (1981): *Poverty and Famines. An Essay on Entitlement and Deprivation.* Oxford: Clarendon Press.

Sen, A. K. (1983): "Poor, Relatively Speaking." *Oxford Economic Papers* 35: 153–169.

Shari, I. (1979): "Estimation of Poverty Lines and the Incidence of Poverty in Peninsular Malaysia, 1973." *Philippine Economic Journal* 18: 418–449.

Shorrocks, A. F. (1980): "The Class of Additively Decomposable Inequality Measures." *Econometrica* 48: 613–625.

Shorrocks, A. F. (1983): "Ranking Income Distributions." *Economica* 50: 3–17.

Smeeding, T. M. (1977a): "The Economic Well-Being of Low Income Households: Implications for Income Inequality and Poverty." In *Improving Measures of Economic Well-Being*, edited by M. Moon and E. Smolensky. New York etc.: Academic Press, pp. 155–183.

Smeeding, T. M. (1977b): "The Antipoverty Effectiveness of In-Kind Transfers." *Journal of Human Resources* 12: 360–378.

Smolensky, E.; Stiefel, L.; Schmundt, M.; and Plotnick, R. (1977): "In-Kind Transfers and the Size Distribution of Income." In *Improving Measures of Economic Well-Being*, edited by M. Moon and E. Smolensky. New York etc.: Academic Press, pp. 131–153.

Stark, T.: (1972): *The Distribution of Personal Income in the United Kingdom 1949–1963*. Cambridge etc.: Cambridge University Press.

Sydenstricker, E., and King, W. I. (1920/21): "The Measurement of the Relative Economic Status of Families." *Quarterly Publication of the American Statistical Association* 17: 842–857.

Szal, R. J. (1977): "Poverty: Measurement and Analysis." World Employment Programme Working Paper 2-23. Geneva: International Labour Office.

Takayama, N. (1979): "Poverty, Income Inequality and their Measures: Professor Sen's Axiomatic Approach Reconsidered." *Econometrica* 47: 747–759.

Thon, D. (1979): "On Measuring Poverty." *Review of Income and Wealth* 25: 429–439.

Thon, D. (1981): "Income Inequality and Poverty: Some Problems." *Review of Income and Wealth* 27: 207–210.

Thon, D. (1983): "A Note on a Troublesome Axiom for Poverty Indices." *Economic Journal* 93: 199–200.

Thon, D. (1984): "A Poverty Measure." *Indian Economic Journal* 30: 55–70.

Townsend, P. (1970): "Measures and Explanations of Poverty in High Income and Low Income Countries: The Problems of Operationalizing the Concepts of Development, Class and Poverty." In *The Concept of Poverty*, edited by P. Townsend. London: Heinemann, pp. 1–45.

Townsend, P. (1974): "Poverty as Relative Deprivation: Resources and Styles of Living." In *Poverty, Inequality and Class Structure*, edited by D. Wedderburn. Cambridge etc.: Cambridge University Press, pp. 15–41.

Townsend, P. (1979a): "The Development of Research on Poverty." In *Social Security Research: The Definition and Measurement of Poverty*, edited by Department of Health and Social Security. London: Her Majesty's Stationery Office, pp. 15–26.

Townsend, P. (1979b): *Poverty in the United Kingdom*. London: Allen Lane and Penguin Books.

US President's Commission on Income Maintenance (1969): *Poverty amid Plenty*. Washington, D.C.: US Government Printing Office.

Vaughan, R. N. (1987): "Welfare Approaches to the Measurement of Poverty." *Economic Journal (Supplement 1987)* 97: 160–170.

Vickery, C. (1977): "The Time-Poor: A New Look at Poverty." *Journal of Human Resources* 12: 27–48.

Watts, H. W. (1967): "The Iso-Prop Index: An Approach to the Determination of Differential Poverty Income Thresholds." *Journal of Human Resources* 2: 3–18.

Watts, H. W. (1968/1977): "An Economic Definition of Poverty." In *On Understanding Poverty*, edited by D. P. Moynihan. New York: Basic Books, pp. 316–329. (Reprinted in *Improving Measures of Economic Well-Being*, edited by M. Moon and E. Smolensky. New York etc.: Academic Press 1977, pp. 19–32.)

Wedderburn, D. (ed.) (1974): *Poverty, Inequality and Class Structure.* Cambridge etc.: Cambridge University Press.

Weisbrod, B. A., and **Hansen, L. W.** (1977): "An Income-Net Worth Approach to Measuring Economic Welfare." In *Improving Measures of Economic Well-Being*, edited by M. Moon and E. Smolensky. New York etc.: Academic Press, pp. 33–50.

Yitzhaki, S. (1979): "Relative Deprivation and the Gini Coefficient." *Quarterly Journal of Economics* 93: 321–324.

Poverty Measures, Inequality and Decomposability

Frank A. Cowell, London, U. K.*

I. Introduction

In recent years the theoretical literature on the measurement of aggregate poverty has grown extensively, particularly with reference to the "aggregation problem": the way in which one combines information about people's incomes into an overall judgment about the extent of poverty *given* that one has already settled the questions of who is to be counted as poor and how their incomes or, living standards are to be measured.[1] However many of the statistical devices that have been used to deal with the aggregation problem — from the elementary devices of "headcounts" and poverty gaps to the more recent sophisticated measures — seem to have an air of arbitrariness about their specification. This appears to be the case even where appeal is made to a set of axioms that seem to capture certain features of what people feel a poverty index ought to do. Indeed, despite their intuitive and logical support, the alternative measures that have emerged in the literature may actually prove to be contradictory in their axiomatic structure as well as in their rankings of income distributions.

The purpose of this paper is to suggest a way in which developments in the theory of inequality measurement can throw light on the problem of poverty measurement. It may also help to quell the uneasy feeling of arbitrariness that is associated with some of the poverty measurement literature. For whilst all axioms are arbitrary and the intellectual prejudices of authors apparent within them, it turns out that rather weak and appealing requirements do impose an interesting and readily interpretable structure on the general mathematical representation of a poverty measure. This structure is a useful vehicle for obtaining general results for poverty measures and, where necessary, for identifying more precisely the nature of the further assumptions required to obtain a specific index. Results on inequality measurement may help to resolve some of the ambiguities in the poverty measurement literature. Although poverty and inequality are distinct concepts,

* I am grateful to Tony Atkinson, Bernd Genser, Nick Stern and an anonymous referee for helpful comments.

[1] See, for example, the surveys in Foster (1985), Hagenaars (1986), Sen (1979).

standard results on the mathematical structure of inequality measures carry over directly to the analysis of poverty indices; in particular we shall find that various types of decomposability by population subgroup are useful in such analysis.

We shall proceed in the following way. In section 2 I explain some preliminary terminology and notation. Section 3 introduces the axioms and derives some basic results on the general form of poverty indices. The central issues here are that the concepts of relative deprivation and absolute deprivation should each be well defined, and that any poverty index should treat incomes of the poor impartially and incomes of the rich impartially — a kind of modified horizontal equity requirement. In sections 4 and 5 I will examine the behaviour of the poverty index based on the theory of decomposable inequality measures in two distinct types of society. Finally section 6 relates the present approach to the literature.

II. Definitions

Let us suppose that each person i in a given population of n persons has associated with him a unique scalar y_i ("income") which completely describes his economic position. We are given a number z and a definition that i is poor if $y_i < z$. Taking a liberty with the language we shall designate as "rich" anyone who is not poor. Without loss of generality we may index the population such that

$$(1) \qquad y_i \leq y_2 \leq \dots y_q \leq z \leq y_{q+1} \leq \dots \leq y_n$$

where q is the number of poor people. Define the *poor set* $N_p \equiv \{1, \dots, q\}$, the *rich set* $N_r \equiv \{q+1, \dots, n\}$ and $N \equiv N_p \cup N_r$. Also define the *poor income vector* $\mathbf{y}_p = (y_1, \dots, y_q)$, the *rich income vector* $\mathbf{y}_r = (y_{q+1}, \dots, y_n)$, the *population income vector* $\mathbf{y} = (\mathbf{y}_p, \mathbf{y}_r)$, and the *relative income set* $Y(q,z) \equiv \{\mathbf{y} \mid$ condition (1) holds$\}$. Write the means of $\mathbf{y}_p, \mathbf{y}_r, \mathbf{y}$ respectively as μ_p, μ_r, μ and define the $(n-1)$-dimensional simplex

$$(2) \qquad S(\mu, n) = \{\mathbf{y} \mid \mathbf{y} \in \mathbb{R}^n_+, \sum_{i=1}^{n} y_i = \mu n\}.$$

A *change in scale* of the income vector $\mathbf{y}$ will be used to denote multiplication of $\mathbf{y}$ (and hence of μ) by a strictly positive scalar λ. Simplices of appropriate dimension and scale changes can of course be defined for subvectors of $\mathbf{y}$.

A *poverty measure* is a function from $\mathbb{R}^{n+1}_+$ to $\mathbb{R}^1_+$ defined thus

$$P = \pi(\mathbf{y}, z).$$

We also need a convenient method of describing changes in the poverty measure caused by mean-preserving changes in $\mathbf{y}$. Hence, consider a distribution $\mathbf{y}'$ formed thus: $y_i' = y_i - \epsilon$, $y_j' = y_j + \epsilon$ and $y_k' = y_k$, $\forall k \neq i, j$. The *transfer effect* for any ϵ is then

$$T_{ij}(\epsilon, \mathbf{y}, z) \equiv \pi(\mathbf{y}', z) - \pi(\mathbf{y}, z). \tag{3}$$

Note that the definition of the transfer effect does not presuppose π to be uniformly differentiable.

III. Basic Results

Let us now impose some fairly basic restrictions on the function π that will enable it to capture the notions of relative and absolute deprivation and of partial equity discussed in the introduction. This step is intended to be in broad agreement with the specific interpretations of these concepts elsewhere in the literature without a prejudicial commitment to a particular functional form for π. We begin with three uncontroversial Axioms.

Axiom A1. (Partial Symmetry)
$\pi(\mathbf{y}, z) = \pi(\mathbf{M}_p\mathbf{y}_p, \mathbf{M}_r\mathbf{y}_r, z)$ $\forall \mathbf{y}, z$ where $\mathbf{M}_p, \mathbf{M}_r$ are arbitrary permutation matrices of appropriate dimension.

Axiom A2. (Smoothness)

(i) $\pi(\mathbf{y}, z)$ is continuous on $Y(q, z)$ for given q, z.

(ii) Partial derivatives of π up to the second order exist for all its arguments and for all distinct distributions $\{\mathbf{y} \mid y_j \neq y_k \ \forall j \neq k\}$ and the commutativity property holds:

$$\pi_{ij}(\mathbf{y}, z) = \pi_{ji}(\mathbf{y}, z)$$

where π_{ij} means $\partial^2\pi/\partial y_i \partial y_j$.

Axiom A3. (Principle of Transfers)
$T_{ij}(\epsilon, y, z) > 0$ if $y_i < y_j$ and $i \in N_p$ and $0 < \epsilon < \frac{1}{2}[y_j - y_i]$.

Axiom (Al) states that identities may be swapped *amongst* the poor or *amongst* the rich without altering the value of the poverty measure; this is a form of "partial horizontal equity". Note that Axiom (A2) imposes continuity in only a limited sense since $Y(q, z)$ is defined *relative* to a given poverty line and poor set: if instead one income of the currently poor population is increased so far that q is decreased by one then $\pi(\mathbf{y}, z)$ may have a discontinuity at that point. However the requirement that the poverty index be continuous throughout the region where everyone is in the same rank order and the poor are still poor seems fairly innocuous. The transfer axiom says that a transfer from a poor man to *anybody* with a higher income will increase poverty whilst we remain, for the moment, uncommitted about transfers amongst the rich. In fact this assumption is stronger than is strictly necessary for all interpretations of poverty since it might be plausibly argued that $T_{ij}(\epsilon, \mathbf{y}) = 0$ if $i, j \in N_p$. I have written Axiom (A3) in this form to capture in an essential way one aspect of *relative deprivation* (RD), namely that widening income differences amongst the poor will increase overall poverty. We shall see below that poverty measures that do not incorporate RD can be obtained as special cases anyway, so that the axiom is not restrictive.

Relative deprivation is a key concept in much of the theoretical work on poverty measurement, and it is interesting to see how this may be explicitly modelled and what essential structure it imposes on π. To do this let us take a limiting form of the transfer effect (3)

$$\begin{aligned} t_{ij}(\mathbf{y}, z) &\equiv Lt_{\epsilon \to 0}[T_{ij}(\epsilon, \mathbf{y}, z)/\epsilon] \\ &= \pi_j(\mathbf{y}, z) - \pi_i(\mathbf{y}, z) \end{aligned}$$

where the subscripts on π denote first order partial derivatives. In view of Axiom (A3), if $i < j < k \leq q$ then we will find that $t_{ik} > t_{ij} > 0$. This implies that a small redistribution between poor people with quite disparate incomes is more effective than a similar redistribution between individuals that are already close. As we have noted, transfers amongst the poor are of interest solely from the point of view of RD and thus it is reasonable to require that the relative effectiveness of such pairwise transfers amongst the poor (between i and j, between i and k, etc.) should be independent of the absolute level of poverty however defined. Without such a requirement the concept of RD is not well-defined: whether the transfer $k \to j$ is more or less effective in terms of reducing poverty than the transfers $j \to i$ would depend on where z was fixed.

So, as a first attempt to capture the concept of RD we may consider the impact of a change in income distribution that affects only the relative incomes of a subset of the poor: a subset that would be classified as poor even if the poverty line were to be varied over a certain range. We shall consider

Axiom A4 (RD)

$\frac{t_{ij}(\mathbf{y})}{t_{ik}(\mathbf{y})}$ is independent of z for all variations of z and $\mathbf{y}$ such that $\{i, j, k\} \subset N_p$.

Notice (A4) does not attempt of itself to define a particular measure of RD, but rather to specify a minimal requirement under which such a measure could be defined. This property will be strengthened below; for the moment we may note

Lemma 1

Axioms (A1)–(A4) imply that the poverty index may be written

$$P = \Phi(I(\mathbf{y}_p), \mathbf{y}_r, z, \mu_p, q) \tag{4}$$

where Φ is increasing in its first argument and I is strongly Schur-convex.

Proof

From (A4), $t_{ij}(\mathbf{y})/t_{ik}(\mathbf{y})$ must be independent also of q since z may be increased arbitrarily. This means that $t_{ij}(\mathbf{y})/t_{ik}(\mathbf{y})$ is independent of $y_{q+1}, \ldots, y_k$. However this is equivalent to requiring that π is decomposable[2] for the subvector $\mathbf{y}_p$ so that (4) holds for some functions I and Φ. Now

$$t_{ij}(\mathbf{y}) = \Phi_I \cdot [I_i(\mathbf{y}_p) - I_j(\mathbf{y}_p)] \qquad \text{if} \quad \{i,j\} \subset N_p. \tag{5}$$

However (A3) implies that (5) is positive iff $y_i > y_j$. Hence if $y_i > y_j$ then either (a) $\Phi_1 > 0$ and $I_i > I_j$, or (b) $\Phi_1 < 0$ and $I_i < I_j$. We make the obvious, conventional choice (a) so that I is indeed Schur-convex.

□

Evidently (A4) imposes only a rather weak requirement on RD, and it is worth exploring this requirement further. Now RD is commonly used to describe the position of an individual with respect to some other person (or group) *above* him, as perceived either objectively or subjectively.[3] Suppose $y_i < y_j < y_k$: i will then be less deprived (relatively) if there is a transfer $j \to i$ or a transfer $k \to i$. In either case (as far as i is concerned) the relative reduction in RD from one or other transfer will be independent of all incomes *less* than y_i, and hence of how many people there are below i. "Relative Deprivation" by its very name implies upward looking; it is not "relative privilege" of the less poor. Also we note that RD should be independent of the scale of the distribution since a simple proportional change in all incomes leaves poor persons in the same position relative to each other and to the rich.[4] Hence we may consider the stronger property:

---

[2] Note that I have not imposed any corresponding condition for $\{i,j,k\} \subset N_r$, so that we cannot, for example, write $P = \phi(I(\mathbf{y}_p), J(\mathbf{y}_r), z, \mu_p, \mu_r, q)$.

[3] See, for example, Townsend in Wedderburn (1974).

[4] If we consider distinct distributions we can always find some change in scale, for fixed q that does not change N_p, N_r.

Axiom A4′ (RD)

$\frac{t_{ij}(\mathbf{y})}{t_{ik}(\mathbf{y})}$ is independent of y_ℓ for all $y_\ell < y_i < y_j < y_k, \quad i \in N_p$.

Axiom A5 (Scale independence of RD)
$t_{ij}(\lambda\mathbf{y})/t_{ik}(\lambda\mathbf{y}) = t_{ij}(\mathbf{y})/t_{ik}(\mathbf{y}), \quad \forall\, \lambda \in (0,\infty)$.

Lemma 2
Axioms (A4′) and (A5) imply that

$$I(\mathbf{y}_p) = f\left(\alpha(\mu_p,q)\sum_{i=1}^{q}\left[\frac{y_i^\kappa}{\kappa^2-\kappa} + \beta(\mu_p,q)\sum_{j=1}^{q} y_j\right];\ \mu_p,q\right)$$

where $\alpha \geq 0$, $\beta \leq 0$, $\kappa \in (-\infty,+\infty)$ is an undetermined parameter[5] and $f(x;\mu_p,q)$ is an increasing function of x.

The proof of this is relegated to the Appendix. The constants α, β and the function f may be chosen purely for the convenience of normalizing the function $I(\cdot)$. Accordingly we may for convenience assume that I takes one or other of the following special forms

(6a) $$I^\kappa(\mathbf{y}_p;q) = \frac{1}{q[\kappa^2-\kappa]}\sum_{i=1}^{q}[y_i^\kappa - \mu_p^\kappa],$$

(6b) $$I^G(\mathbf{y}_p;q) = \frac{1}{2q^2}\sum_{j=1}^{q}\sum_{i=1}^{q}|y_i - y_j|.$$

Note that (6a) and (6b) have been normalised so that if all the y_i were equal, I^κ and I^G would vanish.

We have two further issues to consider: the behaviour of P in response to variations in the rich income vector $\mathbf{y}_r$, and whether it is possible for P to incorporate a well-defined concept of absolute deprivation. Take the former issue. There is a clear case for concern if some of the rich get richer whilst all other incomes remain unchanged; but if all that happens is that the very rich gain at the expense of the moderately rich, leaving the total $\sum_{i=q+1}^{n} y_i$ unaltered then there seems little reason to suppose that P should alter. Hence we extend Axiom (A3) to

Axiom A3′
$T_{ij}(\epsilon,\mathbf{y}) = 0 \quad \text{if} \quad \{i,j\} \subset N_r, \qquad \forall\, \epsilon \geq 0.$

[5] For $\kappa = 0, 1$ the expression $y_i^\kappa/(\kappa^2-\kappa)$ becomes, respectively $-\log y_i$ and $y_i \log y_i$.

Let us turn to the second issue, concerning the concept of absolute deprivation. Clearly this refers to the shortfall of the incomes of the poor below the specified poverty line z, independent of the distribution of the incomes amongst the poor. Now recall that there are two sorts of changes that can affect the index P: (i) Changes in *relative* magnitudes that alter the components of $\mathbf{y}$ that leave the population mean (and hence the scale) unaltered; (ii) changes in *absolute* magnitudes — that leave all the relative magnitudes y_i/y_j unaltered. As an example of such absolute changes consider a small increase in the poverty line ($dz > 0$) and a small increase in the scale of incomes ($d\lambda > 0$): the former could increase the absolute level of poverty, the latter would decrease it. The concept of absolute deprivation (AD) might be interpreted as requiring that these two effects, if combined, should cancel out so that $\partial P/\partial z = \partial P/\partial \lambda$. In fact all we need is the weaker property:

Axiom A6 (AD)

$[\partial P/\partial z] \;/\; \left[\frac{\partial P}{\partial \lambda}\right]$ is independent of $\mathbf{y}$ $\forall\, \mathbf{y}$ such that $\mathbf{y} \in S(\mu, n)$ and $\mathbf{y}_p \in S(\mu_p, q)$ for given μ, μ_p, n, q.

In other words the tradeoff between changing the given poverty line and a proportionate increase in incomes is independent of arbitrary redistributions amongst the poor. Once again this axiom does not attempt of itself to define a particular measure of AD, but merely to specify a minimal requirement for such a concept to be well-defined.

Theorem 1

For a given partition of the population, Axioms (A1)–(A6) imply that $\pi(\mathbf{y}, z)$ may be written

$$P = F(I, B, A), \tag{7}$$

where

$$I = I(\mathbf{y}_p),$$
$$B = B(\mu_p, \mu_r),$$
$$A = A(z, \mu_p, \mu),$$

and $F_I, F_B, F_A > 0$, B is homogeneous of degree zero and is increasing in its second argument, decreasing in its first argument and $A_{\mu_p} < 0$.

Proof

(A3′) implies that for every $\mathbf{y}$ for which equation (4) is defined

$$\frac{\partial \Phi}{\partial y_j} = \frac{\partial \Phi}{\partial y_k} \quad \text{if} \quad j, k \in N_r.$$

Hence we may define a new function $\hat{\Phi}$ where

(8) $$P = \hat{\Phi}(I(\mathbf{y}_p), \mu_r, z, \mu_p, q) \quad \text{iff (4) holds.}$$

For convenience define a new variable $\varsigma \equiv \mu_p/\mu$, and without loss of generality[6] rewrite (8) as

(9) $$P = \tilde{\Phi}(I(\mathbf{y}_p), \varsigma, z, \mu, q).$$

However (A6) implies that $\tilde{\Phi}_z/\tilde{\Phi}_\mu$ is independent of $I(\mathbf{y})$ which is equivalent to a condition for weak separability on the two arguments z and μ. So (9) becomes

$$P = \psi(I(\mathbf{y}_p), \varsigma, q, \hat{A}(z, \mu, \varsigma, q)).$$

For a *given* partition of the population $\langle N_p, N_r \rangle$ we may suppress the q term and, defining $B(\mu_p, \mu_r) \equiv \varsigma$, we have

(10) $$P = F(I(\mathbf{y}_p), B(\mu_p, \mu_r), A(z, \mu_p, \mu)).$$

We know that $F_I > 0$ in view of (A3). Evidently B is homogeneous of degree zero. Now consider an infinitesimal change in $\mathbf{y}$ and that $\mu_p \to \mu_p + dy$, $\mu_r \to \mu_r - \frac{q}{n-q}dy$, $I(\mathbf{y}_p)$ is constant, μ is constant. Differentiating (10) we get

(11) $$\frac{dP}{dy} = F_B \left[B_{\mu_p} - \frac{q}{n-q} B_{\mu_r} \right] + F_A \cdot A_{\mu_p}.$$

Exploiting the homogeneity of degree zero of B we may rewrite (11) as

$$\frac{dP}{dy} = \gamma \cdot F_B B_{\mu_p} + F_A \cdot A_{\mu_p}$$

where $\gamma \equiv \frac{n}{n-q\varsigma}$, a positive number. (A3) requires that the sign of (11) is negative. Evidently we may ensure this by appropriate specification of the functions F, B, A such that $F_B > 0$, $B_{\mu_p} < 0$, $F_A > 0$ and $A_{\mu_p} < 0$. Homogeneity of degree zero of B ensures that $B_{\mu_r} > 0$.

□

[6] Note that $\frac{\mu_r}{\mu} = [1 - qz/n]/[1 - q/n]$, a well-defined function.

The interpretation of Theorem 1 is rather appealing. Given our axioms the aggregate poverty index P is some increasing function of three appropriately specified indices: I an index of inequality *amongst* the poor; B an index of inequality *between* the poor and the rich; and A an index of absolute poverty. It does not appear that we can go further than this without some pretty arbitrary restrictions on the form of $\pi(\mathbf{y}, z)$. We might as well, then, consider what form these restrictions could take.

In the first place we could evidently normalize the function F in some specific way to give a particular weighting to the three components I, B, A. Here it appears that the relationship of A to the other two components is the most troublesome problem. After all I and B can each be regarded as different aspects of the same issue of relative deprivation — the former dealing with mean-preserving transfers from very poor persons to less poor persons, the latter dealing with mean-preserving poor-to-rich transfers. Moreover I and B are each independent of the scale of incomes and (for fixed q) of small variations in z. Not so with A. Hence it may well be worthwhile examining the relationship between I and B more closely and leaving open the question of the role of A.

In the second place we could impose a specific form on the inequality measure I, a practice which has been followed almost universally by previous authors. However, at this stage in the argument there appears to be very little point in making such a specific commitment. Instead the class of inequality measures to which I has *already* been restricted by Lemma 2, namely NODI measures,[7] provides an extremely useful avenue for developing (10).

To see this note that for any arbitrary partition of N into $N_1 = \{1, 2, \ldots, n_1\}$ and $N_2 = \{n_1 + 1, \ldots, n\}$ we have

$$(12a) \qquad I^{\kappa}(\mathbf{y}; n) = \frac{n_1}{n} I^{\kappa}(\mathbf{y}_1; n_1) + \frac{n_2}{n} I^{\kappa}(\mathbf{y}_2; n_2) + I^{\kappa}(\boldsymbol{\mu}; n)$$

$$(12b) \qquad I^{G}(\mathbf{y}; n) = \frac{n_1^2}{n^2} I^{G}(\mathbf{y}_1; n_1) + \frac{n_2^2}{n^2} I^{G}(\mathbf{y}_2; n_2) + I^{G}(\boldsymbol{\mu}; n)$$

where $\mathbf{y}_1$ and $\mathbf{y}_2$ are the subvectors of $\mathbf{y}$ corresponding to N_1 and N_2 respectively, $n_2 = n - n_1$ and $\boldsymbol{\mu}$ is a vector of the first n_1 components equal to μ_1 and the remaining n_2 components equal to μ_2. If we take $n_1 = q$, then evidently the first term in (12a) and (12b) corresponds to $I(\mathbf{y}_p)$ in (10); the second term is irrelevant to the measurement of poverty, consisting merely in the inequality amongst the rich, and the third term is one possible interpretation of $B(\mu_p, \mu_r)$ in (10). In fact there is a powerful argument for normalising F in (10) so that the third component of (12a) and (12b) is *exactly* B.

---

[7] Non-overlapping Decomposition Inequality Measures: see Cowell and Mehta (1982).

For arbitrary n and z define a new vector $\mathbf{y}^*$ in the following manner. Let $q = q(\mathbf{y}, z)$ be the number of components of any given $\mathbf{y}$ with values less than z. Then write

$$\text{(13)} \qquad \left\{ \begin{aligned} y_i^* &= y_i, \quad i = 1, 2, \ldots, q(\mathbf{y}, z) \\ &= \mu_r, \quad i = q(\mathbf{y}, z) + 1, \ldots, n \end{aligned} \right\}$$

where of course $\mu_r = \sum_{i=q(\mathbf{y},z)}^{n} y_i/[n - q(\mathbf{y}, z)]$.

Clearly $\mathbf{y}^*$ has the same mean as $\mathbf{y}$ and is derived from $\mathbf{y}$ by the simple expedient of destroying all information about the distribution amongst the rich. So when we consider poor-to-rich transfers we have in mind a poor person with a *specific* income y_i, and a rich person with the *common* income of the rich μ_r. $\mathbf{y}^*$ thus becomes the relevant income vector for a concept of relative deprivation that is definitionally unconcerned about inequality amongst the rich.

Let us consider an index[8]

$$\text{(14)} \qquad \begin{aligned} R(\mathbf{y}; z) &\equiv \frac{q}{n} I^{\kappa}(\mathbf{y}_p; q) + I^{\kappa}(\boldsymbol{\mu}; n) \\ &= I^{\kappa}(\mathbf{y}^*; n). \end{aligned}$$

Obviously

$$\text{(15)} \qquad \left\{ \begin{aligned} R_j - R_i &= \theta \left[y_j^{\kappa-1} - y_i^{\kappa-1} \right] && \text{if } j \le q \\ &= \theta \left[\mu_r^{\kappa-1} - y_i^{\kappa-1} \right] && \text{if } j > q \\ &= \theta \left[y_j^{*\kappa-1} - y_i^{*\kappa-1} \right] \end{aligned} \right\}$$

where $i \in N_p$ and $\theta \equiv 1/n[\kappa - 1]$. The transfer effect defined on the index R is a function of the y_i^* and y_j^* whether i, j belong to N_p or N_r. Now consider (10) under a small income transfer that leaves A unaltered.[9] Since $\mathbf{y}^*$ is the relevant income vector for the concept of relative deprivation it seems reasonable to require that $t_{ij}(\mathbf{y})$ be proportional to (15) for all i and j. This then requires that $I(\mathbf{y}_p) = I^{\kappa}(\mathbf{y}_p; q)$, $B(\mu_p, \mu_r) = I^{\kappa}(\boldsymbol{\mu}; n)$ and

$$P = F(I, B, A) = P(A, \frac{q}{n} I + B)$$

$$\text{(16)} \qquad \left\{ \begin{aligned} &\Longrightarrow \quad P = P(A, R) \\ &\text{where} \quad R = R(\mathbf{y}; z), \ A = A(z, \mu_p, \mu) \text{ and } P_R, P_A > 0. \end{aligned} \right\}$$

[8] An exactly analogous argument would follow for the alternative $R(\mathbf{y}, z) \equiv I^G(\mathbf{y}^*; n)$.

[9] Such a transfer can always be arranged, with possibly an accommodating adjustment in z, for distinct distributions.

The overall poverty index is thus an increasing function of a relative deprivation index R (a NODI measure defined on the relevant income vector $\mathbf{y}^*$) and an absolute deprivation index A. Since the whole argument has been conducted in terms of a fixed q and n, of course, both the function A and P in (16) may depend on q and n.

IV. The *P(A,R)* Function in Non-destitute Societies

This section examines the usefulness of the component indices A, R and the overall index P in comparing various social states. To do so it is convenient to distinguish two types of society. I shall call a society *destitute* if $\mu < z$; this is equivalent to saying that if all personal incomes were equalized by lump-sum transfers everyone would be below the poverty line.

Now let us consider some of the properties of $\pi(\mathbf{y}, z)$ and of $A(z, \mu_p, \mu)$ we have not yet discussed. Firstly, what happens if z increased? Obviously neither overall poverty, nor the index of absolute poverty should go down. So we require:

$$(17) \qquad \left\{ \begin{array}{l} z_1 > z_0 \Longrightarrow \pi(\mathbf{y}, z_1) \geq \pi(\mathbf{y}, z_0), \quad \forall \mathbf{y} \\ z_1 > z_0 \Longrightarrow A(z_1, \mu_p, \mu) \geq A(z_0, \mu_p, \mu), \quad \forall \mu_p, \mu. \end{array} \right\}$$

If both N_p and N_r are nonempty and n is large and the distribution of income is everywhere dense, we may strengthen the weak inequalities in (17) to strict inequalities, since under such circumstances raising z by \$ 1 definitionally creates new poor families from erstwhile rich ones. This property will be known as *level sensitivity.*

Next, what happens if one person's income is raised *on its own*? If it is a poor person we expect that P and A should decrease. Should the indices have this property, they are said to exhibit *monotonicity.* If the person whose income is increased is rich then we may reasonably require P and A not to decrease.

Summarising it seems to be appropriate to demand the following of the overall (P) and absolute (A) indices:

P nondecreasing in z	A nondecreasing in z	(level senitivity)
$\frac{\partial P}{\partial y_i} \geq 0$ if $i \in N_r$	$A_\mu \geq 0$	
$\frac{\partial P}{\partial y_i} < 0$ if $i \in N_p$	$\left\{ \begin{array}{c} A_\mu + \frac{n}{q} A_{\mu_p} < 0 \\ A_{\mu_p} < 0 \end{array} \right\}$	(monotonicity) .

Accepting these requirements provisionally we may now state the following.

Theorem 2
If relative deprivation is defined as in (14) then absolute deprivation is irrelevant in non-destitute societies for all $\mathbf{y} \in Y(q,z)$ and for arbitrary z.

Proof
Consider first an increase in z. For a sufficiently large increase q will increase to $q+v$ where $y_{q+v} \leq \mu_r$. Recalling that the original vector $\mathbf{y}^*$ was defined as $y_i^* = y_i$ if $i \leq q$ and $y_i^* = \mu_r$ otherwise, the corresponding new income vector $\mathbf{y}^{**}$ is given by

(i) $$y_i^{**} = y_i^* \quad \text{if } i \leq q$$

(ii) $$y_i^{**} = y_i \leq y_i^* \quad \text{if } i = q+1, \ldots, q+v$$

(iii) $$y_i^{**} = \frac{(n-q)\mu_r - \sum_{j=1}^{v} y_{j+q}}{n-q-v} \geq y_i^* \quad \text{if } i = q+v+1, \ldots, n.$$

Clearly the vector $\mathbf{y}^*$ must Lorenz-dominate the vector $\mathbf{y}^{**}$ in view of (ii) and (iii) and the means of $\mathbf{y}^*$ and $\mathbf{y}^{**}$ are identical. Hence $I^\kappa(\mathbf{y}^{**};n) \geq I^\kappa(\mathbf{y}^*;n)$ and $R(\mathbf{y}^*;z)$ must increase or remain constant.

Now consider a change in y_i. Since $\mathbf{y} \in Y(q,z)$ we may take the case where q remains constant.

$$\frac{\partial R(\mathbf{y},z)}{\partial y_i} = \frac{1}{n[\kappa-1]}\left[y_i^{*\kappa-1} - \mu^{\kappa-1}\right]. \tag{18}$$

For a non-destitute society: $i \in N_p \implies y_i^* = y_i < z < \mu$ and (18) is negative; $i \in N_r \implies y_i^* = \mu_r > \mu$ and (18) is positive. Hence for any pair of non-destitute states $(\mathbf{y}^1, z^1)$, $(\mathbf{y}^2, z^2)$

$$\begin{cases} R(\mathbf{y}^1,z^1) > R(\mathbf{y}^2,z^2) \implies A(z^1,\mu_p^1,\mu^1) \geq A(z^2,\mu_p^2,\mu^2) \\ R(\mathbf{y}^1,z^1) = R(\mathbf{y}^2,z^2) \implies A(z^1,\mu_p^1,\mu^1) = A(z^2,\mu_p^2,\mu^2) \end{cases}$$

and hence $\pi(\mathbf{y}^1,z^1) \geq \pi(\mathbf{y}^2,z^2)$ iff $R(\mathbf{y}^1,z^1) \geq R(\mathbf{y}^2,z^2)$ *independently of A.*

□

This result appears to allow for a simplification of the recent literature on poverty measurement. For any society in which mean income is above the poverty line we can take any NODI measure, split the population at the poverty line, ignore all information about the distribution amongst the rich, and write down the value of the inequality statistic.[10] Incidentally we may note that the result does not depend on the choice of NODI measure,[11] nor of course does it make any presupposition that equalising incomes by lump-sum transfers is actually feasible.

V. Destitute Societies

Apart from the dreadful economic problems that destitution implies for a society, there are some obvious difficulties in ranking such societies by degrees of dreadfulness.

To see this technical problem, reconsider equation (18). For a destitute society $\mu < z$, so it is possible that for some particular j we may have $\mu < y_j < z$. In this case $\partial R/\partial y_j > 0$, but in view of the fact that $j \in N_p$ and the monotonicity requirement on A, we have $\partial A/\partial y_j < 0$: the relative and absolute indices move in opposite directions. So Theorem 2 does not hold in this case.

Hence $R(\mathbf{y}, z)$ on its own is not an entirely satisfactory measure of poverty in this case.[12] Does this mean therefore that one must abandon the approach? This is hardly necessary because, firstly, $P(A, R)$ may be suitably normalised so as to eliminate the problem and, secondly, one might as well distinguish explicitly between A and R under these circumstances. Each index provides its own interesting piece of information, and it is not overwhelmingly obvious how these two pieces of information should be combined. Suppose, for example, one has the following situation: there are several million people who are practically starving, a few rich people, and one with an income above the mean, but whose income is slightly below the poverty line. Will we reduce poverty by increasing his income

[10] However recall that this result is established for the vectors $\mathbf{y}$ belonging to $Y(q, z)$. If we consider changes in $\mathbf{y}$ that affect q then dependence of P, A and R on q will obviously have to be taken into account. Note too that if q is not fixed in some cases it is possible for R to fall as a result of a transfer from person i to person q where $i < q$. If there are very few rich people then, when the recipient of the transfer crosses the poverty line, this *may* reduce the perceived average income of the rich in such a way as to reduce the between group component of deprivation B, and thus reduce R — see Thon (1979).

[11] There is one minor qualification for an R-function of type (14b) in footnote 8. If the income of person i is increased we get

$$\text{(18b)} \qquad \frac{\partial R(\mathbf{y}, z)}{\partial y_i} = \frac{2}{2n^2}\left[i - \frac{n+1}{2}\right] \gtrless 0 \quad \text{as} \quad i \gtrless \frac{n+1}{2} \cong \frac{1}{2}n.$$

In other words our criterion of non-destitution must now be z less than *median* income.

[12] See also Sen (1979) for a similar argument against the use of the Takayama-Hamada measures. See also the problems raised by Kundu and Smith (1983).

slightly? The monotonicity axiom replies affirmatively *as long as he remains just below the poverty line*, but this is hardly self-evident. We suggest instead that one simply observes that absolute poverty has declined, but that relative deprivation has definitely increased, (as RD would do if the person were slightly *above* z,) without further arbitrary normalisation.

VI. The Choice of Poverty Measure

In view of the flexibility of the general functional form $F(I, B, A)$ and the more specific form $P(A, R)$ two further questions arise. (i) Do other recent contributions to the theory of poverty measurement fit in with our framework? (ii) Of the various R-functions (6a) and (6b) are there any that merit our special interest?

Turning to the first issue, it appears that in many cases the poverty indices that have been proposed can indeed be written in the general form (7). The most obvious example of this is Blackorby and Donaldson's (1980) measure $\frac{q}{n}[1 - y_{ep}/z]$ where y_{ep} is the "equally distributed equivalent income"[13] for the income vector $\mathbf{y}_p$ given a concave social evaluation function. Note in particular that if the social evaluation function is additive and isoelastic then $y_{ep} = \left[1 - [\kappa^2 - \kappa]\mu_p^\kappa I^\kappa(\mathbf{y}_p; q)\right]^{1/\kappa}$, so that $-y_{ep}$ is ordinally equivalent to our measure I. The Sen-Anand-Thon type of measure also fits this framework,[14] which can easily be seen from Anand's version:

$$P_A = A + B[1 - I]$$

where

$$A \equiv \frac{qz}{\mu n} > 0$$

$$B = -\frac{q\mu_p}{\mu n} < 0.$$

I is the Gini index for y_p and is ordinally equivalent to (6b).

The Takayama-Hamada approach[15] can also be subsumed within our framework. Their method involves the definition of a new vector $\hat{\mathbf{y}}$, defined as $\hat{y}_i = y_i$ if $i \leq q$ and $\hat{y}_i = z$ if $i > q$ and then the measurement of inequality of $\hat{\mathbf{y}}$. Evidently

---

[13] See Atkinson (1970).

[14] Sen (1976), Anand (1977), Thon (1979). Sen and Thon's version can easily be obtained by transforming P_A and can be shown to be $\frac{q}{n}\left[1 + \frac{B}{A}[1 - I]\right]$ and $\frac{q}{n}\left[1 + \frac{B}{A}[1 - \frac{q}{n}I]\right]$ respectively. See also Sen (1979).

[15] See Takayama (1979), Hamada and Takayama (1978).

this is very similar to the definition of our R-measure in terms of the vector $\mathbf{y}^*$, but it ignores all the information about the incomes of the rich, rather than the fact that they are greater than z. Once again, the Takayama-Hamada measure can be shown to be a combination of an index $I(\mathbf{y}_p)$ and an index A that is simply $1 - \mu_p/z$.

Finally, note that the Clark *et al.* (1981) and Foster *et al.* (1984) indices can be obtained from Theorem 1 if Axiom (A5) is replaced by a more general homotheticity requirement as in Cowell (1985).

Now let us turn to question (ii). One further requirement of the poverty index that we may desire is that of *decomposability* which we take to mean the following. Subdivide the poor population into G mutually exclusive and exhaustive groups indexed $g = 1, \ldots, G$ and let the income vector for the q_g members of group g alone be $\mathbf{y}_g$, with mean income μ_g. Noting equation (14) we shall say that the index R is decomposable if it can be written

$$(19) \qquad R(\mathbf{y}, z) = \Lambda(I(\mathbf{y}_1), I(\mathbf{y}_2), \ldots, I(\mathbf{y}_G), \mu_1, \ldots, \mu_G, \mu_r, q_1, \ldots, q_G, n).$$

It is easily seen that only if equation (19) holds may overall relative deprivation be written as a function of relative deprivation in the constituent subgroups. As long as the groups are "non-overlapping" in the sense that each income in group g is less than any income in group $g+1$, every measure of the form (6a) or (6b) will satisfy the property (19) for an arbitrary selection of groups. However if the arbitrary grouping includes *overlapping* groups, measures of type (6b) are ruled out. This then implies that with the exception of Blackorby and Donaldson, Clark *et al.*, Foster *et al.* and some of the Takayama-Hamada creations[16] many of the recent measures proposed do not satisfy the property of decomposability in the general case. This is presumably a serious limitation for an analysis that aims to investigate the structure of inequality by groupings of household size, etc.

Which of the generally decomposable family (6a) should be chosen is a moot point and the issues have been fully discussed in the inequality measurement literature by Bourguignon (1979), Cowell (1980), and Shorrocks (1980). As is well known, the lower the algebraic value of κ (i.e. large negative numbers) the more sensitive the measure is to low incomes. However, given that the index ignores the distribution amongst the rich by definition, it is not self-evident that such sensitivity is of prime importance.[17]

[16] In Takayama and Hamada (1978) both the Gini and the Atkinson index are considered as possible inequality measures.

[17] It should also be noted that large negative values of κ lead to considerable problems in *estimating* $I^\kappa(\mathbf{y}_p; q)$. For a discussion of this see Cowell (1977).

Appendix

Axioms (A4) and (A4′) imply that for all $i = 1, \ldots, q-1$:

$$t_{ii+1}(\mathbf{y}) = \theta \cdot \xi(y_i, y_{i+1})$$

where θ is an expression that may depend on μ_p and q. Hence, since $t_{hj} = t_{ih} + t_{hj}$ by definition of the transfer effect, we find:

$$(2^*) \qquad t_{ik}(\mathbf{y}) = \theta \sum_{h=1}^{k-1} \xi(y_h, y_{h+1}).$$

Consider some $j \in N_p$. From Axiom (A2) and equation (2*) we have

$$(3^*) \quad \pi_{ij} - \pi_{kj} = \theta'[\pi_i - \pi_k] + \theta[\xi_1(y_1, y_{j+1}) + \xi_2(y_{j-1}, y_j)] \qquad \text{if} \quad i < j < k$$

$$(4^*) \quad \pi_{ij} - \pi_{kj} = \theta'[\pi_i - \pi_k] \qquad \text{if} \quad j < i \text{ or } j > k$$

where $\theta' = [\partial\theta/\partial\mu_p]/[\partial\theta/\partial q]$. Assume $i < j < k$. Then we also have

$$(5^*) \qquad \pi_{ki} - \pi_{ji} = \theta'[\pi_k - \pi_j]$$

$$(6^*) \qquad \pi_{jk} - \pi_{ik} = \theta'[\pi_j - \pi_i].$$

But (A2) also implies

$$(7^*) \qquad \pi_{ij} - \pi_{kj} + \pi_{ki} - \pi_{ji} + \pi_{jk} - \pi_{ik} = 0.$$

Hence (3*), (5*)–(7*) imply:

$$(8^*) \qquad 0 = \theta[\xi_1(y_j, y_{j+1}) + \xi_2(y_{j-1}, y_j)].$$

Ignoring the trivial solution $\theta = 0$, (8*) implies

$$\xi(y_j, y_{j+1}) = \overline{\xi} + \phi'(y_{j+1}) - \phi'(y_j).$$

Hence

$$(9^*) \qquad t_{ik}(\mathbf{y}) = \theta[\phi'(y_k) - \phi'(y_i) + \overline{\xi}[k-i]].$$

Application of the results in Bourguignon (1979), Cowell (1980, 1985), Shorrocks (1980, 1984) immediately shows that (A5) implies $\phi'(x) = a + bx^{\kappa-1}$. Integration of (9*) then gives the results.

References

Anand, S. (1977): "Aspects of Poverty in Malaysia." *Review of Income and Wealth* 23: 1–16.

Atkinson, A. B. (1970): "On the Measurement of Inequality." *Journal of Economic Theory* 2: 244–263.

Blackorby, C., and **Donaldson, D.** (1980): "Ethical Indices for the Measurement of Poverty." *Econometrica* 48: 1053–1060.

Bourguignon, F. (1979): "Decomposable Income Inequality Measures." *Econometrica* 47: 901–920.

Clark, S.; **Hemming, R.**; and **Ulph, D. T.** (1981): "On Indices for the Measurement of Poverty." *Economic Journal* 91: 515–526.

Cowell, F. A. (1977): *Measuring Inequality.* Oxford: Philip Allan.

Cowell, F. A. (1980): "On the Structure of Additive Inequality Measures." *Review of Economic Studies* 47: 521–531.

Cowell, F. A. (1985): "Measures of Distributional Change: An Axiomatic Approach." *Review of Economic Studies* 52: 135–151.

Cowell, F. A., and **Mehta, F.** (1982): "The Estimation and Interpolation of Inequality Measures." *Review of Economic Studies* 49: 273–290.

Foster, J. E. (1980): "On Economic Poverty: A Survey of Aggregate Measures." *Advances in Econometrics* 3: 215–251.

Foster, J. E.; **Greer, J.**; and **Thorbecke, E.** (1984): "A Class of Decomposable Poverty Measures." *Econometrica* 52: 761–767.

Hagenaars, A. J. M. (1986): *The Perception of Poverty.* Amsterdam etc.: North-Holland.

Hamada, K., and **Takayama, N.** (1978): "Censored Income Distributions and the Measurement of Poverty." *Bulletin of the International Statistical Institute* 47/1: 617–632.

Kundu, A., and **Smith, T. E.** (1983): "An Impossibility Theorem on Poverty Measures." *International Economic Review* 24: 423–434.

Sen, A. K. (1976): "Poverty: An Ordinal Approach to Measurement." *Econometrica* 44: 285–307.

Sen, A. K. (1979): "Issues in the Measurement of Poverty." *Scandinavian Journal of Economics* 81: 219–231.

Shorrocks, A. F. (1980): "The Class of Additively Decomposable Inequality Measures." *Econometrica* 48: 613–625.

Shorrocks, A. F. (1984): "Inequality Decomposition by Population Subgroups." *Econometrica* 52: 1369–1385.

Takayama, N. (1979): "Poverty, Income Inequality and their Measures. Professor Sen's Axiomatic Approach Reconsidered." *Econometrica* 47: 747–759.

Thon, D. (1979): "On Measuring Poverty." *Review of Income and Wealth* 25: 429–439.

Wedderburn, D. C. (ed) (1974): *Poverty, Inequality and the Class Structure*. Cambridge: Cambridge University Press.

An Introduction to Applied General Equilibrium Tax Modelling

(With a Preliminary Application to the Reform of Factor Taxes in the FRG)

Georg Hirte and Wolfgang Wiegard, Regensburg, West Germany*

Applied General Equilibrium (AGE) Tax Models have become a wide-spread scientific tool, with a steadily increasing importance for the policy debate on tax issues.

Many economists are interested in this new tool kit, but entering the privileged club of AGE modelers is no easy matter. On the one hand, there are excellent survey articles, for example Shoven and Whalley (1984), Shoven (1983) or Whalley (1985). These papers are strongly recommendable to the general reader who wants to get an impression of the basic characteristics and the main results and problems of recent AGE models, but there are no detailed instructions as to how to carry out a concrete AGE study. On the other hand, there are highly sophisticated AGE tax models, too numerous to quote, with a very complex theoretical and empirical structure, the precise details of which are, however, in general only poorly documented — mainly because of space constraints in the relevant journals. This is true for both the subtleties of the theoretical model as well as the complexities of the data base. Essentially, existing AGE tax models remain black boxes to interested readers. All they can do is to "... deliver summary grunts of belief or disbelief but find it difficult to articulate reasons in a disciplined way" (McCloskey, 1983, p. 502).

As a first step to overcome these problems, detailed descriptions of the better known AGE tax models have recently been published; see Ballard, Fullerton, Shoven, and Whalley (1985), Piggott and Whalley (1985). However, reading and understanding these books is hard work and requires a lot of time, and even then some questions will remain leaving the do-it-yourself model builder faced with considerable difficulties.

Therefore, in our opinion there is some need for an introductory article,

* The second author acknowledges help from the Deutsche Forschungsgemeinschaft, financing a visit at the University of Western Ontario, London, Canada. His indebtedness to published and unpublished work of John Whalley is obvious. Useful comments from our discussant, W. Buchholz, are gratefully acknowledged.

explaining in detail how to construct an AGE tax model, and elucidating the strengths and weaknesses of this kind of analysis. Our paper is directed to the interested beginner in Applied General Equilibrium Analysis, with some limited background in Walrasian Economics. We want to provide some help in deciding whether or not to join the AGE club; in the case of a positive answer, with some effort the reader should be able to perform some applied modelling according to his own interest. In our view, despite some shortcomings, AGE tax models are a worthwhile venture to which no real alternatives exist.

Having said this, it should be clear that our paper is not a serious attempt in *empirical* economics; we see its basic contribution in its methodological aspects. A very limited empirical appeal is introduced by illustrating the use of AGE analysis with one aspect of the current tax debate in the FRG: the reform of German factor taxes. In another paper we will tackle the same question with greater emphasis on the *applied* or *empirical* side of the problem, using the input-output statistics of the IFO-Institute with a highly disaggregated production sector etc.

In general, the detail of the empirical data should not obscure the fact that at present the *empirical* side of AGE tax models is still relatively weak. The possible insights afforded by AGE models are clearly stated by John Whalley, probably the most prominent protagonist of AGE analysis, in the following lengthy citation (Whalley, 1985b, p. 4):

> "When used to generate insights rather than precise numbers, ... (the use of AGE models) ... makes explicit the implicit models lying behind various policy positions, and forces policy making to be approached both from an economy wide point of view and in terms of a logically consistent framework. As long as a significant body of economic thought views the Walrasian system as the basic organizational framework for our discipline, nothing could be more natural than to want to use numbers in such analysis. Theoretical analysis usually takes one only part way in policy debate; perhaps identifying the sign of an effect if various conditions hold, or suggesting that several effects enter whose net effect is ambiguous. The need for policy decision making demands more from such analysis, and in the presence of no obviously superior alternative, using numbers in such models (even if in a somewhat rough and ready manner) does not strike me as a bad way to proceed."

Accordingly, one purpose of our paper is to show how AGE models can generate additional insights into tax policy questions, often challenging conventional wisdom that is based on plausibility arguments.

The following flow chart illustrates the typical structure of AGE models.

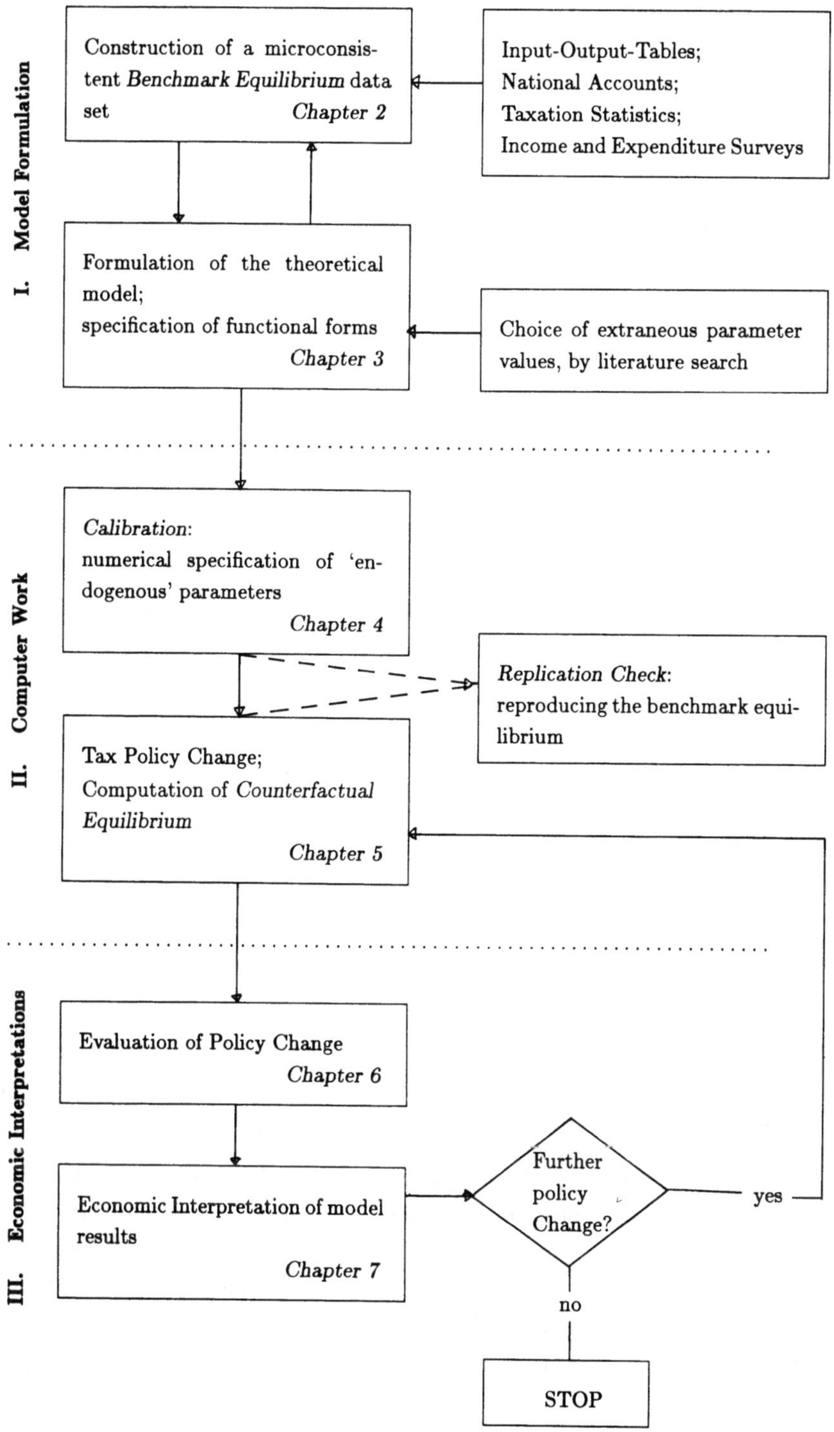

Table 1: Flow Chart for Applied General Equilibrium Tax Models

The different steps are explained in the indicated chapters. In the first chapter we give a short survey of the current tax reform discussion.

I: The Economic Problem: Operationalizing Walras

In this part of our paper, we initially discuss the economic tax reform problem (chapter 1), then describe the data base underlying our numerical calculations (chapter 2) and finally develop a simple theoretical model suitable for the problem at hand (chapter 3).

1: System and Reform of Factor Taxes in the FRG

The reform of local factor taxes, especially that of the trade taxes (Gewerbesteuer), is one of the permanent subjects of tax policy discussion in the FRG.

Up to 1980 trade taxes consisted of three partial taxes: the trade earnings tax (Gewerbeertragsteuer), the trade capital tax (Gewerbekapitalsteuer) and some kind of a payroll tax (Lohnsummensteuer). The latter was abolished with the tax reform act of 1979. We will not outline the details of the tax schedule, which are rather complicated. It suffices to say that the trade taxes form an important part of the federal tax revenue: in the fiscal year 1983, trade tax revenue amounted to approximately DM 26.2 billions or 6.3 % of total federal tax revenue — as in the years before the third largest source of revenue after income and value added taxes.

In accordance with our limited *empirical* pretentions we simply model the payroll tax as a proportional ad valorem tax on wages and the trade earnings and capital taxes as an ad valorem tax on capital income in each production sector.

There are *numerous* objections to the current factor tax system, giving rise to the widespread belief that the utter mess of trade taxes should be replaced by somc lcss disastrous alternative. To simplify matters we will concentrate on the efficiency aspect of the reform debate. As a potential indicator of efficiency losses, consider the ratio of tax liability of the trade earnings tax to capital income, varying from 0.18 % in agriculture, forestry and fisheries to 24.12 % in the mining industry (see Hummel *et al.*, 1985).

According to the literature the main reasons for the assumed allocational inefficiencies of trade taxes are:

- tax exemptions: only the industrial enterprises are assessed by the trade taxes; agricultural enterprises as well as the liberal professions are free from trade taxes, as are the Postal Services, the Federal Railroads and the non-profit organizations;
- tax allowances: these are quite substantial with the consequence that only one third of all industrial enterprises face any tax liability;
- the different average and marginal tax burdens of the different factors of production: the rather low proportional rates of the payroll tax on returns to labour and the considerably higher distorting tax rates of the trade earnings and capital tax on capital income.

Whereas the first two points concern potential distortions in the inter-industry allocation of capital, the last point suggests the possibility of "wrong" factor intensities within a given industry.

By replacing the trade taxes by some equal yield tax alternative it is hoped that competitive distortions can be eliminated. The following tax alternatives are recommended:

1. A broad based local value added tax of the net income type (Nettowertschöpfungsteuer) with a uniform tax rate (proposed, for example, by the Advisory Board to the Treasury — Wissenschaftlicher Beirat, 1982 — or the German Council of Economic Advisers).
2. A tax rate increase of the existing value added tax of the consumption type, with some revenue sharing by the local communities (proposed by the Karl-Bräuer-Institut, 1984, or the Institut Finanzen und Steuern, 1982).

We will calculate the efficiency effects of both tax reform proposals in an AGE setting. Furthermore, we will briefly comment on the somewhat peculiar suggestion of replacing the trade taxes by an equal yield local poll tax (Boss, 1984).

According to the proponents of the first tax alternative, one advantage over the second is to be seen in the fact that a value added tax of the net income type has to apply the destination principle, whereas a value added tax of the consumption type has to be based on the origin principle. This border tax adjustment problem will be dealt with in chapter 7.

In a certain sense, our problem exposition determines the data requirements as well as the basic structure of the theoretical model: to capture the distortions in the allocation of capital between industries, the production sector of the economy has to be sufficiently disaggregated. On the other hand, the imposed restriction on the efficiency aspects of the tax problem in question suggests the assumption of a representative consumer. The foreign sector has to be modelled to deal with the border tax adjustment problem. Finally, consumption and investment demand have to be distinguished in order to comprehend the difference between value added taxes of the net income and of the consumption type.

2: A Micro Consistent Data Set

The essence of AGE economics is the combination of general equilibrium theory with a consistent data set from the National Accounts in order to derive policy insights. In this chapter we describe a micro consistent data set, while the next chapter deals with the theoretical structure of our model.

The basic assumption of most AGE models is that the economy is characterized by a situation of Walrasian equilibrium. In our context the data set in the base year has to comply with the following four equilibrium conditions:

- demands equal supplies for goods and factors;
- all domestic agents satisfy their budget constraints;
- non-positive profits in all industries in long-run equilibrium (residual profit return to equity is treated as a contractual cost)
- zero external sector balance.

It is obvious that the data in current National Accounts do not satisfy these conditions. Various adjustments are necessary in order to construct a *benchmark equilibrium data set*, compatible with the Walrasian system. And as more serious studies show, a lot of work and imagination is involved (see, for example, St.-Hilaire and Whalley, 1983; or St.-Hilaire and Whalley, 1985). Table 2 reports our example of a micro consistent benchmark equilibrium data set. The notation is self-explanatory, but for the sake of completeness is explained in more detail in the appendix. On the whole, these data are aggregated from the input-output statistics 1978 of the "Statistische Bundesamt". But we did not hesitate to 'guesstimate' some numbers, or to draw others out of the hat, whenever necessary. This seems to be acceptable (and is done less obviously even in more serious AGE studies) because our emphasis is on the methodological side of the record.

The data are given in value terms, i.e., they are products of prices and quantities. General Equilibrium Theory requires a separation of prices and quantities. The by now common procedure is to adopt unit conventions on factor quantities, allowing one to translate data on factor incomes into information on physical

Table 2: Benchmark Equilibrium Data Set

Industries:

1: Agriculture, forestry, fisheries
2: Manufacturing
3: Trade, transportation, public utilities
4: Finance, insurance and other services (including housing)
5: Public authorities

Input-Output Table (producer prices)

V_{ij}	1	2	3	4	5	q_iC_i	q_iG_i	q_iI_i	q_iX_i
1	13.90	53.10	0.30	5.70	1.70	7.90	—	0.40	2.30
2	14.40	590.70	42.80	64.00	52.00	271.90	—	231.20	237.00
3	3.90	80.70	18.90	13.00	10.80	122.80	—	12.80	24.40
4	1.90	61.20	31.90	90.80	45.40	139.49	—	6.90	11.10
5	0.40	4.40	1.20	5.30	31.60	—	324.51	—	—
wL_i	5.40	353.90	123.30	75.90	161.10				
rK_i	19.10	91.70	65.70	108.20	64.60				
T_i^L	0.00	2.23	0.68	0.38	0.01				
T_i^K	0.46	12.70	5.50	10.82	0.00				
T_i^Q	−1.76	28.37	−11.48	0.89	0.20				
q_iQ_i	57.70	1279.00	278.80	374.99	367.41				
q_iM_i	27.60	225.00	8.50	13.70	0.00				

Additional data:

Vector of Value Added Taxes on consumption commodities	$T_i^C = [0.62,\ 36.70,\ 4.59,\ 9.39,\ 0.0]$
Income tax revenue	$T^Y = 235.31$
income tax allowance	$A = 127.66$
Transfers to consumers	$Tr = 11.10$

quantities. The most convenient assumption is to choose physical factor quantities such as to earn 1 DM net of all taxes and subsidies in the benchmark equilibrium. Similarly, quantities of commodities are implicitely defined by assuming prices of goods net of consumer taxes to be 1 DM in the base year. The vector of factor and commodity net prices in the benchmark equilibrium consists of 1's only, i.e. $(r, w, q_1, \ldots, q_n) = (1, 1, 1, \ldots, 1)$.

The official input-output statistics report production taxes (minus subsidies) as part of each industry's gross value added, including, among others, excise taxes as well as trade and property taxes. For our purposes it is necessary to remove payroll and trade taxes on earnings and capital stock from these data. This is done by distributing payroll taxes (T_i^L) in proportion to wages and salaries (wL_i) paid by industry i. The distribution of trade earnings and capital taxes by industries was taken from a recent study of the IFO-Institute and updated to the 1978 totals (Hummel *et al.*, 1985). Property taxes A and B, which are levied as a substitute for trade taxes in agriculture and the housing industry were distributed to the first and fourth production sector, respectively. Thus, the T_i^K in the value added quadrant denote the sum of trade and property taxes on an industry level. The negative production taxes (T_i^Q) in industries 1 and 3 indicate subsidies to agriculture (sector 1) and to public utilities, which are included in sector 3.

The distribution of value added taxes over commodities is taken from the input-output statistics and, after some adjustments, imputed to consumption expenditures only.

Let us conclude this chapter with a warning: The reader should not try to reconstruct our benchmark data set, but simply take it as given and as a necessary prerequisite and ingredient for what follows. Our above remarks are thought as a first hint that constructing a complete micro consistent data set for serious *applied* equilibrium studies is loaded with considerable difficulties, mainly because of conceptual differences between Walrasian accounting and the current practice of National Accounts. Indeed, constructing a satisfactory benchmark equilibrium data set is probably the hardest and most time-consuming part of AGE research efforts.

3: The Theoretical Model

The basic structure of our theoretical model is determined by the economic problem on the one hand and by the available data on the other.

a) *Production*

Most AGE studies specify analytically convenient functional forms on the production and consumption side of the economy.

We assume a fixed coefficient technology with respect to intermediate production and value added, and a constant elasticity of substitution (CES) technology between value added and the factor inputs capital and labour.

To be more precise, the production function for sector i is

$$(1) \qquad Q = min\left\{\frac{1}{a_{0i}}f^i(K_i, L_i), \frac{V_{1i}}{a_{1i}}, \ldots, \frac{V_{5i}}{a_{5i}}\right\}, \qquad i = 1, \ldots, 5,$$

where the value added function is given by

$$f^i(K_i, L_i) = \Phi_i\{[\delta_i L_i^{-\mu_i} + (1-\delta_i)K_i^{-\mu_i}]^{-1/\mu_i}\},$$

and where $\mu_i = (1-\sigma_i)/\sigma_i, \qquad (-1 \leq \mu_i \leq \infty).$

Parameter σ_i is the elasticity of substitution, δ_i is a weighting parameter, Φ_i defines units of measurement.

Producer behavior is characterized by cost minimization for a given output.

On the production side of the economy we distinguish two price concepts: producer prices and manufacturing prices, where the first exceed the latter by the production taxes net of subsidies paid per tax assessment unit. The tax base of production taxes is the output valued at *manufacturing prices.* We can avoid a separate symbol for the latter if we compute tax liability as a percentage of output, valued at *producer prices* q_i:

$$T_i^Q = \frac{\tau_i^q}{1+\tau_i^q} q_i Q_i \qquad i = 1, \ldots, 5.$$

For a given output $\overline{Q}_i$ production taxes are fixed. The same is true for purchases of intermediate inputs, i.e. $\sum_j q_j a_{ij} Q_i$ Variable costs of each industry's minimization problem are then given by the sum of capital and labour income, the latter including payroll taxes, the first trade earnings and capital as well as property taxes. Both factor taxes are modelled as sector-specific proportional ad-valorem taxes with (average and marginal) tax rates τ_i^ℓ and τ_i^k.

$$\text{Minimizing} \quad w(1+\tau_i^\ell)L_i + r(1+\tau_i^k)K_i$$
$$\text{subject to} \quad f^i(K_i, L_i) = a_{0i}\overline{Q}_i$$

yields the factor demand requirements

$$(2a) \qquad L_i = \frac{1}{\Phi_i} a_{0i}\overline{Q}_i \left\{\delta_i + (1-\delta_i)\left[\frac{\delta_i r(1+\tau_i^k)}{(1-\delta_i)w(1+\tau_i^\ell)}\right]^{(1-\sigma_i)}\right\}^{1/\mu_i},$$

$$(2b) \qquad K_i = \frac{1}{\Phi_i} a_{0i}\overline{Q}_i \left\{(1-\delta_i) + \delta_i\left[\frac{(1-\delta_i)w(1+\tau_i^\ell)}{\delta_i r(1+\tau_i^k)}\right]^{(1-\sigma_i)}\right\}^{1/\mu_i}.$$

In long-run equilibrium, competition eliminates all "excessive" profits and the zero-profit condition holds:

$$(3) \qquad q_iQ_i - \sum_{j=1}^{5} q_j a_{ji} Q_i - \frac{\tau_i^q}{1+\tau_i^q} q_i Q_i - r(1+\tau_i^k)K_i - w(1-\tau_i^\ell)L_i = 0.$$

The different terms in this equation correspond to the respective column values of our aggregated input-output table.

b) *Private Consumption*

On the consumption side of the economy, too, the model builder has to specify convenient functional forms, which, on the one hand, are easy to handle and, on the other hand, are empirically not implausible.

The most obvious candidate is a Cobb-Douglas utility function. However, these functions imply unitary income and *uncompensated* own-price elasticities, contradicting our empirical observations. The CES generalization suggests itself, but this functional form has the undesirable implication of having approximately the same *compensated* own-price elasticities, provided that budget shares are small. This is particularly disturbing if a variable labour supply is involved. As to other alternatives, the Linear Expenditure System (LES) or Translog Expenditure Function could be considered, but both have their drawbacks in empirical work. Using the Stone-Geary utility function, which gives rise to the LES system, minimum consumption requirements have to be prespecified; the problem with the Translog Expenditure System is to guarantee the usual demand or utility restrictions such as concavity etc.

Anyway, some functional form has to be chosen, balancing the aspects of tractability and plausibility. In this paper we use the concept of a *nested* utility function, combining the virtue of being easy to evaluate in numerical calculations with some degree of flexibility in assigning empirically relevant price elasticities. The standard reference is Keller (1976, 1977).

The outer nest is a CES function over leisure (F) and a composite consumption commodity (C), the inner nest a Cobb-Douglas function defined over the different consumption goods $C_1, \ldots, C_4$. The collective consumption good C_5 is omitted as an argument as will be explained later. More formally:

$$(4a) \qquad U = [(1-\beta)^{1/\nu} C^{(\nu-1)/\nu} + \beta^{1/\nu} F^{(\nu-1)/\nu}]^{\nu/(\nu-1)}$$

and

$$\text{(4b)} \qquad C = \sum_{i=1}^{4} \alpha_i \log C_i \qquad \text{where } \sum_i \alpha_i = 1.$$

This is, in fact, one of the simplest utility tree structures conceivable. With some additional effort more meaningful but more complicated utility trees could be specified. As an illustration, the above structure will suffice.

The optimization problem of our representative consumer can be conceived of as a two stage maximization process: in the first stage, the household chooses leisure F (or labour supply L) and total consumption C by maximizing (4a) subject to

$$\text{(5a)} \qquad pC + wF = [wE + r\overline{K} - T^y + Tr].$$

Here, E is the total time endowment with $E = L + F$, $\overline{K}$ is the fixed supply of capital and p a composite price of consumption C. For later reference we define

$$Y := wE + r\overline{K}$$

as *full income*. The income tax schedule is assumed to be linearly progressive, i.e.

$$T^y = \tau^y[w(E - F) + r\overline{K} - A].$$

A is an income tax allowance, Tr denote transfers.

Substituting T^y into (5a) yields after rearrangement

$$pC + w(1 - \tau^y)F = [(1 - \tau^y)Y + \tau^y A + Tr].$$

Leisure and composite consumption demand are then given by

$$\text{(6)} \quad F = \frac{\beta[(1 - \tau^y)Y + \tau^y A + Tr]}{[w(1 - \tau^y)]^\nu \Omega}; \quad C = \frac{(1 - \beta)[(1 - \tau^y)Y + \tau^y A + Tr]}{p^\nu \Omega}$$

$$\text{where } \Omega = (1 - \beta)p^{(1-\nu)} + \beta[w(1 - \tau^y)]^{(1-\nu)}.$$

In the second stage, (4b) is maximized subject to the remaining income constraint

$$\text{(5b)} \qquad \sum_{i=1}^{4} p_i C_i = (1 - \gamma)[(1 - \tau^y)Y + \tau^y A + Tr - w(1 - \tau^y)F]$$

$$= (1 - \gamma)[wL + r\overline{K} - T^y + Tr]$$

yielding demand functions

$$C_i = \frac{\alpha_i}{p_i}(1-\gamma)[wL + r\overline{K} - T^y + Tr]. \tag{7}$$

Here γ is a constant savings rate out of disposable market income.

Consumer prices p_i are related to producer prices q_i by

$$p_i = q_i(1 + \tau_i^c),$$

τ_i^c being the value added tax rate on the i-th commodity.

As is well known, the elasticity of substition ν in (4a) determines the slope of the indifference curves in (C, F)-space.

The assumption of a constant savings propensity γ introduces a Keynesian element into our neoclassical framework, but seems to be justifiable in static models. By specifying an additional nest of the utility tree between current and future consumption, the analysis could be extended to capture variable savings. This is left to future modelling efforts.

c) *Investment Demand*

Modelling investment demand satisfactorily in a static world is a hopeless undertaking. But it is necessary if one wants to distinguish VAT of the consumption type from VAT of the net income type. Following Piggott and Whalley (1985) we simply assume some kind of a "corporate" consumer. Savings are automatically transferred from the household to the business sector, where the imaginary corporate consumer decides on the composition of investment expenditures according to a Cobb-Douglas function.

Total savings S of the private consumer

$$S = \gamma[wL + r\overline{K} - T^y + Tr]$$

translate into investment demand I_i of the i-th industry by

$$I_i = \frac{\lambda_i}{q_i}S. \tag{8}$$

While savings are a constant fraction of disposable income, there is a limited degree of investment composition variability because of the endogeneity of producer prices.

We interpret savings as current expenditure for future consumption and add the utility of the corporate consumer to that of the private household.

d) *The External Sector*

While modelling the domestic economy by a complete general equilibrium system, we treat the foreign sector in a simple manner, so as to close the model. Our formulation relies heavily on Boadway and Treddenick (1978) with the extensions introduced by Whalley and Yeung (1984). See Goulder, Shoven and Whalley (1983) for alternative foreign sector formulations in AGE models and Whalley (1985b) for a global trade model.

For each of the private producer goods we specify foreign import supply and export demand functions:

$$X_i = \left(\frac{q_i}{d}\right)^{\Theta} \cdot X_i^0 \qquad \infty < \Theta \leq -1,\ i = 1, \ldots, 4, \tag{9a}$$

$$M_i = \left(\frac{q_i}{d}\right)^{\eta} \cdot M_i^0 \qquad 0 \leq \eta < \infty,\ i = 1, \ldots, 4. \tag{9b}$$

The elasticities Θ and η of foreign export demand and import supply with respect to *world* prices (q_i/d) are constant; d being the exchange rate between domestic and foreign prices.

In order to close the general equilibrium system, a trade balance constraint has to be added:

$$\sum_{i=1}^{n} q_i X_i - \sum_{i=1}^{n} q_i M_i = 0. \tag{10}$$

But d is a purely financial magnitude with no real significance for the *real* variables of the system. We can remove it by substituting (9a,b) into the trade balance constraint (10), solving for the exchange rate, and resubstitute into (9a,b) to receive:

$$X_i = \left[\frac{\sum_{j=1}^{4} q_j^{(\Theta+1)} X_j^0}{\sum_{j=1}^{4} q_j^{(\eta+1)} M_j^0}\right]^{\Theta/(\eta-\Theta)} \cdot q_i^{\Theta} X_i^0, \qquad i = 1, \ldots, 4, \tag{11a}$$

$$M_i = \left[\frac{\sum_{j=1}^{4} q_j^{(\Theta+1)} X_j^0}{\sum_{j=1}^{4} q_j^{(\eta+1)} M_j^0}\right]^{\eta/(\eta-\Theta)} \cdot q_i^{\eta} M_i^0, \qquad i = 1, \ldots, 4. \tag{11b}$$

Note that these export demand and import supply functions depend on domestic prices only and imply zero trade balance.

The own-price elasticities with respect to *domestic* prices are also constant and given by

$$\frac{\partial X_i}{\partial q_i}\frac{q_i}{X_i} = \frac{\Theta(1+\eta)}{(\eta-\Theta)}, \qquad \frac{\partial M_i}{\partial q_i}\frac{q_i}{M_i} = -\frac{\eta(1+\Theta)}{(\eta-\Theta)}. \tag{12}$$

The sign restrictions on Θ and η in equations (9) above guarantee that the 'compensated' own price export demand curve is downward sloping, while the import supply curve slopes upward with the own price increasing.

The problem with the interpretation of the equations (11) is that they imply that the i-th commodity is at the same time exported and imported. Even if evident from the trade statistics, the reasons for this "*crosshauling*" are not provided by our model.

e) *The Government Sector*

To a large extent, the modelling of the government sector is restricted by the current practice of National Accounts. There are two broad categories of governmental activities: on the one hand, a collective consumption commodity (commodity 5) is produced by combining labour, capital and intermediate inputs, all of which are bought at market prices. Part of this collective good is subject to user charges and sold to private industries; the other part is defined as 'collective consumption' ($q_5 G_5$) where the quantity G_5 is offered free of charge to the representative consumer. We will assume that the government wants to supply a *constant* quantity $\overline{G}_5$. This is the reason why the collective commodity can be omitted from the domain of the utility function.

On the other hand, the government levies taxes and pays transfers and subsidies, the balance of which has to equal collective consumption $q_5 G_5$. The government budget constraint is therefore given by

$$(13)\qquad \begin{aligned} Tr + q_5 G_5 = &\sum_{j=1}^{5} (\tau_j^k r K_j + \tau_j^\ell w L_j) + \sum_{j=1}^{4} \tau_j^c q_j C_j + \\ &+ \sum_{j=1}^{5} \frac{\tau_j^q}{1+\tau_j^q} q_j Q_j + \tau^y (wL + r\overline{K} - A). \end{aligned}$$

f) *Equilibrium Conditions*

We have to specify equilibrium conditions on markets for factors and privately produced consumption commodities. These are

$$(14)\qquad L = \sum_{j=1}^{5} L_j; \quad \overline{K} = \sum_{j=1}^{5} K_j$$

$$(15)\qquad Q_i + M_i = \sum_{j=1}^{5} a_{ij} Q_j + C_i + G_i + I_i + X_i,$$

or, in matrix notation and after rearranging

$$\mathbf{Q} = (\mathbf{E} - \mathbf{A})^{-1}[\mathbf{C} + \mathbf{G} + \mathbf{I} + (\mathbf{X} - \mathbf{M})]. \tag{16}$$

Here, $\mathbf{Q}$, $\mathbf{C}$, etc. denote suitably dimensioned column vectors, $\mathbf{E}$ is the identity matrix, $\mathbf{A}$ the matrix of input coefficients.

It can easily be checked that demand and supply quantities are invariant to a proportional change of all prices and exogenous income elements. Without any loss of generality we can normalize the price system by choosing labour to be the numeraire and fixing $w = 1$.

For given tax parameters τ_j^k, τ_j^ℓ, τ_j^c, τ_j^q, τ^y, A and constant supply $\overline{G}_5$ we can calculate the solution of our equilibrium system — provided it exists and is unique. When counting variables and equations, note that the above equations are not independent. By Walras law, for example, the government budget is automatically satisfied if all other agents satisfy their budget constraints and if all markets clear.

II: Computer Work: Calibration and Numerical Calculations

In this second part of our paper we will comment on those aspects of AGE models which involve some computational efforts. Firstly, we will show in chapter 4 how to reconcile our benchmark equilibrium data set with the theoretical model developed in the last chapter. Secondly, we will perform some tax policy simulations and compute the respective *counterfactual* equilibria (chapter 5).

4: Calibrating the Model

The theoretical model outlined above could be solved numerically if the precise values of a sufficient number of exogenous parameters were known. But without any further restrictions the computed model solution would not match the empirical data of the benchmark equilibrium.

The problem, therefore, is to determine parameter values such as to exactly reproduce the adjusted data set of the base year. This procedure is known as *calibration*. See Mansur and Whalley (1984) and the comment by Lau (1984) on the pros and cons of numerical parameter specification by calibration methods.

Because of our units convention, equilibrium value transactions can be separated out into price and quantity observations. In benchmark equilibrium, physical quantities of consumption commodities are just as known as are physical factor demands and supplies.

Effective rates of taxes can be calculated from the benchmark equilibrium data set by dividing each agent's tax liability by its tax base, thereby equating marginal and average tax rates. (The importance of distinguishing these rates is stressed by Fullerton, Henderson, and Shoven, 1984, and King and Fullerton, 1984.)

The usual practice is to borrow a sufficient number of extraneous estimates of elasticities or other parameter values from the econometric literature. The remaining parameter values are determined in a nonstochastic manner by solving each agent's equilibrium conditions for the parameters in question using the data on prices and quantities in the benchmark equilibrium data set.

For example, on the production side of the economy we have the following parameters for each industry: σ_i, δ_i and Φ_i. Suppose the econometric literature provides us with some reliable estimates of the elasticities of substitution, σ_i. Then the marginal conditions of each producer's cost minimization problem:

$$\frac{r(1+\tau_i^k)}{w(1+\tau_i^\ell)} = \frac{(1-\delta_i)L_i^{1/\sigma_i}}{\delta_i K_i^{1/\sigma_i}}, \qquad i = 1,\ldots,5$$

can be solved for the share parameters δ_i:

$$\delta_i = \left[\frac{w(1+\tau_i^\ell)L_i^{1/\sigma_i}}{r(1+\tau_i^k)K_i^{1/\sigma_i}}\right] \Big/ \left[1 + \frac{w(1+\tau_i^\ell)L_i^{1/\sigma_i}}{r(1+\tau_i^k)K_i^{1/\sigma_i}}\right], \qquad i = 1,\ldots,5.$$

The values for K_i, L_i, τ_i^k, τ_i^ℓ etc. are known or can be calculated from the benchmark equilibrium data set.

Given σ_i and δ_i, the efficiency parameters Φ_i are immediately derived from the CES value added functions.

On the demand side, with nested utility functions, calibration is slightly more difficult. With the inner nest being Cobb-Douglas functions, share parameters α_i can readily be calculated by solving equations (7):

$$\alpha_i = \frac{p_i C_i}{(1-\gamma)[wL + rK - T^y + Tr]} \cdot$$

Only in the Cobb-Douglas case, parameter values are uniquely determined by the base year's data set.

To solve for the other parameter values we have to specify extraneous elasticity values. The elasticity of substitution in the outer utility nest cannot be known because composite commodity C has no real counterpart. What can be found in the literature are econometric estimates of the *uncompensated* elasticity of labour supply with respect to the net wage rate, e. Given e and the total time endowment E, the elasticity of substition ν as well as the first order share parameter β can be calculated as follows:

Firstly, translate the uncompensated labour supply elasticity into the corresponding elasticity of leisure demand, $\hat{e}$. This is done by combining the definitions

$$e := \frac{\partial L}{\partial w^n} \cdot \frac{w^n}{L} \quad \text{and} \quad \hat{e} := \frac{\partial F}{\partial w^n} \cdot \frac{w^n}{F} \quad \text{where} \quad w^n = w(1-\tau^y).$$

Expanding $\hat{e}$, we get

$$\begin{aligned} \hat{e} &= \frac{\partial(E-L)}{\partial w^n} \cdot \frac{w^n}{(E-L)} \\ &= -\frac{\partial L}{\partial w^n} \cdot \frac{w^n}{E-L} \end{aligned} \tag{17}$$

since $\partial E/\partial w^n = 0$. Define $\varsigma := E/L$. After some manipulations we have

$$\hat{e} = -e\frac{1}{(\varsigma - 1)}. \tag{18}$$

So leisure demand elasticity is given, once the uncompensated labour supply elasticity and either E or ς are known. We will discuss our choice of these parameters below.

The next step is to determine the elasticity parameter ν. This is done by evaluating $\partial F/\partial w^n$ from (6):

$$\frac{\partial F}{\partial w^n} = \frac{\nu F}{w^n} + \frac{\beta E}{(w^n)^\nu \Omega} - \frac{\beta F(1-\nu)}{(w^n)^\nu \Omega}.$$

Substituting into (18) yields

$$\hat{e} = -\nu + \frac{\beta (w^n)^{(1-\nu)} E}{F\Omega} - \frac{\beta(1-\nu)(w^n)^{(1-\nu)}}{\Omega}. \tag{19}$$

Defining the share of leisure 'expenditure' to full disposable income by

$$\begin{aligned} s_f &= \frac{w^n F}{[wE + r\overline{K} - T^y + Tr]} \\ &= \frac{\beta (w^n)^{(1-\nu)}}{\Omega}, \end{aligned}$$

we can solve (19) for the elasticity of substitution after substituting from (6):

$$\nu = (1 - s_f)^{-1}[s_e - s_f - \hat{e}], \tag{20}$$

where $s_e := w^n E/[wE + r\overline{K} - T^y + Tr]$.

All the variables on the right hand side of (20) are either extraneously specified or known from the benchmark data set.

We can now proceed to the determination of the share parameter β. Dividing the demands for leisure and for the composite commodity given by (6), and solving for β yields:

$$\beta = [(w^n)^\nu F/(p^\nu C)] \;/\; \{1 + [(w^n)^\nu F/(p^\nu C)]\}. \tag{21}$$

The unknown values of p and C are obtained by determining the indirect utility function

$$C = (1-\gamma)[wL + r\overline{K} - T^y + Tr] \prod_{i=1}^{4} \left(\frac{\alpha_i}{p_i}\right)^{\alpha_i}.$$

Substituting $pC = [wL + r\overline{K} - T^y + Tr]$ from (5a) gives

$$p = (1-\gamma)^{-1} \prod_{i=1}^{4} \left(\frac{p_i}{\alpha_i}\right)^{\alpha_i}.$$

This completes the calibration of household utility functions.

The parameters of the investment demand function are uniquely determined because of the underlying Cobb-Douglas utility structure.

Specification of parameters for the foreign trade functions (11) involve the elasticity parameters η and Θ and the quantities M_i^0, X_i^0. The latter are equated to the benchmark trade values. Selection of the former will be discussed in the following section.

Specifying Extraneous Parameters

Estimates of the elasticities of substitution in the production sectors are taken from Caddy (1976) as reproduced in Piggott and Whalley (1985, pp. 160–161) and shown in Table 3. These estimates are not very reliable, so we will perform some sensitivity analyses in later chapters.

On the consumer side, we assume that the representative consumer supplies 40-hours out of a possible 70-hour week. The ratio of labour time to total time

Table 3: Calibration (central case)

parameter / agents	extraneously specified	"calibrated"
production	$\sigma_i = [0.7,\ 0.8,\ 0.75,\ 0.75,\ 0.9]$	$\delta_i = [0.1384,\ 0.8270,\ 0.6823,\ 0.3628,\ 0.7341]$ $\Phi_i = [1.5154,\ 1.8072,\ 1.8466,\ 2.0723,\ 1.8046]$
consumption	$e = 0.15$ $\varsigma = 1.75$	$\alpha_i = [0.0144,\ 0.5201,\ 0.2147,\ 0.2509]$ $\nu = 0.9348$ $\beta = 0.3503$
investment		$\lambda_i = [0.0016,\ 0.9200,\ 0.0509,\ 0.0275]$
foreign trade	$\Theta = -10.0$ $\eta = 0.12$	

endowment is therefore given by $\varsigma = 1.75$. We restrain from questioning the 70-hour assumption; a discussion of the economics of sleeping and related activities is beyond our paper. As far as we know there are no serious labour supply estimates for the FRG. Following Ballard, Fullerton, Shoven, and Whalley (1985) we choose $e = 0.15$ as our central case estimate.

Foreign price elasticities of export demand are taken from the compendium of trade elasticities provided by Stern, Francis, and Schumacher (1976). The value of -1.11 given there is satisfied by an infinite number of combinations of η and Θ. To fix ideas we postulate $\Theta = -10.0$, $\eta = 0.12$, implying that German exports are highly sensitive to price.

In the first column of Table 3 we summarize the extraneous specifications of parameter values; the second column shows the calibrated values of the remaining parameters.

By performing some sensitivity analysis around this central case specification we are able to isolate the key factors determining the results.

Let us close this chapter with a final remark on the shortcomings of calibration procedures. Presumably, to the econometrician parameter determination by calibration is unacceptable. There is no statistical test of the model specification, there is a serious underidentification problem and there is a lack of "flexibility" of the assumed functional forms of utility and production functions. The econometric approach to AGE, described for example by Jorgenson (1984) seems to be superior to calibration, but this is a very difficult and time-consuming undertaking. In the meantime, some policy advice is required, and calibration is a convenient procedure for a quick answer. As Lawrence Lau (1984, p. 136) puts it: "It is a useful shortcut for a modeler in a hurry".

5: Numerical Policy Simulations

After having finished calibration, the theoretical model should exactly reproduce the benchmark equilibrium data set with the calibrated parameter values. So, as a first check on the accuracy of the programming code the model should be solved with the solution already known. This is called the *replication check*. After passing this internal consistency check, policy simulations can be performed by changing tax rates or other policy instruments. A new equilibrium is calculated (the *counterfactual* equilibrium) for each policy change. Policy conclusions are derived by comparing the endogenous variables in the counterfactual equilibria with those of the benchmark equilibrium. Usually one concentrates on various summary statistics such as the Hicksian Equivalent Variation (HEV) or the Gini-index in distributional studies. This is the numerical counterpart of comparative statics analysis.

The tax problem we want to deal with is the substitution of trade taxes by an equal yield value added tax of the net income type with a uniform rate structure. Trade taxes are thus reduced to zero and a new proportional tax rate on value added is calculated yielding the same tax revenue. Here 'equal yield' is understood as the tax revenue which allows the same quantity $\overline{G}_5$ of the public consumption good and the same transfer payments to the household sector. To determine this 'real' equality of transfer payments we use the Laspeyres price index to correct for price changes. See Shoven and Whalley (1977) for a more detailed discussion of equal yield tax alternatives.

Tax liability under the new VAT is calculated by the addition method in adding up all factor payments and applying the relevant tax rate to this sum.

Table 4 displays the counterfactual equilibrium in quantity and value terms for our central case parameter specifications. The intermediate input flows are not reproduced but can easily be calculated using the input coefficients.

Table 4: Central Case Counterfactual Equilibrium Quantities and Values

Replacement of trade and property taxes by a VAT of the net income type

quantities

						C_i	G_i	I_i	X_i
						7.73	—	0.39	1.79
						269.57	—	229.22	238.63
						121.23	—	12.64	23.54
						138.71	—	6.86	11.51
L_i	5.36	347.99	121.32	74.58	163.64	—	324.51	—	—
K_i	18.47	94.76	65.31	108.66	62.09				
Q_i	56.11	1271.82	275.35	373.40	367.33				
M_i	27.68	224.98	8.50	13.69	—				

values ($w = 1.0$; $r = 1.0632$;
$q_i = [1.0496, 1.0227, 1.0271, 1.0197, 1.0465]$)

						q_iC_i	q_iG_i	q_iI_i	q_iX_i
						8.01	—	0.41	1.88
						275.69	—	236.42	244.05
						124.51	—	12.98	24.18
wL_i	5.36	347.99	121.32	74.58	163.64	141.44	—	7.00	11.74
rK_i	19.64	100.75	69.44	115.53	66.02	—	339.60	—	—
T_i^Q	−1.80	28.85	−11.65	0.90	0.21				
T_i^W	1.00	17.91	7.61	7.59	9.17				
q_iQ_i	58.89	1300.70	282.81	380.75	384.42				
q_iM_i	29.06	230.09	8.73	13.96	—				

Additional data:

Value added taxes on consumption	$T_i^C = [0.63, 37.20, 4.66, 9.51, 0.0]$
Income tax revenue	$T^Y = 239.15$
Transfers to consumers	$Tr = 11.36$

We will comment on these results in a later chapter.

Numerically solving general equilibrium models is not a trivial problem. We used Merrill's variant of Scarf's algorithm (1973, 1984), which seems to be the most widely used fixed point algorithm. For a user oriented description of Merrill's algorithm the reader is referred to Wiegard (1985). But generally Newton-type methods will do the job just as well. Meanwhile, black-box algorithms are available — PLALGO by M. Todd (1985), OCTASOLV by M. Broady (1985) or MPS/GE by T. Rutherford (1985) —, freeing the general AGE modeler from the necessity of writing his own solution code.

A survey of different methods of computing economic equilibria is provided by Todd (1984) or Preckel (1985). In any case, the availability of numerical solution methods is no longer an effective constraint on AGE modelling activities.

III: Economic Interpretation of Simulation Results

In principle, it is possible to trace all factor and commodity movements caused by the policy change by simply comparing the respective numbers in the benchmark and counterfactual equilibria. More commonly, the valuation of efficiency gains or losses following tax reforms is based on some summary statistics. In an one consumer economy the Hicksian Equivalent Variation (HEV) is the best candidate if a sequence of possible counterfactual equilibria has to be considered. The HEV is defined as the amount of additional income at benchmark equilibrium prices that would just enable the consumer to reach the utility level realized in the counterfactual equilibrium. This definition implies that a positive HEV indicates a welfare gain and vice versa. We calculate the HEV for the CES function between leisure demand and composite consumption. For homogeneous functions the HEV is given by

$$HEV = \left(\frac{U^1 - U^0}{U^0}\right) I^0,$$

where superscripts $0, 1$ denote values in the benchmark and counterfactual equilibrium, respectively, and I is full disposable income.

6: Efficiency Aspects of Replacing Trade Taxes

In this chapter we will check how far theorizing takes us in determining the qualitative results of the tax proposals in question. According to the literature, the substitution of trade taxes by a uniform VAT of the net income type is supposed to result in a clear efficiency gain, the main reason being the elimination of inter- and intra-industry distortions caused by trade taxes.

But the Theory of Second Best tells us that some caution is required with too rough and ready conclusions. The value added tax of the net income type is not neutral in an efficiency sense, but distorts the choice between leisure and consumption just as the income tax does. And it is a frequent fallacy to draw a conclusion from the number of distortions involved about its severities. Possibly, some of the distortions introduced by trade taxes compensate for others so that the overall efficiency loss is less than the single one introduced by a uniform VAT.

But the theory gives some further hints. We have imposed a specific functional form on utility nests, implying strong separability and homotheticity. In this case it is known from optimal taxation theory that a uniform rate structure is optimal. In a strict sense this only holds in a second-best optimum. As Dixit (1975) and others have shown for tax reform proposals, even a switch from distortionary taxes to a lump sum tax can *reduce* welfare if the full optimum is not achieved. Furthermore, these tax rules are valid in a closed economy, but not necessarily when international trade flows are taken into account. Nevertheless, all in all our economic intuition suggests that in tendency the switch from trade taxes to a uniform equal yield VAT of the net income type raises domestic welfare.

But there is (at least) one other important feature that may be crucial for the results of our model. This is the *terms-of-trade* effect which domestic factor taxes can induce. Whalley (1980) has shown that current factor tax structures can produce significant terms-of-trade gains, with welfare losses ocurring if factor tax distortions are removed. The reason is that factor taxes can act as incomplete substitutes for the use of optimal tariffs, which are prevented under the GATT rules. Vandendorpe (1972) has shown that a second best optimum implies a production tax on exportables. A quick glance at our data set shows that the heaviest burden of trade taxes is indeed on those commodities of which the FRG is a net exporter. Abolishing trade taxes may therefore restrict the indirect exercise of monopoly power implicit in the current system of trade taxes. The terms of trade will deteriorate if trade taxes are replaced, inducing a loss in national welfare.

Theoretical reasoning thus identifies two presumably opposing welfare effects when replacing trade taxes by a uniform value added tax of the net income type, namely: a domestic efficiency gain by reducing domestic distortions of trade taxes, but a welfare loss due to a worsening of national terms-of-trade. The overall effect is ambiguous. For our central case parameter specification, Table 5 indicates an overall welfare loss, contradicting traditional views. In the next chapter we will try to gain some further insights by running some simulation experiments.

Table 5: Efficiency Effects of Replacing Trade taxes

	Substitution of trade tax by ...	
	VAT of the net income type (uniform tax rate)	VAT of the consumption type (differentiated tax rate)
central case parameter specification	Equivalent variation (HEV):	
	− 4.66	−12.48
	HEV as a percentage of tax revenue (absolute values)	
	14.26	32.92
	Prices	
	$w = 1.0$ $r = 1.0632$ q_i = [1.0496, 1.0227, 1.0271, 1.0197, 1.0465]	$w = 1.0$ $r = 1.0641$ q_i = [1.0098, 0.9837, 0.9880, 0.9810, 1.0066]

As to the second alternative, i.e., replacing trade taxes by an equal yield tax rate adjustment of the existing VAT of the consumption type, we would expect an even clearer welfare loss for the following reasons: firstly, the differentiated rate structure of current VAT is itself distorting, between both consumption and leisure and between the different consumption commodities. Secondly, as Vandendorpe (1972) has shown, when international trade flows are taken into account, an optimal consumption tax requires a subsidy on exportables. However, in our benchmark equilibrium exportables are subject to a high value added tax rate, implying additional welfare losses if increased even further. The counterfactual data for this tax reform case confirm our intuition (Table 5).

The precise numbers of our central case counterfactual equilibria should not be overemphasized; in our view, the broad themes emerging from the simulation results are much more important. In the next chapter, we will elaborate on this point in some more depth.

In addition, we performed some sensitivity analyses with the elasticities of substitution σ_i. We gradually increased all elasticities up to 1.3 and calculated the HEVs for various combinations. The changes in the HEVs were surprisingly small and are clearly dominated by the effects of alternative labour supply elasticities as well as price elasticities of foreign trade. That is why we do not reproduce the simulation results for different σ_i's.

7: The Economics of AGE Tax Models

A more common critique of national planning models, to which AGE models clearly belong, reads as follows: economic policy degenerates to the computation of fixed points, which itself is done by a computer. Each student, knowing how to operate the computer, could numerically solve the policy models and become a perfect adviser on taxation problems in less than a month (for example, Besters, 1981, p. 187).

This critique, of course, ignores the essential point. Indeed, exactly the contrary is true. An important economic part of the exercise just starts after the numbers have been produced. Numbers are not very interesting from an economic point of view. In AGE models, they can be wrong for various reasons: there may be simple coding errors, data can be misread, some arithmetic operations may be incorrectly specified, etc. The replication check serves as a first test in detecting logical errors, but the most important check of the validity of the numbers is the test against economic intuition. And this, of course, requires an intimate knowledge of economic theory. Furthermore, the choice of different simulation runs depends heavily on economic insights into the nature of the problem.

The following sections should illustrate these points.

The Importance of Labour Supply Elasticities

Our central case labour supply elasticity with respect to the net wage was 0.15, averaged from slightly negative elasticities for prime age males and positive values around 1 for secondary workers.

One central message of modern taxation theory is that it is not the uncompensated but the *compensated* elasticity of labour supply which is relevant for tax induced efficiency losses. The reason, of course, is that the income effects cancel out if equal yield tax alternatives are considered.

Decomposing labour supply changes with respect to the net wage into a substitution and an income effect yields the familiar Slutsky equation (see, for example, Atkinson and Stiglitz, 1980, p. 61):

$$\frac{\partial L}{\partial w^n} = \left.\frac{\partial L}{\partial w^n}\right|_u + L\frac{\partial L}{\partial I}. \tag{22}$$

Defining price and income elasticities by

$$e := \frac{\partial \, log \, L}{\partial \, log \, w^n}; \quad e_u := \left.\frac{\partial \, log \, L}{\partial \, log \, w^n}\right|_u; \quad e_{LI} := \frac{\partial \, log \, L}{\partial \, log \, I}$$

the elasticity form of (22) is

$$e = e_u + \frac{wL}{I} e_{LI}.$$

Substituting

$$\begin{aligned} e_{LI} = \frac{\partial(E-F)}{\partial I} \frac{I}{E-F} &= -\frac{\partial F}{\partial I} \frac{I}{(E-F)} \\ &= -\frac{\partial F}{\partial I} \frac{I}{F} \frac{F}{E-F} \\ &= -\frac{\partial F}{\partial I} \frac{I}{F}(\varsigma - 1) \end{aligned}$$

gives

$$e = e_u - \frac{wL}{I}(\varsigma - 1)\hat{e}_{FI},$$

with the definition

$$\hat{e}_{FI} := \frac{\partial F}{\partial I} \frac{I}{F}.$$

For CES utility functions, the income elasticity of leisure demand equals one and we can solve for the compensated labour supply elasticity

$$e_u = e + \frac{wL}{I}(\varsigma - 1).$$

We can generate different compensated elasticities by suitable combinations of parameters e and ς. However, there is one important restriction on these possible combinations: it has to be guaranteed that the compensated elasticity is positive; a negative value would be in contradiction with the usual assumptions of neoclassical theory of the household.

As is well known from the literature on labour supply and taxes (for example Hausman, 1981, 1985), higher absolute values of compensated labour supply elasticities generally induce higher efficiency losses. This can be considered as a first test on the reliability of our numerical results. Table 6 illustrates that lower values of e and/or ς, implying lower compensated elasticities e_u, indeed increase economic welfare. This is true for both tax alternatives, the substitution of factor taxes by a VAT of the net income type and one of the consumption type.

Let us briefly comment on the parameters chosen for our simulations. If ς is set at 1.25, this reflects the assumption that the normal employee supplies a 40-hour week out of a possible 50 hours. This is assumed by Piggott and Whalley (1985, p. 269). The negative uncompensated elasticity of -0.4, reported by Killingsworth, results in a *negative* substitution effect of labour supply when combined with either $\varsigma = 1.75$ or $\varsigma = 1.25$ and has to be discarded. Instead, we experimented with $e = -0.04$. The case $e = 0$ and $\varsigma = 1.001$ approximates a zero compensated labour supply elasticity. In this case a uniform VAT is equivalent to a lump sum tax, and welfare gains should be maximal or welfare losses minimal. A final simulation run was made with $e = 0.0$ and $\varsigma = 1.75$. This is to illustrate that welfare losses occur even if the *uncompensated* labour supply is completely inelastic. All that matters for efficiency questions is the elasticity of the *compensated* labour supply. The numerical results are in accordance with this intuition.

So far so good; but the HEV is still negative and we have to explain why.

The Importance of Trade Elasticities

In this section we will elaborate on our hypothesis that a country can realize a welfare gain by suitably imposing factor taxes such as the German trade taxes.

Let us simplify our model to a two commodity world, where only net trade flows are considered. The essential argument can then be captured in a simple offer-curve diagram. In Figure 1, let X_2 denote the quantity of the home country's (FRG) export commodity 2; M_1 is the quantity of the home country's importable. T_0^H stands for the home country's free trade offer curve, T_0^F for that of the foreign country (rest of the world). The curvature of T_0^F is due to the assumed value of own price elasticity of foreign export demand (-1.11), indicating some monopoly power

Table 6: Simulation Analysis: The Importance of Trade and Labor Supply Elasticities

'Large' economy $\epsilon^{FD} = 1.11$ / 'Small economy' $\epsilon^{FD} \longrightarrow -\infty$		*HEV* values when substituting trade taxes by ... uniform VAT (net income type)	differentiated VAT (consumption type)
central case	large	−4.66	−12.43
$e = 0.15$, $\varsigma = 1.75$	small	−3.24	−10.78
$e = 0.15$	large	−3.28	−11.73
$\varsigma = 1.25$	small	−1.93	−10.22
$e = -0.04$	large	−2.76	− 8.81
$\varsigma = 1.75$	small	−1.76	− 7.40
$e = -0.04$	large	−1.35	− 7.68
$\varsigma = 1.25$	small	−0.30	− 6.48
$e = 0.00$	large	−3.33	− 8.52
$\varsigma = 1.75$	small	−2.07	− 7.24
$e = 0.00$	large	−0.41	− 7.61
$\varsigma = 1.001$	small	0.57	− 6.52

of the FRG in international trade relations. The free trade price ratio of exports and imports (terms-of-trade) is given by the slope of the line $0P_0$, connecting the origin with the intersection of the two countries free trade offer curves. U_0^H is the home country's trade-indifference curve associated with free trade equilibrium point P_0.

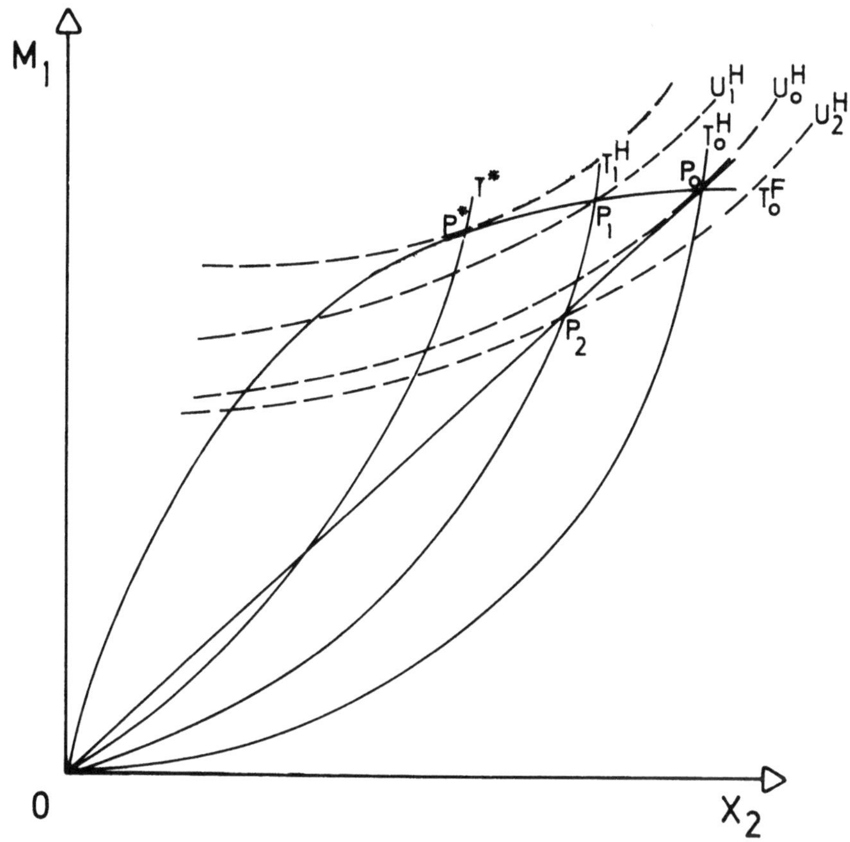

Figure 1: Welfare Effects of Trade Taxes

The home country could improve its terms-of-trade and realize a welfare gain if unilateral optimal tariffs (or equivalent combinations of production and consumption taxes) were allowed and possible: In Figure 1 the home country's offer curve is shifted to the left (T^*) by restricting the imports until point P^* is reached. But by assumption optimal tariffs are ruled out.

Now consider differentiating factor taxes as a second (or third) best alternative to optimal tariffs. Georgakopoulos (1974) has shown that if the home country levies a production tax on the commodity of which it is a net exporter, its offer curve will be shifted to the left of its free trade counterpart. The same effect appears if the factors employed in the production of the export commodity are taxed more heavily than those used in the production of importables. T_1^H is a possible offer curve position with improved terms-of-trade given by the slope of the straight line $0P_1$ (not drawn) and increased trade-indifference level U_1^H. On the other hand, if the heavier taxation of factors used in the production of exportables is abolished and a uniform rate structure introduced, the offer curve is shifted to the right, with a terms-of-trade and welfare loss associated. Let us finally add that levying production taxes is equivalent to applying the origin principle of taxation.

True, our theoretical model is much more complex, but the basic insights of simple diagrams can often be applied to more 'realistic' structures. As our benchmark data show, the FRG is a net exporter of manufactured goods produced in sector 2 and this industry is more heavily taxed under the current factor tax system. Presumably, existing trade taxes change the terms-of-trade in favor of the FRG.

Figure 1 suggests a simple cross-check in order to determine the importance of this terms-of-trade effect. Assume the FRG economy is modelled as a small open economy, with — by definition — no influence on world prices. In this case the foreign offer curve coincides with the straight line $0P_0$. The intersection with the trade tax offer curve of the home country is in P_2 implying a welfare loss as compared to P_1. But this is in accordance with our intuition because the terms-of-trade effect is eliminated.

In a two commodity world the elasticity of the foreign offer curve is given by $\epsilon^{FD}/(\epsilon^{FD} - 1)$, where ϵ^{FD} is the own price elasticity of foreign export demand (see Johnson, 1954). A linear foreign offer curve through the origin implies an offer curve elasticity of -1. This can be generated by assuming high own price elasticities of foreign export demand.

This is exactly what we did in some simulation runs. Assuming $\Theta = -25$ and $\eta = 10$ gives a foreign export demand elasticity of -7.86 according to our equation (12). This strongly weakens the terms-of-trade effect and, according to our reasoning above, should raise welfare as compared to the central case specification. The figures reproduced in the first column of Table 6 confirm this reasoning.

However, a positive HEV only appears in the extreme case that the compensated elasticity of labour supply is approximately zero. So we still have to explain the negative HEV of the replacement of factor taxes by a uniform VAT of the net income type even if the terms-of-trade effect is negligible.

Before that we will briefly comment on our second tax alternative, the abolition of factor taxes and equal yield tax rate increase of the existing VAT of the consumption type. As is well-known, this tax is levied according to the destination principle. Consider the second column of Table 6. The figures show that the HEVs are much less than their counterparts in the first column. This is as it should be. Firstly, we would expect a higher welfare loss associated with the domestic reallocation of resources. As was mentioned above, in the presence of international trade flows an optimal consumption tax system is characterized by a subsidy of the export commodity. Our benchmark equilibrium data set indicates just the opposite: the VAT tax burden is higher on net exportables. So even if there is no terms-of-trade effect we would expect some welfare losses. These losses should diminish when the compensated elasticity of labour supply diminishes (generated by lower values of e and/or ς), but remain negative. The 'small-open-country' case in Table 6 validates this presumption. As to the second point, a higher negative terms-of-trade welfare loss seems to be plausible. This is illustrated by Figure 2.

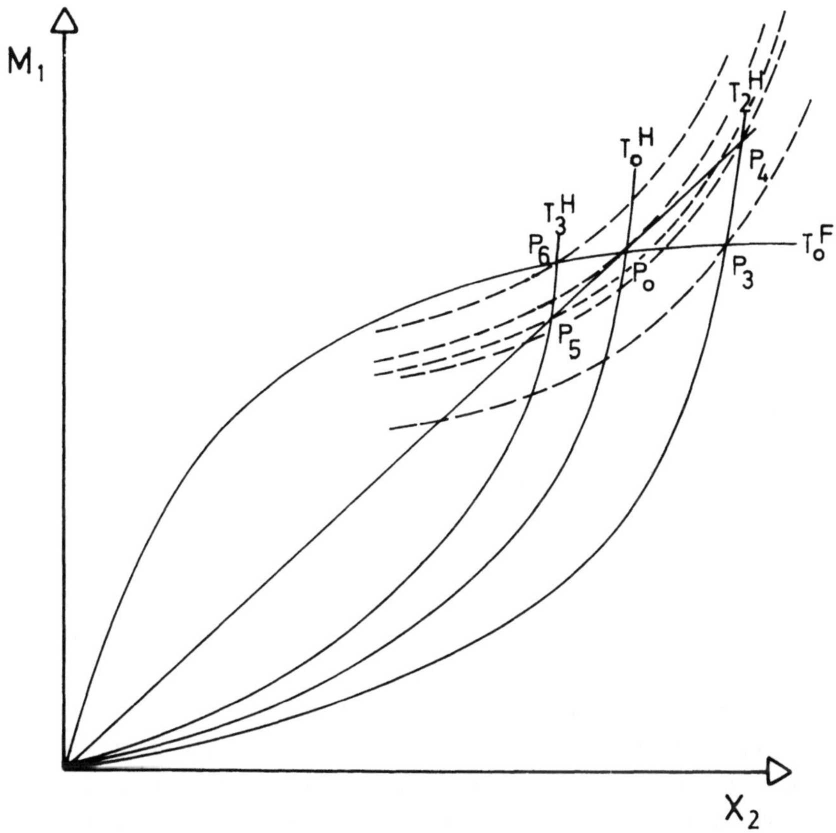

Figure 2: Welfare Effects of Substituting Trade Taxes by Differentiating VAT of the Consumption Type

As in Figure 1, T_0^H is the home country's free trade offer curve, T_3^H is the offer curve when trade taxes are levied. Suppose now that a consumption tax on the export commodity is introduced whereas the imported good remains untaxed. This will shift the free trade offer curve T_0^H to the right (see Georgakopoulos,

1974). Let the new offer curve be given by T_2^H. Replacing the trade taxes by the consumption tax will worsen the terms-of-trade for the home country from the slope of the line $0P_6$ to that of line $0P_3$ (both not drawn). Even with constant terms-of-trade, the tax substitution moves the economy from P_5 to P_4, implying a loss in national welfare. But as Figure 2 indicates, the welfare loss should be higher if terms-of-trade can be influenced by the home country.

We will close this chapter by trying to explain the welfare loss even if trade taxes are replaced by a uniform VAT of the net income type and even if terms-of-trade are (approximately) constant. Initially, we had expected a welfare gain because with a CES utility function defined over leisure and the composite commodity a uniform production or consumption tax is optimal. But this only holds for a closed economy. In an open economy the optimal tax structure seems to be driven by different factors. The exact causal relation still has to be worked out; our results indicate some need for additional research efforts.

Conclusions

With our paper we wanted to illustrate the basic procedure of AGE analysis; some limited empirical appeal was introduced by considering an aspect of the ongoing tax reform debate in the FRG: the replacement of trade taxes by some equal yield tax alternatives. For a more serious empirical study both the theoretical model and the data base have to be improved. This is left to another paper. Even if the precise numbers are not very reliable, some lessons emerged which presumably will also hold in more 'realistic' models. In our opinion, the central message is that — contrary to widespread belief — the abolition of trade taxes will result in efficiency and welfare *losses*. Only in one rather special case a welfare gain could be demonstrated, namely if terms-of-trade are constant and compensated labour supply elasticity is approximately zero. In this case, a uniform VAT of the net income type is equivalent to a lump-sum tax and the appearance of efficiency gains is self-evident. But the substitution of trade taxes by lump-sum taxes is by no means sufficient to guarantee an improvement in resource allocation (as Boss, 1984, suggests). Adopting the trade elasticities from the compendium by Stern, Francis, and Schumacher (1976), welfare losses occur if trade taxes are removed.

Our analysis seems to challenge conventional wisdom in two respects: Firstly, as far as we can see, the terms-of-trade gain associated with the current factor tax system has been neglected in the vast majority of the literature. Secondly, the allocational disincentive effects of trade taxes seem to have been badly exaggerated.

In fact, there is some reason to believe that current trade taxes are an acceptable proxy for optimal factor taxes if international trade flows are taken into account.

On the other hand, if trade taxes should be replaced for whatever reasons, a uniform VAT of the net income type (Nettowertschöpfungssteuer) seems to be clearly preferable to an adjustment of existing VAT tax rates. Furthermore, when considering the *effective* rates of current VAT, fairly high efficiency losses appear. The reason is that in an international trade setting our existing VAT does not at all approximate an optimal indirect tax structure. Our results suggest that more care should be given to the calculation of effective rates of value added taxes in future modelling efforts.

In our opinion, these results will remain valid in more complex environments. Anyway, we have presented a complete and analytically rigorous, if simple applied tax model. Anyone who disagrees with our conclusions will have to show which model assumptions are invalid, or which parameter values are misspecified; and in a next step that changing assumptions or parameters will change results. Thus, AGE tax models have the nice effect of shifting the onus onto those who disagree with the model results.

Appendix: Glossary of Notation

w	price of labour
r	price of capital
q_i, p_i	producer and consumer price of the i-th commodity
d	exchange rate
L_i, K_i	use of labour and capital, respectively, in the i-th industry
L, $\overline{K}$	supply of labour and capital (fixed)
F	leisure
E	total time endowment
C_i	quantity of the i-th consumption commodity
C	composite consumption
p	price of composite consumption
S	savings
G_i	quantity of the i-th collective consumption commodity
I_i	quantity of the i-th investment commodity
X_i, M_i	quantity of exports and imports of the i-th commodity
X_i^0, M_i^0	values of exports and imports in the base year
Q_i	domestic production of the i-th commodity
V_{ij}	intermediate demand of the i-th industry for the j-th commodity
a_{0i}, a_{ij}	fixed technology coefficients
T_i^L, τ_i^ℓ	revenue and ad valorem tax rate of payroll taxes of the i-th industry
T_i^K, τ_i^k	revenue and ad valorem tax rate of trade and property taxes
T_i^Q, τ_i^q	revenue and ad valorem tax rate of production taxes

T_i^C, τ_i^c	revenue and ad valorem tax rate of VAT of the consumption type
T^y, τ^y	revenue and marginal tax rate of income taxes
A	tax allowance
Tr	transfers to consumers
Φ_i, β_i, σ_i	production function parameters
α_i, β, ν	utility function parameter
λ_i	parameters of investment demand
Θ, η	trade elasticities
γ	average (= marginal) savings rate
ς	E/L
e	elasticity of labour supply with respect to the net wage rate
$\hat{e}$	elasticity of leisure demand with respect to the net wage rate
ϵ^{FD}	(compensated) elasticity of foreign export demand with respect to its own price
s_e, s_f	expenditure shares of full income E and leisure demand F to full disposable income

References

Atkinson, A. B., and **Stiglitz, J. E.** (1980): *Lectures on Public Economics.* London etc.: McGraw-Hill.

Ballard, C. L.; **Fullerton, D.**; **Shoven, J. B.**; and **Whalley, J.** (1985): *A General Equilibrium Model for Tax Policy Evaluation.* Chicago etc.: University of Chicago Press.

Besters, H. (1981): *Neue Wirtschaftspolitik durch Angebotslenkung.* 2nd edition. Baden-Baden: Nomos.

Boadway, R., and **Treddenick, J. M.** (1978): "A General Equilibrium Computation of the Effects of the Canadian Tariff Structure." *Canadian Journal of Economics* 2: 424–446.

Boss, A. (1984): "Zur Reform der Gemeindesteuern." Working Paper 216. Kiel: Institut für Weltwirtschaft.

Bundesministerium der Finanzen (1984): *An ABC of Taxes in the Federal Republic of Germany.* Bonn.

Caddy, V. (1976): "Empirical Estimation of the Elasticity of Substitution: A Review." Working Paper. Melbourne: Industries Assistance Commission.

Dixit, A. K. (1975): "Welfare Effects of Tax and Price Changes." *Journal of Public Economics* 4: 103–123.

Feldstein, M. (ed.) (1983): *Behavioral Simulation Methods in Tax Policy Analysis.* Chicago etc.: University of Chicago Press.

Fullerton, D., and **Gordon, R. H.** (1983): "A Reexamination of Tax Distortions in General Equilibrium Models." In *Behavioral Simulation Methods in Tax Policy Analysis*, edited by M. Feldstein. Chicago etc.: University of Chicago Press, pp. 369–426.

Fullerton, D.; **Henderson, Y. K.**; and **Shoven, J. B.** (1984): "A Comparison of Methodologies in Empirical General Equilibrium Models of Taxation." In *Applied General Equilibrium Analysis*, edited by H. E. Scarf and J. B. Shoven. Cambridge etc.: Cambridge University Press, pp. 367–410.

Georgakopoulos, T. (1974): "The 'Excess Burden' Controversy in a Trading World: A Case for Special Indirect Taxes." *Public Finance* 29: 152–167.

Goulder, L.; **Shoven, J. B.**; and **Whalley, J.** (1983): "Domestic Tax Policy and the Foreign Sector: The Importance of Alternative Foreign Sector Formulations to Results from a General Equilibrium Tax Analysis Model." In *Behavioral Simulation Methods in Tax Policy Analysis*, edited by M. Feldstein. Chicago etc.: University of Chicago Press, pp. 333–364.

Hausman, J. A. (1981): "Labor Supply." In *How Taxes Affect Economic Behavior*, edited by H. J. Aaron and J. A. Pechman. Washington, D.C.: Brookings Institution, pp. 27–72.

Hausman, J. A. (1985): "Taxes and Labor Supply." In *Handbook of Public Economics, Vol. I*, edited by A. J. Auerbach and M. Feldstein. Amsterdam etc.: North-Holland, pp. 213–263.

Hummel, M.; **Körner, J.**; and **Leibfritz, W.** (1985): *Strukturelle Auswirkungen des Steuersystems*. München: Ifo-Institut. (Ifo-Studien zur Finanzpolitik, 33.)

Institut Finanzen und Steuern (1982): "Modell für die Ablösung der Gewerbesteuer durch einen Gemeindeanteil an der Umsatzsteuer." Brief 211. Bonn.

Johnson, H. G. (1954): "Optimum Tariffs and Retaliation." *Review of Economic Studies* 21: 142–153.

Jorgenson, D. W. (1984): "Econometric Methods for Applied General Equilibrium Analysis." In *Applied General Equilibrium Analysis*, edited by H. E. Scarf and J. B. Shoven. Cambridge etc.: Cambridge University Press, pp. 139–203.

Karl-Bräuer-Institut des Bundes der Steuerzahler (1984): "Abbau und Ersatz der Gewerbesteuer — Darstellung, Kritik, Vorschläge." Heft 57. Wiesbaden.

Keller, W. J. (1976): "A Nested CES-Type Utility Function and its Demand and Price-Index Functions." *European Economic Review* 7: 175–186.

Keller, W. J. (1977): "Savings, Leisure, Consumption and Taxes. The Household Expenditure System." *European Economic Review* 9: 151–167.

King, M. A., and **Fullerton, D.** (eds.) (1984): *The Taxation of Income from Capital*. Chicago etc.: University of Chicago Press.

Lau, L. J. (1984): "Comments." In *Applied General Equilbrium*, edited by H. E. Scarf and J. B. Shoven. Cambridge etc.: Cambridge University Press, pp. 127–137.

Manne, A. S. (ed.) (1985): *Economic Equilibrium: Model Formulation and Solution.* Amsterdam etc.: North-Holland. (Mathematical Programming Study 23.)

Mansur, A., and **Whalley, J.** (1984): "Numerical Specification of Applied General Equilibrium Models: Estimation, Calibration, and Data." In *Applied General Equilibrium Analysis*, edited by H. E. Scarf and J. B. Shoven. Cambridge etc.: Cambridge University Press, pp. 69–127.

McCloskey, D. N. (1983): "The Rhetoric of Economics." *Journal of Economic Literature* 21: 481–517.

Piggott, J., and **Whalley, J.** (1985): *UK Tax Policy and Applied General Equilibrium Analysis.* London etc.: Cambridge University Press.

Preckel, P. V. (1985): "Alternative Algorithms for Computing Economic Equilibria." In *Economic Equilibrium: Model Formulation and Solution*, edited by A. S. Manne. Amsterdam etc.: North-Holland, pp. 163–172. (Mathematical Programming Study, 23.)

Scarf, H. (1973): *Computation of Economic Equilibria.* New Haven: Yale University Press.

Scarf, H. (1984): "The Computation of Equilibrium Prices." In *Applied General Equilibrium Analysis*, edited by H. E. Scarf and J. B. Shoven. Cambridge etc.: Cambridge University Press, pp. 1–49.

Scarf, H. E., and **Shoven, J. B.** (eds.) (1984): *Applied General Equilibrium Analysis.* Cambridge etc.: Cambridge University Press.

Shoven, J. B. (1983): "Applied General Equilibrium Tax Modeling." *IMF Staff Papers* 30: 394–420.

Shoven, J. B., and **Whalley, J.** (1977): "Equal Yield Tax Alternatives. General Equilibrium Computational Techniques." *Journal of Public Economics* 8: 211–224.

Shoven, J. B., and **Whalley, J.** (1984): "Applied General-Equilibrium Models of Taxation and International Trade." *Journal of Economic Literature* 22: 1007–1051.

St.-Hilaire, F., and **Whalley, J.** (1983): "A Microconsistent Equilibrium Data Set for Canada for Use in Tax Policy Analysis." *Review of Income and Wealth* 29: 175–204.

St.-Hilaire, F., and **Whalley, J.** (1985): "A Microconsistent Data Set for Canada for Use in Regional General Equilibrium Policy Analysis." Working Paper 8533 C. London, Canada: University of Western Ontario.

Stern, R. M.; Francis, J.; and **Schumacher, B.** (1976): *Price Elasticities in International Trade: An Annotated Bibliography.* London: Macmillan.

Todd, M. J. (1984): "Efficient Methods of Computing Economic Equilibria." In *Applied General Equilibrium Analysis*, edited by H. E. Scarf and J. B. Shoven. Cambridge etc.: Cambridge University Press, pp. 51–68.

Vandendorpe, A. (1972): "Optimal Tax Structures in a Model with Traded and Non-traded Goods." *Journal of International Economics* 2: 235–256.

Whalley, J. (1980): "Discriminatory Features of Domestic Factor Tax Systems in a Goods Mobile-Factors Immobile Trade Model: An Empirical General Equilibrium Approach." *Journal of Political Economy* 88: 1177–1202.

Whalley, J. (1985a): *Trade Liberalization among Major World Trading Areas*. Cambridge etc.: MIT Press.

Whalley, J. (1985b): "Operationalizing Walras: Experience with Recent Applied General Equilibrium Tax Models." Working Paper 8434 C. London, Canada: CSIER, University of Western Ontario.

Whalley, J., and **Yeung, B.** (1984): "External Sector 'Closing' Rules in Applied General Equilibrium Models." *Journal of International Economics* 16: 123–138.

Wiegard, W. (1985): "Die Algorithmen von Scarf und Merrill zur numerischen Berechnung allgemeiner Gleichgewichte. Eine Einführung mit Beispielen aus der Steuerpolitik." *Zeitschrift für Wirtschafts- und Sozialwissenschaften* 105: 709–741.

Wissenschaftlicher Beirat beim Bundesministerium der Finanzen (1982): *Gutachten zur Reform der Gemeindesteuern in der Bundesrepublik Deutschland*. Bonn.

Incidence Effects of Changing the German Income Tax Rate Schedule

Manfred Rose, Hans Kungl, and Bernhard Kühn, Heidelberg, West Germany*

I. Introduction

As a result of the income tax rate reform, which is planned for the period 1986–1988 and which in part has already been implemented, the marginal tax rates in the progression ranges of the personal income tax are lowered and higher basic tax exemptions are granted in the Federal Republic of Germany. To evaluate the long run incidence of such a tax change it is necessary to acquire knowledge about the induced long run changes of the welfare for various household groups in the society of Western Germany.

West Germany's Minister of Finance Mr. Stoltenberg is of the opinion that the rate adjustment will not lead to a redistribution from bottom to top, as the oppositional parties have claimed.[1] To this extent Stoltenberg refers to the formal-statutory incidence of income tax payments, i.e. to the new shares which result from the new rates and which the various groups contribute to the total yield of the income tax. However, in the final outcome the decisive point is the effective incidence. It takes into account all effects which the tax impulse brings about in the total economic system and which ends in new incomes of all households. Furthermore, it is known from welfare theory that the disposable income of an individual accounts for a great part but not for all of its welfare level. Hence, in determining the welfare incidence effects of a tax change we have to take into account not only the induced changes in individual incomes but, for example, also the new burdens from consumption taxes concerning each group of households.

In turning attention to the so-called longer-run effects of tax policy measures, the applied general equilibrium tax analysis is going to be a more and more ap-

---

* This paper contains results of a research project supported by the Deutsche Forschungsgemeinschaft within the Sonderforschungsbereich 5.
We are grateful to Irene Rößler for her help in forming the decision structure of households, and to Tomas Farken for forming simulation programmes. Furthermore, we are indebted to Dr. Carsten Stahmer and Dr. Klaus Schüler from the Statistisches Bundesamt Wiesbaden for generously providing us with detailed statistics.

[1] See Minister of Finance Stoltenberg in Presse- und Informationsamt der Bundesregierung (1985, p. 9).

propriate tool to deal with these questions. The main advantage of the applied general equilibrium tax models as introduced by Shoven and Whalley extending the traditional two-sector models of Harberger and others[2] is — compared with a partial equilibrium analysis of tax effects — the inclusion of second-round effects: hence the ability to get some insights into the long run incidence, i.e. to look at the point at which tax burdens come to rest. Despite this advantage there is no question that a general equilibrium model of the German economy as presented in this paper cannot be used to estimate the observable outcome of changing the German tax system.

Nevertheless, we agree with the statement of Shoven and Whalley how applied general equilibrium tax models can be used in supporting tax policy decisions:

> "As with all such modeling efforts, policy statements generated by these models have to be treated with an appropriate degree of caution. However, our view is that these models have already contributed to policy debate, and if used sensibly can make further important contributions. This is especially so with estimates of combined efficiency and distributional effects of policies where, prior to these models, no wholly satisfactory way of simultaneously quantifying these effects existed."[3]

The plan of the paper is as follows. Part II gives a short description of our 'general equilibrium model of the West German economy in its international trade context' with respect to the assumed structure of the interdependence of the commodity and factor markets as well as to the chosen structure of the input-output flows.

Part III was designed to specify the fundamental system equations by modelling the decision structure of households, firms and the government assumed to be valid in the German economy and in the Rest of the World economy. Market equilibrium conditions are used to getting a complete general equilibrium model.

To get a solvable applied general equilibrium model one has to work on a consistent data set (i.e. on constructing of a benchmark equilibrium data set) and on choosing suitable values of the model parameters so as to achieve a general equilibrium in the reference year (calibration). What we have done in this context is described in part IV of the paper.

The results of simulating an exchange of the income tax rate schedule in force in 1980 for the tax rates effective as from 1988 in conjunction with three alternative kinds of balancing the government's budget are presented in part V.

[2] See Shoven and Whalley (1984) or Shoven (1983).
[3] Shoven and Whalley (1984, p. 1048).

Here, we mainly refer to measuring labour supply effects, trade effects, and some types of both the individual income and the individual welfare incidence.

II. Essential Characteristics of the General Equilibrium Model Used

A. Market Structures and International Trade

The tremendous external integration of the West German economy leads one to expect that the allocation effects of domestic tax reforms are determined to a significant extent by changing foreign trade flows via the international price dependence.[4] This has prompted us to pay special attention to adequately covering foreign trade in the very first version of our model. In addition to the German economy, there is also a foreign economic bloc. It represents the so-called rest of the world (ROW) and is relatively large in comparison to the Federal Republic of Germany (FRG) with respect to the total production and the total factor input. The economic bloc designated as the rest of the world and contrasted with the Federal Republic of Germany is viewed as a unit and — as far as decision-making theory is concerned — is modeled with the same amount of detail as the German economic system is. In this way the essential economic processes (production, demand, supply, etc.) are controlled by qualitatively equal basic economic structures in both economic blocs[5] in a consistent manner.

The information flow diagram in Figure 1 illustrates the modeled market re-

[4] For this subject see Whalley (1980) or Wiegard (1985).

[5] A different method often used in general equilibrium analysis is to describe foreign trade relation via incorporation of a rudimentary external sector closing rule. For the problems of the elasticity of imports and exports implicitly generated hereby see Whalley (1985). As opposed to this, in our model export supply and import demand are directly derived from domestic and foreign household utility maximizing and firms' profit maximizing decisions. This procedure implies that utility and production functions contain domestic and foreign products as separate arguments. Such approaches are used in the multicountry models by Whalley (1980, 1982) or Deardorff and Stern (1981). These models contain tradables as well as non tradable goods and allow for international capital movements and tariffs. Moreover, the model used by Deardorff and Stern distinguishes sectors for home and export production in each industry that produces tradables. In our analysis no tariffs exist and factors are regarded as internationally immobile. All products are assumed to be tradables. Apart from these differences the basic structure concerning markets, production and consumption in the model presented here is similar to those quoted above. In comparison with our model, however, the models mentioned above show a much higher degree of disaggregation with respect to the number of countries, products and agents. Moreover, the functional forms of utility and production functions are more elaborate in these models. E.g. we use fixed input coefficients for the description of the input-output structure, while these allow for substitutability between intermediate products.

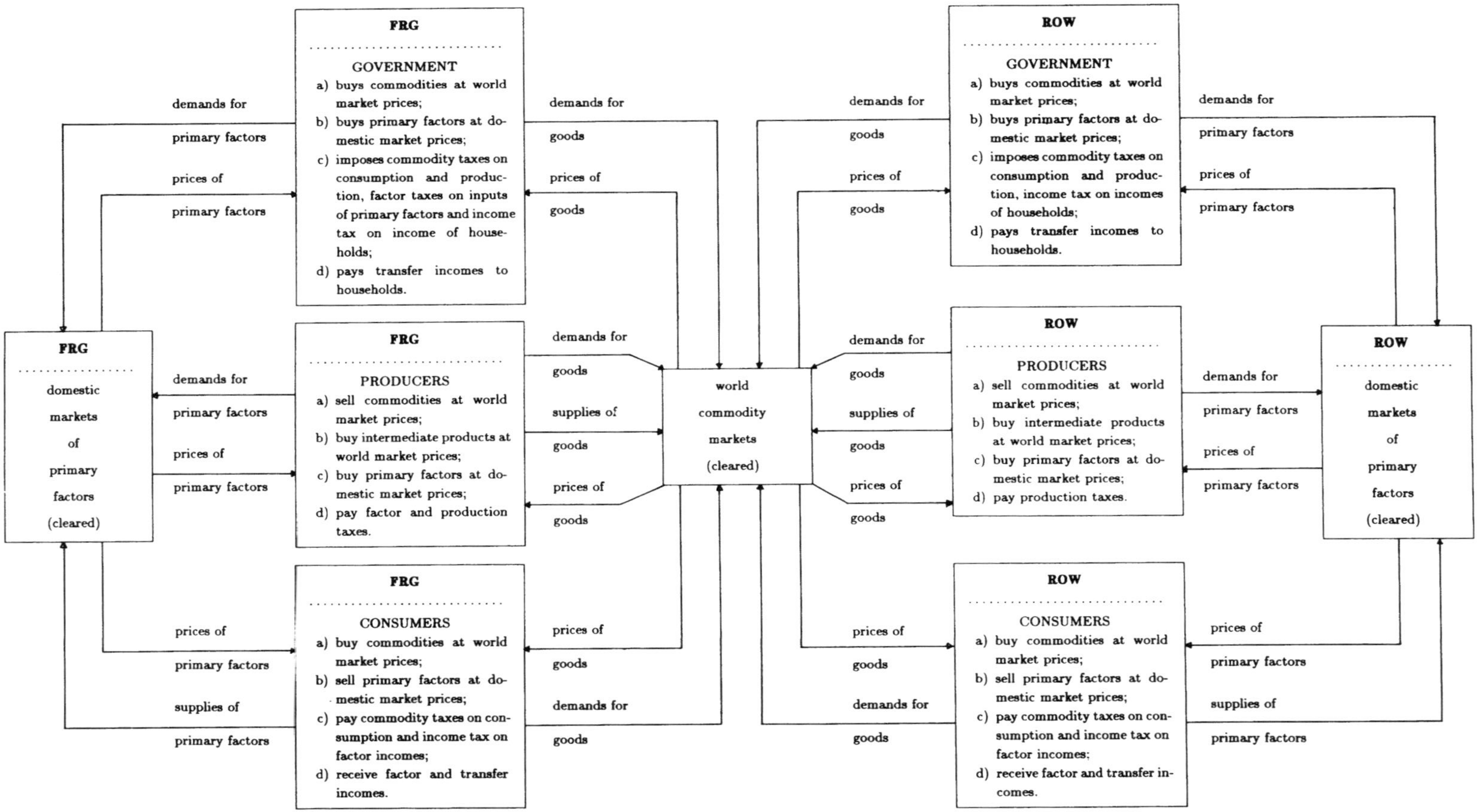

Figure 1: Market Structures of the FRG/ROW General Equilibrium Model

lations in the international context. All goods produced by domestic and foreign companies are traded on world commodity markets. A total of twenty-four of these exist since there are twelve production sectors in the German economy and twelve in the rest of the world. Goods of the same physical and technical nature produced in Germany and in the rest of the world are regarded as heterogeneous. This makes allowance for the empirical fact that consumers and producers in the Federal Republic of Germany as well as in other countries throughout the world simultaneously demand goods with similar physical and technical properties produced both domestically and abroad. Each of the goods traded on world markets is produced either only in Germany or only in the rest of the world. The domestic production of an imported good of a certain type (e.g. Fiat brand cars) of a good category (e.g. cars) is absolutely ruled out,[6] but different variations (such as, for example, cars made by Mercedes) of the same category of products can be manufactured and exported domestically, according to the actual situation in world production and in world trade.

Domestic and foreign households buy goods for personal use on world commodity markets. The demand for goods produced domestically and for imported goods of the same type is subject to different price elasticities. Domestic and foreign producers demand the same goods — taking into account different but always fixed production coefficients — as intermediate products, i.e. as means of production. Additional demand on the world commodity markets is created by the government of the Federal Republic of Germany and the governments of the rest of the world. The various governments use the goods purchased at world market prices to produce and supply public goods; a small portion of these goods goes to the sector of private production as intermediate inputs whereas the larger share is available to domestic households for use free of charge. The world market prices of the goods are producers' prices of the individual countries, i.e. the destination principle is applicable for levying consumption taxes. In each case, the consumption of domestically produced goods and imported goods of the same physical and technical nature is charged at the same consumption tax rate. Exported goods leave each of these countries consumption-tax free. Customs duties and similar charges are not explicitly dealt with.

The primary production factors are labour and capital in the production process with full mobility between the industries and equal prices before factor taxes for each industry. The stock of productively usable primary inputs is in the hands of the households. They offer the entire capital stock on the domestic capital market only to the domestic companies and to their government for production-

[6] Modelling foreign trade relations via heterogeneous goods comes from Armington (1969).

related use. The labour output of the households is not traded internationally either. The variable labour supply is always below the maximum possible working time since leisure time is viewed by the households as a positively valued consumer good. All households in each economic bloc receive the same gross wage rate per working time unit. Since the primary production factors are not traded internationally, their prices before taxes can also differ from one country to the next.

In conclusion, it must be mentioned that the trade balance, the current account balance and the balance of payments are identical and are always balanced according to the conditions of a general equilibrium.

B. Input-Output Structure of the Model

The goods integration inherent in the model is shown in Figure 2. Twelve product aggregates are produced in the Federal Republic of Germany and twelve in the rest of the world. The intermediate product input always occurs with fixed input coefficients. In the Federal Republic of Germany's production sector, which is divided into 12 sectors, for example, intermediate inputs X_G^G from domestic production and imported intermediate inputs X_R^G from production in the ROW are used. The input of labour and capital in the FRG as well as in the ROW occurs with variable (price-dependent) input coefficients.

The gross value added V_G^G in FRG and V_R^R in ROW goes only to economic units of each individual country. This illustrates the assumed international immobility of the primary production factors labour and capital. In statistical terms, the item of gross wages and salaries describes the payment for labour employment in the reference year. The gross value added percentage of the production factor capital is recorded by the statistical parameter gross operating surplus. The remaining parts of the overall economic gross value added are bound up in the input of labour or capital and in production-related taxes. Due to inadequate statistical information, only taxes linked to production are distinguished according to production sectors in the rest of the world. A share E_G^R of the total production Q_G in the Federal Republic of Germany goes for final use to households in the rest of the world. The goods volume E_G^G is available to the German consumer for final uses. Correspondingly, the final consumers in the Federal Republic of Germany take up a share E_R^G of the total production Q_R of ROW.

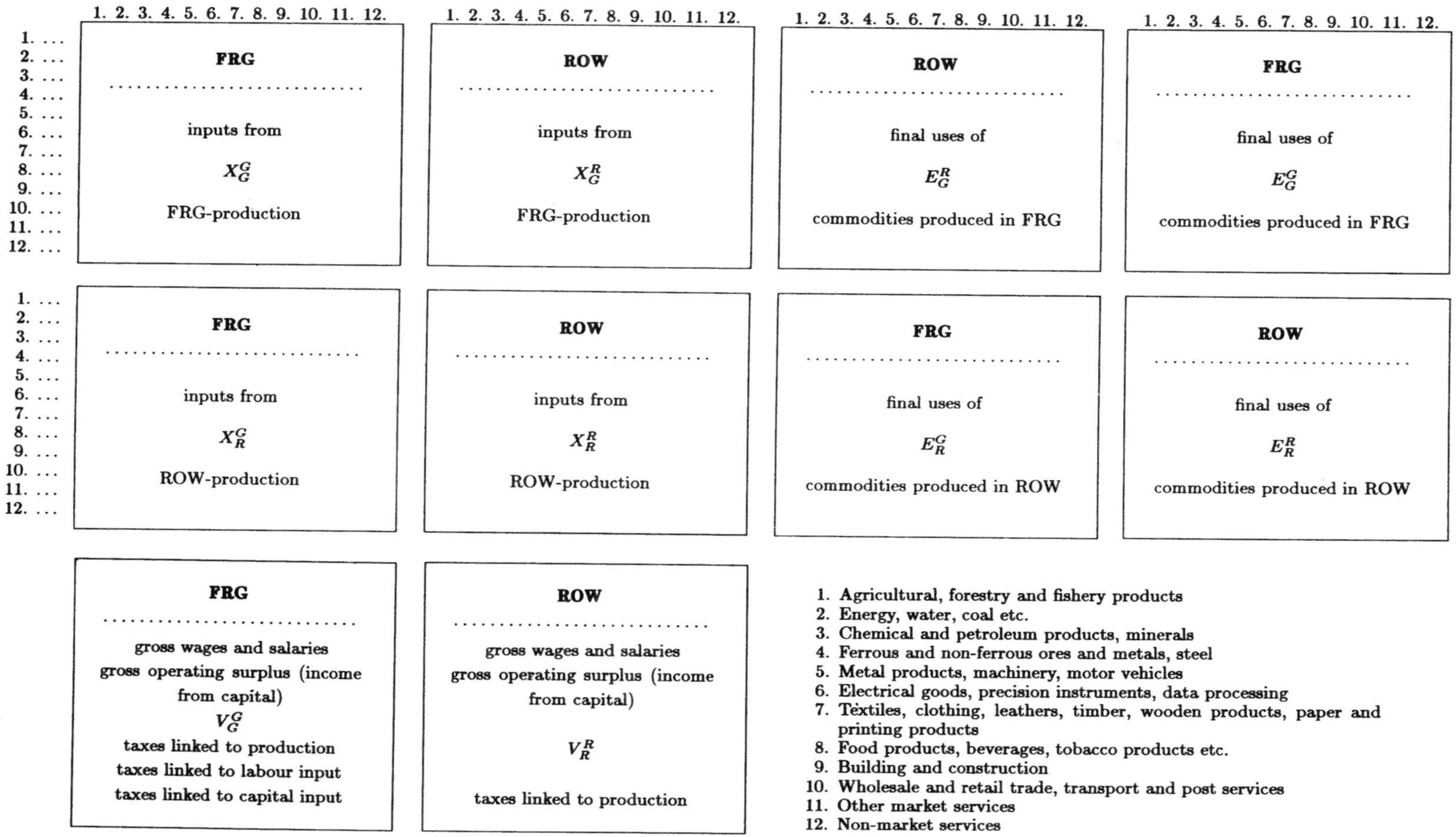

Figure 2: Input-Output Structure of the FRG/ROW General Equilibrium Model

III. Specification of the Fundamental System Equations of the FRG/ROW General Equilibrium Model

A. Goods Demand and Labour Supply Functions of the Consumers

In the household sector of the FRG, all households are assigned to one of four income classes, depending on the level of their net income. Let us assume that each of them has demand functions that are homogeneous of degree zero in all consumer prices and in its exogenously given income. The demand is for eleven goods produced by domestic companies and for eleven goods imported from ROW. Moreover, each group offers services on the labour market and, since utility satiation is precluded, offers its entire sum of productively usable capital to the competitively organized capital market. The aggregation of the demand over all of the household groups results in the market-related demand of the household sector. For the sake of simplifying the symbols, the variables and parameters are not marked with the household group identification index n in the text below.

We assert that the consumer of each income class engages in a constrained maximizing behavior, the objective of which is to maximize the well-behaved utility function

$$U = U(x_0, x_1, \ldots, x_{11}, E^{\mathrm{St}}, x_{13}, \ldots, x_{23}) \tag{1}$$

where x_0 is the demand for leisure time, $x_1, \ldots, x_{11}$ are goods produced domestically by private companies, E^{St} is a vector of public consumption goods and $x_{13}, \ldots, x_{23}$ are imported consumer goods from private production abroad.

The budget constraint the consumer (i.e., every household of each income group) faces when maximizing its utility is

$$(2) \qquad y_{max} = (1 - \Theta_y) w x_0 + \sum_{i=1}^{11} [(1 + \Theta_{c,i}) p_i x_i + (1 + \Theta_{c,i}) p_{i+12}\, x_{i+12}]$$

$$y_{max} = (1 - \Theta_y)[w l_{max} + r k_{max}] + s + \Theta_y f$$

where y_{max} denotes the maximum disposable income, Θ_y is the marginal tax rate of the income tax, $\Theta_{c,i}$ is the consumption tax rate on product i, l_{max} denotes the maximum working time (leisure time), k_{max} denotes the maximum capital supply (= amount of salable capital), s is the individual transfer income and f is the effective exemption applying the income tax rate formula.

We specify the utility functions of consumers according to (1) to have the form of the following three-stage utility tree:

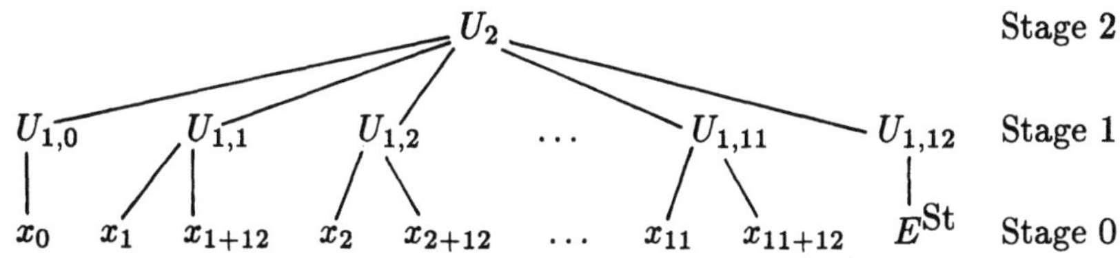

(3)
$$\begin{aligned} U_2 &\equiv U(x_0, x) \\ U_2 &= \left\{ \tau_0^{1-\delta} U_{1,0}^{\delta} + \sum_{i=1}^{11} \tau_i^{1-\delta} U_{1,i}^{\delta} \right\}^{1/\delta} + U_{1,12} \\ U_{1,i} &= \mu_i^{-\mu_i} (1-\mu_i)^{-(1-\mu_i)} x_i^{\mu_i} x_{i+12}^{(1-\mu_i)} \\ &= \left\{ \frac{x_i}{\mu_i} \right\}^{\mu_i} \left\{ \frac{x_{i+12}}{1-\mu_i} \right\}^{1-\mu_i} ; \quad i = 1, \ldots, 11 \\ U_{1,12} &= g(E^{St}); \quad U_{1,0} \equiv 1; \ \delta = (\sigma - 1)/\sigma; \\ & \tau_j > 0; \ \sum_{j=0}^{11} \tau_j = 1; \ 0 < \sigma < \infty; \ \mu_i > 0. \end{aligned}$$

σ is the elasticity of the substitution of $U_{1,0}$ by $U_{1,i}$. With respect to the utility from the consumption of public goods E^{St} and the utility from the consumption of goods x_i that are only available on the market or the utility from leisure time x_0, the utility function is strictly separable.

With the quantity index

(4)
$$m_i = \left\{ \frac{x_i}{\mu_i} \right\}^{\mu_i} \left\{ \frac{x_{i+12}}{1-\mu_i} \right\}^{1-\mu_i},$$

$U(x, E^{St})$ can also be represented as

(5)
$$U(x_0, m, E^{St}) = \left\{ \tau_0^{1-\delta} x_0^{\delta} + \sum_{i=1}^{11} \tau_i^{1-\delta} m_i^{\delta} \right\}^{1/\delta} + g(E^{St}).$$

On the basis of a proposition by Green (1964, p. 25), a consistent two-stage utility maximization is possible with m_i, since m_i is linearly homogeneous in x_i, x_{i+12}, $i = 1, \ldots, 11$.

Hence, at the first stage, the first-order conditions of maximizing

(6)
$$\mathcal{L}(x_0, m, \Gamma_1) = U(x, m, E^{St}) + \Gamma_1 \left[y_{max} - (1 - \Theta_y) w x_0 - \sum_{i=1}^{11} \Pi_i \, m_i \right]$$

can be simplified to give the following demand system:

$$(7) \qquad m_i = \tau_i \Pi_i^{-\sigma} \Pi^{\sigma-1} y_{max} = \tau_i \left[\frac{\Pi}{\Pi_i}\right]^\sigma \frac{y_{max}}{\Pi}, \quad i = 1, \ldots, 11,$$

$$(8) \qquad x_0 = \tau_0[(1-\Theta_y)w]^{1-\sigma} \frac{y_{max}}{(1-\Theta_y)w} \Pi^{\sigma-1} = \tau_0 \left[\frac{\Pi}{(1-\Theta_y)w}\right]^\sigma \frac{y_{max}}{\Pi},$$

where the specific price index, Π_i, appertaining to its quantity index, m_i, is defined as

$$(9) \qquad \Pi_i = (1+\Theta_{c,i})\, p_i^{\mu_i}\, p_{i+12}^{1-\mu_i}, \quad i = 1, \ldots, 11$$

and the general price index, Π, is defined as

$$(10) \qquad \Pi = \left\{ \tau_0[(1-\Theta_y)w]^{1-\sigma} + \sum_{i=1}^{11} \tau_i \Pi_i^{1-\sigma} \right\}^{\frac{1}{1-\sigma}} .$$

The Lagrange formulation of the second maximization stage

$$(11) \qquad max \quad \mathcal{L}(x_i, x_{i+12}, \Gamma_2) = \left\{\frac{x_i}{\mu_i}\right\}^{\mu_i} \left\{\frac{x_{i+12}}{1-\mu_i}\right\}^{1-\mu_i} + \Gamma_2[\Pi_i m_i - \\ - (1+\Theta_{c,i})(p_i x_i + p_{i+12}\, x_{i+12})]; \quad i = 1, \ldots, 11$$

gives first-order conditions resulting in the Marshall demand functions

$$(12) \qquad x_i = \tau_i \mu_i \left[\frac{\Pi}{\Pi_i}\right]^\sigma \left[\frac{p_{i+12}}{p_i}\right]^{1-\mu_i} \frac{y_{max}}{\Pi}; \quad i = 1, \ldots, 11$$

$$(13) \qquad x_{i+12} = \tau_i (1-\mu_i) \left[\frac{\Pi}{\Pi_i}\right]^\sigma \left[\frac{p_i}{p_{i+12}}\right]^{\mu_i} \frac{y_{max}}{\Pi}; \quad i = 1, \ldots, 11.$$

Since the utility function is strictly separable between the private goods and the public goods, the quantities contained in E^{St} made available to the consumers free of charge by the government do not influence the market-related demand for goods by the households either.

Demand functions of the form (9), (12) and (13) also apply to the one-consumer household sector in the rest of the world. Since the government in the ROW levies a proportional income tax, $f = 0$ holds true in (2).

B. Factor Demand Functions of the Producers

Let us say that in each production sector $j = 1, \ldots, 12$ of the German economy, a representative firm maximizes its profit under the assumption that all output can be sold on the world markets at the given producers' prices p_j. Quantities of labour L_j and capital K_j can be substituted within the framework of a CES production function with constant returns to scale, and they effect a total input of primary inputs with a constant relationship $a_{0,j}$ to the industry output Q_j. Intermediate inputs from domestic (foreign) production are entered with a fixed share $a_{k,j}$ ($a_{k+12,j}$), $k = 1, \ldots, 12$, of Q_j. The government levies production taxes on the firms at a rate of $\Theta_{Q,j}$ on their sales proceeds (net of their production tax payments). Furthermore, domestic companies have to pay factor taxes on the wage total at a rate of $\Theta_{L,j}$ and on the paid-out capital income at a rate of $\Theta_{K,j}$. From the first-order conditions of maximizing

$$(14)\quad \mathcal{L}(L_j, K_j, \Gamma) = p_j Q_j - (1+\Theta_{L,j}) w L_j - (1+\Theta_{K,j}) r K_j -$$

$$- \frac{\Theta_{Q,j}}{1+\Theta_{Q,j}} p_j Q_j - \sum_{k=1}^{12} p_k\, a_{k,j}\, Q_j - \sum_{k=1}^{12} p_{k+12,j}\, a_{k+12,j}\, Q_j +$$

$$+\Gamma \left\{ a_{0,j} Q_j - \Phi_j \left[\epsilon_j L_j^{\delta_j} + (1-\epsilon_j) K_j^{\delta_j} \right]^{1/\delta_j} \right\}; \qquad j = 1, \ldots, 12$$

$$\Phi_j > 0;\ \delta_j = (\sigma_j - 1)/\sigma_j,\ 0 < \sigma_j < \infty;\ 0 < \epsilon_j < 1$$

one gets the factor demand functions

$$(15)\quad L_j = f_j(w,r) Q_j$$

$$= \frac{1}{\Phi_j} a_{0,j} \left\{ \epsilon_j + (1-\epsilon_j) \left[\frac{\epsilon_j}{1-\epsilon_j} \, \frac{1+\Theta_{K,j}}{1+\Theta_{L,j}} \, \frac{r}{w} \right]^{1-\sigma_j} \right\}^{\frac{\sigma_j}{1-\sigma_j}} Q_j$$

$$(16)\quad K_j = g_j(w,r) Q_j$$

$$= \frac{1}{\Phi_j} a_{0,j} \left\{ 1 - \epsilon_j + \epsilon_j \left[\frac{1-\epsilon_j}{\epsilon_j} \, \frac{1+\Theta_{L,j}}{1+\Theta_{K,j}} \, \frac{w}{r} \right]^{1-\sigma_j} \right\}^{\frac{\sigma_j}{1-\sigma_j}} Q_j .$$

$f_j(w,r)$ and $g_j(w,r)$ are the factor unit demand functions. Perfect competition on all markets and constant returns to scale in production do not permit any pure business profit to accrue. All of the proceeds from sales are thus used up in paying for the primary inputs, for the intermediate inputs imported and produced by other domestic firms and for paying taxes on the wage sum, on the expenditures for acquiring capital to use it in producing commodities and on the total revenue. Therefore, the profit definition on the right side of equation (14) and the factor demand functions according to equations (15) and (16) lead to the price = marginal costs relationships

$$(17) \qquad p_j\left[1-\frac{\Theta_{Q,j}}{1+\Theta_{Q,j}}\right]-\sum_{k=1}^{12}p_k\,a_{k,j}-\sum_{k=1}^{12}p_{k+12}\,a_{k+12,j}= \\ [1+\Theta_{L,j}]wf_j(w,r)+[1+\Theta_{K,j}]rg_j(w,r);\quad j=1,\ldots,12.$$

Since equations (15) and (16) are also valid for the twelfth production sector, the factor demand of the public enterprise is subject to the same regularity as that of private firms. (17) shows that the public enterprise producing output Q_{12} does not realize any net profit. Outputs Q_j, $j = 13,\ldots,24$ are produced in the rest of the world. Structurally speaking, the same factor demand functions and the same price = marginal costs relationships exist as in the Federal Republic of Germany.

C. Government Budget Constraints

On the revenue side, in the government budget constraints of the Federal Republic of Germany, the revenue accruing from the levying of consumption taxes, income taxes, production taxes and factor taxes must be taken into account. On the expenditure side, there are the transfer expenditures S, of which every household group n receives a share Ω^n, as well as the expenditures resulting from constant final demands of the government E_j^{St}. Thus in the FRG, we have the government budget constraint

$$(18)\ \sum_{n=1}^{4}\Theta_y^n\{wL^n+rK^n-F^n\}+\sum_{i=1}^{11}\Theta_{c,i}\left[p_i\sum_{n=1}^{4}E_i^n+p_{i+12}\sum_{n=1}^{4}E_{i+12}^n\right]+ \\ +\sum_{j=1}^{12}\frac{\Theta_{Q,j}}{1+\Theta_{Q,j}}p_jQ_j+\sum_{j=1}^{12}\Theta_{L,j}\,wL_j+\sum_{j=1}^{12}\Theta_{K,j}\,rK_j\;=\;\sum_{j=1}^{24}p_jE_j^{\mathrm{St}}+S,$$

where L^n represents the labour supply, K^n is the capital supply (= capital endowment), F^n is the deduction from gross taxable income and E_j^n is the final demand for goods j of household group n. The latter is the result of the aggregation of all individual goods demands x_j^n within each household group n.

The first term on the right side of equation (18) makes it clear that the government in the Federal Republic of Germany also buys goods from foreign production on the world market.

In the rest of the world there is only one consumer and no factor taxes. Moreover, the income of the representative household is assumed to be taxed at a constant average rate. Thus in the ROW, the government budget constraint is

$$(19)\quad \Theta_y\{wL + rK\} + \sum_{i=1}^{11} \Theta_{c,i}\left[p_i E_i^H + p_{i+12}\, E_{i+12}^H\right] + \sum_{j=13}^{24} \frac{\Theta_{Q,j}}{1+\Theta_{Q,j}} p_j Q_j$$
$$= \sum_{j=13}^{24} p_j E_j^{\mathrm{St}} + S.$$

As can be seen from the addends on the right side of equation (19), on the world market the foreign government only demands goods from its own production. This is a simplified model assumption, made for data-related reasons.

For the sake of simplifying the symbols, the variables were not marked with G for the Federal Republic of Germany and with R for the rest of the world.

D. Market Equilibrium Conditions and General Equilibrium

The world commodity markets are in a state of equilibrium when — for each industry output produced in the Federal Republic of Germany Q_j, $j = 1, \ldots, 12$ and for each industry output produced in the rest of the world Q_j, $j = 13, \ldots, 24$ — a corresponding goods demand from both economic regions exists at prevailing market prices. Here, in addition to the final demand made by the households and the public institutions, it is also necessary to consider the demand for intermediate products made by the production sectors. Thus the goods market equilibrium conditions are

$$(20)\quad Q_j = E_j^{G,H}(p, w^G, r^G, S^G, \Theta_c^G) + E_j^{R,H}(p, w^R, r^R, S^R, \Theta_c^R)$$
$$+ \sum_{k=1}^{12} a_{j,k} Q_k + \sum_{k=1}^{12} a_{j,k+12}\, Q_{k+12}$$
$$+ E_j^{G,St} + E_j^{R,St}.$$

goods produced in FRG
$j = 1, \ldots, 12$

goods produced in ROW
$j = 13, \ldots, 24$

The market demand of German households $E_j^{G,H}$ is obtained by aggregation over the goods demand of the four consumer groups. Θ_y^G and F^G are vectors consisting of the marginal income tax rates and the effective deductions from taxable income for every household group in the FRG. Θ_y^R is the uniform income tax rate in the ROW. The consumption tax rate vectors Θ_c^G and Θ_c^R each contain 11 components and the vector of producer prices contains 22. In the case where $j \leq 12$, $E_j^{R,St} = 0$.

The markets of the internationally immobile primary production factors labor and capital are in a state of equilibrium when for the

factors offered and used in the FRG

$$L^G(p, w^G, r^G, S^G, \Theta_c^G) = \sum_{j=1}^{12} L_j = \sum_{j=1}^{12} f_j^G(w^G, r^G) Q_j \tag{21}$$

$$K^G = \sum_{j=1}^{12} K_j = \sum_{j=1}^{12} f_j^G(w^G, r^G) Q_j \tag{22}$$

factors offered and used in the ROW

$$L^R(p, w^R, r^R, S^R, \Theta_c^R) = \sum_{j=13}^{24} L_j = \sum_{j=13}^{24} f_j^R(w^R, r^R) Q_j \tag{23}$$

$$K^R = \sum_{j=13}^{24} K_j = \sum_{j=13}^{24} g_j^R(w^R, r^R) Q_j. \tag{24}$$

L^G is the aggregate on the labour supply of all four domestic household groups.

Equation (17), in the versions for the FRG and the ROW, and equations (18) to (24) describe the general equilibrium of our small world model. If we select a numeraire good, e.g. through $w^G = 1$, the system may be assumed to have a clear-cut solution in all variables. Hence, unique general equilibrium values for the central systems variables w^G, r^G, w^R, r^R and one instrument variable from the government budget equation (e.g., S^G and S^R) may also exist.

IV. Data Set and Calibration to Solve General Equilibria for the German Economy and for the Economy of the Rest of the World

The basis of the planned comparative-static analysis of welfare and incidence effects of alternative tax reform programs is the selection of a reference year in which one assumes that the conditions of a general equilibrium are met. To start with, the value-dimensioned data of the market and the budgets of all of the economic units covered in the model are to be determined in a consistent manner from various statistical sources and to be adjusted in such a way that they could have occurred in a general equilibrium of the economy (construction of a benchmark equilibrium data set).

The next step is to break down the market sales into a price and a quantity component so that the central economic variables of the general equilibrium can also be interpreted empirically. For this purpose, the producers' prices p as well as the factor prices w and r of the supposedly observed equilibrium are fixed at 1 DM. Thus, each product unit is defined in such a manner that it was sold on the world markets for 1 DM in the reference year. In the FRG as well as in the ROW, households receive 1 DM per factor quantity unit before income tax on the domestic factor markets for labour and capital.

Then the parameters of the model are to be determined so that a general equilibrium with the values of the reference year can be achieved (calibration).

A. Construction of a Consistent Data Set

The empirical status of the model is based on the data of the year 1980 for the Federal Republic of Germany and the rest of the world.

A significant special feature of the data basis is to be seen in the integrated representation of the input-output tables of the two economies, FRG and ROW, within a closed system as already roughly outlined in Figure 2. This makes it possible, in addition to the requirement made of an input-output table concerning equality of the total input and of the total output of goods for each production sector, to assure that within this system, the foreign trade of the two countries remains in a state of equilibrium.

The matrices pertaining to X_G^G, X_R^G, E_R^G, E_G^G and V_G^G were taken from the input-output tables 1 and 2 of the Statistisches Bundesamt Wiesbaden (1984). The final demand of the German companies, i.e. the private investment demand, has been included in the vector of the final demand of the household sector. Since the general equilibrium does not allow an unbalanced trade balance, the foreign trade deficit of the year 1980 also had to be distributed over the final demand of the German households. The public investments were included in the vector of the public consumption demand appearing as final demand.

The taxes in the gross value added V_G^G were distributed according to the appropriate structural data from table 3.41 of the national income accounts of the Statistisches Bundesamt Wiesbaden (1985). Corporation income tax, business tax

(Gewerbesteuer), property taxes, inheritance tax and capital income withholding tax have been regarded as taxes linked to the capital input. The key used for distributing the tax accrual among the 12 domestic production sectors was the distribution of the income from business activities and assets as taken from the input-output table. The contributions to social security paid by employees and employers were considered as taxes on the labour input. Here we used the distribution of the labour income as taken from the input-output table as the key for distributing the tax accrual among the 12 domestic production sectors.

The matrices pertaining to X_G^R and E_G^R describe the distribution of the German exports among the individual groups of goods within the intermediate and final demand from abroad. The structural information basis for this as well as for the matrices pertaining to X_R^R, E_R^R and V_R^R came from the input-output table of 1975 for the EC of the Statistisches Amt der Europäischen Gemeinschaft (1983a). For the reference year 1980, these tables have been updated by means of the RAS algorithm[7] using level data — taken from the Yearbook of National Accounts Statistics of the United Nations (1981) and from the national income accounts of the Statistisches Amt der Europäischen Gemeinschaft (1983b) — related to a bloc of countries which purchases approx. 84 % of the West German exports and from which the FRG in turn buys 83 % of its imports.

Statistics on the group-specific modeling of the household sector were taken from the income and consumption random sample of 1978 of the Statistisches Bundesamt Wiesbaden (1982). This caused coordination problems in gathering a consistent data set since the input-output tables on the one hand and the income and consumption random sample on the other hand use different goods classifications. Converting the data from one system to the other was done by means of a table[8] showing the correlation between private consumption referring to the intended use and private consumption referring to the groups of goods. Coordination problems also arise through the use of different price systems within the various statistics. Whereas the input-output tables are based mainly on the ex-factory price, the income and consumption random sample uses the concept of the acquisition price.[9] Therefore it was necessary to neutralize differences between the price system by means of a consistent transfer of the entries for trade and transportation services.

In the household sector, the consumption tax payments accruing from the

[7] Concerning the RAS-algorithm see Bacharach (1971).

[8] We used table 4.2 in Statistisches Bundesamt Wiesbaden (1984).

[9] The acquisition price (Anschaffungspreis) is the sum of the producer price, the unit costs of wholesale and transportation and the VAT. See Statistisches Bundesamt Wiesbaden (1984, p. 18).

value-added tax and the tax payments from the levying of income tax (withholding wage tax and assessed income tax) are considered as being endogenous to the model. The effective consumption tax rates of the year 1980 were calculated on the basis of data in table 7 of the Statistisches Bundesamt Wiesbaden (1984). The total income tax yield recorded in the national income accounts was distributed among four net income classes according to a key which is defined by the distribution of the income tax payments according to the income and consumption random sample. Each given income tax payment by a household group n was established on the basis of a tax liability resulting from the taxation of a gross income in 1980. Thus it is assumed that the actual given payments of tax arrears from tax liabilities of the households before 1980 exactly balance out the actual tax prepayments on tax liabilities of the year 1980 that have not yet been assessed.

First of all, the taxable income y_t^n was determined by taking the rate stated in the basic table as the basis and using the statistically given income tax payment t_y^n of a household of income class n. According to the statutory tax assessment formula, there is a marginal tax rate Θ_y^n belonging to y_t^n, and in the model this rate is constant for each household group. Thus in turn, a first exemption f_1^n determined by the tax rate can be figured out, and this guarantees the actual tax yield t_y^n at the fixed marginal tax rate. The gross income $y^{g,n}$ that can be calculated on the basis of the data of the income and consumption random sample deviates from the taxable income y_t^n because of numerous legal and illegal tax evasion possibilities by the amount of another exemption f_2^n.[10] Applying the basic rate in a linear approximation, the income tax payment for a household of group n would be

$$(25) \qquad t_y^n = \Theta_y^n[y^{g,n} - f_1^n - f_2^n] = \Theta_y^n[wl^n + rk_{max}^n - f^n].$$

In actual fact, however, for a number of households it is not the basic table that is applicable but rather the splitting table. According to the splitting rate, the tax liability of a married-couple household is calculated by applying the basic rate to half of the total income of the household and doubling the resulting amount. Taking into consideration that a portion b^n of the number B^n of all households in group n pays taxes according to the splitting rate, the representative household of class n would then have an average tax yield function of

$$(26) \qquad \begin{aligned} t_y^n =& \{\Theta_y^{n,1} b^n + \Theta_y^{n,2}(1-b^n)\}[y^{g,n} - f_2^n] - \{2\,\Theta_y^{n,1}\, b^n f_1^{n,1} + \\ &+ \Theta_y^{n,2}(1-b^n) f_1^{n,2}\}; \qquad n = 1,\ldots,4. \end{aligned}$$

[10] For a detailed disaggregated description of these deductions see Albers (1974).

The marginal tax rate $\Theta_y^{n,2}$ and the tax exemption $f_1^{n,2}$ are calculated for the taxable income y_t^n in the same way as when the basic rate is applied. The smaller marginal tax rate $\Theta_y^{n,1}$ and tax exemption $f_1^{n,1}$ for married-couple households caused by the tax progression is calculated by the rate formula at the position $y_t^n/2$. Table 1 documents the parameters of the individual tax yield functions of all household groups when the basic rate is applied and when the taxation is proportional according to the splitting rate. Let us assume

$$\hat{\Theta}_y^n = \Theta_y^{n,1} b^n + \Theta_y^{n,2}(1-b^n) \tag{27}$$

$$\hat{f}^n = f_2^n + \frac{1}{\hat{\Theta}_y^n}\left\{ 2\,\Theta_y^{n,1}\, b^n f_1^{n,1} + \Theta_y^{n,2}(1-b^n) f_2^{n,2} \right\}. \tag{28}$$

Table 1: Tax Parameters of the Model Applying the 1980 Income Tax Rate Schedules

(Marginal Tax Rates in %; Taxable Income, Deductions and Income Tax Payments in DM)	Groups of Households with a Yearly Net Income (in 1 000 DM) per Household of			
	less than 16.8	16.8–48	48–120	120 or more
Gross Income and Income Tax Payments				
$y^{g,n}$	4 516	35 656	98 246	298 536
t_y^n	382	4 893	15 951	63 042
Tax Parameters Partially Applying the Splitting Schedule				
$\hat{\Theta}_y^n$	13.20	27.95	42.22	54.58
$\hat{f}^n$	1 622	18 154	60 464	183 047

Since precise information is not yet available as to the proportion of married-couple households in each income class, we have figured out the data configuration for the general equilibrium in the reference year 1980 using the example of the proportional coefficients $b^1 = 0.4$, $b^2 = 0.6$, $b^3 = b^4 = 0.8$. On the basis of data from the income tax statistics of 1980, this configuration seemed to be a first reasonable approximation.

B. Calibration

In the calibration process, one uses the conditions for the optimization of the producers' and consumers' decisions in the reference equilibrium in order to numerically fix a number of parameters. Particularly estimated values for substitution elasticities are taken from econometric studies.

Values for the parameters ϵ_j and Φ_j of the production functions $h_j(L_j, K_j)$ of our model can be calculated for the given substitution elasticities σ_j as follows. According to the first-order conditions of maximizing the firms' profit (14), we get the result

$$(29) \qquad \frac{\epsilon_j}{1-\epsilon_j}\left[\frac{K_j}{L_j}\right]^{1/\sigma_j} = \frac{w(1+\Theta_{L,j})}{r(1+\Theta_{K,j})}; \qquad j = 1, \ldots, 12.$$

K_j, L_j as well as the production factor tax rates $\Theta_{L,j}$ and $\Theta_{K,j}$ are known from the data for the equilibrium in the reference year. Since the factor prices $w = r = 1$ are applicable there, one can determine the ϵ_j according to

$$(30) \qquad \epsilon_j = \frac{\left[\frac{K_j}{L_j}\right]^{1/\sigma_j} \frac{1+\Theta_{L,j}}{1+\Theta_{K,j}}}{1 + \frac{1+\Theta_{L,j}}{1+\Theta_{K,j}} \left[\frac{K_j}{L_j}\right]^{1/\sigma_j}}.$$

The level parameters Φ_j can then be figured out from the production functions. The substitution elasticities σ_j documented along with ϵ_j and Φ_j in Table 2 were taken from Mansur and Whalley (1980).

Table 2: Parameters of the Production Sector and Quantities of Primary Factors Used in the Reference Year 1980

Production Branches	σ_j	ϵ_j	Φ_j	L_j (in mill. units)	K_j (in mill. units)
1	0.607	0.0776	1.4354	4063	22189
2	0.827	0.4860	2.0510	15745	22091
3	0.806	0.7734	1.9257	35021	17679
4	0.827	0.8435	1.6255	18696	6421
5	0.780	0.8736	1.5635	63152	18587
6	0.843	0.8118	1.6861	39867	15183
7	0.950	0.7400	1.8097	28690	14313
8	0.908	0.5377	2.2128	14442	16485
9	0.820	0.6679	1.9181	41749	29272
10	0.800	0.5926	1.9416	90549	85621
11	0.800	0.2595	1.8315	56638	167518
12	0.800	0.9693	1.1997	187188	11811

In the demand functions (9), (12) and (13) that are linked to the 'nested' utility functions (3), the parameters τ_i and μ_i still have to be calibrated. The division of equation (12) by equation (13) results in the determination equations for each consumer group n,

$$\mu_i = \frac{p_i x_i^n}{p_i x_i^n + p_{i+12}\, x_{i+12}^n}, \quad i = 1, \ldots, 11 \tag{31}$$

in the equilibrium of the reference year. The consumer expenditures specified in equation (31) were taken from the income and consumer random samples which were adjusted to the input-output table.

By dividing equation (12) by equation (9), taking into account equation (7) and $p_j = 1$, $j = 1, \ldots, 24$, one gets the equation system

$$\frac{\tau_i^n}{\tau_0^n} = \left[\frac{1 - \Theta_y^n}{1 + \Theta_{c,i}}\right]^{-\sigma^n} \frac{x_i^n}{\mu_i^n x_0^n}, \quad i = 1, \ldots, 11. \tag{32}$$

However, with the normalization condition $\sum \tau_i^n = 1$, all τ_i^n, $i = 0, 1, \ldots, 11$ can only be determined when the substitution elasticities σ^n, $n = 1, \ldots, 4$ and the leisure time demands x_0^n are known. For the equilibrium in the reference year 1980, a value for the maximum leisure time l_{max}^n of the representative household in each income class n must be selected. With empirical information on the direct wage elasticitiy of the labour supply, ϕ^n, a plausible value for the substitution elasticity σ^n can be found.[11]

From equation (9) one gets

$$\phi^n = \sigma^n \left[1 - \tau_0^n \left(\frac{w(1 - \Theta_y^n)}{\Pi^n}\right)^{1-\sigma^n}\right] \frac{x_0^n}{l^n} - \tau_0^n \left(\frac{w(1 - \Theta_y^n)}{\Pi^n}\right)^{1-\sigma^n} \tag{33}$$

where the first term on the right hand represents the compensated elasticity of the labour supply, $\tilde{\phi}^n$, and the second term comes from the total income effect of changing the net wage $w(1 - \Theta_y^n)$.

Becausc of the gap of information, the long run labour supply pattern of German households concerning the values of all parameters which must be chosen respectively are arbitrary estimates. The representative consumer of each group of households is assumed not to work more than one additional day per week,

---

[11] Mansur and Whalley (1984, p. 108): "Literature estimates on this elasticity vary sharply by the group involved, with prime-age males having low if not negative elasticities, and secondary and older workers having higher elasticities (around) 0.5."

whatever the level of the net wage is. Thus, with respect to an average five day and forty hour work week we fix the maximum of the potential labour supply at 20 % of the total labour supply of the year 1980. An equivalent interpretation for this is that the quantity of leisure in the reference year 1980 which might have been given up for income yielding labour supply mounts up to 20 % of the labour force of this year. Thus, keeping l^n_{max} for every household at a constant value in all simulations we have $l^n_{max} = 1.2\ l^n_{1980}$ throughout. The elasticities of substitution σ^n all are fixed at the value 0.55 so as to generate an uncompensated net wage elasticity of labour supply $\tilde{\phi}^n$ in the reference year 1980 close to a value of 0.10 for the households in every income class. Hence, the uncompensated net wage elasticity of labour supply will differ with consumers of different income groups according to the intensity of the total income effect.

The parameters of the utility and demand functions as well as the net wage elasticities of the labour supply generated by the assumed values of l^n_{max} and σ^n are documented in Table 3.

Table 3: Parameters of Demand Functions of Consumers

Commod-ities	$\tilde{\phi}^1 = 0.1085$ $\phi^1 = 0.0948$ τ_i^1	$\tilde{\phi}^2 = 0.1015$ $\phi^2 = 0.0245$ τ_i^2	$\tilde{\phi}^3 = 0.1031$ $\phi^3 = 0.0400$ τ_i^3	$\tilde{\phi}^4 = 0.1088$ $\phi^4 = 0.0977$ τ_i^4	μ_i
0	0.0152	0.0915	0.0825	0.0164	
1	0.0224	0.0154	0.0118	0.0048	0.5016
2	0.0446	0.0224	0.0167	0.0096	0.9594
3	0.0714	0.0646	0.0648	0.0456	0.8245
4	0.0018	0.0053	0.0094	0.0195	0.9565
5	0.0446	0.0952	0.1425	0.2334	0.8334
6	0.0390	0.0479	0.0635	0.0946	0.7691
7	0.0949	0.0801	0.0761	0.0548	0.7208
8	0.1764	0.1161	0.0851	0.0295	0.8908
9	0.0444	0.0973	0.1661	0.2964	1.0000
10	0.1410	0.1719	0.1119	0.0942	0.9957
11	0.3042	0.1921	0.1697	0.1010	0.9988

V. Computing General Equilibria for Alternative Tax Systems

A. Description of the Reform Approaches

In the framework of comparatively static analyses, the effects of the introduction of the income tax rate which is to go into force in 1988 were determined, and the empirical configuration of the year 1980 with the tax rates valid at that time served as the reference equilibrium.[12] In order to indirectly model the income tax progression, the linear rate appoximations according to the tax amount function (25) were used with the tax parameters listed in Table 4.

Table 4: Tax Parameters of the Model Applying the 1988 Income Tax Rates

(Marginal Tax Rates in %; Taxable Income, Deductions and Income Tax Payments in DM)	Groups of Households with a Yearly Net Income (in 1 000 DM) per Household of			
	less than 16.8	16.8–48	48–120	120 or more
Gross Income and Income Tax Payments				
$y^{g,n}$	4 516	35 656	98 246	298 536
t_y^n	268	4 375	13 679	56 717
Tax Parameters Partially Applying the Splitting Schedule				
$\hat{\Theta}_y^n$	13.20	24.83	34.58	52.07
$\hat{f}^n$	2 487	18 041	58 691	189 607

As measures to assure a balanced domestic government's budget, we have examined the following three alternatives:

1. Budget balancing only by means of a proportional change of all effective value added tax rates $\Theta_{c,i}$.
2. Budget balancing only by means of lowering the public expenditure for final products E_j^{St}.
3. Budget balancing by means of lowering the public expenditure for final products E_j^{St} by the amount of the expected loss in the yield from the income tax in conjunction with a corresponding adjustment of the value added tax rates.

[12] The equilibrium solutions of the model were computed by using a decomposition variant of the Merill algorithm. See Merill (1972).

Carrying out the income tax rate schedule 1988 in conjunction with one of these compensation rules, we have a specific new tax system in the Federal Republic of Germany in each of these cases. Hence, in the following we will speak of a new tax system with or established by the reform alternatives 1, 2 or 3, referring to the rules of balancing the government's budget as characterized above.

Finally, the government in the rest of the world is assumed to balance its budget by means of an appropriate adjustment of its transfer expenditures S^R, i.e. in a non-distortionary way.

Whereas the introduction of the income tax rate in 1988 on the basis of the income situation in 1980 must inevitably lead to a lower income tax yield, it is by no means clear a priori that such a rate change must, in fact, finally result in lower income tax payments by the households. However, a lower income tax yield (see Table 5) actually did result for all three compensation alternatives for the parameter configuration shown in Tables 2–4. Thus, in order to finance the income tax rate reduction, in the case of using the compensation alternative 1, the value added tax yield has to be raised correspondingly by means of an increase in the value added tax rates, or when applying the balancing rule 2 the public

Table 5: Income Tax Payment by Income Class (Total and Changes from Reference Year 1980 in Mill. DM)

	Groups of Households with a Yearly Net Income (in 1 000 DM) per Household of				
	less than 16.8	16.8–48	48–120	120 or more	$\sum$
Tax System of the Year 1980					
T_y^n	1 413	74 974	66 532	10 591	153 510
Tax System with Reform Alternative 1					
T_y^n	1 006	67 727	58 352	9 766	136 850
ΔT_y^n	– 407	–7 247	–8 180	– 825	–16 660
Tax System with Reform Alternative 2					
T_y^n	1 020	68 047	58 936	10 010	138 014
ΔT_y^n	– 393	–6 927	–7 596	– 581	–15 500
Tax System with Reform Alternative 3					
T_y^n	1 038	68 423	59 620	10 294	139 376
ΔT_y^n	– 375	–6 551	–6 912	– 297	–14 130

goods expenditure, i.e. the final demand brought to effect by the government has to be curtailed. Table 6 shows that the government using the third compensation alternative is overcompensating a postiori when it reduces the expenditures for public goods by the amount of the expected reduction in the income tax payments. The value added tax rates have to be lowered in order to meet the government budget; hence, a lower consumption tax yield will accrue in the new equilibrium.

Table 6: VAT Payment by Income Class (Total and Changes from Reference Year 1980 in Mill. DM)

	Groups of Households with a Yearly Net Income (in 1 000 DM) per Household of				
	less than 16.8	16.8–48	48–120	120 or more	$\sum$
Tax System of the Year 1980					
T_c^n	5 754	54 231	32 946	3 519	96 450
Tax System with Reform Alternative 1					
T_c^n	6 542	62 143	38 374	4 103	111 162
ΔT_c^n	788	7 912	5 428	584	14 712
Tax System with Reform Alternative 2					
T_c^n	5 800	55 090	34 087	3 654	98 632
ΔT_c^n	45	859	1 141	136	2 182
Tax System with Reform Alternative 3					
T_c^n	4 937	46 887	29 078	3 127	84 030
ΔT_c^n	– 818	–7 344	–3 867	– 391	–12 420

B. Labour Supply Effects

Changes of the households' labour supply have an impact on the level of their income and welfare. Hence, it seems reasonable to focus on what comes from the new tax system relating to this. Despite these questions it may be interesting to acquire some knowledge about the tax reform induced labour supply effects in the long run from an employment point of view.

To get first information on the major forces determining the direction of the labour supply change let us differentiate equation (8) as follows:

$$\frac{dx_0}{x_0} = \frac{d(y_{max}/\Pi)}{y_{max}/\Pi} - \sigma \frac{d(w(1-\Theta_y)/\Pi}{w(1-\Theta_y)/\Pi}. \tag{34}$$

We denote y_{max}/Π as the maximum real income and $w(1-\Theta_y)/\Pi$ as the real net wage rate. From equation (34) and $l = l_{max} - x_0$, it is straightforward to observe that the individual labour supply l is negatively linked with the maximum real income and positively linked with the real wage rate. To get deeper insights referring to what is behind these effects, we regard the total differentials of the maximum real income and the real net wage rate in equation (34) and obtain, after some rearrangements, the relative change of the individual demand for leisure as shown in figure 3.

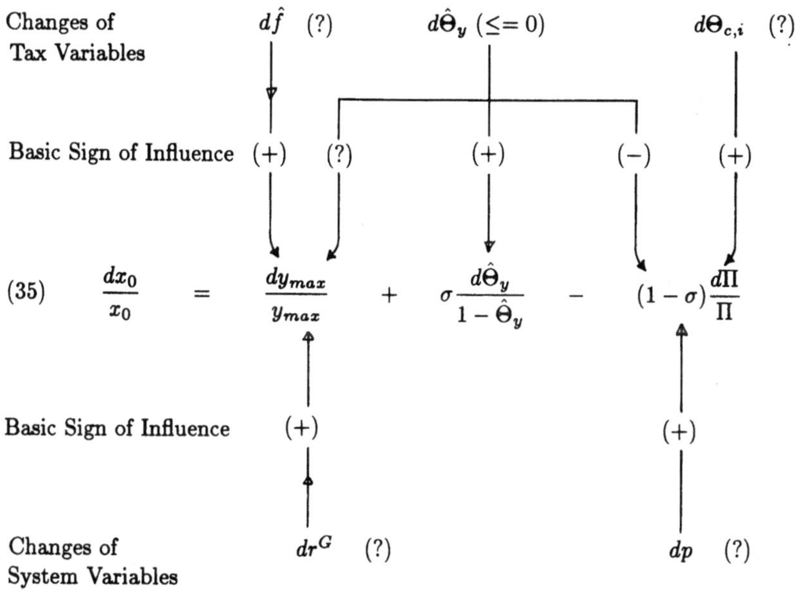

Figure 3: Factors Influencing the Demand for Leisure

This diagram points at the basic factors determining changes of leisure time and this way of labour supply. Moreover, one can see what is usually neglected arguing with results derived from a partial equilibrium analysis.

To begin with, the deduction $\hat{f}$ of the linearized tax amount function, see equations (26) to (28), applying the income tax 1988 might be lower or higher compared with that according to the tax schedule valid in the reference year 1980. From the tax parameters reported in table 1 and table 4 one can see that for the relatively poorest and richest consumers a higher deduction $\hat{f}$ applies after passing to the new income tax of 1988. But for the households in group 2 and 3 which mostly benefit from lower marginal income tax rates the linearization of the tax functions is jointly responsible for smaller deductions. Hence, higher thresholds will stimulate consumers in group 1 and 4 to reduce their labour supply. In contrast to that, households in group 2 and 3 are motivated to extend their labour supply.

Due to the normalization $w = 1$, the net price of leisure time goes up absolutely for all households for which the rate adjustment brings about a reduction in the marginal income tax rate $\hat{\Theta}_y$ that is applicable to them. For household groups 2, 3 and 4, this would stimulate a higher labour supply because the second and the third term on the right hand of equation (35), where we assume $\sigma < 1$, determine the final result.

Changes of the consumption tax rates $\Theta_{c,i}$ do affect the consumers' leisure demand only in the cases of the tax reform alternatives 1 and 3. Balancing the government's budget only by means of value added tax parameters one expects to get higher effective consumer tax rates. But even with constant producer prices r^G and p, i.e. following ways of partial equilibrium analysis, such consequences are by no means compelling. If the consumers decide to work more both the taxable income and the base of the value added tax will enlarge so as to compensate the smaller public revenue accruing from the reduced income tax rates. Of course, a priori we do not know how the effective consumption tax rates must be changed when introducing tax reform alternative 3 either. Referring to these questions, the results of our simulation as reported in table 7 are that the tax reform approach 1 requires higher, and the tax reform alternative 3 asks for lower levels of the effective consumption tax rates. Hence, herewith the labour supply will be stimulated in exactly the same directions, assuming $\sigma < 1$ again.

Ultimately, the a priori unknown system effects via the induced changes of the interest rate r^G, and the commodity prices p are to be taken into account. As can be seen from table 7, r^G rises by introducing the income tax 1988 despite the assumed different means of balancing the government's budget. Thus, this would decrease the labour supply of all households.

The effects of changed commodity prices p emerge in the new levels of the general individual price index Π^n. The results appearing eventually are a clear-cut increase of Π^n for all groups in the case of reform alternative 1, higher price indices in the case of reform alternative 2 as well but comparably not on a large scale, and a significant decrease of Π^n simulating the reform alternative 3.

Table 7: Net Wage Rates, Consumer Price Indices, Interest Rate, Level of Effective Consumption Tax Rates ($\Theta^*_{c,i} = \Theta_{c,i}/\Theta^0_{c,i}$), Maximum Income (in Mill. DM) for Alternative Tax Systems (T0, T1, T2 and T3)

	Groups of Households with a Yearly Net Income (in 1 000 DM) per Household of			
	less than 16.8	16.8–48	48–120	120 or more
Nominal Net Wage Rates				
*T*0	0.868	0.7205	0.5778	0.4542
*T*1–*T*3	0.868	0.7517	0.6542	0.4793
Level of Consumption Tax Rates				
*T*0, *T*2	1.00000	1.00000	1.00000	1.00000
*T*1	1.14509	1.14509	1.14509	1.14509
*T*3	0.83652	0.83652	0.83652	0.83652
Interest Rate				
*T*1	1.00998	1.00998	1.00998	1.00998
*T*2	1.02055	1.02055	1.02055	1.02055
*T*3	1.03288	1.03288	1.03288	1.03288
Consumer Price Indices Π^n				
*T*0	1.09143	1.05532	1.04963	1.08814
*T*1	1.10745	1.07273	1.07276	1.10463
*T*2	1.09325	1.05976	1.05840	1.08842
*T*3	1.07741	1.04528	1.04237	1.07032
Nominal Maximum Income				
*T*0	67 737	696 919	390 504	38 887
*T*1	68 258	708 488	404 512	40 191
*T*2	68 362	709 869	405 871	40 421
*T*3	68 483	711 480	407 457	40 689
Real Maximum Income				
*T*0	62 063	660 389	372 037	35 737
*T*1	61 635	660 456	377 078	36 384
*T*2	62 531	669 842	383 475	37 137
*T*3	63 563	680 663	390 895	38 016
Real Net Wage Rates				
*T*0	0.7953	0.6827	0.5721	0.4174
*T*1	0.7838	0.7007	0.6098	0.4339
*T*2	0.7940	0.7093	0.6181	0.4793
*T*3	0.8056	0.7191	0.6181	0.4404

Summing up, no conclusion can be drawn a priori as well as a postiori from all factors working via the real income effect or the real wage effect as to the direction of the final labour supply change.

As reported in table 8, households located in the lowest income class reduced their labour supply also in those cases where the real income and the real wage effect worked oppositionally. For consumers in group 3 the wage effect dominated the income effect so as to raise their labour supply in all cases. Referring to households in group 2 and 4 the results are ambiguous.

Table 8: Supply of Labour by Income Class for Alternative Tax Systems (Total and Changes from Reference Year 1980 in Mill. Units)

— Results from General Equilibrium Analysis: GEA —

— Results from Partial Equilibrium Analysis: PEA —

Tax System of Year 1980				
L^n	5 358	372 501	213 200	4 741
Tax System with Reform Alternative 1				
ΔL^n: PEA	1.0	1 224.6	1 945.8	9.2
ΔL^n: GEA	−1.2	1 052.7	1 787.2	3.3
Tax System with Reform Alternative 2				
ΔL^n: PEA	−6.5	752.8	1 662.3	2.1
ΔL^n: GEA	−9.1	505.7	1 400.8	−8.4
Tax System with Reform Alternative 3				
ΔL^n: PEA	−7.5	692.1	1 625.9	1.2
ΔL^n: GEA	−18.1	−122.8	954.3	−22.1

We now turn to the question of how the labour supply effect drawn from partial equilbrium analysis is to be seen in the light of the results from simulating with the general equilibrium tax model. Here, a partial equilibrium basis is called for to focus on taxes directly affecting the decisions of households. With reference to a well-established tradition in tax incidence analysis, let us define the concerned partial equilibrium setting as systems where all domestic consumers are in the state of equilibrium and all producer prices p and r^G are constant throughout. Because it makes no sense to allow for an unbalanced government budget we further assume the alternative compensating rules as elaborated above. Hence, the consumers as well as the government are assumed to get what they want to buy on commodity markets and to sell on factor markets. Thus, in a partial equilibrium tax model we totally abstract from the consequences of unbalanced budgets of domestic firms and all foreign decision units.

Comparing the changes of the labour supply computed by solving general equilibria with those which one can derive from the partial equilibrium analysis the concerned results as reported in table 8 differ substantially. Arguing from a point of view of a partial equilibrium setting especially the second round income effect is neglected. Thus, disregarding the effects of changed factor and commodity prices, we would postulate a considerably too high increase in the supply of labour. From table 8, one can further derive that the results which the partial equilibrium analysis brings about in some cases would even give us false information on the direction of the labour supply change in the long run.

C. Trade Effects

We now turn to the far more difficult question of how to explain the direction of trade effects.

From the theory of optimal tariffs we know that one country which has a monopoly power in trade with another country can restrict trade so as to improve its terms of trade and welfare at the expense of its trading partner. And it is well known, see for example Vandendorpe (1968), that imposing appropriate taxes is a qualitatively similar way to realize such gains from trade. If consumer taxes are at disposal, the exploitation of the rest of the world might be realized by subsidizing the domestic consumption of exportables and taxing the domestic consumption of importables. Taking this into account the higher level of consumption tax rates required with the tax reform alternative 1 works in favor of the rest of the world. But we also have to observe changes of the terms of trade induced by the curtailed income tax rates. The higher labour supply caused by this, for example, works to raise the interest rate r^G, i.e. the factor price of capital. This way all domestic households get higher capital incomes which stimulate their demand for goods so as to generate higher producer prices of commodities produced by firms in the Federal Republic of Germany.

Summing up, a priori we cannot derive information on the direction of how prices and quantities change on various world commodity markets due to performing the tax reform alternative 1 in the Federal Republic of Germany. In the cases of carrying out the tax reform alternatives 2 and 3 some a priori conjectures concerning the direction of the trade effects cannot be drawn from the basic structure of the specified general equilibrium model either. Thus, to get some knowledge about the trade effects involved in all of the considered tax reform measures we depend upon the relevant results from computed general equilibria completely.

Space limitation allows only to report the trade effects of introducing the income tax schedule 1988 in connection with a tax yield compensation by means of a change in the value added tax rates. As can be derived from table 9, with a declining monetary foreign trade volume there is an improvement of the foreign trade conditions for the German economy. This positive foreign trade effect is, in fact, documented by the general increase in the domestic producers' prices and the general decrease in the foreign producers' prices. As can also be seen in table 9, in the new equilibrium the economy of the Federal Republic of Germany tends to lose fewer goods to the economy of the ROW through export business. Furthermore, a larger share of the foreign production is available to the West German households and firms due to almost consistently increased imported goods volumes from all foreign production sectors.

The German economy also gains from the rest of the world carrying out the tax alternatives 2 and 3. The prices of commodities produced by firms in the rest of the world would drop largest introducing the income tax 1988 in conjunction with the third form of balancing the government's budget in the Federal Republic of Germany. It should be pointed out that this tax reform alternative brings about the largest, although overestimated, cut in public expenditure and lower consumption tax rates simultaneously.

D. Income Effects

In order to demonstrate how the individual incomes change due to performing the income tax rate schedule 1988, we focus on the disposable income of a consumer in each of the four groups of households. Referring to a concept of measuring the income available to consumers to purchase commodities at their market prices we define such a disposable income of a consumer according to

$$y^n = (1 - \Theta_y^n)[wl^n + rk^n] + \Theta_y^n f^n + s^n. \tag{36}$$

Hence, in comparison to the observed values $y^{n,0}$ of the reference year 1980, the absolute incidence of the individual income results from

$$yv^n = y^n - y^{n,0}, \quad n = 1, \ldots, 4. \tag{37}$$

In order to throw some light on how the income incidence changes from a partial equilibrium setting to the general equilibrium framework we computed both

Table 9: Export and Import (in Mill. DM) of FRG by Production Sectors and World Market Prices (in DM)

Production Sectors	Export 1980	Real Export / Reform Alternative 1	Nominal Export / Reform Alternative 1	World Market Prices / Reform Alternative 1
1	2 581	2 576	2 587	1.0044
2	6 718	6 717	6 735	1.0027
3	63 176	63 169	63 164	1.0000
4	29 555	29 544	29 561	1.0006
5	109 724	109 326	109 442	1.0011
6	48 689	48 509	48 571	1.0013
7	24 282	24 223	24 253	1.0012
8	14 273	14 229	14 264	1.0024
9	7 207	7 184	7 199	1.0021
10	40 312	40 289	40 427	1.0034
11	10 795	10 791	10 847	1.0052
12	526	526	526	1.0013
$\sum$	357 836		357 575	

Production Sectors	Export 1980	Real Export / Reform Alternative 1	Nominal Export / Reform Alternative 1	World Market Prices / Reform Alternative 1
13	29 472	29 613	29 448	0.9944
14	58 588	58 705	58 393	0.9947
15	67 452	67 672	67 318	0.9948
16	28 329	28 407	28 254	0.9946
17	38 795	39 205	38 988	0.9945
18	32 822	33 031	32 849	0.9945
19	47 143	47 343	47 085	0.9945
20	22 834	23 013	22 888	0.9946
21	5 005	5 023	4 996	0.9945
22	11 482	11 545	11 480	0.9944
23	15 817	15 866	15 777	0.9943
24	99	100	100	0.9943
$\sum$	357 836		357 575	

of the concerned values of the measure yv^n. These results of effective incidence can be confronted with a formal-statutory incidence defined as the change in the individual tax payment which will occur when applying the new tax rates to the individual tax base of the reference year 1980. Hence, in this case yv^n measures the income variation that would come about as the result of carrying out the new tax system before any adjustments occur and proceed throughout the economy until a new equilibrium is reached.

A characteristic result of the examined tax reform is that in the new general equilibria all households have a higher nominal gross income and, at the same time, have lower income tax payments. In some cases of a decreasing labour income, the total nominal factor income still increases, because the higher interest income here overcompensates for the loss of income in the area of wages.

With all of the considered rules of balancing the government's budget the gain in disposable income induced by carrying out the income tax rates 1988 in the reference year 1980 rises from the lowest to the uppermost consumer group (see table 10). One of the main determinants of this result is an unchanged marginal tax rate in the lowest income class, and the application of the cuts in the marginal tax rates to higher taxable income going from consumer group 2 to consumer group 4.

It may be of some interest to look at what happens to the individual disposable incomes if households adjust to the new tax system so as to reach a new state in a partial equilibrium. Hence, we are going to compare differences between the formal-statutory incidence and the concerned results from a partial equilibrium point of view.

At first, we do not always observe the lowest income increases measuring from a formal-statutory point of view. Consumers in the first income class lose in disposable income due to own adjustments, as carried out in the partial equilibrium setting, in response to implementing the tax reform alternatives 2 and 3. The concerned households will reduce their labour supply, see figure 3 and table 8, due to the higher deduction $\hat{f}^1$. Hence this adjustment leads to lower wage incomes and this way to reduced disposable incomes. Choosing the third compensating procedure the lower consumption tax rates are effective in the same direction. On the other hand when applying the first tax reform alternative, higher consumption tax rates tend to increase the consumer's labour supply so as to stimulate higher disposable incomes.

The change from this first round effective incidence to the second round effective incidence which is the result of various adjustments throughout the economy until a new general equilibrium is reached is far more difficult to explain. One of

Table 10: Individual Disposable Income by Consumer Groups: Changes from Reference Year 1980 in DM

— Results from Partial Equilibrium Analysis: PEA —

— Results from General Equilibrium Analysis: GEA —

	Groups of Households with a Yearly Net Income (in 1 000 DM) per Household of			
	less than 16.8	16.8–48	48–120	120 or more
Formal-Statutory Incidence Related to All Tax Reform Alternatives				
	114.1	518.2	2 272.1	6 324.6
Effective Incidence Related to Reform Alternative 1				
PEA:	114.3	578.3	2 577.3	6 350.8
GEA:	140.4	654.9	2 860.0	7 626.9
Effective Incidence Related to Reform Alternative 2				
PEA:	112.6	555.1	2 532.8	6 330.7
GEA:	166.7	718.2	3 125.2	8 962.5
Effective Incidence Related to Reform Alternative 3				
PEA:	112.3	552.1	2 527.1	6 328.1
GEA:	197.4	792.5	3 435.5	10 521.4

the major forces which might have been responsible for a higher disposable income in the new general equilibrium is the risen interest rate. But, just this system effect gives rise to reduce the households' labour supply, see, for example, such cases as reported in table 8, through which lower levels of the households' disposable incomes follow. In the end, the higher income from capital via the increase of r^G was dominant for every household leading to a higher disposable income for all of the considered tax reform measures.

E. Welfare Effects

In order to measure the welfare effects of carrying out the new tax system, we select the individual Hicks equivalent variation[13] *ev*, which has proven to be a utility-consistent standard.

[13] For proof that the equivalent variation is a suitable measure of individual welfare see Ahlheim and Rose (1984).

At first, it should be mentioned that we only focus on measuring changes of the individual welfare from consuming private goods x_i, x_{i+12}; $i = 0, 1, \ldots, 11$. Hence, the concerned utility level U_* we are interested in is the utility U reduced by the utility from the consumption of public goods E^{St}, i.e. we have

$$(38) \qquad U_* = U - g(E^{\mathrm{St}}).$$

Now, using the individual expenditure functions $e(\tilde{w}, \tilde{p}; U_*)$, where $\tilde{w}$ and $\tilde{p}$ are consumer prices according to

$$(39) \qquad \tilde{w} = (1 - \Theta_y)w; \quad \tilde{p}_i = (1 + \Theta_{c,i})p_i; \quad \tilde{p}_{i+12} = (1 + \Theta_{c,i})p_{i+12}; \\ i = 1, \ldots, 11,$$

the appropriate equivalent variation for a consumer of group n is defined as

$$(40) \qquad ev^n = e^n(\tilde{w}^{n,0}, \tilde{p}^0; U_*^n) - y_{max}^{n,0}.$$

Here, e^n are the minimum expenditures for achieving the utility level U_*^n after the tax reform, and $y_{max}^{n,0}$ is the maximum available income in the initial period 0 before the reform measure. $w^{n,0}$ is the group-specific domestic net wage rate, and $\tilde{p}^0$ is the consumer price vector of the reference year, thus before a tax reform.

The expenditure functions $e(\tilde{w}, \tilde{p}; U_*)$ can be formed for the utility function assumed for equation (3) as follows. By minimizing the consumer's expenditures under the restriction of his utility function with U_* keeping constant, the first-order conditions of the Lagrange formulation

$$(41) \quad min\, \mathcal{L}(x_0, m, \Gamma) = \tilde{w}x_0 + \sum_{i=1}^{11} \Pi_i m_i + \Gamma \left[U_* - \left(\tau_0^{1-\delta} x_0^\delta + \sum_{i=1}^{11} \tau_i^{1-\delta} m_i^\delta \right)^{1/\delta} \right]$$

result in the Hicks demand functions

$$(42) \qquad x_0 = \tau_0 \tilde{w}^{-\sigma} \Pi^\sigma U_*$$

$$(43) \qquad m_i = \tau_i \Pi_i^{-\sigma} \Pi^\sigma U_*; \quad i = 1, \ldots, 11.$$

If one puts the Hicks demands according to equations (42) and (43) into the total expenditures as defined in equation (40) and, furthermore, if one regards the term for Π according to equation (10), then one will find the very simple expenditure function

$$(44) \qquad e(\tilde{w}, \tilde{p}, U_*) = \Pi(\tilde{w}, \tilde{p}) U_*.$$

One can also verify, comparing the equations (8) and (41) for example, that U_* derived from the related indirect utility function is given as

$$U_* = \frac{y_{max}}{\Pi}. \tag{45}$$

Thus the equivalent variation from equation (40), taking into account the equations (44) and (45), is determined according to

$$ev^n = \Pi^{n,0} \frac{y^n_{max}}{\Pi^n} - y^{n,0}_{max}. \tag{46}$$

The first term on the right hand side of equation (46) can be interpreted as an individual money metric of the utility which the consumer has after the implementation of the tax reform and the concerned adjustments to this were carried out.

To get some information on how the welfare levels are changed by the new structure of the consumer prices $\tilde{w}^n$, $\tilde{p}_i$, $\tilde{p}_{i+12}$, $i = 1, \ldots, 11$, it furthermore seems reasonable to compute an incidence basing on the consumption expenditure net of taxes which is defined as

$$c = wx_0 + \sum_{i=1}^{11} p_i x_i + p_{i+12}\, x_i. \tag{47}$$

One then gets the concerned incidence we are interested in from

$$cv^n = c^n - c^{n,0}, \tag{48}$$

where $c^{n,0}$ denotes the net consumption expenditure in the reference year 1980. A detailed comparison of the used money metric of utility with the net consumption expenditure shows that differences between ev^n and cv^n will mainly arise from a change in the relative consumer prices affecting Π^n.

Having established how welfare effects are measured, first of all it might be interesting to look at those factors which primarily determine the equivalent variation. Referring to this, we differentiate equation (46), and obtain

$$\frac{dev^n}{ev^n} = \frac{dy^n_{max}}{y^n_{max}} - \frac{d\Pi^n}{\Pi^n}. \tag{49}$$

Comparing equation (35) with equation (48) one can conclude that the tax reform induced change of y^n_{max} and Π^n almost equally determine both the direction of the leisure demand effect and the welfare effect.

But, the relative change of the price index Π^n affects considerably less the relative change of leisure than the change of the welfare. The cause for this is the weight $(1 - \sigma^n)$ the value of which we fixed at 0.45 when finishing the calibration procedure. This may produce the result that the leisure time and the welfare are moved in different directions. Hence, this argument helps to explain that for the consumers in the first income class the equivalent variation and the change of labour supply have equal signs in the case of financing the income tax reform by means of increasing the consumption tax rates.

Further differences in the effects we are discussing arise from the change in the marginal income tax rates. Curtailing Θ_y^n has a direct negative effect on the wanted leisure time, see equation (35). Thus it seems reasonable that for consumers in group 3 the effective income tax rate of which is reduced most of all, a positive welfare incidence is accompanied by a higher labour supply.

The characteristic welfare incidence of the examined tax reforms is that the equivalent variation rises from bottom to top of the consumer groups, see table 11. Against the income incidence as described and discussed above, the household-specific burdens from changed consumer prices are also relevant in addition to the change in gross income and income tax payments. Let us focus on variations of consumer prices which mainly arise from changed consumption tax rates as in the case of carrying out the income tax reform in conjunction with a revenue-loss compensating increase of the value added tax rates. The extent to which the influences stemming from the changed consumption tax burdens can go in this context, becomes clear from the simulation results for the lowest income class, for instance. Here, the increase in consumption tax burdens arising from higher consumption tax rates leads to a situation where — in spite of rising gross income and falling income tax burden — the incidence with respect to the equivalent variation is negative. This is also valid for consumers of group 2 after adjustments we have to take into account in a partial equilibrium analysis. Only consumers of the two upper income classes can be sure that both the disposable income and the utility level go up, which is shown by positive equivalent variations.

The results of simulating the tax reform alternative 2 also show that divergences between the income incidence on the one hand and the incidence on the basis of a reliable welfare measure on the other hand are empirically relevant. For households of group 1, 2 and 3 the disposable income increases more than the money metric of utility, i.e. the concerned ev^n is smaller than the corresponding yv^n.

The extent of the welfare gain or welfare loss which may arise from the tax

Table 11: Individual Welfare and Net Consumption Expenditures by Consumer Groups: Changes from Reference Year 1980 in DM

— Results from Partial Equilibrium Analysis: PEA —

— Results from General Equilibrium Analysis: GEA —

	Groups of Households with a Yearly Net Income (in 1 000 DM) per Household of			
	less than 16.8	16.8–48	48–120	120 or more
Implementing Tax Reform Alternative 1				
PEA: cv^n	−151.6	−137.8	552.1	2 196.4
PEA: ev^n	−170.8	−133.4	810.5	2 408.3
GEA: cv^n	−72.1	69.8	1 130.1	4 131.3
GEA: ev^n	−126.2	4.7	1 270.2	4 187.6
Implementing Tax Reform Alternative 2				
PEA: cv^n	104.6	459.2	1 906.2	5 738.7
PEA: ev^n	114.1	518.1	2 778.6	6 323.0
GEA: cv^n	156.9	629.1	2 515.8	8 204.8
GEA: ev^n	138.0	651.1	2 880.1	9 065.2
Implementing Tax Reform Alternative 3				
PEA: cv^n	137.8	536.4	2 081.5	6 197.4
PEA: ev^n	150.9	602.2	2 468.4	6 829.5
GEA: cv^n	423.3	1 279.8	4 133.9	12 982.0
GEA: ev^n	442.4	1 396.4	4 747.3	14 757.8

reform induced change of the relative consumer prices can be seen from table 11 comparing the results for ev^n and cv^n.

First of all, there are no clear-cut characteristic results to report referring to this question. Only in the case of carrying out the tax reform alternative 3 which, as we know, is accompanied by the greatest cut in public expenditure and lower consumption tax rates as well, all consumers would gain additional welfare both from a partial equilibrium and a general equilibrium point of view. It is furthermore noteworthy, that in three cases consumers in the lowest income class do lose welfare because of the changed relative consumer prices. A value added tax financing of the income tax reform 1988 might also have the consequence that the relative price effect brings about welfare losses for consumers of group 2.

If there is an interest in totally evaluating the considered tax reform alternatives from a welfare point of view, one would have to take into account possible welfare changes which are produced by lowering the level of the public goods' provision when carrying out the government's budget balancing rules 2 and 3. We refrained from computing the corresponding welfare effects because we do not know any acceptable way how to deal with the concerned measurement problem.

But nevertheless, it may be of some interest to know that the change in public expenditure per household is −345.0 DM in the case of compensating a loss in public revenue by means of public expenditure, and mounts up to −769.1 DM balancing the government's budget according to the third rule described above.

Finally, a brief comment on the question of setting out social welfare effects of the examined income tax reform should not be left out. Regarding the developed standard of measuring welfare effects of fiscal policy programmes it would only seem reasonable to focus on equal-yield tax reforms. Thus, only the examined tax reform alternative 1 can be analyzed with respect to its social welfare effects, and one could think of using the equivalent variation as a basis for solving the concerned aggregation problem.

But, since the ev^n are utility parameters measured in money, strictly speaking, their aggregation via the households in group n or via all households in the Federal Republic of Germany is only possible presupposing their cardinality and interpersonal comparability. These prerequisites will probably hardly be given. However, if statements on the overall welfare effect of tax reform alternatives from a political point of view should be desired, this would only be possible by means of the introduction of a convention with regard to aggregation. The basis of such a metric convention can be the individual equivalent variation or the respective individual money metric of utility. There are various suggestions[14] made on this in the literature but we cannot deal with them here. Since so far, no metric convention concerning a social money metric of utility has become widely accepted, we refrained from analyzing the social welfare effects referring to the discussed tax reform case. Sometimes however, authors use the well-known aggregated metric by Harberger[15] which is most simply defined as the sum of all individual equivalent variations. Thus, some readers might be interested to know that the income tax rate reduction 1988, along with compensation for the tax yield losses by raising the value added tax rates creates in our general equilibrium model a social welfare gain of 5.6 billion DM in the sense of Harberger.

[14] See for example Deaton (1980), King (1983), McKenzie (1983) and Jorgenson and Slesnick (1983).

[15] See Harberger (1971).

VI. Final Remarks

The actual financing of the income tax rate change of 1988 cannot be identified empirically, particularly since the West German Federal government has not submitted an alternative budget for the situation without the tax rate reform. To a certain extent, this is not even possible since the yield of the individual taxes cannot be forecast.

For this reason, we have analyzed three financially feasible compensation alternatives within the scope of a model. It is possible at any time to use the model to figure out other financially interesting alternative compensation policies and then — for instance on the basis of a given social equivalent variation and/or a distribution metric — to make the desired comparison of the alternatives. Of course, the incidence effects related to income and/or welfare would then have to be interpreted in far greater depth than we have been able to do here in this limited space, especially also from the standpoint of equitable distribution.

Our main objective was to introduce the empirical model of a general equilibrium developed for the Federal Republic of Germany and to demonstrate how it works on the basis of several tax reform alternatives. There is no doubt that the basic structure of the model is still inadequate in a number of ways and in need of expansion. It should be pointed out that it is necessary to move on from the static version to an intertemporal-dynamic version. The modeling of the income tax rate structure also needs to be formulated in detail; however, this will only be possible once a consistent tax data basis exists with regard to the integration of the income tax statistics and the income and consumption random sample.

Notation

FRG	Federal Republic of Germany
G	label of variables related to FRG
ROW	rest of the world
R	label of variables related to ROW
H	label of variables related to the household sector
St	label of variables related to the government sector
0	label of variables related to the reference year 1980
n	label of variables and parameters related to one of the consumer groups in the FRG
j	label of variables related to one of the production sectors
i	label of variables related to one of the consumption goods
E_k^m	final uses in $m = G$, R, H, St or n of an output produced in $k = G$, R or j
V_k^k	value added in region $k = G, R$

X_k^m	intermediate input in region $m = G, R$ of an output produced in region $k = G, R$
U	utility level of a household
U_*	utility level of a household reduced by the utility from public goods
U_k	total utility level on stage k of the utility tree
$U_{k,i}$	utility level on stage k from consumption of goods of type i
x_0	leisure demand of a household
x_i	quantities of goods consumed by a household
μ_i, τ_i, δ_i	parameters of the utility function
σ	elasticity of substitution of leisure by commodities
w	gross wage rate
r	gross interest rate
$y_{\max}$	maximum disposable income
$l_{\max}$	endowment of leisure
$k_{\max}$	endowment of capital
s	individual transfer income
S	public transfer expenditures
Ω	share of a household group in S
f	effective personal exemption related to income taxation
$\Theta_{c,i}^k$	consumption tax rate on commodity i in region k
F	aggregate effective exemption related to income taxation
Θ_y	marginal income tax rate
m_i	quantity index of consumption of good i and $i + 12$
Π_i	price index of consumption of good i and $i + 12$
Π	general price index of consumption goods
L	aggregate labour supply
K	aggregate capital supply
Q_k	total output of region $k = G, R$
Q_j	output of sector j
p_j	producer price of commodity j
$a_{k,j}$	input coefficient of commodity k in sector j
$\epsilon_j, \Phi_j, \delta_j$	parameters of the production functions
σ_j	elasticity of substitution of L_j by K_j
$\Theta_{L,j}$	rate of tax on labour income in production sector j
$\Theta_{K,j}$	rate of tax on capital income in production sector j
$\Theta_{Q,j}$	rate of tax on sales receipts in sector j
t_y	individual income tax payment
y^g	individual gross factor income
y_t	individual taxable income
$\hat{\Theta}_y$	marginal income tax rate partially applying the splitting schedule
$\hat{f}^n$	effective personal exemption partially applying the splitting schedule
b	share of married couples within a household group
B	number of households
ϕ	net wage elasticity of labour supply
$\tilde{\phi}$	compensated net wage elasticity of labour supply
T_y	aggregate income tax payments
T_c	aggregate consumption tax (VAT) payments
l	individual labour supply
y	individual disposable income

yv	changes of y from reference year 1980
c	individual consumption expenditure net of taxes
cv	change of c from reference year 1980
$\tilde{w}$	net wage rate
$\tilde{p}_j$	consumer prices of commodities
ev	individual equivalent variation (change of the money metric of utility from reference year 1980)

References

Ahlheim, M., and **Rose, M.** (1984): "Alte und neue Maße individueller Steuerlasten." *Finanzarchiv, N.F.* 42: 274–349.

Albers, W. (1974): "Umverteilungswirkungen der Einkommensteuer." In *Öffentliche Finanzwirtschaft und Verteilung*, edited by W. Albers. Berlin: Duncker & Humblot.

Armington, P. S. (1969): "A Theory of Demand for Products Distinguished by Place of Production." *IMF Staff Papers* 159–176.

Bacharach, M. (1971): *Bi-proportional Matrices and Input-Output Change*. Cambridge etc.: Cambridge University Press.

Deardorff, A. V., and **Stern, R. M.** (1981): "A Disaggregated Model of World Production and Trade: An Estimate of the Impact of the Tokyo Round." *Journal of Policy Modelling* 3: 127–152.

Deaton, A. (1980): "The Measurement of Welfare: Theory and Practical Guidelines." LSMS Working Paper No. 7. Washington, D.C.: The World Bank Development Research Center.

Green, H. A. J. (1964): *Aggregation in Economic Analysis: An Introduction Survey*. Princeton, N.J.: Princeton University Press.

Harberger, A. C. (1971): "Three Basic Postulates for Applied Welfare Economics: An Interpretative Essay." *Journal of Economic Literature* 9: 785–797.

Jorgenson, D. W., and **Slesnick, D. T.** (1983): "Individual and Social Cost of Living Indexes." Discussion Paper Series 973. Cambridge, Mass.: Harvard University, Harvard Institute of Economic Research.

King, M. A. (1983): "Welfare Analysis of Tax Reforms Using Household Data." *Journal of Public Economics* 21: 183–214.

Mansur, A., and **Whalley, J.** (1984): "Numerical Specification of Applied General Equilibrium Models: Estimation, Calibration, and Data." In *Applied General Equilibrium Analysis*, edited by E. Scarf and J. B. Shoven. Cambridge etc.: Cambridge University Press.

McKenzie, G. W. (1983): *Measuring Economic Welfare: New Methods*. Cambridge etc.: Cambridge University Press.

Merrill, O. H. (1972): *Applications and Extensions of an Algorithm that Computes Fixed Points of Certain Upper Semicontinuous Point to Set Mappings.* Diss. University of Michigan.

Presse- und Informationsamt der Bundesregierung (1985): *Steuerentlastung 1986/1988. Weniger Staat — mehr Einkommen.* Bonn.

Shoven, J. B. (1983): "Applied General Equilibrium Tax Modeling." *IMF Staff Papers* 30: 394–420.

Shoven, J. B., and **Whalley, J.** (1984): "Applied General-Equilibrium Models of Taxation and International Trade: An Introduction and Survey." *Journal of Economic Literature* 22: 1007–1051.

Statistisches Bundesamt Wiesbaden (1982): *Wirtschaftsrechnungen. Fachserie 15. Einkommens- und Verbrauchsstichprobe 1978. Heft 4. Einkommen und Ausgaben privater Haushalte.* Stuttgart etc.: Kohlhammer.

Statistisches Bundesamt Wiesbaden (1984): *Volkswirtschaftliche Gesamtrechnungen. Fachserie 18. Reihe 2. Input-Output-Tabellen 1980.* Stuttgart etc.: Kohlhammer.

Statistisches Bundesamt Wiesbaden (1985): *Volkswirtschaftliche Gesamtrechnungen. Fachserie 18. Reihe S.8. Revidierte Ergebnisse 1960–1984.* Stuttgart etc.: Kohlhammer.

Statistisches Amt der Europäischen Gemeinschaften (1983a): *Volkswirtschaftliche Gesamtrechnungen ESVG. 1970–1981.* Luxembourg.

Statistisches Amt der Europäischen Gemeinschaften (1983b): *National Accounts ESA. Input-Output Tables 1975.* Luxembourg.

United Nations (1983): *Yearbook of National Accounts Statistics 1981. Vol. 1. Part 1/2.* New York.

Vandendorpe, A. (1972): "Optimal Tax Structures in a Model with Traded and Nontraded Goods." *Journal of International Economics* 2: 235–256.

Whalley, J. (1980): "Discriminatory Features of Domestic Factor Tax Systems in a Goods Mobile Factors Immobile Trade Model. An Empirical General Equilibrium Approach." *Journal of Political Economy* 81: 1177–1202.

Whalley, J. (1980): "General Equilibrium Analysis of US–EEC–Japanese Trade and Trade Distorting Policies: A Model and Some Initial Findings." *Economie Appliquée* 33: 191–230.

Whalley, J. (1982): "An Evaluation of the Tokyo Round Trade Agreement Using General Equilibrium Computational Methods." *Journal of Policy Modelling* 4: 341–361.

Whalley, J. (1984): "External Sector 'Closing' Rules in Applied General Equilibrium Models." *Journal of International Economics* 16/17: 123–138.

Wiegard, W. (1985): "Besteuerungsanalysen im Rahmen der empirischen allgemeinen Gleichgewichtsökonomie — Vorläufige Berechnungen zur Substitution der Gewerbesteuer." Mimeo. University of Regensburg.

Income Tax Reduction and the Quantification of Welfare Gains — An Applied General Equilibrium Analysis

Klaus Conrad and Iris Henseler-Unger, Mannheim, West Germany

I. Introduction

Recently a growing number of studies of the applied general equilibrium model type have been used to quantify and to simulate strategies in fiscal, economic and energy policy. In analyzing the impact of such programs on the total economy, models of the Keynesian type have lost their attraction. Their black box character with respect to the allocation mechanism of prices in the structure of production, sectoral employment and income distribution makes it difficult to evaluate the outcome of the simulation. Some well-known studies of applied general equilibrium models used in evaluating fiscal policy measures are those by Shoven and Whalley (1972, 1973), Whalley (1975), Fullerton, King, Shoven, and Whalley (1981), Fullerton, Shoven, and Whalley (1983) and by Ginsburgh and Waelbroeck (1981). As a result of criticisms of these models, viz. the unrealistic assumptions on which these models are based, the restriction of perfectly competitive markets has been partially replaced by an assumption of imperfect competition. In addition, institutional conditioning factors are also considered (see Harris, 1985).

In this paper we relax the unrealistic assumption that all variables adjust immediately to their long-run optimal values by treating some factors of production as fixed in the short-run so that the economy is in a temporary equilibrium or short-run disequilibrium. A temporary equilibrium may occur when unexpected demand shocks lead to underutilization or overutilization of capacity, or when sudden changes in factor prices result in short-run relative factor usage which is inappropriate in the long-run. With quasi-fixed inputs, the economy is in a temporary equilibrium; it will not reach the long-run equilibrium as long as exogenous shocks like energy prices, government expenditure programs or discontinuities in population growth result in non-optimal usage of temporarily fixed inputs such as the capital stock, for example. If the actual capital stock is larger than the optimal capital stock there is underutilization. This is equivalent to a situation where potential output is larger than actual output. In such a situation a reduction in income taxes can lead to an expansion in demand and production. This will reduce welfare losses which arise when the actual level of production remains below the potential level.

A further objective of this paper is that of developing an appropriate measure of the welfare economic consequences of a tax reduction which reduces the under-utilization of existing economic capacities. The quantification of welfare gain will be based on the measure of equivalent income variation.

It is well known that Marshall's consumer surplus is hardly appropriate for measuring changes in welfare. If the price system changes, the problem with the path dependency of the integration emerges. Closely related to this problem is the untenable assumption of a constant marginal utility of income. Equivalent and compensating income variations, however, are welfare measures which are based on the compensated demand function and are, therefore, path independent. These also rank different bundles of commodities in such a way that the result turns out to be a correct transformation of the underlying ordinal preference system.

Another welfare gain from an income tax reduction is the smaller dead weight loss due to a better utilization of production capacities in the case of an increase in producers' surplus resulting from an increase in production. Finally, welfare gains originate if disappointed expectations are reduced as a result of a movement of the economy towards a long-run equilibrium situation. Entrepreneurs expect the long-run internal rate of return to be equivalent to the interest rate on government bonds. They obtain a lower rate of return on their invested capital only in a temporary equilibrium. In the short-run, firms bear an imaginary loss which will only disappear in the long-run equilibrium when the ex-ante expected rate of return coincides with the ex-post realized rate of return.

The paper is organized as follows: in Section II we present the concept of a temporary equilibrium based on short-run restricted cost functions. In Section III we outline the structure of our model and in Section IV explain the construction of our set of welfare measures. Empirical results are presented in Section V and in Section VI we present our conclusion based on this analysis.

II. The Specification of a Temporary Equilibrium Model

In this paper we do not set out in detail the framework and specifications of our long-run equilibrium model. This has already been done in several other papers (Conrad, 1982; Conrad and Henseler-Unger, 1984, 1986; Henseler-Unger, 1985). What we want to do is to present the modifications which are required if a long-run equilibrium model is to be interpreted as a special case of a temporary equilibrium model. The main modification results from dropping the assumption of short-run variability of sectoral capital stocks. Figure 1 gives an overview of the structure of the model. There is a parallel determination of a suboptimal short-run solution, given in terms of quantities and prices, and an optimal long-run solution where full flexibility of all capital stocks is assumed. The ratio of the short-run output level to the optimal long-run output level can then be used to measure capacity utilization in diverse sectors of the economy.

The core of the temporary equilibrium model is the input-output matrix containing forty-five industries, a system of forty-five prices as the solution to a simultaneous equation system of forty-five average cost functions, and a price-dependent input structure. A standard characteristic of these models is the decomposition of total supply into intermediate industrial goods and final goods, all expressed in constant and current market prices, including value added taxes and subsidies. Total supply of an industry consists of domestic production and of competitive imports. Finally, total supply from the flow-of-product account equals the value of primary and secondary inputs of factor costs using a cost-flow approach.

Crucial for determining the economic effects within an applied general equilibrium model is the specification of the unit cost system and its price-impact on supply and demand. We define the variable costs VC_j of industry j to be

$$VC_j = \sum_{i=1}^{n} PY_i \cdot X_{ij} + PL_j \cdot L_j \tag{1}$$

where X_{ij} are intermediate goods delivered to industry j by industry i, PY_i is the price of industry i, and PL_j is the price of labor in industry j.[1] Given domestic production X_j and with capital fixed at the end level of a previous period, the variable (or restricted) cost function

$$VC_j = VC_j(X_j, K_j; PY, PL_j) \tag{2}$$

characterizes a technology at a short-run equilibrium. VC_j denotes the minimum possible costs of producing output X_j, given capital stock K_j and the vector $PY = (PY_1, \ldots, PY_n)$ of prices for intermediate goods and the price PL_j of labor.

From Shephard's Lemma, we know that under cost-minimizing behavior, the cost elasticity with respect to input prices is equal to the cost share:

$$\frac{\partial \ln VC_j(\cdot)}{\partial \ln PY_i} = \frac{PY_i X_{ij}}{VC_j}, \qquad i = 1, \ldots, n+1 \qquad \text{with } n+1 \text{ for labor } L_j. \tag{3}$$

[1] To simplify the presentation we do not explicitly introduce taxes on production (e.g. taxes on crude oil), price differentiation and factor augmenting technical change. The computer program, however, contains all these refinements.

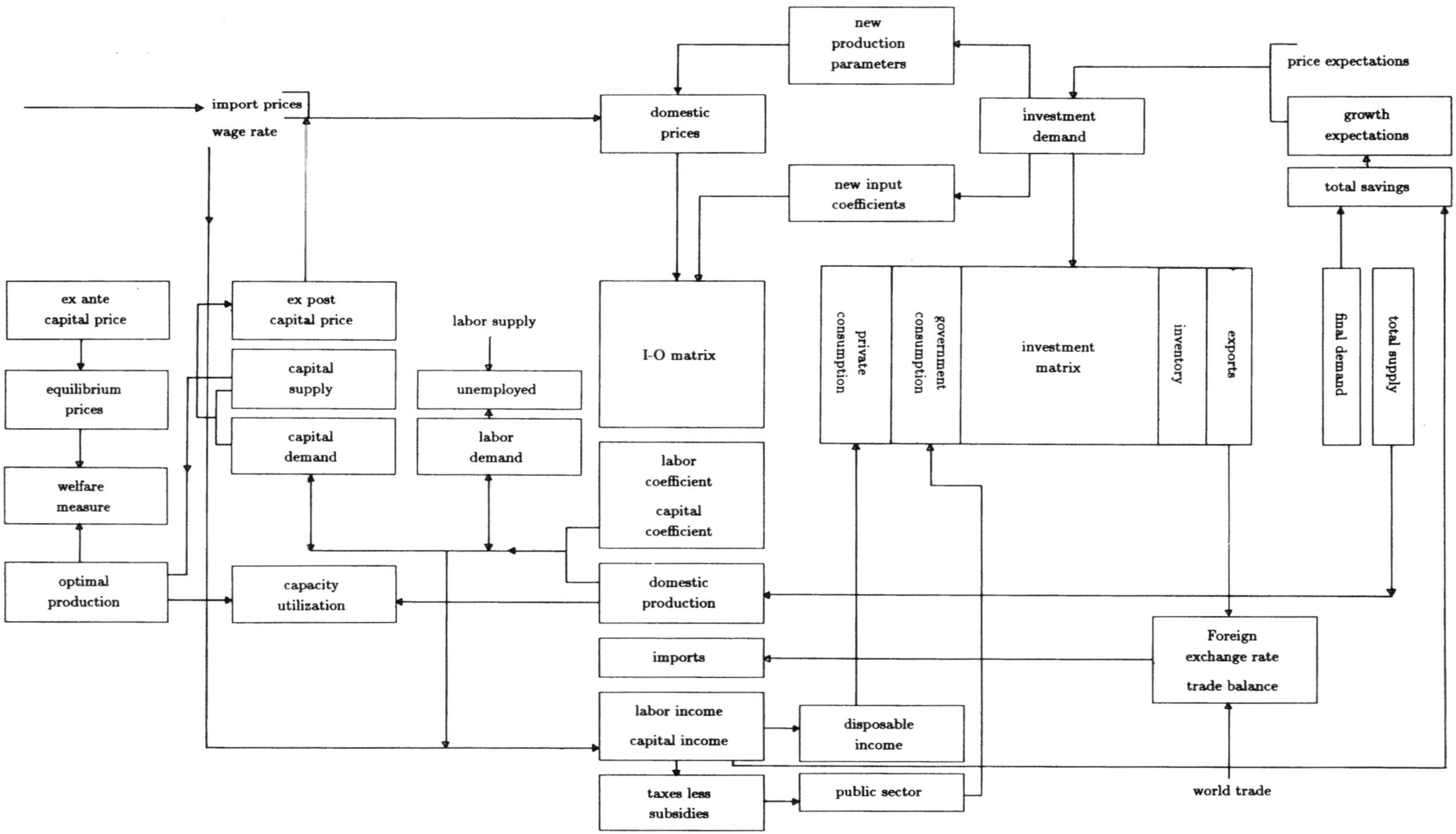

Figure 1: The Structure of the Temporary Equilibrium Model

Rewriting (3) we obtain a set of price-dependent input coefficients

$$(4) \qquad \frac{X_{ij}}{X_j} = \frac{\partial\, ln\, VC_j}{\partial\, ln\, PY_i} \cdot \frac{AVC_j(\cdot)}{PY_i}, \qquad i = 1, \dots, n+1,$$

where $AVC_j(\cdot)$ is the average variable cost function. The input coefficients can be calculated if a variable cost function has been specified and if cost elasticities have been empirically estimated.

In order to determine an input coefficient for fixed capital, we calculate the shadow price ZK of the quasi-fixed capital. This is the reduction in variable costs incurred by having one more unit of K, i.e.[2]

$$(5) \qquad ZK_j = -\frac{\partial VC_j(\cdot)}{\partial K_j}.$$

The shadow price ZK_j is endogenous and reflects the best firms can do for their shareholders in the short-run, given the exogenous restrictions (X_j, K_j, PY, PL_j). From (5) we obtain the short-run capital coefficient

$$(6) \qquad \frac{K_j}{X_j} = \left(-\frac{\partial\, ln\, VC_j(\cdot)}{\partial\, ln\, K_j}\right) \frac{AVC_j(\cdot)}{ZK_j}.$$

After having derived the price-dependent input structure in (4) and (6), we next determine the price system. The domestic capital stock price is denoted by PX_j and the price of total capital supply Y_j is given by PY_j. PY_j is a price index vector expressed as a function of PX_j and import prices PM_j, $PY_j = f_j(PX_j, PM_j)$. From the profit maximizing rule that price be equal to marginal cost, i.e. $PX_j = \partial VC_j / \partial X_j$, after rearranging we obtain

$$(7) \qquad PX_j = \epsilon^j_{VC,X} \cdot AVC_j(X_j, K_j; PY_1, \dots, PY_n, PL_j), \quad j = 1, \dots, n,$$

where $\epsilon^j_{VC,X} = \frac{\partial\, ln\, VC_j}{\partial\, ln\, X_j}$ is the cost elasticity with respect to output.

The simultaneous system (7) must be solved for prices $PX_1, \dots, PX_n$, when the average cost function is specified, given industrial wage rates PL_j and the cost elasticities with respect to output. The average cost functions in (7) can be substituted into the input coefficients (4) and (6) resulting in the following expressions

$$(8) \qquad a_{ij} := \frac{X_{ij}}{X_j} = \frac{\epsilon^{j,i}_{VC,PY}}{\epsilon^j_{VC,X}} \frac{PY_j}{PY_i}, \quad a_{K_j} := \frac{K_j}{X_j} = \frac{\epsilon^j_{VC,K}}{\epsilon^j_{VC,X}} \frac{PY_j}{ZK_j}$$

[2] See Berndt and Fuss for the shadow price interpretation in order to distinguish between a long-run and short-run equilibrium.

where $\epsilon^{j,i}_{VC,PY}$ and $\epsilon^{j}_{VC,K}$ are the elasticities of variable costs with respect to PY and K, respectively.

Furthermore, we assume constant returns to scale in the long-run so that the variable cost function VC_j is linear homogeneous in K_j and X_j. Using Euler's Theorem and (5) we obtain

$$(9) \qquad PX_j \cdot X_j - ZK_j \cdot K_j = VC_j.$$

There are no profits or losses in a temporary equilibrium if firms accept as a fact the ex post shadow price ZK_j of capital. This temporary equilibrium is a long-run equilibrium if the realized ex post price of capital ZK_j corresponds to the expected ex ante price of capital calculated by the firm, which is based on the risk-free interest rate on government bonds. Let PK_j be the ex ante price of capital. A temporary as well as a long-run market equilibrium exists for good j if the endogenous price of capital is equal to the exogenous price PK_j,[3] i.e.

$$(10) \qquad PK_j = ZK_j.$$

In this case total cost TC_j is

$$(11) \qquad TC_j = VC_j + PK_j \cdot K_j.$$

According to (9), total cost TC_j is equal to total revenue $PX_j \cdot X_j$ if $PK_j = ZK_j$. Therefore, only in long-run equilibrium is the total cost TC_j equal to the shadow cost STC_j, where the shadow cost is defined as follows:

$$(12) \qquad STC_j = VC_j + ZK_j \cdot K_j.$$

It has been shown by Berndt and Hesse (1985) that a necessary condition for minimizing average total cost $ATC_j = TC_j/X_j$ with respect to X_j is (10), i.e.

$$(13) \qquad PK_j = -\frac{\partial}{\partial K_j} VC_j(X_j^*, K_j, PY_1, \ldots, PY_n, PL_j),$$

where X_j^* is the output at full-capacity given the quasi-fixed capital stock K_j. Hence the long-run equilibrium characterizes a state where output has reached a level which minimizes total average costs on the basis of the expected ex ante price of capital PK_j. With the capital price PK_j as given, we can calculate X_j^* from (13). For PK_j we specify that

$$(14) \qquad PK_j = PI \cdot (r + \delta_j),$$

[3] See Berndt and Fuss (1986), Berndt and Hesse (1985) and Morrison (1985) for this condition.

where r is the interest rate on government bonds, PI is the price of investment goods and δ_j is the rate of replacement. It is easy to see from the property of monotonicity that $PK_j > ZK_j$ implies that $X_j^* > X_j$, and $PK_j < ZK_j$ implies $X_j^* < X_j$. Hence X/X^* can be used as a measure of capacity utilization with $X/X^* < 1$ when the capital stock K is underutilized.

For a comparison of the temporary equilibrium with the long-run equilibrium, both prices and quantities in the long-run equilibrium are of interest. We obtain these magnitudes by solving systems (7) and (13) in $2n$ equations for the n quantities X_j^* and for the n prices PX_j^*. Before solving for PX_j^*, the n supply prices PY_j have to be replaced by $PY_j = f_j(PX_j, PM_j)$ for $j = 1, \ldots, n$, and the input prices PM_j are exogenous. This long-run equilibrium will serve as a point of reference for evaluating a fiscal policy measure with respect to its ability to bring the economy closer to the long-run equilibrium.

In what follows we outline some more or less traditional properties and characteristics of models of the applied general equilibrium type. Our price system consists of a CES unit cost function nested in an energy (ten industries) and non-energy (thirty-five industries) price index. The sub-price function for non-energy industries is based on the average variable cost function mentioned above, and is of the Cobb-Douglas type. Hence the cost elasticities in (7) and (8) are constant and are functions of the elasticities of production. Parameter estimates of the functions are point estimates of the input-output table for the base year 1978. The elasticities of substitution are assumed to be 0.5 in all industries.

For the components of final demand we have developed small submodels. Disposible income enters into the macroeconomic consumption function and aggregate consumption is allocated to consumer demand by sector using Stone's linear expenditure system. Sectoral export functions are based on CES specifications, government consumption is exogenous, and investment demand by origin has been derived from investment demand by destination based on price-dependent investment coefficients. Investment demand by industry has been transformed into industrial investment goods through a distribution matrix for investment demand. Our approach guarantees that the ex post equality of savings and investments is satisfied in each year. An additional feature of our model of investment demand is a putty-clay concept with vintage technologies which influence prices and input coefficients. Furthermore, supply and demand of foreign currency determines the foreign exchange rate. The rate of inflation and changes in labor productivity of the previous year determine the change in the wage rate.

Finally, we calculate domestic production similar to Leontief's inverse procedure. However, our model is neither linear nor recursive but interdependent in its structure. In addition, we employ the Gauß-Seidel method for solving it iteratively. The driving force of the model is a set of exogenous data which consists of import prices, tax rates, technical change, volume of world trade, government expenditure, and labor supply. The model's solution has domestic prices and production per industry, imports, exports, disposible income, private consumption, and number of unemployed persons as components.

III. The Welfare Loss of a Temporary Equilibrium

A graphical analysis may help us determine the welfare losses which we want to measure. Figure 2 shows average total cost $ATC_j(PK) = TC_j/X_j$ with TC_j defined in (11). ATC_j reaches its minimum at the capacity output X_j^*. In addition, the figure shows average total cost as based on the ex post price of capital ZK_j with $ATC_j(ZK_j) = STC_j/X_j$ and STC_j defined in (12). Since a temporary equilibrium is characterized by zero profits (as based on ZK), price and quantity is determined through the intersection of the marginal cost curve (MC_j) and the $ATC_j(ZK)$ curve. A long-run equilibrium occurs when price equals long-run average cost as calculated through the ex ante expected price of capital PK. As with the price-equals-marginal-cost rule, production occurs where the average cost curve is at its minimum, i.e. at the capacity output X_j^*, given any capital K_j. Figure 2 shows a situation with underutilization of the quasi-fixed capital stock. If capacity output is situated to the left of the temporary equilibrium output X_j^0, we have a situation of overutilization of the capital stock.

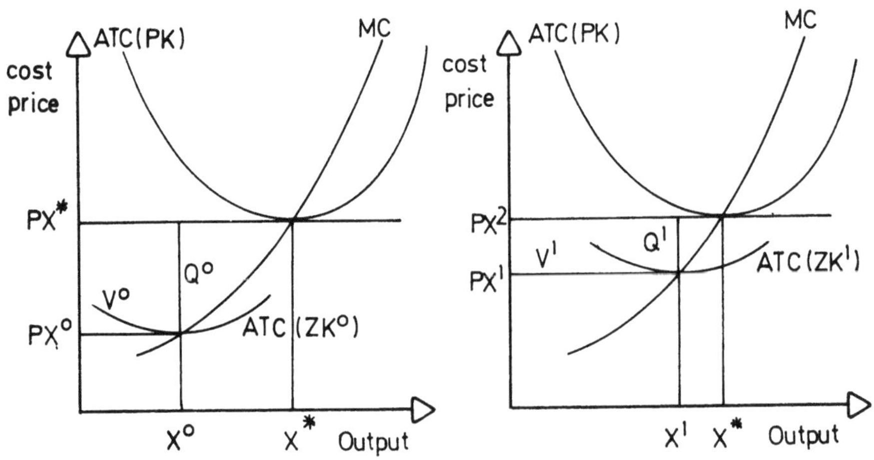

Figure 2: Welfare Losses of a Temporary Equilibrium

In the case where the capital stock is underutilized, the welfare loss of a temporary equilibrium can be measured as follows. First, we realize that unit cost and price will be higher if costs are based on the ex ante expected higher rate of return. Firms will, therefore, have to accept a reduction in revenues due to the nonrealized higher rate of return. This reduction V_j^0 is given as

$$V_j^0 = (PX_j^* - PX_j^0)X_j^0. \tag{15}$$

This will, however, be completely compensated through the amount saved due to lower cost of production, as prices are equal to ATC:

$$V_j^0 = (ATC_j(PK_j) - ATC_j(ZK_j))X_j^0.$$

However, a welfare loss emerges in terms of a reduction in producers' surplus which is smaller in the temporary equilibrium than in the long-run equilibrium (Q_j^0 in Fig. 2). We approximate this triangle by

$$Q_j^0 = 0.5(PX_j^* - PX_j^0)(X_j^* - X_j^0) \tag{16}$$

where Q_j^0 is the welfare loss of industry j, as given from the producers' point of view.

As a measure of changes in welfare from the consumers' point of view we employ Hicks's measure of equivalent income variation (EV).[4] The equivalent variation of an economic policy measure which helps us approach the long-run equilibrium is equal to either the minimum income the consumer must receive to come into a temporary equilibrium ($EV > 0$) or the maximum amount a consumer must pay ($EV < 0$) in order to be able to realize an optimal consumption plan under the original price vector PX^0 which is equivalent to the new consumption plan in the X^* state. This measure also takes into account the change in the distribution of income from Y^0 in the temporary equilibrium to Y^* in the long-run equilibrium,[5] such that

$$EV = E(PX_1^0, \ldots, PX_n^0, U^*) - E(PX_1^*, \ldots, PX_n^*, U^*) + Y^* - Y^0. \tag{17}$$

$E(\cdot)$ is the expenditure function of the consumer and U^* is the level of utility achieved in the long-run equilibrium.[6] If $EV > 0$, then the long-run equilibrium

[4] See Ahlheim and Rose (1984) for a comprehensive survey on welfare measures of tax burdens.

[5] To be correct Y should be that part of income spent for consumption. The computer program takes care of this difference but in this paper income is synonomous with consumption expenditure.

[6] To simplify the notation, we did not distinguish here between domestic prices (PX), prices of total supply PY (including import prices) and market prices (including indirect taxes). Of course this has been done in the computer program.

situation is preferable. With U^0 as the utility level in the temporary equilibrium, the expression in (17) can be rewritten as

$$EV = E(PX_1^0, \dots, PX_n^0, U^*) - E(PX_1^0, \dots, PX_n^0, U^0). \tag{18}$$

Hence, EV represents the difference in the minimal expenditure under the price system PX^0 in the temporary equilibrium necessary for the consumer to achieve the former utility level U^0 on the one hand, and the new utility level U^* on the other.

The difference in income can easily be calculated as

$$Y^* - Y^0 \equiv PL \cdot L^* + PK \cdot K - PL \cdot L^0 - ZK \cdot K,$$

where L is the hours worked in all industries and PL is the corresponding wage rate $(PL \cdot L = \sum PL_j \cdot L_j)$. Similarly $PK \cdot K$ represents the sum of sectoral capital income. After rearranging the terms we obtain

$$Y^* - Y^0 = PL(L^* - L^0) + (PK - ZK) \cdot K. \tag{19}$$

If there is underutilization in temporary equilibrium, we get $PK > ZK$ and $L^* > L^0$ as $PL/PK < PL/ZK$. The wage rate does not change in our welfare comparison. PL depends on predetermined variables and is not endogenous within one year. $Y^* - Y^0$ is, therefore, positive.

As our demand system is based on an aggregated utility function of the Stone-Geary type, we obtain as expenditure function

$$E(PK_1^k, \dots, PK_n^k, U^*) = C_B^k + U^* \prod_{i=1}^{n} c_i{}^{-c_i} (PX_i^k)^{c_i}, \quad k = 0, *$$

with the value of the indirect utility function, $U^* = (Y^* - C_B^*) \prod_{i=1}^n c_i{}^{c_i} PX_i^{*-c_i}$. γ_i is the minimum required quantity of good j, $C_B^k = \sum_j PX_j^k \gamma_j$ is the subsistence income and c_i is the marginal budget share of good i.

The price-affected disadvantage of the long-run equilibrium is represented as

$$E(PX^0, U^*) - E(PX^*, U^*) = C_B^0 - C_B^* + (Y^* - C_B^*) \cdot \left[\prod_{i=1}^{n} \left(\frac{PX_i^0}{PX_i^*} \right)^{c_i} - 1 \right]. \tag{20}$$

Since the price level in long-run equilibrium is higher than PX^0 because $PK > ZK$ in the case of underutilization in the temporary equilibrium, the expression in (20) is negative. In contrast to this price-affected disadvantage, there is an income advantage in the long-run equilibrium, which we have already calculated in (19). Rearranging (17) we obtain

$$EV^0 = C_B^0 - C_B^* + (Y^* - C_B^*) \cdot \left[\prod_i \left(\frac{PX_i^0}{PX_i^*} \right)^{c_i} - 1 \right] + PL(L^* - L^0) + (PK - ZK)K.$$

Since we have assumed an underutilization of capacity in the temporary equilibrium, we expect to move towards the production levels of the long-run equilibrium if an income tax reduction is introduced. As we measure the welfare effect only for the year of the tax reduction (1986), we assume that the wage rate remains unchanged and, therefore, the equilibrium solution from (7) and (13) is the same before and after the tax reduction. The picture on the right in Figure 2 shows the new temporary equilibrium under the tax reduction. Instead of Q_j^0, we now have to calculate the smaller area Q_j^1. The welfare gain from an income tax reduction results, therefore, from a reduction of the "triangle" Q_j and from the difference in the equivalent variations. Hence, the welfare gain WG can be calculated as

$$\begin{aligned} WG &= \sum_{j=1}^{n} (Q_j^0 - Q_j^1) + (C_B^0 - C_B^*) + (Y^* - C_B^*) \cdot \left(\prod_{i=1}^{n} \left(\frac{PX_i^0}{PX_i^*} \right)^{c_i} - 1 \right) + \\ &\quad + PL(L^* - L^0) + (PK - ZK^0)K - [C_B^1 - C_B^* + (Y^* - C_B^*) \cdot \\ &\quad \cdot \left(\prod_{i=1}^{n} \left(\frac{PX_i^1}{PX_i^*} \right)^{c_i} - 1 \right) + PL(L^* - L^1) + (PK - ZK^1)K]. \end{aligned}$$

Cancelling out several terms we obtain

$$\begin{aligned} WG &= \sum_{j=1}^{n} (Q_j^0 - Q_j^1) + C_B^0 - C_B^1 + (Y^* - C_B^*) \cdot \left[\prod_{i=1}^{n} \left(\frac{PX_i^0}{PX_i^*} \right)^{c_i} - \right. \\ &\quad \left. - \prod_{i=1}^{n} \left(\frac{PX_i^1}{PX_i^*} \right)^{c_i} \right] + PL(L^1 - L^0) + (ZK^1 - ZK^0)K. \end{aligned}$$

We observe that the price effect turns out to be negative; this represents a deterioration if the economy approaches the long-run equilibrium. The income effect is, however, positive and signals an improvement as $L^1 > L^0$ and $ZK^1 > ZK^0$ because $PL/ZK^1 < PL/ZK^0$ as a result of better capacity utilization ($ZK^1 > ZK^0$).

IV. Empirical Results

A reference framework with 1978 assumed to be the equilibrium base year was set up for the German economy to quantify the welfare effects under tax reductions. Using this equilibrium assumption, it was possible to "estimate" all parameters of the CES and Cobb-Douglas cost functions as well as the factor demand functions (input coefficients) using base year data. The ex post industrial internal rates of return for this year were interpreted as being expected ex ante, and the factors of proportionality to the interest rate on government bonds were considered "normal". We used these factors of proportionality together with the interest rates on government bonds since 1978 to calculate ex ante prices of capital. These prices PK_j play a crucial role in the determination of capacity outputs levels (see (13)). Internal ex post rates of return have been derived endogenously as shadow prices of capital (see (5)); they enter into calculation of the capital coefficients and the investment functions.

In our first simulation we calculated the temporary equilibrium prior to the year 1986. The capital stock was assumed to be quasi-fixed in each year, which means that the capital stock is changed over time by investment, but only on a lagged basis. At the same time, this simulation permits calculation of the long-run equilibrium. The associated equilibrium quantities and prices are based on the hypothetical construction that, given fixed capital stocks, capacity outputs have already been produced, and that equilibrium prices include the ex ante expected rate of return. We then compared the price and quantity system of the temporary equilibrium to that of the long-run equilibrium using some indexes of performance to receive a quantitative impression of the welfare loss in a temporary equilibrium.

In the first column of the following table some of those welfare measures are shown. The welfare loss from lower revenues due to smaller rates of return in a temporary equilibrium with underutilization is labeled V_j^0 in Figure 2. These amount to 321 billion German marks (DM) accrued from all industries. This additional amount of money could have been earned by all industries if in temporary equilibrium the higher prices based on the higher expected rate of return had been charged. This amount is also equal to the lower cost of production due to the lower ex post rate of return accepted in the short run. Therefore, the net effect for total welfare is zero. Next, the sum of differences between producers' surplus in a temporary and a long-run equilibrium summed over all j, that is Q_j^0 in Fig. 2, is 36.6 billion DM if the income tax is unchanged.

The price effect for consumers is negative as expected, and equal to −76.4 billion DM if the higher prices in the long-run equilibrium were to be paid. The

1986 Welfare Effects from a 10 Percent Income Tax Reduction (in Bill. DM)

Advantage (+) or disadvantage (-) of the long-run equilibrium	Income tax unchanged	Income tax reduction of ten percent	Difference[g]
Increase in revenue from higher returns[a] or cost reduction, respectively	321	269.8	51.2
Loss of producer surplus[b]	36.6	31.8	4.8
Price effect[c]	-76.4	-57.1	-19.3
Income effect[c]	252.3	195.4	56.9
Equivalent income variation[d]	157.8	119.9	37.9
Welfare loss of a temporary equilibrium[e]	194.4	151.8	42.6
Capacity utilization $CU = X/X^*$	0.858	0.863	

income effect is positive, as shown in the preceding section, and amounts to 252 billion DM, which is three times as high in absolute terms as the price effect. This signals considerable changes in gross value added if a temporary equilibrium approaches a long-run equilibrium. Hence, the income effect more than compensates for the negative price effect, and the equivalent income variation of 158 billion DM shows a remarkable improvement in welfare for consumers in the case of full capital utilization.

The welfare gain for the total economy from a transition to a full equilibrium can be determined by adding up the welfare gain of the consumers and the changes

[a] $\sum(PX_j^* - PX_j^k)X_j^k$ (see (15)), $k = 0, 1$.

[b] $Q_j^k 0.5(PX_j^* - PX_j^k)(X_j^* - X_j^k)$.

[c] $C_B^0 - C_B^* + (Y^* - C_B^*) \cdot \left[\prod_{j=1}^n \left(\frac{PX_j^0}{PX_j^*}\right)^{c_i} - 1\right]$, (see (20)).

[d] $Y^* - Y^k$. (see (19)).

[e] Sum of c and d.

[f] Sum of b and e.

[g] Realized advantage (+) or disadvantage (−) (1. colum ./. 2. column).

in producers' surplus. This total welfare gain is 194 billion DM. The last row in this table gives the endogenously determined capacity utilization as calculated from weighted sectoral capacity utilizations. These are defined as X_j/X_j^*.

In a second simulation run identical to the first run for the years 1978–1985, we have introduced an income tax cut of 10 percent. At the same time government expenditure has been reduced so that goverment budget deficits in the first and second run are the same. Hence, effects from the income tax reduction on the economy will be partly offset by the government budget consolidation policy. In order to achieve the unchanged budget deficit, aggregate government consumption C_G has been lowered by the difference between the base-run deficit and the lower-tax-run deficit. The contributions of the 45 industries to the components of C_G are, therefore, reduced by a certain percentage. On the other hand, consumers' disposable income and, therefore, aggregate private consumption increases after the tax cut. This, in turn, has a growth effect on the contributions of the 45 industries to the components of private consumption.

We expect that the redistribution of final demand from government consumption to private consumption will not only cause structural effects, but it will also have an expansive impact.[7] In this case, the actual production level X^1 should approach the optimal level X^*, and the actual price level PY^1 should move towards the optimal price level PY^*. Hence, all measures which capture the deviation of the new temporary equilibrium under the tax cut from the long-run equilibrium should be smaller in absolute terms.

Column 2 of our table shows the effects of an income tax cut accompanied by a simultaneous consolidation of the government budget. Effects are as expected and the quantitative relation of the figures remain approximately the same. Column 3 expresses the change between welfare in the first run (without an income tax cut) to the second run (with an income tax cut of ten percent) as the difference between the first two columns. The rate of change between run one and run two varies from negative ten percent to negative thirty percent, depending on the welfare measure used. We observe that the gain in welfare of 42.6 billion DM from the income tax reduction results mainly from an improvement of consumers' well-being (about 90 percent); only 10 percent of the welfare gain can be attributed to the reduction

[7] As there is a joint reduction in taxes and government consumption, one would a priori expect a contractive Haavelmo effect. However, higher private savings after the tax cut will ex post show up as higher investment. As our model has no submodel for the monetary sector, we modelled a decline in the rate r on government bonds by multiplying this rate r by (I/S) in the formula for user cost of capital $PK = PI(r(I/S) + \delta)$. If, due to a tax cut, $I < S$, then the interest rate $r(I/S)$ will drop and the lower user cost of capital stimulates investment. The model iterates until $I = S$.

of the loss in producers' surplus.[8] In addition to this 5 billion DM reduction in dead weight loss, our table also shows a reduction of non-realized revenues by 51.2 billion DM. This reduction is compensated, however, by an increase in costs by the same amount. Along with this transaction comes a redistribution in terms of higher revenues along with increasing capital income. Finally, we observed a small improvement of capacity utilization from 0.858 to 0.863.

We conclude, therefore, that a ten percent income tax cut will have positive welfare effects in spite of a consolidation of the government budget (by an amount smaller than the tax cut). These positive effects result mainly from an improvement of consumers' well-being via raised income levels before and after tax. But producers also improve their performance; producers' surplus increases and the costs of being away from the long-run equilibrium, measured in terms of losses in producers' surplus, become smaller. Opportunity costs from underutilization of the existing capital stock shrink.

References

Ahlheim, M., and **Rose, M.** (1984): "Alte und neue Maße in der Lehre von den Steuerlasten." *Finanzarchiv* 42: 274–349.

Berndt, E. R., and **Fuss, M. A.** (1986): "Productivity Measurement with Adjustments for Variations in Capacity Utilization and Other Forms of Temporary Equilibria." *Journal of Econometrics* 33: 7–29.

Berndt, E. R., and **Hesse, D. M.** (1986): "Energy Price Increases, Capacity Utilization, and Productivity Growth in the Manufacturing Sectors of OECD Countries." *European Economic Review* 30: 961–989.

Conrad, K. (1982): "Die Anpassung der Volkswirtschaft beim Übergang zu neuen Energieversorgungssystemen: Die theoretischen Grundlagen eines Energiemodells für die Bundesrepublik Deutschland." In *Reaktionen auf Energiepreissteigerungen*, edited by Horst Siebert. (Staatliche Allokationspolitik im marktwirtschaftlichen System 6.) Frankfurt etc.: Lang, pp. 1–37.

Conrad, K., and **Henseler-Unger, I.** (1984a): "Die internationale Wettbewerbsfähigkeit der Bundesrepublik mit und ohne Kernkraftwerke: eine dynamische Input-Output-Studie." In *Quantitative Ansätze zur Modellierung des Energiesektors*, edited by Horst Siebert. Tübingen: Mohr, pp. 87–119.

[8] For an evaluation of the size of the welfare gain it is important to note that government consumption as component of final demand does not enter into our measures of welfare gain. It enters indirectly via the creation of jobs and income. There is no utility function which measures the welfare aspect of highways, museums or military expenditure.

Conrad, K., and **Henseler-Unger, I.** (1984b): "Der Einfluß alternativer Technologien in der Elektrizitätswirtschaft auf sektorale Preisstrukturen und langfristige Allokation der Produktionsfaktoren." In *Intertemporale Allokation*, edited by Horst Siebert. (Staatliche Allokationspolitik im marktwirtschaftlichen System 10.) Frankfurt etc.: Lang, pp. 551–579.

Conrad, K., and **Henseler-Unger, I.** (1986): "Applied General Equilibrium Modelling for Longterm Energy Policy in the Fed. Rep. of Germany." *Journal of Policy Modelling* 8: 531–549.

Fullerton, D.; **King, A. T.**; **Shoven, J. B.**; and **Whalley, J.** (1981): "Corporate Tax Integration in the United States: A General Equilibrium Approach." *American Economic Review* 71: 677–691.

Fullerton, D.; **Shoven, J. B.**; and **Whalley, J.** (1983): "Replacing the U. S. Income Tax with a Progressive consumption Tax." *Journal of Public Economics* 20: 3–23.

Ginsburgh, V. A., and **Waelbroeck, J. L.** (1981): *Activity Analysis and General Equilibrium Modelling.* Amsterdam etc.: North-Holland.

Harris, R. (1985): "Applied General Equilibrium Analysis of Small Open Economies with Scale Economies and Imperfect Competition." *American Economic Review* 74: 1016–1032.

Henseler-Unger, I. (1985): *Ein dynamisches Modell des allgemeinen Gleichgewichts als Energiemodell für die Bundesrepublik Deutschland.* Frankfurt etc.: Lang.

Morrison, C. (1986): "Productivity Measurement with Nonstatic Expectations and Varying Capacity Utilization: An Integrated Approach." *Journal of Econometrics* 33: 51–74.

Shoven, J. B., and **Whalley, J.** (1972): "A General Equilibrium Calculation of the Effect of Differential Taxation of Income from Capital in the U. S." *Journal of Public Economics* 1: 281–321.

Shoven, J. B., and **Whalley, J.** (1973): "General Equilibrium with Taxes: A Computational Procedure and an Existence Proof." *Review of Economic Studies* 60: 475–490.

Whalley, J. (1975): "A General Equilibrium Assessment of the 1973 United Kingdom Tax Reform." *Economica* 42: 139–161.

On the Evaluation of Tax Systems

Udo Ebert, Bonn, West Germany*

I. Introduction

This paper is concerned with the excess burden from taxation. A simple definition of this concept is given by Auerbach in his recent survey: 'The deadweight loss from a tax system is that amount that is lost in excess of what government collects' (Auerbach, 1986, p. 67). At the same time he states 'Unfortunately, while this definition makes intuitive sense, it is too vague to permit a *single* interpretation' (emphasis added). Therefore there are many different definitions of excess burden in the literature (e.g. Mohring, 1971; Diamond and McFadden, 1974; Kay, 1980; Pazner and Sadka, 1980; Zabalza, 1982). But a more careful investigation shows that essentially one can find only two types of measures.

One measure is based on the Hicksian compensating variation, the other one on the equivalent variation. Diamond and McFadden define the excess burden as the 'loss or excess of income we must give a consumer to restore him to his pretax indifference curve over the tax revenue collected from him' (Diamond and McFadden, 1974, p. 11). This definition is based on the pretax situation and leads to a formula which uses the compensating variation. A similar one is proposed by Zabalza (1982) as well. On the other hand Kay's excess burden gives an 'answer to the question how much more would the taxed consumer be willing to pay in a lump sum rather than as commodity taxes?' (Kay, 1980, p. 115). The suggestion lays emphasis on the post-tax situation and implicitly employs the equivalent variation. This proposal can also be found in Mohring (1971), Pazner and Sadka (1980), and Zabalza (1982). In all these papers the concept of excess burden is mostly treated verbally, by means of formal expressions, and/or by means of diagrams. Thus it is not always easy to see which properties the excess burden possesses.

It is the aim of this paper to derive measures of excess burden by a simple axiomatic approach. The investigation is based on the fact that we are not interested in the entire welfare change of the consumer but rather in the change in excess of revenue collected. Thus in a first step we have to evaluate the tax paid

* I thank Michael Ahlheim, participants of the Klosterseminar at Neresheim, and an anonymous referee for most valuable comments.

by the consumer *and* the change of his welfare implied by the imposition of a tax. Afterwards both evaluations have to be combined in order to measure the excess burden. Thus we employ two concepts: one is the measure of welfare change, the other is the amount of tax paid. It will be shown that some few axioms suffice to characterize a measure of excess burden uniquely. It turns out that the only measure which satisfies the axioms proposed is (a generalization of) Kay's excess burden.

In the second part of the paper the results are generalized to the multi-consumer case. It is well known that there are difficulties in measuring the excess burden in this case (cf. Auerbach, 1986, p. 79). Here it is assumed that a social welfare function is given which allows to evaluate the welfare changes. We use the concept of the 'constrained social expenditure function' introduced by Pollak (1981). Measuring welfare changes we suppose that the income distribution remains constant either in a 'relative' or in an 'absolute' sense. This leads to two forms of the excess burden which can be considered as generalizations of Kay's measure to the many consumers case. The analysis demonstrates that the difficulties discussed by Auerbach can be surmounted.

Furthermore the axiomatic approach leads implicitly to the conclusion that Diamond and McFadden's excess burden which is based on the compensating variation is not a sensible measure of excess burden. It does not satisfy the properties proposed below; particularly one can easily see that it is not consistent with the optimal taxation problem; i.e. minimizing Diamond and McFadden's excess burden does not imply the same result as maximizing the individual's utility. In the meantime this result is well-known in the literature (cf. Kay, 1980; Pazner and Sadka, 1980); but the axiomatic approach reveals it automatically.

II. Model

There are n commodities. A vector $x = (x_1, \ldots, x_n) \in \mathbb{R}^n$ denotes a commodity bundle. Positive components x_i belong to goods demanded by the consumer, negative components x_i mean that these quantities are supplied. Let $p = (p_1, \ldots, p_n) \in \mathbb{R}^n_{++}$ be the vector of producer prices which are supposed to be constant; i.e., the production possibility frontier is assumed to be linear. This assumption implies that the producer prices are not changed by taxation. The price system p prevails if no tax is implemented. $q \in \mathbb{R}^n_+$ denotes an arbitrary price system.

At first we consider one consumer. He or she possesses a preference ordering $\succeq$ on the set $\mathbb{R}^n$ of all commodity bundles. This ordering is represented by the direct utility function U, the indirect utility function V, and the expenditure function E. It is assumed that $\succeq$, U, V, and E have the usual properties (cf. e.g. Blackorby, Primont, and Russell, 1978). Moreover the consumer gets an exogenous income $m > 0$ which is not affected by taxation and which is fully spent on consumption. Let $x(q,m) = (x_1(q,m), \ldots, x_n(q,m))$ denote the ordinary and $x^c(q,u) = (x_1^c(q,u), \ldots, x_n^c(q,u))$ the compensated demand (supply) functions.

A tax system (t,T) is described by a vector $(t_1, \ldots, t_n, T) \in \mathbb{R}^{n+1}$ consisting of the commoditay taxes $t = (t_1, \ldots, t_n)$ and the lump sum tax T. The tax system leads to post-tax prices $p + t$ and post-tax income $m - T$. If commodity i is a good (factor) which is demanded (supplied) a positive sign of t_i means that this commodity is burdened (subsidized) by taxation. If the sign of t_i is negative the opposite holds.

Measuring the excess burden which is associated with the tax system (t,T) we have to compare the utility (or welfare) level of the consumer in the no-tax situation S_0 (when he or she faces the price system p) and in the post-tax situation $S(t,T)$ when prices $p+t$ prevail and a lump sum tax T is raised. Moreover we have to take into account the tax payments in situation $S(t,T)$. We denote the welfare change by $I(t,T)$. Its sign reflects the kind of change. If $I(t,T)$ is positive the consumer is better off, if it is negative utility decreases, and if it equals zero utility is unchanged. All three cases can occur since any sign of the lump sum tax T and of the taxes t_i is allowed as long as $p+t > 0$ and $m-T > 0$. It should be emphasized that actually $I(t,T)$ compares *two* situations, namely the no-tax situation S_0, characterized by producer prices p and *no* taxation, and the new situation $S(t,T)$, characterized by the tax vector t and the lump sum tax T. Since the situation S_0 is *always* kept fixed in the following we use the notation $I(t,T)$ instead of the more clear, but also more cumbersome notation $I(S_0, S(t,T))$. Let $R(t,T)$ be the amount of taxes paid by the consumer.[1] A detailed definition (characterization) of $I(t,T)$ and $R(t,T)$ will be given later. In the moment it is supposed that $I(t,T)$ and $R(t,T)$ are continuous functions of (t,T) and are determined somehow. They can take every real value.

Now we introduce the concept of excess burden EB. It must be a continuous function of the welfare change I and the tax revenue R, namely $EB(I,R) = g(I,R)$. To be more precise, we assume that the function g is defined on a connected subset Σ of $\mathbb{R}^2$. In the next section we obtain explicit expressions for EB

[1] The same remark applies here: $R(t,T)$ is an abbreviation of $R(S_0, S(t,T))$.

by postulating some reasonable properties and deriving their consequences for the form of EB.[2]

We list the two kinds of excess burden which were discussed in the introduction since they will be referenced later on. The definitions given here are slightly broadened in order to include the lump sum tax.

Diamond and McFadden, and Zabalza propose[3]

$$\begin{aligned} EB_C(t,T) &:= E(p+t,u_0) - E(p,u_0) - tx^c(p+t,u_0) \\ &= -CV(S_0,S(t,T)) - tx^c(p+t,u_0) - T \end{aligned} \tag{1}$$

where u_0 is the consumer's utility level in the pre-tax situation and $CV(S_0, S(t,T))$ denotes the compensating variation. Mohring, Kay, Pazner and Sadka, and Zabalza suggest an excess burden based on the equivalent variation EV:

$$\begin{aligned} EB_E(t,T) &:= E(p+t,u(t,T)) - E(p,u(t,T)) - tx^c(p+t,u(t,T)) \\ &= -EV(S_0,S(t,T)) - tx^c(p+t,u(t,T)) - T \end{aligned} \tag{2}$$

where $u(t,T)$ is the utility level in the post-tax situation $S(t,T)$. In a certain way both definitions are symmetric. (1) lays emphasis on the status quo, the pre-tax situation, (2) emphasizes the post-tax situation.

III. Concept of Excess Burden

In this section the concept of excess burden is discussed on condition that the welfare change I implied by the tax and the revenue R ensuing from the tax are known. The way these latter measures may depend on the tax system is treated in the next sections. But it is assumed that I and R are comparable, i.e. that the welfare change and the tax revenue are measured by the same measuring rod. For the moment we are only interested in the size of I and R; therefore the reference to the corresponding (t,T) is dropped. This simplification allows to take Auerbachs definition as a basis for the following considerations. For the moment the excess burden is *completely* determined by the welfare change and the tax

[2] Actually one has to distinguish between the concept of excess burden which is based on the *function* $g(I,R)$, the *measure* of welfare change $I(t,T)$, and the *definition* of tax revenue $R(t,T)$, on the one hand, and the function $g(I,R)$, which is defined for given *values* I and R, on the other hand.

[3] $EB(t,T)$ denotes the excess burden implied by the tax system (t,T). Here again the status quo S_0 is not referenced explicitly in order to simplify notation.

revenue. Furthermore it plays no role whether we consider a single consumer or many consumer economy.

The most important property of a measure of excess burden is its consistency, i.e. its relationship to the welfare change. Given a fixed amount of tax revenue R the size of the excess burden $EB(I,R)$ must reflect the change of the consumer's utility level or the consumers' welfare level. The greater the welfare loss, the greater should be the excess burden. This postulate is expressed by

Property EC (Consistency)

$$\forall\ (\overline{I},R),(\overline{\overline{I}},R)\in\Sigma:\ EB(\overline{I},R)<EB(\overline{\overline{I}},R)\iff\overline{I}>\overline{\overline{I}}.$$

Interpreting this property one has to remember the meaning of the sign of the welfare measure. If for example both $\overline{I}$ and $\overline{\overline{I}}$ are negative, i.e., if they indicate a loss of welfare, $\overline{I}>\overline{\overline{I}}$ means that the loss $|\overline{\overline{I}}|$ (in absolute terms) is greater than the loss $|\overline{I}|$. If property EC is satisfied and if the welfare measure I is *properly* chosen it makes no difference for optimal taxation whether one maximizes the utility (welfare) function or minimizes the excess burden in order to collect an a priori fixed revenue.

Of course we are able to postulate an analogous property EM.

Property EM (Monotonicity)

$$\forall\ (I,\overline{R}),(I,\overline{\overline{R}})\in\Sigma:\ EB(I,\overline{R})<EB(I,\overline{\overline{R}})\iff\overline{R}>\overline{\overline{R}}.$$

Consistency EC is concerned with the case in which the tax revenue is constant and distinct welfare changes have to be compared. Property EM deals with a fixed welfare change and distinct tax revenues. Monotonicity requires that the excess burden is the smaller, the more revenue is collected.

In a certain sense both properties discussed until now imply that the excess burden $EB(I,R)$ is monotone with respect to I and R. Of course, the properties EC and EM are sufficient as long as one compares only tax systems which either lead to the same revenue or to the same welfare change. The excess burden increases if in the first case the corresponding welfare loss increases or if in the second case the tax revenue decreases. But suppose that a tax system is given and that the government wants to raise more or less revenue by means of a *new* tax system then in general different welfare losses and different tax revenues are implied if we take the no tax situation as common status quo. Now the question arises how e.g. a simultaneous *increase* of the welfare loss and the tax revenue should be reflected by EB.

The next property corresponds to the idea that the excess burden measures the gain or loss occurred to the consumer(s) in *excess* of revenue collected.

Property ET (Trade off)

$$\forall\ (I,R) \in \Sigma,\ \ \alpha \in \mathbb{R}^1:\ \ EB(I,R) = EB(I-\alpha, R+\alpha).$$

This property is concerned with the trade off between the welfare change and the tax revenue. Suppose one wants to calculate the excess burden from two different tax systems, one leading to the welfare change I and tax revenue R and one leading to $I-\alpha$ and $R+\alpha$. (Here one has to remember the fact that I and R $[I-\alpha$ and $R+\alpha]$ are *comparable*.) Since the welfare loss changes by an amount α and since the revenue collected changes by the same amount α, the excess burden should be the same for both tax systems. In this case the additional welfare loss α is traded off against the additional revenue α. Thus the (net) deadweight loss remains constant. Auerbach's definition of excess burden cited above is reflected by Property ET.

It is easy to see the consequences of these properties. We have

Proposition 1
EB satisfies the properties EC [EM] and ET if and only if there exists a continuous strictly decreasing function such that

$$EB(I,R) = f(I+R).$$

Proof
Choose $\alpha := I$ and apply ET. The monotonicity of f is implied by EC [EM].

□

Obviously one of the properties EC and EM and property ET suffice to derive the above structure of EB. The excess burden is additively separable in I and R.

Finally one has to determine the function f. The following rule suggests itself.

Property EN (Normalization)

$$\forall\ (I,0) \in \Sigma:\ \ EB(I,0) = -I.$$

If a tax system distorts the prices p and/or levies a lump sum, but if it yields no (net) revenue only the welfare level of the consumer(s) is changed. Then the excess burden should be equal to the welfare change (and the sign of I has to be corrected according to the definition of EB). Property EN provides a rule for the normalization of the excess burden EB.

Now we are in a position to present an axiomatization of the general concept of excess burden. We obtain

Theorem 2
The excess burden EB satisfies the properties EC [EM], ET, EN[4] if and only if

$$EB(I,R) = -I - R. \tag{3}$$

It should be emphasized again that the sign of I reflects the kind of welfare change; e.g. I is positive if welfare increases, i.e. if the individual(s) is (are) better off. Theorem 2 provides a definition of excess burden. Investigating EB_E and EB_C one easily realizes that both excess burdens possess the form (3). On the basis of theorem 2 special measures of deadweight loss can be derived by specifying definite welfare measures and concrete formulae for the tax revenue. This will be done in the following sections.

IV. One Consumer

At first we consider a single consumer. We have to propose a sensible measure of welfare change $I(t,T)$ and an expression for $R(t,T)$.

The derivation of the welfare measure is the more difficult part. It is very important that the measure reflects the change in the consumer's utility.[5] Therefore we require

Property UR (Ranking)

$$\forall\ (\bar{t},\overline{T}),(\bar{\bar{t}},\overline{\overline{T}}) \in \Sigma :\ I(\bar{t},\overline{T}) \leq I(\bar{\bar{t}},\overline{\overline{T}}) \iff u(\bar{t},\overline{T}) \leq u(\bar{\bar{t}},\overline{\overline{T}}).$$

If a welfare measure $I(t,T)$ possesses property UR it is possible to compare the utility implied by the two tax systems $(\bar{t},\overline{T})$ and $(\bar{\bar{t}},\overline{\overline{T}})$. The magnitude of $I(t,T)$ allows to *rank* the tax systems. The greater welfare change uniquely corresponds

[4] The properties EC [EM], ET, and EN are not independent. ET and EN imply EC [EM] since property ET yields $EB(I,R) = EB(I+R,0)$ and property EN already implies $EB(I+R,0) = -(I+R)$. I owe this insight to the unknown referee.

[5] For an axiomatization of more general measures see Ebert (1984) and Ebert (1987b, chapter 2).

with the higher level of utility. The reader may be reminded that the welfare measure $I(t,T)$ evaluates the (welfare) difference between the status quo S_0 *and* the new situation $S(t,T)$ in which the individual faces the prices $p+t$ and has to pay the lump sum tax T. Since the status quo is the same for all comparisons it is not referred to explicitly.

In a next step one has to find the measuring stick which determines the scale of $I(t,T)$. Two different axioms suggest themselves, both dealing with specific tax systems. Of course a normalization rule is necessary since we have to express the welfare change in monetary units. (Remember property ET. I and R have to be comparable). The first rule is the following.

Property UN (Normalization)

$I(t,0) = \frac{m}{1+\lambda} - m \qquad \forall\, t = \lambda p,\ \lambda > -1.$

Here we consider tax systems having the special form $t = \lambda p$ and $T = 0$. The vector of taxes t is a multiple of the vector of producer prices p which belong to the status quo S_0. Since there is no lump sum tax it follows that the introduction of such a tax system is equivalent to the multiplication of all prices by the factor $(1+\lambda)$. In this case the welfare change $I(t,0)$ can be described by a corresponding change of the exogenous income m. (This income is not affected by taxation!) The commodity taxes t can be replaced by a tax on the exogenous income m. Facing the prices $(1+\lambda)p$ and having the income m the consumer is as well off as facing the prices p and having the income $\frac{m}{1+\lambda}$. Thus we get the welfare change $I(t,0)$ as the difference between the 'after tax' income $\frac{m}{1+\lambda}$ and the before-tax income m:

$$I(t,0) = \frac{m}{1+\lambda} - m = -\frac{\lambda}{1+\lambda}m.$$

If for example $\lambda = 1$, i.e. if prices double this change is equivalent to loosing half of the income m. Therefore this rule is plausible.

Another simple tax system is one which levies only a lump sum tax on the consumer. We formulate

Property UNL (Normalization for lump sum tax)

$I(0,T) = -T \qquad \forall\, T \in \mathbb{R}_1,\ m - T > 0.$

It is obvious that the consumer's welfare loss equals T if he or she has to pay a lump sum tax T and if all prices remain constant. Thus property UNL is a sensible requirement. Moreover it turns out that both normalization rules are equivalent.

Proposition 3: Assume UR.
A welfare measure $I(t,T)$ satisfies UN if and only if it satisfies UNL.

Proof
Consider the following equations which hold since the indirect utility function is homogeneous of degree zero.

$$V(p+\lambda p, m) = V\left(p, \frac{m}{1+\lambda}\right) = V\left(p, m - \frac{\lambda}{1+\lambda}m\right).$$

Because of UR the welfare measure $I(t,T)$ does not depend on the tax system (t,T) directly, but only on the utility level $u(t,T)$ (cf. Ebert, 1984, Lemma 1), i.e. the following equivalence holds

$$I(\bar{t},\bar{T}) = I(\bar{\bar{t}},\bar{\bar{T}}) \iff u(\bar{t},\bar{T}) = u(\bar{\bar{t}},\bar{\bar{T}}). \tag{4}$$

Therefore we have

$$I(\lambda p, 0) = I\left(0, \frac{\lambda}{1+\lambda}m\right).$$

From this the above assertion follows immediately.

□

The properties UR and UN [UNL] already suffice to determine the welfare measure $I(t,T)$ exactly.

Proposition 4
$I(t,T)$ satisfies UR and UN if and only if it is equal to the equivalent variation:[6]

$$\begin{aligned} I(t,T) &= EV(S_0, S(t,T)) \\ &= E(p,u(t,T)) - E(p+t,u(t,T)) - T. \end{aligned}$$

Proof
Assume UR and UN and choose any arbitrary tax system (t,T). We define

$$m(t,T) := E(p, V(p+t, m-T)) = E(p, u(t,T)).$$

$m(t,T)$ is the minimum amount of income which allows the consumer to attain the utility level $u(t,T)$ if prices p prevail. Thus it follows from the definition of the expenditure function and the homogeneity of the indirect utility function that

$$V(p+t, m-T) = V(p, m(t,T)) = V\left(\frac{m}{m(t,T)}p, m\right).$$

[6] Compare proposition 2 in Ebert (1984). That result is given for welfare measures in a world without taxation.

Therefore we have

$$u(t,T) = u\left(\left(\frac{m}{m(t,T)} - 1\right)p, 0\right).$$

Using the equivalence (4) and property UN we obtain

$$I(t,T) = I\left(\left(\frac{m}{m(t,T)} - 1\right)p, 0\right) = m(t,T) - m$$

and

$$\begin{aligned} I(t,T) &= E(p, u(t,T)) - E(p, u_0) \\ &= E(p, u(t,T)) - E(p+t, u(t,T)) - T \end{aligned}$$

since $E(p+t, u(t,T)) = E(p, u_0) - T$.

The converse is obvious.

□

Proposition 4 once more gives support to the experience that generally two properties are sufficient to characterize a welfare measure for a single consumer uniquely (cf. Ebert, 1984, 1985b). All one needs is a property which specifies the ranking of two situations with respect to a common status quo and a property which provides a normalization. Furthermore in the light of proposition 3 it does not matter whether one chooses property UN or Property UNL as normalization rule. It should be stressed that choosing a normalization different from UN and UNL does in general not imply the equivalent variation if it is combined with the ranking property UR. But the resulting welfare measure is ordinally equivalent to the equivalent variation as long as we evaluate all welfare changes with respect to a common status quo.

Finally we have to define $R(t,T)$. Since the welfare measure $I(t,T)$ coincides with the equivalent variation and since the EV evaluates the changes by means of the price system p it suggests itself to use the *same* measuring stick for the tax revenue. In real terms the tax revenue can be expressed by the difference between the pre-tax commodity bundle $x(p,m)$ and the post-tax bundle $x(p+t, m-T)$. Evaluating this difference by the price system p yields

$$\begin{aligned} p(x(p,m) - x(p+t, m-T)) &= m - px(p+t, m-T) \\ &= tx(p+t, m-T) + T \end{aligned}$$

since $(p+t)x(p+t, m-T) = m - T$.

Therefore we choose

Definition RT (Tax revenue)

$R(t,T) = p(x(p,m) - x(p+t, m-T)).$

The results derived above can be combined. We summarize

Theorem 5
The excess burden EB, the welfare measure I, and the tax revenue R satisfy EC [EM], ET, EN, UR, UN [UNL], and RT if and only if

$$\begin{aligned} EB(I(t,T), R(t,T)) &= -I(t,T) - R(t,T) \\ &= -EV(S_0, S(t,T)) - tx^c(p+t, u(t,T)) - T. \end{aligned}$$

This theorem[7] presents an axiomatization of the excess burden EB_E which coincides with Kay's definition if no lump sum tax is introduced. Insofar it is a generalization of Kay's excess burden. Theorem 5 reveals a set of important properties which are fulfilled by EB_E and which determine it uniquely.

Our derivation demonstrates that EB_E is based on the equivalent variation and that the properties EC and UR are satisfied (cf. Pazner and Sadka, 1980, and Auerbach, 1986, for a discussion of the properties of EB_E). Combining these properties we obtain the following equivalences:

$$\forall\ (\bar{t}, \overline{T}), (\bar{\bar{t}}, \overline{\overline{T}}) \in \Sigma \text{ such that } R(\bar{t}, \overline{T}) = R(\bar{\bar{t}}, \overline{\overline{T}}):$$

$$EB_E(\bar{t}, \overline{T}) < EB_E(\bar{\bar{t}}, \overline{\overline{T}}) \iff I(\bar{t}, \overline{T}) > I(\bar{\bar{t}}, \overline{\overline{T}}) \iff u(\bar{t}, \overline{T}) > u(\bar{\bar{t}}, \overline{\overline{T}}).$$

That means that one can either minimize $EB_E(t,T)$ or maximize $u(t,T)$ if one intends to collect a fixed revenue $R(t,T) = \overline{R}$; the excess burden is really consistent with the optimal taxation problem. It should be obvious that this statement is wrong for an excess burden based on the compensating variation (like EB_C, proposed by Diamond and McFadden) since the compensating variation does *not*[8] satisfy UR (cf. e.g. Ebert, 1984). But it took some years to discover this property of EB_C (Kay, 1980; Pazner and Sadka, 1980; and Pauwels, 1984). Employing an axiomatic approach one realizes from the beginning that a consistent excess burden must be based on an equivalent variation. This result demonstrates the merits of this kind of proceeding.

---

[7] Cf. footnote 4.

[8] Of course the compensating variation satisfies UR for *specific* types of preferences (cf. Chipman and Moore, 1980).

V. Many Consumers

One has to extend the notation introduced in section II to this case. We assume that there are $k > 1$ individuals. In the following all symbols possessing a superscript i $(1 \leq i \leq k)$ denote the respective function which belongs to individual i. Furthermore we suppose that a social welfare function W is given which indicates a decision maker's attitude towards the social welfare of society.[9] This function $W = W(U^1, \ldots, U^k)$ is to be continuous, individualistic, i.e. based on the individuals' utilities U^i, concave, and strictly increasing in U^i. (t, T) denotes a tax system again. The lump sum tax T is levied on each individual.

Pollak (1981) proposed the concept of a constrained social expenditure function. It denotes the minimum amount of money which is necessary to attain a level $\overline{w}$ of social welfare if prices q prevail *and* if a given constraint on the distribution of incomes is satisfied. We consider two specific constraints. The first one requires that the income distribution remains constant in relative terms, i.e. all incomes can be changed only in the same proportion:

$$E_w^r(q, \overline{w}; m^1, \ldots, m^k) := \min_{\substack{\rho \in \mathbb{R}_+^1 \\ W(V^1(q,\rho m^1),\ldots,V^k(q,\rho m^k)) \geq \overline{w}}} \sum_{i=1}^{k} \rho m^i.$$

Therefore each individual's share of total income $\rho m^i / \sum_{j=1}^k \rho m^j$ remains the same. Moreover calculating E_w^r one keeps the proportion of two incomes m^i and m^j constant.

In the second case all incomes are allowed to be changed by the same amount. Here the income distribution is not altered in an absolute sense. The difference between two incomes m^i and m^j remains constant. We define[10]

$$E_w^a(q, \overline{w}; m^1, \ldots, m^k) := \min_{\substack{\alpha \in \mathbb{R}^1 \\ W(V^1(q,m^1+\alpha),\ldots,V^k(q,m^k+\alpha)) \geq \overline{w}}} \sum_{i=1}^{k} m^i + k \cdot \alpha.$$

Both constrained social expenditure functions play an important role below.

As already discussed in section III the properties EC, ET, and EN do not depend on the number of individuals. Therefore we postulate them for a definition

---

[9] Instead of employing a social welfare function it is also possible to use the (weighted) sum of the individual equivalent variations (cf. Ebert, 1987a, 1986). The relationship between the sum of Hicksian measures and Debreu's coefficient of resource utilization is investigated in Ebert (1985a).

[10] In the following it is always assumed that E_w^a is correctly defined, i.e. $m^i + \alpha > 0$ for all $i = 1, \ldots, k$.

of the excess burden EB in this section as well. But we have to change, or to be more precise, we have to adapt the properties UR, UN [UNL], and RT.

We begin with UR which is easily translated to

Property WR (Ranking)

$\forall\ (\bar{t},\overline{T}), (\bar{\bar{t}},\overline{\overline{T}}) \in \Sigma:\ I(\bar{t},\overline{T}) \leq I(\bar{\bar{t}},\overline{\overline{T}}) \iff w(\bar{t},\overline{T}) \leq w(\bar{\bar{t}},\overline{\overline{T}})$
where $w(t,T) = W(u^1(t,T),\ldots,u^k(t,T))$.

That means that the individual utility function U in UR is replaced by the social welfare function W. WR requires that the magnitude of a welfare change is perfectly correlated with the associated level of social welfare.

As in the single consumer's case we consider two special tax systems in order to determine the scale of the measure of welfare change $I(t,T)$. It suggests itself to sum up the individual evaluations.

Property WN (Normalization)

$$I(t,0) = \sum_{i=1}^{k} \left(\frac{m^i}{1+\lambda} - m^i\right) \qquad \forall\, t = \lambda p,\ \lambda > -1.$$

Property WNL (Normalization for lump sum tax)

$$I(0,T) = -k \cdot T \qquad \forall\, T \in \mathbb{R}_1,\ min_{i=1,\ldots,k} \quad (m^i - T) > 0.$$

Since the interpretation of WN and WNL is analogous to that of UN and UNL it is not repeated here.

But there is one important contrast to the above analysis. A connection between WN and WNL which is analogous to the assertion of proposition 3 does in general *not* exist. It can be proved only if all incomes m^i $(i = 1,\ldots,k)$ are equal.[11] Here we come to the core of our problem. A welfare measure (and of course also a measure of excess burden) for *many* consumers requires that we keep the income distribution constant somehow (cf. Auerbach, 1986). Otherwise we are confronted with an additional redistribution of income. This idea is reflected by the properties WN and WNL. Here the income distribution remains constant in relative terms (Property WN) and in absolute terms (Property WNL), respectively. Therefore we get *distinct* welfare measures (measures of excess burden) if we require WN and WNL, respectively.

We obtain

[11] An analogous proposition can also be proved if distinct lump sum taxes T_i are allowed for all individuals and if the income distribution is kept fixed in relative terms, i.e. if $m^i - T^i = m^i/(1+\lambda)$. I owe this comment to Michael Ahlheim.

Proposition 6

a) $I(t,T)$ satifies the properties WR and WN if and only if

$$\begin{aligned} I(t,T) &= E^r_w(p,w(t,T);m^1,\dots,m^k) - \sum_{i=1}^k m^i \\ &= E^r_w(p,w(t,T);m^1,\dots,m^k) - E^r_w(p,w_0;m^1,\dots,m^k) \\ &\qquad =: EV^r(S_0,S(t,T)) \end{aligned}$$

where $w_0 = W(u_0^1,\dots,u_0^k)$.

b) $I(t,T)$ satisfies the properties WR and WNL if and only if

$$\begin{aligned} I(t,T) &= E^a_w(p,w(t,T);m^1,\dots,m^k) - \sum_{i=1}^k m^i \\ &= E^a_w(p,w(t,T);m^1,\dots,m^k) - E^a_w(p,w_0;m^1,\dots,m^k) \\ &\qquad =: EV^a(S_0,S(t,T)). \end{aligned}$$

Obviously proposition 6 presents a characterization of two types of 'social equivalent variation'. EV^r [EV^a] evaluates the welfare change between situation S_0 and situation $S(t,T)$ by the additional amount of income which is necessary to attain the welfare level $w(t,T)$ if all incomes are changed simultaneously in the same proportion [by the same lump sum]. Therefore these measures are direct generalizations of the ordinary equivalent variation to the multi-consumer case.

The proof of proposition 6 runs along similar lines as the proof of proposition 4.

Proof

a) Assume WR and WN. Because of WR we get

$$I(\bar{t},\overline{T}) = I(\bar{\bar{t}},\overline{\overline{T}}) \iff w(\bar{t},\overline{T}) = w(\bar{\bar{t}},\overline{\overline{T}}), \tag{5}$$

i.e. $I(t,T)$ depends only on the *level* of social welfare.

For every (t,T) we define

$$\mu(t,T) := \frac{E^r_w(p,w(t,T);m^1,\dots,m^k)}{\sum_{i=1}^k m^i}.$$

Using $\mu(t,T)$ we have

$$\begin{aligned} w(t,T) &= W(V^1(p+t,m^1-T),\dots,V^k(p+t,m^k-T)) \\ &= W(V^1(p,\mu(t,T)m^1),\dots,V^k(p,\mu(t,T)m^k)) \\ &= W\left(V^1\left(\frac{p}{\mu(t,T)},m^1\right),\dots,V^k\left(\frac{p}{\mu(t,T)},m^k\right)\right). \end{aligned}$$

Equation (5) and property WN imply

$$\begin{aligned} I(t,T) &= I\left(\left(\frac{1}{\mu(t,T)}-1\right)p,0\right) \\ &= \sum_{i=1}^{k}\mu(t,T)m^i - \sum_{i=1}^{k} m^i \\ &= E_w^r(p,w(t,T);m^1,\ldots,m^k) - E_w^r(p,w_0;m^1,\ldots,m^k). \end{aligned}$$

The converse is obvious again.

b) Here one defines

$$\nu(t,T) := \frac{E_w^a(p,w(t,T);m^1,\ldots,m^k) - \sum_{i=1}^k m^i}{k}.$$

Then one gets

$$\begin{aligned} w(t,T) &= W(V^1(p+t,m^1-T),\ldots,V^k(p+t,m^k-T)) \\ &= W(V^1(p,m^1+\nu(t,T)),\ldots,V^k(p,m^k+\nu(t,T)) \end{aligned}$$

and

$$\begin{aligned} I(t,T) &= I(0,-\nu(t,T)) = k\cdot\nu(t,T) \\ &= E_w^a(p,w(t,T);m^1,\ldots,m^k) - E_w^a(p,w_0;m^1,\ldots,m^k). \end{aligned}$$

□

Lastly we propose a measure of tax revenue. We simply add up the individual tax burdens.

Definition RT (Tax Revenue)*

$R(t,T) := \sum_{i=1}^k p(x^i(p,m^i) - x^i(p+t,m^i-T))$.

The tax burden is determined by the difference in demand and supply between pre-tax and post-tax situation and by the prices of the pre-tax situation.

Now it is possible to derive a result which is analogous to theorem 5.

Theorem 7
The excess burden EB, the welfare measure I, and the tax revenue T satisfy EC, ET, EN, WR, WN [WNL], and RT* if and only if

$$EB(I(t,T), R(t,T)) = -I(t,T) - R(t,T)$$
$$= -EV^r(S_0, S(t)) - \sum_{i=1}^{k} tx^{ci}(p+t, u^i(t,T)) - kT$$
$$\left[= -EV^a(S_0, S(t)) - \sum_{i=1}^{k} tx^{ci}(p+t, u^i(t,T)) - kT \right].$$

Thus theorem 7 presents two generalizations[12] of the excess burden EB_E to the many consumers case. One point must be emphasized. The excess burdens are consistent with the social welfare function. This property is implied by EC and WR; i.e. we obtain the following equivalence

$$\forall\ (\bar{t},\overline{T}), (\bar{\bar{t}},\overline{\overline{T}}) \text{ such that } R(\bar{t},\overline{T}) = R(\bar{\bar{t}},\overline{\overline{T}}) :$$
$$EB(I(\bar{t},\overline{T}), R(\bar{t},\overline{T})) < EB(I(\bar{\bar{t}},\overline{\overline{T}}), R(\bar{\bar{t}},\overline{\overline{T}})) \iff w(\bar{t},\overline{T}) > w(\bar{\bar{t}},\overline{\overline{T}}).$$

If we compare two tax systems $(\bar{t},\overline{T})$ and $(\bar{\bar{t}},\overline{\overline{T}})$ which yield the same revenue $R(\bar{t},\overline{T}) = R(\bar{\bar{t}},\overline{\overline{T}})$ then the tax connected with the smaller excess burden implies the higher level of welfare. Of course this relationship can be seen directly as well. Minimizing the excess burden for a given value of $R(t,T)$ amounts to maximizing the social equivalent variation which in turn is equivalent to maximizing $w(t,T)$.

VI. Conclusion

The derivation reveals the advantages of using axioms. The properties EC, ET, EN establishing the form of (the function) EB are the same in both cases. Furthermore the other properties UR, UN [UNL], and RT can be easily changed to WR, WN [WNL], and RT*, respectively. Moreover this generalization demonstrates the importance of the initial distribution of exogenous income and the implications of WN and WNL to the welfare measure.

The analysis of this paper can be extended in various ways. E.g. different rules of normalization can be introduced. If one chooses a commodity as numeraire

[12] Cf. footnote 4.

one can normalize the welfare measure in such a way that $I(t,T)$ becomes the equivalent surplus (Pauwels, 1985). In this case one gets further new measures of excess burden. Moreover the characterization can easily be generalized to a situation in which a tax system is changed (i.e. in which a tax system already exists).

References

Auerbach, A. J. (1986): "The Theory of Excess Burden and Optimal Taxation." In *Handbook of Public Economics, Vol. I*, edited by A. J. Auerbach and M. Feldstein. Amsterdam etc: North-Holland, pp. 61–127.

Blackorby, C.; Primont, D., and **Russell, R. R.** (1978): *Duality, Separability, and Functional Structure.* New York etc.: North-Holland.

Chipman, J. S., and **Moore, J. C.** (1980): "Compensating Variation, Consumer's Surplus, and Welfare." *American Economic Review* 70: 933–949.

Diamond, P. A., and **McFadden, D. L.** (1974): "Some Uses of the Expenditure Function in Public Finance." *Journal of Public Economics* 3: 3–21.

Ebert, U. (1984): "Exact Welfare Measures and Economic Index Numbers." *Zeitschrift für Nationalökonomie/Journal of Economics* 44: 27–38.

Ebert, U. (1985a): "On the Relationship Between the Hicksian Measures of Change in Welfare and the Pareto Principle." *Social Choice and Welfare* 1: 263–272.

Ebert, U. (1985b): "Non-transitive Representations of Transitive Orderings." *Economics Letters* 18: 109–112.

Ebert, U. (1986): "Equity and Distribution in Cost-benefit Analysis." In *Welfare Economics of the Second Best*, edited by D. Bös and C. Seidl. Vienna etc.: Springer, pp. 67–78. (*Journal of Economics/Zeitschrift für Nationalökonomie*, Supplementum 5.)

Ebert, U. (1987a): "Axiomatic Foundations of Hicksian Measures of Welfare Change." Forthcoming in *Journal of Public Economics.*

Ebert, U. (1987b): *Beiträge zur Wohlfahrtsökonomie — Effizienz und Verteilung.* Berlin etc.: Springer. (Studies in Contemporary Economics.)

Kay, J. A. (1980): "The Deadweight Loss from a Tax System." *Journal of Public Economics* 13: 111–120.

King, M. A. (1983): "Welfare Analysis of Tax Reforms Using Household Data." *Journal of Public Economics* 21: 183–214.

Mohring, H. (1971): "Alternative Welfare Gain and Loss Measures." *Western Economic Journal* 9: 349–368.

Pauwels, W. (1984): "Correct and Incorrect Measures of the Deadweight Loss of Taxation." Discussion Paper. Antwerp: University of Antwerp.

Pauwels, W. (1985): "Measuring Welfare Changes in Quantity Constrained Regimes." Discussion Paper 85/174. Antwerp: University of Antwerp.

Pazner, E. A., and **Sadka, E.** (1980): "Excess-burden and Economic Surplus as Consistent Welfare Indicators." *Public Finance* 35: 437–449.

Pollak, R. A. (1981): "The Social Cost of Living Index." *Journal of Public Economics* 15: 311–336.

Zabalza, A. (1982): "Compensating and Equivalent Variations, and the Deadweight Loss of Taxation." *Economica* 49: 255–359.

Comprehensive versus Neutral Income Taxation

Wolfram F. Richter, Dortmund, West Germany*

The income definition that has undoubtedly received most support from German and American tax theorists is the Schanz-Haig-Simons concept of demanding comprehensiveness (cf. Goode, 1977, p. 7). The idea is that all income should be taxed alike, irrespective of the source. If at all other income concepts are considered, then the discussion typically narrows down to an act of choice between competing tax bases. Thus, Goode's otherwise commendable survey of income concepts ends with "the conclusion that the S-H-S definition of income is much better for tax purposes than other definitions" (Goode, 1977, p. 28). It is not that conceptual and administrative problems were played down or even denied, it is that other concepts such as the Hicksian (1939, 1968) economic yield of capital, are seen as posing even more problems.

The impression I gain from this kind of analysis is that the question as to what is the best definition of income is not very fruitful. We can only have ad hoc answers as long as we have no clear understanding of the objective of income taxation. Stating it positively, we should focus on objectives. The question of the adequate tax base is a subordinate issue. This paper is written in this spirit.

It is taken for granted that the primary function of income taxation is fund raising. However, once we move beyond this classical fiscal function, views may easily diverge. An income tax may be seen to serve definite distributional or allocational goals. Or one may share the view that tax provisions should interfere with private efforts and decisions to earn income as little as possible. In this paper, we follow the latter line. Neutrality is taken to be the guiding objective. We ask how the tax base should be chosen so as to ensure neutrality with respect to investment decisions.

The key to the answer is the neutrality theorem from Johansson (1961, 1969) and Samuelson (1964) which demands "tax deductibility of economic depreciation to insure invariant (investment) valuations". According to this theorem, to a certain extent there is no contradiction between comprehensive and neutral taxation.

---

* **This paper benefited considerably by intensive discussions with W. Buchholz and H.-W. Sinn. Herewith I would like to thank both colleagues. It is only in the process of printing that Fane (1987) came to my attention. The reader might wish to consult this reference in connection with section 5.**

However, important conceptual differences become apparent when considering uncertainty, market imperfections, gratuitous receipts, and so forth. In such borderline cases the suggestion of comprehensive income taxation is often heavily rejected by tax specialists. Conversely, the neutrality objective tends to suggest solutions that might meet with more approval. In this paper we wish to substantiate this claim for selected classes of revenue. Thus we shall see that under the neutrality objective, income from life annuities is best defined by Hicks. Alternatively, an argument can be made for taxing the returns from human capital upon realization, which is the common practice, but difficult to reconcile with the S-H-S income concept. Or, to give one last example, the neutrality objective well accommodates the common practice of excluding from income gratuitous receipts in the form of gifts and inheritances.

In this paper we first reproduce Johansson's and Samuelson's neutrality theorem and provide it with a choice-theoretic foundation. This not only has expository advantages, but allows us to generalize the neutrality theorem to investments with risky returns, which is a prerequisite for treating the taxation of life annuities. In the closing section we discuss conceptual differences between neutral and comprehensive income taxation.

The paper heavily draws on two of my earlier works (1986, 1987) in German. The material, however, has been condensed from the original German versions and reorganized to emphasize different questions and conclusions.

1. The Investor's Decision

Let us consider a non-corporate investor initially endowed with K_0 units of wealth. The question is how this stock of value is optimally invested, explicitly regarding tax regulations. The decision problem is one of partial analysis and the model is highly stylized. Uncertainty is excluded, at least in the beginning. An analysis of investments with risky returns is deferred to a later section.

There are two investment alternatives, a financial and a real one. The share of initial wealth devoted to financial investments is denoted by a, i.e. aK_0 is lent at the interest rate i. The financial market is perfect in the sense that the same rate applies to lending and borrowing. The real investment is characterized by its produced cash flow. An initial cost of K_0 at time 0 promises some (net-)return R_τ at time $\tau = 1, 2, \ldots$. There are no restrictions on the tradability of the asset, i.e. the real investment has a resale value of K_1 at $\tau = 1$. The end-of-period wealth before tax amounts to

$$a(1+i)K_0 + (1-a)[R_1 + K_1].$$

We now add income taxation to the picture. The tax shall be of the general type, applying equal rates to incomes from interest and from real investment. Losses from one source may be fully offset by positive returns from the other. Let B_1 denote the (unsplit) tax base which applies to the real investment at time $\tau = 1$. Hence $R_1 - B_1$ stands for tax depreciation. Tax depreciation need not coincide a priori with economic depreciation. The latter requires that $B_1 = R_1 - (K_0 - K_1)$ which amounts to taxation upon accretion. If w denotes exogenous wage income, taxable income is given by

$$aiK_0 + (1-a)B_1 + w =: Y_1. \tag{1}$$

Let $T(Y_1)$ denote tax liability. The investor is assumed to maximize end-of-period wealth after tax of

$$a(1+i)K_0 + (1-a)[R_1 + K_1] + w - T(Y_1)$$

with respect to a. Note that Y_1 is constant in a iff $B_1 = iK_0$. In this case $(1+i)K_0 = R_1 + K_1$ seems to be a condition of investment equilibrium. In the other case where, for instance $iK_0 < R_1 + K_1 - K_0$, investors would have an incentive to make unrestricted real investments by borrowing an infinite amount of money ($a = -\infty$). Hence we can say that in equilibrium, taxable income Y_1 is independent of the investors decision iff the real investment is taxed upon accrual, $B_1 = iK_0 = R_1 + K_1 - K_0$.

In the other case where $B_1 \neq iK_0$, taxable income $Y_1 = Y_1(a)$ is a function of a and, assuming a strictly monotonically increasing marginal tax rate T', end-of-period wealth is a strictly concave function of a. Hence, any optimal choice $\overline{a}$ is uniquely determined if a maximum is reached at all. In general, of course, the optimization need not have a finite solution. One may think of cases where the before-tax rates of return on real and financial investments deviate to such an extent that even a discriminatory tax system cannot close the margin. However, such a situation would appear to be one of disequilibrium. We hence limit our consideration to the case where a finite $\overline{a}$ maximizes end-of-period wealth. The first-order condition is then

$$(1+i)K_0 - [R_1 + K_1] = [iK_0 - B_1]T'(Y_1(\overline{a})). \tag{2}$$

Investments are made to the point where before-tax return differentials are offset by tax load differentials. Assuming $T' \in (0,1)$ we obtain

$$0 < \frac{(1+i)K_0 - R_1 - K_1}{iK_0 - B_1} < 1.$$

Restricting consideration to $iK_0 > B_1$, which, in a deterministic world seems to be more relevant than $iK_0 < B_1$, the inequality chain can be rewritten as $iK_0 > R_1 + K_1 - K_0 > B_1$. Hence we have a situation where a financial investment yields a higher return before tax than a real investment. The lower profitability is compensated, however, by a noncomprehensive tax base. For real investments, accrued income exceeds taxable income. One may think of favourable depreciation allowances for housing or of the failure to tax capital gains.

It should be clear that the given assumptions are not able to guarantee $0 \leq \bar{a} \leq 1$. The case when $\bar{a} \notin [0,1]$ must, therefore, be suitably interpreted. In this event $\bar{a} > 1$ stands for a short sale of real assets where the proceeds are used for financial investment.

2. Valuing Investment Projects

We have shown that (2) is an equilibrium condition when end-of-period wealth is to be maximized. (Note that (2) equally characterizes the case where $iK_0 = B_1$ if only marginal tax rates are positive by assumption.) In deriving (2) we have assumed that K_0 and K_1 are exogenous. Let us give up this assumption now and interpret K_0 as today's subjective value of the real asset and K_1 as its expected resale value tomorrow. K_0 and K_1 are endogenously determined by the arbitrage condition (2). If both values violate (2), we cannot speak of an investor's equilibrium. The investor would have an incentive to regroup his portfolio. More precisely,

Definition:
$K_\tau(T) = K_\tau(T, w) \quad (\tau = 0, 1)$ is called a *private (equilibrium) valuation* if

(3) $$(1+i)K_0(T) - [R_1 + K_1(T)] = [iK_0(T) - B_1]T'(Y_1)$$

holds, where $Y_1 = Y_1(K_0, K_1, B_1, T, i, w)$ denotes the investor's taxable income.

One might think of defining Y_1 in terms of (1). However, the precise specification of Y_1 is largely irrelevant in what follows.

We first notice that under proportional taxation the *discounting of cashflows always generates a private equilibrium valuation* — irrespective of what depreciation formula $B_1, B_2, \dots$ applies. This is proved by setting $T(Y) := tY$ and verifying that

$$K_\tau(T) := \sum_{n \geq 1} \frac{R_{\tau+n} - tB_{\tau+n}}{(1+(1-t)i)^n}$$

conforms (3). When taxation is non-proportional we have to replace t by the marginal tax rate $T'(Y_{\tau+n})$ to ensure a private equilibrium valuation.

Consider (3) for the special case where $T = 0$. The right hand-side then vanishes. After rearranging the terms we obtain

$$(3^0) \qquad iK_0(0) = R_1 - [K_0(0) - K_1(0)]$$

(cf. Samuelson, 1936/37, p. 485).

The left-hand side may equally be interpreted as interest income or *economic yield of capital* (Hicks, 1939, 1968; Lindahl, 1933). Without taxation (and in the absence of uncertainty), a private equilibrium valuation is characterized by the equality of accrued income and the economic yield of capital. Here the Hicksian income concept coincides with the S-H-S definiton. Since this equality is independent of personal characteristics w, we may call $K_\tau(0)$ a *social (equilibrium) valuation* if (3^0) is met.

We are now in the position to specify the notion of an income tax that ensures investment neutrality. It is advisable to differentiate between static and dynamic investment neutrality. We speak of static neutrality if private and social valuation coincide at time $\tau = 0$. Dynamic neutrality holds whenever the equality of private and social valuation is preserved across time.

Definition:
With respect to income taxation, we speak of

a) *static (investment) neutrality*
   if $K_0(T, w) = K_0(0)$ for all w ; and

b) *dynamic (investment) neutrality*
   if $K_0(T, w) = K_0(0)$ holds for all w
   if and only if $K_1(T, w) = K_1(0)$ for all w.

In the literature there is a tendency to speak of "production efficiency" when investment neutrality is actually meant, e.g., see Bradford (1981), Kovenock and Rothschild (1983) or Seidl (1985). I prefer not to follow their example. Although neutrality will guarantee intersectoral production efficiency, the condition remains one of *valuation* the importance of which extends to the equity objective.

3. Johansson's and Samuelson's Neutrality Theorem

This theorem tells us in essence that *economic depreciation ensures investment neutrality* and that no other rule would do the same. The crucial assumption is that $K_\tau(T,w)$ and $K_\tau(0)$ denote private and social equilibrium valuations, respectively. Income upon accrual thus equals the economic yield of capital per assumption. The immediate implication is that permitting economic depreciation is equivalent to taxing the economic yield of capital.

Theorem:

a) If $T'(Y_1) > 0$, static and dynamic neutrality together require economic depreciation.

b) If $T'(Y_1) \leq 1$, economic depreciation implies dynamic neutrality.

The proofs are straightforward.

a) Employing (3^0), the assumptions given above, and (3), we obtain

$$\begin{aligned} 0 &= (1+i)K_0(0) - R_1 - K_1(0) \\ &= (1+i)K_0(T,w) - R_1 - K_1(T,w) \\ &= [iK_0(T,w) - B_1]T'(Y_1). \end{aligned}$$

As $T'(Y_1)$ is positive, $B_1 = iK_0(T,w) = iK_0(0)$ which has been asserted.

b)

$$\begin{aligned} &(1+i-iT'(Y_1))[K_0(T,w) - K_0(0)] \\ &= (1+i-iT'(Y_1))K_0(T,w) - (1+i-iT'(Y_1))K_0(0) \\ &= (1+i)K_0(T,w) - R_1 - [iK_0(T,w) - B_1]T'(Y_1) - (1+i)K_0(0) + R_1 + \\ &\qquad + [iK_0(0) - B_1]T'(Y_1) \\ &= K_1(T,w) - K_1(0) + 0. \end{aligned}$$

The assumptions (3), (3^0), and the one of economic depreciation all entered into the last equality. The theorem is confirmed when the extreme left and right-hand sides of the equality chain are compared. Note that the inverse discount factor $1 + i - iT'(Y_1) = 1 + (1 - T'(Y_1))i$ is positive.

4. Static versus Dynamic Neutrality

In some of the literature, for example in Johansson (1969) and Schneider (1970, 1980), there is a focus on the static dimension of neutrality. The above theorem, however, suggests that dynamic neutrality is the truly important property attributable to economic depreciation. This gains further support through the following observation. If a real asset wears out after a finite number of periods with the consequence that $K_n(T,w) = 0 = K_n(0)$ holds for some distant n, then, by backwards induction, dynamic neutrality implies static neutrality, i.e. $K_n(T,w) = K_n(0)$ implies $K_{n-1}(T,w) = K_{n-1}(0)$ and so forth until we end up with $K_0(T,w) = K_0(0)$. This leads us to the following corollary:

Corollary: For real assets with finite lives and $T'(Y_1) \in (0,1]$ dynamic neutrality is insured if, and only if, economic depreciation is applied.

It should be clear that dynamic neutrality cannot imply static neutrality if the earnings power never fades out. Consider a perpetual annuity of constant return R. Set $K_\tau(T) := R/(1-t)i$ and interpret this to mean that income from the annuity is tax free, i.e. $B_\tau = 0$ for all τ, whereas interest income is liable to the constant tax rate t. Static neutrality is then violated, i.e. $K_0(T) \neq K_0(0) = R/i$, whereas dynamic neutrality is a void requirement and thus ensured in some purely logical sense. Note that $K_\tau(T)$ and $K_\tau(0)$ nevertheless define equlibrium valuations. On the other hand, static neutrality is too weak to ensure dynamic neutrality. This is easy to show by way of examples. Choose a proportional tax, and let

$$K_\tau(T) := \sum_{n\geq 1} \frac{R_{\tau+n} - tB_{\tau+n}}{(1+(1-t)i)^n} \quad ,$$

$0 = B_2 = B_3 = \ldots$; B_1 is determined by requiring that

$$K_0(T) = K_0(0).$$

The significance of investment neutrality is best elucidated by a tax system which violates it. In the case where there is no static neutrality, private equilibrium valuation may crucially depend on private characteristics. Valuation differences, however, open up possibilities for advantageous arbitrage.

Samuelson (1964) has indicated the possibility of "tax swaps". Assume a situation where, in contrast to dynamic neutrality,

$$K_0(T,w_1) = K_0(T,w_2) \quad \text{but} \quad K_1(T,w_1) < K_1(T,w_2).$$

This requirement ensures that if w_1 carries out a real investment at time 0 and sells it a period later to w_2 at a price determined by supply and demand within the range delimited by private valuations the transaction will be profitable. The effect is increased business activity motivated by the sole objective of collecting a tax rent at the cost of general revenues. The practice of income taxation is full of examples.

5. Risky Returns

The return to investments suffers under uncertainty. If this real world feature is explicitly regarded, it is no longer clear whether or not economic depreciation will ensure investment neutrality. It becomes necessary, therefore, to inspect the investor's decision-making problem taking riskiness into special consideration.

We treat K_0, i, w, and a as deterministic variables as their values are known at time 0. Sure information is lacking ex ante on the return $\widetilde{R}_1$, the resale value $\widetilde{K}_1$, and the tax base $\widetilde{B}_1$, with the tilde denoting random variables. There are no markets to insure the risks.

The investor is assumed to be risk-neutral. This assumption is made since risk aversion tends to destroy any neutrality which might result. The income tax heavily affects the decision of risk-averse investors. (Extensive literature on this subject is recorded in Bamberg and Richter, 1987.) The risk-neutral investor maximizes

$$a(1+i)K_0 + (1-a)E[\widetilde{R}_1 + \widetilde{K}_1] + w - ET(\widetilde{Y}_1)$$

where $\widetilde{Y}_1 := aiK_0 + (1-a)\widetilde{B}_1 + w$ and E is the expectation operator. The first-order condition is

$$(1+i)K_0 - E[\widetilde{R}_1 + \widetilde{K}_1] = E[(iK_0 - \widetilde{B}_1)T'(\widetilde{Y}_1)]$$

which motivates the following:

Definition: $K_0(T) = K_0(T, w)$ and $\widetilde{K}_1(T) = \widetilde{K}_1(T, w)$ are called a *private (equilibrium) valuation* if

$$(1+i)K_0(T) - E[\widetilde{R}_1 + \widetilde{K}_1(T)] = E[(iK_0(T) - \widetilde{B}_1)T'(\widetilde{Y}_1)].$$

For $T = 0$ the equality reduces to

$$iK_0(0) = E[\widetilde{R}_1 + \widetilde{K}_1(0)] - K_0(0).$$

In other words, the economic yield of capital equals the *expected* income accretion, a condition we call a *social (equilibrium) valuation.*

The notion of *static neutrality* clearly needs no adaption to the stochastic framework. On the other hand, *dynamic neutrality* requires that

$$\begin{aligned} K_0(T,w) &= K_0(0) \quad \text{for all } w \\ \text{iff} \quad E\widetilde{K}_1(T,w) &= E\widetilde{K}_1(0) \quad \text{for all } w. \end{aligned}$$

Theorem:

a) If static and dynamic neutrality hold, then

$$(4) \qquad E[(iK_0(0) - \widetilde{B}_1)T'(\widetilde{Y}_1)] = 0, \qquad \text{and}$$

b) if $ET'(\widetilde{Y}_1) \leq 1$, then (4) implies dynamic neutrality.

The proof parallels the one given before and thus has been omitted.

The question now is what definitions of $\widetilde{B}_1$ ensure the validity of condition (4)? Three prominent cases deserve special notice. First we may choose to tax income ex post, in which case there are two variants: 1) we either follow Schanz, Haig, and Simons and tax accrued income ex post, $\widetilde{B}_1 := \widetilde{R}_1 + \widetilde{K}_1(0) - K_0(0)$, or 2) we tax interest income ex post, $\widetilde{B}_1 := i(\widetilde{R}_1 + \widetilde{K}_i(0))/(1+i)$ as found in Apel's (1938) proposal. In both cases, the marginal tax rate must be constant if neutrality is to be guaranteed. Alternatively, we may follow Hicks and tax income as it is expected ex ante. In equilibrium expected income accretion equals interest income ex ante, $\widetilde{B}_1 := iK_0(0)$. The advantage of the Hicksian income definition is that it ensures neutrality even under variable marginal tax rates. However, this advantage has to be weighed against liquidity gains produced by ex-post taxation in a world of imperfect capital markets. All three income concepts suffer more or less equally from problems of assessment, which I therefore prefer to refrain from discussing.

A strong case can be made for taxing the Hicksian economic yield of capital in case of life annuities.

6. Life Annuities

If the income from life annuities is taxed ex post upon accrual let us say it is taxed according to the S-H-S-rule. Similarly, let "Apel" stand for the taxing of interest income ex post and "Hicks" for the taxing of interest income ex ante. (Interestingly enough, Apel is an insurance mathematician who developed his tax proposal for life annuities. Instead of arguing in economical terms, however, he contended himself simply with deriving mathematical formulas.)

If adjustments for inflation and growth are neglected, annuities yield relatively sure, steady income. The liquidity argument for taxation ex post is then less convincing. Even more, the assertion of neutrality becomes lost if the fact that annuities expire in case of death is taken into account. This is easily seen in the case of the S-H-S-rule. Note that accrued income from life annuities is a random variable having one of two possible realizations: either the recipient survives till the end of the period, in which case accrued income is $R_1 + K_1 - K_0$; or death causes the annuity to expire, in which case accrued income is $R_1 - K_0$. If dead people do not file income tax declarations (as in Germany) the capital loss K_0 cannot be offset against positive returns. The same argument pertains to Apel's rule. The obvious result is that taxation ex post becomes taxation on survival, which destroys neutrality. The conclusion hence is that *life annuities should be taxed according to the Hicksian rule to ensure neutrality.*

The rule that is commonly addressed by "*the annuity rule*" (cf. Sunley, 1977, p. 80/81, e.g.) is something different. Under the German income tax system it is the rule that applies to private life annuities as well as to social insurance benefits. It assumes a constant annuity payment $R := R_1 = R_2 = \ldots = R_n$ until the *expected* expiration time n. Consequently, the present value $K_{0,n}$ of this finite annuity differs from the actuarial value of the underlying life annuity. Life expectancy n is clearly contingent on the age when the annuity starts. The idea behind the annuity rule is to pay out $K_{0,n}$ in n equal shares. Thus $K_{0,n}/n$ is the fictious return of capital and $R - K_{0,n}/n$ return to capital. Only the latter defines taxable income under the annuity rule. It results in a systematic underreporting of the economic yield of the annuity capital. (See below.)

The subtle economical question in the taxation of life annuities is the choice of the discount rate. As this question, however, concerns all rules equally I will not discuss it here. Prior to 1982, the German income tax used a discount rate of 4 per cent. Since 1982 this has been increased to 5.5 per cent. These are also the rates used as the basis of the following table.

This table gives us an idea of quantitative implications. It shows the percentage of a constant life annuity R that is treated as taxable income under the respective rules. In contrast to the simplified presentation above, the fact that the annuity is paid at the beginning of each month has been explicitly considered. (For details see Richter, 1987.) All numbers are based on West-German mortality tables of 1970/72.

The first two broad rows show the impact of interest rate changes; the first

Taxable Income in Percentage

	age of first payment	S-H-S	Apel	Hicks	annuity rule
male $i = 0.055$	20 40 60 80	93.6 81.9 70.5 78.2	87.9 74.9 48.9 21.4	87.7 74.7 47.9 18.8	64.4 50.6 29.9 10.7
male $i = 0.04$	20 40 60 80	87.4 73.0 63.4 76.0	81.5 65.8 40.1 16.6	81.3 65.6 39.3 14.6	55.4 41.7 23.3 8.0
female $i = 0.055$	20 40 60 80	94.2 85.2 70.4 72.6	90.7 80.1 57.3 24.1	90.6 80.0 56.7 21.8	67.4 55.1 35.7 12.5
actuarial present value of tax bases: male, $i = 0.055$	20 40 60 80	1486.0 1141.9 736.6 390.9	[a]	1338.3 902.0 373.8 74.2	936.4 589.4 228.1 41.8

and the third rows show the impact of different mortality risks. In comparing the columns it should be kept in mind that under the annuity rule the taxable income ratio is fixed for the full duration, whereas under the other rules this ratio is adjusted from year to year. For this reason, in the last broad row displayed, the actuarial present values of the tax bases have been computed to allow comparability among the rules.

One might expect taxable income to decrease when getting older. However, this is not the case under the S-H-S rule. Here, the ratio of yearly taxable income is v-shaped, with a minimum around 60 for men and around 70 for women. It should be stressed that this is just a reflection of biological survival probabilities. It would not be correct to interpret this effect as a "fair" compensation for supernormal long lives.

[a] Numbers not available at the time of print.

7. Conceptual Differences between Comprehensive and Neutral Income Taxation

Various noteworthy conclusions may be drawn from the above discussion. The starting point was that comprehensiveness of income is a property that can hardly claim approval in itself. It is an ad-hoc concept wherein the dominant objective is not identified (see, for example, the early critique of Neumark, 1947, p. 40). Comprehensiveness is definitely not the right criterion if investment neutrality is to be ensured. Admittedly, comprehensiveness guarantees neutrality under the ideal assumptions of the original theorem of Johansson and Samuelson. However, these assumptions blur all notional differences between the S-H-S income definition and other concepts, such as that from Hicks. Differences arise when uncertainty is taken into consideration. The S-H-S concept is then identified with accrued income ex post. In equilibrium the Hicksian economic yield of capital, on the other hand, equals the ex ante expected accrued income. The argument in favour of taxation ex post is based on liquidity considerations. The Hicksian notion, however, has the advantage that it ensures neutrality even under variable marginal tax rates. Furthermore, it is the only notion neutralizing investments in life annuities.

Differences between comprehensive and neutral taxation become even more apparent when market failure is taken into consideration. Due, however, to space limitations, only a cursory treatment is possible here. The interested reader is referred to Richter (1987). Some differences shall be outlined here by looking at human capital.

Human capital is a perfect example of market incompleteness. It defines a nontradable "asset" where investments are irreversible. According to Goode (1977, p. 12), the S-H-S concept does not include accretions in human wealth. He does not, however, supply a cogent justification for the exclusion. Mitschke (1976, p. 92), e.g., insists on including such gains in principle. Horizontal equity would require one to do so.

The difficulties for consistent reasoning on S-H-S grounds arise from a notable asymmetry between gains and losses in human wealth. The former accrue mainly in youth. They are a reflection of increased individual earnings expectations and, in absence of markets, are fundamentally difficult to value. The valuation problem is far less serious in the case of those losses accrued towards the end of life as a reflection of depletion in earnings. The value of losses can be determined relatively easily with the help of actuarial tables. The crucial point is that there is nothing in the pure S-H-S concept that allows for human wealth losses during old age to be simply offset against the gains accrued during youth. Losses and gains have to be treated separately in the periods of their respective accrual. Accepting this view leads to the following suggestion. Consistant with common practice, the income of young, active earners should be taxed upon realization because necessary information about accretions in human wealth is lacking. The aged should, however, be permitted to deduct from their earned income an actuarially fair depreciation allowance. As a result of this asymmetric provision human capital investments would enjoy highest preferential treatment.

The solution is quite different if we agree to pursue the neutrality objective. We then obtain a rather convincing argument for offsetting human wealth losses against respective gains, i.e. for uncompromising taxation upon realization. The argument is that since human capital is nonmarketable (except in slavery), the only decision is whether to invest in human capital or in non-human capital. This decision is irreversible. There is no "switching out" of human wealth. As a consequence, neutral taxation has to consider the full life span. There is no point in preserving neutrality with respect to each year. It is the original decision to invest into human wealth alone that has to be neutralized.

Perfect neutralization is clearly impossible in view of valuation difficulties inherent to gains in human wealth. However, there is much appeal to the argument that we should come as close as possible to neutral taxation. This is presumably done by uncompromisingly taxing human wealth upon realization. Let us be aware that taxation upon realization favours human capital investments in comparison to financial alternatives that cause no deferred yields. This is true because human wealth undergoes a life-cycle. Depreciation comes only after accumulation. Hence taxation upon realization results in tax deferral. It is as if the taxpayer obtained an interest free loan.

The fact that non-accrual income taxation may raise the capital value of investments is found in the literature as the so-called "tax-paradox" (see Schneider, 1970, 1980, p. 278, and Diamond, 1975, p. 235). The application to human capital investment is nothing but a special case. Note that the tax induced incentive to invest in human capital does not require inflation for getting operative. Strong anticipated inflation can only reinforce relatively preferential taxation of human capital.

Once the assertion that human wealth already enjoys preferential treatment by taxation upon realization has been accepted, the argument for deducting extra depreciation allowances at old age loses its thrust.

Let us turn to a last example that demonstrates conceptual differences between comprehensive and neutral taxation. This example concerns gratuitous receipts. There seems to be no doubt that "the S-H-S concept calls for including in income gratuitous receipts in the form of gifts and bequests" (Goode, 1977, p. 19).

However, as Goode admits, few tax specialists would really want to go so far. We need not weigh their arguments (see McDaniel et al., eds., 1985, Guideline 2). We also need not enter into the fruitless discussion of which transfers really qualify as gratuitous. For economists in the Chicago tradition there seems to be almost nothing like a gratuity. (For a recent example of this view see Bernheim et al., 1985.) My point is that the neutrality objective makes it possible to exclude those receipts from income that cannot be connected with some conscious investment decision (in its broadest sense). Where no investment decision is made there is no need to ensure tax neutrality.

References

Apel, R. (1938): "Gerechte Besteuerung von Leibrenten." *Neumanns Zeitschrift für Versicherungswesen*: 692–693 and 807–808.

Bamberg, G., and **Richter, W. F.** (1987): "Risk-Taking under Progressive Taxation: Three Partial Effects." Forthcoming in *Measurement in Economics: Theory and Application of Economic Indices*, edited by W. Eichhorn et al. Heidelberg: Physica.

Bernheim, B. D.; **Shleifer, A.**; and **Summers, L. H.** (1985): "The Strategic Bequest Motive." *Journal of Political Economy* 93: 1045–1076.

Bradford, D. F. (1981): "Issues in the Design of Savings and Investment Incentives." In *Depreciation, Inflation, and the Taxation of Income from Capital*, edited by C. R. Hulten. Washington, D.C.: Urban Institute Press, pp. 13–47.

Diamond, P. A. (1975): "Inflation and the Comprehensive Tax Base." *Journal of Public Economics* 4: 227–244.

Fane, G. (1987): "Neutral Taxation under Uncertainty." *Journal of Public Economics* 33: 95–106.

Goode, R. (1977): "The Economic Definition of Income." In *Comprehensive Income Taxation*, edited by J. A. Pechman. Washington, D.C.: Brookings Institution, pp. 1–30.

Hicks, J. R. (1939, 1968): *Value and Capital*. 2nd ed., Oxford: Clarendon Press.

Johansson, S.-E. (1961): *Skatt-investering-värdering*. Stockholm: Företagsekonomiska Forskningsinstitutet. (Appendix in English.)

Johansson, S.-E. (1969): "Income Taxes and Investment Decisions." *Swedish Journal of Economics* 71: 104–110.

Kovenock, D. J., and **Rothschild, M.** (1983): "Capital Gains Taxation in an Economy with an 'Austrian Sector'." *Journal of Public Economics* 21: 215–256.

Lindahl, E. (1933): "The Concept of Income." In *Economic Essays in Honour of Gustav Cassel*. London, pp. 399–407. (Reprinted in *Readings in the Concept and Measurement of Income*, edited by R. H. Parker and G. C. Harcourt. Cambridge etc.: Cambridge University Press, 1969, pp. 54–62.)

McDaniel, P. R., and **Surrey, S. S.** (eds.) (1985): *International Aspects of Tax Expenditures: A Comparative Study*. Deventer: Kluwer.

Mitschke, J. (1976): *Über die Eignung von Einkommen, Konsum und Vermögen als Bemessungsgrundlagen der direkten Besteuerung*. Berlin: Duncker & Humblot.

Neumark, F. (1947): *Theorie und Praxis der modernen Einkommensbesteuerung*. Bern: Francke.

Richter, W. F. (1986): "Das Johansson-Samuelson-Theorem bewertungsneutraler Abschreibung langlebiger Wirtschaftsgüter bei Einkommensbesteuerung." *Finanzarchiv* N.F. 44: 435–449.

Richter, W. F. (1987): "Neutrale Ertragsanteilsbesteuerung von Renten." To appear in *Deutsche Rentenversicherung*.

Samuelson, P. A. (1936/37): "Some Aspects of the Pure Theory of Capital." *Quarterly Journal of Economics* 51: 469–496.

Samuelson, P. A. (1964): "Tax Deductibility of Economic Depreciation to Insure Invariant Valuations." *Journal of Political Economy* 72: 604–606.

Schneider, D. (1970, 1980): *Investition und Finanzierung*. 5th Edition, Wiesbaden: Gabler.

Seidl, C. (1985): "Effizienz und Steuerreform: Umfassende Einkommensteuer oder Konsumsteuer?" *Das öffentliche Haushaltswesen in Österreich*: 180–197.

Sunley, E. M., Jr. (1977): "Employee Benefits and Transfer Payments." In *Comprehensive Income Taxation*, edited by J. A. Pechman. Washington, D.C.: Brookings Institution, pp. 75–106.

Neutral Taxation of Risky Investment

Wolfgang Buchholz, Tübingen, West Germany*

1. Introduction

Since John Stuart Mill (1886), the venerable "leave-them-as-you-find-them"-rule is primarily interpreted as an efficiency requirement. Taxes should be levied in such a manner that scarce resources are not diverted from more to less productive employments.[1] This view by far dominates the modern neoclassically oriented Theory of Public Finance, where allocative neutrality serves as the fundamental benchmark for the evaluation of tax measures and tax systems. A tax design, for example, is investigated which avoids perturbations of the real and financial decisions of a firm.[2] But in this context until the present time a rather important topic has only been treated superficially. Rather independently from the mainstream analysis of investment behaviour, a particular branch of the literature has developed in which the risk dimension of investment decisions is emphasized.[3] This paper presents a discussion of the question of tax neutrality within this framework. Above all, the question of which taxes can be neutral if a certain structure of individual risk preferences is assumed will be examined. In principle, this question was already put forward by Feldstein (1969) in his pioneering article about tax effects on risk taking. His considerations were restricted to the case of utility functions with constant relative risk aversion.[4]

In this paper, however, only general assumptions will be made about the degree of risk aversion of the underlying utility function. This makes it clearly impossible to determine specific tax functions. The analysis must instead be content with the derivation of general properties of a tax formula. First, conditions will be

* I am indebted to Wolfram Richter and Hans-Werner Sinn for helpful comments.

[1] Mill (1886, p. 490). A modern and more general formulation of his conception is provided by Musgrave and Musgrave (1984, p. 225): "Taxes should be chosen so as to minimize interference with economic decisions in otherwise efficient markets".

[2] See e.g. Atkinson and Stiglitz (1980, pp. 128–159), Auerbach (1983, pp. 33–55), Sinn (1985a).

[3] The most important references are Domar and Musgrave (1944), Stiglitz (1969), Feldstein (1969). For recent surveys see Sandmo (1985) and in the German literature, Cansier (1985).

[4] See also the short remark in Schneeweiss (1967, p. 87), where the case of constant absolute risk aversion is also considered. In a nontechnical way the neutrality question is also hinted at by Elschen and Hüchtebrock (1983, pp. 275–280).

sought which guarantee that every neutral tax function (with respect to a given utility function on a certain interval) is progressive. In the second step, an attempt is made to completely solve Feldstein's problem. All tax functions are described explicitly, which fulfill the neutrality requirement for a certain utility function exhibiting constant absolute or constant relative risk aversion. Some reflections about the reverse question are included. In some special cases the question as to if a given tax function can be neutral with respect to any utility function will be examined. Finally, a new connection between distributive and allocative neutrality is outlined, as the well-known absolute and relative sacrifice prescriptions for the design of a 'just' income tax can be seen as special cases of the neutrality postulate for decisions under risk.

2. The Model

It is assumed that an individual has to rank investment projects with uncertain outcomes. These are characterized by real-valued income variables Z_i. The "states of nature" in which the different outcomes of a given Z_i occur are to be well-defined with known probabilities, such that a risk situation in the sense of Knight is present. To describe decision-making in this situation, the framework of expected utility theory is used, i.e. the risk preferences of an investor are given by a utility function $u(\cdot)$ defined on an interval $D \subseteq \mathbb{R}$. $u(\cdot)$ is assumed to be twice differentiable with $u'(z) > 0$ and $u''(z) \leq 0$ for all z in the interior of D, i.e. the investor is risk neutral or risk averse for all income levels. Risky projects are then evaluated by their expected utility with respect to the given $u(\cdot)$. If Z_1 to Z_2 denote two risky projects, the investor (weakly) prefers Z_1 to Z_2 if and only if $Eu(Z_1) \geq Eu(Z_2)$, where $E(\cdot)$ is the expectation operator. The effect of this ordering by an income tax $T(\cdot)$, which transforms gross income z into net income $S(z) := z - T(z)$,[5] is subsequently examined. To simplify the exposition, the tax formula $T(\cdot)$ shall also be twice differentiable with $T'(z) \geq 0$ and $T'(z) \leq 1$ for all income levels for which $T(\cdot)$ is defined. The tax burden never decreases with increasing income and the tax increment never exceeds the additional income. With regard to the net income function, these conditions mean $S'(z) \leq 1$ and $S'(z) \geq 0$ for all z where $S(\cdot)$ is defined.

In this framework, neutrality of taxation simply means that the ordering of

[5] With respect to this particular description of the tax effects on risk-taking, cf. Feldstein (1969), Schneider (1977), Bamberg and Richter (1984, 1987), Buchholz (1985).

risky projects made by an investor is preserved after a tax function $T(\cdot)$ has been applied. Stated formally

Definition 1: A tax function $T(\cdot)$ is called neutral with respect to a utility function $u(\cdot)$ and an interval I if and only if $Eu(S(Z_1)) \geq Eu(S(Z_2))$, whenever $Eu(Z_1) \geq Eu(Z_2)$, where Z_1 and Z_2 are risky projects defined only within I.

Above all, tax functions fulfilling this neutrality criterion with respect to a given $u(\cdot)$ are to be determined. But the opposite question may also be of some interest. In general, the interest of this paper will be in the description of the sets $N(u(\cdot), I)$ and $N(T(\cdot), I)$, as defined below.

Definition 2: If a utility function $u(\cdot)$ and an interval I are given, $N(u(\cdot), I)$ denotes the set of all tax functions which are neutral with respect to $u(\cdot)$ and I. Conversely, $N(T(\cdot), I)$ contains all utility functions for which $T(\cdot)$ is neutral in I.

The first lemma says that neutrality defined in this sense is, in fact, a property of linear classes of utility functions.

Lemma 1: If $u(\cdot)$ and I are given then $N(u(\cdot), I) = N(cu(\cdot)+d, I)$ for every $c > 0$ and every $d \in \mathbb{R}$.

Proof: If Z_1 and Z_2 with $Ecu(Z_1) + d \geq Ecu(Z_2) + d$ are given, $c > 0$ implies $Eu(Z_1) \geq Eu(Z_2)$. For any $T(\cdot) \in N(u(\cdot), I)$ neutrality leads to $Eu(S(Z_1)) \geq Eu(S(Z_2))$ or, equivalently, $Ecu(S(Z_1))+d \geq Ecu(S(Z_2))+d$. Hence $N(u(\cdot), I) \subseteq N(cu(\cdot) + d, I)$. The other conclusion can be proved in the same manner.

□

3. The Basic Criterion for Neutrality

The key to all specific results regarding the neutrality of tax functions is provided by the following theorem which relates how the utilities of gross and net incomes have to be connected if neutrality is to be ensured. In a certain way this result is rather trivial. It is based on a striking idea, which was developed only recently, of combining net income functions and utility functions.

Theorem 1: $T(\cdot) \in N(u(\cdot), I)$ if and only if there are two constants $a > 0$ and b such that $u(S(z)) = au(z) + b$ for all $z \in I$.

Proof:[6] The basic idea is to interpret $u(S(\cdot))$ as a new (auxiliary) utility function.[7] The result follows then immediately from two general propositions which are well known in expected utility theory:

a) Two utility functions $u_1(\cdot)$ and $u_2(\cdot)$ defined on the same interval I lead to the same ordering of risky projects (with outcomes in I) if and only if they exhibit the same degree of absolute risk aversion everywhere on I, i.e. $-u_1''(z)/u_1'(z) = -u_2''(z)/u_2'(z)$ for all $z \in I$.[8]

b) The degrees of absolute risk aversion are identical for two utility functions on a certain interval I if and only if they can be represented as linear transformations of each other where the multiplicative component has to be strictly positive.

Assertion a) is at the heart of the theory of risk aversion, whereas b) is simply proved by integrating $(\log u_i'(z))' = u_i''(z)/u_i'(z)$, $(i = 1,2)$ and then taking the exponential values.

□

With the help of Theorem 1 it becomes very easy to give an explicit description of all tax functions in a certain $N(u(\cdot), I)$. Obviously, $T(\cdot) \in N(u(\cdot), I)$ if and only if $S(z) = z - T(z) = u^{-1}(au(z) + b)$ where $(a, b) \in \mathbb{R}^+ \times \mathbb{R}$ has to be chosen such that $au(z) + b \in D$ for all $z \in I$ and $T(\cdot)$ has the two properties required for a tax function.

On closer look, it turns out that in Theorem 1 the sufficient conditions for the representation formula are unnecessarily strong. To arrive at $u(S(z)) = au(z) + b$, the postulate for full neutrality can be replaced by the following less demanding assumption:

Definition 3: Let a utility function $u(\cdot)$ and an open interval I be given. A tax function $T(\cdot)$ is called partially neutral with respect to a certain $r \in I$ if and only if $Eu(r) = Eu(Z)$ always implies $Eu(S(r)) = Eu(S(Z))$, where Z is a risky project only defined within I.

The following theorem says that partial neutrality defined in this way is in fact sufficient to imply the representation formula:

---

[6] Cf. Borch (1968, pp. 28–29) to see that such a proof is not necessarily as simple as is suggested by the following argumentation.

[7] This approach was hinted at by Fellingham and Wolfson (1978) and fully developed by Bamberg and Richter (1987).

[8] See Pratt (1964).

Theorem 2: Let $u(\cdot)$ and an open I be given. A tax function is partially neutral with respect to a certain $r \in I$ if and only if $u(S(z)) = au(z) + b$ for all $z \in I$ with $a > 0$.

Proof: Obviously the representation formula implies partial neutrality. For the proof of the converse of the theorem let two values $z_1, z_2 \in I$ be given with $z_1 < r < z_2$. p denotes the probability for which $pu(z_1) + (1-p)u(z_2) = u(r)$. (Such a $p \in]0,1[$ always exists, as $u(\cdot)$ was assumed to be strictly increasing.) For this p, a function $\tilde{z}(\cdot)$ is defined by $pu(z) + (1-p)u(\tilde{z}(z)) = u(r)$ for all $z < r$. Implicit differentation of this formula leads to $\tilde{z}'(z) = -p/(1-p) \cdot u'(z)/u'(\tilde{z}(z))$. If $u(S(\cdot))$ is abbreviated by $v(\cdot)$, partial neutrality means that $pv(z) + (1-p)v(\tilde{z}(z)) = v(r)$ must also be valid for all $z < r$. Hence, by implicit differentiation $\tilde{z}'(z) = -p/(1-p) \cdot v'(z)/v'(\tilde{z}(z))$ for all $z < r$. This implies that

$$v'(z)/v'(\tilde{z}(z)) = u'(z)/u'(\tilde{z}(z))$$

for all $z < r$.[9] Especially in cases where $z = z_1$ and $\tilde{z}(z_1) = z_2$, this leads to

$$v'(z_1)/u'(z_1) = v'(z_2)/u'(z_2).$$

As z_1 and z_2 (with $z_1 < r < z_2$) were arbitrarily chosen, $v'(z)/u'(z)$ must be constant ($= a$) for all $z \in I$, which is easily seen to be equivalent to $v(z) = au(z)+b$ for all $z \in I$.

□

Leaving the framework of decision theory, this result has an important application for the construction of redistributive tax-subsidy schemes over a set M of different units (e.g. individual members of a community or states in a federal union). If $T(\cdot)$ is a (closed) tax-subsidy scheme distributed over M, i.e. $ET(Z) = 0$ for all distributions Z on M which have the same mean value r, then $T(\cdot)$ must be a linear function of z. This immediately follows from Theorem 2 by assuming a linear utility function.[10]

As neutrality is in fact defined with respect to linear classes of utility functions, the mathematical formulations of Theorem 1 and Theorem 2 can be reduced to the following:

Theorem 3: If $T(\cdot) \in N(u(\cdot), I)$, there is a positive linear transformation of $u(\cdot)$

[9] See also Buchholz (1986) for this line of argumentation.

[10] A similar result was proved by Buhl and Pfingsten (1986) in quite a different manner.

such that

(I) $u(S(z)) = u(z) + b,$ or

(II) $u(S(z)) = au(z)$ with (IIa) $a < 1,$ *or*

(IIb) $a > 1.$

Proof: Following Theorem 1, let $\tilde{u}(S(z)) = \tilde{a}\tilde{u}(z) + \tilde{b}$. Then either $\tilde{a} = 1$ such that (I) is obtained, or $\tilde{a} \neq 1$. Replacing $u(\cdot)$ by $\tilde{u}(\cdot) + \frac{\tilde{b}}{a-1}$, with $a := \tilde{a}$, implies that

$$u(S(z)) = \tilde{u}(S(z)) + \frac{\tilde{b}}{a-1} = a\tilde{u}(z) + \tilde{b} + \frac{\tilde{b}}{a-1} = a\tilde{u}(z) + \frac{a\tilde{b}}{a-1}$$
$$= a\left(\tilde{u}(z) + \frac{\tilde{b}}{a-1}\right) = au(z).$$

□

4. Progressivity of Neutral Tax Functions

Which conditions are sufficient for the progressivity of tax functions, which are neutral with respect to a utility function $u(\cdot)$ on an interval I, will now be determined. Here only the case where $I \subseteq \mathbb{R}_0^+$ is considered, i.e. only non-negative income levels are allowed. As usual, a tax function $T(\cdot)$ will be called (weakly) progressive on an interval I if and only if the average tax rate $T(z)/z$ is nondecreasing in z. Obviously, this is equivalent to the postulate that $S(z)/z$ is nonincreasing on I, which means $(S(z)/z)' = \frac{S'(z)z - S(z)}{z^2} \leq 0$ or $\frac{S'(z)z}{S(z)} \leq 1$. In other words, the elasticity of net income with respect to gross income must not exceed one if progressivity is to be ensured.

All results about progressivity of neutral taxes are now based on the following consideration: if $T(\cdot) \in N(u(\cdot), I)$ then, following Theorem 1, there is a representation $u(S(z)) = au(z) + b$ for all $z \in I$. Taking the derivative with respect to z yields $u'(S(z))S'(z) = au'(z)$, i.e.

$$\frac{S'(z)z}{S(z)} = \frac{au'(z)z}{u'(S(z))S(z)}.$$

Hence, progressivity of $T(\cdot)$ is guaranteed if $a \leq 1$ and $u'(z)z \leq u'(S(z))S(z)$. If all negative taxes are excluded for the moment (i.e. $T(z) \geq 0$ is additionally required for a tax function), the second condition is fulfilled if $u'(z)z$ is nonincreasing in z, which means $(u'(z)z)' = u''(z)z + u'(z) \leq 0$ for all $z \in I$. This inequality can be transformed to $-u''(z)z/u'(z) \geq 1$, i.e. the relative risk aversion of $u(\cdot)$ must not be less than one for all $z \in I$. But one is just the value of the relative risk aversion of the Bernoullian utility function $u(z) := ln\, z$. This implies the following:

Lemma 2: Let $I \subseteq \mathbb{R}^+$. If $u(\cdot)$ is at least as risk averse as the Bernoullian utility function for all $z \in I$, then every nonnegative tax function in $N(u(\cdot), I)$ which belongs to an $a \leq 1$ must be progressive.

This assertion already covers cases (I) and (IIa) of Theorem 3. To exclude case (IIb), i.e. $a > 1$, different assumptions about $u(\cdot)$, I and $T(\cdot)$ have to be made.

Theorem 4: Given an interval $I := [z_1, z_2[$ and an utility function $u(\cdot)$, which is at least as risk averse as the Bernoullian utility function, every $T(\cdot) \in N(u(\cdot), I)$ with $T(z_1) = 0$ and $T(z) \geq 0$ for all $z \in I$ must be progressive.

Proof: Assume that there is an utility function $u(\cdot)$ and $a > 1$ such that $u(S(z)) = au(z)$ for all $z \in I$. For $z = z_1$ we get $S(z_1) = z_1$, i.e. $u(z_1) = au(z_1)$ which implies $u(z_1) = 0$. Then $u(z) \geq 0$ for all $z \in I$, as $u(\cdot)$ was assumed to be strictly increasing. Hence, $u(S(z)) = au(z) > u(z)$ for all $z \in I$, which is a contradiction to $S(z) \leq z$ or, equivalently, $T(z) \geq 0$. Therefore $a \leq 1$ is guaranteed, which makes Lemma 2 applicable.

□

Quite similarly another criterion is obtained:

Theorem 5: Let $I \subseteq \mathbb{R}^+$ be an interval unbounded on the right and $u(\cdot)$ an utility function which is unbounded from above and at least as risk averse as the Bernoullian utility function. Then all $T(\cdot) \in N(u(\cdot), I)$, with $T(z) \geq 0$ for all $z \in I$ are progressive.

Proof: As $u(\cdot)$ is unbounded from above, there exists a $\hat{z}$ with $u(\hat{z}) > 0$. If $u(S(z)) = au(z)$ with $a > 1$ the inequality $u(S(\hat{z})) > u(\hat{z})$ i.e. $S(\hat{z}) > \hat{z}$ would be implied, which is in contradiction with $T(z) \geq 0$ for all $z \in I$.

□

This result covers the Bernoullian utility function itself as well as all utility functions which can be represented as $v(ln(\cdot))$, for z sufficiently great where $v(\cdot)$ is some concave function unbounded from above.

However, with respect to the more important case of utility functions bounded from above,[11] no definite answer can be reached with the help of Lemma 2. If $u(z) < 0$ for all $z \geq 0$ it is possible to have $u(S(z)) \leq au(z)$ with $a > 1$, without violating $S(z) \leq z$ for all z. For the treatment of this case another way has to be chosen: the representation formula is solved for $a = \frac{u(S(z))-b}{u(z)}$, such that the condition of Lemma 2 can be written as

$$\frac{S'(z)z}{S(z)} = \left(1 - \frac{b}{u(S(z))}\right) \frac{u'(z)z/u(z)}{u'(S(z))S(z)/u(S(z))} \leq 1.$$

Then the condition for (weak) progressivity is fulfilled if $b/u(S(z)) \geq 0$ and $u'(z)z/|u(z)| \leq u'(S(z))z/|u(S(z))|$. This leads to the following auxiliary result:

Lemma 3: Let $I \subseteq \mathbb{R}^+$. Every tax function in $N(u(\cdot), I)$ must be (weakly) progressive if either $b \geq 0$, $u(z) > 0$ for all $z \in I$ and $u'(z)z/u(z)$ is nonincreasing on I, or $b \leq 0$, $u(z) < 0$ for all $z \in I$ and (the negative-valued function) $u'(z)z/u(z)$ is nondecreasing in I.

For a utility function $u(\cdot)$ with $u(z) < 0$ for all $z > 0$, a nondecreasing elasticity of utility with respect to income is equivalent to the postulate that $-ln(-u(\cdot))$ is a concave utility function which is locally at least as risk averse as the Bernoullian utility function. (This is easily seen, as the relative risk aversion of $-ln(-u(\cdot))$ at z can be expressed as $-\left(\frac{u''(z)}{u'(z)} - \frac{u'(z)}{u(z)}\right) z$, which is not less than one if and only if $(u''(z)z + u'(z))u(z) - u'(z)^2 z \geq 0$. After some straightforward calculations it turns out that the expression on the left side of this inequality coincides with the numerator of $(u'(z)z/u(z))'$, which proves the assertion.) On the basis of this consideration a further criterion for progressivity can be derived:

Theorem 6: For a utility function $u(\cdot)$ bounded from above let $u_0(\cdot)$ denote that positive linear transformation of $u(\cdot)$ for which $lim_{z\to\infty}\, u_0(z) = 0$. If $-ln(-u_0(\cdot))$ is a concave utility function which is at least as risk averse as the Bernoullian utility function then every $T(\cdot) \in N(u(\cdot), I)$ with $T(z) \geq 0$ for all $z \in I$ is progressive, where I is an interval unbounded on the right.

Proof: The underlying assumption with respect to $u_0(\cdot)$ obviously implies that $u_0'(z)z$ is nonincreasing, i.e. $-u_0''(z)z/u_0'(z) \geq 1$ for all $z > 0$. As the degrees of relative risk aversion coincide, the same holds true for $u(\cdot)$. Then cases (I) and

[11] Arrow (1971, p. 69), claims that only such bounded utility functions can be allowed if the St. Petersburg-Paradox is to be avoided in any case ("Utility Boundedness Theorem"). But his view is not uncontroversial, as other plausible restrictions are possible which serve the same purpose. See e.g. Ryan (1974), Sinn (1983).

(IIa) of Theorem 3 are covered by Lemma 2. Case (IIb), i.e. $u(S(z)) = au(z)$ with $a > 1$ for all $z \in I$, remains to be considered. As $S(z) \leq z$ for all $z \in I$ and the unboundedness of I on the right were assumed, $u(z) < 0$ for all $z > 0$ must be fulfilled. Hence, the second part of Lemma 3 applies (with $b = 0$) if $u'(z)z/u(z)$ is nondecreasing in z. But this follows from the postulate that $-\,ln(-u_0(\cdot))$ is at least as risk averse as $ln(\cdot)$. It has only to be shown by simple differentiation that $(u_0'(z)z/u_0(z))' \geq 0$ implies $(u_0'(z)z/(u_0(z) + d))' \geq 0$ whenever $d \leq 0$.

□

But Lemma 3 can also be used to relax the conditions for progressivity if $u(\cdot)$ is unbounded from above.

Theorem 7: Let an interval $I := [z_1, z_2[$ $(z_2 \leq \infty)$ and $u(\cdot)$ be given. Then every $T(\cdot) \in N(u(\cdot), I)$ with $T(z_1) = 0$ is progressive if $ln\, u(\cdot)$ is at least as risk averse as $ln(\cdot)$ in I.

Proof: With regard to Lemma 3 it has only to be noted that $u(z) \geq 0$ for all $z \geq z_1$ (because $u(S(z_1)) = u(z_1) = 0$) and $(u'(z)z/u(z))' \geq 0$ for all $z \in I$ is equivalent to the statement that $ln(u(\cdot))$ is at least as risk averse as $ln(\cdot)$ in I.

□

If $u(\cdot)$ is bounded from below this result can be extended to all tax functions which are neutral for all $z \geq 0$. Without loss of generality $u(0) = 0$ can be assumed. (If a neutral tax function on $\mathbb{R}^+$ is represented by $u(S(z)) = au(z) + b$, it is impossible to have $b < 0$. Otherwise $lim_{z \to 0}\, u(S(z)) = b < 0$ which would contradict $u(z) > u(0) = 0$ for all $z > 0$.) But with $b \geq 0$ progressivity of all neutral tax functions on $\mathbb{R}_0^+$ is ensured by Lemma 3 if $(u'(z)z/u(z))' \leq 0$ for all $z > 0$.

Theorem 8: If $u(\cdot)$ is bounded from below let $u_0(\cdot)$ be the positive linear transformation of $u(\cdot)$ with $u_0(0) = 0$. If $ln\, u_0(\cdot)$ is at least as risk averse as the Bernoullian utility function, every $T(\cdot) \in N(u(\cdot), \mathbb{R}^+)$ is progressive.

Sometimes progressivity of a tax function is not defined in terms of the average, but in terms of the *marginal* tax rate. So "progressive" is also used for tax fomulas whose marginal tax rate increases with z. To avoid any confusion about terminology,[12] the notion "progressive" will be restricted to the case of a nondecreasing average tax rate, whereas all tax functions with a nondecreasing marginal

[12] Recently, the discussion between Fellingham and Wolfson (1978, 1984) and Schneider (1980) about the risk effects of progressive taxes is at least partly due to such a confusion.

tax rate will be called "convex". It is a well-known result that in most important cases the convexity of a tax function will imply its progressivity. Here, instead, convexity arises as an implication of progressivity if some further assumptions are added.

Theorem 9: If $u(\cdot)$ exhibits nondecreasing relative risk aversion,[13] every progressive $T(\cdot) \in N(u(\cdot), I)$ (with an arbitrarily chosen I and $T(z) \geq 0$ for all $z \in I$) will be convex.

Proof: Taking the derivative of $S'(z) = au'(z)/u'(S(z))$ yields

$$S''(z) = a(u''(z)u'(S(z)) - u'(z)u''(S(z))S'(z))/u'(S(z))^2.$$

Obviously $S''(z) \leq 0$ if and only if

$$\frac{u''(z)}{u'(z)} - \frac{u''(S(z))}{u'(S(z))}S'(z) \leq 0$$

which can be transformed into

$$-\frac{u''(S(z))}{u'(S(z))}S(z)\frac{S'(z)z}{S(z)} \leq -\frac{u''(z)z}{u'(z)}.$$

But progressivity implies $S'(z)z/S(z) \leq 1$, whereas (because $S(z) \leq z$) nondecreasing relative risk aversion leads to

$$-\frac{u''(S(z))S(z)}{u'(S(z))} \leq -\frac{u''(z)z}{u'(z)}.$$

□

5. Application to Particular Utility Functions

The most important classes of utility functions are characterized by the assumptions of constant absolute and constant relative risk aversion.[14] As the Bernoullian utility function (with a constant relative risk aversion equal to one) was used as

---

13 This assumption was advocated by Arrow (1971, p. 96).

14 As it is sometimes held (see e.g. Sinn, 1983, 1985b) that only constant relative risk aversion provides a realistic description of human behaviour, this special case is distinguished, among other reasons, by its easy tractability.

a standard of comparison throughout the last section, it seems obvious to first determine the neutral tax functions belonging to $u(z) = ln\, z$.

If an interval $I \subset \mathbb{R}^+$ is given, Theorem 2 says that for every $T(\cdot) \in N(ln(.), I)$, there must be a pair $(a, b) \in \mathbb{R}^+ \times \mathbb{R}$ such that $ln\, S(z) = a\, ln\, z + b$, i.e. $S(z) = Bz^a$ with $B = e^b > 0$ for all $z \in I$. But to obtain a real tax function, $S'(z) = aBz^{a-1} \leq 1$ has to be fulfilled for all $z \in I$. Just as in the general analysis before, let I be an unbounded interval, i.e. $I := [z_0, \infty[$. Then $a > 1$ is excluded, as otherwise $lim_{z \to \infty} S'(z) = \infty$.

A tax function is obtained if $a \leq 1$ is selected arbitrarily and, additionally, $B \leq z_0^{1-a}/a$. As $lim_{z_0 \to 0}\, z_0^{1-a} = 0$ if $a < 1$, $a = 1$ is required for every tax function to be neutral for all $z \geq 0$, i.e. $N(ln(\cdot), \mathbb{R}^+)$ consists only of proportional functions.

The other utility functions with constant relative risk aversion are either given by $u(z) = z^r$ with $r \in]0, 1]$, or $u(z) = -z^r$, with $r < 0$. In both cases the index of relative risk aversion equals $1 - r$.[15] The representative formulas for neutral tax functions are now given by $S(z) = (az^r + b)^{1/r} = z(a + (b/z^r))^{1/r}$ if $r \in]0, 1]$ and $S(z) = (az^r - b)^{1/r} = z(a - (b/z^r))^{1/r}$ for $r < 0$. Therefore, for every interval the progressivity of a neutral tax function depends only on the sign of b. For $r > 0$ a neutral tax will be progressive if and only if $b \geq 0$. For $r < 0$, on the other hand, progressivity is obtained if and only if $b \leq 0$. But the cases $r > 0$ and $r < 0$ are not as symmetric as it seems at first. This is seen if all tax functions which are neutral on unbounded intervals are determined.

For $r \in]0, 1]$ the relevant condition $S'(z) = a(a + (b/z^r))^{(1-r)/r} \leq 1$ is violated for every $a > 1$ if a large enough z is chosen. But if a certain $a < 1$ is given for every $z_0 > 0$, negative as well as positive values of b can be selected such that $S(z) = (az^r + b)^{1/r}$ describes the net income function belonging to a neutral tax, as $S'(z) \leq 1$ for all $z > z_0$ turns out to be equivalent to $b \leq (a^{-1} - a)z_0^r$. For such a b and every $a < 1$, the condition $S(z) \leq z$ is obviously valid, too. Thus neutral tax functions may occur which are regressive even on an unbounded interval. (As the relative risk aversion of $u(\cdot)$ is $1 - r < 1$, a first counter-example to Theorem 4 is provided in this way.) This is no longer possible if $I = \mathbb{R}^+$. Then, $b < 0$ can be excluded because corresponding neutral tax functions cannot be defined for income levels sufficiently small. For $b > 0$, on the other hand, $S'(z)$ would tend to infinity as z approaches zero. Thus $S(z) = a^{1/r}z$ with $a \leq 1$ is implied, i.e. only proportional taxes are contained in $N(z^r, \mathbb{R}^+)$ whenever $r > 0$. In particular $N(z^r, \mathbb{R}^+)$ is the same, irrespective of which particular $r \in]0, 1]$ has been chosen.

---

[15] This case was considered by Feldstein (1969, p. 763), but he developed only the most simple features of the problem.

By taking the limits, the case $r = 0$ can be identified with the Bernoullian utility function. Thus this result formally holds for every $r \in [0,1]$.

Turning to $r < 0$, the situation is completely changed. Here all tax functions neutral on an unbounded interval must be progressive as $b > 0$ is excluded. (Otherwise $S(z)$ would not be defined for large enough values of z.) If $b \leq 0$ is assumed, a sufficient condition for $S'(z) = a(a - (b/z^r))^{(1-r)/r} \leq 1$ to be true is that $a \geq 1$. Then $S(z) \leq z$ is automatically fulfilled. For a tax function neutral on $\mathbb{R}^+$, $a \geq 1$ is even necessary. Otherwise $lim_{z \to 0}\ S'(z) = a \cdot a^{(1-r)/r} = a^{1/r} = 1$ would be implied. For $b = 0$ the proportional taxes are obtained again, but here only as a subclass of $N(-z^r, \mathbb{R}^+)$, with $(r < 0)$. The shape of the corresponding neutral tax functions, however, is quite different for $b < 0$. For a given $a > 1$, it has the same gradient as the proportional tax belonging to a if z approaches zero. But, quite opposite from the case $b = 0$, $S(\cdot)$ does not approach infinity, but is bounded by $(-b)^{1/r}$, thus showing a very strong form of progressivity. This upper bound obviously gets smaller if b increases. Having established in Theorem 6 that $S(\cdot)$ must be concave, the net income functions fulfilling the neutrality condition can be depicted as follows:

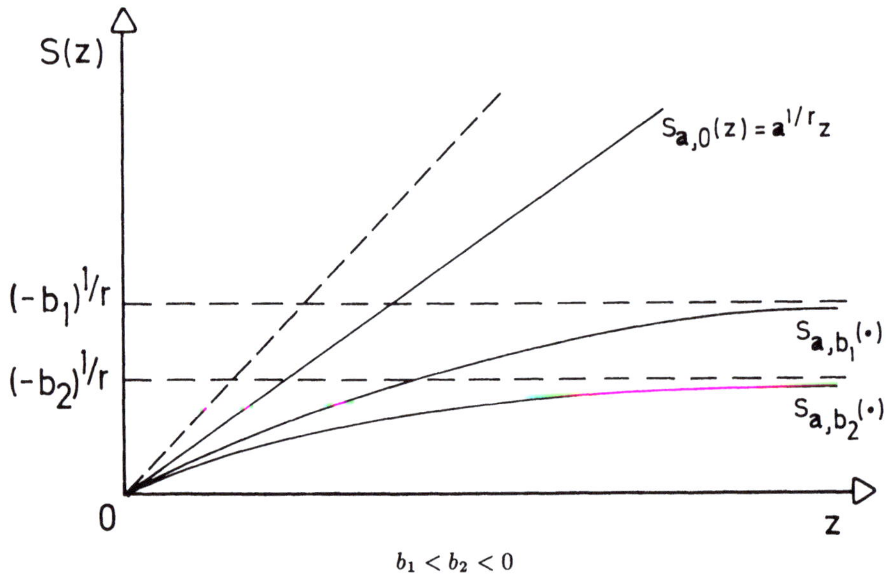

Figure 1

The analysis becomes more intricate for nonlinear utility functions exhibiting constant absolute risk aversion. In their most simple form these utility functions are given by $u(z) = -e^{-Rz}$ with $R > 0$. Here, R denotes the index of absolute risk aversion. The representation formula now implies that for every $T(\cdot) \in N(u(\cdot), I)$ there is a pair $(a,b) \in \mathbb{R}^+ \times \mathbb{R}$ such that $S(z) = -(ln(ae^{-Rz} - b))/R$ for all

$z \in I$. As $S'(z) = ae^{-Rz}/(ae^{-Rz} - b) = 1/(1 - (b/a)e^{Rz})$ it is obvious that $b \leq 0$ has to be fulfilled if $S'(z) \in [0,1]$ is to be obtained. In this case $S(\cdot)$ is defined for all $z > 0$. Then the convexity of a corresponding neutral tax function is also ensured, i.e. $S''(z) < 0$ for all $z \in I$. To fulfill the additional condition $S(z) \leq z$, the class of admissible parameters is further restricted. The relevant condition is $ln(ae^{-Rz} - b) \geq -Rz$ for all $z \in I$, which is easily transformed into $(a-1)e^{-Rz} \geq b$. To fulfill this condition for all $z \geq z_0$, the parameters a and b as well as z_0 must be selected such that $(a-1)e^{-Rz_0} \geq b$ is valid. Contrary to the other examples, it is still possible to have $S(z) < 0$, i.e. $T(z) > z$, for all $z > z_0$. To exclude this case, it is required that $ae^{-Rz_0} \leq 1 + b$. With $ae^{-Rz_0} = 1 + b$, a neutral tax function results which is convex, but not progressive everywhere in $[z_0, \infty[$. (Cf. Fig. 2.) Thus a counter-example to Theorem 5 is found, as the utility function exhibits a relative risk aversion greater than one for all $z > z_0$ whenever $z_0 > 1/R$. Especially when $b = 0$, lump-sum taxes are obtained as the most common taxes in $N(-e^{-Rz}, [(ln\, a)/R, \infty[)$ if a certain $a > 1$ is given. The tax amount is $(ln\, a)/R$.

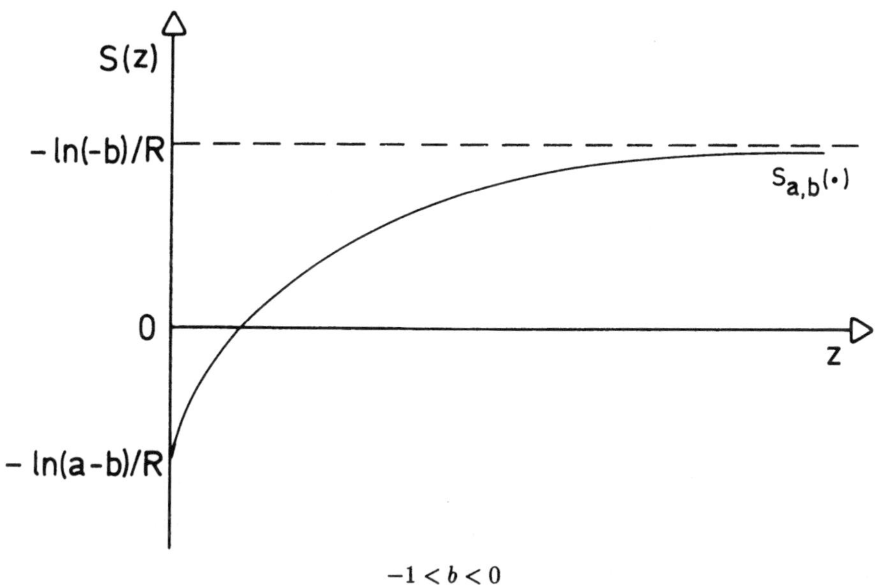

Figure 2

To reach $S(z) \leq z$ for all $z > 0$, $S(0) = -ln\,(a-b)/R \leq 0$ is required, i.e. $a \geq 1 + b$. Additionally, if $S(z) \geq 0$ is to be valid for all $z > 0$, the parameter a must coincide with $1 + b$. Seen from another point of view, these conditions are rather obvious as the range of all net income functions fulfilling the neutrality requirement with respect to nonlinear utility functions with constant absolute risk aversion is bounded below by $-ln\,(a-b)$ and by $-ln\,(-b)$ from above.

6. The Reverse Question: Neutrality of Given Tax Functions

The problem of determining $N(T(\cdot), I)$ for a given $T(\cdot)$ may be regarded as fundamental for the whole theory of risk aversion as the concepts of constant absolute and relative risk aversion can be introduced in the following way. A utility function $u(\cdot)$ can be said to exhibit constant absolute (relative) risk aversion on a certain interval $I \subset \mathbb{R}^+$ if and only if $u(\cdot) \in N(T(\cdot), I)$ for all lump-sum (proportional) taxes defined in I.[16] It is not very difficult to see that this definition corresponds to the conventional ones. This result can be improved if it is assumed a priori that absolute and relative risk aversion are monotonic functions of income. It is then sufficient to postulate $u(\cdot) \in N(T(\cdot), I)$ for one single lump-sum (proportional) tax if the constancy of absolute (relative) risk aversion is to be ensured.

The general problem is that of determining which properties a tax function must have if it is to be neutral with respect to a concave utility function. Until now no convincing solution has been reached which restricts considerations to the treatment of a rather simple particular case. Furthermore, a situation is described where $N(T(\cdot), I)$ is empty. As both examples are interpreted clearest in cases where income losses occur, the assumption applicable in the last section, i.e. $z \geq 0$, is now dropped.

The most prominent case in the theory of tax effects on risk-taking is considered first, i.e. a proportional income tax with full loss offset.[17] If the tax rate is denoted by t, the net income function is given by $S(z) = sz$ (with $s := 1 - t$), irrespective of whether z is positive or negative. Let an open interval $I \subset \mathbb{R}$ with $0 \in I$ be given. To attain neutrality with respect to a certain utility function $u(\cdot)$ in I, there must be $(a, b) \in \mathbb{R}^+ \times \mathbb{R}$, such that $u(sz) = au(z) + b$ for all $z \in I$. As $0 \in I$, i.e. $u(0) = au(0) + b$, $a = 1$ is impossible if $b \neq 0$. Then, by Theorem 3, $u(\cdot)$ can be chosen such that $u(sz) = au(z)$ for all $z \in I$, which implies $u(0) = 0$. Differentiation leads to $su'(sz) = au'(z)$, which for $z = 0$, implies $s = a$. Thus $u'(sz) = u'(z)$ for every $z \in I$. By iteration $u'(s^n z) = u'(z)$ is obtained for every $n \in \mathbb{N}$ and all $z \in I$. But as $lim_{n \to \infty}\ s^n z = 0$ and $u'(\cdot)$ was assumed to be continuous, $u'(z) = lim_{n \to \infty}\ u'(s^n z) = u'(0)$ is implied, i.e. $u(\cdot)$ must be a proportional function.

Theorem 10: If an open interval I with $0 \in I$ is given, every $u(\cdot) \in N(sz, I)$ $(s < 1)$ must exhibit risk neutrality.

[16] See also Schneeweiss (1967, pp. 85–87).

[17] In a certain way, the treatment of this case is just the beginning of the theoretical analysis in this field. See Domar and Musgrave (1944).

The polar case is described by the absence of all loss-offset opportunities. A tax function $T(\cdot)$ defined for an open interval I with $0 \in I$ is said to allow no loss offset at all if $T(z) = 0$, i.e. $S(z) = z$, for all $z \leq 0$. Now the following impossibility theorem can be derived:

Theorem 11: Let an open interval I with $0 \in I$ be given. A non-zero tax function $T(\cdot)$ without loss offset opportunities cannot be neutral with respect to any concave or linear utility function $u(\cdot)$ and the given interval I, i.e. $N(T(\cdot), I) = \emptyset$.

Proof: Just as in the proof of the last theorem, $a = 1$ is impossible as $S(0) = 0$ if $T(\cdot)$ is nonzero. Then, without any loss of generality, $u(S(z)) = au(z)$ can be assumed. If a $\hat{z} \in I$ with $\hat{z} < 0$ is given, $u(\hat{z}) = au(\hat{z})$ is implied by $S(\hat{z}) = \hat{z}$. As $u(\cdot)$ is strictly increasing, $a = 1$ must hold, which leads to a contradiction.

□

7. A Distributional Interpretation of Risk Neutrality

At least in a purely formal way there is a narrow connection between the theory of tax neutrality under risk presented here and much older topics in the theory of Public Finance. Hence, the absolute and proportional sacrifice prescriptions for the design of a just income tax can be seen as special cases of the tax neutrality condition if $u(\cdot)$ is not considered as a von Neumann-Morgenstern utility function, but as an index of individual welfare. Equal proportional sacrifice (PS)[18] means that an income tax $T(\cdot)$ leads to a proportional reduction of all individual welfare levels, i.e. $u(S(z)) = au(z)$ is valid for all income levels for which $u(\cdot)$ is defined. Obviously this identity results for $b = 0$ in the representation formula. Quite analogously, equal absolute sacrifice (AS)[19] requires $u(S(z)) = u(z) + b$, where $b < 0$ denotes the utility loss of each taxpayer implied by taxation. To get this AS-condition, $a = 1$ and $b < 0$ have to be substituted into the representation formula. If consideration is restricted to nonnegative income levels and $T(z) \geq 0$ is required for all $z > 0$, Theorem 3 says that neutrality is even equivalent to either AS or PS.

However, this formal identity is questionable for two reasons. First, the equal proportional sacrifice prescription only makes sense if the underlying utility in-

[18] See e.g. Cohen-Stuart (1889), who examined mathematically whether the PS-rule really implied income tax progressivity.

[19] See Mill (1886, p. 484). For a modern treatment of equal sacrifice concepts cf. Samuelson (1947, p. 227), Smith (1968), Richter (1983).

dices do not take on negative values.[20] This postulate is obviously violated by many important utility functions, e.g. for those with a constant relative risk aversion exceeding one. As shown before, it is even possible to have $a > 1$ which does not fit the intuitive conception of utility sacrifice. This difficulty can be easily overcome if the narrow sacrifice concepts are generalized to a postulate of *distributional* neutrality.[21] For this purpose, the differences between the utility levels of all individuals in a given economy are taken as the starting point of the analysis. All utility profiles leading to the same distributional structure of these differences with respect to the Lorenz curve criterion are then identified. In this respect, distributional neutrality simply means that all equivalence classes defined in this way are preserved by taxation.[22] This postulate, however, directly leads to the representation formula. If it is assumed that functions of individual welfare are determined only up to linear transformations, this approach to distributional neutrality seems very conclusive. In this case, the ratios of differences between the different utility levels constitute the only data available for the characterization of utility profiles.

Coping with the second objection is more difficult. One could ask if it is really possible to equate von-Neumann-Morgenstern utility functions, which are used to describe decisions under uncertainty, with utility functions indicating individual levels of well-being. Sometimes such an equivalence is implicitly assumed without any attempt at justification.[23] In other instances it is explicitly advocated.[24] Here, a pragmatic view is taken. In general, it is not at all clear what is meant by individual welfare. It is this conceptual difficulty which leads to the most fundamental objection to the sacrifice concept. The expected utility theory, on the other hand, has at least the advantage of giving a well-defined meaning to utility. This implies that it is possible to give a distributional meaning to neutrality with respect to decisions under risk. Thus, allocative and distributional neutrality converge in a certain way. Or, as seen from the other side, interpreting welfare indices as von-Neumann-Morgenstern utility functions leads to an embedding of the AS- and PS-concepts in the framework of decision theory. Thus the problem of defining indicators of well-being is avoided.

[20] This problem is neglected in the recent contribution of Young (1987).

[21] Tax neutrality originally referred to distributional rather than allocative aspects. Cf. Mann (1937, p. 158), who quotes Petty (1662): "For men (...) if the Estates of them all were either halfed or doubled, would in both cases remain equally rich."

[22] See e.g. D'Aspremont and Gevers (1977, p. 200), where this assumption is conceived as axiom of "co-cardinality".

[23] Cf. Young (1987).

[24] Sometimes it is even believed that this identity is more than formal. See e.g. Borch (1968, p. 27), who claims that $u(z)$ can be interpreted as "utility of money". For a clear statement of the opposite position see e.g. Schneeweiss (1967, pp. 67–73).

Interestingly, the idea of combining allocative and distributive neutrality can be traced back to Pigou. The framework of his analysis, however, was quite different, as he considered tax effects on the incentive to work: "The condition that the amount of work done shall not be altered by the announcement effects of taxation is that the satisfaction derived from increasing a gross income x by a small increment is not altered by the imposition of a tax."[25] Formally, this means $(u(z))' = (u(S(z)))'$, which leads to constant absolute sacrifice. However, this simple but lucid idea was not taken up again.

8. Summary

The main results of this paper can be summarized as follows:

- A tax function $T(\cdot)$ does not change the ordering of risky projects implied by a utility function $u(\cdot)$ if and only if $u(S(\cdot))$ is a positive linear transformation of $u(\cdot)$. But it is not necessary to define full neutrality in this way in order to imply the representation formula. A much weaker condition will do, i.e. that all projects with a given expected utility remain equivalent after the application of the tax.
- If progressivity of all tax functions which are neutral for a given $u(\cdot)$ on an unbounded interval $I \subset \mathbb{R}^+$ is to be ensured, a key role is played by the assumption that $u(\cdot)$ is at least as risk averse as the Bernoullian utility function $ln(\cdot)$. But this condition alone is not sufficient for progressivity. Interestingly, for utility functions whose degree of risk aversion is so great that they are bounded from above, regressive taxes may be neutral on unbounded intervals.
- Convexity of progressive tax functions is guaranteed if the Arrowian assumption of nondecreasing relative risk aversion is added.
- With respect to utility functions exhibiting a constant relative risk aversion ρ, the cases $\rho \leq 1$ and $\rho > 1$ are sharply distinguished. With $\rho \leq 1$ neutrality in $\mathbb{R}^+$ can only be achieved by proportional net income functions, whereas with $\rho > 1$ net income functions bounded from above may also be neutral in $\mathbb{R}^+$.
- Proportional income taxes with either full loss offset or without any loss offset cannot be neutral with respect to a concave utility function.

[25] Pigou (1928, p. 86).

- Neutrality of taxation under risk, as it was described here, provides a new approach for the interpretation of the traditional constant absolute and constant relative sacrifice prescriptions in normative tax theory.

The analysis could be extended in the following ways:

- Other possible relaxations of the neutrality postulate could be considered. For example, fixed distributions of probabilities over a finite set of "states of the world" might serve as a point of departure.
- It would be interesting to determine the conditions a tax function must fulfill if it is to be neutral with respect to at least one concave utility function.
- Finally, the underlying neutrality concept could be changed. Instead of treating all projects in the same manner, one might try to "skim the cream" on a project-specific base, i.e. to tax away those parts of the project's income which are not necessary to induce a certain investment project. Following this different neutrality conception "rent taxes" would be suggested which seem particularly attractive for the taxation of exhaustible resources.[26]

References

Arrow, K. J. (1971): *Essays in the Theory of Risk-Bearing.* Amsterdam etc.: North-Holland.

Atkinson, A. B., and **Stiglitz, J. E.** (1980): *Lectures on Public Economics.* London etc.: McGraw-Hill.

Auerbach, A. J. (1983): *The Taxation of Capital Income.* Cambridge, Mass., etc.: Harvard University Press.

Bamberg, G., and **Richter, W. F.** (1984): "The Effects of Progressive Taxation on Risk-Taking." *Zeitschrift für Nationalökonomie/Journal of Economics* 44: 93–102.

Bamberg, G., and **Richter, W. F.** (1987): "Risk-Taking under Progressive Taxation: Three Partial Effects." Forthcoming in *Measurement in Economics*, edited by W. Eichhorn et al. Heidelberg: Physica.

Borch, K. (1968): *The Economics of Uncertainty.* Princeton, N.J.: Princeton University Press.

[26] See e.g. Garnaut and Clunies Ross (1983) and Korn (1984). Especially for the analysis of risk effects in this context also cf. Meyer (1984). But this alternative neutrality conception was already sketched by Musgrave (1969, p. 140).

Buchholz, W. (1985): "Die Wirkung progressiver Steuern auf die Vorteilhaftigkeit riskanter Investitionen." *Zeitschrift für betriebswirtschaftliche Forschung* 37: 882–890.

Buchholz, W. (1986): "Die Elastizität des Grenznutzens als Determinante optimaler Allokation." *Jahrbücher für Nationalökonomie und Statistik* 201: 66–80.

Buhl, H. U., and **Pfingsten, A.** (1986): "Eigenschaften von Verfahren für einen angemessenen Länderfinanzausgleich in der Bundesrepublik Deutschland." *Finanzarchiv N.F.* 44: 98–109.

Cansier, D. (1985): "Steuern und Investitionsrisiko." In *Öffentliche Finanzen, Kredit und Kapital — Festschrift für Werner Ehrlicher zur Vollendung des 65. Lebensjahres*, edited by D. Cansier and D. Kath. Berlin: Duncker & Humblot, pp. 255–283.

Cohen-Stuart, A. J. (1889): "On Progressive Taxation." (Reprinted in: *Classics in the Theory of Public Finance*, edited by R. A. Musgrave and A. T. Peacock. London: Macmillan 1958, pp. 48–71.)

D'Aspremont, D., and **Gevers, L.** (1977): "Equity and the Informational Basis of Collective Choice." *Review of Economic Studies* 44: 199–209.

Domar, E. D., and **Musgrave, R. A.** (1944): "Proportional Income Taxation and Risk-Taking." *Quarterly Journal of Economics* 58: 388–422.

Elschen, R., and **Hüchtebrock** (1983): "Steuerneutralität in Finanzwissenschaft und Betriebswirtschaftslehre." *Finanzarchiv N.F.* 41: 253–280.

Feldstein, M. S. (1969): "The Effects of Taxation on Risk-Taking." *Journal of Political Economy* 77: 755–764.

Fellingham, J. C., and **Wolfson, M. A.** (1978): "The Effects of Alternative Income Tax Structures on Risk-Taking." *National Tax Journal* 31: 339–347.

Fellingham, J. C., and **Wolfson, M. A.** (1984): "Progressive Income Taxes and the Demand for Risky Assets." *National Tax Journal* 37: 127–129.

Garnaut, R., and **Clunies Ross, A.** (1983): *Taxation of Mineral Rents.* Oxford: Clarendon Press.

Korn, M. (1984): *Ökonomische Beurteilung spezieller Abgaben für Rohstoffproduzenten.* Frankfurt etc.: Lang.

Mann, F. K. (1937): *Steuerpolitische Ideale.* Jena: Gustav Fischer.

Mayer, A. (1984): "Besteuerung von erschöpfbaren Ressourcen: Die Rohstoffrentensteuer." In *Intertemporale Allokation*, edited by H. Siebert. Frankfurt etc.: Lang, pp. 367–394.

Mill, J. S. (1886): *Principles of Political Economy.* London: Longman, Green and Co.

Musgrave, R. A. (1969): *Finanztheorie.* 2nd ed., Tübingen: Mohr.

Musgrave, R. A., and **Musgrave, P. B.** (1984): *Public Finance in Theory and Practice*. 4th ed., New York etc.: McGraw-Hill.

Petty, W. (1662): *A Treatise of Taxes and Contributions*. London.

Pigou, A. C. (1928): *A Study in Public Finance*. (3rd. ed. 1956) London: Macmillan.

Pratt, J. W. (1964): "Risk Aversion in the Small and in the Large." *Econometrica* 32: 122–136.

Richter, W. F. (1983): "From Ability to Pay to Concepts of Equal Sacrifice." *Journal of Public Economics* 20: 211–229.

Ryan, T. M. (1974): "The Use of Unbounded Utility Functions in Expected-Utility Maximization." *Quarterly Journal of Economics* 88: 133–135.

Samuelson, P. A. (1947): *Foundations of Economic Analysis*. Cambridge, Mass.: Harvard University Press.

Sandmo, A. (1985): "The Effects of Taxation on Savings and Risk-Taking." In *Handbook of Public Economics, Vol. 1*, edited by A. Auerbach and M. Feldstein. Amsterdam etc.: North-Holland, pp. 265–311.

Schneider, D. (1977): "Gewinnbesteuerung und Risikobereitschaft: Zur Bewährung quantitativer Ansätze in der Entscheidungstheorie." *Zeitschrift für betriebswirtschaftliche Forschung* 29: 633–666.

Schneider, D. (1980): "The Effects of Progressive and Proportional Income Taxation on Risk-Taking." *National Tax Journal* 33: 67–76.

Schneeweiss, H. (1967): *Entscheidungskriterien bei Risiko*. Berlin etc.: Springer.

Sinn, H.-W. (1983): *Economic Decisions under Uncertainty*. Amsterdam etc.: North-Holland.

Sinn, H.-W. (1985a): *Kapitaleinkommensbesteuerung*. Tübingen: Mohr.

Sinn, H.-W. (1985b): "Psychophysical Laws in Risk Theory." *Journal of Economic Psychology* 6: 185–206.

Smith, P. E. (1968): "The Ability-to-Pay Principle and Equal Proportional Sacrifice." *Public Finance* 23: 485–491.

Stiglitz, J. E. (1969): "The Effects of Income, Wealth and Capital Gains Taxation on Risk-Taking." *Quarterly Journal of Economics* 83: 262–283.

Young, H. P. (1987): "Progressive Taxation and the Equal Sacrifice Principle." *Journal of Public Economics* 32: 215–230.

On Measuring the Welfare Cost of Public Expenditure: A Simple General Equilibrium Approach

Wilhelm Pfähler, Koblenz, West Germany*

I. Introduction

Economists have long been aware that taxes produce a welfare cost (efficiency loss, excess burden) to the economy by distorting resource allocation. In view of the concern of economists over resource allocation, it is surprising how few studies attempt to calculate this welfare cost. The pioneer in this work has been Harberger (1964a, 1964b, 1966, 1974) who has drawn on Hotelling's (1938) earlier formulations and provided calculations of the welfare costs of a number of tax distortions.

In recent years, this work has been carried further through more complex models constructed to evaluate the interacting effects of tax distortions in various economies. Moreover, the focus has shifted from the measurement of *total welfare costs* of existing taxes as compared with lump-sum taxes of equal yield to the assessment of the *marginal welfare costs* of raising extra revenue from already existing distorting taxes. The literature now provides empirical estimates of the marginal welfare cost of tax-induced labor supply distortions,[1] of tax-induced savings distortions,[2] of tax-induced interindustry distortions of capital use,[3] as well as of the whole tax subsidy system.[4]

This paper once more addresses the question of the marginal welfare cost of taxing income from labor. The available estimates of the marginal welfare cost of labor income taxation do not explicitly take into account the spending of tax revenue on public expenditure or redistributive transfers. They therefore neglect

* I thank the participants of the Klosterseminar at Neresheim and two anonymous referees for valuable comments and discussions. The paper was inspired by many fruitful discussions with Art Snow. The usual disclaimer applies.

[1] See, e.g., Harberger (1964); Browning (1976); Hausman (1981a, 1981b, 1983a, 1983b); Stuart (1984); Hansson and Stuart (1985); Wildasin (1984); Ballard, Shoven, and Whalley (1982, 1985).

[2] See, e.g., Hall (1968); Mieszkowski (1978); Fullerton, Shoven, and Whalley (1983); Summers (1979).

[3] See, e.g., Harberger (1964, 1966); Shoven (1976); Fullerton, King, Shoven, and Whalley (1981).

[4] See Ballard, Shoven, and Whalley (1985).

the possible additional income and substitution effects the use of the tax revenue may have on labor supply which, in turn, may significantly influence the marginal welfare cost of labor income taxation. These estimates, thus, are based on *partial equilibrium models of labor supply.*

A *general equilibrium model of labor supply*, in contrast, would have to incorporate the repercussions of public expenditure on labor supply and, hence, on the welfare cost of labor income taxation. The general equilibrium effect of public expenditure on labor supply has already been addressed by Friedman (1949), Goode (1949), and Bailey (1954). Their argument is that, in the appropriate balanced-budget framework, a spending change must accompany the tax change and will induce an income effect that dissipates the partial equilibrium income effect of the tax change. Recently, while discussing the Laffer curve relationship, Lindbeck (1982), Gwartney and Stroup (1983), Wilde (1984), and Snow and Warren (1985) have revived the analysis of this general equilibrium effect. However, all these authors, with the notable exception of Snow and Warren, consider special cases only, as will be shown. Atkinson and Stern (1974), followed by Wildasin (1979, 1984), were the first, to my knowledge, to discuss explicitly the significance of this effect for the welfare cost of taxation and public expenditure.

The purpose of this paper is to pick up on this discussion and to reconsider the marginal welfare cost of taxes on income from labor on the basis of a simple second-best general equilibrium model of public expenditure and taxation. In particular, I will reconsider the marginal welfare cost of an incremental addition to pure public goods supply financed by a higher marginal tax rate of a linear-progressive (or flat rate) tax on income from labor. In doing this, special emphasis is placed on clearly identifying and defining the various types of welfare benefits and costs as well as their determinants and their pattern of interaction. The balanced-budget framework of analysis allows for a clear-cut evaluation of the assumptions made implicitly in recent literature with regard to the repercussions of public expenditure on labor supply and on the marginal welfare costs of public funds.

The plan of the paper is as follows: In sec. II a simple second-best general equilibrium model of public good supply is presented. On the basis of this model, the marginal welfare effects of a tax-financed expansion in pure public goods supply will be analysed in detail in sec. III. Sec. IV contains a reappraisal of some relevant literature in light of the general equilibrium view of the welfare cost of taxation. Sec. V concludes the paper.

II. A Simple Second-best General Equilibrium Model of Public Good Expenditure

From a general equilibrium perspective, the second-best welfare analysis of public expenditure and taxation comprises four aspects:

1. the *direct social benefit* of public expenditure;
2. the *direct opportunity cost* of production;
3. the *indirect social cost/benefit of distortionary finance*;
4. and the *indirect social cost/benefit of public expenditure.*

The *direct social benefit* and *direct opportunity cost* of public expenditure are considered in Samuelson's (1954, 1969) first-best theory of public expenditure and taxation. This theory also lies at the foundation of applied benefit-cost analysis of public expenditure. The *indirect social cost/benefit of financing public good supply by distortionary taxation* has in theory been addressed by Pigou (1947), Stiglitz and Dasgupta (1971), and, most rigorously, by Atkinson and Stern (1974). The indirect welfare cost of public funds is the primary object of the aforementioned empirical estimates.[5] The *indirect social cost/benefit of public expenditure*, however, which in theory was first addressed by Atkinson and Stern (1974), is as yet not taken into account in these empirical estimates. This omission reflects implicit hypotheses on the effects of public goods supply on the various tax bases which should and will be made explicit.

All four welfare aspects, the direct and indirect social cost and benefit of public expenditure and distortionary taxation, as well as their determinants and pattern of interaction are simultaneously revealed in a second-best general equilibrium welfare analysis. Such a second-best analysis has two characteristic features: first of all, the government's budget policy is regarded as exogenous to the consumers' economic decision making. This, in turn, also precludes a first-best Lindahl (quasi-market) equilibrium of public expenditure and taxation, as defined in Samuelson (1969). Secondly, lump-sum taxes to finance public expenditure are regarded as not being feasible, so that distortionary taxes have to be used to finance public expenditure.

A simple second-best general equilibrium model of (pure) public good expenditure and taxation with linear technology and a linear tax on labor income suffices to meaningfully and operationally specify most of the relevant welfare aspects of a balanced-budget increase in public good supply. Assume that there are H households, each with a twice continuously differentiable strictly quasi-concave

[5] See fn. 1 to 4 above for some examples of this literature.

utility function $u^h(x^h, z, L^h)$, defined over private numeraire good consumption, $x^h > 0$ (where $\sum x^h = x$ and $p_x = 1$), public good consumption, $z > 0$ (where $z = z^h$), and consumption of leisure, $L^h > 0$. Everyone is endowed with E^h units of time which can be allocated either to market work as labor, ℓ^h, or to non-market activities as leisure, L^h, i.e. $E^h = \ell^h + L^h$.[6]

Labor is the only factor and is assumed to have a constant marginal product in private and public goods production. Thus, production technology is assumed to be linear, implying constant direct (real) opportunity cost of the public good, $MRT = -dx/dz = p_z$, and a constant (gross-of-tax) wage rate, w. It also implies zero pure economic profits as well as automatic good and factor market clearance, $\sum_h x^h = x$ and $\sum_h \ell^H = \ell$. As a consequence, the social production possibility frontier is determined by

$$(1)\quad w\sum_h L^h + \sum_h p_x x^h + p_z z = w\sum_h E^h \quad \text{or}$$
$$\sum_h p_x x^h + p_z z = w\sum_h (E^h - L^h) = w\sum_h \ell^h \quad (p_x = 1).$$

Macroeconomic considerations, such as unemployment and inflation, as well as dynamic issues of capital accumulation, growth, and debt finance, shall not enter into the analysis. This simplification dictates that the fiscal budget be balanced. Given a single linear-progressive (or flat rate) tax with a constant marginal rate, t, on labor income exceeding an untaxed threshold, D, a balanced budget requires

$$(2)\qquad T = \sum_h T^h = \sum_h t(w\ell^h - D) = p_z z = G$$

where T and G are total tax revenue and total public goods expenditure, respectively.

The government is assumed to act as an exogenous agent that determines the budget policy (t, D, z). Each household takes this budget policy as given and chooses labor supply so as to maximize utility, subject to the household's budget constraint

$$(3)\qquad I^h = (1-t)wE^h + tD = p_x x^h + (1-t)wL^h \qquad (\text{with } p_x = 1)$$

where I^h is the household's total spending on private good consumption and on leisure. From the source side, I^h is defined as the sum of the net-of-tax value

[6] Alternatively, one could model $u(x, y, z)$ with total time endowment being devoted to taxed uses x (i.e. to the taxed sector) and to untaxed uses y (i.e. to the untaxed sector), where the latter uses would encompass time devoted to (resource using) home production, leisure, as well as to "on-the-job-leisure" and to activities leading to tax evasion and fringe benefits. See, for example, Stuart (1984).

of the total time endowment, $(1-t)wE^h$, and the value of the implicit transfer accruing to the household by being granted a tax threshold, tD.[7] Net of tax labor income is given as $(1-t)w\ell^h + tD$.

With the government's budget policy taken as exogenous, the household's labor supply (or demand for leisure) is determined by the first order condition

$$(4) \qquad (\partial u^h/\partial L^h) \;/\; (\partial u^h/\partial x^h) = (1-t)w$$

and the budget constraint (3). The ordinary (Marshallian) supply function of labor, conditional on a given budget policy (t, z, D), is then given as

$$(5) \qquad \ell^h = \ell^h(p_x, (1-t)w, z, I^h) \qquad \text{(with } p_x = 1\text{)}$$

Note that due to eqs. (3) and (5) the marginal tax rate in combination with the tax threshold determines the household's total spending on private good consumption and leisure. Households adjust their labor supplies (or demands for leisure) and their private good demands in response to the public good provision. With public good provision given exogenously, ℓ^h is completely determined and each household's indirect utility function can be written as

$$(6) \qquad V^h(p_x, (1-t)w, z, I^h) = \max_{x^h, L^h} u(x^h, z, L^h) \quad \text{s. t.} \quad I^h = (1-t)wE^h + tD = p_x x^h + (1-t)wL^h$$

In equilibrium, the conditional demand price for the public good, p_z^h, is the household's marginal valuation of the public good; that is,

$$(7) \qquad p_z^h = (\partial u^h/\partial z) \;/\; (\partial u^h/\partial x^h) = MRS^h.$$

Consequently, the household's "full income", including imputed income for public good expenditure, can be written as

$$(8) \qquad I^{h*} = I^h + MRS^h \cdot z$$

which, of course, does not include the consumer's surplus on inframarginal units of the public good.[8]

---

[7] Suppose the household supplies all its time as labor. Then, if there were no tax threshold, the tax bill would be twE^h. With a tax threshold the tax bill is $tw(E^h - D) = twE^h - tD$, i.e. the value of the tax relief is tD. This tax relief can be interpreted as an implicit (lump-sum) transfer or, in Hausman's (1981) terminology, as "virtual income".

[8] This is in line with the imputation procedure for the incidence of public good benefits developed by Aaron and McGuire (1970).

Let us, for simplicity, also eliminate all equity considerations by assuming distributional neutrality in the sense of equal social marginal utilities of the consumption of the numeraire good, i.e. $dW/dI^h = (\partial W/\partial V^h)(\partial V^h/\partial I^h) = m$ for all h.[9] Given all these assumptions and definitions, the simplified second-best general equilibrium model, by Walras' law, need only consist of an indirect (utilitarian) social welfare function

$$W = \sum\nolimits_h V^h(p_x, (1-t)w, z, I^h) \tag{9}$$

and the government's budget constraint (2).[10] This simplified model contains most of the relevant aspects of the problem at hand. It neglects, for example, public expenditures for public inputs as well as mixed goods.

III. Marginal Welfare Costs and Benefits of Public Expenditure in Second-best Analysis

The second-best condition for a welfare-enhancing increase of the public good supply, financed by a higher marginal tax rate on taxable labor income, then, is derived from maximizing (9) subject to (2) with respect to t and z.[11] For expository purposes, however, we rather state the following formula for the second-best condition:[12]

$$\frac{dW/dz}{dW/dI^h} = \sum\nolimits_h \frac{\partial V^h/\partial z}{\partial V^h/\partial I^h} - \sum\nolimits_h (-)\frac{\partial V^h/\partial t}{\partial V^h/\partial I^h} \cdot \frac{dt}{dz}. \tag{10a}$$

The left side of this formula expresses, in monetary terms,[13] the *social net value of a marginal balanced-budget expansion in public good supply*, $(dW/dz)\,/\,(dW/dI^h)$.

---

[9] Note that in the household's optimum the marginal utility of consuming the numeraire good is $\partial u^h/\partial x^h = m^h p_x = m^h = \partial V^h/\partial I^h$ (because of $p_x = 1$), where m^h is the private marginal utility of income. It is, of course, paradoxical to assume identical social marginal utilities within a second-best framework. Either lump-sum taxes/transfers can be used to achieve this identity, in which case we do not have to bother with distortionary taxation, or lump-sum taxes/transfers are not feasible, and then we cannot meaningfully eliminate the equity issue.

[10] The asssumption of lincar technology guarantees automatic goods and factor market clearance, and the households' budget constraints are taken into account in the indirect utility functions.

[11] Alternatively, one could consider financing the one-unit increase in public good supply by lowering the tax threshold.

[12] The following formula is obtained from totally differentiating W with respect to z and t and by dividing it by dz and by m, where m denotes the social marginal utility of household income (assumed to be equal for all households).

[13] By division by the marginal utility of income all marginal utilities are transformed into monetary units.

It is obtained as the difference between the *direct marginal social benefit* of the incremental public good supply and its *marginal social cost* of financing it by a higher marginal tax rate. In the second-best optimum, the marginal social net value, of course, must be zero. Both the direct marginal social benefit and, in particular, the marginal social cost will now be analysed in some detail.

Direct Marginal Social Benefit

The *direct marginal social benefit* can easily be shown to equal the sum of the households' marginal rates of substitution between the private numeraire good and the public good, i.e.[14]

$$\sum\nolimits_h \frac{\partial V^h/\partial z}{\partial V^h/\partial I^h} = \sum\nolimits_h MRS^h. \tag{11}$$

Thus, the change in utility from an increased public good supply equals its direct marginal effect on utility. While the household may change its other purchases and factor supplies in response to a change in public good supply, these changes will have no further effect on utility.

Marginal Social Cost

According to Samuelson's first-best welfare (or efficiency) criterion $\sum_h MRS^h = MRT$, an extra unit of a public good is desirable as long as the direct social marginal benefit is greater than the direct social marginal opportunity cost of the resources used up in providing this extra unit of a public good. In a second-best environment, in contrast, the marginal social cost comprises more than simply the direct marginal social opportunity cost MRT.

For an exogenous one-unit increase in public good supply, financed by a distortionary tax on income from labor, the *marginal social cost* (MSC) is instead defined as

$$MSC = \sum\nolimits_h (-)\frac{\partial V^h/\partial t}{\partial V^h/\partial I^h} \cdot \frac{dt}{dz} = \sum\nolimits_h (w\ell^h - D) \cdot \frac{MRT - (\partial T/\partial z)_{\bar{t}}}{(\partial T/\partial t)_{\bar{z}}} \tag{12a}$$

[14] The equality $(\partial V^h/\partial z)$ / $(\partial V^h/\partial I^h) = (\partial u^h/\partial z)$ / $(\partial u^h/\partial x^h)$ follows from the partial derivative $\partial V^h/\partial z$ of the dual, taking into account the budget restraint (3), totally differentiated with respect to z, as well as from the first-order optimality condition (4) of the primal of the consumer problem (with $p_x = 1$).

i.e. as the product of the monetary social marginal cost of a one-percentage-point increase of the tax rate, $\sum_h (\partial V^h/\partial t)/(\partial V^h/\partial I^h)$, and the actually required number of percentage points by which the marginal tax rate has to be increased in order to finance a one-unit increase in public good supply, taking into account all general equilibrium repercussions, dt/dz.

According to Roy's identity, the monetary marginal social cost of a one-percentage-point increase of the marginal tax rate equals one unit of total taxable income, i.e. $\sum_h (\partial V^h/\partial t)/(\partial V^h/\partial I^h) = -\sum_h (w\ell^h - D)$. The actual tax hike required for this balanced-budget operation, dt/dz, is determined by (1.) the direct social opportunity cost, MRT, (2.) the tax revenue effect of a tax rate increase, holding public good supply constant, $(\partial T/\partial t)_{\bar{z}}$, and (3.) the tax revenue effect of an expanded public good supply, holding the tax rate constant, $(\partial T/\partial z)_{\bar{t}}$, i.e. $dt/dz = (MRT - (\partial T/\partial z)_{\bar{t}})/(\partial T/\partial t)_{\bar{z}}$.

In order to facilitate a more conventional and more convenient economic interpretation, it is useful to decompose the marginal social cost of a balanced-budget operation, as defined in (12a), into the marginal social cost elements attributable to taxation and to public expenditure, respectively. Thus, let $MSCG = d(G - T_{\bar{t}})/dz$ be the *net marginal social cost of an incremental public good supply*, as measured by the budget deficit $G - T_{\bar{t}}$ incurred, if the public good supply is incrementally expanded while the tax rate is held constant. Assuming a balanced-budget framework, the only source of revenue available in order to finance this budget deficit are taxes. Hence, $d(G - T_{\bar{t}}) = dT_{\bar{z}}$ in taxes is needed to finance the deficit.[15]

On the other hand, let $MSCT = \sum_h (w\ell^h - D)dt/dT_{\bar{z}}$ be the *indirect marginal social cost of distortionary finance* of one additional tax DM (or \$) by increasing the marginal tax rate, while holding the public good supply constant. The *social marginal cost of a balanced-budget operation*, MSC, can then equivalently be expressed as the following product:

$$\text{(12b)} \qquad MSC = \frac{\sum_h (wl^h - D)dt}{dT_{\bar{z}}} \cdot \frac{d(G - T_{\bar{t}})}{dz} = MSCT \cdot MSCG.$$

Each component of MSC will now be investigated in turn.

---

[15] From the government's budget constraint $T = G$ in (2) the total differential is obtained as

$$dT = (\partial T/\partial t)_{\bar{z}} dt + (\partial T/\partial z)_{\bar{t}} dz = dT_{\bar{z}} + dT_{\bar{t}} = dG,$$

such that $d(G - T_{\bar{t}}) = dT_{\bar{z}}$.

Marginal Social Cost of Distortionary Finance

Let us first analyse in some detail the *indirect marginal social cost/benefit of distortionary tax finance MSCT*. It is defined as the monetary value of the social marginal welfare cost of an additional DM (or \$) tax revenue from a higher marginal tax rate, i.e.

$$(13) \qquad MSCT = \sum\nolimits_h (-)\frac{\partial V/\partial t}{\partial V/\partial I^h} \cdot \frac{dt}{dT_{\bar{z}}} = \frac{\sum_h (w\ell^h - D)}{\sum_h (w\ell^h - D) + tw\sum_h (\partial \ell^h/\partial t)}.$$

The tax hike required to collect an additional DM (or \$) tax revenue, while holding public good supply constant, is determined by $dt/dT_{\bar{z}}$. Its reciprocal is the tax revenue effect $dT_{\bar{z}}/dt = \sum_h (w\ell^h - D) + tw\sum_h(\partial \ell^h/\partial t)$; it is composed of the exogenous "arithmetic" effect of a higher tax rate applied to a given tax base, $\sum_h(w\ell^h - D)$, and the endogenous economic effect of an increased tax rate on labor supply and, hence, on the tax base, $tw\sum_h(\partial \ell^h/\partial t)$.[16] The interaction of the "arithmetic" and the economic effect, of course, is captured in the (nowadays) so-called Laffer curve.

Obviously, according to (13), the indirect social marginal cost of distortionary finance of an additional tax DM (or \$) depends critically on the economic tax base effect $\partial \ell^h/\partial t$. If each household's ordinary (or Marshallian) labor supply is completely inelastic with respect to a tax-induced change of the net wage rate, or, equivalently, if the labor income tax is (at least locally) a lump sum-type of tax, the indirect social marginal cost of financing an additional tax DM (or \$) by a linear tax on labor income is precisely that DM (or \$), i.e. $MSCT = 1$ if $\partial \ell^h/\partial t = 0$ for all h. On the other hand, if households reduce/increase their labor supplies with rising marginal tax rates, the indirect social marginal cost of an additional DM (or \$) will exceed/fall short of that DM (or \$), i.e. $MSCT > / < 1$ if $\partial \ell^h/\partial t < / > 0$ for all h.

More specifically, the household's labor supply reaction to an increased marginal tax rate of a linear tax on labor income is derived from (5) as

$$\begin{aligned}(14a) \quad \partial \ell^h/\partial t &= (\partial \ell^h/\partial w_n)(\partial w_n/\partial t) + (\partial \ell^h/\partial I^h)_{une}(\partial I^h/\partial t)\\ &= (\partial \ell^h/\partial w_n)(-w) + (\partial \ell^h/\partial I^h)_{une} D\end{aligned}$$

or as

$$\begin{aligned}(14b) \quad \partial \ell^h/\partial t &= (\partial \ell^h/\partial w_n)_{\overline{U}}(-w) + (\partial \ell^h/\partial I^h)_e(-wE^h) + (\partial \ell^h/\partial I^h)_{une} D\\ &= -wS^h - (\partial \ell^h/\partial I^h)_{une+e}(wE^h - D).\end{aligned}$$

---

[16] That is, from $T = tB(t)$ it follows that $dT/dt = B + t(\partial B/\partial t)$, where $B(t)$ is the "arithmetic" effect and $t(\partial B/\partial t)$ the economic effect. B is the total tax base.

Thus, there exist two tax-induced labor supply effects. One is the usual *direct price (net wage rate) effect*, $\partial \ell^h / \partial w_n$, which is composed of a substitution effect, $S^h = (\partial \ell^h / \partial w_n)_{\overline{U}}$, and an *earned income effect*, $(\partial \ell^h / \partial I^h)_e$. The earned income effect results from the devaluation of the monetary value $(1-t)wE^h$ of the total time endowment in response to a higher marginal tax rate. The other effect is a *pure unearned income effect*, $(\partial \ell^h / \partial I^h)_{une}$; it results here from the revaluation of the implicit transfer value tD of the tax threshold.[17]

In theory, the direct price (net wage rate) effect is ambiguous in sign; while the substitution effect of a lower net wage rate discourages labor supply, the earned income effect stimulates labor supply (if leisure is normal). The pure unearned income effect of a tax hike, in contrast, discourages labor supplies of the income recipients above the tax threshold (if leisure is normal), whereas those below the tax threshold remain unaffected.[18]

Traditionally, it is assumed that the substitution effect dominates the earned income effect of a higher marginal tax rate such that the ordinary labor supply curve is sloped positively. In this case, a higher marginal tax rate discourages ordinary labor supply and the unearned income effect of the higher valued tax threshold reinforces this disincentive. Depending on the magnitude of this effect for the entire economy, this negative economic tax base effect may or may not outweigh the positive "arithmetic" tax rate effect on tax revenue so that the economy is located on the downward-sloping or upward-sloping segment of the Laffer curve. Empirical research, however, casts doubt on this traditional assumption and rather indicates vertical or even backward bending ordinary labor supply schedules of married prime-age males.[19]

Empirical estimates of the marginal welfare cost of distortionary taxes have traditionally been based on a *partial equilibrium Pigou-Harberger-type analysis*. In this type of analysis real income (utility) is kept constant by assuming that the involved income effects are compensated by (non-distortionary) rebating the tax revenue. Consequently, the substitution effect along the *compensated labor supply curve* is of sole interest; and since the substitution effect clearly discourages labor supply, there are indeed *indirect social marginal costs of compensated distortionary tax finance*. That is, the marginal social cost per DM (or \$) of ad-

[17] An additional unearned income effect would result from a change in non-labor income taxation.

[18] Note that creating a tax threshold leads to a kinked budget constraint with different marginal tax rates in two brackets.

[19] (Normal) Labor supply schedules of female workers, in contrast, reveal significant positive elasticities.

ditional compensated tax revenue will exceed that DM (or \$), $(MSCT)_{\overline{u}} > 1$, as argued by Pigou (1947).

In a *general equilibrium analysis* of a balanced-budget operation, in contrast, the tax revenue will not be rebated but rather funneled into public goods expenditure or redistributive transfers. In this case, one has to refer to the *ordinary labor supply curves* to assess the indirect marginal social cost of distortionary finance. It may then well be the case that the earned income effect dominates the substitution and unearned income effect such that the ordinary labor supply curve increases with higher marginal tax rates. In this special case, which was first explicitly considered by Atkinson and Stern (1974) in a balanced-budget framework, there will be an *(indirect) social marginal benefit*, rather than a social marginal cost, *of (non-compensated) distortionary tax finance.* That is, the social marginal cost per DM (or \$) of additional tax revenue will be less than that DM (or \$), i.e. $MSCT < 1$.

More specifically, if the tax revenue is funneled into redistributive lump-sum transfers everyone's supply of labor decreases (if leisure is a normal good), implying a reduction in aggregate labor supply. In this case we can derive the household's *ordinary general equilibrium supply curve* of labor as

$$d\ell^h/dt = -wS^h/(1 - tw(\partial \ell^h/\partial I^h)) < 0 \qquad (14c)$$

i.e. each household's labor supply is reduced by an amount that is proportional to but smaller than the substitution effect.[20]

---

[20] In this pure transfer case in which consumption externalities of transfers are neglected the household's and the government budget constraints read as, respectively,

$$I^h = (1-t)wE^h + tD + TR^h \qquad (3^*)$$

$$T = \sum_h t(w\ell^h - D) = \sum_h TR^h = TR. \qquad (2^*)$$

By differentiating the conditional ordinary supply function of labor $\ell^h(p_x, (1-t)w, z, I^h)$ with respect to t, one obtains

$$d\ell^h/dt = -w(\partial \ell^h/\partial w_n)_{\overline{U}} - (wE^h - D)(\partial \ell^h/\partial I^h) + (\partial \ell^h/\partial I^h)(dTR^h/dt).$$

Assuming head transfers $TR^h = TR/H$, such that $dTR^h/dt = (dTR/dt)/H$ and, for simplicity, identical households one obtains from the above government budget constraint

$$dTR^h/dt = (w\ell^h - D) + tw(d\ell^h/dt)).$$

Substituting into $d\ell^h/dt$ and simplifying yields equation (14c). This pure transfer case is also considered by Lindbeck (1982) as his Case 1, by Gwartney and Stroup (1983), and by Snow and Warren (1985).

Net Marginal Social Cost of Public Good Supply

If the tax revenue, in contrast, is used to expand the public good supply (rather than for redistribution), *net marginal social cost of public good supply MSCG* enters into the picture. This cost element is defined as

$$(15)\quad MSCG = d(G - T_{\bar{t}})/dz = MRT - (\partial T/\partial z)_{\bar{t}} = MRT - tw \sum_h (\partial \ell^h/\partial z)_{\bar{t}}$$

i.e. as the difference between the *direct marginal social opportunity cost, MRT* (> 0), and the *indirect marginal social cost/benefit of public good supply, $\partial T/\partial z$* ($> / < 0$). The latter cost component, which was first addressed by Atkinson and Stern (1974), is of paramount interest here, since it is generally disregarded in theoretical and applied welfare analysis. It is determined by the endogenous change in tax revenue caused by the general equilibrium "cross-price" effect of public good supply on labor supply, $(\partial \ell^h/\partial z)_{\bar{t}}$, and, hence, on the labor income tax base, while holding the tax rate constant.

The "cross-price" effect is itself the result of a substitution and an (imputed) income effect. This decomposition has recently been shown by Wildasin (1979, 1984), and similarly by Lindbeck (1982) and Snow and Warren (1985), to read as:

$$(16)\quad \partial \ell^h/\partial z = (\partial \ell^h/\partial z)_{\bar{U}} + MRS^h(\partial \ell^h/\partial I^{h\bullet}).$$

The substitution effect between labor (or leisure) and public good consumption, $(\partial \ell^h/\partial z)_{\bar{U}}$, assumes that with a one-unit increase in public good supply "full income" is simultaneously adjusted downward by the imputed income, MRS^h, in order to keep utility constant.[21]

In general, the sign of the substitution effect is not restricted, it can be positive or negative, allowing for public good consumption and labor supply to be Hicks- (or compensated) complements (> 0), Hicks-independent ($= 0$), or Hicks-substitutes (< 0).[22] The income effect has the usual negative sign. Depending on the interaction of the substitution and income effect, the "cross-price" effect, $\partial \ell^h/\partial z$, may be positive, zero, or negative, implying public good consumption and labor supply to be Edgeworth-complements (> 0), Edgeworth-independent ($= 0$), or Edgeworth substitutes (< 0).

Hicks-independence of public goods and labor is the implicit assumption made by Friedman (1949), Goode (1949), Bailey (1954) and Gwartney and Stroup (1983)

[21] A one-unit increase in z increases the household's real income by MRS^h, since this is the amount of numeraire that would have to be taken away to keep utility constant as z rises.

[22] In this respect, it is unlike the Slutsky equation with its necessarily negative own-substitution term.

who — *cum grano salis* — argue that the partial equilibrium substitution effect of a tax change is of primary or even sole importance because the income effect of the spending change partially or even totally dissipates the partial equilibrium income effect of the tax change. The substitution effect between public goods and labor is completely neglected in that line of argument.

If public good consumption and labor supply are Edgeworth-substitutes/complements such that a one-unit increase in public good supply curtails/enlarges the labor income tax base, then there are indirect social costs/benefits supplementing/diminishing the direct social opportunity cost of public good supply, i.e. $\partial T/\partial z > / < 0$. On the other hand, if public good consumption and labor supply are Edgeworth-independent, the effects of the change in public spending are irrelevant to the labor/leisure choice and labor supply depends only on the opposing substitution and income effects that arise in the partial equilibrium analysis. In this very special case of Edgeworth-independence, there only exist indirect marginal welfare costs of distortionary finance, but not of public expenditure, i.e. $\partial T/\partial z = 0$ such that $MSCG = MRT$ and $MSC = MSCT \cdot MRT$.

Summary and Pattern of Interaction

Substituting (11)–(16) into (10a) and rearranging terms yields the following equivalent expression for the net marginal social value of a tax financed one-unit increase in public good supply (see also Wildasin, 1984):

$$\text{(10b)} \quad \frac{dW/dz}{dW/dI} = \sum_h MRS^h - \frac{\sum_h (w\ell^h - D)\left(MRT - tw\sum_h(\partial \ell^h/\partial z)\right)}{\sum_h w\ell^h\left[1 - \frac{t}{1-t}e^h\right] - \sum_h D\left[1 - \frac{t}{1-t}w_n\left(\frac{\partial \ell^h}{\partial I^h}\right)_{une}\right]}$$

where $e^h = d\log \ell^h / d\log w_n$ is the net wage rate elasticity of labor supply.[23]

Thus, if we are given a linear labor income tax schedule, a one-unit increase in public good supply financed by an increased marginal tax rate has *five interacting*

[23] If the incremental public good supply is financed by a strictly proportional tax (with $D = 0$), such that the unearned income effect does not appear, this expression simplifies to the formula:

$$\text{(10c)} \quad \frac{dW/dz}{dW/dI} = \sum_h MRS^h - \frac{MRT - tw\sum_h(\partial \ell^h/\partial z)}{1 - \frac{t}{1-t}e^h}.$$

substitution and income effects on *ordinary labor supply* (but, of course, only two interacting substitution effects on compensated labor supply). They determine whether and to what extent the indirect social cost/benefit has to be taken into account in addition to the direct cost/benefit known from first-best theory. Only empirical investigation will tell what the net result of these effects on labor supply and, hence, on indirect social cost/benefit will be.

A closer inspection of (10b) reveals the pattern of interaction between the various components and determinants of the marginal social costs and benefits of a balanced-budget expansion in public good supply. In particular, the marginal social costs of a tax financed increment in public good supply, MSC, are higher when

- the direct opportunity cost is higher, or, since in general the direct cost increases with public good supply, the existing provision with public good supply is larger;
- labor is more easily substituted for public good consumption, or, equivalently, leisure is more complementary with public good consumption;
- the prevailing level of marginal tax rates is higher;
- the labor supplies are more positively elastic with respect to the net wage rate;
- the negative unearned income effect on labor supplies is stronger;
- and, finally, the initial tax threshold is higher.[24]

If the model were more general and contained more taxable private consumption goods and taxed factors of production there would exist, of course, additional cross price effects on labor supply due to tax-induced product and factor price changes.[25] They would also bear on the indirect marginal welfare cost/benefit of distortionary finance and public good expenditure. In particular, the labor income tax, including the employee portion of the social security payroll tax, is but one tax falling on income from labor. Sales and excise taxes as well as the employer portion of the payroll tax and, in some countries, state and local income taxes also distort the income-leisure choice and, hence, contribute to the marginal welfare cost of labor income taxation.[26] It is true, as already noted by Browning (1976,

[24] But note the counteracting effect of: the less people experiencing the unearned income effect, the higher the tax threshold.

[25] The formulae for the most general (static) second-best theory of public expenditure and proportional (sic!) *ad valorem* commodity and factor taxation is developed in Diamond (1975).

[26] This effect occurs regardless of whether sales and excise taxes are shifted forward or backward. The real wage rate is reduced either if these taxes depress the nominal gross-of-tax wage

p. 290; 1985, p. 1026), that we cannot identify part of the *total* welfare cost as "the" welfare cost attributable to a subset of these taxes; but it is nevertheless possible and of interest to evaluate the *marginal* welfare cost of a specified change in the tax system.

Finally, if production technology exerted increasing marginal opportunity cost, there would exist an additional general equilibrium effect on the gross-of-tax wage rate. In principle, the gross-of-tax wage rate will then be lower such that this general equilibrium labor market effect tends to mitigate the marginal social cost of distortionary finance.[27]

IV. Implicit Hypotheses of Empirical Estimates of the Welfare Cost of Labor Income Taxation

The indirect social marginal cost of distortionary taxation is the primary object of empirical measurement in economic literature. Typically it is expressed as the social *marginal excess burden*, defined as $MEB = MSCT - 1$.

In the partial-equilibrium approach to the measurement of the marginal social cost of labor income taxation, pursued in the seminal contributions of Harberger (1964) and Browning (1976), the dependence of the marginal social cost on the use of marginal tax revenue fails to show up. Browning explicitly assumes "that the expenditure programs themselves do not distort labor supply decisions at the margin — that is, they can be viewed as lump sum transfers" (p. 284). The Harberger-Browning compensated marginal excess burden formula is defined as

$$MEB_c = \frac{\begin{array}{c}\text{marginal loss}\\ \text{of surplus}\end{array} - \begin{array}{c}\text{marginal gain}\\ \text{of tax revenue}\end{array}}{\begin{array}{c}\text{marginal gain}\\ \text{of tax revenue}\end{array}} = MSCT_c - 1$$

and intends to measure the cost of failing to use lump-sum taxation. As such, the formula makes use of compensated (or Hicks) labor supply functions and, strangely enough, does not recognize the economic tax base effect.[28] If looked at the Harberger-Browning approach from a general equilibrium perspective, this

rate without raising product prices, or if these taxes raise product prices while leaving the nominal wage rate constant.

[27] To this point see also Browning (1976, p. 286, n. 4; 1985, p. 1032 passim).

[28] See Browning's (1976) equations (4) and (5). This point has also been criticized by Stuart (1984, p. 353) and by Wildasin (1984, p. 238), among others.

partial equilibrium approach is conceptually valid only if one of the following two scenarios is implicitly assumed:

1. The additional tax revenue is spent on public (or publicly provided) goods which are Hicks-independent of labor supply and exert a positive income effect that just matches the negative (earned) income effect of the tax hike.
2. The additional tax revenue is spent on lump-sum transfers.

If public good consumption is not Hicks-independent of labor supply and if, at the same, the increase in public good spending is valued more or less than the foregone private spending, the Browning-Harberger formula is conceptually inadequate. This also holds true if the redistribution is of a negative income tax variety such that it distorts the labor supply decisions of receivers and givers.

Hausman (1981a, 1981b, 1983a, 1983b) attempts to estimate the monetary compensation required to offset the utility difference between the present income tax system and a lump-sum tax of equal yield. He also uses a partial equilibrium approach. However, as criticized most recently by Browning (1985), Hausman is in fact estimating the marginal welfare cost of a specific reduction in the effective marginal tax rate on labor income and his method of estimating this change in welfare cost is incorrect. According to Browning, this is because he does not take into account the *cross-price effects of other taxes on labor supply.* Moreover, Hausman follows the Harberger-Browning tradition of not taking into account the *cross-price effect of public expenditure.*

Stuart's (1984) criticizes the partial-equlibrium estimates of Harberger and Browning and provides estimates of the marginal excess burden per $ of additional tax revenue in the United States on the basis of a simple static, two-sector (taxed and untaxed sector), one-factor (labor) general equilibrium model. It is very similar to the model presented in sect. II. except that it explicitly allows for tax revenue to be expended on either government consumption or (lump-sum) redistribution or even on a mixture of the two. Redistributed tax revenue is treated as a perfect substitute for private consumption of taxed-sector output (or, equivalently, for net labor income).

Government consumption, however, does not explicitly enter into the household (Stone-Geary generalized CES) utility functions, which are defined over consumption of taxed-sector output and untaxed-sector output only. Thus, the implicit assumption is that public goods enter utility in an additively separable way, yielding Edgeworth-independence $\partial \ell^h / \partial z = 0$. In this special case, the effect of the change in public spending is irrelevant to the labor/leisure choice and labor supply depends only on the direct price effect and the unearned income effect of the higher marginal tax rate. This, in turn, implies that the presumably negative income effect of public good provision on labor supply is just compensated by a positive substitution effect and that labor (leisure) and public goods are Hicks-complements (substitutes).

In Stuart and Hansson (1985) the same type of static general equilibrium model is used to estimate the marginal excess burden of public funds in Sweden. The model in this co-authored contribution is extended to include taxable income from the supply of capital. Moreover, the co-authors now explicitly introduce an additively separable utility function $U(C_1, C_2, Z, X) = V(C_1, C_2) + W(Z, X)$, defined over two privately consumed outputs, C_1 and C_2, and separable government expenditure benefits, Z, as well as other factors influencing utility (including, for example, external consumption externalities from redistributional spending), X.

The authors argue that assuming (additive) separability between private and government consumption might be a good approximation for some government expenditures. Examples are defense expenditure, government expenditure on international affairs, administration of justice, general government. All of these expenditures most likely do not affect individual private consumption behavior at the margin. In his 1984 paper, however, Stuart also (implicitly) includes into the category of marginally neutral government expenditures such items as highways expenditure, (one half of) energy expenditure, expenditure on community and regional development and so forth. This is undoubtedly an heroic assumption. Most of these expenditures are funneled into public inputs and outputs which serve as complements or substitutes to private (labor and capital) inputs or private consumption expenditure. For example, a rapid transit system providing cheap and time-saving access to downtown firm locations not only serves (to a certain degree) as a substitute to private car transportation but also induces labor supply by considerably lowering the costs of labor supply.

Assuming that all marginal tax revenue is funneled into government consumption rather than (lump-sum) redistribution, Stuart's (1984) calculated 1976 value of the marginal excess burden per additional dollar labor income tax drops from 20.7 cent to 7.2 cent. The reason for this marked and politically significant difference is, of course, that Stuart's model takes account of the negative unearned income effect of (lump-sum) redistributions on labor supply whereas the "cross-price" effect of government expenditure on labor supply is (implicitly) assumed to be zero. If government consumption would be assumed to be a complement to (substitute of) leisure (labor supply) the difference of the marginal excess burdens of alternative uses would be less dramatic than revealed by Stuart's data.

The most complex model applied to estimate the marginal welfare costs of taxes is the multisector, dynamic computational general equilibrium model used in Fullerton, King, Shoven, and Whalley (1981); Fullerton, Shoven, and Whalley (1983); and in Ballard, Shoven, and Whalley (1985). In the 1981- and 1983-applications of this model, the authors use the conventional differential incidence approach holding constant the size of government. In the most recent 1985-application the authors announce to analyze the balanced-budget incidence of higher taxes; but actually they proceed to calculate in a conventional way the marginal excess burden (*MEB*) per additional dollar of revenue, as measured by the ratio $(HEV - dT)/dT = MSCT - 1$ (where HEV = Hicksian equivalent variation). Unfortunately, even in this complex model publicly provided goods do not enter into household utility functions. Thus, the implicit assumption is again that public goods enter utility in an additively separable way, yielding (Edgeworth-) independence $\partial \ell^h / \partial z = 0$.

Wildasin (1984) provides some illustrative examples that reveal the potential significance of the "cross price" effect of public expenditure for the marginal welfare costs of public funds. He first corrects Browning's (1976) original data for the missing economic tax base effect and then recalculates these data under the alternative assumption that labor supply and public goods are either Edgeworth (ordinary) independents or Hicks (compensated) independents. For example, Browning's (1976) estimate for the compensated MSC_c per additional tax \$ raised by a linear progressive (or flat rate) tax is \$ 1.18. The corrected value under the (logically consistent) assumption of Hicks-independence is a stunning \$ 1.85.

V. Conclusions

Lump sum taxation is not one of the alternatives available for raising an additional dollar of tax revenue by an income tax. Consequently, measuring the cost of failing to use lump sum taxation by the compensated marginal social cost of distortionary taxation is not a very fruitful line of research. What we are interested in (in a comparative static analysis without debt finance) is the change in social welfare when the economy moves from an equilibrium before a balanced-budget operation to one after this operation. This interest is served if *all* general equilibrium repercussions of this balanced-budget operation on social welfare are taken into account, including the income and substitution effects of government spending of additional tax money on the various tax bases. It should be recalled that the government raises tax money not for its own sake but rather in order to finance distortionary redistributive transfers, subsidies to firms and exhaustive public expenditure on intermediate goods and final goods. The very rationale of a noticeable share of public outlays is to deliberately influence private activities in one way or another. One would simply miss the point if this influence were not taken into account in the assessment of the welfare cost of taxation.

Of course, incorporating all general equilibrium repercussions of government spending of tax money into welfare analysis is a formidable task to accomplish. There are many different public goods in real economies, and each affects taxed goods and factors differently. Moreover, there are also "cross-price" effects between different types of publicly provided intermediate and final goods. Nevertheless, macroeconomists do not hesitate to portray the full economic picture in their simulation models for the effect of balanced-budget operations on NNP, employment and prices. Why should microeconomists settle for less ambituous efforts in measuring welfare and efficiency effects of fiscal policy programmes; simply because they try to live up to higher standards of theoretical consistency and depth?

References

Aaron, H. and **McGuire, M.** (1970): "Public Goods and Income Distribution." *Econometrica* 38: 907–920.

Atkinson, A. B. and **Stern, N. H.** (1974): "Pigou, Taxation and Public Goods." *Review of Economic Studies* 41: 119–128.

Bailey, M. J. (1954): "The Marshallian Demand Curve." *Journal of Political Economy* 62: 255–261.

Ballard, C. L.; Shoven J. B., and **Whalley, J.** (1982): "The Welfare Cost of Distortions in the United States Tax System: A General Equilibrium Approach." Working Paper no. 1043, Cambridge, Mass.: N.B.E.R.

Ballard, C. L.; Shoven J. B., and **Whalley, J.** (1985): "General Equilibrium Computations of the Marginal Welfare Costs of Taxes in the United States." *American Economic Review* 75: 128–138.

Boskin, M. J. (1981): "Comments." In *How Taxes Affect Economic Behavior*, edited by H. J. Aaron and J. A. Pechman. Washington, D.C.: Brookings Institution, pp. 84 ff.

Browning, E. K. (1976): "The Marginal Cost of Public Funds." *Journal of Political Economy* 84: 283–298.

Browning, E. K. (1985): "A Critical Appraisal of Hausman's Welfare Cost Estimates." *Journal of Political Economy* 93: 1025–1034.

Diamond, P. A. (1975): "A Many Person Ramsey Tax Rule." *Journal of Public Economics* 4: 335–342.

Friedman, M. (1949): "The Marshallian Demand Curve." *Journal of Political Economy* 57: 463–495.

Fullerton, D.; King, T. A.; Shoven, J. B., and **Whalley, J.** (1981): "Corporate Tax Integration in the United States: A General Equilibrium Approach." *American Economic Review* 71: 677–691.

Fullerton, D.; Shoven, J. B., and **Whalley, J.** (1983): "Replacing the U.S. Income Tax With a Progressive Consumption Tax: A Sequenced General Equilibrium Approach." *Journal of Public Economics* 20: 3–23.

Goode, R. (1949): "The Income Tax and the Supply of Labor." *Journal of Political Economy* 57: 428–437.

Gwartney, J., and **Stroup, R.** (1983): "Labor Supply and Tax Rates: A Correction of the Record." *American Economic Review* 73: 446–451.

Hall, R. (1968): "Consumption Taxes versus Income Taxes: Implications for Economic Growth." In *Proceedings of the National Tax Association.* Columbus, Ohio: The Association, pp. 125 ff.

Hansson, I., and **Stuart, C.** (1985): "Tax Revenue and the Marginal Cost of Public Funds in Sweden." *Journal of Public Economics* 27: 331–353.

Harberger, A. C. (1964a): "Taxation, Resource Allocation and Welfare." In *The Role of Direct and Indirect Taxes in the Federal Revenue System*, edited by J. Due. Princeton, N.J.: Princeton University Press, pp. 25–81.

Harberger, A. C. (1964b): "The Measurement of Waste." *American Economic Review, Papers and Proceedings* 54: 58–76.

Harberger, A. C. (1966): "Efficiency Effects of Taxes on Income from Capital." In *Effects of Corporation Income Tax*, edited by M. Krzyaniak. Detroit, Ill.: Wayne State University Press, pp. 107 ff.

Harberger, A. C. (1974): *Taxation and Welfare.* Boston, Mass.: Little Brown.

Hausman, J. A. (1981a): "Labor Supply." In *How Taxes Affect Economic Behavior*, edited by H. J. Aaron and J. A. Pechman. Washington, D.C.: Brookings Institution, pp. 27–83.

Hausman, J. A. (1981b): "Income and Payroll Tax Policy and Labor Supply." In *The Supply-Side Effects of Economic Policy*, edited by L. H. Meyer. Boston, Mass., etc.: Kluwer-Nijhoff, pp. 173–202. (Center for the Study of American Business, Formal publication 39.)

Hausman, J. A. (1983a): "Stochastic Problems in the Simulation of Labor Supply." In *Behavioral Simulation Methods in Tax Policy Analysis*, edited by M. Feldstein. Chicago, Ill.: Chicago University Press (for N.B.E.R.).

Hausman, J. A. (1983b): "Taxes and Labor Supply." Working Paper no. 1102, Cambridge, Mass.: N.B.E.R.

Heckman, J. J. (1983): "Comment." In *Behavioral Simulation Methods in Tax Policy Analysis*, edited by M. Feldstein. Chicago, Ill.: Chicago University Press (for N.B.E.R.), pp. 70–82.

Hotelling, H. (1938): "The General Welfare in Relation to Problems of Taxation and of Railway and Utility Rates." *Econometrica* 6: 242–269.

Lindbeck, A. (1982): "Tax Effects versus Budget Effects on Labor Supply." *Economic Inquiry* 20: 473–489.

Mieszkowski, P. (1978): "The Choice of Tax Base: Consumption Taxes versus Income Taxes." In *Federal Tax Reform: Myth and Realities*, edited by M. J. Boskin. San Francisco: Institute for Contemporary Studies, pp. 27 ff.

Perloff, J. M. (1981): "Discussion of the Hausman Paper." In *The Supply-Side Effects of Economic Policy*, edited by L. H. Meyer. Boston, Mass., etc.: Kluwer-Nijhoff, pp. 231–236. (Center for the Study of American Business, Formal publication 39.)

Pigou, A. C. (1947): *A Study of Public Finance*. 3rd. ed., London: Macmillan.

Samuelson, P. A. (1954): "The Pure Theory of Public Expenditure and Taxation." *Review of Economics and Statistics* 36: 387–389.

Samuelson, P. A. (1969): "Pure Theory of Public Expenditure and Taxation." In *Public Economics*, edited by J. Margolis and H. Guitton. London: Macmillan, pp. 98–123.

Shoven, J. B. (1976): "The Incidence and Efficiency Effects of Taxes on Income from Capital." *Journal of Political Economy* 84: 1261–1283.

Snow, A., and **Warren, R. S.** (1985): "Labor Supply and Tax Rates in General Equilibrium." Mimeo, Department of Economics, University of Virginia.

Stiglitz, J. E., and **Dasgupta, P.** (1971): "Differential Taxation, Public Goods and Economic Efficiency." *Review of Economic Studies* 38: 151–174.

Stuart, C. (1984): "Welfare Costs per Dollar of Additional Tax Revenue in the United States." *American Economic Review* 74: 352–362.

Summers, L. H. (1979): "Capital Taxation and Accumulation in a Life Cycle Growth Model." Paper presented at the Conference on the Taxation of Capital, Nov. 16–17, 1979. Cambridge, Mass.: N.B.E.R.

Wildasin, D. E. (1979): "Public Good Provision with Optimal and Non-optimal Commodity Taxation." *Economics Letters* 4: 59–65.

Wildasin, D. E. (1984): "On Public Good Provision with Distortionary Taxation." *Economic Inquiry* 22: 227–243.

Wilde, J. A. (1984): "Labor Supply and Tax Rates: Comment." *American Economic Review* 74: 1103–1107.

Welfare Effects of Privatizing Public Enterprises

Dieter Bös, Bonn, West Germany*

1. Introduction

If a public firm is privatized, most probably the productive efficiency of the firm will increase. The efficiency gains will improve welfare. However, the privatized firm will tend to increase profit. Then a welfare optimum is achieved only if the firm operates in a perfectly competitive environment. Otherwise the profit maximization reduces welfare. However, the profit can be redistributed among consumers as dividend payments which increase incomes and thereby increase welfare. Part of the increased profit, moreover, may remain in the public budget and be used to increase government expenditures. And the revenue from selling the shares will also be spent as government expenditures. The increasing expenditures will increase the welfare. Given the different welfare effects of privatization: how many shares of a public firm shall be sold and what are the economic consequences of an optimum privatization?

We assume that the profits of the privatized firm cannot be held low by market entry. Either there are not enough market entrants, or the privatized firm still holds special patents, or particular legal barriers to entry are not abolished in spite of the privatization. Hence, the privatized firm should remain regulated even if part of its shares or all shares have been sold to the public. British Telecom is a good example of a regulated privatized firm, at least with respect to many of its services. "Like it or not, we have here the beginning of a public regulatory process" (Beesley, 1981).

It is the main objective of the present paper to explain in which way the dividend incomes influence the optimum policy on privatization. It would be possible to assume that the issue price to be paid for the shares of the privatized firm is equated to the expected dividends. Then there would be no net incomes from dividends. In the present paper, however, positive net incomes from dividends are considered. We show in which way the positive influence of both income effects

* I gratefully acknowledge the comments of Wolfgang Peters, Ray Rees, Wolfram Richter, the participants in the Neresheim seminar and an anonymous referee.

and efficiency effects from privatization counteract the negative influence of profit (price) effects.

The paper is organized as follows. We model privatization in the general framework which is due to Boiteux (1956, 1971).[1] In section 2 we describe the economic agents of the model, namely consumers, the privatized firm and the government. Then, in section 3, we present the optimization approach and the relevant first-order conditions. The subsequent sections interpret the results: section 4 deals with the optimal issue price of the shares and the optimal extent of privatization. Section 5 explicitly introduces into the model the welfare effects of spending the government revenues from privatization. Section 6 is devoted to the pricing policies of the privatized firm. Section 7 summarizes and concludes the paper.

2. The Economic Agents

2.1 Consumers

Each consumer maximizes utility as depending on the consumed quantities $x_h = (x_{0h}, \ldots, x_{nh})$. Positive quantities denote demand, negative quantities supply, in particular labor supply x_{0h}. The utility function $u_h(x_h)$ has the usual neoclassical properties. Given the non-labor income r_h and the prices $p = (1, p_1, \ldots, p_n)$, the consumer proceeds as follows:

$$(1) \qquad \max_{x_h} \; u_h(x_h) \text{ subject to } px_h = r_h \qquad h = 1, \ldots, H.$$

A condensed description of the optimal consumption choice is given by the indirect utility function $v_h(p, r_h)$.

The non-labor income r_h consists of an exogenously given part r_{0h} and the income the consumer draws from his newly acquired shares of the privatized firm. Let the shares of the privatized firm be evenly spread among the consumers. Every consumer owns a percentage Θ/H of the privatized firm. To get the shares the consumer pays a price $(\Theta/H)S$. The ownership of the shares entitles the consumer to get dividends $(\Theta/H)\Pi$, where Π is the profit of the privatized firm. The dividends exceed the price of the shares, otherwise the consumer would not buy

[1] This framework has intensively been used to analyze public sector pricing, particularly by Drèze (1964, 1984), Drèze and Marchand (1976), Hagen (1979), Marchand, Pestieau, and Weymark (1982), Bös (1985, 1986a) and Sheshinski (1986).

the shares. We assume that the consumer also buys the shares if he has no net income from dividends. In that case the issue price the consumer has to pay for the shares is equated to the expected dividend payments. Hence the consumer's non-labor income is

$$r_h = r_{0h} + \frac{\Theta}{H}(\Pi - S), \qquad (\Pi - S) \geq 0. \tag{2}$$

On the basis of the consumer utilities we can define the welfare in the economy according to

$$W\big(v(p, r_0 + \frac{\Theta}{H}(\Pi - S))\big). \tag{3}$$

The vector $v = (v_1, \ldots, v_H)$ denotes the indirect utilities. We assume $W_h = \partial W/\partial v_h > 0$ for all h.

2.2 The Privatized Firm

If $\Theta = 0$, we have a public firm. If $\Theta = 1$, we have a fully privatized firm. If $0 < \Theta < 1$, we will speak of partial privatization. The firm will be called "privatized", regardless of whether its shares are owned publicly and privately, or wholly privately.

2.2.1 *Privatization and the Objectives of the Firm*

Privatization changes the objectives of the firm. In theoretical abstraction a fully public firm maximizes welfare, a fully privatized firm maximizes profit. With increasing extent of privatization, therefore, the firm switches from welfare maximization to profit maximization. As we describe in Bös and Peters (1987), there is a bargaining process at the board of the firm, where the representatives of the government and of the private shareholders negotiate about the welfare-profit trade-off which can be achieved by the firm's policy. We can assume that at the board of the firm $100 \cdot (1 - \Theta)\,\%$ government representatives plead for welfare maximization, whereas $100 \cdot \Theta\,\%$ private owners plead for profit maximization. However, when maximizing welfare, the government representatives are restricted by that profit level which must be conceded to the private shareholders,

$$P = \Pi(\Theta), \qquad \Pi_\Theta := \frac{\partial \Pi}{\partial \Theta} > 0. \tag{4}$$

The profit level Π depends on the bargaining power of the representatives of private owners. This bargaining power is higher, the more shares have been sold. Due to this higher emphasis on the profit motive, the profit monotonically increases in Θ.

On the other hand, the intended profit maximization of the private shareholders is restricted by that welfare level which must be conceded to the government representatives

$$(5) \qquad W = \Omega(\Theta), \qquad \frac{\partial \Omega}{\partial \Theta} \gtreqless 0.$$

It is surprising that a reduction in government ownership may decrease or increase the welfare level Ω. The reason is the following. The efficiency gains can be used to produce at lower costs and to sell at lower prices in such a way that both profit and welfare are improved. Only if increasing Θ enables the private shareholders to enforce profits in excess of the cost savings which result from privatization, welfare will be decreasing in Θ.

Bös and Peters (1987) deal with bargaining solutions which are technologically feasible, market clearing, and "rational". The latter means that the two groups of representatives agree to choose only points at the profit-welfare frontier, where profit can only be increased at the expense of welfare and vice versa. Then the optimization problem of the government representatives ($max\ W$ s.t. $\Pi(\Theta)$) is dual to the optimization problem of the private shareholders ($max\ P$ s.t. $\Omega(\Theta)$). Hence it suffices to describe the firm's decision by only one of the two optimization approaches mentioned in the foregoing sentence.

Applying the Bös-Peters approach, in this paper the pricing decisions at the board of the firm are derived from the maximization of a Bergson welfare function subject to the profit constraint set by the bargaining power of the private shareholders.[2] Note that this description of the firm's decision on prices is equivalent to the derivation of prices from the maximization of profit given a welfare constraint.

The instruments available to the board of the enterprise are as follows. A subset of all prices is controlled by the board. These prices are denoted p_e where $e \in E \subset I, I = \{0, \ldots, n\}$. There may exist also non-regulated prices of goods which are supplied or demanded by the privatized firm. In those cases the privatized firm has to accept prices which are set by private enterprises or by government agencies outside our model. We exclude regulation of wages, p_0. All uncontrolled prices $p_i, i \notin E$, are exogenously given.

[2] Taking into account technological feasibility and market clearing constraints.

2.2.2 *Privatization and the Efficiency of the Firm*

The transition to profit maximization will change the efficiency of the firm. Profit maximization, in practice, provides a better incentive towards efficiency than welfare maximization.

Let the firm sell or buy netputs $z = (z_0, \ldots, z_n)$. Positive quantities are outputs, negative quantities are inputs, in particular labor inputs $z_0 < 0$. We describe the production possibilities of the firm by the labor requirement function. This function determines the minimal labor input which is necessary given a vector of outputs and non-labor inputs $z_1, \ldots, z_n$. We assume that the minimal labor requirement directly depends on the extent of privatization

$$z_0 = z_0(z_1, \ldots, z_n, \Theta). \tag{6}$$

The strict equality characterizes the production as technically efficient,[3] given the extent of privatization. Moreover, efficiency also varies with the extent of privatization: if $\partial z_0/\partial\Theta > 0$, efficiency increases in Θ because less labor input is needed given all other netputs. If $\partial z_0/\partial\Theta < 0$, the contrary is valid. Many empirical studies, which compare the efficiency of private and public firms, suggest that $\partial z_0/\partial\Theta > 0$ is more probable. However, there are empirical studies which illustrate the contrary.

We denote the derivatives[4]

$$-\frac{\partial z_0}{\partial z_i} =: c_i(z_1, \ldots z_n, \Theta). \tag{7}$$

c_i is a shadow price which measures the marginal labor costs of producing output $z_i > 0$, or a marginal rate of transformation between labor and some input $z_i < 0$. The values of c_i depend on the extent of privatization. This is an advantage of our general formulation of the technology. We allow for the possibility that privatization changes the marginal rates of transformation between the various netputs other than labor. Such effects would have been excluded if we had chosen an additive structure of the labor requirements

$$z_0 = z_0(z_1, \ldots, z_n) + I(\Theta). \tag{6'}$$

[3] For the terminology see Marchand, Pestieau, and Tulkens (1984).

[4] For the rationale of this terminology see Boiteux (1956, 1971), Bös (1986a, pp. 81–85), Peters (1986).

Let us now define "*privatization efficiency*". For the various extents of privatization Θ we can find the envelope of the labor requirement $max_\Theta\, z_0(z_1, \ldots, z_n, \Theta)$. We denote this envelope by $Z(z_1, \ldots, z_n)$. If the firm produces at the envelope, we call the production privatization efficient. Otherwise $z_0 < Z$ and the production is privatization inefficient.

Privatization efficiency implies minimal labor requirement with respect to Θ given all other netputs except labor. Hence, privatization efficiency can be described by the following optimization approach

$$(8) \qquad \max_{\Theta}\; z_0(z_1, \ldots, z_n, \Theta) \qquad \text{subject to} \quad 0 \le \Theta \le 1.$$

It can easily be seen that this optimization leads to the following conditions for privatization efficiency

$$(9.1) \qquad \frac{\partial z_0}{\partial \Theta} \le 0 \quad \text{for} \quad \Theta^* = 0$$

$$(9.2) \qquad \frac{\partial z_0}{\partial \Theta} = 0 \quad \text{for} \quad 0 < \Theta^* < 1$$

$$(9.3) \qquad \frac{\partial z_0}{\partial \Theta} \ge 0 \quad \text{for} \quad \Theta^* = 1.$$

It is privatization efficient not to sell any shares of the public firm if doing so increases the labor requirement. Partial privatization is privatization efficient if selling more shares or selling less shares increases the labor requirement. In the case of total privatization no more shares can be sold. Hence it is privatization efficient to sell all shares if selling less than 100% of the firm implies a higher labor requirement.

2.3 The Government

We impute to the government the objective of maximizing a Bergson welfare function of the type (3). Hence, the same objective function is relevant for both the government body who decides on the extent of privatization by selling shares, and for the board of the privatized firm. Moreover, the government has to accept the profit constraint (4) which is set by the private shareholders, and has to consider the technology of the firm and the market clearing conditions. The same objective function and the same constraints are relevant for both the government privatization body and the board of the firm.

The government's instruments are

- the extent of privatization Θ and
- the issue price of shares S.

Setting Θ in a welfare-optimal way means a decision on the profit of the firm and on its efficiency. The profit increase is acceptable for the government if the implied efficiency gains allow both profit and welfare to be increased. The welfare gain can be achieved in a twofold way. First by lower prices due to efficiency gains. Second by higher non-labor incomes of the consumers. Here the second instrument of the government becomes important too. The non-labor incomes can be increased by increasing Θ and by reducing the issue price S. However, the policy maker faces a political constraint when reducing the issue price. He would be exposed to harsh criticism by both the opposition and the media if he subsidized the acquisition of shares of public firms. Hence a negative issue price cannot be chosen for political reasons even if it might be the correct policy to privatize public firms which work under permanent deficit. Typically, the policy maker will also avoid giving the shares away free of charge. So there exists some political threshold which must be taken care of,

$$S \geq \overline{S} \tag{10}$$

where the threshold $\overline{S}$ is positive. The actual issue price will be somewhere between $\Pi(\Theta)$ and $\overline{S}$. It must be weakly lower than the profit as mentioned in (2). Otherwise nobody would buy the shares. And it must be weakly higher than the threshold $\overline{S}$. Otherwise there would be too much political opposition against the privatization.

Public deficit firms are not privatized. Hence we assume $\Pi(0) > \overline{S}$ which implies $\Pi(\Theta) > \overline{S}$ because $\Pi_\Theta > 0$.

Thus we have three regimes of an issue price:

(i) High issue price: $\Pi(\Theta) = S > \overline{S}$

(ii) Medium issue price: $\Pi(\Theta) > S > \overline{S}$

(iii) Low issue price: $\Pi(\Theta) > S = \overline{S}$.

Net incomes from dividends increase from case (i) to (ii) and (iii) respectively.

For the moment we do not consider how government revenues from privatization are spent as public expenditures. That problem will be treated explicitly in section 5 below.

When deciding on privatization, the government should always explicitly consider how the prices of the privatized firm change depending on the extent of privatization. This problem is dealt with in the following way. As both the privatization body and the board of the firm choose the same objective function, both agents can optimize welfare given the relevant constraints, with respect to the same variables, namely netput prices, issue price of shares and extent of privatization. By solving the optimization approach with respect to all those variables, every agent always considers the optimal adjustment of the other agent to his policy. Then, on the basis of solving this optimization approach, the board of the firm sets netput prices, whereas the government privatization body sets the optimal extent of privatization and the issue price of the shares. It is the advantage of this procedure that the optimal adjustment of netput prices to the privatization policy is implicitly taken into account in the decision on privatization without explicitly dealing with price trajectories $\partial p/\partial \Theta$ which can only be interpreted in very simple models.[5]

3. The Optimization Approach

The objective function of the board of the firm and of the government privatization body is given by

$$W\left((v(p, r_0 + \frac{\Theta}{\Pi}(\Pi(\Theta) - S))\right). \tag{3}$$

The lump-sum incomes r_{0h} are exogenously given; controlled prices, issue price and extent of privatization are endogenously determined. The welfare maximization is restricted

- by the bargaining solution at the board of the firm which constitutes $P = \Pi(\Theta)$, as defined in (4),
- by the political constraints on the relation between profit and issue price, $\Pi(\Theta) \geq S \geq \overline{S}$, as defined in (2) and (10),
- by the labor requirement function of the firm, as defined in (6), and
- by the markets in which the firm operates.

The analysis can be simplified if some constraints are substituted into the others. We proceed as follows. When maximizing welfare according to (3), both the board of the firm and the government privatization body explicitly consider the markets

[5] See Bös (1986c).

in which the firm operates. Hence the supply of, or demand for, any non-labor netput is defined as

$$(11) \quad z_i(p,S,\Theta) := \sum_{h=1}^{H} x_{ih}\left(p, r_{0h} + \frac{\Theta}{H}(\Pi(\Theta) - S)\right) - \sum_{j=1}^{J} y_{ij}(p), \quad i = 1,\ldots,n.$$

In this equation $x_{ih}(\cdot)$ denotes consumer demand or supply, $y_{ij}(p)$ denotes the demand or supply of the j-th private firm. $z_i(\cdot)$ as defined in (11) is a definition: in fact only $x_{ij}(\cdot)$ and $y_{ij}(\cdot)$ enter the model, but $z_i(\cdot)$ can be used as an abbreviation for the sake of simplicity. Using the demand and supply functions $z_i(\cdot)$ is an implicit consideration of the market equilibria in all markets $i = 1,\ldots,n$. Note that an explicit consideration of market equilibria would request a specification of z_i as instrument variables which only at the optimum depend on netput prices, issue price and extent of privatization. The specification we have chosen in this paper leads to a considerable simplification of all derivations.[6]

We consider market equilibria in all netput markets except labor. This assumption implies the very customary regulation of the "cover-all-demand" rule: public firms are often instructed to sell as much net outputs as consumers and private firms demand. Moreover, in our model, we have a "buy-all-supply" rule: the firm is instructed to buy as much net inputs as consumers and private firms offer. The latter instruction can be justified by a responsibility for their suppliers which in practice often is imposed on public purchasers.

Equilibrium in the labor market is not postulated. This assumption is meaningful from the empirical point of view. Even a large privatized firm cannot accept the sole responsibility for the equilibrium in the labor market. Hence we intentionally avoided to introduce the equilibrium in the labor market.[7]

By differentiating (11) we obtain the price effects

$$(12.1) \qquad \frac{\partial z_i}{\partial p_e} = \sum_h \frac{\partial x_{ih}}{\partial p_e} - \sum_j \frac{\partial y_{ij}}{\partial p_e}$$

and the income effects

$$(12.2) \qquad \frac{\partial z_i}{\partial r_h} = \frac{\partial x_{ih}}{\partial r_h}.$$

[6] Usually in the Boiteux tradition the netputs z_i are chosen as instruments. For details see Bös (1986a, chapter 3).

[7] It may be of interest for the reader that in one of the drafts of this paper the author explicitly formulated the problem in a framework which postulates equilibrium in all markets, labor market included. The qualitative results do not change if such a modelling is chosen.

It will be convenient to abbreviate

$$\frac{\partial z_i}{\partial r} = \sum_h \frac{\partial z_i}{\partial r_h}. \tag{13}$$

The profit of the privatized firm can be defined by using the demand and supply functions $z_i(\cdot), i = 1, \ldots, n$, and the labor requirement function $z_0(\cdot)$

$$P := \sum_{i=1}^{n} p_i z_i(p, S, \Theta) + z_0(z_1(\cdot), \ldots, z_n(\cdot), \Theta). \tag{14}$$

This profit must be equated to the political profit constraint $\Pi(\Theta)$. Hence, the relevant optimization approach is as follows

$$\max_{S,\Theta,p_e} \quad W\left(v(p, r_0 + \frac{\Theta}{H}(\Pi(\Theta) - S))\right)$$

subject to

$$\begin{aligned} &\Pi(\Theta) = \sum_{i=1}^{n} p_i z_i(p, S, \Theta) + z_0(z_1(\cdot), \ldots, z_n(\cdot), \Theta) \qquad (\alpha) \\ &\Theta \leq 1 \qquad (\beta) \\ &S \leq \Pi(\Theta) \qquad (\gamma) \\ &\overline{S} \leq S \qquad (\delta). \end{aligned} \tag{15}$$

To solve this optimization approach we write down the following Lagrangean function.[8]

$$\begin{aligned} L &= W(\cdot) - \alpha\left(\Pi(\Theta) - \sum_{i=1}^{n} p_i z_i(\cdot) - z_0(z_1(\cdot), \ldots, z_n(\cdot), \Theta)\right) - \\ &\quad - \beta(1 - \Theta) - \gamma(\Pi(\Theta) - S) - \delta(S - \overline{S}). \end{aligned} \tag{16}$$

In order to simplify the presentation of the first-order conditions we substitute $c_i = -\partial z_0/\partial z_i$ and introduce a variable A which stands for

$$A = \frac{1}{H}\left[\sum_{h=1}^{H} W_h \frac{\partial v_h}{\partial r_h} + \alpha \sum_{h=1}^{H}\sum_{i=1}^{n}(p_i - c_i)\frac{\partial z_i}{\partial r_h}\right]. \tag{17}$$

[8] See Panik (1976, p. 297). The non-negativity condition for Θ is not treated as structural constraint but appears explicitly in the necessary optimum conditions.

We then obtain the following conditions

$$L_S = -A\Theta + \gamma - \delta = 0 \tag{18}$$

$$L_\Theta = A[(\Pi - S) + \Theta\Pi_\Theta] + \alpha\left(\frac{\partial z_0}{\partial \Theta} - \Pi_\Theta\right) + \beta - \gamma\Pi_\Theta \leq 0 \tag{19}$$

$$L_\Theta \Theta = 0 \tag{20}$$

$$\beta(1-\Theta) = 0;\ \beta \leq 0;\ 0 \leq \Theta \leq 1 \tag{21}$$

$$\gamma(\Pi - S) = 0;\ \gamma \leq 0;\ S \leq \Pi(\Theta) \tag{22}$$

$$\delta(S - \overline{S}) = 0;\ \delta \leq 0; \overline{S} \leq S\ . \tag{23}$$

Moreover, we have to consider the marginal conditions which result from differentiating the Lagrangean function with respect to the prices p_e:

$$L_{p_e} = \sum_h W_h \frac{\partial v_h}{\partial p_e} + \alpha\left(z_e + \sum_{i=1}^{n}(p_i - c_i)\frac{\partial z_i}{\partial p_e}\right) = 0, \quad e \in E. \tag{24}$$

It should be noted that $\alpha \geq 0$ can be learned from an alternative Kuhn-Tucker formulation of an optimization approach, assuming $\Pi \leq \sum_1^n p_i z_i + z_0(\cdot)$. We will assume $\alpha > 0$ results from the behavior of the privatized firm.

4. The Optimal Privatization Policy

4.1 The Optimal Issue Price

The issue price is bounded from below and from above

$$\overline{S} \leq S \leq \Pi(\Theta) \tag{25}$$

with the associated Lagrangean multipliers γ and δ. Hence the economic properties of the optimal issue price can be dealt with by interpreting the L_S condition

$$A\Theta = \gamma - \delta. \tag{26}$$

Let us begin with the *left-hand side* of (26). To begin with, we must exclude $\Theta = 0$. If no shares are sold, the question about an issue price has no relevance at all. There are no income effects regardless of any arbitrarily chosen issue price. It is of no importance whether the imprint on the shares is \$ 5 or \$ 10 if no share is sold. Hence we restrict the analysis to the case $\Theta > 0$.

Next, we must interpret A. Fortunately a nice economic meaning can be given to A: it measures the welfare effects of a change in the individual incomes. Let us start from the definition

$$A = \frac{1}{H}\left[\sum_{h=1}^{H} W_h \frac{\partial v_h}{\partial r_h} + \alpha \sum_{h=1}^{H}\sum_{i=1}^{n}(p_i - c_i)\frac{\partial z_i}{\partial r_h}\right]. \tag{17}$$

An increase in the income r_h affects welfare in a twofold way. First the individual utility increases and so does welfare. Hence the first term in (17) measures the marginal social benefits of the income change. This term always is positive. Second, if individual incomes change, both consumer demand for outputs and consumer supply of inputs will change. The additional demand and supply go to the privatized firm only: demand for, and supply of, netputs of the private firms depend on prices only, not on incomes. Hence welfare is affected as far as the profit of the privatized firm changes

$$\partial\left(p_0 z_0 + \sum_{i=1}^{n} p_i z_i\right) / \partial r_h = \sum_{h=1}^{H}\sum_{i=1}^{n}(p_i - c_i)\frac{\partial z_i}{\partial r_h}. \tag{27}$$

Therefore the second term in (17) measures the feedback of the dividends on the profit of the firm which pays the dividends, evaluated in welfare units. This term can either be positive or negative. There is a trade-off between consumption and input substitution effects.

The consumption effects typically are positive as increasing income will increase the consumption of outputs, $\partial x_{ih}/\partial r_h = \partial z_i/\partial r_h > 0$. These income effects are multiplied by price-cost deviations which will be positive for the consumption goods. It is improbable that the privatized firm sets prices below marginal labor costs, because in our model the firm never runs at a deficit ($\Pi(\Theta) > \overline{S} > 0$). It is also improbable that private firms set prices below marginal labor costs.

The input substitution effects typically are negative. Increasing income will reduce the supply of inputs, $\partial x_{ih}/\partial r_h = \partial z_i/\partial r_h > 0$. (Recall $z_i < 0$ for inputs.) These income effects are multiplied by the difference of factor prices and marginal rates of substitution which will be negative for reasons of profit maximization.

The total welfare effects of income changes, A, are positive if the associated marginal social benefits and the consumption effects outweigh the input substitution effects. When will that happen? It will depend on the distribution of incomes.

For a rather suboptimal distribution of incomes both the welfare effects and the income effects of changes in r_h will be high. So both consumption and input substitution effects will be high, but even if they wash out, the high welfare evaluation will imply a positive A. The "better" the income distribution, the lower the welfare effects and the higher the probability that the income substitution effects outweigh the welfare and consumption effects.

How A depends on the income distribution can most clearly be shown by dealing with the *hypothetical* case of an optimal distribution. Let the government set lump-sum transfers r_{0h} so as to maximize welfare on the basis of the Lagrangean function (16). Then the government applies first-order conditions

$$W_h \frac{\partial v_h}{\partial r_h} + \alpha \sum_{i=1}^{n} (p_i - c_i) \frac{\partial z_i}{\partial r_h} = 0. \tag{28}$$

Hence the welfare effects of income changes, A, would be equated to zero if the income distribution were chosen optimally. However, this is a theoretical limiting case without great empirical relevance. Moreover, the lump sum incomes r_{0h} are not chosen as instruments in our model.

The considerations of the preceding paragraph make clear that much depends on the income distribution and if there is enough inequality aversion in the government's welfare function, in our model a positive A is a very probable case.

We have now interpreted the left-hand side of (26) and are in the position to deal with the properties of the optimal issue price S. We distinguish three regimes.

(i) High issue price

The issue price is kept as high as possible, it is equated to the profit of the firm

$$\overline{S} < S = \Pi, \qquad \text{i.e. } \delta = 0, \ \gamma \leq 0. \tag{29}$$

This case occurs if the welfare effects of income changes are negative, $A \leq 0$. Because of the negative welfare effects the policy maker absorbs all dividends by choosing the high issue price $S = \Pi$. So the gains in productive efficiency, which result from privatization, can be exploited, but net incomes from dividends are excluded. However, as mentioned earlier, negative welfare effects of income changes are not very probable.

(ii) Medium issue price

The issue price is somewhere between the lower and the upper boundary

$$\overline{S} < S < \Pi, \qquad \text{i.e. } \delta = 0, \ \gamma = 0. \tag{30}$$

This case holds if the welfare effects of income changes are nil, $A = 0$. At the optimum, in this case, welfare cannot be increased by changing the dividend incomes.

(iii) Low issue price

The issue price is kept as low as possible, the firm's profit exceeds the issue price

$$\overline{S} = S < \Pi, \qquad \text{i.e. } \delta \leq 0, \;\gamma = 0. \tag{31}$$

This case can only be given if $A \geq 0$. The economic rationale is straightforward. If income changes have a positive welfare effect, the net incomes from dividends should be chosen as high as possible. This can be achieved by choosing the issue price as low as possible. Note that we consider $A > 0$ as a very probable case. Hence the low issue price $\overline{S}$ is a very probable outcome of our model. So the model gives a welfare economic explanation of low issue prices in the case of privatization. Such an explanation is of interest, because in the practice of privatization the issue price typically is chosen low and many policy makers have been accused of throwing away national property because of their choosing a low issue price of shares. Our model offers proof of the fact that such a low issue price can well be the result of a welfare oriented policy.

4.2 The Optimal Extent of Privatization

The optimal extent of privatization is characterized by a trade-off between allocative and distributional effects.

The allocative effects depend on the efficiency changes from privatization, $\partial z_0/\partial\Theta$, and on the profit increases which must be conceded to the private shareholders if privatization proceeds, $\Pi_\Theta > 0$. From the allocative point of view privatization is desirable if $\partial z_0/\partial\Theta > \Pi_\Theta$. In such a case the efficiency gains in the production are high enough to allow an increase both in profit and in welfare. Therefore the policy maker is willing to accept the profit increases as the price which has to be paid for the efficiency gains which allow to increase welfare.

The distributional effects depend on how net incomes from dividends influence welfare. These effects are measured by A as dealt with in the preceding subsection. From the distributional point of view privatization is desirable if $A > 0$.

The trade-off between allocative and distributional effects decisively depends on the issue price of the shares. This can be shown by substituting (18) into (19) to obtain

$$A(\Pi - S) - \delta\Pi_\Theta + \beta \leq \alpha\left(\Pi_\Theta - \frac{\partial z_0}{\partial\Theta}\right). \tag{32}$$

On the basis of this inequality let us now deal with the optimal extent of privatization, given the various regimes of issue prices.

(i) High issue price ($S = \Pi$)

In this case there are no net incomes from dividends, $\Pi - S = 0$. Hence there are no distributional effects which must be traded-off against the allocational effects and we obtain the following special case of (32)[9]

$$\beta \leq \alpha \left(\Pi_\Theta - \frac{\partial z_0}{\partial \Theta} \right) . \tag{33}$$

This condition implies

(34.1) $$\Pi_\Theta \geq \frac{\partial z_0}{\partial \Theta} \quad \text{for } \Theta = 0$$

(34.2) $$\Pi_\Theta = \frac{\partial z_0}{\partial \Theta} \quad \text{for } 0 < \Theta < 1$$

(34.3) $$\Pi_\Theta \leq \frac{\partial z_0}{\partial \Theta} \quad \text{for } \Theta = 1 .$$

No privatization takes place if the profit increases exceed the efficiency gains. Otherwise shares are sold until the profit increases are equated to the efficiency gains, or until 100 % are sold.

(ii) Medium issue price ($\overline{S} < S < \Pi$)

In that case the welfare effects of income changes are zero, $A = 0$ and the net incomes from dividends are chosen so as to direct demand to the products which provide the best opportunities for efficiency increases. Hence there are allocational effects only and once again we obtain

(33) $$\beta \leq \alpha \left(\Pi_\Theta - \frac{\partial z_0}{\partial \Theta} \right) .$$

The interpretation is equal to the case of a high issue price.

(iii) Low issue price ($S = \overline{S}$)

In this case there are positive net incomes from dividends, $\Pi - S > 0$, which have positive distributional consequences, $A \geq 0$. Hence distributional effects matter, in contrast to the cases of the high and the medium issue price. We are left with

---

[9] Recall $\delta = 0$ because $S > \overline{S}$.

that trade-off between allocation and distribution which is exhibited in the original formula (32). How this trade-off works, can best be seen if we restrict the analysis to partial and total privatization, $\Theta > 0$. Then (32) becomes an equality which, in turn, can be transformed into an inequality by dropping $\beta \leq 0$. We obtain

$$A(\Pi - S) \geq (\alpha + \delta)\Pi_\Theta - \alpha \frac{\partial z_0}{\partial \Theta}. \tag{35}$$

No further shares are sold if the distributional term on the left-hand side of (35) becomes smaller than the allocative term on the right-hand side. The allocative term may be high because of high profit increases or low efficiency gains.

The policy maker accepts profit increases because they can be used to increase welfare by paying dividends to the consumers. The accepted profit increases may be substantial as compared with the efficiency gains, because the profit increases are weighted by $(\alpha + \delta)$, the efficiency gains by α and $\alpha + \delta \leq \alpha$.

Finally, for all regimes of issue prices we must investigate whether *privatization efficiency* is achieved or not. If we compare (32) with the conditions for privatization efficiency (9), we have to realize that there is no case at all where privatization efficiency holds. The increase in profits Π_Θ disturbs the achievement of privatization efficiency. In the case of a low issue price, moreover, the distributional effects have to be considered. Not even in the case of no privatization or total privatization do our efficiency conditions (9) hold. This is in striking contrast to other papers on the topic (Bös 1986b, Bös and Peters 1987) where at least some cases of privatization efficiency occur.

5. Public Expenditures

Until now we have neglected that government revenues from privatization will be used to finance public expenditures. The government revenues R consist of the revenues from selling shares and of that part of the profit which the government earns as the owner of $100 \cdot (1 - \Theta)\,\%$ of the shares

$$R = \Theta S + (1 - \Theta)\Pi(\Theta). \tag{36}$$

To consider the welfare effects of the public expenditures we shall analyze the effects of the following policy. We assume that all government revenues from privatization are used to finance a public good. Hence revenue R is the demand for the public good which is covered by the supply G,

$$G = \Theta S + (1 - \Theta)\Pi(\Theta)\ . \tag{37}$$

We refrain from explicitly modelling the production of G,[10] but assume the supply function G to be given. Remember that for private firms we have proceeded in a similar way.

The public good enters the consumers' utility functions in the usual way

(38) $$v_h = v_h(p, r_h, G), \ \partial v_h/\partial G > 0 \ .$$

Let us now apply the same optimization approach as in section 3 above. The differentiation with respect to S and Θ leads to[11]

(39) $$L_S = -(A-B)\Theta + \gamma - \delta = 0,$$

(40) $$L_\Theta = (A-B)[(\Pi - S) + \Theta\Pi_\Theta] + \alpha\left(\frac{\partial z_0}{\partial\Theta} - \Pi_\Theta\right) + \beta + (B-\gamma)\Pi_\Theta \leq 0,$$

where

(17) $$A = \frac{1}{H}\left[\sum_{h=1}^{H} W_h \frac{\partial v_h}{\partial r_h} + \alpha \sum_{h=1}^{H}\sum_{i=1}^{n}(p_i - c_i)\frac{\partial z_i}{\partial r_h}\right],$$

(41) $$B = \sum_{h=1}^{H} W_h \frac{\partial v_h}{\partial G} + \alpha \sum_{i=1}^{n}(p_i - c_i)\frac{\partial z_i}{\partial G}.$$

A is the welfare effect of changes in the consumers' net incomes from dividends, abbreviated the private welfare effect. B is the welfare effect of changes in the government expenditures G, abbreviated the public welfare effect.

The economic interpretation of B is similar to A. An increase in G affects welfare in a twofold way. First the individual utilities increase and so does welfare. Second both consumer demand for outputs and consumer supply of inputs change. Both consumption and input effects may be positive or negative.

If the amount of public expenditures were first best, $B = 0$ would result. This can be seen by the following hypothetical optimization. Let us forget for the

---

[10] Explicit modelling of the production of G is possible in a model of the Boiteux framework. However, the model becomes much more complicated and the benefits from this complication, in terms of economic insight, are minimal.

[11] The p_e-marginal conditions remain unchanged because G is functionally independent of any price.

moment that G is determined endogenously and let the government choose G so as to maximize welfare. Then

$$(42) \qquad L_G = 0, \ L_{GG} < 0.$$

Hence $B = 0$ if the public expenditures are first best. Assuming that $L_G = 0$ has a unique solution, we can rely on the second-order condition to conclude that $B > 0$ if the public expenditures are too low and $B < 0$ if the public expenditures are too high.

The *optimal issue price* can easily be determined on the basis of condition (39)[12]. We obtain the result:

(i) high issue price if $(A - B) \leq 0$

(ii) medium issue price if $(A - B) = 0$

(iii) low issue price if $(A - B) \geq 0$.

The result depends on the trade-off between the private welfare effect A and the public welfare effect B. The net effect $A - B$ is decisive because any increase in the share price S takes from the consumers and gives to the government whence we have to trade off the welfare effects of reduced consumer incomes and the welfare effects of increased government expenditures.[13]

If the net effect $A - B$ is negative, the issue price is equated to the profit. The government applies a "skimming policy". As $S = \Pi$, the public expenditures are equal to the profit of the privatized firm. Note that in our model the exclusion of net incomes from dividends does not mean that public expenditures are equated to zero. The profit Π still is spent as public expenditure although the welfare effects of such an expenditure are negative. As we shall see, however, these welfare effects influence the optimal extent of privatization.

In the case of a medium issue price the private and the public welfare effects wash out. Once again, at the interior optimum welfare cannot be increased by changing the dividend incomes.

If the net effect $A - B$ is positive, the lowest possible issue price is chosen. The government applies a "dividend policy". Government revenues from selling shares are reduced, consumers' net incomes are increased.

The reader will have realized the close similarity between the issue price in the public expenditure case and in the no-expenditure case. In the expenditure

[12] As in section 4.1 we exclude the case of $\Theta = 0$.

[13] Recall that we are interpreting eq. (39). Hence we argue for constant Θ.

case the issue price depends on both the private and the public welfare effect, $A - B$. In the no-expenditure case the issue price only depends on the private welfare effect A. Otherwise in both cases the decision on the share price follows the same pattern.

Let us now turn to the *optimal extent of privatization* which can be discussed on the basis of condition (40).

If a high issue price is chosen, there are no net incomes from dividends. We have $\Pi - S = 0$ and condition (40) reduces to

$$B\Pi_\Theta + \beta \leq \alpha\left(\Pi_\Theta - \frac{\partial z_0}{\partial \Theta}\right). \tag{43}$$

This condition implies

$$\Pi_\Theta(\alpha - B) \geq \alpha\frac{\partial z_0}{\partial \Theta} \qquad \text{for } \Theta = 0 \tag{44.1}$$

$$\Pi_\Theta(\alpha - B) = \alpha\frac{\partial z_0}{\partial \Theta} \qquad \text{for } 0 < \Theta < 1 \tag{44.2}$$

$$\Pi_\Theta(\alpha - B) \leq \alpha\frac{\partial z_0}{\partial \Theta} \qquad \text{for } \Theta = 1. \tag{44.3}$$

Compared with the no-expenditure case (34), the policy maker is willing to accept higher profit increases if there are positive welfare effects of public expenditures.

If a medium issue price is chosen, the private and the public welfare effect cancel out, $A - B = 0$, and once again the condition (43) holds.

Finally, we come to the case of a low issue price. There are positive net incomes from dividends, $\Pi - S > 0$, and there are positive distributional consequences of dividends and public expenditures, $A - B \geq 0$. We are back at the trade-off between distribution and allocation which is exhibited in the original condition (40). A nice interpretation of this condition can be given if we restrict the analysis to the cases of partial and total privatization, $\Theta > 0$, as we did in section 4 above. Then we obtain[14]

$$(A - B)(\Pi - S) \geq (\alpha - B + \delta)\Pi_\Theta - \alpha\frac{\partial z_0}{\partial \Theta} \tag{45}$$

which can be compared with inequality (35) of the no-expenditure case. As we expected, the private welfare effect A is replaced with the difference of the private

[14] Substitute $(A - B)\Theta = \gamma - \delta$ from (39). Excluding $\Theta = 0$, (40) becomes an equation. After dropping $\beta \leq 0$ we have an inequality again.

and the public welfare effects $A - B$. However, the "pure profit effect" $B\Pi_\Theta$ also influences the decision on the extent of privatization.

Once again, the policy maker may accept profit increases. He does so if they can be used to increase welfare by consumer dividends and public expenditures. The accepted profit increases may be substantial as compared with the efficiency gains. The weight $(\alpha - B + \delta)$ is lower the higher the welfare effects of the public expenditures. Hence higher profit increases are accepted the higher the welfare effects of the public expenditures.

6. Optimal Prices[15]

For the following elaboration we consider the pricing of an output good, $x_e, z_e > 0$. Substituting Roy's identity, $\partial v_h/\partial p_e = -x_{eh}(\partial v_h/\partial r_h)$ into (24) we obtain the following pricing structure

$$\sum_{i=1}^{n}(p_i - c_i)\frac{\partial z_i}{\partial p_e} = -z_e + F_e x_e, \quad e \in E \tag{46}$$

where $x_e = \sum_h x_{eh}$. The "distributional characteristics" F_e are a distributionally weighted sum of individual consumption shares

$$F_e := \sum_h \frac{W_h}{\alpha}\frac{\partial v_h}{\partial r_h}\frac{x_{eh}}{x_e}, \quad e \in E. \tag{47}$$

The social valuation of changes in the individual non-labor incomes will be a decreasing function of individual incomes, thereby bringing about the distributional weighting mentioned above. For a similar reasoning see Feldstein (1972a,b,c) and Atkinson and Stiglitz (1980, pp. 387, 469).

For *intermediate goods*, $x_e = 0$, and the monopoly type of pricing applies. The neglect of distributional concern is surprising because the intermediate goods are used by other firms to produce consumption goods and the distributional valuations in $W(\cdot)$ refer to consumers and hence to their consumption. The reason for this surprising result is the omission of explicit production functions of the

[15] This section can be skipped by the reader who is familiar with the usual results of public sector pricing. The qualitative result of this section is identical to the well-known Feldstein prices although, of course, all variables and functions in (46) depend on Θ and on S. For details on Feldstein pricing see Bös (1986a, chapter 10).

private firms in our model whence there is no feedback relating to the welfare importance of intermediate goods.

When selling *consumption goods*, however, the privatized firm explicitly considers distributional objectives in the pricing structure. Let us first consider consumption goods which are supplied only by the privatized firm. In that case $\sum_j y_{ej} = 0$[16] and $z_e = x_e$. The equation (46) reduces to

$$(48) \qquad \sum_{i=1}^{n}(p_i - c_i)\frac{\partial z_i}{\partial p_e} = -(1-F_e)z_e, \quad e \in E.$$

A general interpretation of the distributional price structure (48) can be given by comparing this price structure with that of a perfect monopolist.[17] The board of the privatized firm behaves as if it were a monopolist who inflates each price elasticity of demand by $1/(1-F_e)$.[18] The operation of this procedure can be illustrated most easily if we neglect cross-price effects. Then the pricing rule is as follows

$$(49) \qquad (p_e - c_e)\frac{\partial z_e}{\partial p_e} = -(1-F_e)z_e, \quad e \in E.$$

If we exclude positive price effects, then the price of good e will exceed the marginal costs if $1 > F_e > 0$ and fall below marginal costs if $F_e > 1$. For a price above marginal costs the inflating factor $1/(1-F_e)$ will exceed unity and will increase with increasing F_e. The demand elasticity must therefore be overestimated and the degree of over-estimation increases with increasing social valuation of individual consumption as reflected in F_e. Above all, the price elasticities of necessities must be over-estimated because monopolistic pricing always implies greater care in the pricing of goods with higher demand elasticities. If, on the other hand, the price falls below marginal costs, the inflating factor $1/(1-F_e)$ will be negative and will again increase with increasing F_e. This implies once again a tendency to reduce the price of necessities.

If the privatized firm is not the only supplier of the consumption good e, the equation (46) can be transformed into

$$(50) \qquad \sum_{i}(p_i - c_i)\frac{\partial z_i}{\partial p_e} = -(1-F_e)x_e + \sum_j y_{ej}, \quad e \in E.$$

---

[16] where $e \in E$ is taken as the index of outputs sold by the privatized firm at the prices p_e. We exclude $\sum_j y_{ej} > 0$ by the assumption of monopolistic supply z_e and we exclude $\sum_j y_{ej} < 0$ by the assumption that e refers to consumption goods only.

[17] This sort of interpretation is due to Drèze and Marchand (1976).

[18] See Bös (1986a, pp. 216–218).

This formula shows that prices are not only reduced for distributional reasons but also because of competition by other firms. This trade-off can be seen directly by looking at equation (50). Cheaper prices for necessities are brought about by lower $(1 - F_e)x_e$. The price of good e is also reduced if $\sum y_{ej}$ increases, i.e. if the consumption from other firms' supply is greater (for outputs $y_{ej} > 0$).

7. Summary

It has puzzled me for many years that the issue price of shares typically is chosen very low if public enterprises are privatized. Does this mean that the government frivolously wastes national property? In this paper I give a welfare economic explanation of why such low issue prices can be consistent with rational behavior of a policy maker.

If the welfare effects of the net incomes from dividends are positive, the policy maker chooses the lowest issue price which is politically feasible. Then, in choosing the optimal extent of privatization, the distributional effects of net incomes from dividends are traded-off against the allocative effects of privatization, namely the profit increases and the gains in the productive efficiency.

A different situation arises if the net incomes from dividends have negative or zero welfare effect. If the effect is negative, the policy maker chooses the highest possible issue price, i.e. he absorbs all dividends by equating issue price and profit. No income effects occur. If the welfare effect is zero, net incomes from dividends are chosen so as to direct demand to those goods with the highest potential for efficiency gains in the production.

In both cases of the preceding paragraph there are no distributional effects of privatization: either no net income from dividends occurs, or if it occurs it has no distributional consequences. The extent of privatization, then, is chosen so as to cope with the remaining issues, i.e. the allocation problems. The gains in productive efficiency from privatization must be high enough to offset the profit increases.

A more general analysis includes not only the net incomes from dividends, but also the public expenditures which result from privatization. The latter consist of the revenues from selling the shares and of the government's share in the firm's profit. The rationale of low issue prices remains the same as in the no-expenditure case. However, the combined welfare effects of public expenditures and of net incomes from dividends must be taken care of.

References

Atkinson, A. B., and **Stiglitz, J. E.** (1980): *Lectures on Public Economics.* London etc.: McGraw-Hill.

Beesley, M. E. (1981): "Liberalisation of the Use of British Telecommunications Network." Report to the Secretary of State, Department of Industry, London.

Bös, D. (1985): "Public Sector Pricing." In *Handbook of Public Economics, Vol. I,* edited by A. Auerbach and M. Feldstein. Amsterdam etc.: North-Holland, pp. 129–211.

Bös, D. (1986a): *Public Enterprise Economics.* Amsterdam etc.: North-Holland. (Advanced Textbooks in Economics, 23.)

Bös, D. (1986b): "A Theory of the Privatization of Public Enterprises." In *Welfare Economics of the Second Best,* edited by D. Bös and Ch. Seidl. Vienna etc.: Springer, pp. 17–40. (*Journal of Economics / Zeitschrift für Nationalökonomie,* Supplementum 5.)

Bös, D. (1987): "Privatization of Public Enterprises." *European Economic Review* 31: 352–360.

Bös, D., and **Peters, W.** (1987): "A Normative Approach to Privatization." Mimeo. Bonn: University of Bonn.

Boiteux, M. (1956, 1971): "Sur la gestion des monopoles astreints à l'équilibre budgétaire." *Econometrica* 24: 22–40. English edition: "On the Management of Public Monopolies Subject to Budgetary Constraints." *Journal of Economic Theory* 3: 219–240.

Drèze, J. H. (1964): "Some Postwar Contributions of French Economists to Theory and Public Policy with Special Emphasis on Problems of Resource Allocation." *American Economic Review* 54, No. 4, Part 2 (Supplement): 1–64.

Drèze, J. H. (1984): "Second-best Analysis with Markets in Disequilibrium: Public Sector Pricing in a Keynesian Regime." In *The Performance of Public Enterprises,* edited by M. Marchand, P. Pestieau, and H. Tulkens. Amsterdam etc.: North-Holland, pp. 45–79.

Drèze, J. H., and **Marchand, M.** (1976): "Pricing, Spending, and Gambling Rules for Non-profit Organizations." In *Public and Urban Economics, Essays in Honor of William S. Vickrey,* edited by R. E. Grieson. Lexington, Mass.: Heath, pp. 59–89.

Feldstein, M. S. (1972a): "Distributional Equity and the Optimal Structure of Public Prices." *American Economic Review* 62: 32–36. (Corrected version of p. 33, footnote 7: *American Economic Review* 62: 763.)

Feldstein, M. S. (1972b): "Equity and Efficiency in Public Sector Pricing: The Optimal Two-part Tariff." *Quarterly Journal of Economics* 86: 175–187.

Feldstein, M. S. (1972c): "The Pricing of Public Intermediate Goods." *Journal of Public Economics* 1: 45–72.

Hagen, K. P. (1979): "Optimal Pricing in Public Firms in an Imperfect Market Economy." *Scandinavian Journal of Economics* 81: 475–493.

Marchand, M., Pestieau, P., and **Weymark, J. A.** (1982): "Discount Rates for Public Enterprises in the Presence of Alternative Financial Constraints." In *Public Production*, edited by D. Bös, R. A. Musgrave, and J. Wiseman. Vienna etc.: Springer, pp. 27–50. (*Zeitschrift für Nationalökonomie / Journal of Economics*, Supplementum 2.)

Marchand, M., Pestieau, P., and **Tulkens, H.** (1984): "The Performance of Public Enterprises: Normative, Positive and Empirical Issues." In *The Performance of Public Enterprises*, edited by M. Marchand, P. Pestieau, and H. Tulkens. Amsterdam etc.: North-Holland, pp. 3–42.

Panik, M. J. (1976): *Classical Optimization: Foundations and Extensions.* Amsterdam etc.: North-Holland.

Peters, W. (1986): "Cost-Inefficiency and Second-best Pricing." Mimeo. Bonn: University of Bonn.

Sheshinski, E. (1986): "Positive Second-best Theory." In *Handbook of Mathematical Economics, Vol. III*, edited by K. J. Arrow and M. D. Intriligator. Amsterdam etc.: North-Holland, pp. 1251–1280.

Measuring Environmental Benefits: A Comparison of Hedonic Technique and Contingent Valuation

Werner W. Pommerehne, Berlin, West Germany, and Zurich, Switzerland*

1. Introduction

As it is well known there is a substantial gap between the rigorous and elegant definition of welfare change and benefits derived from theoretical welfare economics and their empirical estimate. This holds especially in the case of public goods such as, e.g., environmental improvements originating in reduced air or water pollution and noise reduction, all of them characterized by non-divisibility and non-rivalness in consumption. Consequently, there are no markets, no customers, no sales and, thus, no cheap information on the benefits of environmental improvement. However, it is important for decision makers in the public sector to have an idea about individual demand of such public goods and their related benefits. This information is necessary to undertake benefit-cost analysis, which is the major tool for evaluating and selecting those policy alternatives which contribute to more effective resource utilization.[1]

So far a number of attempts has been undertaken in the last two decades to determine the demand for public goods and the related benefits:[2]

(1) The application of the *hedonic price technique* can be considered as the best known and most accepted empirical approach. It involves the analysis of market data from transactions in private goods and services which are in turn complementarily related to the characteristics of the public good under consideration. For example, it is assumed that housing values ceteris paribus

* The author is indebted to Willi Brammertz, Reiner Eichenberger and Thomas Steinemann for research assistance, and to Heinz Buhofer and Peter Zweifel (all University of Zurich) as well as to Kai Fürntratt and Anselm Roemer (both Free University of Berlin) for useful comments on an earlier draft. Additional helpful comments were received from the participants of meetings at Amsterdam, Geneva, Linz, Louvain, Maastricht, Madison, Munich, Neuchâtel and Paris. The study also benefited from most useful suggestions of the participants of the Neresheim seminar and of two anonymous referees. They are, of course, not implicated in any remaining errors.

[1] If the benefits of public goods cannot be evaluated on the basis of individual preferences, cost-effectiveness analysis may be the second best approach. However, it has the disadvantage that only alternatives with (nearly) identical output can be compared.

[2] See Pommerehne (1987) for a more detailed presentation and discussion of the following as well as of a number of further (though in this concrete context perhaps less adequate) approaches.

reflect spatial variation in the quality of environmental goods (such as climate, air pollution, noise level). Therefore, it should be possible to estimate a house price function and, by calculating its partial derivative, to compute the marginal implicit price of any house-related characteristic. An evaluation of environmental improvement, thus, can be undertaken. This indirect approach has proven to be quite useful.[3]

(2) An alternative is to ask individuals to state their willingness-to-pay for environmental improvement directly, using a survey questionnaire to acquire information. Central to this method, now commonly referred to as *contingent valuation* is the construction of a hypothetical allocation procedure for the public good under consideration. This direct approach, based on work of Davis (1963), Bradford (1970), Bohm (1971) and others, has been successfully applied in valuing a number of environmental commodities (air pollution, scenic visibility etc.).[4]

The purpose of this paper is to apply these two approaches to the same problem, i.e., the measurement of the demand for a concrete public good: Noise reduction in the city of Basle (Switzerland). In contrast to some other pollutants which are imperceptible to the point where behavior is not influenced by changes in the level of pollution, noise has the advantage of being readily perceived, which, as a consequence, makes a comparison of different approaches most meaningful. In addition, while noise is without doubt the cause of hearing impairment, it has no long-run cumulative effects in the environment, as is the case with air pollution, which make benefit-cost evaluations so difficult.[5]

The main reason for the application of two different approaches is that each one has some specific strengths and weaknesses. For instance, the contingent valuation approach has the advantage that it generates its own data and does not depend upon pre-existing market observations and, therefore, can be used to value *any* public good within a benefit-cost framework. However, it has been criticized for a variety of potential biases, in particular due to the hypothetical decision-making situation and the inherent incentive for strategic behavior of respondents, which may render the resulting willingness-to-pay figures as non-interpretable. The hedonic price approach, in contrast, has the advantage of relying on market data, i.e., on revealed behavior of individuals making rather well informed decisions under a budget constraint and, therefore, considering the consequences of

[3] See, among others, Hoch and Drake (1974), Harrison and Rubinfeld (1978) and Nelson (1978, 1981) for successful applications of this method.

[4] For a survey of recent applications see Schulze, d'Arge and Brookshire (1981).

[5] See Pearce (1976) for a detailed elaboration of these perception and accumulation problems.

faulty behavior. The major disadvantage of this approach consists in the rather strong assumptions which must be made[6] and its failure in a number of important instances like the evaluation of some specific environmental commodities as, for instance, the remote and unique scenic vista of a sparsely inhabited mountain area. In this case, lack of sufficient (variance among the available) data inhibits the use of the hedonic price approach. Other important cases where this technique cannot be used relate to potential optional, bequest and prestige values of the public good in question, for which, due to the lacking link to any market good, simply no market data exist.

The results achieved so far by the use of the hedonic price approach and the contingent valuation method appear to be, internally consistent, replicable and in line with demand theory. However, only few work is done on external validation.[7] Therefore, one purpose of this study is to report on an experiment designed to validate the contingent valuation method by direct comparison to the hedonic price approach, using in the first case a sample of more than 200 households in the city of Basle and in the latter a data set referring to the various characteristics of the respective over 200 dwellings. If both methods are compatible, the contingent valuation approach seems to be applicable to the valuation of those public goods where no well developed hedonic market exists. However, "compatibility" in this context does not mean that the results should be identical. As discussed later, there are theoretical reasons why the expected results of one approach will deviate from those of the other and, in particular, why the monthly willingness-to-pay derived from market data must exceed the estimates of household willingness-to-pay from survey data for the same amount of noise reduction.[8]

Section 2 briefly reviews the theoretical base of the hedonic price approach and discusses a number of specification issues. Then, it provides empirical findings and simulation results for the willingness-to-pay for noise reduction, based on a sample of dwelling data for the city of Basle. Section 3 deals with the primary features of the survey instrument used — the contingent valuation experiment. It discusses the compatibility of its findings with those of the hedonic price technique, and presents empirical estimates and simulation results based on survey data of

[6] See Mäler (1977) for a critical discussion of the theoretical assumptions of the hedonic price approach.

[7] A well known exception is the study of Brookshire, Thayer, Schulze, and d'Arge (1982) on the reduction of air pollution in a number of Californian regions. However, their comparison suffers from the fact that the samples used in both approaches are not identical. Nevertheless, that study heavily influenced the present research in which, moreover, one and the same sample (of dwellings and inhabitants) is used in order to minimize potential sampling biases.

[8] Moreover, in contrast to the study of Brookshire et al. (fn. 7) where only one kind of disamenity is considered, the present research provides a double-check of this hypothesis because a distinction is made between different types of noise.

the households of the respective dwellings. Section 4 contrasts the main results of both approaches and discusses the implications of the empirical findings. The final section 5 contains some concluding remarks.

2. Valuing Noise Reduction from Market Data: The Hedonic Price Approach

2.1 Theoretical Base

The basic idea behind the hedonic price approach is that a dwelling can be characterized through a bundle of *attributes*: the number, size and quality of rooms; size of the garden; characteristics of neighborhood, like proximity to shops, school and parks; accessibility to city center and so on. The level of noise is one more attribute and indeed, can be thought of as a negative attribute. The dwelling price or rent is then some combination of the implicit, or hedonic prices of various attributes. Since noise is a negative attribute it should have a negative price. Alternatively, the inverse of noise, "peace and quiet" can be regarded as a positive attribute and, therefore, should have a positive price. The household is assumed to have an utility function of the form

(1) $$U = U(X, c_i) \qquad i = 1, \ldots, n$$

where X describes the bundle of non-housing goods consumed (e.g. food, clothes) and c_i is a vector of any dwelling-related characteristic i. The budget constraint is given by

(2) $$Y = P_X \cdot X + \sum_{i=1}^{n} P_i \cdot c_i$$

where Y is income, P_X is the price of non-housing goods, and P_i is the implicit price of the i-th attribute. Maximizing (1) with respect to (2) yields an expenditure function (3), linking the dwelling-related characteristics and other goods and services to expenditure levels:

(3) $$f(c_i, X, Y) = 0.$$

If the utility function (1) is separable between dwelling-related characteristics and the consumption of other (non-housing) goods, (3) can be expressed as

(4) $$g(c_i, E) = 0$$

where E is dwelling expenditure ($E = Y - P_X \cdot X$). The implicit function (4) can be expressed in explicit form

$$(5) \qquad E = e(c_i)$$

and indicates that dwelling expenditure E (expressed in rental terms)[9] is a function of the various characteristics of the dwelling.

The *marginal* valuation of any dwelling-related characteristic i is given by $\partial E/\partial c_i$, measuring the marginal willingness-to-pay for an extra unit of the respective attribute. This is the marginal implicit or hedonic price, other things being equal. Function (5) may be linear or non-linear, that is, the value of $\partial E/\partial c_i$ may or may not depend on quantities of characteristics being purchased.[10] Due to tie-ins and indivisibilities, non-linear relationships seem to describe the dwelling market best.

Dwelling rents, of course, reflect both supply and demand, and the same should also hold for the implicit price of characteristics. Therefore, it should be noted that estimates of equation (5) do not directly represent the underlying structural equations. Rather, observed marginal implicit prices are determined by the distribution of consumer tastes and producer cost, and are, thus, outcomes of equilibrium. Figure 1 illustrates the demand for a dwelling-related characteristic i, where w_{i_j} is the implicit marginal valuation or willingness-to-pay function of the j-th household and where $\partial E/\partial c_i$ is assumed to be decreasing in c_i.[11]

Households increase their consumption of the attribute i as embodied in the various dwellings as long as $w_{i_j} > \partial E/\partial c_i$, i.e. an implicit or hedonic price function

---

[9] Converted to present-value (PV) terms (5) leads to $PV = E/r = (1/r) \cdot e(c_i)$, where r is the interest rate, i.e. the capitalized value of the dwelling rent depends upon the level of the attributes of the dwelling.

[10] If utility function (1) is linear, the form of equation (5), the equation to be estimated, will be

$$(5a) \qquad E = a_1 \cdot c_1 + a_2 \cdot c_2 + \ldots a_n \cdot c_n$$

where the a's are constants and, since $\partial E/\partial c_i = a_i$, these constants are themselves the marginal implicit/hedonic prices. If instead, for example, a multiplicative utility function is chosen, the respective log-linear regression equation is

$$(5b) \qquad \log E = a_1 \cdot \log c_1 + a_2 \log c_2 + \ldots a_n \cdot \log c_n$$

where the coefficients are no longer the hedonic prices, but $\partial E/\partial c_i = (\partial \log E/\partial \log c_i)\cdot(E/c_i) = a_i(E/c_i)$, i.e. the marginal implicit price depends on both the dwelling rent E and the level of the attribute c_i.

[11] For the discussion of the supply-side of an implicit market for an attribute see Freeman (1979, chap. 6).

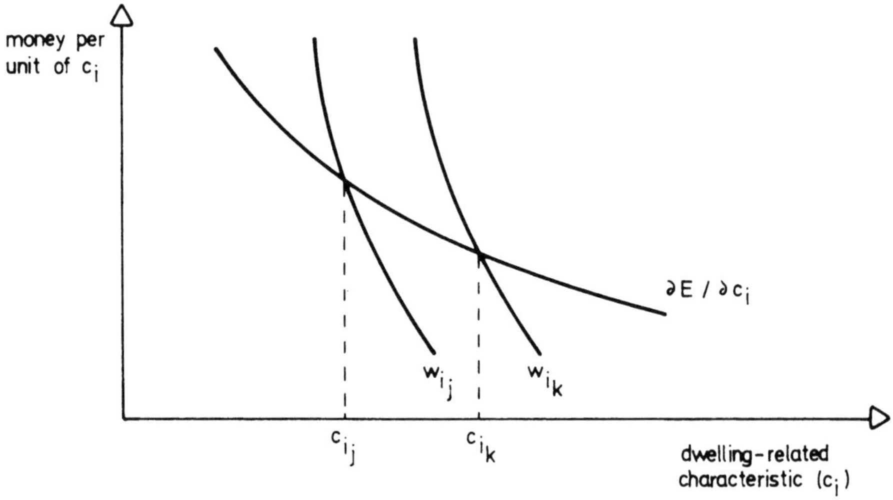

c_1 is defined as a positive dwelling-related attribute e.g. level of "peace and quiet"

Figure 1: Marginal Implicit Price Function and Willingness-to-Pay for a Dwelling-related Characteristic

is a locus of equilibrium willingness-to-pay, and households locate themselves in attribute spaces so that price differences between characteristics are equalizing only at the margin (c_{i_j} and c_{i_k} , respectively). How useful this information appears, depends in part on the circumstances in question:

First, market adjustments are assumed to occur sufficiently quickly so that all potential consumer surplus is fully captured in the form of higher dwelling rents; second, for equation (5) to be directly applied to benefit evaluation, it must be possible to treat reductions of noise as marginal improvements. The circumstances under which the first assumption holds have been discussed extensively[12] and it will be considered later in what direction the estimates are biased if mobility of households is restricted. The second assumption may be less appropriate for current noise reduction policies in such medieval cities like Basle. Therefore, and because partial equilibrium assumptions may not hold, the estimated implicit marginal rents will be used as the dependent variable in a second-step estimation of a demand function for 'peace and quiet'.[13]

[12] A summary is given in Pearce (1978, chap. 2).

[13] See Rosen (1974, p. 50) and, for an earlier attempt to apply this two-stage procedure, Harrison and Rubinfeld (1978).

2.2 Specification of the Rent Function

In general form the following rent function can be established

(6) $$p_m = p(D_{m_s}, H_{m_t}, L_{m_u}, N_m)$$

where p_m is the monthly *net rent of dwelling m*, D_{m_s} is a vector of specific characteristics ($s = 1, \ldots, w$) of *dwelling m* (e.g. number of rooms, quality of dwelling,...), H_{m_t} is a vector of characteristics ($t = 1, \ldots, x$) of residential *house m* (distance to school, bus stop, ...), L_{m_u} is a vector of characteristics ($u = 1, \ldots, y$) of *locality m* (size of the open area, neighborhood characteristics, ...) and N_m is the *traffic noise* with dwelling m.

The concrete specification of this reduced form equation rises a number of problems:

The first issue to deal with relates to the *adequate measure of noise nuisance.* The relevant noise level is the individually perceived and not the objectively measured noise level. However, there are major difficulties measuring subjectively perceived disamenities. Fortunately, in the case of noise damage there seems to be no large inter-individual differences in perception, though the relationship between the individually felt and the objectively measured noise level seems to be an exponential relationship: sound level measurements are based on a logarithmic scale, and perceived traffic noise loudness tends to double every ten decibels (the standard measure of physical sound pressure of traffic noise). A subjective annoyance rating plotted on a log scale therefore will approximate a linear relationship with the perceived noise level in decibels.[14] Taking into account this relationship, suppose equation (6) is represented by

(7) $$p_m = a_0 \cdot Z_m^{a_1} \cdot N_m^{a_2} \cdot e_1$$

where p_m is the monthly dwelling rent, Z_m is a set of all other physical and locational dwelling attributes, N_m is subjective nuisance due to traffic noise, and e_1 is a stochastic error term. Subjective annoyance, in turn, is expressed by

(8) $$N_m = b_0 \cdot exp\,(b_1 \cdot dB_m) \cdot e_2$$

where dB_m refers to the objective sound level measurement in decibels and e_2 is a stochastic error term. Taking natural logs at both sides of equation (7) and substituting for $ln\ N_m$, it follows

(9) $$ln\ p_m = d_0 + d_1\ ln\ Z_m + d_2\, dB_m + e_3$$

---

[14] See Starkie and Johnson (1975, chap. 1), Walters (1975, chap. 2), Nelson (1978, chap. 2), and Sinn (1983, chap. 3) for further evidence.

where $d_0 = ln\ a_0 + a_2\ ln\ b_0$, $d_1 = a_1$, $d_2 = a_2 \cdot b_1$ and $e_3 = a_2\ ln\ e_2 + ln\ e_1$. The coefficient of d_2 (times 100) represents the percentage change in a given dwelling rent due to a decibel change in noise. The implicit marginal price of traffic noise is given by $\partial p_m / \partial dB_m = d_2 \cdot p_m$, the noise elasticity is $d_2 \cdot dB_m$.

A second specification issue refers to the perception of *different kinds of noise*, different with respect to the intensity of the sound and pressure waves. Road traffic noise, being rather smoothed, seems to be perceived in quite a different way than aircraft noise, the latter being characterized by shorter durage, but very high frequencies of sound pressure. In order to distinguish between these two major noise nuisances, two distinct measures are used: (i) the level of *road traffic noise* (in decibel), and (ii) the level of *aircraft noise*, measured by the Noise-and-Number-Index (*NNI*).[15] In addition, an interaction term is introduced in order to capture potential interrelationship between both kinds of noise nuisance.

A sample of 223 dwellings spread over the city of Basle is chosen, covering dwellings in one family house, those in multi family houses, houses which are solely used as a residental house, others with mixed (residential/commercial) use and so on. In total, for each dwelling data are collected on more than 70 characteristics of the dwellings itself, the residential houses, the locality and, finally, of traffic noise.[16] A summary of the main variables considered, the empirical proxies used and the expected sign of the respective coefficient is given in Table A (appendix). This table also describes the concrete specification of the estimation equation finally used.[17]

---

[15] The *NNI*-index for loudness also represents a logarithmic relation with physical sound pressure, though sound waves are differently weighted as compared to the decibel-scale. Of course, both measures relate to each dwelling and each measure has been taken at the same time during the day.

[16] Most data on the structural characteristics of each individual dwelling and the respective residential house have been taken from a broad survey among the owners of the houses, kindly provided by Professor Tobias Studer (University of Basle). This information has been checked as well as expanded by a (repetitive) survey among the tenants. Data on the structural characteristics of the locality of each dwelling-house have been collected from various official statistics and especially from a detailed quantitative description of the 60 statistical units of the city of Basle (BNM Planconsult 1982). Measures of air pollution by district (two different indicators) have been kindly provided by the Federal Bureau of Environment (Berne). Data on the amount of road traffic noise at each individual dwelling [expressed on the base of 'equivalent permanent noise level' (in *dB*)] have been provided by Rapp Consulting Incorporation (Basle). Finally, the level of aircraft noise at each dwelling has been calculated from maps with detailed iso-loudness pressure lines, provided by the Federal Testing Laboratory (Zurich).

[17] As in most cases of large scale quantitative research, a number of linear and non-linear specifications has been applied with respect to the estimation equation, as well as to a number of explanatory variables.

2.3 Empirical Results

In this section the main OLS estimation results are presented, based on the assumption that there exists a log-linear relationship between the individually perceived and the objectively measured noise level.[18] Therefore, both traffic noise variables enter the regression equation in absolute values (*dB*, *NNI*); the dependent variable consists in the natural logarithm of the monthly net dwelling rent in Swiss Francs (SFr) in 1983.

(10)	*ln* net dwelling rent (in SFr) =	6.962 (12.720)	constant term
		0.663^{**} (11.621)	*ln* number of standardized rooms
		0.028^{**} (3.465)	quality index (-9 = very bad to $+9$ = very good)
		0.127^{**} (4.401)	dummy variable: pure dwelling house = 1 (otherwise = 0)
		0.205^{**} (3.267)	dummy variable: one family house = 1 (otherwise = 0)
		$0.111^{(*)}$ (1.829)	dummy variable: avenue with trees = 1 (otherwise = 0)
		0.279^{**} (3.537)	dummy variable: situated on the Rhine = 1 (otherwise = 0)
		-0.00049^{**} (-4.737)	*ln* distance to next shopping center (meters)
		-0.00020^{*} (-2.120)	*ln* distance to next public playground (meters)
		$-0.00021^{(*)}$ (-1.989)	*ln* distance to next bus/tramway stop (meters)

[18] This equation retains only those explanatory variables from Table B (appendix) which do not seem to be highly correlated with other independent variables (the simple correlation coefficients among these variables are given in Table C, appendix) and contribute significantly to the explanatory power of the model.
In fact, there is a serious multicollinearity problem when both measures of air pollution appear in the same equation. However, even when this problem is simplified by including only a single pollutant measure (as in equations (1) and (2) of Table B) there remains some multicollinearity among a number of characteristics of the house (especially among distance measures), of locality, and of traffic noise (though the two measures of traffic noise are not correlated). Therefore, a number of these variables are eliminated and ridge-regression technique is applied in order to find out whether the parameter estimates, given in equation (3) of Table B do alter. This is not the case. Moreover, the matrix of independent variables is decomposed in its singular values. The relatively high singular values obtained indicate that there are no further near-linear dependencies among the remaining variables. Therefore, it can be concluded that there is no serious multicollinearity problem inhibiting the estimation of the dwelling rent function.

$0.0010^{(*)}$ (1.988)	*ln* open area (in % of total space)
-0.0038^{**} (−3.420)	*ln* industrial area (in % of total space)
-0.0125^{**} (−3.479)	road traffic noise (*dB*)
-0.0020^{*} (−2.001)	aircraft noise (*NNI*)

$\overline{R}^2 = 0.713$; F-value = 37.210; d.f.= 209.

The figures in parentheses below the parameter estimates denote the respective $\hat{t}$-value. Two asterisks show statistical significance at the 99 %-, one asterisk (in parentheses) indicates significance at the 95 %-(90 %-)confidence level, using a two-tailed-test.

Measured by conventional test statistics the regression results have to be considered as quite good. More than 70 % of the variation in dwelling rents can be statistically explained by the variation in the independent variable set. All coefficients possess the expected relationship to the dependent variable (discussed in Table A, appendix) and all are — often highly — statistically significant. Both traffic noise variables have the expected negative influence on dwelling rent; moreover the results confirm the hypothesis that both kinds of noise nuisance are perceived quite differently and independently.[19]

In total, the results are quite plausible: doubling the number of (standardized) rooms from 3 to 6 would increase the mean net dwelling rent of 560 SFr by 66.3 %, to 930 SFr, ceteris paribus. This price increase, less than 100 %, is consistent with observed scale economies. Similarly, the payment for a dwelling with a "very high" (instead of mean) quality is 140 Sfr higher (700 instead of 560 Francs), whereas a dwelling with a "very bad" quality costs only 440 instead of 560 Sfr, ceteris paribus. Living in a pure dwelling house (as compared to a multiple used building) increases the net rent by some 70 Sfr; in a similar way, the rent payment for a dwelling in a one family house (instead of a several families one) is some 100 Sfr higher, ceteris paribus. A much higher price (720 instead of 560 Francs) must be paid if the dwelling is situated on the Rhine-stream promenade. On the contrary, the rent payment becomes the lower, the more industry is located in the respective district. Increased distances to the next shopping center, to the next public playground and to the next bus/tramway stop, all have a dampening influence on the net dwelling rent, though the quantitative impact is rather modest (for instance, doubling the

[19] As shown in Table B (appendix), the coefficients of the interaction variable are always far from any significance level; see also Table C of the appendix.

mean distance to the next shopping center, i.e. 800 instead of 400 meters, results in a reduction of the mean net rent by only 25 Francs). Finally, an increase of road traffic noise by one unit (one *dB*) is linked to a net rent decrease of 1.25 %. In the case of aircraft noise the respective price decrease is 0.22 % for an additional unit of *NNI*.

These results can be compared to those of other hedonic price studies on the impact of noise on rental/housing prices. Such a comparison is presented elsewhere in more detail (Pommerehne, 1987a) and indicates that the results based on rental data of the city of Basle are quite in line with those for other cities. For a great number of American cities, for instance, the range of price depreciations (expressed as a percentage of the respective price) due to increased road traffic noise extends from 0.65 % to 1.33 % (for each additional unit of *dB*), with a mean depreciation rate of 0.99 %. The respective rate of 1.25 % for Basle comes rather close.

With respect to the impact of aircraft noise, the price depreciation rate due to an increase of *NNI* by one unit is 0.22 % in the case of Basle, whereas a dozen of other studies come to results in the range of 0.26 to 0.35 % (mean value of 0.30 %). Again the discrepancy is not very large, though, this time, it runs exactly into the opposite direction as compared to the case of road traffic noise. Yet, these systematic deviations are quite plausible. Road traffic noise seems to be much more burdensome in such a medieval and urban city (with a high density) like Basle as compared to most U.S. cities. The reverse conclusion is definitively true for aircraft noise: whereas the mean aircraft noise level is as low as 30 *NNI* in the case of Basle, it varies for the set of other places studied between 55 and 75 *NNI*.[20]

However, these systematic deviations in the computed impact of traffic noise increases may indicate another problem. The depreciation due to an increase of the noise level by one unit may be not linear, but may also depend on the initial (high/low) noise level of the respective dwelling. In order to test this conjecture, a reestimation of the rent function is done by non-linear techniques, allowing that the exponent in the noise relationship [equation (8)] may have a value other than 1.

The maximum-likelihood estimates lead to the following results:

(11)	*ln* net dwelling rent (in SFr) =	7.321^{**} (13.237)	constant term
		0.663^{**} (11.321)	*ln* number of standardized rooms

[20] In fact, the situation of Basle is perhaps unique because the airport is ten miles distant from the city border.

0.030** (3.479)	quality index (−9 = very bad to +9 = very good)
0.131** (4.510)	dummy variable: pure dwelling house = 1 (otherwise = 0)
0.213** (3.272)	dummy variable: one family house = 1 (otherwise = 0)
0.122(*) (1.928)	dummy variable: avenue with trees = 1 (otherwise = 0)
0.271** (3.378)	dummy variable: situated on the Rhine = 1 (otherwise = 0)
−0.00037** (−4.536)	*ln* distance to next shopping center (meters)
−0.00019* (−2.383)	*ln* distance to next public playground (meters)
0.00022(*) (−1.936)	*ln* distance to next bus/tramway stop (meters)
−0.0012* (2.120)	*ln* open area (in % of total space)
−0.0042** (−3.537)	*ln* industrial area (in % of total space)
$-0.002943^{**} \cdot dB^{1.3}$ (−3.720)	road traffic noise (dB)
$-0.001471^{*} \cdot NNI^{1.1}$ (−2.141)	aircraft noise (NNI)

$\overline{R}^2 = 0.762$; F-value = 38.397; d.f.= 209.

These results are better than those of equation (10): the $\overline{R}^2$ improves by 4.5 percentage points to 76.2 % and the $\hat{t}$-value of both traffic noise coefficients increases. Moreover, the marginal rent depreciation doesn't seem to be constant, but rather depends on the respective noise level of the dwelling considered. Thus, $\partial p/\partial N = -0.00383 \cdot dB^{0.3}$ in the case of road traffic noise and $-0.00162 \cdot NNI^{0.1}$ in the case of aircraft noise increase (by one unit). In figure 2 these differences in the impact of both specifications of the noise relationship are illustrated for the case of road traffic noise.

The ordinate measures the decrease of the dwelling rent (in percentage) due to an increase of road traffic noise by one unit of dB; the abscissa shows the initial noise level. The dotted line (non-linear relationship) indicates that the net dwelling rent decreases by some 1.5 % if the level of road traffic noise increases from 70 to 71 dB, whereas this decrease is only about 1 % in the case of an initial noise level of 30 dB (and an increase to 31 dB). In contrast, the log-linear specification provides a constant price decline of 1.25 % per any additional unit of road traffic noise, independently of the respective noise level.

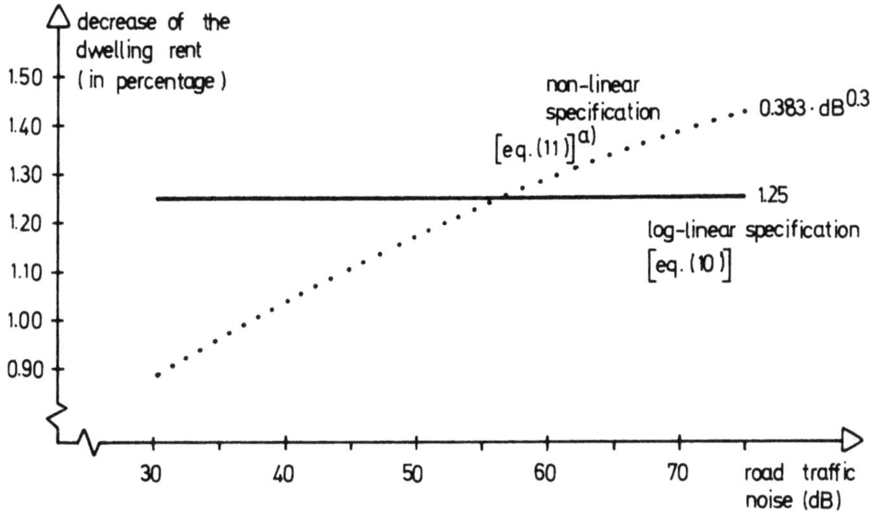

[a] Partial derivative of equation (11) with respect to road traffic noise.

Figure 2: Percentage Decrease of Monthly Net Dwelling Rent due to Increase of Road Traffic Noise by one Unit

Basically the same picture holds for the increase of aircraft noise (not shown here). However, the deviations from the constant price depreciation (0.20 %) are rather small: whereas the net rent decrease is some 0.23 % if the level of aircraft noise increases from 40 to 41 *NNI*, it is still 0.18 % if the noise level increases from 20 to 21 *NNI*.

2.4 Willingness-to-Pay for "Peace and Quiet"

The results based on the non-linear specification of the noise-relationships allow to proceed further than most noise studies and to estimate a schedule relating the willingness-to-pay for non-marginal noise reductions to the actual levels of traffic noise and a number of other demand-related variables.

In order to be able to compare the results with those of the contingent evaluation approach the net rent function, equation (11), is used to simulate the willingness-to-pay for a reduction of the actual noise level by the half for each individual dwelling.[21] These willingness-to-pay figures constitute the dependent,

[21] This includes a simulation using variable coefficients. The willingness-to-pay (*WTP*) for a noise reduction of 50 % equals the difference between the theoretical levels of the net rent which would have to be paid if the proposed noise level (N) would be 50 % lower than the actual level (N^*), $\hat{p}(0.5\,N^*)$, and of the net rent which must be paid at the actual noise level, $\hat{p}(N^*)$, that is: $WTP_{0.5} = \hat{p}(0.5\,N^*) - \hat{p}(N^*)$.

a number of demand variables the independent variables. Household income, the initial noise level of each dwelling, the number of rooms per person and a series of other potentially relevant determinants are considered as demand factors. The results of the OLS-estimates,[22] retaining the significant variables, are given in Table 1.[23]

The results of both equations measured by conventional test statistics, are quite acceptable, in particular if one takes into account that both are estimates of the effects of second order. All coefficients have a sign consistent with our expectations, i.e., in both equations household income has a positive impact on the willingness-to-pay for peace and quiet, and the same holds for the level of actual traffic noise.[24] Figure 3 (see p. 378) shows the relationship between the willingness-to-pay and these two key variables for the case of road traffic noise reduction, and figure 4, respectively, for aircraft noise reduction.[25]

Turning to figure 3, the curves illustrate the willingness-to-pay as a function of the actual road traffic noise level for three income levels. The positive slope indicates that the households' willingness-to-pay is the greater the higher the actual road traffic noise level. For instance, a middle income household earning 4000 SFr monthly and living in a dwelling exposed to a low noise level (of 30 *dB*) would be willing to pay somewhat less than 60 SFr for a noise reduction by half, while this willingness-to-pay figure would increase to about 95 SFr in the case of a high noise level (75 *dB*).

Figure 3 also indicates that the willingness-to-pay for noise reduction rises with increasing income, ceteris paribus. Whereas a low income household (2500 SFr per month) exposed to an average noise level of 55 *dB* would be willing to pay about 65 SFr, a high income household (in the same noise situation) would

---

[22] The willingness-to-pay equations are estimated under the assumption that the supply of traffic noise is perfectly inelastic at each location. This assumption is plausible in a short-run cross-section analysis; therefore, the ordinary least squares technique seems to be reasonable.

[23] This table only presents the results of the equations postulating a log-log relationship between the willingness-to-pay for a noise reduction by half and a set of independent variables. Other formulations, assuming a linear or a log-linear relationship, performed somewhat less satisfactory. Again, due to multicollinearity among some characteristics of households, a number of explanatory variables are eliminated and various techniques (see fn. 18) have been applied in order to test whether any further serious multicollinearity problem inhibits the estimation of the willingness-to-pay functions.

[24] It has also been tested whether the actual level of the, respectively, other kind of traffic noise has a significant (positive) impact on the willingness-to-pay for noise reduction. However, this was not the case, a result which is consistent with prior estimates [equations (1) and (2) in Table B, appendix].

[25] When simulating these figures, all other independent variables are kept constant at their mean value.

Table 1: Willingness-to-Pay for Noise Reduction by 50 % Derived from Market Data; Log-log Relationship; OLS Estimates; City of Basle, 1983/84[a]

Independent variables	Willingness-to-pay for reduction of:[b]	
	road traffic noise	aircraft noise
constant term	−1.991 (−2.371)	−1.920 (−1.872)
ln household net income (SFr)	0.490** (8.472)	0.530** (8.791)
ln number of rooms per person	0.142* (2.218)	0.217** (2.793)
dummy variable: household with child under age 15 = 1 (otherwise = 0)	0.317* (2.423)	—
ln road traffic noise (dB)	0.542* (2.015)	—
ln aircraft noise (NNI)	—	0.150* (2.027)
$\overline{R}^2$	0.531	0.352
F-value	32.265	20.638
degrees of freedom	218	219

[a] The dependent variable is *ln* monthly willingness-to-pay for noise reduction by half of the actual level, computed with the help of a simulation using variable coefficients.
[b] The figures in parentheses below the parameter estimates denote the respective $\hat{t}$-value. Two asterisks indicate statistical significance at the 99 %-, one asterisk (in parentheses) shows significance at the 95 %- (90 %-) confidence level, using a two-tailed-test.

pay a premium of roughly 95 SFr for the same amount of noise reduction. Finally, the differential in the premiums becomes smaller (larger) the lower (higher) the noise level considered. For example, whereas it is about 12 SFr at a noise level of 30 dB, it jumps to nearly 20 SFr at a level of 75 dB. So, the premium that high income households are willing to pay increases as the actual noise level rises or, in other words, households in different income groups have different elasticities of willingness-to-pay with respect to the noise level.

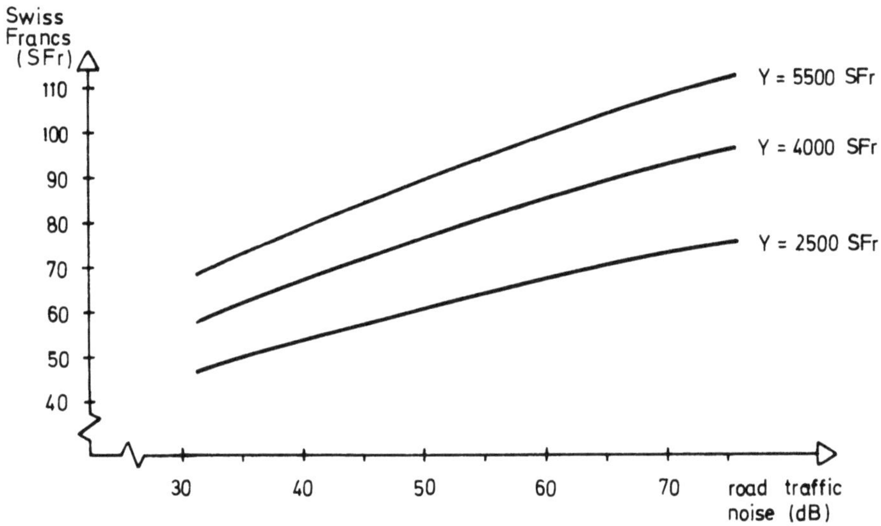

Figure 3: Willingness-to-Pay for Road Traffic Noise Reduction by 50 %; Simulation Results Based on Market Data

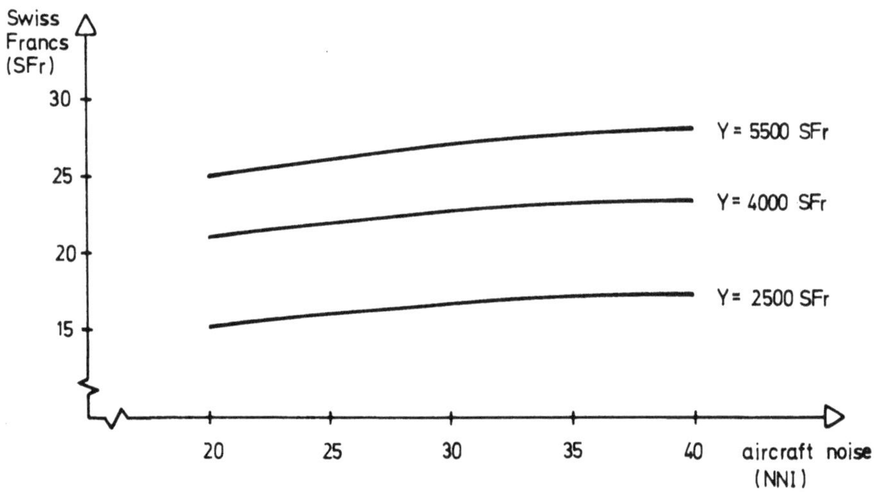

Figure 4: Willingness-to-Pay for Aircraft Noise Reduction by 50 %; Simulation Results Based on Market Data

The willingness-to-pay for aircraft noise reduction, shown in Figure 4, can be interpreted in a similar way. However, the slope of the curves indicates that there is only a weak positive dependence of the premium for peace and quiet on the respective actual aircraft noise level. Nevertheless, again there is a positive and significant influence of household income on willingness-to-pay for aircraft noise reduction, i.e., these results, too, are in line with the a priori expectations.

Summarizing this part: it can be concluded that the hedonic price approach applied to the problem of traffic noise comes to concrete results which are internally consistent, in line with standard demand theory, and intuitively plausible. However, there remains a number of caveats with respect to the functional form of the hedonic price equation chosen, to the omission of specific variables and, in consequence, to the willingness-to-pay estimate for the non-marginal reduction of traffic noise.[26] Moreover, this benefit measure is derived from a usual (Marshallian) willingness-to-pay function, which includes not only the price effect, but also the income effect on welfare change. The correct measure would be one based on a (Hicksian) income-compensated willingness-to-pay function. However, up to now there seems no way to derive such a function, compensated to keep the utility level constant, from market data.

3. Valuing Noise Reduction by Non-Market Data: The Contingent Valuation Approach

3.1 Theoretical Base

By using a survey the estimation of an income-compensated willingness-to-pay function is in principle possible. Therefrom a measure of welfare change can be derived where utility level is kept constant. The survey should cover standard concepts of consumer surplus (equivalent/compensating variation) and also focus on the possibility of strategic behavior. The latter often causes economists' reservation towards the use of survey techniques. However, considerable evidence, both in experimental economics[27] and in survey work,[28] is now available suggesting that the influence of strategic bias may be less important than previously thought.

[26] As shown before in some detail, the marginal implicit price of noise is quite sensitive to the conrete form of the dwelling rent function. However, once the relatively best specification has been determined, the benefit estimates based on this "basic equation" showed to be quite robuste to modifications of the functional form of the willingness-to-pay relationship and of the concrete specification of the variables included in the equations.

[27] See Grether and Plott (1979), Schneider and Pommerehne (1981), Pommerehne, Schneider, and Zweifel (1982); for a survey on these and further experiments see Pommerehne (1987, chap. 8).

[28] See Bishop and Heberlein (1979), Rowe, d'Arge, and Brookshire (1980), Carson and Mitchell (1983), and Throsby and Withers (1986). In a study comparing a number of earlier survey works Schulze, d'Arge, and Brookshire (1981, p. 70) conclude that "the strategic bias in revealing consumer preferences is not likely to be a major problem".

Especially due to the hypothetical nature of the questions asked in survey analysis, it seems that incentives for strategic behavior are substantially weakened. But the hypothetical nature of the questions may also weaken the incentive to provide an accurate answer concerning the willingness-to-pay for a public good such as environmental improvement by noise reduction. Yet, as illustrated later, there is the possibility to reduce this potential bias by the creation of a realistic decision-making situation in which the participants seriously take their budget constraint into account and, thus, provide a reliable answer. Given that there is no other major bias in the responses, these answers should provide information on the willingness-to-pay, holding constant the initial utility level of each individual (equivalent variation). Moreover, as hypothesized by Brookshire, Thayer, Schulze, and d'Arge (1982), excluding the income effect, this measure of welfare change should be lower than the willingness-to-pay figure derived from market data. This point is demonstrated with the help of Figure 5. At the same time, it provides the theoretical background for a comparison of the contingent valuation method with the hedonic price approach and, thus, finally allows a test of the external validity of both welfare measures.

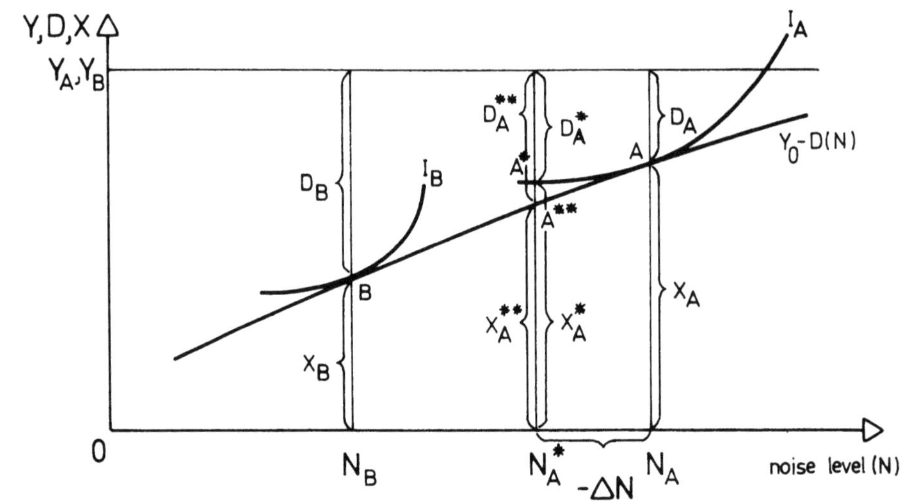

Y = household net income
D = dwelling rent
X = expenditure on composite commodity

Figure 5: Willingness-to-Pay for Noise Reduction Based on Two Methods of Measurement

The abscissa shows the noise level (N); the ordinate measures household net income (Y), household expenditure on all other goods (X) except housing, where one unit of the composite commodity is standardized at the price of unity, and household expenditure on the dwelling (D), where $D(N)$ describes the continuously differentiable dwelling rent gradient ($\partial D/\partial N < 0$). Each household maximizes its utility, $U(X, N)$, where $\partial U/\partial X > 0$ and $\partial U/\partial N < 0$, subject to the budget constraint $Y - X - D(N) = 0$.

Graphically the first order conditions are fulfilled at point A where the marginal rate of substitution between noise and the composite commodity equals the slope of the rent gradient, $\partial D/\partial N$. Thus, a household with income Y_A and tastes given by indifference curve I_A chooses to locate at noise level N_A, to consume X_A and to pay the dwelling rent D_A. Another household B with the same income $Y_B = Y_A$, but tastes given by I_B, would choose point B, i.e. locating at N_B, paying a higher rent D_B and consequently allowing only for a lower consumption X_B, ceteris paribus. If both households' incomes should increase (not shown in the figure), the budget constraint would shift vertically and each household would relocate to a new equilibrium on the left of the initial optimum, choosing a still lower noise level (higher dwelling rent) and a higher consumption of the composite commodity. In short, both tastes and income are crucial for the location decisions over noise levels.[29]

Given an equilibrium situation, as depicted in point A of Figure 5, the contingent valuation survey now asks how much, at most, the respective household would be willing to pay for a noise reduction by half ($-\Delta N$), as compared to the noise level at the site where the household presently resides (N_A). Thus, the household is asked how much the dwelling rent could increase to experience N_A^* instead of N_A while being on the same utility level. Of course, given an indifference curve as assumed in the figure, the household will be indifferent between A and A^* , i.e., its willingness-to-pay for noise reduction will be $D_A^* - D_A$. However, this willingness-to-pay obtained from survey data must be smaller than the willingness-to-pay derived from market data. The latter, based on the estimated rent gradient function, includes the income effect and equals $D_A^{**} - D_A$, where $D_A^{**} - D_A > D_A^* - D_A$.[30] Therefore, if survey data are a valid measure of willingness-to-pay, then the stated willingness-to-pay must be lower than the respective rent differential, while the latter should be interpreted as an upper bound of the benefit from noise reduction.

---

[29] For a more elaborated discussion, also considering differences in other characteristics of households, see Brookshire, Thayer, Schulze, and d'Arge (1982).

[30] This result evidently depends on the shape of the rent gradient function. However, the gradient function does not need to be strictly convex, but may also be concave, given that the function lies below the relevant indifference curve. Yet, Anderson's (1985) computations of the eigenvalue of housing prices in various empirical studies indicate a predominance of a convex rent gradient.

3.2 Empirical Results

Of course, the survey actually used in the city of Basle did not directly ask for the willingness-to-pay for a noise reduction by half. Instead, the 223 households were told to be involved in a larger study on environmental problems, initiated by the Swiss National Science Foundation and guided by the University of Basle. This research needed information on the environmental situation as perceived by households. Therefore, the survey included a number of specific questions but also provided some background information on the environment, including a detailed description of the actual noise situation of the respective household, the noise situation nearby and at other well known places in Basle. Moreover, indicating to these other places (nearby and/or well known), alternatives were chosen where the noise level was lower by 50% as compared to the respective actual noise level.[31]

In a next step households were informed that they could improve their actual housing situation by moving into another dwelling being identical, but situated in a neighboring street where traffic noise is reduced by half. Moving costs, was said, would be financed out of a special fund of city government. After that, households were asked about their actual net rent and the maximum accepted increase for the alternative dwelling. Thus, the households' decision-making situation looks quite realistic, but, nevertheless creates no major incentive for strategic behavior. Moreover, it provides a good knowledge about the present budget constraint (household income, actual dwelling rent payment) and may even give some incentive to reflect seriously on the consequences of faulty decisions. Therefore, the answers given can be taken as a quite reliable measure of the willingness-to-pay for noise reduction.[32] Again, these figures constitute the dependent variable while the independent ones are the same as used in Table 1. The only additional variable is a dummy indicating whether the respective dwelling is insulated against noise.[33] The OLS estimates are given in Table 2, once more retaining only the significant variables.

Measured in terms of $\overline{R}^2$, these results, based on survey data, are better than those derived from market data (given in Table 1).[34] Again, all coefficients have the expected sign. In total, the contingent valuation estimates seem to be quite

[31] In order to keep the survey manageable a distinction is made between 3 classes of road traffic noise and 3 classes of aircraft noise, thus allowing a grouping of the households into 9 classes.

[32] It should be noted that the survey did not ask for the willingness-to-pay for a combined reduction of road traffic and aircraft noise, but splitted this question into two independent ones.

[33] This additional variable is included for the reason of consistency, because, in both approaches, the *perceived* noise level counts.

[34] However, this may especially be due to the fact that these estimates are those of the effects of *first* order.

Table 2: Willingness-to-Pay for Noise Reduction by 50 % Derived from Survey Data; Log-log Relationship; OLS Estimates; City of Basle, 1983/84[a]

Independent variables	Willingness-to-pay for reduction of:[b]	
	road traffic noise	aircraft noise
constant term	−4.011 (−2.123)	−2.213 (−1.927)
ln household net income (SFr)	0.680** (6.210)	0.597** (5.136)
ln number of rooms per person	0.101(*) (1.832)	0.133(*) (1.723)
dummy variable: household with child under age 15 = 1 (otherwise = 0)	0.419** (2.693)	—
dummy variable: insulation of the dwelling against noise = 1 (otherwise = 0)	−0.175(*) (−1.737)	−0.207(*) (−1.812)
ln road traffic noise (*dB*)	0.640* (2.181)	0.029(*) (1.692)
ln aircraft noise (*NNI*)	—	0.181* (2.046)
$\overline{R}^2$	0.613	0.410
F-value	38.274	21.830
degrees of freedom	217	217

[a] The dependent variable is *ln* monthly willingness-to-pay for noise reduction (by half of the actual level) as responded to the contingent survey.

[b] The figures in parentheses below the parameter estimates denote the respective $\hat{t}$-value. Two asterisks indicate statistical significance at the 99 %-, one asterisk (in parentheses) shows significance at the 95 %- (90 %-) confidence level, using a two-tailed-test.

similar to those based on the hedonic price function, that means, this approach creates concrete results which are internally consistent, in accordance with standard demand theory, and intuitively plausible. However, a more detailed comparison of both measures will be undertaken in the next section.

4. Contrasting Both Approaches

4.1 Comparison of Simulation Results

Since both approaches have been applied to the same sample of dwellings and households, the central hypothesis that the willingness-to-pay figures based on survey data must be lower than those derived from market data can be easily tested.[35] It suffices to undertake a comparison of the respective simulation results to those presented in the Figures 3 and 4. Such a comparison is shown in the following two figures in which, again, a distinction is made between different actual noise and different income levels.

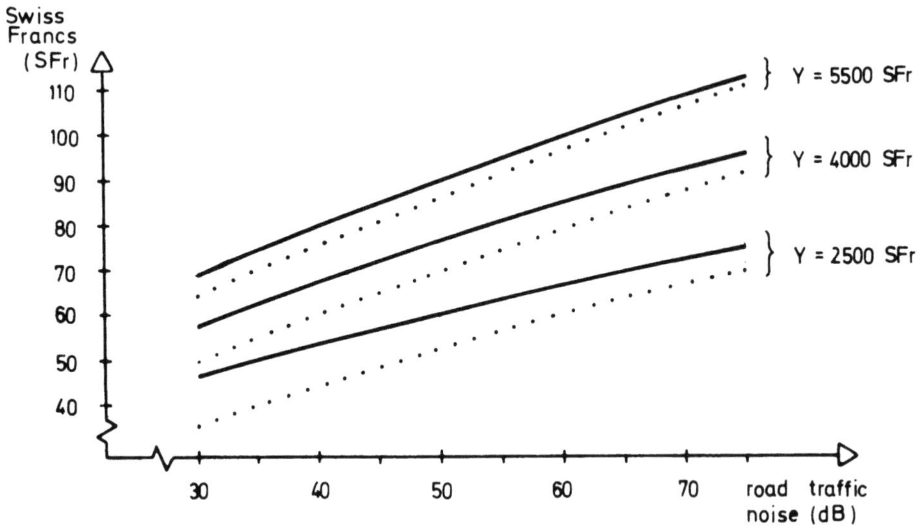

Figure 6: Willingness-to-Pay for Road Traffic Noise Reduction by 50%; Simulation Results Based on Market Data (Full Lines) and on Survey Data (Dotted Lines)

As presented in Figure 6 for the case of road traffic noise each dotted line, expressing the simulated willingness-to-pay obtained from survey data, lies below the respective full line which corresponds to the simulated willingness-to-pay derived from market data.[36] Since this differential is statistically significant (at

[35] Otherwise, if the samples used are not identical, the test would consist in a pairwise comparison of results, ordered by the respective household income and the respective noise levels.

[36] Referrring to the mean value of the relevant variables the difference in the willingness-to-pay figures is about 7 SFr, i.e. 8% in terms of the Marshallian consumer surplus measure. This differential is larger than the maximum bound calculated by Willig's (1976) rule of thumb. According to his formula and based on the measured consumer surplus of 2% of household income (81 SFr./4000 SFr.) and on the income elasticity of demand for peace and quiet, ϵ_Y of 0.90 [ϵ_Y = (1/elasticity of willingness-to-pay with respect to noise reduction)$\cdot$ elasticity of

the 95 %-confidence level), the central hypothesis of the validity of the contingent valuation approach cannot be rejected.

However, as shown in Figure 7, the same conclusion cannot be drawn for an aircraft noise reduction.

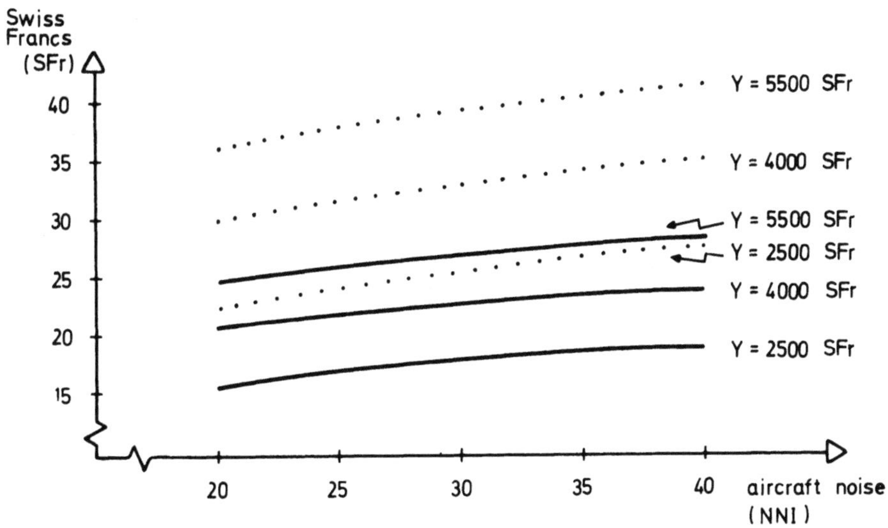

Figure 7: Willingness-to-Pay for Aircraft Noise Reduction by 50 %; Simulation Results Based on Market Data (Full Lines) and on Survey Data (Dotted Lines)

In this case the central hypothesis of a ceteris paribus lower willingness-to-pay obtained from survey data clearly is rejected. Evidently the opposite is true, the differential between both measures of welfare change being statistically significant at the 99 %-confidence level.[37]

4.2 Examination of the Results

It is not easy to explain why the central hypothesis on the expected differential in the willingness-to-pay figures has been confirmed in the case of road traffic noise, but rejected with respect to aircraft noise reduction. However, it should be kept in mind that both approaches are based on a number of critical assumptions. Therefore, the results of both methods have to be examined.

willingness-to-pay with respect to household income = $(1/0.542) \cdot 0.490 = 0.90$; see Table 1], this differential should not exceed 1 % (see Willig, 1976, Table 1). However, his formula does not take into consideration transaction costs. If transaction costs are explicitely considered, the maximum differential can be considerably larger; see Randall and Stoll (1980).

[37] Considering again the mean value of the relevant variables, the differential in the willingness-to-pay figures now becomes 10 SFr that is, an equivalent consumer surplus being 44 % *larger* than the Marshallian one!

First, it can be asked to what degree the resulting willingness-to-pay figures reflect the influence of transaction costs, i.e., of monetary as well as of psychical costs of removal. As discussed by Mishan (1976, chap. 48) these costs may have a dampening impact on the benefit measure derived from market data, i.e., this (net) measure does not cover the full welfare change due to a 'pure' noise reduction. In contrast, when asking households for their willingness-to-pay for noise reduction, it has been stressed that the monetary costs of removal will be paid by a special city government program.[38] Given that the (expected) costs are sizeable, but nevertheless have been almost ignored by the participants of the contingent survey, it even is astonishing that the test of the central hypothesis didn't fail in *both* cases.

A second reason why the test did not fully succeed may consist in the hypothetical decision-making situation in the survey context in which, moreover, only one and, in addition, fictitious issue has to be decided on instead of a greater number of issues, each having real consequences, as in the case of market decision. In line with this conjecture is the fact that the slope of the willingness-to-pay curves based on survey data (Table 1) is steeper than the slope of the respective curves derived from market data (Table 2). The same is true for the differential impact of household income.

A third and related reason can be that both approaches measure something more than just the welfare change due to noise reduction, though to a *different* amount. In the case of road traffic noise an additional dummy variable enters both willingness-to-pay equations (Tables 1 and 2), indicating whether the respective household has a younger child. In both equations the coefficient of this dummy is statistically significant, suggesting that a household with children considers traffic noise reduction not only as a decrease of noise nuisance, but also as a reduction of the danger from road traffic for their child.[39] If so, it can be expected that households with children, when asked in a survey, take a decision which is more pronounced in favor of noise reduction than their effective location decisions on the market. Again, this conjecture is not contradicted by empirical estimates.[40]

---

[38] Moreover, the survey has been framed in such a way as to keep psychical costs minimal. For instance, the dwellings proposed were said to be located nearby. Therefore, benefits from households' investment in neighborhood relationships would not be lost by a change of the dwelling.

[39] Of course, an alternative interpretation could be the existence of intergeneration utility interdependency. However, the same dummy variable did never become statistically significant in the two equations explaining the willingness-to-pay for aircraft noise reduction.

[40] According to the estimates based on survey data the differential between the willingness-to-pay for road traffic reduction is 34 SFr (for a household having a young child compared to one without child). The same differential, when computed from willingness-to-pay equation based on market data, is only 25 SFr (all simulations refer to the mean value of the relevant variables).

Finally, the failure of our test in the case of aircraft noise reduction may be due to the specific situation of Basle. It cannot be excluded that the participants, when asked for their willingness-to-pay for aircraft noise reduction, did not reflect the extraordinary low noise level in their city but, instead, were influenced by reports on the more dramatic noise nuisance of Geneva or Zurich. Unfortunately, no specific test has been developed in order to examine this potential source of a systematic response bias. However, there is no comparable information in the media with respect to road traffic noise — and also no sign for an evident overstatement of welfare change in that case.

To summarize this section: the main hypothesis that the willingness-to-pay obtained from survey data are lower than those derived from market data has been confirmed in the case of road traffic, but rejected for aircraft noise reduction. But, as discussed at the end, both estimates might be somewhat biased. Those obtained from market data presumably are underestimates, whereas those based on survey data seem to be upward biased. Nevertheless, even if no adjustment is made for any identified biases, the two different approaches yield related findings. Moreover, the results of each method consistently differ with respect to the kind of noise nuisance: the willingness-to-pay for a reduction of road traffic noise compared to aircraft noise is 3.6:1 (81 SFr : 22.3 SFr at the mean values) in the case of the hedonic price approach, and 2.3:1 (74.9 SFr : 32.2 SFr) when the contingent valuation method is applied. This small difference between the ratios is well within plausible boundaries of accuracy. In total we may conclude that the contingent valuation method is a most useful instrument, especially in all those cases where no alternative measurement approach is available.

5. Concluding Remarks

One conclusion is obvious. High levels of road traffic and aircraft noise seem to create significant disamenities for those urban residents who are exposed to them. Of course, this is evident for anyone who has lived in a noisy region and from traditional concern for regulating traffic noise. However, for a long time, the benefits from traffic noise reduction have not been quantitatively measured, but only been described as 'intangible' — and for that reason often been neglected in the political-administrative process.

Therefore the usefulness of the approaches applied here lies in the potential which the estimates of welfare change from environmental improvement has for benefit-cost analysis, as well as for the process of collective decision-making. These estimates make the benefits 'tangible' and provide information which has hitherto not been available. At the same time this information urges the participants of the political process to take the benefits from public goods more consequently into account.

Appendix

Table A: Specification of the Dwelling Rent Equation

theoretical variable	empirical proxy used	expected sign of coefficient
Dependent variable:	natural logarithm (*ln*) of monthly net dwelling rent (in SFr)	
Explanatory variables:		
I. *Characteristics of dwelling*		
number of rooms (*NR*)	*ln* number of standardized rooms; *NR* represents spaciousness and, in a certain sense, quantity of housing; it should be positively related to dwelling rent	positive
quality of dwelling (*QUAL*)	sum of a number of dummy variables each with the value of 1 if major repairs and renovations have been made (otherwise 0) during the last five years with respect to kitchen, plumbing, sanitary, insulation and so on (in total 9 items), minus the sum of a number of dummy variables, each with the value of 1 if the respective repairs and renovations are planned for the next five years. For each dwelling (built before 1975) the difference of both sums is taken as an indicator of quality, with "very low quality" (−9) if none of the nine kinds of repairs was done in the past, but all are planned and "very high quality" (+9) if all kinds of repairs and renovations were done and no one is planned for the next five years. For dwellings constructed after 1975 (less than 10 % of the sample) a "high quality" is assumed. Of course, quality should be positively related to dwelling rent	positive

Table A: continued

theoretical variable	empirical proxy used	expected sign of coefficient
II. *Characteristics of house*		
age of the house (*AGE*)	*ln* number of years since the house has been built; with the possible exception of historic houses (see *HH*) age should be negatively related to dwelling rent	negative
historic house (*HH*)	dummy variable with the value of 1, if the house under consideration is a "historic house", mentioned in the list of 'historic houses of the city of Basle' (otherwise 0); living in a historic house may create some pleasant effects, but it also is more constrained by regulations on the use of the house, the type of renovation and modernization allowed and so on; therefore no clear impact on dwelling rent is expected	ambiguous
pure dwelling house (*PDH*)	dummy variable with the value of 1, if the house is solely used as a dwelling house (otherwise 0); a mixed use (commercial activities/dwellings) may create additional problems; therefore a positive influence on dwelling rent is expected in the case of pure dwelling house	positive
one family house (*OFH*)	dummy variable with value of 1, if the house is a one family house (otherwise 0); though there are less constraints on the home activities of a household (with respect to the neighbors) living in a one family house, as compared to a multi family house, there also are higher complementary costs of heating, cleaning of sidewalks and so on per household — therefore no clear impact on dwelling rent is expected	ambiguous
number of floors (*NF*)	*ln* number of floors of the house; *NF* represents a higher amount of trouble in a multi floor (multi family) house, an increased constraint on home activities of a household, but also lower complementary costs for heating, cleaning of sidewalks etc.; due to the countervailing effects no clear impact on dwelling rent is expected	ambiguous

Table A: continued

theoretical variable	empirical proxy used	expected sign of coefficient
garden for tenants (*GAT*)	dummy variable with the value of 1, if the house has a garden which can be utilized by the tenants; *GAT*, being another aspect of quality (otherwise 0) should be positively related to dwelling rent	positive
condition of plaster (*CD*)	dummy variable with the value of 1, if the plaster of the house is renovated during the last eight years (otherwise 0); *CD* represents pleasant visual effects, and thus, it should be positively related to dwelling rent	positive
avenue with trees (*AT*)	dummy variable with the value of 1, if the house is situated in an avenue with trees (on both sides of and/or between the roadways, otherwise 0); *AT*, reflecting a further aspect of quality, should be positively linked to dwelling rent	positive
Rhine-stream-promenade (*RSP*)	dummy variable with the value of 1, if the house is situated on the Rhine-stream-promenade; *RSP* represents a free view on the stream, an excellent possibility for 'in-door' recreation and may also cover a potentially important positive prestige value; all these amenities should have a positive impact on dwelling rent	positive
park and/or forest (*PF*)	dummy variable with the value of 1, if the house borders upon a recreational park and/or a forest (otherwise 0); *PF* represents the close accessibility to a recreational area and, thus, should be positively related to dwelling rent	positive
blind alley (*BA*)	dummy variable with the value of 1, if the house is situated in a blind alley (otherwise 0); *BA* reflects the amenities of reduced traffic flow and, therefore, should positively affect dwelling rent	positive
distance to shopping center (*DSC*)	*ln* distance (in meters) to next shopping center; *DSC* reflects — as well as the following distance measures — the higher time/travelling cost for reaching more distant places; therefore, they all should negatively affect the dwelling rent	negative

Table A: continued

theoretical variable	empirical proxy used	expected sign of coefficient
distance to public playground (*DPP*)	*ln* distance (in meters) to next public playground for children	negative
distance to public kindergarten (*DPK*)	*ln* distance (in meters) to next public kindergarten	negative
distance to public schools (*DPS*)	*ln* distance (in meters) to next public primary school	negative
distance to recreational park/forest (*DRPF*)	*ln* distance (in meters) to next public recreational park/forest	negative
distance to bus/tramway stop (*DBTS*)	*ln* distance (in meters) to next bus/tramway stop	negative
distance to public sporting ground (*DPSG*)	*ln* distance (in meters) to next public sporting ground	negative
distance to public swimming pool (*DPSP*)	*ln* distance (in meters) to next public swimming pool	negative
distance to central city (*DCC*)	*ln* distance (in meters) to central city as the employment center; according to traditional theories of urban rent gradients, the dwelling rent should be higher near the employment center; thus, *DCC* should be negatively related to dwelling rent	negative
III. *Characteristics of locality*		
historic district (*HD*)	dummy variable with the value of 1, if the respective locality is part of the historic district of Basle (otherwise 0); *HD* may reflect some pleasant effects, therefore it should be positively related to dwelling rent	positive
no-parking area (*NPA*)	dummy variable with the value of 1, if the district is part of a no-parking area (otherwise 0); parking regulations for public ground/streets will impede the access to the own house, to shops in the district and so on; thus, *NPA* should negatively affect dwelling rent	negative

Table A: continued

theoretical variable	empirical proxy used	expected sign of coefficient
open area (OA)	*ln* open area of the locality (in % of total space of the district); OA may reflect positive externalities related to open areas such as play grounds, green belts, and recreational parks and, therefore, should have a positive impact on dwelling rent	positive
industrial area (IA)	*ln* non retail business area of the locality (in % of total space of the district); IA serves as a proxy for negative externalities associated with industry (heavy traffic, unpleasant visual effects), and, thus, should be negatively related to dwelling rent	negative
medical care (MC)	number of general medical doctors per capita of inhabitants of the respective district; MC reflects the accessibility to medical care and, therefore, should positively affect dwelling rent	positive
school quality (SQ)	pupil-teacher ratio in primary schools in the district; the relation of the pupil-teacher ratio to school quality is not entirely clear, although a higher ratio should imply that each pupil receives less individual attention; therefore, a negative sign for the coefficient of SQ is expected	negative
proportion of foreigners (PF)	proportion of foreigners (in % of total population) by district; at low to moderate levels of PF, an increase in PF should have a negative impact on dwelling rent if foreigners are regarded as less desirable neighbors by Swiss population. But, market discrimination means that dwelling rents may be higher at high levels of PF. Therefore, a parabolic relationship could be expected between proportion of foreigners in local neighborhood and dwelling rent: PF should have a negative impact on the dwelling rent,	negative
	whereas the squared value of PF should have a positive effect.	positive
proportion of lower status (PLS)	population without some high school education (in % of total population). As in the case of PF, a parabolic relationship could be ex-	

Table A: continued

theoretical variable	empirical proxy used	expected sign of coefficient
	pected between *PLS* and dwelling rent. Therefore, *PLS* should be negatively related to dwelling rent,	negative
	whereas the squared value of *PLS* should positively affect the dwelling rent	positive
crime rate (*CR*)	crime rate by district; assuming that *CR* is generally proportional to people's perception of danger, it gauges the threat to well-being that households perceive in the various districts of the city of Basle; therefore, *CR* should have a negative effect on dwelling rent	negative
air pollution I (*AP*)	*ln* particle concentration (annual average concentration in milligrams per hundred cubic meters) by district; *AP*, being a disamenity, should negatively affect the dwelling rent	negative
air pollution II (NO_2)	*ln* nitrogen dioxide concentration (annual average concentration in parts per hundred million) by district is used as an alternative measure of air pollution; accordingly, a negative effect on dwelling rent is expected, too	negative
sunny weather (*SW*)	*ln* altitude (deviation from minimal altitude of the city area, in meters) by district serves as a proxy for the frequency of absence of fog and the number of sunny days; *SW* being an amenity, a positive impact on dwelling rent can be expected	positive
IV. *Noise nuisance*		
road traffic noise (*RTN*)	measured in decibels (*dB*); as discussed in the text, *RTN* should have a negative effect on dwelling rent	negative
aircraft noise (*AN*)	measured by the noise-and-number index (*NNI*); as in the case of *RTN*, a negative impact is expected for *AN*	negative

Table B: Estimation Results for the Dwelling Rent Function; Various Specifications; OLS Estimates; City of Basle; 1983/84[a]

Independent variables[b]		(1)	(2)	(3)
I. *Characteristics of dwelling*				
number of rooms	(*NR*)	0.638** (11.312)	0.642** (11.410)	0.662** (11.563)
quality of dwelling	(*QUAL*)	0.030** (3.729)	0.030** (3.699)	0.028** (3.479)
II. *Characteristics of house*				
age of house	(*AGE*)	−0.098 (−0.098)	−0.102 (−0.099)	—
historic house	(*HH*)	0.142 (0.987)	0.137 (0.889)	—
pure dwelling house	(*PDH*)	0.138** (3.254)	0.129** (3.436)	0.126** (4.392)
one family house	(*OFH*)	0.292** (3.838)	0.263** (3.629)	0.207** (3.307)
number of floors	(*NF*)	−0.033 (−0.589)	−0.048 (−0.621)	—
garden for tenants	(*GAT*)	0.029 (0.378)	0.021 (0.355)	—
condition of plaster	(*CD*)	0.018 (0.279)	0.016 (0.199)	—
avenue with trees	(*AT*)	0.168* (2.204)	0.157* (2.102)	0.110(*) (1.821)
Rhine-stream promenade	(*RSP*)	0.236** (3.109)	0.241** (3.129)	0.275** (3.495)

[a] The dependent variable is *ln* net dwelling rent (in SFr). For the concrete specification of the independent variable see Table A (appendix).

[b] The figures in parentheses below the parameter estimates denote the respective $\hat{t}$-value. Two asterisks indicate statistical significance at the 99 %-, one asterisk (in parentheses) shows significance at the 95 %- (90 %-) confidence level, using a two-tailed-test.

Table B: continued

Independent variables[b]		(1)	(2)	(3)
park/forest	(*PF*)	0.058 (0.354)	0.042 (0.342)	—
blind alley	(*BA*)	0.019 (0.340)	−0.012 (−0.120)	—
distance to shopping center	(*DSC*)	−0.00035** (−3.210)	−0.00037** (−3.392)	−0.00049** (−4.762)
distance to public playground	(*DPP*)	−0.00013(*) (−1.920)	−0.00012(*) (−1.892)	−0.00021* (−2.312)
distance to public kindergarten	(*DPK*)	−0.000072 (−0.230)	0.000021 (0.035)	—
distance to public school	(*DPS*)	0.000091 (0.217)	0.00012 (0.612)	—
distance to recreational park/forest	(*DRPF*)	−0.000012 (−0.035)	0.0000032 (0.005)	—
distance to bus/tramway stop	(*DBTS*)	−0.00016(*) (−1.682)	−0.00018* (−1.721)	−0.00021(*) (−1.987)
distance to public sporting ground	(*DPSG*)	0.000037 (0.097)	−0.000041 (−0.101)	—
distance to public swimming pool	(*DPSP*)	0.000091 (0.018)	0.000072 (0.012)	—
distance to central city	(*DCC*)	0.000021 (0.763)	0.000018 (0.689)	—
III. *Characteristics of locality*				
historic district	(*HD*)	0.092 (0.137)	−0.0021 (−0.031)	—
no-parking area	(*NPA*)	−0.077 (−0.731)	−0.069 (−0.682)	—
open area	(*OA*)	0.0013(*) (1.934)	0.0011(*) (1.783)	0.0010* (2.030)
industrial area	(*IA*)	−0.043** (−3.558)	−0.039** (−3.320)	−0.0040** (−3.478)
medical care	(*MC*)	0.00072 (0.797)	0.00069 (0.691)	—
school quality	(*SQ*)	−0.015 (−0.310)	−0.017 (−0.319)	—

Table B: continued

Independent variables[b]		(1)	(2)	(3)
proportion of foreigners	(PF)	−0.023 (−1.176)	−0.022 (−1.092)	—
	$(PF)^2$	0.0073 (1.203)	0.0091 (0.987)	—
proportion of lower status	(PLS)	−0.0041 (−0.731)	−0.0039 (−0.701)	—
	$(PLS)^2$	0.00025 (0.078)	−0.00030 (−0.029)	—
crime rate	(CR)	−0.0011 (−0.031)	−0.0012 (−0.027)	—
air pollution	(AP)	−0.0012 (−0.632)	—	—
	(NO_2)	—	−0.0014 (−0.982)	—
sunny weather	(SW)	0.0090 (0.432)	0.0082 (0.398)	—
IV. *Noise nuisance*				
road traffic noise	(RTN)	−0.0123** (−3.219)	−0.0121** (−3.072)	−0.0126** (−3.500)
aircraft noise	(AN)	−0.0019(*) (−1.982)	−0.0017(*) (−1.789)	−0.0023* (−2.039)
interaction variable	$(RTN) * (AN)$	−0.00035 (−0.098)	−0.00034 (−0.102)	−0.00019 (−0.031)
V. *Constant term*		7.321 (12.921)	7.138 (12.370)	6.930 (12.631)
$\overline{R}^2$		0.672	0.669	0.710
F-value		29.721	28.928	36.729
degrees of liberty		184	184	208

	(1)	(2)	(3)	(4)	(5)	(6)	(7)	(8)	(9)	(10)	(11)	(12)	(13)
(1) *NR*	1.000												
(2) *QUAL*	0.011	1.000											
(3) *PDH*	−0.132	0.080	1.000										
(4) *OFH*	0.477	0.005	−0.110	1.000									
(5) *AT*	0.079	−0.070	−0.116	0.027	1.000								
(6) *RSP*	0.010	0.029	0.350	0.179	0.098	1.000							
(7) *DSC*	0.194	−0.085	−0.211	0.279	0.129	0.029	1.000						
(8) *DPP*	−0.008	−0.039	0.208	−0.162	0.132	−0.125	0.021	1.000					
(9) *DBTS*	0.104	−0.032	0.085	0.170	−0.035	−0.029	0.039	−0.141	1.000				
(10) *OA*	−0.019	0.036	−0.057	0.027	0.048	−0.007	−0.112	−0.204	−0.021	1.000			
(11) *IA*	−0.025	−0.102	0.039	−0.092	−0.117	−0.210	0.032	−0.079	0.069	−0.170	1.000		
(12) *RTN*	−0.016	0.021	0.216	−0.081	0.030	0.098	−0.005	0.026	−0.223	0.031	0.432	1.000	
(13) *AN*	−0.065	0.028	0.046	−0.035	−0.027	0.036	−0.073	−0.039	−0.139	−0.078	0.128	0.007	1.000

Table C: Matrix of Simple Correlations among the Independent Variables of the Dwelling Rent Function

References

Anderson, J. E. (1985): "On Testing the Convexity of Hedonic Functions." *Journal of Urban Economics* 18: 334–337.

Bishop, R. C., and **Heberlein, T. A.** (1979): "Measuring Values of Extramarket Goods: Are Indirect Measures Biased?" *American Journal of Agricultural Economics* 61: 926–930.

BNM Planconsult (1982): *Bewertung der Wohnqualität von Basel-Stadt mit Hilfe von Indikatoren*, Vols. 1 and 2. Basle: Amt für Kantons- und Stadtplanung Basel-Stadt.

Bohm, P. (1971): "An Approach to the Problem of Estimating Demand for Public Goods." *Swedish Journal of Economics* 73: 55–66.

Bradford, D. F. (1970): "Cost-Benefit Analysis and Demand Curves for Public Goods." *Kyklos* 23: 775–791.

Brookshire, D. S., and **Crocker, T.** (1981): "The Advantages of Contingent Valuation Methods for Benefit-Cost-Analysis." *Public Choice* 36: 235–252.

Brookshire, D. S.; **Randall, A.**; and **Stoll, J. R.** (1980): "Valuing Increments and Decrements in Natural Resource Service Flows." *American Journal of Agricultural Economics* 62: 478–488.

Brookshire, D. S.; **Thayer, M. A.**; **Schulze, W. D.**; and **d'Arge, R. C.** (1982): "Valuing Public Goods: A Comparison of Survey and Hedonic Approaches." *American Economic Review* 72: 165–177.

Carson, R. F., and **Mitchell, R. C.** (1983): "Observation on Strategic Bias and Contingent Valuation Surveys." Working Paper. Berkeley: University of California, and Madison: University of Wisconsin.

Davis, R. K. (1963): "Recreation Planning as an Economic Problem." *National Resources Journal* 3: 239–249.

Freeman, A. M. (1979): *The Benefits of Environmental Improvement: Theory and Practice*. Baltimore etc.: John Hopkins University Press.

Grether, D., and **Plott, C.** (1979): "Economic Theory and the Preference Reversal Phenomenon." *American Economic Review* 69: 623–638.

Harrison, D., and **Rubinfeld, D. L.** (1978): "Hedonic Housing Prices and the Demand for Clean Air." *Journal of Environmental Economics and Management* 5: 81–102.

Hoch, I., and **Drake, J.** (1974): "Wages Climate, and the Quality of Life." *Journal of Environmental Economics and Management* 1: 268–295.

Mäler, K.-G. (1977): "A Note on the Use of Property Values in Estimating Marginal Willingness to Pay for Environmental Quality." *Journal of Environmental Economics and Management* 4: 355–369.

Mishan, E. J. (1976): *Cost Benefit Analysis.* 2nd ed. New York: Praeger.

Nelson, J. P. (1978): *Economic Analysis of Transportation Noise Abatement.* Cambridge, Mass.: Ballinger.

Nelson, J. P. (1981): "Measuring Benefits of Environmental Improvements: Aircraft Noise and Hedonic Prices." In *Advances in Microeconomics, Vol. 1*, edited by V. K. Smith. Greenwich, Conn.: JAI Press, pp. 51–75.

Pearce, D. W. (1976): "The Limits of Cost-Benefit-Analysis as a Guide to Environmental Policy." *Kyklos* 29: 97–112.

Pearce, D. W. (ed.) (1978): *The Valuation of Social Cost.* London: Allen and Unwin.

Pommerehne, W. W. (1987): *Präferenzen für öffentliche Güter: Ansätze zu ihrer Erfassung.* Tübingen: Mohr.

Pommerehne, W. W. (1987a): "L'évaluation des gains et des pertes d'aménités: le cas du bruit de trafic." In *Services publics locaux: demande, offre et financement*, edited by P. Burgat and C. Jeanrenaud. Paris: Economica, pp. 197–220.

Pommerehne, W. W.; Schneider, F.; and **Zweifel, P.** (1982): "Economic Theory of Choice and the Preference Reversal Phenomenon: A Reexamination." *American Economic Review* 72: 569–574.

Randall, A., and **Stoll, J. R.** (1980): "Consumer's Surplus in Commodity Space." *American Economic Review* 70: 449–455.

Rosen, H. S. (1974): "Hedonic Prices and Implicit Markets: Product Differentiation in Pure Competition." *Journal of Political Economy* 82: 34–55.

Rowe, R.; d'Arge, R. C.; and **Brookshire, D. S.** (1980): "An Experiment on the Economic Value of Visibility." *Journal of Environmental Economics and Management* 7: 1–19.

Schneider, F., and **Pommerehne, W. W.** (1981): "Free Riding and Collective Action: An Experiment in Public Microeconomics." *Quarterly Journal of Economics* 46: 689–704.

Schulze, W. D.; d'Arge, R. C.; and **Brookshire, D. S.** (1981): "Valuing Environmental Commodities: Some Recent Experiments." *Land Economics* 57: 151–172.

Sinn, H.-W. (1983): *Economic Decisions under Uncertainty.* Amsterdam etc.: North-Holland.

Starkie, D. N. M., and **Johnson, D. M.** (1975): *The Economic Value of Peace and Quiet.* Westmead: Saxon House.

Throsby, C. D., and **Withers, G. A.** (1986): "Strategic Bias and Demand for Public Goods: Theory and an Application to the Arts." *Journal of Public Economics* 31: 307–327.

Walters, A. A. (1975): *Noise and Prices.* Oxford: Clarendon Press.

Willig, R. D. (1976): "Consumer Surplus without Apology." *American Economic Review* 66: 587–597.

Economic Impact of Emission Standards: A Computational Approach to Waste Water Treatment in Western Europe

Gunter Stephan, Heidelberg, West Germany*

1. Introduction

Pollution, in its many forms, is widely regarded as our major environmental problem. As the entropy law tells us, the industrial process is inescapably connected with a continuous flow of pollution and causes irreversible ecological change. Economic growth means, among other things, that more and more raw materials and energy have to be put into circulation, producing an increasing amount of waste which is then discharged into the environment. Without some kind of pollution control, nature's assimilative capacities could be reached or even surpassed in the long-run and an irreversible degeneration of the ecological system might be the consequence.

Faced with this problem, economic theory has developed a great body of methods and techniques on the optimal use of natural resources. The principal idea these solutions are based upon is that environmental detoriation is due to externalities and market failure. Environmental resources, such as clean air and water, are usually not under private ownership and generally have been regarded as free. Nobody, however, has an economic incentive to avoid polluting the environment or to pay for cleaning up pollution as long as no costs are assigned for environmental protection or to repair ecological damage. It has been suggested, consequently, that this type of market failure, namely the lack of inclusion of environmental costs, should be corrected by governmental intervention.

Economists generally argue that prices and taxes are the best policy tools for controlling externalities (see Baumol and Oates, 1975; Harford and Oguga, 1983): via the invisible hand, prices guarantee an efficient and Pareto-optimal allocation of resources. They encourage firms to lower pollution, whereas quantity rules, such as standards, tend to allocate production inefficiently and provide no economic incentive for emission reductions. Despite the advantage of the price system, governments continue to use standards as their major policy instrument

* I am grateful to Malte Faber, Joachim Neipp, Gerhard Wagenhals and two anonymous referees for helpful comments and suggestions. The usual disclaimer applies.

for environmental regulations. One reason might be that lawmakers have revealed an aversion to prices and distrust the invisible hand. A second, more serious reason, however, is that even from a theoretical viewpoint quantity rules tend to be superior to price regulations in cases in which imperfect competition, technical change or process innovation is observed (see for a discussion Mendelsohn, 1984).

This paper analyzes the intertemporal economic impacts of environmental regulations by emission standards. In particular, a computable equilibrium model is used to examine in a counterfactual analysis how different waste water standards affect economic growth, the development of emissions and the time pattern of savings, investment and consumption.

Analyzing these effects strongly invites methodologies which are based upon an equilibrium framework (see for example Mäler, 1974; Pethig, 1975): pollution control has an impact on the whole economic system. It generates a set of feedbacks that influence the economic development, the final allocation of resources and the distribution of income. The most consistent way to capture these interactions qualitatively as well as quantitatively is to model all agents in a computable equilibrium framework. No other numerical tool has the ability (1) to trace the consequences of a change of policy through the entire economy, (2) to provide an unified framework for analyzing the tradeoffs between economic efficiency and equity, and (3) to illustrate the operation of an economic system in which all decisions are implemented on a decentralized level.

Despite this advantage, computable equilibrium models are unsatisfactory in many respects. For example there is no easy way to incorporate time and dynamics into this approach. And if the neoclassical intertemporal equilibrium framework is employed, it has at least two important drawbacks:

(1) It is difficult to solve and requires additional data. To the author's knowledge, the papers of Bovenberg (1985), Chao, Kim, and Manne (1982), Heady and Mitra (1985), Manne and Preckel (1985) are the only contributions to computable intertemporal equilibrium models.

(2) By definition, in an intertemporal equilibrium framework it is assumed that consumers and producers are clairvoyant. Hence they forecast future equilibrium prices correctly. Plans are coordinated for the present based on a complete set of future markets. Consequently, intertemporal equilibrium models can only be used to study smooth adjustments and economic developments which are based upon long-run equilibrium price formations (see Arrow, 1983), whereas short-run adjustment and production process innovations cannot be treated in this framework (see Stephan, 1986, for a detailed discussion).

In this paper an alternative approach is used. It shares with an intertemporal equilibrium model the assumption that all economic agents are clairvoyant and make consistent projections of future prices. In this way the time pattern of consumption, savings and investment is determined the same as in an intertemporal equilibrium model, i.e. in a logically consistent manner. Hence, the well-known welfare properties of a Walrasian model hold true within this framework. But in contrast to the Walrasian model, this model is designed to explain short-run frictions in adjustment and production process innovation. For this purpose market imperfections and time-consuming gestation processes for capital goods are incorporated into a computable equilibrium framework.

Section 2 contains the formulation of the theoretical approach. Since this is a simplified version of a general dynamic multisector model as developed in Stephan (1986), only the most important elements of the model formulation are reported. (A detailed description of the general model, a discussion of its properties and a proof of existence for a long-run equilibrium can be found in Stephan, 1986.) In Section 3 the model is applied in an empirical study of waste water treatment in Western Europe. It is shown that (1) emission standards have important distributional effects; (2) they lead to a significant reduction of waste water emissions; and (3) they encourage implementation of less polluting production techniques in the long-run. This is in contrast to many studies which conclude that emission standards provide no economic incentive for reducing pollution (see Baumol and Oguga, 1975; Endres, 1985).

2. The Model and Key Assumptions

This section highlights the theoretical approach used in this analysis. It is a simplified three region version of a general dynamic multisector model (see Stephan, 1986). It focuses upon economic growth and environmental regulations by effluent standards and is characterized by two important features:

(1) In order to determine the long-run behavior of economic agents in a logically consistent way, a conventional market equilibrium framework is employed as far as possible. That means: all individuals have identical and certain price expectations and behave as price takers. Households optimize intertemporal utilities, producers maximize short-run profits and investors maximize present values. Money is neutral and the system is driven by relative prices between regions and over time. In each region environmental regulations are imposed by emission standards which have to be obeyed by every producer at any time.

(2) In order to allow for time lags in adjustment and process innovations there is, however, an important point of departure from the neoclassical paradigm. Within an intertemporal equilibrium model it is assumed that all commodities are dated and can be traded on a complete set of perfect present and future markets. This implies that future development is anticipated correctly by all agents, markets clear in each period, adjustment is smooth, instantaneous and timeless. In this analysis we use a different institutional framework. The set of all commodities is divided into two disjunct subsets. Complete and well-organized present and future markets exist for all nondurables such as consumption goods, labor, imports and exports, but do not exist for all durables such as used or semi-finished capital goods. By this assumption markets do not clear in each period and prices can be rigid in the short-run. Durable factors of production might be tight and restrict production possibilities in the short-run. Hence, time is required to adjust to changes in prices or exogenous parameters.

Figure 2.1 provides an overview of the structure of economic decisions over time.

Since used capital goods are not marketable and time is required to build up new ones, capital stocks are fixed in the short-run and restrict production possibilities within each period. Supply and demand for marketable commodities such as labor, consumption goods, exports and imports result from short-run profit maximization by producers (see Section 2.4.2) and utility maximization by consumers (see Section 2.3). In each single period, supply and demand are coordinated by a market mechanism such that a market-(flow)-equilibrium is achieved. Although fixed in the short-run, capital stocks can be changed in the long-run via capital construction processes (see Section 2.4.3). The investment criterion is the maximization of present value. Since producers have correct price expectations, capital stocks are implemented such that in the long-run, production is adjusted to changes in prices and environmental regulations (see Stephan, 1986, for details).

Obviously the above distinction between marketable and non-marketable commodities simplifies reality and only seems reasonable in an aggregated framework. But in this way at least two types of economic irreversibilities are captured which prohibit smooth and instantaneous adjustment processes and demonstrate short-run disequilibria. The first one is due to the lack of markets for used capital goods and implies irreversible investment. The second one is caused by the fact that more than one period is required to change production capacities, since capital markets are imperfect and finished capital goods are only part of a productive capital stock (see Faber, Niemes, and Stephan, 1983).

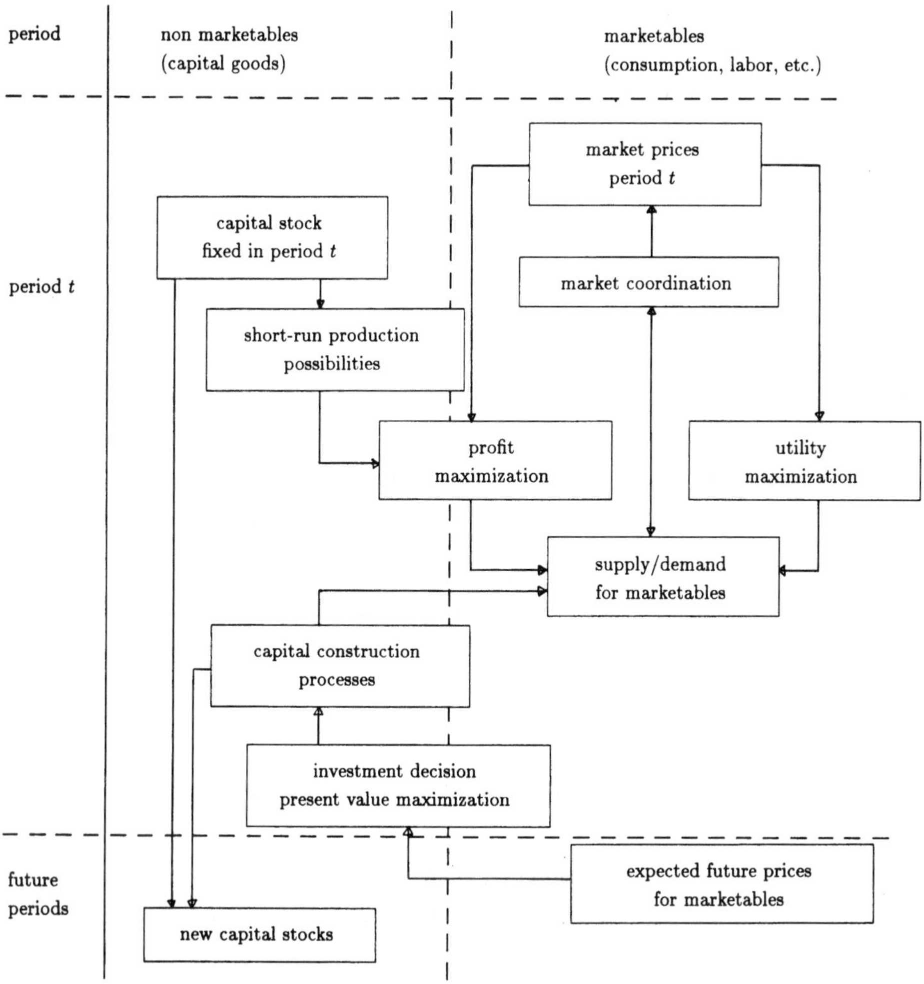

Figure 2.1 Structure of Economic Decisions

2.1 Single Period Constraints for Marketable Commodities

The spatial disaggregation of the analysis distinguishes three regions. Each region is viewed as a single point in space. Goods are characterized by date of availability and region of origin. The time horizon is divided into a sequence of T periods. For vividness region 1 refers to the northern, highly industrialized Western European nations of the United Kingdom, France, Belgium, the Netherlands, West Germany, Switzerland and Austria. Region 2 includes the southern, less industrialized countries of Portugal, Spain, Italy and Greece. Region 3 covers Western Europe's main trade partners, including the US and Japan.

It is assumed that each region $i = 1, 2, 3$ produces a specific good which can be consumed, exported, used as an intermediate factor for waste water treatment or builds up domestic capital stocks. Hence, in each period there are three different types of produced goods which are traded within or among regions under a complete system of perfect present and future markets.

The material balances of the produced goods are written for each region $i = 1, 2, 3$ and every period $t = 1, \ldots, T$

$$Y(i,t) \geq C(i,t) + I(i,t) + \sum_j X(i,j,t) + F(i,t). \tag{2.1}$$

$Y(i,t)$ symbolizes the gross output, $C(i,t)$ the aggregate consumption and $I(i,t)$ the aggregate inputs into construction processes for capital goods of different vintages in region i (see Section 2.4.3). $X(i,j,t)$ are the exports to region $j = 1, 2, 3$ with $X(i,j,t) = 0$ and $F(i,t)$ denotes the inputs into a waste water treatment system (see Section 2.2).

Labor is supplied exogenously in each region and cannot be transferred between regions. Hence, we observe for each region i and every period t the constraint

$$L(i,t) \leq \overline{L}(i,t). \tag{2.2}$$

$\overline{L}(i,t)$ denotes the amount of labor supplied exogenously and $L(i,t)$ is the labor input into production.

As (2.1) indicates, each region's exports are viewed as intermediate factors rather than final goods. That is, imports enter directly into production but not into consumption. In this way each region's export prospects are related to the other's production propensities and an Armington (1969) approach of substitution between imports from individual regions of origin is employed. Other nonenvironmental production inputs are the services from capital goods of different vintages and labor. Since this analysis focuses upon the economic impact of waste water regulations, water is considered as the only environmental input into production.

2.2 Waste Water Regulations and Treatment

Waste water policy in West Germany is an example of a mixed strategy between state-controlled regulations through standards and a market conform polluter-pays principle. Under the 1973 revision of the Wasserhaushaltsgesetz, it is required, for example, that the biochemical oxygen demand (BOD_5) of waste water be reduced by approximately 80 % before it is discharged into the environment. In principle, if a producer is not able to meet this requirement, he will not be allowed to operate his enterprise. Note that until 1973 no minimal BOD_5 waste water standard was in force. But in practice, waste water was treated as if a 60 % BOD_5 reduction had been required (see Bower, Barre, Kuchner, and Russell, 1981).

An 80 % BOD_5 standard, however, is too low to obtain the surface water quality regarded as socially optimal in the Umweltprogramm of the federal government (see Faber, Niemes, and Stephan, 1983). To reach this goal, at least a 90 % to 95 % removal is necessary. The Abwasserabgabengesetz which has been in force since 1981 defines an effluent charge which provides an economic incentive for a 95 % reduction in the average BOD_5.

During the early 1970s, the European Community (EC) and the Organization for Economic Cooperation and Development (OECD) have tried to urge their member nations to adopt prices and a polluter-pays principle for environmental control. Despite West Germany's experiences with the Abwasserabgabengesetz, there is no realistic basis to assume that the polluter-pays principle will be used in other countries. On the contrary, it seems reasonable that effluent standards will be imposed for waste water regulation in the rest of Western Europe, the US and Japan. The 1972 Federal Water Pollution Control Act in the US and the 1973 revision of West Germany's Wasserhaushaltsgesetz may serve as a rational basis for expecting that in the US, Japan and Western Europe the biochemical oxygen demand of waste water (BOD_5) effluents has to be reduced by 95 %.

Engineering analyses of such end-of-the-pipe treatment systems suggest that the principal determinants of purification are the volume of the waste water stream $E(i,t)$, the concentration of waste and the effluent standard $R(i)$ (see Fraas and Munley, 1984). For a fixed standard $R(i)$, waste water treatment is characterized by economies of scale. Hence, marginal costs of treatment decline with increasing flow size. For fixed volumes $E(i,t)$, however, marginal costs gradually increase, if the standard $R(i)$ is raised. This reflects increasing difficulties of waste extraction. (For a detailed discussion of the costs of waste water treatment systems see Faber, Niemes, and Stephan, 1983; Fraas and Munley, 1984).

To cope with this technical relationship, a two argument, three parameter function is used to express the input requirements for an end-of-the-pipe treatment system

$$F(i,t) = E(i,t)^{æ}(c - b \cdot ln(100 - R(i))). \tag{2.3}$$

For simplification purposes, the index i is omitted in (2.3). For $æ < 1$ waste water purification exhibits increasing returns to scale, if the waste water standard is regarded as fixed. The parameters c and b determine marginal costs of waste extraction depending upon the waste water standard $R(i)$ only.

2.3 Intertemporal Consumption Choices

As mentioned above, consumers and producers are clairvoyant and forecast prices correctly. Supply of and demand for consumption goods are coordinated on a complete set of perfect markets (see Figure 2.1).

To simplify the analysis, a Ramsey criterion is employed for determinig each region's time pattern of consumption and savings. This means it is supposed that (1) within each region there is a representative consumer who maximizes his intertemporal utility expressed as the sum of discounted logarithms of consumption; (2) it is expected that all economically relevant variables grow at the same (post terminal) rate along the time horizon T; and (3) since waste water quality is regulated by standards and standards are the result of a political process, emission standards $R(i)$ reflect consumers' satisfaction from preserving the environment. Therefore, environmental quality does not enter as an argument into the utility function.

Let $\Theta(i)$ denote the one period utility discounting factor. Suppose that the expected post terminal consumption growth rate is $\Omega(i)$. Each region's maximand is then written by

$$U(C(i,1),\ldots,C(i,T)) = \sum_{t}^{T-1} \Theta(i)^t \, log(C(i,t)) + \sum_{T}^{\infty} \Theta(i)^t \, log(C(i,T))(1+\Omega(i))^{t-T}. \tag{2.4}$$

Each region's intertemporal consumption and savings choices are optimized subject to its individual wealth constraint, expressed in present value prices. To calculate the individual intertemporal budget, it is assumed that each region owns its initial capital stock and its labor resources.

2.4 Production, Investment and Adjustment

In this analysis it is assumed that: (1) there are well-organized present and future markets for consumption goods, labor, exports, imports and intermediate factors;

(2) there are no markets for used capital goods; and (3) time is required to produce new capital goods. Hence, there is no perfect coordination or adjustment of existing capital stocks to changes in prices or exogenous parameters and the short-run flexibility of an economic system is low in contrast to its long-run adjustment potential.

To capture these assumptions an extreme and sharp formulation of intertemporal production flexibility is used which has become known as the putty-clay hypothesis (see Johansen, 1972): at any point of time, the production possibilities are solely determined by previous investment decisions. This means, in each period production possibilities are fixed. No changes are possible ex post and short-run substitution elasticities are close to zero. Ex ante, however, there is a free choice among the set of production processes which are technically feasible. This enables flexible adjustment to price changes or environmental regulations in the long-run.

To formalize these ideas two sets of production possibilities have to be introduced: (1) ex ante production possibilities, which reflect engineering knowledge and data that are known at the beginning of the time horizon. These determine the set of all production processes which are technologically feasible in the long-run; and (2) ex post production possibilities, which solely depend upon the set of production possibilities and capacities introduced in prior periods. As such, ex post production possibilities determine what is feasible in the short-run.

2.4.1 *Ex Ante Production Possibilities*

To reduce the efforts of econometric estimations (see Section 3) nested CES production functions have been employed to characterize the ex ante production possibilities for each region i. This means, a production process

$$a(i) = (k(i), \ell(i), x(i,j),\ j = 1,2,3,\ y(i), e(i)) \tag{2.5}$$

is technically feasible in region i in the long-run if

$$y(i) = \left\{A(i)\left[k(i)^{\alpha}\ell(i)^{\beta}\pi_j x(i,j)^{\tau}\right]^{\delta} - B(i)e(i)^{\delta}\right\}^{1/\delta} \tag{2.6}$$

where the subscripts are omitted for region i.

$k(i)$ denotes the capital stock, which is specific for production process $a(i)$. That is, $k(i)$ is technically necessary and determines the production capacity of process $a(i)$ in the sense of Koopmans (1977). Output $y(i)$ is produced by means of labor input $\ell(i)$ and imports $x(i,j)$ from regions $j = 1,2,3$ with $x(i,i) = 0$, if the capital stock $k(i)$ is fully utilized. $e(i)$ denotes waste water generation of process $a(i)$.

This formulation assumes that it is technically feasible to combine the nonenvironmental production factors of labor, imports and services of capital goods like in a Cobb-Douglas production function. In turn, this index of inputs is linked with waste water generation through a CES formulation. Hence, in the long-run there is an unitary elasticity of substitution between different nonenvironmental goods and a constant elasticity of substitution (typically less than one) between water and nonenvironmental factors.

2.4.2 *Ex Post Production Possibilities*

To characterize the ex post production possibilities, it is assumed (see Koopmans, 1977) that: (1) capital stocks must not be fully utilized, hence production processes can be carried out at a lower level than full capacity; and (2) capital goods decay exponentially at the same rate independent of their vintage.

Following Hildenbrand (1981), the ex post production possibilities of region i at each date t are then described by a finite family of production processes which represents the full history of choices from the set of ex ante production possibilities in the past up to period t. To be more precise, let $a(i)_s$ denote a production process (see (2.5)) which has been chosen from the set of ex ante production possibilities in period $s < t$. Let $\{a(i)_s | s < t\}$ be the family of production processes which represents the full history of choices prior to period t. Then the set of short-run production possibilities is defined by the zonotope $V(i,t)$ (see Hildenbrand, 1981, for a detailed discussion)

$$(2.7) \qquad V(i,t) = \left\{a(i,t) \mid a(i,t) = \sum_s^t a(i)_s \sigma^{t-s} z_s, \quad 0 \le z_s \le 1\right\}.$$

z_s, $0 \le z_s \le 1$ is a real number and determines the level at which the production process $a(i)_s$ is carried out in period t. σ^{t-s} denotes the fraction of the capital stock of vintage s that has survived in period t. Note that capital goods of different vintages are considered to be distinct.

In each period production decisions are based upon prices, existing ex post production possibilities, restrictions of the labor force (see (2.2)) and constraints by exports (see (2.1)). This means, if the prices for consumption goods, exports, the wage rate for labor and the marginal costs of the waste water treatment are given, in each period t a profit maximizing mix of the existing production processes is chosen from the zonotop $V(i,t)$. Since this choice is restricted to a finite set of production processes which are characterized by fixed coefficients and fixed capacities, waste water generation and capital are complements during the short-run. They are, however, substitutes in the long-run, for with each successive vintage of capital goods and investment, less polluting production techniques can be introduced.

2.4.3 *Long-run Adjustment and Innovation*

How can the short-run production possibilities be changed and less polluting production techniques be implemented? Since each production process needs a specific capital stock, new short-run production processes can be employed only after the technically necessary capital stocks have been constructed.

In modelling the capital gestation processes it is assumed that S periods are required to construct each type of capital goods. This means, if a technically feasible production process $a(i)$ should be used for production in period t, in each period $t-s$, $1 \leq s \leq S$, a fraction of the capital stock $k(i)$ has to be invested. Let $h(i, t-s)$ for $1 \leq s \leq S$ be the fraction of produced resources allocated to the capital construction process s period from completion of capital stock $k(i)$, then the vector

$$H(t, k(i)) = (h(i, t-S), \ldots, h(i, t-1), k(i)) \tag{2.8}$$

formally denotes the intertemporal capital construction process.

The criterion for implementation of new production processes is present value maximization. That is, producers choose those production processes from the set of ex ante production possibilities which maximize expected profits for constructing the technically required capital stock (see Figure 2.1).

How will polluters react to an effluent standard? Note that the explicit distinction between ex ante and ex post production possibilities allows different strategies to be analyzed which can be employed, depending upon the time horizon. In the short-run it might be possible only to cut back the level of production and consumption or to change the amount of raw and intermediate material inputs. In the long-run, however, implementation of new production processes and substitution of existing by less polluting capital equipment enables environmental and ecological damage to be reduced.

3. Numerical Inputs and Results

The results reported in this section can only be regarded as preliminary. Because of lack of data, all calculations are based upon stylized facts rather than econometrically estimated equations. Only for the base year are the gross domestic products, exports and waste water generation taken directly from the original statistics (Statistische Jahrbücher, 1976, 1985). All other data are benchmarked against these values. For solving the dynamic model numerically, as given in Section 2, a revised and enlarged version of the 3RT code (see Manne and Preckel, 1985) and Broadie's (1985) OCTASOLV algorithm have been employed.

3.1 Numerical Inputs and Assumptions

The time horizon is subdivided into six periods, each of a five year length except for the first one, which contains seven years. The base year for calculations is 1973, the first year reported is 1980 and the last year reported is 1995.

To run the model, the following numerical inputs have to be specified for each region: (1) for the base year, the gross domestic products, the exports, the waste water quantities as well as the treatment prices, and the initial (base year) capital stocks; (2) for each period, the putty-clay decay factors, the annual growth rates of the labor force, the utility discount factors and the post terminal growth rates; and (3) the coefficients of the capital gestation processes (2.8), the parameters of the ex ante production function (2.6) and the parameters of the waste water treatment function (2.3).

Table 3.1 shows for each region the base year gross domestic products, exports and waste water generation as taken directly from the original source (see Statistische Jahrbücher, 1976, 1985). Assuming a capital to gross national product ratio of 3.0, a capital to output ratio between 2.1 and 2.8 is implied for the initial capital stocks (base year vintage) across the regions. As the analysis of Bower, Barre, Kuchner, and Russell (1981) reports, until 1973, industrial waste water was purified in Western Europe and the US as if a 60 % BOD_5 reduction standard had been imposed (see Section 2.2). Hence, for the base year waste water treatment prices are set equal to marginal costs of 60 % BOD_5 waste water purification, as have been calculated by Ewringmann, Kibat, and Schafhausen (1980).

Table 3.2 shows the data for the annual putty-clay decay factors, the post terminal rates and the annual growth rates of the labor force. Annual putty-clay decay factors are set at 94 % for each region. Given this assumption, capital equipment of each vintage has to be replaced at least every 20 years on the average.

Table 3.1: Base Year Inputs from the Original Source

	Region 1	Region 2	Region 3
Gross domestic product (billion DM)	2791.4	1210.0	10090.0
Waste water production (million cbm)	101.3	50.9	405.5
Capital stocks	7505.7	2517.9	29215.5
Exports from	Region 1	Region 2	Region 3
to Region 1	0.0	90.7	298.8
to Region 2	70.5	0.0	100.2
to Region 3	264.0	88.0	0.0
Waste water treatment price (DM/cbm)	0.25	0.25	0.25

In contrast to the World Bank's (1981) long term prospects on world population, lower growth rates for the labor force are assumed in this analysis: 2 % in region 1, 3 % to 2 % in region 2 and 4 % to 2 % in region 3. For consistency, the post terminal growth rates for all regions are set equal to the growth rates of the labor force at the end of the time horizon, and the one period utility discount factors. Hence, it is supposed that consumers discount at a 2 % basis each year. This checks closely with the numerical results from a continuous infinite time horizon model (see Manne, 1981).

Table 3.2: Putty-clay Factor, Growth Rate, Discount Factor

	Region 1	Region 2	Region 3
Putty-clay decay factor	0.94	0.94	0.94
Growth rate labor force	2 %	3 %–2 %	4 %–2 %
Utility discount factor	2 %	2 %	2 %
Post terminal growth rate	2 %	2 %	2 %

Capital goods in our model reflect all types of tangible capital, including stocks of plants and equipment, consumer durables and housing. Different types of capital goods have different construction periods and patterns of input requirement. As a vintage approach is employed, capital goods are distinguished by date of invention, but for each vintage there is only one type of capital good. Since the findings of Hall (1977) and Mayer (1960) suggest an average construction period of nearly two years for plants, as a compromise a two year gestation period is assumed for each type of capital goods. Hence, with five year time periods and a two year investment to capital good construction period, at each date of report t five different vintages of capital goods can be introduced: three for which the construction process has been started in the five year interval $(t-1, t)$ and two for which the starting point of gestation dates back to the previous interval $(t-2, t-1)$.

To estimate the ex ante production possibilities for each region, it is assumed that in the base year inputs and outputs were optimally adjusted to a long-run equilibrium. Thus, the relationship (2.6) has to be met in the base year and the technical parameters can be benchmarked. That is, exhaustion of product and first order optimality conditions are used to derive the constants A, B, α, β, τ for each region. Table 3.3 reports these benchmark values.

Table 3.3: Ex Ante Technology Parameters

Technology parameters	Region 1	Region 2	Region 3
CES parameter	−0.66	−1.50	−1.22
Capital exponent	0.24	0.33	0.27
Labor exponent	0.61	0.36	0.69
Import exponent from	Region 1	Region 2	Region 3
to Region 1	0.00	0.22	0.02
to Region 2	0.02	0.00	0.01
to Region 3	0.10	0.08	0.00

To complete the description of the ex ante production possibilities an additional numerical input has to be specified exogenously. Empirical studies (see for example Ewringman, Kibat, and Schaffhausen, 1980) show that in West Germany, industrial waste water generation was reduced by more than 50 % between 1973 and 1977. Since West Germany's domestic production accounts to more than one-third of the total annual gross product of region 1, it is assumed that in the northern part of Western Europe (region 1) waste water generation can be reduced by 55 % in the long-run. For the southern countries in Western Europe (region 2), a 35 % reduction potential is assumed. For region 3, a 45 % reduction potential is supposed. These assumptions crosscheck with the observations that, in general, waste water generation could be reduced by 30 % to 60 % using existing technology (see Faber, Niemes, and Stephan, 1983). Based upon these assumptions, the values of the elasticity of substitution between non environmental and environmental inputs are calculated (Table 3.3).

Finally, the parameters æ, b, and c for the waste water treatment function (2.3) are directly estimated from the literature. As a survey shows (see for example Eckenfelder, 1966), the exponent æ ranges from 0.58 to 1.07. Since it is difficult to incorporate increasing returns to scale into an equilibrium framework, æ is set equal to one. The calculations of the parameters b and c are based upon Faber, Niemes, and Stephan (1983), as well as Unser and Made (1977). b and c are determined such that with a 95 % BOD_5 removal marginal cost of waste water treatment would be 0.91 DM/cbm (expressed in 1973 DM). This is in the upper range of the values which are estimated for the actual waste water treatment costs in West Germany. Note that with a 60 % BOD_5 reduction, which characterizes the real situation in 1973, the estimated marginal costs are 0.25 DM/cbm. These are exactly the waste water treatment prices used in this analysis for the base year (see Table 3.1).

3.2 Results and Numerical Output

In this section the numerical results for the years 1980, 1985, 1990 and 1995 are reported. For a counterfactual analysis, calculations are carried out under two different scenarios. (1) For reference case calculations it is supposed that in all periods and each region, 60 % of the biochemical oxygen demand (BOD_5) of waste water is reduced at the effluent. This means, no additional waste water regulation to the existing ones are imposed. (2) For the alternative case it is assumed that in every region a 95 % BOD_5 emission standard is enforced, beginning in 1980. Hence, for the alternative calculations exactly those regulations are used which are expected to be implemented in reality (see Section 2.2).

In Table 3.4 the annual gross domestic products and in Table 3.5 the present value prices for produced and traded commodities are printed for both scenarios.

Under reference case assumptions, i.e. a 60 % BOD_5 reduction in all regions and periods, in each region gross domestic production is growing continuously over time (see Table 3.4). The highest growth rates are obtained for region 3, which

Table 3.4: Annual Gross Domestic Production

Gross domestic product: 60 % BOD_5 reduction (billion 1973 DM)					
Region/year	1973	1980	1985	1990	1995
1	2791.4	3874.0	4122.5	4523.9	4958.4
2	1210.0	1322.9	1361.1	1399.8	1467.1
3	10090.5	15968.0	19396.4	22952.3	26186.2
total	14091.9	21164.9	24880.0	28875.0	32611.7

Gross domestic product: 95 % BOD_5 reduction (billion 1973 DM)					
Region/year	1973	1980	1985	1990	1995
1	2791.4	3952.8	4195.3	4644.5	5124.3
2	1210.0	1181.9	1252.5	1313.7	1399.1
3	10090.5	15886.0	19316.2	22876.3	26141.3
total	14091.9	21020.8	24764.1	28834.5	32664.7

Table 3.5: Present Value (Equilibrium) Prices

Present value prices: 60 % BOD_5 reduction					
Region/year	1973	1980	1985	1990	1995
1	1.00	0.49	0.31	0.31	0.29
2	0.12	0.12	0.11	0.09	0.09
3	0.23	0.17	0.13	0.09	0.09

Present value prices: 95 % BOD_5 reduction					
Region/year	1973	1980	1985	1990	1995
1	1.00	0.56	0.45	0.37	0.35
2	0.15	0.14	0.13	0.12	0.11
3	0.34	0.25	0.18	0.14	0.14

covers the US and Japan as Western Europe's main trade partners. Average annual economic growth in this region is close to 4.5 %. The lowest growth rates are reported for the southern part of Western Europe (region 2). On the average they stay below 1 %. The growth rates in the northern countries of Western Europe lie midway between the growth rates of region 3 and region 2, but always keep significantly below 3 % per year. Total economic development for all regions is around 4 % annually. Hence, the reported rates seem to be relatively optimistic. But they are in the range of the growth rates as projected in the World Bank's World Development Report (1981).

As one expects, Table 3.4 and Table 3.5 indicate that tightening the waste water standards leads to a slight increase of the present value prices of traded products, but has little impact on economic growth and production in total. Overall economic growth is still close to 4 % annually if a 95 % BOD_5 emission standard is imposed in all regions.

There are, however, important differences across single regions after the waste water standards have been changed. Region 2 and region 3 are worse off if a 95 % BOD_5 standard is enforced. In the southern part of Western Europe (region 2), the long-run economic growth is cut back almost by half, whereas region 3, this means primarily Japan and the US, suffers only a slight reduction in economic development. In contrast to these two regions, Table 3.4 reports that the domestic production and the economic growth are increased in the northern countries of Western Europe (region 1) if a 95 % BOD_5 reduction standard is required. Moreover, the calculations show that compared to the reference case, the northern part of Western Europe has extended its exports to the other regions under the 95 % BOD_5 reduction scenario. In region 2 and region 3, tightening waste water standards has the opposite effect on export prospects. Hence, a distributional effect across regions is observed.

A look at the numerical assumptions (see Section 3.1) may help to explain this result. Based upon the historical development, it is assumed that in the long-run waste water generation can be technically reduced by 55 % in region 1, 35 % in region 2 and 45 % in region 3. Hence, the northern part of Western Europe is characterized by the highest potential to react to changes in waste water regulation in the long-run. The south of Western Europe, however, has the lowest adjustment potential. The differences in the technologically determined potential to adjust to new waste water standards explain the observed distributional effects.

Though tightening waste water regulation affects production only slightly, it has an important impact upon the time pattern of emissions, as Table 3.6 indicates. Under both scenarios a gap between economic growth and the development of

Table 3.6: Annual Waste Water Emissions

Waste water emissions: 60 % BOD_5 reduction (Million cbm)					
Region/year	1973	1980	1985	1990	1995
1	101.3	111.7	119.1	137.1	164.9
2	50.9	53.4	54.9	57.5	63.1
3	405.5	532.1	637.2	788.4	881.5

Waste water emissions: 95 % BOD_5 reduction (Million cbm)					
Region/year	1973	1980	1985	1990	1995
1	101.3	110.7	107.1	107.0	106.9
2	50.9	47.7	46.8	45.3	45.3
3	405.5	428.5	469.2	514.3	569.0

waste water generation is observed. But a significant reduction of waste water emissions in the long-run can be obtained only if the 95 % BOD_5 effluent standard is imposed in each region. Under reference case assumptions, i.e. either no change in the existing waste water regulations or a 60 % BOD_5 emission standard, waste water emissions develop at almost the same rates as economic production: at 2 % in region 1, at 0.6 % in region 2 and at approximately 4 % in region 3. If it is required, however, that 95 % of the biochemical oxygen demand (BOD_5) of waste water effluent be reduced beginning in 1980, the overall picture changes significantly. Only region 3 is still characterized by increasing aggregate waste water emissions. In Western Europe as a whole, the aggregate volume of annual waste water generation is declining over time, but with a different time path in each region. In the northern part (region 1) a peak in waste water generation is calculated for 1980, whereas in southern Western Europe (region 2), waste water emission will be reduced continuously over the whole time horizon.

How can the drastic reduction of waste water emissions under the 95 % BOD_5 emission standard be explained? What are the reasons for the 1980 peak in waste water generation?

As discussed at the end of Section 2, in principle, there are two sets of strategies which may reduce waste water generation. In the short-run this might be possible through input substitution. This means a higher percentage of foreign produced goods would be used as inputs into production, hence an export of environmental pollution to other regions. In the long-run one would typically expect a change of production possibilities and implementation of less polluting processes.

This explicit distinction between short-run and long-run strategies serves as an explanation for the 1980 waste water peak in northern Western Europe. It follows from the model formulation that time is required to adjust to a change in environmental regulations for two reasons (see Section 2): (1) construction of capital goods consumes time and investment decisions have to be set at least two periods ahead; and (2) capital stocks and production possibilities are fixed in the short-run and cannot be abandoned. Consequently, until 1980 the time span had been too short to construct a sufficient amount of new and less waste water intensive capital equipment to adjust to the imposed waste water regulations. Hence, in 1980 production is mainly based on the old techniques and a short-run reduction strategy has been applied. But with each investment, less polluting production processes can be implemented, and a long-run strategy is employed in subsequent periods. This explains why imposing a 95 % BOD_5 emission standard in 1980 is followed by a drastic reduction of emissions in the long-run.

To support this argumentation Table 3.7 reports the emission coefficients for the sequence of production processes introduced over the time span 1973–1995.

Table 3.7: Development of Emission Coefficients

Waste water emission coefficients: 60 % BOD_5 reduction					
Region/year	1973	1980	1985	1990	1995
1	0.036	0.032	0.029	0.033	0.039
2	0.042	0.038	0.043	0.043	0.043
3	0.040	0.038	0.032	0.036	0.036
Waste water emission coefficients: 95 % BOD_5 reduction					
Region/year	1973	1980	1985	1990	1995
1	0.036	0.021	0.019	0.017	0.016
2	0.042	0.031	0.029	0.027	0.027
3	0.040	0.028	0.023	0.020	0.020

To allow for comparison between different vintages, production processes are normalized to produce one unit of the specific regional output. Table 3.7 shows that emission coefficients do not change significantly over time in the reference case. Obviously, a 60 % BOD_5 emission standard is too low to enforce the implementation of less polluting production techniques during the time horizon of the analysis. But, if a 95 % BOD_5 emission standard is imposed, from period to period there is a decrease in the waste water coefficients for each region. Hence in all regions, less polluting production processes are implemented over time.

4. Concluding Remarks

In summary, the numerical analysis shows at least two important results.

(1) Tightening environmental standards has almost no impact on economic development as a whole, but has significant distributional effects. International trade as well as imports and export prospects of single regions may change significantly, as the counterfactual analysis indicates.

(2) In contrast to the conclusions of most theoretical studies (see for a reference Endres, 1985), emission standards provide a dynamic incentive to reduce waste water generation in the long-run and to implement less polluting production techniques. However, the time path of adjustment and innovation depends upon how the temporal structure of the production system and its flexibility to react to price changes and environmental regulations are modeled. Even in this highly aggregated analysis it is obvious how complex the interactions between environmental protection and economic development are if time and dynamics are explicitly taken into account.

References

Armington, P. S. (1969): "A Theory of Demand for Products Distinguished by Place of Production." *International Monetary Fund Staff Papers* 16: 159–178.

Arrow, K. (1983): "The Future and Present in Economic Theory." In *Collected Papers: General Equilibrium*. Oxford: Basil Blackwell, pp. 275–289.

Baumol, W., and **Oates, W.** (1975): *The Theory of Environmental Policy*. Englewood Cliffs, N.J.: Prentice Hall.

Bovenberg, L. (1985): "Dynamic General Equilibrium Tax Models with Adjustment Costs." In *Mathematical Programming Study 23.* Amsterdam etc.: North-Holland, pp. 40–55.

Bower, T. C.; Barre, R.; Kuchner, J.; and **Russell, C.** (1981): "Incentives in Water Quality Management." Mimeo. Washington, D.C.: Environmental Protection Agency.

Broadie, M. (1985): "An Introduction to the Octasolv Algorithm." In *Mathematical Programming Study 23.* Amsterdam etc.: North-Holland, pp. 121–143.

Chao, H.; Kim, S.; and **Manne, A. S.** (1982): "Computation of Equilibria for Nonlinear Economies." *Journal of Policy Modeling* 4: 24–43.

Eckenfelder, W. W. (1966): *Industrial Water Pollution Control.* (McGraw-Hill Series in Water Resources Engineering.) New York etc.: McGraw-Hill.

Endres, A. (1985): *Umwelt und Ressourcenökonomie.* Darmstadt: Wissenschaftliche Verlagsanstalt.

Ewringmann, D.; Kibat, K.; and **Schafhausen, F. J.** (1980): *Die Abwasserabgabe als Investitionsanreiz.* Berlin: Schmitt.

Faber, M.; Niemes, H.; and **Stephan, G.** (1983): *Umweltschutz und Input-Output-Analyse: Mit zwei Fallstudien aus der Wassergütewirtschaft.* Tübingen: Mohr.

Fraas, A. G., and **Munley, V. G.** (1984): "Municipial Waste Water Costs." *Journal of Environmental Economics and Management* 11: 28–38.

Hall, R. E. (1977): "Investment, Interest Rates and Effects of Stabilization." *Brookings Papers on Economic Activity* 6: 61–121.

Harford, J., and **Oguga, S.** (1983): "Pollution Taxes and Standards." *Journal of Environmental Economics and Management* 11: 1–17.

Heady, C. J., and **Mitra, P. K.** (1985): "A Computional Approach to Optimal Public Policy." In *Mathematical Programming Study 23.* Amsterdam etc.: North-Holland, pp. 95–120.

Hildenbrand, W. (1981): "Short-run Production Functions Based on Microdata." *Econometrica* 49: 1095–1125.

Johansen, L. (1972): *Production Functions.* New York etc.: North-Holland.

Koopmans, T. C. (1977): "Examples of Production Relations Based on Microdata." In *The Microeconomic Foundation of Macroeconomics*, edited by G. C. Harcourt. Amsterdam etc.: North-Holland, pp. 145–171.

Mäler, K. G. (1974): *Environmental Economics: A Theoretical Inquiry.* Baltimore etc.: Johns Hopkins University Press.

Manne, A. S. (1981): "A Three Region Model of Energy and Economic Growth." Staff Working Paper 474. Washington, D. C.: World Bank.

Manne, A. S., and **Preckel, P.** (1985): "A Three Region Model of Energy and Capital Flows." In *Mathematical Programming Study 23.* Amsterdam etc.: North-Holland, pp. 56–65.

Mayer, T. (1960): "Plant and Equipment Lead Times." *Journal of Business* 33: 127–132.

Mendelsohn, R. (1984): "Endogenous Technical Change and Environmental Regulation." *Journal of Environmental Economics and Management* 11: 185–197.

Pethig, R. (1975): "Umweltverschmutzung, Wohlfahrt und Umweltpolitik in einem Zwei-Sektoren-Gleichgewichtsmodell." *Zeitschrift für Nationalökonomie* 35: 99–124.

Statistische Jahrbücher (1976, 1985). Wiesbaden: Statistisches Bundesamt.

Stephan, G. (1986): *Umweltstandards und Ablösung von Techniken: Ein berechenbarer Gleichgewichtsansatz.* Habilition thesis. To appear as *Microeconomic Study*, Berlin etc.: Springer.

Unser, K. and **Made, E.** (1977): "Kosten für industrielle und kommunale Abwässer." *Korrespondenz Abwasser* 24: 45–53.

World Bank (1981): *World Development Report 1981.* Washington, D.C.: World Bank.

Addresses of Authors

Dr. Michael **Ahlheim**, Alfred-Weber-Institute, University of Heidelberg, Grabengasse 14, D-6900 Heidelberg 1, West Germany.

Prof. Dr.Dr. Dieter **Bös**, Institute of Economics, University of Bonn, Adenauerallee 24–42, D-5300 Bonn 1, West Germany.

Priv.-Doz. Dr. Wolfgang **Buchholz**, Quentedtstraße 32, D-7400 Tübingen, West Germany.

Prof. Dr. Klaus **Conrad**, Institute of Economics, University of Mannheim, Seminargebäude A5, D-6800 Mannheim 1, West Germany.

Dr. Frank A. **Cowell**, Reader in Economics, London School of Economics, Houghton Street, London WC2A 2AE, United Kingdom.

Priv.-Doz. Dr. Udo **Ebert**, Institute of Economics, University of Bonn, Adenauerallee 24–42, D-5300 Bonn 1, West Germany.

Dr. Iris **Henseler-Unger**, Bundesministerium für Wirtschaft, Ref. IA2, Villemombler Straße, D-5300 Bonn 1, West Germany.

Dipl.-Vw. Georg **Hirte**, Hemauer Straße 16, D-8400 Regensburg, West Germany.

Dr. Bernhard **Kühn**, Handschuhsheimer Landstraße 84, D-6900 Heidelberg, West Germany.

Dipl.-Vw. Hans **Kungl**, Blumenstraße 41, D-6900 Heidelberg, West Germany.

Prof. George **McKenzie**, Ph.D., Department of Economics, The University, Southampton S09 5NH, United Kingdom.

Prof. Dr. Wilfried **Pauwels**, Department of Economics, University of Antwerp, Prinsstraat 13, B-2000 Antwerp, Belgium.

Prof. Dr. Wilhelm **Pfähler**, Koblenz School of Corporate Management, Zwickauer Strasse 23, D-5400 Koblenz, West Germany.

Prof. Dr. Werner W. **Pommerehne**, FB 10 Economics, Free University Berlin, Boltzmannstraße 20, D-1000 Berlin 33, West Germany.

Prof. Dr. Wolfram **Richter**, Institute of Economics, University of Dortmund, P.O. Box 50 05 00, D-4600 Dortmund 50, West Germany.

Prof. Dr. Manfred **Rose**, Alfred-Weber-Institute, University of Heidelberg, Grabengasse 14, D-6900 Heidelberg 1, West Germany.

Prof. Dr. Christian **Seidl**, Institute of Public Economics, University of Kiel, Olshausenstraße 40, D-2300 Kiel 1, West Germany.

Prof. Dr. Hans-Werner **Sinn**, Institute of Economics, University of Munich, Ludwigstraße 33/III, D-8000 Munich 22, West Germany.

Priv.-Doz. Dr. Gunter **Stephan**, Alfred-Weber-Institute, University of Heidelberg, Grabengasse 14, D-6900 Heidelberg 1, West Germany.

Prof. Dr. Wolfgang **Wiegard**, Institute of Economics, University of Regensburg, P.O. Box 397, D-8400 Regensburg, West Germany.

MIX
Papier aus verantwortungsvollen Quellen
Paper from responsible sources
FSC® C105338

If you have any concerns about our products,
you can contact us on
ProductSafety@springernature.com

In case Publisher is established outside the EU,
the EU authorized representative is:
Springer Nature Customer Service Center GmbH
Europaplatz 3, 69115 Heidelberg, Germany

Printed by Libri Plureos GmbH
in Hamburg, Germany